MICROECONOMICS

MICROECONOMICS

SECOND EDITION

Steven T. Call
Metropolitan State College
Denver, Colorado

William L. Holahan
University of Wisconsin
Milwaukee, Wisconsin

Wadsworth Publishing Company
Belmont, California
A Division of Wadsworth, Inc.

To Janean and Mary, who humored us in our desire to write this book, and to Mark, David, Stephanie, Michelle, Daniel, two Heathers, and Phillip, who will love to see their names in print.

Economics Editor: Bill Oliver

Production: Del Mar Associates

Designer: John Odam

Manuscript Editor: Rebecca Smith

Technical Illustrators: Richard Carter, Kim Fraley

Printed in the United States of America

1 2 3 4 5 6 7 8 9 10—87 86 85 84 83

ISBN 0-534-01314-7

Library of Congress Cataloging in Publication Data

Call, Steven T.
  Microeconomics
  Includes bibliographies and index.
  1. Microeconomics. I. Holahan, William L.
II. Title
HB172.C34   1983   338.5   82-13573
ISBN 0-534-01314-7

Contents

Applied Micro Theories

Preface

There is a great myth abroad in the land: Macroeconomics is more interesting and relevant than microeconomics. To be sure, inflation and unemployment are important and fascinating topics. But microeconomics has a unique power and a thoughtful, logical method of attacking problems. It deals with exciting issues that are every bit as relevant and that you ultimately have far more control over. Furthermore, understanding macroeconomics requires a solid foundation in microeconomic reasoning.

In an effort to bolster the popularity of microeconomics, we have tried to provide intermediate students with a rich treatment of modern price theory and its applications. This second edition has benefited from hundreds of solicited and unsolicited suggestions from colleagues and students. It retains from the first edition the basic structure and overall organization. It also retains our emphasis on applications that are closely aligned with modern problems and actual concerns. But we have discarded material that seemed to lack contact with the real world or was too advanced for intermediate courses.

To Mathephobes

Mathephobes (those of you exhibiting an irrational and persistent fear of mathematics) have been discouraged from taking any math or analytical courses, either out of a genuine fear or on the advice of a teacher or guidance counselor somewhere in the dim past. Now you find yourself reading the preface of a book that will develop your analytical skills and put your mathephobia to the test. If you close the book and select nonanalytical courses, you automatically sever yourself from the fascinating study of economics and its power to explain the world's problems. You may also cut yourself off from the many lucrative occupations that open up to people with analytical training. One result is that you may be consigned to already-overcrowded majors and occupations. Our experience with students convinces us that analytical training can be an important source of liberation for those who want satisfying careers.

Our graphic and verbal analysis, with occasional use of elementary algebra, is within the reach of nearly everyone and can be an invaluable aid to logical thinking. We believe all students can benefit from a careful presentation of economics that uses elementary mathematical techniques.

To Mathephiles

Mathephiles (those of you favorably disposed toward mathematics) will learn the material in this book easier than mathephobes will.

Your experience in analytical thinking and in modeling gives you an edge. You have the opportunity to penetrate the subject deeply and quickly. However, do not be overconfident; overconfidence may insulate you from the richness of economic reasoning contained in a verbal, graphic approach. Our book establishes a solid foundation for mathematical extension in subsequent courses. It will also be useful to students whose first exposure to economics took place in a mathematical context.

All Ph.D. economists need substantial training and intuition in mathematics to participate in the development of new knowledge. Anyone contemplating a career in economics or a related field is well advised to get a solid foundation in math. You have a head start here. But we feel strongly that there are other ways to approach the study of economics. Hence we have purposely kept this book at the graphic and verbal level.

To the Instructor

Student interest must be engaged before any real learning can take place. In order to accomplish this prerequisite, we have tried to apply microeconomic theory in stimulating ways. A complete list of the applications follows the contents.

Applications are important, but so is the theory itself. Here is a list of topics that were well received in the first edition because they show the relevance of theory to actual markets and real behavior.

> *Perfect competition versus pure competition:* This distinction makes it possible to analyze competitive industries that are not characterized by identical firms but that are still governed by price-taking behavior.
>
> *Multiplant analysis:* Firms commonly operate from numerous plants. This extension draws students closer to the world they see outside the classroom.
>
> *Cartel analysis:* A natural bridge exists between multiplant analysis and cartels, and it unifies the analysis of multiplant monopoly and cartels.
>
> *Consumer surplus:* This topic is especially rich in applications.
>
> *Dominant-firm analysis and applications:* This model is a complete description of the incentives of firms operating at the competitive fringe. It is used to analyze the decision in the "cellophane case."
>
> *Joint products and externalities:* Joint product theory is the core of externalities.

Level of Theory and Applications

Theoretical presentations and applications should be the same level of difficulty. It is pointless to present elegant theory if the applications do not require that much elegance. Moreover, students become frustrated when the applications are more difficult than the theory. In this book, we have emphasized a uniform level of presentation so that students are neither overloaded with unnecessary theory nor presented with applications that they are not prepared for.

Improvements in the Second Edition

We have tried in this edition to engage student interest right from the start. Part of this effort shows in the analytical content of the book. Another part shows in the design and format. This edition features the following improvements:

A thorough rewriting of the entire manuscript.

Imaginative and pleasing design to enhance learning.

A second color, where necessary, to clarify discussions and diagrams.

Completely redrawn and simplified diagrams.

Extensive explanatory figure captions.

Thirty new applications.

Reorganization of some material for smoother presentation and more orderly development of ideas.

Many new end-of-chapter problems.

A new Instructor's Manual, which answers all end-of-chapter questions and provides additional problems and answers.

An end-of-book glossary defining all terms highlighted in the book.

We hope that you enjoy teaching from our book and that your students receive a worthwile and stimulating exposure to microeconomics. Please address your comments on our efforts either to us directly at our respective universities or to Wadsworth Publishing Company.

Acknowledgments

The preparation of this book has been enormously stimulating and a labor of love throughout. We thank Bill Oliver and his capable staff for their excellent editorial assistance along the way. We are grateful to the following reviewers for their suggestions on the manuscript: Ross M. LaRoe, Kalamazoo College; T. S. Ulen, University of Illinois; Harry E. Frech III, University of California, Santa Barbara. Joyce Miezin, our bionic typist, is unexcelled. Thanks also are due to Sandra Craig and Nancy Sjoberg for supervising the editing and production of this book. Rebecca Smith provided excellent copyediting. John Odam designed the book and its cover. Richard Carter supervised the team of artists. Of course, words cannot adequately convey our indebtedness to our wives and children for their constant encouragment and endless patience.

Finally, we extend sincere thanks to our many teachers who have helped us appreciate microeconomic theory. Steven Call's greatest debt is to Richard Wirthlin and Dean Rickenbach, who sparked his interest in economics, and to James Witte and Elmus Wicker, whose superior scholarship and masterful teaching fanned the spark to full flame. Bill Holahan is especially grateful to John Prather Brown for demonstrating the wide applicability of the theory as a device for organizing thoughts and to Martin Beckmann for teaching elegant sneak-attack problem solving. We gratefully acknowledge our many benefactors who, as teachers, colleagues, students, and historical and contemporary scholars, have molded our thinking and deepened our commitment to economic science.

MICROECONOMICS

The Study of Microeconomics

Microeconomic reasoning offers rich insights into human behavior. Thus it can aid us in solving important individual and social problems. It can also be a stimulating field of study, perhaps even the basis for a fulfilling career.

Modern life and contemporary events demand resourcefulness in approaching our chief economic problem—scarcity. Formally, economics is the study of how society chooses to allocate its scarce resources among the relatively unlimited wants of society's members. But focusing narrowly on this formal definition fails to capture the breadth of economic inquiry. Microeconomics encompasses topics like these: (1) the effect of the OPEC cartel and the Mexican oil reserves on the price of gasoline and oil in the United States; (2) ways to price products with irregular demands, such as electricity and mass transit; (3) how price controls on storable resources, such as petroleum, can actually increase current period supplies, thus obscuring and worsening future shortages; (4) the relative work-incentive effects of government programs, such as wage subsidies and negative income taxes, designed to supplement the earnings of poor families; (5) the role of profit as a means of social control and the means by which the search for profits reduces profits; and (6) the most suitable pricing policies in the control of such externalities as pollution and highway congestion. These are only some of the problems that economic analysis can help resolve.

The activities and components of an economic system may be viewed from several perspectives. For example, every economy must answer four basic questions: (1) *What* output is to be produced? (2) *How* is the output to be produced? (3) *When* will the output be produced? (4) *For whom* is the output produced? The first three questions refer to production, and the fourth is a matter of distribution of output among the members of the economy. These basic activities are interconnected and central to a viable economic system.

Another way to inventory the functions of an economy is to scrutinize how it (1) *motivates* its members, (2) *coordinates* their activities, and (3) *distributes* the resulting output. In a free-enterprise system, these functions are performed by a network of legal systems, markets, governments, and a social system made up of families, churches, clubs, and neighborhoods. The members of a free-enterprise system determine not only the quantity of each good to be produced but also the institution that will produce and distribute it. The relationships between markets and society's other institutions are important and often neglected facets of economic inquiry.

1

In the final analysis, economics is a social science that employs the scientific method in studying the economic choices that people make and the consequences of those choices. However, human choices are so complex and interrelated that they cannot be understood without simplification. In response to the need to simplify, economists have developed **theories** and **models,** in which certain assumptions are made in order to reduce problems to manageable and understandable proportions. A road map is a model of the terrain between cities; it is not the terrain itself. And yet a map contains enough information for the purpose at hand—to help drivers reach their destinations. The economist's road map is the model employed to simplify real problems. Some economic models are household words: "supply and demand" and "diminishing returns" no doubt lead the list in name recognition.

Models perform several functions. They simplify and summarize relationships and facts, organize thoughts, and generate testable predictions. Thus models aid and guide learning. Even if the data to test the models do not exist, models can still be useful. All decisions are based on incomplete information, because information is expensive to collect and analyze. Thus economists often use untested models to shape their thinking, organize their thoughts, and aid them in decisionmaking while they wait for the necessary data.

The following chapters present many applications of economic models under the heading "Applied Micro Theory." Some of these applications use theories that have been tested and measured empirically; others suggest ways of tackling particular problems even when the data to test the models are not accessible. Later in your study of economics you may delve into statistics and econometrics, which provide methods of testing theoretical hypotheses. These methods are an important part of economic science. But if you limited yourself to studying only tested theories, you would be restricted to an extremely small subset of the useful models that economists have produced.

Every introductory chapter sould contain one solid piece of advice to students. Here is ours: Economics should be studied in a hard wooden chair—and not during a TV show! With this counsel, we invite you to turn the page and begin to study economics in earnest.

Suggested Readings

Friedman, Milton. "The Methodology of Positive Economics." In *Essays in Positive Economics*, pp. 3–46. Edited by Milton Friedman. Chicago: University of Chicago Press, 1953.

Lange, Oscar. "The Scope and Method of Economics." *Review of Economic Studies* 8 (1945–1946): 12–32.

Wicksteed, Philip H. "The Scope and Method of Political Economy." *Economic Journal* 24 (1914): 1–23.

Supply and Demand

The concepts and applications embodied in the economist's model of supply and demand are among the most important ideas currently being taught in any university. The model of supply and demand facilitates study of the behavior of economic agents in pursuit of their self-interests and provides direction in the formulation of economic policy. It is the cornerstone of economic anaylsis.

This chapter presents an intuitive analysis of supply and demand, leaving rigorous analysis and sophisticated applications to later chapters.

Scarcity, Choice and Opportunity Cost

Two elementary facts face the world and every individual in it: limited resources and relatively unlimited wants. The combination of these two facts creates **scarcity** and the need for individuals and society to make choices among the virtually limitless possible activities that can be undertaken and goods that can be enjoyed. Robert Frost's poem "The Road Not Taken" portrays the inherent need to choose; the horseman could not travel both roads. Likewise, a football player who also plays trumpet cannot play both football and trumpet in the pep band; he must choose. Nor can individual consumers and entire societies produce and consume all they would like. Resource limitations simply do not permit fulfillment of all wants. Thus a college student may have to choose between a summer trip and a new stereo system if she cannot afford both; a city may spend money on rat control and wastewater treatment, but no community has sufficient resources to kill every rat and return all its wastewater to pristine condition. Choice among alternatives is a fact of daily life imposed on us by scarcity.

This need to choose gives rise to a key word in economics—**substitutes.** Consumers, business firms, and governments must constantly evaluate substitute activities, determining what they must give up in order to purchase a good or engage in an activity. Two fundamental constraints on their activities are income and time. Both are limited.

The income constraint enters decisionmaking in a variety of ways. Current income can be spent or saved, and people can borrow against future income. People can invest in their brains (students), brawn (athletes), or beauty (movie starlets) to increase their incomes; or they can choose an esthetic, meaningful inner life and content themselves with lower incomes (university professors). Some people have high incomes and others low, but no one is released from the constraint that a limited income imposes on the enjoyment of goods and services.

2

A prominent church recently constructed a skyscraper on Manhattan Island. The first two floors of the building are used as office space and local headquarters for the church; the rest of the building, except for the third floor, is rented apartment space. The third floor contains a worship chapel for the use of church members on Manhattan Island. What is the opportunity cost of reserving the third floor of this skyscraper for a worship chapel that is used, at most, 10 hours a week?

Many people, unschooled in thinking about costs in terms of alternatives forgone, are inclined to say that the opportunity cost of the chapel is low because the revenue from the rented apartments easily covers the cost. But this response confuses benefits with costs. The cost of the chapel is the highest-valued forgone use of the third floor, which most likely is additional apartment or office space. Of course, the benefits of such a location may exceed these opportunity costs, but we must never mix benefits and costs. It is important to see opportunity costs for what they are—the value of the most preferred forgone option.

The time constraint also enters decisions in numerous ways. Each person has 24 hours per day to divide between daytime and nighttime activities. The average person lives about 70 years. These facts place boundaries on our activities. Within narrow limits, weight reduction and jogging one's cardiovascular system into good condition can relax these time constraints. The constraints can also be tightened considerably by overeating. Or one can combine the two strategies: stay in perfect condition (jog) but terrible shape (overeat) and hope to last 70 years.

In any case, all activities require some income and/or some time, which leads to a second key concept in economics. **Opportunity (alternative) cost** is the value of the best forgone option. When you select one among many substitute ways of spending your limited income and time, you choose the most valuable option and leave a rather long list of alternative wants unfulfilled. Suppose you go to a movie, spending $5 for a ticket and 2 hours in time. You have many other uses for that income and time, but you chose the movie. The most sensible and complete way of describing the cost of the movie is to measure the value of the best forgone option. Your money and time have alternative uses that you forgo by going to the movie. The value of your time and money in their next most valuable and forgone use is the opportunity cost of the movie. Even if your best friend is the ticket taker and lets you in free, the opportunity cost is not zero, because your time could have been spent in other valuable ways. The money price of an activity may be zero, but the opportunity cost is never zero as long as alternatives exist.

Resources have not only alternative uses in the current period but also alternative time periods of use. Consumers decide what proportion of their incomes to spend on goods and services in the current period and what proportion to save for future consumption. Sellers decide whether to sell all their available inventories in the current period or to hold some back for future sale. Decisions like these cannot be made effectively without evaluating the benefits and opportunity costs of particular choices. But the opportunity cost is the same as before: Using a resource in one time period forecloses the option of using the resource in the next most valuable time period. Opportunity costs are always measured by the value of forgone options.

The opportunity costs of goods are usually measured in terms of their money prices. But even under ideal market circumstances, prices reflect full opportunity costs only if the time costs of consumption are negligible and if the price accurately reflects the costs of the goods. Exceptions abound: Monopolists charge prices in excess of money costs; bus fares alone don't measure passenger costs, because they do not include time costs; the price of an energy source may fail to reflect the costs of environmental damage incurred as a by-product of production. Thus prices are only a rough

Price versus Cost

<table>
<tr><td>APPLIED
MICRO
THEORY

2.2</td></tr>
</table>

Learning about economics often requires one to distinguish between the ordinary meanings of words in everyday English and the specific, scientific meanings of those words when they are used formally by economists. For example, the words *price* and *cost* are often used interchangeably in ordinary English. But they mean different things to economists. **Price** is the amount of money (or goods in a barter economy) that a buyer gives to a seller in exchange for a good or service. In contrast, **cost** is the forgone value in other uses of the resources devoted to the production of a good or service. Price represents a money payment, whereas cost measures the value of opportunities forgone. Under some circumstances, product price equals the opportunity cost of production. In many circumstances, however, price and

cost are not the same. Consider the following examples, which will be described in more detail throughout the book.

Electricity Pricing
The cost of producing electric power is low during periods of slack demand (3:00 A.M.) and higher during periods of peak demand (11:00 A.M. on weekdays). When electricity is priced at a fixed rate, without regard to the actual cost of generation at time of use, price does not reflect cost.

Price Controls
Price ceilings hold down money prices but produce shortages, which in turn raise customers' costs. Consider the time wasted

standing in line, the inconvenience of not knowing whether a product will be available, higher search costs, the need to buy less-preferred products in order to reduce waiting time and aggravation, reductions in product quality, and discrimination against surplus buyers because of race, age or sex.

Monopoly Pricing
Firms with monopoly power often set prices far above costs. Hence monopoly and cartel prices do not reflect the value of the resources devoted to producing the product.

Pollution
Many firms dump their waste materials into the air and water without paying any fee. The price of such pollution to these firms is zero, even though the cost of pollution to society, measured in terms of the environmental damages and forgone opportunities, may be immense.

guide to opportunity costs; there are occasions when money prices need to be adjusted in order to evaluate the full opportunity cost of certain activities.

Much of economics consists of evaluating the benefits and (opportunity) costs of alternative actions. Consider the drug safety law of 1962, which complicated the research and testing processes required prior to putting a drug on the market. There are two types of errors in drug marketing: placing harmful drugs on the market too soon and delaying the marketing of good drugs too long. The 1962 law had the benefit of increasing the safety of drugs available to consumers but also imposed the cost of delaying helpful drugs. One investigator estimated that this law, which tended to delay the marketing of new drugs an average of two years, imposed an opportunity cost approximately ten times greater than the associated benefits.[1] Unless there is waste in the system, we cannot lessen one error without enlarging the other. We must always evaluate the tradeoffs, keeping in mind the concepts of opportunity cost and substitution in response to scarcity.

1. Sam Peltzman, "An Examination of Consumer Protection Legislation: The 1962 Drug Amendments," *Journal of Political Economy* 81 (1973): 1049–1091.

Demand

Consider a familiar product, McDonald's Big Mac. Someone who was thinking of buying a Big Mac would have some alternatives, including other fast foods (the Colonel's fried chicken, for example), medium-speed food (restaurants with tablecloths and waitresses), slow food (home cooking), or no food (dieting or fasting). Even the most ardent Big Mac devotee would rely more heavily on these substitutes if the money or time cost of the Big Mac rose while the costs of the substitutes stayed the same. Consumers buy fewer Big Macs at high prices than at low prices. This inverse relationship between product price and the amount consumers purchase is observed so regularly that it is called the **law of demand.**

Let's consider another example, natural gas. Table 2.1 lists the uses of natural gas and substitutes in the event that the price of natural gas rises. Although there may be no substitutes for using natural gas in an existing furnace, hot water heater, stove, or appliance, there are substitute ways to heat and cook. It is also possible to reduce or eliminate some uses. In time, the existing furnace or stove may even be replaced by one that uses less gas or a different fuel.

Table 2.1
Uses and Substitutes for Natural Gas

Uses	Possible Substitutes
Home heating	Reduce heat in some rooms Lower thermostat and wear sweater Insulate house Use oil heat Use coal heat Use solar heat Move to the Sun Belt
Heating domestic hot water	Reduce water temperature Turn off water heater at night Use electric razor for shaving Take showers instead of tub baths Take fewer showers (when cleanliness is costly, some filth is optimal)
Running clothes dryer	Use clothes line Use electric dryer Buy drip-dry clothes Wash clothes less frequently
Cooking	Cook more stove-top meals Buy new, smaller oven Cook in microwave oven Use electric stove Use wood stove Eat cold food Cook meals that use less energy (eggs instead of turkey) Cook in bulk and save leftovers for cold meals
Lighting decorative gas lamps	Switch to electric lamps Use decorative lamps less often

People become interested in substitutes for natural gas because the law of demand is at work in the natural gas market. When natural gas prices rise, consumers seek relatively less costly substitutes; when prices drop, buyers shift away from gas substitutes and toward natural gas. Note the central role of substitutes in deriving the law of demand.

The Big Mac and natural gas examples emphasize the importance of price in consumers' buying decisions. Yet there are other factors that influence these decisions as well. We need a definition of demand that takes into account all the factors that influence consumer buying. Equation 2.1 is a useful beginning point:

$$Q_d = f(P, P^s, P^c, I, N, \ldots) \tag{2.1}$$

where

Q_d = quantity demanded of the good
P = product price
P^s = price of substitutes
P^c = price of complements
I = consumer income
N = number of consumers
$\ldots$ = all other factors not mentioned explicitly

This demand equation indicates that the quantity of a good consumers wish to buy depends on many factors, including the price of the good, the prices of substitutes and complements, consumer income, the number of consumers demanding the good, and a variety of other factors. The ellipsis dots in Equation 2.1 emphasize that demand is ordinarily affected by many more factors than the few listed explicitly in the equation, including fads, time to adjust, expectations of price changes, laws, regulations, and customs. This demand equation stresses an important fact: **Demand** is the multidimensional relationship between the quantity consumed and the factors that determine how much is consumed.

The diagrammatic representation of the demand equation is a **demand curve.** And here we face a problem common to nearly every aspect of microeconomics and macroeconomics: How can a multidimensional relationship be illustrated in two dimensions? Equation 2.2 illustrates the analytic technique involved:

$$Q_d = f(P, \underbrace{P^s, P^c, I, N, \ldots}_{\substack{\text{shift} \\ \text{parameters}}}) \tag{2.2}$$

movement
parameter

The determinants of demand are divided into two groups: a **movement parameter** (price) and **shift parameters** (all demand deter-

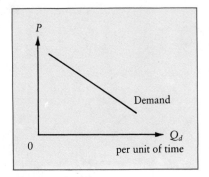

Figure 2.1
The Demand Curve

The demand curve is negatively sloped because consumers seek out less costly substitutes when price rises, *ceteris paribus.*

minants except price). Holding the values of all shift parameters constant, we can trace out a two-dimensional relationship between the movement parameter (P) and quantity demanded (Q_d). The visual result is the demand curve, illustrated in Figure 2.1. Price is measured on the vertical axis and quantity demanded on the horizontal axis.

Note that the curve in Figure 2.1 is negatively sloped. This slope is the graphic expression of the law of demand: Consumers buy less at higher prices. The demand curves for Big Macs and natural gas are negatively sloped like the demand curve in Figure 2.1. Holding all shift parameters constant, price and quantity demanded are inversely related.

We now have a precise definition of the demand curve: the relationship between the quantities of a good that consumers are willing to buy and all possible prices, in a specified time period, *ceteris paribus.* The phrase in *a specified time period* emphasizes that demand is a flow of purchases over time. Any specific quantity demanded occurs in a specific time period. The Latin phrase **ceteris paribus** means "others things constant." Holding the shift parameters constant allows us to focus on the relationship between price and quantity and to draw a demand curve in two dimensions.

Table 2.2 shows that the information contained in a demand curve can be summarized in a table, although only a few data points can be shown. The demand curve and its tabular equivalent remind us that demand is not a single number (say 2000 cubic feet of natural gas); rather, it encompasses the number of units desired at each price, *ceteris paribus.*

Table 2.2
Quantity Demanded for Natural Gas

Price of Natural Gas per 1000 Cubic Feet	Quantity of Natural Gas Demanded per Specified Time Period
70¢	1200 cu. ft.
60	1600
50	2000
40	2400
30	2800

$\times$ Now consider the solid demand curve, D_0, in Figure 2.2. If the price rises from P_0 to P_1, consumers will cut purchases from Q_0 to Q_1. The price increase causes a movement from point A to point B along the same demand curve. This is not a change in demand, because demand encompasses all points on the curve, *ceteris paribus.* It is true, however, that the higher price reduces the quantity demanded from Q_0 to Q_1. Movement along a stationary demand curve is a change in **quantity demanded,** not a change in demand.

Demand changes only when the entire demand curve shifts, as illustrated by the shift from demand curve D_0 to D_1. The demand curve shifts only when the values of the shift parameters change. We will study the specific causes of demand shifts later. For now, recognize that a change in demand means only one thing: Consumers want to purchase a different amount of output than before *at each price*. At point C on demand curve D, consumers have reduced the quantity demanded from Q_0 to Q_1 at the same price P_0. Point A and point C lie on different demand curves at the same price (P_0) and therefore indicate a change in demand. In essence, the original demand curve, D_0, disappears and is replaced with a new price-quantity relationship, D_1.

This discussion about demand has made a distinction that is of incalculable significance: Movement along a stationary demand curve is caused *only* by a change in price (the movement parameter), holding all shift parameters constant. Price is the movement parameter because only changes in price cause movements along the demand curve. It is conventional to call movement along a stationary demand curve a **change in quantity demanded.** Shift of the demand curve is caused *only* by a change in one or more of the shift parameters and appears as a shift of the entire demand curve. The shift parameters are so named because changes in their values shift the demand curve. It is conventional to call a shift of a demand curve a **change in demand.**

Demand has now been described in four ways: verbally, graphically (Figure 2.1), as a schedule (Table 2.2), and as a function (Equation 2.2). You must learn to recognize the demand concept in any of its many disguises.

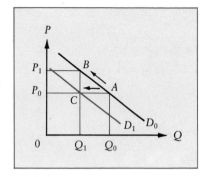

Figure 2.2
The Demand Curve: Movements versus Shifts

The movement from A to B along demand curve D_0 is a reduction in quantity demanded due to a price increase. The shift from demand curve D_0 to D_1 is a reduction in demand, because consumers want to purchase less at each price.

Supply

We can approach the subject of supply intuitively by returning to our Big Mac example. What is McDonald's supply response to higher prices for fast food? The central concept is again substitution—in this case, substitute methods of producing more Big Macs. Some of the possibilities are

More grill and storage space for Big Macs.

More restaurant locations.

More-expensive equipment.

More-expensive and better-trained workers.

More workers per Big Mac.

Faster service.

When Big Mac prices are low compared to costs, McDonald's has little profit incentive to sell many Big Macs or to engage in high-cost production techniques. However, at higher prices the firm has the incentive to adopt some higher-cost production methods. Firms reevaluate alternative production and sales techniques and increase the quantities supplied when product price rises, *ceteris paribus*. Output usually cannot be increased without increasing average production costs. Thus firms are usually unwilling to increase costs by expanding production unless they have reasonable expectations of higher prices.

On the supply side of the natural gas market, the following production substitutes may be induced by higher prices:

1. Sell to different markets
   a. Home
   b. Industry
   c. Agriculture

2. Explore more
   a. Offshore
   b. In Alaska
   c. Off New York coast
   d. Near known sources

3. Extract more from existing wells
   a. Dig deeper
   b. Explode rock formations

4. Transfer natural gas being saved for future sales to the current market

5. Import more from Russia and Malaysia

As the price rises, natural gas suppliers get the message, communicated by profit impulses, to increase the quantity of gas supplied by engaging in production methods that would not be profitable at lower gas prices.

Now a formal definition of the **supply curve:** the relationship between the quantities of a good that suppliers are willing to sell and all possible prices, for a specified time period, *ceteris paribus*.

The definition of supply, the depiction of the supply curve, the distinction between movement along a stationary supply curve and a shift in the supply curve, and the problem of illustrating a multi-dimensional supply concept in two dimensions closely parallel the demand discussion. In functional notation, supply may be represented as

$$Q_s = f(P, \underbrace{w, r, T, \ldots}_{})$$ (2.3)

movement parameter   shift parameters

where

Q_s = quantity supplied
P = product price
w = price of labor
r = price of capital
T = level of technology

As with demand, **supply** is the multidimensional relationship between the **quantity supplied** and all of its determinants. Such an unwieldy concept is made tractable by breaking it into its component parts—the movement parameter and shift parameters. Like demand, the movement parameter for supply is price. However, the supply shift parameters usually differ from the demand shift parameters. Equation 2.3 includes three specific shift parameters: the price of labor, the price of capital, and the level of technology. The three ellipsis dots allow for the inclusion of other relevant supply determinants, such as weather, transportation costs, government regulation, taxes, producer expectations, and so forth.

The supply curve is the two-dimensional relationship between the movement parameter (P) and the quantity supplied (Q_s), holding all shift parameters constant. Supply curve S_0 in Figure 2.3 is drawn with a positive slope. The movement from point A to point B is movement along a stationary supply curve or, alternatively, a **change in quantity supplied** (in this case, an increase). It results from an increase in the movement parameter, which is price. On the other hand, the shift from supply curve S_0 to S_1 is a **change in supply** (also an increase) resulting from improvements in technology, reductions in price of the factors of production, or similar cost-reducing changes in other shift parameters. When production costs fall, the firm has a profit incentive to sell more output *at each price*. This is the meaning of an increase in supply. Movement from point A to point C represents an increase in supply; more is offered for sale at the same price. But remember: For supply to increase at a given price, one or more of the shift parameters must change.

As with demand, supply may be expressed verbally, graphically, as a schedule, and in functional form. One pleasing feature of microeconomics is that analytical methods learned in one context often carry over into others. If you understand demand, supply should be child's play.

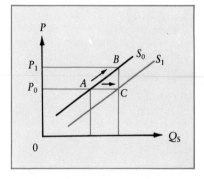

Figure 2.3
The Supply Curve: Movements versus Shifts

The movement from A to B along supply curve S_0 is an increase in quantity supplied due to a price increase. The shift from supply curve S_0 to S_1 is an increase in supply, because firms wish to sell more at each price.

Market Equilibrium, Shortages, and Surpluses

Thus far we have encountered two market forces—supply and demand. Although each is influenced by price, neither supply nor demand by itself can determine price. Actual market prices are determined by the balance of these two market forces.

Figure 2.4
Market Equilibrium

Equilibrium price is P_e and equilibrium quantity is Q_e. All shortages and surpluses are eliminated in equilibrium.

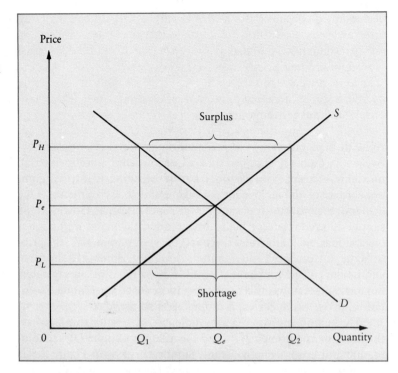

Figure 2.4 combines supply and demand curves. Is there one price toward which the market will move, or is the actual price random? As a matter of fact, the price tends to approach P_e, the **equilibrium price.** Equilibrium describes a state of balance, a position of rest, or a position that can be maintained if achieved. Why is the price P_e the only possible price "at rest," or the only price that can last?

Consider price P_L, a price below the equilibrium price. At price P_L the quantity demanded, Q_2, exceeds the quantity supplied, Q_1. This difference is an excess demand, or **shortage.** At price P_L firms have little profit incentive to produce, even though consumers wish to purchase in large quantities because they regard this good favorably in comparison to its relatively more expensive substitutes. But only Q_1 units will be available at P_L, because the supply decisions of firms limit availability. The price P_L cannot be maintained, because the disappointed buyers will begin to bid for the limited supplies by offering higher prices. Shortages tend to disappear in uncontrolled markets by the upward price haggling of disappointed consumers. As price rises, there are movements along both curves: Price increases encourage firms to sell more and consumers to buy less. In this way the shortage is eliminated. The price P_e is the limit of this price increase because at price P_e the quantity demanded equals the quantity supplied, both Q_e. At price P_e there are no disappointed consumers (or sellers), and the previous forces urging price increases have run their course. With all market participants satisfied, the price P_e is sustainable; the market is in equilibrium.

Suppose the price rises temporarily above P_e, to P_H. Now there is an excess supply, or **surplus.** At price P_H, firms wish to sell many units in order to increase profits, whereas the high price discourages buyers and pushes them toward more attractive substitutes. Thus the firms will be unable to sell their desired quantities, and unwanted inventories will accumulate. But the surplus will be eliminated as firms lower their prices in order to reduce unwanted inventories. These price reductions eliminate the surplus partly by inducing firms to produce less but also by increasing the quantities demanded by consumers. As before, the price will stop falling once a price is achieved that balances the desires of both buyers and sellers. This occurs only at price P_e.

The process by which prices are bid up and down can be simple or complex. The simplest bidding process is an auction, where buyers and sellers bid personally in response to shortages and surpluses. In the stock market, buyers and sellers make bids through an agent—the stockbroker. In most other markets, such as food, drugs, clothing, and hardware, long strings of intermediaries between the original manufacturer and the final consumer make personal bidding impossible. Still, a shortage is evidence to sellers of buyers' willingness to pay higher prices rather than go without some units of the good. Thus shortages send signals to sellers, all the way from retail stores to the manufacturer, to raise prices, even though buyers are not personally offering higher prices. And as prices rise, shortages are eliminated.

Equilibrium price is usually not achieved and maintained immediately after a market disturbance, as in the movement of an arrow to its target; rather, equilibrium is a central tendency, a price toward which the market moves. Just as a marble dropped into a fruit bowl will roll around before it reaches a resting position (equilibrium), so may market prices tend to overshoot or undershoot as they move ever closer to an equilibrium position.

Demand and supply are written in functional form as follows:

$$\text{Demand} = Q_d = f(P, P^s, P^c, I, N, \ldots) \qquad \textbf{(2.4)}$$

$$\text{Supply} = Q_s = f(P, w, r, T, \ldots) \qquad \textbf{(2.5)}$$

Holding all nonprice shift parameters constant, Equations 2.4 and 2.5 are the algebraic equivalents of the demand and supply curves.

Equilibrium is achieved by finding the price that equates the quantity supplied and the quantity demanded. Equilibrium price is found by setting Equations 2.4 and 2.5 equal and solving for price.

$$Q_s = Q_d \tag{2.6}$$

equilibrium condition

The price that satisfies Equation 2.6 eliminates shortages and surpluses. Equation 2.6 is the algebraic equivalent of the intersection of supply and demand curves. It is the solution to the system of simultaneous equations contained in Equations 2.4 and 2.5.

To summarize, undesired inventories force prices down whenever price exceeds equilibrium, whereas unsatisfied consumer demands force prices up when price is less than equilibrium. In a free market, surpluses and shortages tend to be self-eliminating as the market pushes toward equilibrium. Price—the movement parameter—plays the dominant role in market analysis because it is the only economic variable that always influences both the supply and demand sides of the market.

Demand and Supply Curve Shifts

Consider the following demand function for natural gas:

$$Q_d = f(P, P^s, P^c, I, \text{weather}, \ldots) \tag{2.7}$$

Figure 2.5
Shift of the Demand Curve

(a) The demand for natural gas increases (shifts) when the price rises for number-2 heating oil, a substitute. (b) A price increase results in a reduction in the quantity demanded of number-2 heating oil.

For initial values of the shift parameters P^s (prices of substitutes), P^c (prices of complements), I (income), weather, and all other factors, there is a two-dimensional relationship between price and quantity demanded. Equation 2.7 delineates the solid demand curve for natural gas, labeled D_0 in Figure 2.5a. Let's see how the demand curve

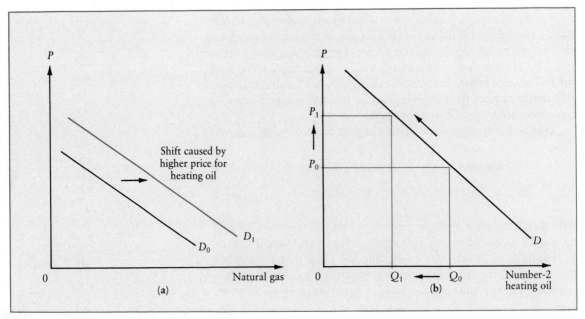

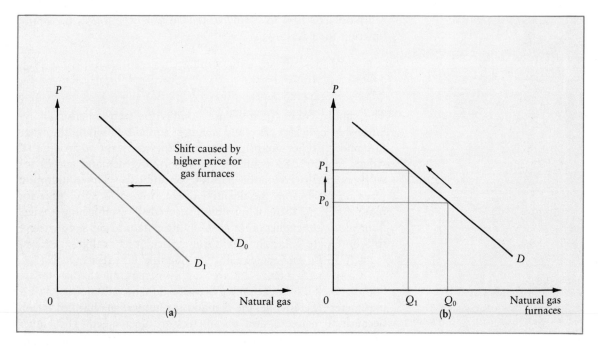

(a)   (b)

shifts when the values of these shift parameters change.

Suppose that the price of number-2 heating oil, a substitute for natural gas, rises from P_0 to P_1 in Figure 2.5*b*. Consumers will purchase less heating oil than before and, as a result, will want more natural gas at each price of natural gas. The higher price of the substitute shifts the natural gas demand curve from D_0 to D_1 (to the right in Figure 2.5*a*).

If the price of a **complement** (a good used in conjunction with the good in question) rises, the demand curve shifts to the left. Thus an increase in the price of gas furnaces from P_0 to P_1 reduces consumers' desire to buy natural gas at each price, as illustrated in Figure 2.6.

Finally, nothing alters one's appreciation for natural gas as a home-heating fuel so much as changes in the weather. In Figure 2.7, the natural gas demand curve for a warm winter, D_0, shifts to D_1 for a normal winter and to D_2 for a cold winter.

A full discussion of the income shift parameter will be postponed until Chapter 3 because of its special role in economic analysis. Suffice it to say that an increase in income may shift the demand curves for chicken necks and caviar differently. People may reduce their consumption of chicken necks when their incomes rise because they can afford higher-quality and more-expensive foods. If so, chicken necks are considered "inferior goods." On the other hand, higher incomes may induce greater consumption of caviar, a "normal good." (See Chapter 3 for a more technically precise discussion of normal and inferior goods.)

Figure 2.6
Shift of the Demand Curve

(a) The demand for natural gas falls (shifts) when the price rises for gas furnaces, a complement. (b) When prices increase, there is a reduction in the quantity demanded of gas furnaces.

Figure 2.7
Shift of the Demand Curve

The demand for natural gas is greater during a cold winter than a warm winter.

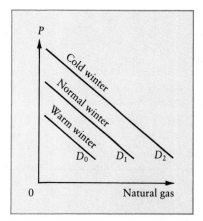

Now let's turn to supply shifts. Consider the following supply function for natural gas:

$$Q_s = f(P, w, \ldots) \tag{2.8}$$

The supply curve S_0 in Figure 2.8a is the two-dimensional relationship between price and quantity supplied, holding the wage rate and all other nonprice supply factors constant at their initial values. Figure 2.8b contains the supply and demand curves for workers employed in the natural gas industry. The equilibrium wage w_0 establishes the position of the original supply curve for natural gas, S_0. If the labor union succeeds in establishing a wage floor of w_1, the higher labor costs shift the natural gas supply curve to S_1 in Figure 2.8a. The equilibrium price of natural gas increases from P_0 to P_1, and the equilibrium quantity falls from Q_0 to Q_1.

Caution: In Figure 2.8 the supply of natural gas has fallen. Suppliers sell less at each price because of higher labor costs, a shift parameter. Meanwhile, the demand for natural gas has not fallen, because all demand shift parameters are unchanged. The higher price causes a movement along the stationary demand curve, D_0. Thus quantity demanded has fallen; demand has not.

Figure 2.8
Shift of the Supply Curve

(a) The supply of natural gas falls (shifts) when wage costs rise, resulting in a rise in price. (b) The wage rises from w_0 to w_1 through union bargaining.

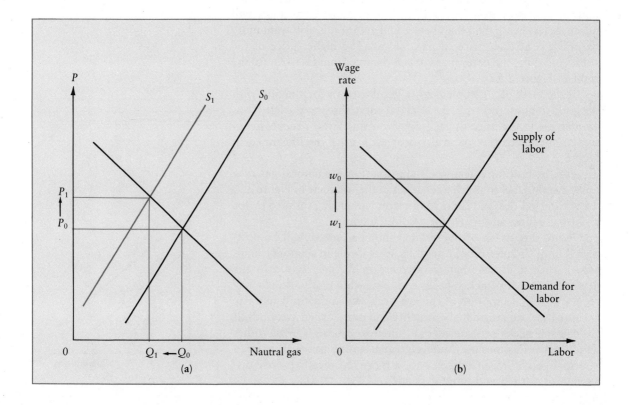

(a)   (b)

The Fallacy of Composition

APPLIED MICRO THEORY

2.3

One fallacy of logic that often plagues economic analysis is the **fallacy of composition**. This fallacy is committed when someone argues that what is true of the part must also be true of the whole. For example: "Any one individual can exit the theater in less than 30 seconds. Thus all individuals can exit the theater in less than 30 seconds." To argue that what is true of one individual (the part) when acting alone is necessarily true of all individuals (the whole) when acting together is to commit the fallacy of composition.

Say that Farmer Brown tries to increase his income by planting an additional field of corn. Assuming constant weather, rain, and other growing conditions, he may well be able to increase his income. But it is foolish to extend the argument and say that all farmers can increase their incomes by increasing corn acreage. Farmer Brown is such a small component of the corn market that his decision cannot affect market price. Thus he may be able to sell more corn at a constant price and thereby increase his income. But if all farmers simultaneously increase corn acreage, the effect will be to increase the corn supply, reduce the market price of corn, and increase the quantity of corn sold. The possibility exists that more corn sold at a lower price could actually reduce total farm income.

Economic analysis is replete with similar situations. Indeed, the next several chapters will develop market demand and supply curves from individual demand and supply curves. The process of aggregation is important in economics, so we must be careful not to allow the fallacy of composition to interfere with clear thinking.

Comparative Statics

APPLIED MICRO THEORY

2.4

Comparative statics, a term used frequently in this book and all other microeconomic books you will read, is a method of comparing different equilibrium positions. For example, if the original demand and supply curves are D_0 and S_0 in the accompanying figure, the initial equilibrium price and equilibrium quantity sold are P_0 and Q_0. Now suppose that the demand curve shifts to the right, to D_1. The increase in demand increases both price and quantity sold, to P_1 and Q_1. By changing one shift parameter at a time, we can compare the initial equilibrium with the new equilibrium. This comparison is comparative statics. Use of the word *statics* emphasizes that we are interested in only the beginning and ending equilibrium values and not in the dynamic processes of adjustment. The dynamics of change, such as the timing of the adjustment, are important but not relevant in static analysis.

Comparative static analysis is also applicable with multiple changes in shift parameters, although qualitative predictions may become clouded. For example, if supply falls to S_1 at the same time that demand increases to D_1, equilibrium price could increase to P_2. But these shifts would have an ambiguous effect on equilibrium quantity. Under these conditions, information about the relative magnitude of the demand and supply shifts is necessary in order to determine the comparative static effect on quantity sold.

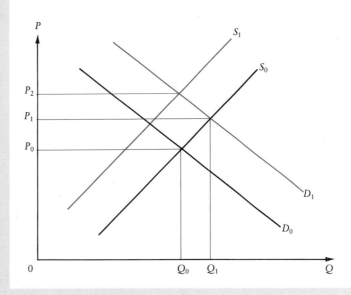

Comparative statics is the comparison of market equilibria before and after a market disturbance.

Comparative Statics in Related Markets

APPLIED
MICRO
THEORY

2.5

Changes in the static equilibrium of one market may set off a chain reaction among closely related markets. Suppose that the supply of labor available for drilling petroleum falls from S_0^L to S_1^L, as shown in Figure A. The static equilibrium readjusts to a higher wage rate and lower quantity of labor. However, the wage rate is a shift parameter in the supply curve of petroleum, as shown in Figure B. When wages rise, the supply of petroleum falls from S_0^P to S_1^P, and the equilibrium price rises from P_0^P to P_1^P. In turn, the supply of antifreeze is affected by all input prices, one of which is the price of petroleum. Thus when wages rise, antifreeze supply falls and its equilibrium price rises, as seen in

Figure C. In short, when the static equilibrium solution values are shift parameters in other markets, a change in one market rattles around the system and disturbs all equilibrium values in a chain reaction.

Figure A

A reduction in the labor supply increases wages.

Figure B

Higher wages reduce the supply of petroleum and increase the price of petroleum.

Figure C

Higher petroleum prices reduce the supply of antifreeze and increase antifreeze prices.

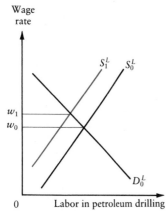

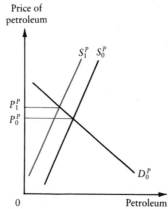

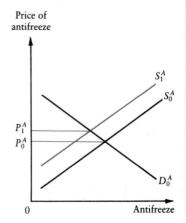

Can Subsidies Provide a Free Lunch?

APPLIED
MICRO
THEORY

2.6

The verity "There is no such thing as a free lunch" expresses succinctly the essence of opportunity cost: You cannot get something for nothing, because everything has an alternative use. However, governments often attempt to give us a "free lunch" by subsidizing the production or consumption of various goods. A **subsidy** is the difference between the price that buyers pay and the price that sellers receive. Supply and demand theory helps us investigate the effects of subsidies.

In the figure, the presubsidy supply and demand curves, S_0 and D_0, establish the initial equilibrium values for price and quantity, P_0 and Q_0. Whether the government chooses to subsidize the producers or the consumers, the results will be the same.

Let's begin with a subsidy paid to suppliers. Say that the seller receives a total payment equal to the price the consumer pays augmented by the per-unit subsidy. This subsidy increases the supply curve from S_0 to S_1. As a result, a larger quantity of output than before will be supplied at each consumer price. The new supply curve lies below the old one by exactly the amount of the per-unit subsidy. The subsidy therefore reduces the consumer price to P_1 and raises output to Q_1. Direct consumer expenditure on the good is now $0P_1 \cdot 0Q_1$, or the area $0P_1LQ_1$. The total subsidy is the per-unit subsidy times units sold, $P_1P_2 \cdot 0Q_1$, or the area P_1P_2RL. But the subsidy must be paid from taxes, an indirect consumer payment. Thus the total consumer expenditure for the good—the direct payment plus the taxes to cover the subsidy—equals the area $0P_2RQ_1$. This amount is larger than the presubsidy expenditure, $0P_0NQ_0$, as you can easily see in the figure. Subsidies,

by encouraging expenditures in select markets, transfer resources from other markets. Thus they do not provide a free lunch. The fact that the direct price the consumer pays is lower than before should not blind us to the true opportunity costs of expanding output in subsidized markets.

The results are the same when the government subsidizes consumers instead of producers.

The subsidy shifts the demand schedule D_0 to D_1, the vertical distance between D_0 and D_1 being the per-unit subsidy to buyers. The new demand curve must pass through point R, because R lies vertically above L by the amount of the subsidy. In equilibrium, price and quantity increase to P_2 and Q_1. But these equilibrium results are the same as when the subsidy is given to the producer.

Now is a perfect time to distinguish between price and cost. Subsidies cannot provide a free lunch in the sense of giving us more output at a lower cost. All they can do is provide a low-priced lunch that costs a lot.

Per-unit subsidies achieve the same results, whether given to buyers or sellers. Consumer subsidies shift the demand curve, and producer subsidies shift the supply curve.

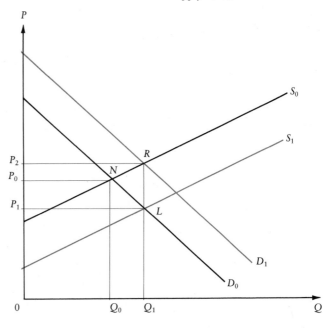

The Functions of the Market

Now that we have seen how market forces determine prices, let's study the social significance of prices. In the process of determining prices and output, a market system provides guidance, rationing, information, impersonality, allocation of tasks, and freedom.

Guidance

To understand the guidance function of the market, suppose that the supply and demand for honey (see Figure 2.9) determine the initial equilibrium price P_0 and quantity Q_0. Now assume that the market for honey rises from D_0 to D_1. The initial shortage AB is eliminated by price adjustments as the new price P_1 and output Q_1 are approached. Higher honey prices encourage profit-motivated producers to increase their production and sales of honey. Thus the increased consumer demand for honey is communicated to suppliers via price adjustments, and these price adjustments encourage firms to produce the additional honey that consumers demand.

In this way society's scarce resources are channeled toward uses that consumers prefer. Resources are guided by the pricing mechanism; price adjustments signal firms to increase production when increases in demand raise prices and to decrease production when reductions in demand reduce prices. Prices coordinate the commu-

Figure 2.9
The Market Guidance Function

An increase in demand raises price and attracts resources into the market.

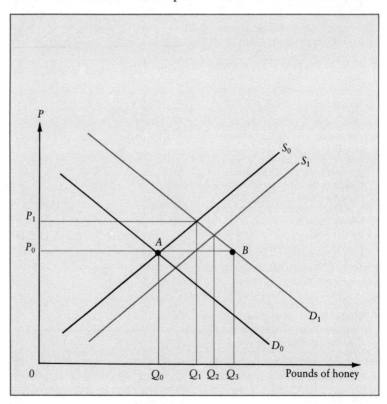

nication between buyers and sellers, communication that must take other forms in nonmarket economies.

In the honey example, the output of existing firms will tend to rise in the short run from Q_0 to Q_1. In the longer run, higher prices may even attract new firms from other industries if expected profits in the honey industry exceed the profits in their present occupations. If new firms are attracted into the industry, the output of honey will increase to Q_2, and prices will fall.

In summary, increases in consumer demand increase prices, which gives established honey-producing firms the incentive to increase production in the short run and also attracts new honey producers in the longer run. Resources are directed toward honey production and away from alternative uses, and the guiding mechanism is price.

Rationing

In Figure 2.9 the initial increase in the demand for honey from D_0 to D_1 causes a shortage, AB. The sellers' quantity supplied of Q_0 units places a limit on the amount of honey that consumers can buy at price P_0, even though they want to purchase the larger quantity Q_3 at that price. How is it decided which customers to disappoint and which uses of honey to forgo? This is clearly a **price rationing** problem.

The most straightforward rationing device is price rationing, under which prices would rise. Honey producers would increase their quantities of honey supplied at higher prices, whereas consumers would reduce their quantities demanded by switching to honey substitutes and by eliminating less important uses of honey. In Figure 2.9, when the price rises to P_1, the initial shortage AB is rationed among buyers by price adjustments and, in the process, is eliminated. In nonmarket or controlled-market economies, other means must be used to allocate such shortages among consumers.

Information

The price system provides information to market participants at low cost. Producers use market prices to determine consumer interest in their products. Consumers decide on the quantity and variety of goods to buy by checking their relative prices. In addition, the market provides information about the location and availability of goods. If you know the location of a gas station, you usually know the location of gas. However, this was not true in 1979, when gas shortages induced by price controls and the associated waiting lines, quotas, and unexpected closings of gas stations made it very difficult to know where to buy gasoline. The search and information costs for determining the location, availability, and quality of goods rise whenever nonprice rationing systems are substituted for price rationing.

Impersonality

The price system operates on money transactions. Any buyer who can pay the asking price can buy the good. This impersonal nature of market transactions has two important implications. First, the market satisfies demands, not needs. Goods and services are obtained by those who can pay for them, even though legitimate needs and wants of other consumers remain unfulfilled because of their inability to pay market prices. The market responds strictly to purchasing power and, in this sense, has no conscience.

The second aspect of impersonal markets is the anonymity with which goods are bought and sold. At the equilibrium price, the quantity supplied equals the quantity demanded, so there are no extra customers in the market, as there are during shortages. Thus sellers cannot refuse to serve customers without sacrificing profits, because customers who are turned away can go elsewhere to purchase their goods. During shortages, sellers typically refuse to sell to some customers for two reasons: (1) discrimination against the customer based on personal characteristics (such as race, religion, or sex) and (2) discrimination against the customer based on "worthiness" (which customers are the most important?). Under price controls, waiting lines of unsatisfied customers make it possible for sellers to pick and choose among customers without loss in profits. Thus the impersonality of the market system, where goods must be sold to anyone with enough money, serves as an imperfect but important check on discriminatory behavior and, in general, protects against the abuse of power.

Allocation of Tasks

When buyers and sellers can use prices as signals, they can readily calculate and compare benefits and costs arising from their choices. All consumers and firms must decide whether to rely on the market to provide goods, services, training, and opportunities or whether to seek a degree of **vertical integration** by owning goods outright and providing services themselves. For example, consumers can hire all their typing services in the marketplace, or they can buy a typewriter and learn to type. Firms can rely on markets to provide the resources needed for production, or they can vertically integrate by producing and storing the necessary resources themselves. An efficient balance between vertical integration and market reliance depends on the benefits and costs of the alternatives. The benefits and costs are conveyed by market prices.

Freedom

No economic system can free its citizens from the scarcity imposed on society by limited resource and time constraints. But within these constraints, the market system allows its participants the freedom to make buying and selling decisions based on the relative prices of goods and services. Choices concerning where to work, where to live, when and where to go to school, and what goods and services to buy are individual decisions. Of course, free agency brings a corresponding responsibility for one's own acts, and people either enjoy or suffer the consequences of their economic decisions. Still, a market system functions most effectively when its participants are free to change occupation, residence, and purchasing patterns as prices change.

Buyer and Seller Response to Nonprice Rationing

To further emphasize the services that the market provides, let's examine consumers' and sellers' responses to shortages caused by **nonprice rationing.**

The General Response of Consumers to Shortages

Suppose that the initial equilibrium price of gasoline is P_0 in Figure 2.10 and that the quantity sold is Q_0. Assume further that demand increases from D_0 to D_1. Finally, suppose that the government imposes a price ceiling at P_0 to assure that the price of gasoline does not rise. How do customers respond to such price controls?

At price P_0, there is an initial shortage of AB. Where possible, consumers respond to shortages by **hoarding,** which is an effort to lower the risk of not finding future supplies. For example, during

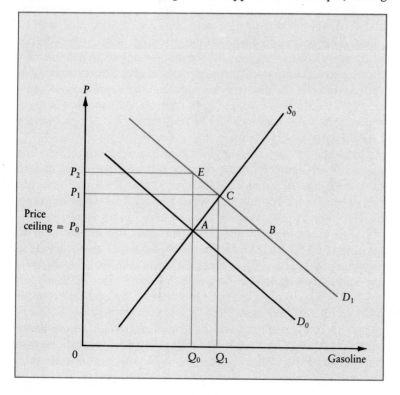

Figure 2.10
Buyer and Seller Response to Price Controls

Buyers respond to shortages by hoarding, making illegal payments, wasting time in queues, and increasing information costs. Sellers shift production to unregulated markets, eliminate low-price products, reduce product quality, and increase discrimination.

the 1973–1974 gas shortages, it was estimated that the average gas tank, kept one-quarter full before the price controls, was kept three-quarters full. If the average tank holds 20 gallons, there was an average increase in gasoline storage of 10 gallons. With about 100 million cars in the United States, the increase in hoarding in gas tanks alone was a billion gallons in the first two weeks of the price controls. The sudden increase in demand caused by hoarding exacerbated the shortage.

In Figure 2.10, quantity Q_0 sets the limit on the gas that consumers can buy at the controlled price, P_0. But consumers are willing to pay price P_2 for quantity Q_0. This fact, and the prevailing shortage AB at price P_0, suggests that the real price of buying gasoline will rise even if the money price is constant.

Suppose that the shortage AB is rationed by queue pricing—that is, first come, first served. In order for a quasi equilibrium to be achieved, the quantity supplied must equal the quantity demanded. Ignoring illegal (black market) payments for now, we would find that consumers would be willing to pay as much as P_2 for quantity Q_0. Because consumers could legally pay only P_0, they would have to pay the difference in nonmoney terms (such as waiting time). Thus the market would achieve a kind of equilibrium: Buyers and sellers are both satisfied when buyers pay a total price of P_2 per unit of gas purchased. P_0 is money price, and P_0P_2 is the value of waiting time spent per unit of gasoline. Two observations are now appropriate. First, the total real price paid, P_2 (money price plus waiting time), is higher than the equilibrium price that would be reached if prices were free to fluctuate, P_1. Second, the dollars that consumers transfer to oil companies during periods of high prices can be reinvested, either in the discovery of additional oil supplies or in some alternative economic investment. In contrast, the time that customers waste in waiting lines cannot be transferred; it is a "dead-weight loss" of a valuable resource.

Another consumer response to shortages is to offer illegal side payments. In Figure 2.10, the distance P_0P_2 may represent, instead of waiting time, illegal black market payments. These payments can take subtle forms. For instance, when rent controls create shortages in rental housing, prospective renters, who cannot legally make a rent offer above the controlled level, may offer to purchase an extra set of keys for $200. Such an offer gives the renter an advantage in obtaining scarce housing space. Customers who make such offers are said to belong to the "key club." During gasoline shortages, customers who join the "rabbit's foot club" (buy a rabbit's foot for $50) or the "battery club" (buy a worn-out battery for $50) can obtain special treatment from the station owner and assure themselves of gas supplies. In similar fashion, financial institutions with names like Murder, Inc. loan money to borrowers at interest rates in excess of the maximum legal rates set by usury laws.

We have already learned that shortages cause an increase in information costs. One such cost is the behavior of frustrated customers waiting in line for gasoline, which reached its worst level in 1973 and again in 1979 when customers with frayed nerves shot and killed other customers. Less dramatic responses to customer frustration were evident in every gas waiting line in the country.

To summarize: The basic consumer responses to shortages are hoarding, illegal side payments, increases in information costs, and time wasted both on waiting in line and in figuring out which lines to wait in.

The General Response of Sellers to Shortages

Again, Figure 2.10 indicates that firms would sell Q_1 units if the price could rise to P_1 but would sell the smaller quantity, Q_0, if prices were controlled at P_0. In other words, the firm's initial response to price controls is to reduce its output by comparison with its uncontrolled output. A related response may be to use the price-controlled inputs to increase the quality of goods not subject to regulation. For example, petroleum products may be used to increase the quality of clothing or of antifreeze, whose prices may not be controlled. Also, when firms produce several lines of a product, they may eliminate their low-priced lines and produce the high-priced lines, whose prices are controlled at higher levels.

Shortages tend to reduce the quality of the good whose price is controlled. In the case of gasoline, the ancillary filling station services, such as tire pressure checks, free maps, and restroom stops, were curtailed during the 1979 gas shortages. The equivalent response in rent-controlled housing markets is to reduce repairs, upkeep, and renovation. Profit-motivated firms, when restricted from increasing their revenues by price adjustments, tend to reduce costs by quality reductions. And because of the waiting list of customers, the firms can get away with such actions.

Firms facing long lines of customers who cannot all be served are put in the position of deciding which customers are important. In the case of gas shortages, the decision to sell only to commuters or only to familiar faces allows the seller of gas to make arbitrary decisions concerning who will be served. In short, the gasoline station manager becomes the "maharaja of petroleum." In a closely related point, prejudices are exercised during shortages because of the power that circumstances give to sellers. Such prejudices can be exercised without loss of profits during shortages.

These responses to shortages on the supply and demand side of the market make it doubtful that price controls can achieve even their primary purpose—holding prices down. True prices (opportunity costs) usually rise.

Toilet Paper Shortages: Not Funny

APPLIED
MICRO
THEORY

2.7

Economists use the term *shortage* in a special way. It refers to the excess of quantity demanded over quantity supplied *at a given price*. Therefore, both the supply and demand sides of the market contribute to the shortage. When the price is below equilibrium, sellers reduce their quantities supplied and buyers increase their quantities demanded by comparison to equilibrium values. Thus suppliers and consumers both contributed to the toilet paper shortage of 1973.

During the summer and fall of 1973, many markets, including the market for paper pulp, experienced shortages created by price controls. Shortages of newsprint caused some newspaper publishers to adopt smaller print to conserve paper. Toilet paper producers, unable to buy the amounts of paper needed to satisfy all their customers, needed to decide which of their customers to disappoint. They decided to disappoint the buyers of the lowest-grade toilet paper because prices and profits were higher for the perfumed and decorated high-grade product. When production shifted to the higher-grade lines, the toilet paper industry did indeed contribute to a shortage of low-grade toilet paper by the economist's definition: At

the controlled price, quantity demanded exceeded quantity supplied. Buyers of low-grade toilet paper were left with a considerable problem.

One of the major purchasers of low-grade toilet paper is the military, which was experiencing difficulty buying its usual brand. What was a garden-variety shortage (with the potential of upgrading military toilet paper) became an all-out crisis when Johnny Carson, extrapolating the military's problem to the entire country, said it looked like the United States faced a toilet paper shortage. The "Tonight Show" audience was silent, and Carson changed the subject. But the next morning, toilet paper shelves were gutted by consumer hoarding. Attempts to ration supplies with one-to-a-customer limits merely prompted people to bring their spouse, parents, children, and neighbors' children, each counting as one customer.

Sources close to the toilet paper industry claimed there was no shortage, but the empty shelves put the lie to such claims. Many people presumed that the shortage was artificially induced by the industry in order to justify higher prices. But for whatever cause, people were now going to the neighbors to borrow toilet paper. The shortage of low-grade paper, affecting the military primarily,

was extended to all users of toilet paper by consumer hoarding.

It is probable that Carson could have cleared up the confusion right when it began if his audience had laughed at the first line and encouraged more on the subject. But toilet paper shortages are not funny; they represent disappointed customers. Thus the 1973 toilet paper shortage began in the government's decision to control prices, was helped along by suppliers' decisions to put limited paper supplies into the higher-grade products, and was further accelerated by consumer hoarding in response to Carson's monologue. Buyers *and* sellers contributed to the shortage.

This example illustrates another effect of price controls. Price controls are often advanced as a means to aid the poor. But as we have seen, price controls on paper products forced the low-grade toilet paper off the market. In the same vein, low-grade weiners were forced off the market because meat packers, faced with short supplies, used scarce meat in the more expensive preparations, including bratwursts and Polish sausages. Thus price controls often discourage production of the low-grade commodities that the poor rely on.

Summary

"Supply and demand" is a model that allows us to study the results of many buyers and sellers interacting with one another in the production and sale of a given product. Substitution by buyers and sellers is the key concept in an intuitive development of supply and demand curves. When shortages or surpluses occur at a given price, they are eliminated and equilibrium achieved by suitable price adjustments.

Product price is important to both buyers and sellers. For this reason, price is treated as the movement parameter for both supply and demand curves. Price controls interfere with the self-adjustment of market price and distort the adjustment of the only parameter that is always of key importance to both suppliers and demanders: price. Thus price controls limit the ability of price to (1) guide scarce resources to their most valuable uses, (2) ration supplies among consumers, (3) provide low-cost information to market participants, (4) maintain market transactions on an impersonal basis, (5) achieve an efficient allocation of tasks, and (6) allow economic agents the greatest possible freedom of choice within the bounds set by scarcity.

Problems

1. Consider the market for wheat in the United States.
   a. List five substitutes for wheat.
   b. Using shorthand notation, write the demand equation for wheat, identifying the movement parameter and the shift parameters.
   c. List the factors that affect the supply of wheat. (If you are not a farmer, use your imagination. Your ability to manipulate the curves is what is important.)
   d. Write the supply equation for wheat that corresponds to your list in part *c*. Identify the movement parameter and shift parameters.
   e. Put the supply and demand curves together and identify the equilibrium price and quantity for wheat.
2. Assume that there is a crop failure in the U.S. wheat market due to bad weather. Show the impact of the bad weather on the wheat market by describing the effect on shift parameters and on the equilibrium values of price and quantity.
3. Show the effect of a crop failure in the Soviet Union. How does this case differ from a U.S. crop failure?
4. Corn is a substitute for wheat. Analyze the effects in the corn market that would result from the crop failures described in questions 2 and 3.
5. Assume that the price of gasoline in Saudi Arabia is 10 cents per gallon and that the price in the United States is 60 cents. Assume that the transport cost from Saudi Arabia to the United States is 1 cent per gallon. Now distinguish between the price and the cost of gasoline in Saudi Arabia.
6. Assume that, due to price controls, gasoline is selling for 50 cents a gallon and that long waiting lines form at the gas stations. In periods of shortages like this, managers often limit purchases to, say, 10 gallons per customer.
   a. What is the price of gas? What is the cost of gas?
   b. How does the 10-gallon limit affect costs? Does it affect all people the same way?
7. Many freeway projects are designed to save time for shippers and commuters. Does an hour saved have the same value if it comes all at once as when it comes in 120 segments 30 seconds long? (Hint: What can you do with the time?)
8. Northwestern Mutual Life Insurance Company provides a free lunch for its approximately 2000 employees who work in the home office in Milwaukee, Wisconsin. In what sense is this a free lunch? Distinguish clearly between price and cost.

Key Terms

9. Dental care can usually be obtained at university dental clinics for about half the price of going to a dentist in private practice. It is observed that most of the patients at such dental clinics are either children, women, or elderly persons. Can you develop an explanation for this observation using the concept of opportunity cost?

10. Board chairmen of large corporations occasionally proclaim their support for wage/price guideposts and controls. Can you explain why such captains of industry would approve of government interference in the marketplace?

11. Say that your boss asks you to prepare a speech extolling the virtues of price controls as "Protector of the Little Guy." The boss will deliver the speech at the annual meeting of the National Independent Meatcutters Trade Association. After telling him you're not sure that small butchers fared very well during the 1972–1973 controls on meat, your boss says, "Well, then just write a speech about price controls that makes me look good." What theoretical arguments would be useful? What data would you look for? Suppose your boss gave you a $200 budget for telephone calls. Whom would you call? What questions would you ask?

12. Draw a demand curve for attendance at a private college. Analyze separately the impact of a tuition increase, a tuition subsidy at the nearby state college, and the discovery that the private college's graduates seldom get jobs.

13. Let's say that the government decides to promote jobs for teenagers.
    a. Use supply and demand curves to develop a list of effects for the establishment of minimum wages above the market wage. Do you think minimum wages help teenage workers?
    b. Use supply and demand curves to analyze the impact of a Job Tax Credit, under which the government pays employers 50% of the cost of hiring unskilled teenage workers.

14. Who rents a dwelling instead of owns? Why? What are the predictable effects of rent controls? Do rent controls protect the little guy?

15. You are given the assignment of pricing tickets for the New York Yankees. What are the likely effects of setting prices so low that there is excess demand for tickets? Would you expect your fans to appreciate the low prices? Do scalpers serve any economic purpose?

16. Distinguish between price and cost in these cases:
    a. You drive your car on the freeway system for free at 3:00 A.M.; you drive free at 7:00 A.M.
    b. Suburbanites are allowed to purchase sewage and water hookups at the same price as central-city homeowners.
    c. The city zoo has no admission charge.
    d. XYZ Brewery dumps waste into Lake Erie without charge.

Suggested Readings

Baumol, W. J., and Blinder, A. S. *Economics: Principles and Policy.* New York: Harcourt Brace Jovanovich, 1979, chap.4.

Marshall, Alfred. *Principles of Economics,* book 5. 8th ed. New York: Macmillan, 1961, chap.3.

Consumer Behavior, Demand, and Elasticity

Every market transaction requires a buyer and a seller. The behavior of buyers determines the demand forces in a market, and the behavior of sellers determines the supply forces. When demand and supply forces interact, markets move toward equilibrium, as discussed in Chapter 2. In this chapter we study the behavior of the individual economic agents who create demand forces. In later chapters we will explore the seller's individual behavior in equal detail.

Economists have long attempted to develop testable hypotheses about consumer behavior, about the economic choices that consumers make—such as what goods to buy, how many hours to work, and how much income to spend. You may wonder if it is possible to develop hypotheses like these in view of the fact that consumers are so varied in their needs. Although economists cannot create a consumer's eye view of the world, they have constructed theoretical models with which they can explain and predict consumer behavior. For example, the individual demand curve, developed intuitively in Chapter 2, is one important end product of any theory of consumer behavior.

Cardinal Utility

To begin with, we can assume that consumers arrange their expenditure and consumption patterns so as to create for themselves the maximum satisfaction. The technical name for measures of consumer satisfaction is **utility**. The words *utility, satisfaction, welfare, happiness,* and *well-being* are more or less synonymous.

Nineteenth-century economists introduced the concept of **cardinal utility,** which presumed that consumers are capable of measuring the utility they derive from the consumption of a good or service. Cardinal utility derived its name from cardinal numbers, which express amount, such as 1, 2, or 3. The unit of measurement was the mystical util; thus a moated castle may have generated 500 utils (units of satisfaction) to the king and a flowered courtyard may have yielded 200 utils to the queen. Jeremy Bentham taught that society was best served when it achieved "the greatest good for the greatest number," a concept that seemed to suggest that utility could be added. Hence the total utility of the castle and courtyard would be 700 utils.

The impossibility of measuring utils for one consumer—let alone adding utils together meaningfully or comparing utility levels

3

for different people—caused economists to abandon cardinal utility in large part. Nevertheless, the demand curve was derived from assumptions of cardinal utility. Furthermore, considerations of cardinal theory introduced concepts and language that still play key roles in economic analysis.

Total Utility, Marginal Utility, and Diminishing Marginal Utility

Picture yourself sitting by a campfire with a bag of marshmallows in one hand and a toasting stick in the other. Assuming you are able to calculate the utils of satisfaction derived from each marshmallow you eat, start eating and recording utils. Your tally sheet will probably exhibit characteristics similar to one of the columns in Table 3.1: Either you record the total utils accumulated by eating a certain quantity of marshmallows (**total utility**) or the additional utils that each marshmallow bestows (**marginal utility**). The two measures are related, of course, because the total utility of any given number of marshmallows must equal the sum of the individual marginal utilities up to that level of consumption. For example, the total utility generated by four marshmallows is

$$U(4) = \sum_{i=1}^{4} MU_i = 30 + 10 + 5 + 3 = 48 \qquad (3.1)$$

Given data on marginal utility, the schedule of total utilities can be derived easily in this way.

Figure 3.1 depicts the relationship between total utility and marginal utility curves. Panel a shows that increases in the consumption of good X causes total utility to rise up to a consumption level X_1 but that beyond level X_1 additional purchases of X reduce total utility. Panel b measures marginal utility on the vertical axis. Economists have a convenient method of deriving the marginal utility curve. Note that the slope[1] of the total utility curve is

Table 3.1
Total and Marginal Utility from Consuming Marshmallows

Number of Marshmallows	Total Utility	Marginal Utility
1	30	30
2	40	10
3	45	5
4	48	3
5	48	0
6	45	-3

1. The slope of any curve is rise/run. Throughout this book, the Greek delta symbol, Δ, is used to refer to a small change in a variable.

$$\text{Slope} = \frac{\text{change in total utility}}{\text{change in purchase of } X} = \frac{\Delta U}{\Delta X} \qquad (3.2)$$

Conveniently, the economist's definition of marginal utility is

$$\text{MU} = \frac{\text{change in total utility}}{\text{change in purchase of } X} = \frac{\Delta U}{\Delta X} \qquad (3.3)$$

As you can see, the mathematical definition of the slope of the total utility curve equals the economist's definition of marginal utility. Hence, each point on the marginal utility curve in Figure 3.1b equals the slope of the total utility curve at that rate of consumption of X. Marginal utility diminishes for each unit consumed up to X_1, because the total utility curve rises at a decreasing rate and therefore becomes flatter and flatter. Marginal utility is zero at X_1, because the slope of the total utility curve is zero at point A. Beyond X_1, marginal utility is negative, because the slope of the total utility curve is negative in that range of consumption. Thus total and marginal utility curves are tied together by a convenient mathematical property—the marginal curve is the slope of the total curve.

Figure 3.1 displays a basic assumption of cardinal utility theory—**diminishing marginal utility.** The first unit consumed yields the most satisfaction, and each subsequent unit provides less additional satisfaction than the last. According to the concept of diminishing marginal utility, the more of a good that one already possesses, the less additional utility another unit can add.

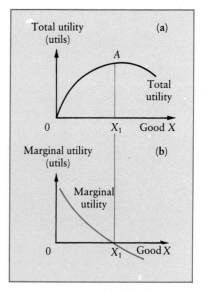

Figure 3.1
**Total Utility and
Marginal Utility Curves**
(a) The greatest total utility occurs at consumption level X_1. (b) The slope of the total utility curve at a given rate of consumption equals the marginal utility of the last unit consumed. Both total and marginal curves exhibit diminishing marginal utility.

Utility Maximization

The consumer's utility depends on the quantity of goods consumed, as expressed in this simple utility function:

$$U = f(X, Y) \qquad (3.4)$$

where

   U = total utility derived from goods X and Y
   X = the good under investigation
   Y = a composite good representing all goods other than X
      (it is convenient to define Y as the money income the
      consumer spends on all goods other than X)

The assumed properties of this cardinal utility function are (1) diminishing marginal utility of good X and (2) constant marginal utility of money income Y. We have already studied the rationale behind the assumption of diminishing marginal utility. The marginal utility of money income is considered constant because money income Y, the substitute for X, is a composite of a large number of alternative goods, the purchase of no single one of which would be significantly altered by a change in the price of X. For this reason changes in utility resulting from changes in the purchase of Y (or money income used to buy any good other than X) can effectively be ignored.

Under what conditions do consumers maximize their satisfaction, subject to the limitations of money income and the prices paid for goods X and Y? Logically, utility maximization occurs only when consumers allocate their money income among all possible uses so that the marginal utility per dollar spent on any one good is equal to the marginal utility per dollar spent on any other good. This utility-maximizing condition may be expressed as

$$\frac{MU_X}{P_X} = \frac{MU_Y}{P_Y} \tag{3.5}$$

Suppose Equation 3.5 is not satisfied, so that $MU_X/P_X > MU_Y/P_Y$. The consumer would switch expenditures toward X and away from Y because the per-dollar marginal utility of X (utility gained by purchasing more X) exceeds the per-dollar marginal utility of Y (utility given up by purchasing less Y). The net effect of buying more X and less Y is to increase total utility. When the ratios in Equation 3.5 are equal, no further increases in utility can be achieved by shifting expenditures between X and Y; total utility is maximized.

Cardinal Utility and the Demand Curve

A downward-sloping demand curve can be derived from the assumed properties of the utility function in Equation 3.4 and the utility-maximizing condition of Equation 3.5. Suppose the utility-maximizing condition is achieved when the consumer purchases X_1 units of X at price P_{X1}. This quantity demanded is plotted as point A in Figure 3.2. Now let the price of X fall to P_{X2}, *ceteris paribus*. The optimizing equality of Equation 3.5 is no longer satisfied and is replaced by

$$\frac{MU_X}{P_{X2}} > \frac{MU_Y}{P_Y} \tag{3.6}$$

The per-dollar marginal utility of X has risen due to the lower price, but the per-dollar marginal utility of Y remains constant. (The marginal utility of money income, MU_Y is constant by assumption, and the price of Y, P_Y, is held constant by the *ceteris paribus* change in the price of X.) The equality of Equation 3.5 can be reattained at the lower price of X only if the marginal utility of X is reduced. But due to diminishing marginal utility, this can be accomplished only by purchasing more X. Thus the consumer will buy the larger quantity, X_2, when the price of X falls in order to equate per-dollar marginal utilities at the new price of X—and restore the condition

Figure 3.2
The Demand Curve and Cardinal Utility

Each point on the demand curve is a price-quantity combination at which the consumer equates the marginal utility per dollar spent on X with the marginal utility per dollar spent on all other goods.

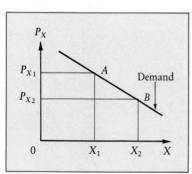

in Equation 3.5. The new quantity demanded at price P_{X2} is plotted as point B in Figure 3.2. Combining points A and B and all other points similarly derived produces a negatively sloped demand schedule. The logic is flawless, given the assumptions.

Ordinal Utility

Cardinal utility would no doubt be a prominent tool in studying consumer behavior but for one major flaw: Utility cannot be measured cardinally. Enter **ordinal utility**, a theory of consumer behavior that yields about the same results as cardinal theory but that requires less information and has broad application to public policy and private market decisions. Ordinal utility derives its name from ordinal numbers, which express ranking in a series, such as first, second, and third. Accordingly, the use of ordinal utility requires only that consumers be able to rank their preferences for goods rather than attach quantifiable units of satisfaction to them.

Axioms of Consumer Behavior

Axioms of consumer behavior are the assumptions that economists make about the way consumers act. They are assertions that are accepted without proof in order to study their consequences. Axioms lead to theoretical predictions that can be tested. Scientists often judge the validity of a theory by its ability to make accurate predictions rather than by the realism of the axioms (assumptions). The microeconomic model of consumer behavior rests on three particular axioms.

AXIOM 1: ORDERING OF BUNDLES   Economists assume that consumers can rank alternative bundles of goods according to their preferences. For example, in a simple two-good world of Twinkies and Clark candy bars, a consumer might be confronted with the following two commodity bundles:

> *Bundle A:* three Twinkies and two Clark bars
> *Bundle B:* two Twinkies and three Clark bars

The consumer can make only one of three possible responses:

> A is preferred to B.
> B is preferred to A.
> A and B yield equal utility. The consumer is indifferent.

According to this axiom, consumers need not measure the utility derived from each bundle of commodities but only compare the two bundles and rank them according to their preferences.

Figure 3.3
Number Line Illustrating Intransitive Choices

This consumer's preference rankings are inconsistent, resulting in the absurd inference that bundle C is preferred to itself.

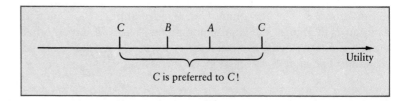

AXIOM 2: TRANSITIVITY   The transitivity axiom simply states that consumers are consistent in their choices. If a consumer prefers commodity bundle A to B and B to C, then consistency requires that the consumer prefer A to C. If C is preferred to A (see Figure 3.3), then by implication C is preferred to C, which is impossible. Similarly, if Goldilocks prefers beds to rocking chairs and rocking chairs to porridge, the consistency of her choices, or transitivity, requires that she prefer beds to porridge. If she preferred porridge to beds under these circumstances, her choices would have no identifiable order—and we could not predict her behavior.

AXIOM 3: NONSATIATION   The nonsatiation axiom asserts that consumers prefer more to less. Adding one unit of a good to any commodity bundle yields a preferred bundle. Thus any consumer would prefer a bundle of ten Twinkies and five Clark bars to a bundle of ten Twinkies and four Clark bars.

The consumer axioms underpin the main analytical tool in ordinal utility theory—the **indifference curve**. An indifference curve shows all of the commodity bundles that give the consumer equal utility.

Indifference curves have four essential properties; the first three are deduced from the axioms and the fourth is based on an observable generalization.

1. Indifference curves are negatively sloped.

2. Indifference curves are nonintersecting.

3. Indifference curves are everywhere dense.

4. Indifference curves are convex to the origin.

PROPERTY 1: INDIFFERENCE CURVES ARE NEGATIVELY SLOPED   The curve labeled U_0 in Figure 3.4 is an indifference curve showing the various combinations of Twinkies and Clark bars that yield equal utility. Any commodity bundle in the shaded area northeast of commodity bundle A (point A on the graph) will be considered preferable to bundle A because of the nonsatiation axiom. Any bundle in the shaded area southwest of bundle A will be considered

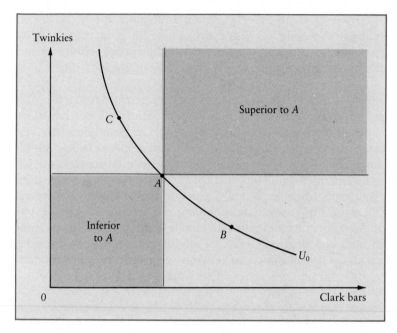

Figure 3.4
**Indifference Curves are
Negatively Sloped**

The shaded areas are either superior or inferior to A. Bundles yielding equal utility, like B and C, must lie only in the unshaded areas.

inferior. An indifference curve containing point A as one bundle cannot therefore contain any points in the two shaded areas. The only bundle that logically can yield the same utility as bundle A must lie in the unshaded quadrants, as do points B and C. Because a movement along the curve must contain less of one good and more of the other, the indifference curve must therefore be negatively sloped.

The slope of the indifference curve is so important analytically that it has its own name. The **marginal rate of substitution (MRS)** is the rate at which the consumer is willing to trade one good for another and stay on the same indifference curve. In Figure 3.5, imagine the move from A to B to be an infinitesimally small change that we have enlarged with a magnifying glass. To remain on the same indifference curve, the consumer gives up ΔY units of Y in exchange for ΔX units of X. Thus,

$$\text{MRS} = \frac{\Delta Y}{\Delta X}\bigg|_{U_0} = \text{slope of indifference curve} \qquad (3.7)$$

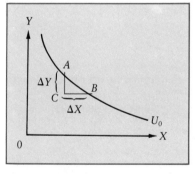

Figure 3.5
The Marginal Rate of Substitution

The slope of the indifference curve—the MRS—represents the number of units of Y that the consumer is willing to give up to obtain a unit of X: $\text{MRS} = \Delta Y/\Delta X = AC/CB$ in range AB.

The notation $A|_{(x,\ y,\ z,\ \ldots)}$ means that whatever the A expression is, its calculation takes place holding the values of $(x, y, z, \ldots)$ fixed. Thus Equation 3.7 measures the slope of the curve along which utility, U_0, is fixed.[2]

2. This is, of course, only an approximation, and it improves the closer that A and B become. When the slope of the curve is taken at a point (using differential calculus), the approximation is exact.

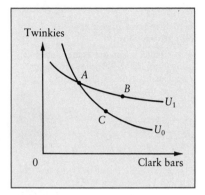

Figure 3.6
Indifference Curves Cannot Intersect

Curves U_1 and U_2 intersect, leading to the inference that bundles B and C yield equal utility, a violation of the nonsatiation axiom. Transitivity and nonsatiation conflict when indifference curves intersect.

For each small move along an indifference curve, the loss in utility from having less Y is exactly offset by the increase in utility from having more X. Note that the MRS is negative because ΔY and ΔX have opposite signs.

PROPERTY 2: INDIFFERENCE CURVES ARE NONINTERSECTING   It is easiest to demonstrate the second property of indifference curves by showing the logical impossibility of making them intersect. Consider the two intersecting indifference curves in Figure 3.6, for example. Bundles A and C yield equal utility on indifference curve U_0, as do bundles A and B on curve U_1. Therefore, the transitivity axiom requires that bundles B and C generate identical utility. However, following the nonsatiation axiom, the consumer should unambiguously prefer bundle B to bundle C, because B contains more of both commodities than C. Therefore, intersecting indifference curves create contradictions between axioms and must be ruled out.

PROPERTY 3: INDIFFERENCE CURVES ARE EVERYWHERE DENSE   Pick a commodity bundle at random, such as bundle A in Figure 3.7. It is on an indifference curve because there are equally desired bundles. Bundle B also lies on an indifference curve, as does C. In fact, every commodity bundle lies on an indifference curve; commodity space is full of indifference curves. This is the mathematical meaning of indifference curves being "everywhere dense." The family of indif-

Figure 3.7
Indifference Curves Are Everywhere Dense

The indifference map comprises all indifference curves. Utility rises in the direction of the arrow.

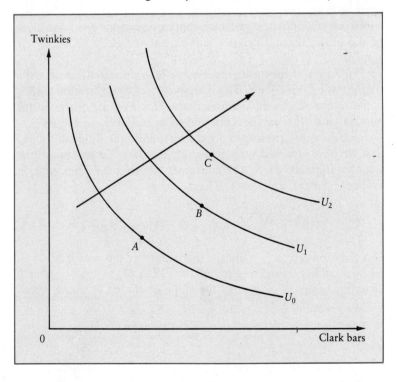

ference curves is the consumer's **indifference map.**

Figure 3.7 depicts three of the infinite number of indifference curves in one consumer's map. All are negatively sloped and non-intersecting. Bundle B is preferred to bundle A by the nonsatiation axiom. Transitivity requires that all bundles that yield the same utility as bundle B—in other words, those along indifference curve U_1—be preferred to all bundles that yield the same utility as bundle A, or those along curve U_0. By moving to the northeast from one indifference curve to another, as illustrated by the arrow in Figure 3.7, the consumer will find increased utility.

Conceptual problems with this axiom arise when goods are not infinitely divisible. How can the indifference curve touch each point in commodity space if one of the goods is, say, automobiles, which can only be measured by integers? Although we can think of $2\frac{1}{2}$ gallons of gasoline, an infinitely divisible good, it does not seem to make sense to think of $2\frac{1}{2}$ cars. But this problem is solved and the axiom rescued by measuring indivisible commodities in flow terms. That is, we cannot think of $2\frac{1}{2}$ cars, but we can think of 5 cars in two years or $2\frac{1}{2}$ cars per year. Then we can use indifference curves to study the tradeoff of any rate of auto replacement with any other commodity.

PROPERTY 4: INDIFFERENCE CURVES ARE CONVEX FROM THE ORIGIN
The marginal rate of substitution is the slope of the indifference curve. The convexity property asserts that the slope of the indifference curve will get smaller in absolute value (flatter) as more X is obtained. To demonstrate, let $FE = CB$ in Figure 3.8. The con-

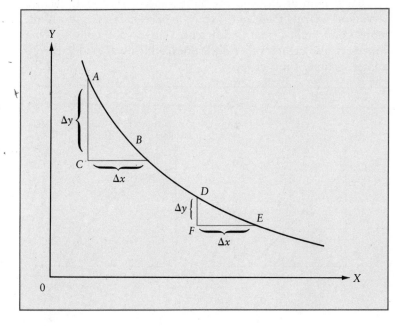

Figure 3.8
Indifferences Curves are Convex from the Origin

The diminishing marginal rate of substitution means that the willingness to give up Y to obtain X falls as the consumer's endowment of Y falls and X expands. The slope of the indifference curve gets smaller in absolute value in moving downward and to the right.

sumer is willing to give up *AC* units of *Y* to obtain *CB* units of *X* when, at point *A,* he or she already possesses a large quantity of *Y.* However, starting from a lower endowment of *Y,* such as point *D,* he or she is willing to give up only *DF* units of *Y* to obtain the same changes in *X* as before. This is so because *Y* and *X* are imperfect substitutes and *Y* has become scarce compared to *X.* There is a growing reluctance to trade *Y* for *X* when *Y* becomes relatively scarce. The curve therefore bows out and the slope, $\Delta Y / \Delta X$, becomes smaller in absolute value as more *X* is obtained. Formally, this convexity property is referred to as the **diminishing marginal rate of substitution.**

The linear indifference curve shown in Figure 3.9*a* indicates that the consumer is indifferent in a choice between Twinkies and Clark bars; they are perfect substitutes. This consumer is willing to trade them one for one whether he or she already has 1000 Twinkies and 0 Clark bars or whether the reverse is true. Although this may be so for goods that are perfect substitutes, such as different brands of gasoline or cement, it is not true for most goods. Indeed, microeconomics is the study of how economic agents make choices between imperfect substitutes. Such choices are ruled out by linear indifference curves. Moreover, indifference curves that are concave from the origin, or curves that appear to be pushed up from below, as in Figure 3.9*b*, offend our sensibilities even more. They imply that the consumer is more willing to trade Twinkies for an extra Clark bar when he or she has few Twinkies and many Clark bars (area *B*) than when he or she has many Twinkies and few Clark bars (area *A*).

Because linear and concave indifference curves contradict observation, we rule them out (except in special cases) and assume, more comfortably, that indifference curves are convex. Nonconvexity also creates other difficulties, which will be discussed in a later section of this chapter.

Figure 3.9
Linear and Concave Indifference Curves

(a) Twinkies and Clark bars are perfect substitutes if the indifference curve is linear. (b) Concavity implies an increasing marginal rate of substitution: The more Twinkies the consumer has, the fewer he or she will give up to obtain a Clark bar.

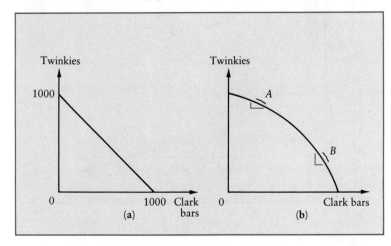

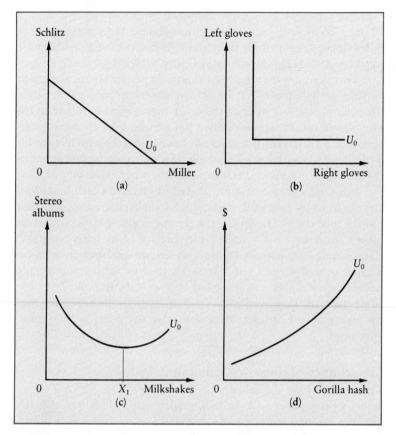

Figure 3.10
Special Cases of Indifference Curves
(a) Different brands of beer are perfect substitutes. (b) Right and left gloves are perfect complements. (c) The consumer is satiated with milkshakes at X_1. (d) Gorilla hash is an economic "bad."

Figure 3.10 illustrates some special cases of indifference curves. Panel *a* is the case of the previously discussed perfect substitutes: The consumer likes beer but isn't fussy about brands.

If goods are perfect complements and must be used in a fixed ratio, indifference curves like that in Figure 3.10*b* emerge. If the two goods are left and right gloves, there is no rate of substitution of one for the other that will keep utility constant. One right and ten left gloves provide no greater utility than one right and one left glove. The nonsatiation axiom has been relaxed in this instance.

A portion of the indifference curve in Figure 3.10*c* has a positive slope. Again the nonsatiation axiom has been relaxed. The consumer is satiated with milkshakes at X_1. More milkshakes will reduce utility, a loss that must be made up by more stereo albums in order to maintain constant utility.

Figure 3.10*d* describes a related case. With dollars as one good, the positive slope throughout indicates that the good on the horizontal axis is not a good at all, but a "bad." Thus the consumer is saying, "You would have to pay me to eat gorilla hash." This kind of indifference curve has been used primarily in financial portfolio theory where an investor selects points of indifference between the

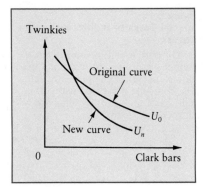

Figure 3.11
Shifting the Indifference Map

The consumer's preferences have strengthened for Clark bars; at each point, the MRS is greater than before.

expected return on a bond portfolio and the associated risk. Risk is a "bad," so more expected return must compensate for more risk in order to keep the investor indifferent. Hence the indifference curve would be positively sloped, as in Figure 3.10d.

Now consider the effect of a change in preference for the goods in question. In Figure 3.11, let the original indifference curve be U_0. This curve, together with all the other curves corresponding to the same tastes (which are not drawn but which make up the indifference map), represents a statement of the consumer's preference for Twinkies and Clark bars. The slope (MRS) defines the rate at which the consumer is willing to trade one for the other. Now suppose that the consumer's preferences are altered in favor of Clark bars. This change in tastes alters the slope of the indifference curve. The new indifference curve, U_n, depicts the change in tastes as the consumer grows up to the more mature preference for Clark bars. Note that the indifference curves in Figure 3.11 do not intersect; instead, U_0 disappears and U_n takes its place. The key point is that changing preferences changes the marginal rate of substitution. The consumer now requires a larger compensation of Twinkies in exchange for giving up a Clark bar than before at any point in the preference map.

Constraints Facing the Consumer

Thus far we have described a theoretical model illustrating a consumer's preferences with an indifference map, which conceptually contains an infinite number of potential levels of consumer utility. Which of these utility levels will the consumer be able to achieve? The answer, of course, lies in the **budget constraints** that limit the consumer's ability to purchase commodities.

One important limitation is the consumer's money income (I). Other things equal, a higher income means an increased ability to purchase goods. But the quantity of goods that can be purchased from a given money income depends on the prices of the goods. Thus the consumer is limited by money income and by the prices of goods. In a simple, two-good world, these limitations on purchasing power may be expressed in the form of a budget constraint equation:

$$I = P_Y Y + P_X X \tag{3.8}$$

where

$$I = \text{money income}$$
$$Y \text{ and } X = \text{the units of each good purchased}$$
$$P_Y \text{ and } P_X = \text{the prices of } Y \text{ and } X, \text{ respectively}$$

This budget equation divides consumer income between income spent on good Y ($P_Y \cdot Y$) and the income spent on good X ($P_X \cdot X$).

Let's assume for ease that consumers spend all their income on the two goods in the current period. Solving Equation 3.8 for Y rearranges the budget equation to

$$Y = \frac{I}{P_Y} - \frac{P_X}{P_Y}X \qquad (3.9)$$

Equation 3.9 is a linear equation, where I/P_Y is the intercept coefficient (the value of Y when $X = 0$) and $-P_X/P_Y$ is the slope of the **budget line**. Figure 3.12 illustrates.

When the consumer purchases all Y and no X, the maximum number of units of Y obtainable is I/P_Y. This is the vertical intercept in Figure 3.12 and also the value of Y for $X = 0$ in Equation 3.9. Similarly, if the consumer purchases all X and no Y, I/P_X represents the maximum units of X obtainable, which is the intercept of the horizontal axis in Figure 3.12 and also the value of X when $Y = 0$ in Equation 3.9. Commonly, the consumer will choose to buy some combination of goods rather than specialize in only one good; and the alternative combinations available to the consumer may be visualized by connecting the two intercepts with a straight line, the slope of which is $-P_X/P_Y$, as Equation 3.9 verifies.

The area of the triangle bounded by 0, I/P_Y, and I/P_X is the consumer's **choice set**, a concept closely related to the consumer's standard of living. Given income I and prices P_Y and P_X, the individual can choose any combination of X and Y within the choice set triangle. Thus the size of the triangle limits the consumer's standard of living. The consumer could select any interior point, such as A in Figure 3.12, because it lies within the domain of the choice set. But in the following discussion, let's rule out such interior points, because they do not exhaust the consumer's income, an assumption we should maintain for the present. Any point outside the choice set, such as B, is unobtainable due to income and price constraints. Thus the consumer seeks positions that lie on the budget line.

The budget line will shift if any of its parameters—I, P_X, or P_Y—change. If income I increases while prices remain constant, the intercept values will rise, and more of each good can be purchased than before. The budget line will shift upward and to the northeast, as illustrated in Figure 3.13a. The new budget line is parallel to the old one, indicating that the slopes are the same. This must be true inasmuch as the price ratio is unaffected. The income increase from I_0 to I_1 increases the consumer's standard of living by expanding the choice set triangle.[3]

Now let's see how a change in relative prices affects the budget line. Let the price of X increase from P_{X_0} to P_{X_1}, holding income and

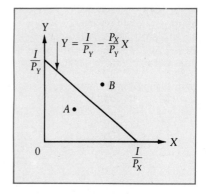

Figure 3.12
The Budget Constraint Line

The linear equation is $Y = I/P_Y - P_X/P_Y \cdot X$. Each point *on* the line is available. Each point *off* the line is either unobtainable (B) or represents unspent income (A).

3. Note that the parallel displacement of the budget line in Figure 3.13a could be achieved with a constant money income I and a proportional reduction in the prices of X and Y, which also keeps the slope of the budget line constant and expands the choice set.

Figure 3.13
Shifting the Budget Line

(a) A parallel shift is caused by a change in income, holding the price ratio constant. (b) A nonparallel shift rotating around the Y axis is caused by an increase in the price of X, holding income and the price of Y constant.

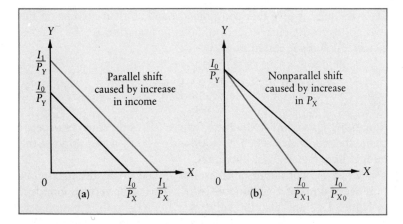

the price of Y constant. The choice set is now reduced to the smaller triangle in Figure 3.13b as the horizontal intercept falls to I/P_{X_1}. The absolute value of the slope of the budget line, $|P_X/P_Y|$, has increased, reflected by the greater steepness of the new budget line. The consumer's standard of living has fallen.

You are left with the exercise of shifting the budget line for income decreases, reductions in the price of X, and changes in the price of Y. How is the consumer's choice set affected by changes in these constraints?

Consumer Optimization: Individual Decisionmaking

Thus far we have considered separately the consumer's preferences (the indifference map) and the constraints in realizing these preferences (the budget line). We may now combine these two concepts in order to answer a very simple question: How do consumers allocate their limited budgets between the purchase of goods X and Y? This decision is up to the individual consumers, who take prices, incomes, and other market-determined variables as given and make the choices, given these parameters, to maximize utility. The model of individual decisionmaking is a major building block toward our ultimate goal of understanding the market mechanism.

Figure 3.14 combines the indifference map with the linear budget line. The consumer is able to purchase any combination of goods along the budget line, but what combination will be purchased? By choosing the combination X_0 and Y_0, or commodity bundle C, the consumer attains the highest possible indifference curve and thereby achieves the highest possible utility, given the income and price constraints. At point C the budget line is tangent to the indifference curve U_2. The consumer is able to purchase bundles A, B, C, or any other bundle on the budget line. However, choosing bundle B pushes the consumer to the lower indifference curve U_1 and choosing bundle A to the still lower indifference curve U_0. Any change in

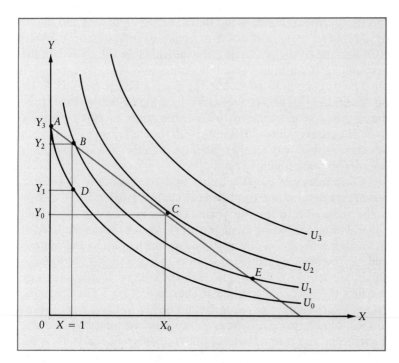

Figure 3.14
Consumer Optimization
Utility is maximized at C where |MRS| = |P_X/P_Y|.

purchases away from point C in either direction worsens utility. Point C is the consumer optimum because it represents the greatest utility available, given I, P_X, and P_Y.

Now we can proceed to a formal statement of **consumer optimization,** using the slopes of the indifference curve and the budget line. Both have negative slopes, so it is convenient to use their absolute values. The slope of the indifference curve, $\Delta Y/\Delta X$ = |MRS|, is the rate at which the consumer *is willing* to trade Y and X without altering utility. The slope of the budget line, $\Delta Y/\Delta X$ = |P_X/P_Y|, is the rate at which the consumer *is able* to trade Y for X. The market exchange rate is given by the ratio of prevailing prices. The tangency at point C means that the two slopes are equal, or that

$$|\text{MRS}| = \left|\frac{P_X}{P_Y}\right| \qquad (3.10)$$

Consider a nonoptimum position where Equation 3.10 is not satisfied, such as point A in Figure 3.14. Point A is a **corner solution,** where $X = 0$ and indifference curve U_0 is achieved. At point A the absolute slope of the indifference curve is greater than the absolute slope of the budget line, or |MRS| > |P_X/P_Y|. The economic interpretation is that the rate at which the consumer *is just willing* to trade away Y in order to obtain a unit of X (MRS) is greater than the rate at which he or she *is able* to trade Y for X (the price ratio).

Specifically, the consumer is indifferent between points A and D and would trade $Y_3 - Y_1$ units of Y to obtain the first unit of X. However, because of the price ratio, the individual is able to obtain the first unit of X on more favorable terms; only $Y_3 - Y_2$ units of Y must be forgone in order to buy the first unit of X. Because B lies on the budget line and is intersected by a higher indifference curve than A, the consumer improves his or her utility by moving from A to B. Thus the condition $|MRS| > |P_X/P_Y|$ implies that exchanges can be accomplished with smaller sacrifices than the consumer requires in order to remain indifferent.

Consumers can increase utility by buying more X and less Y whenever the slope of the indifference curve is greater than the slope of the budget line in absolute terms. Therefore, B cannot be optimal either, because the same inequality of slopes persists as occurred at A. Further movements down the budget line by purchasing more X and less Y will yield further increases in utility as higher indifference curves are achieved. When C is reached, $|MRS| = |P_X/P_Y|$: The rate at which the consumer is willing to substitute X for Y just equals the rate at which market prices force him or her to make such substitutions. No further gains from substitution are possible, and any movement away from C reduces utility. Indifference curve U_2 is the highest utility obtainable given the consumer's income and price constraints. Can you prove the other half of the tangency proposition, that more Y and less X whould be purchased whenever $|P_X/P_Y| > |MRS|$, as at E?

Earlier in this chapter, convexity was listed as a property of the indifference curve. This property is not derived from the consumer axioms per se but is nevertheless assumed because it is implausible that indifference curves would be either concave or linear. Now we can rationalize convexity through an understanding of consumer optimization.

Let's begin by assuming that indifference curves are concave, as illustrated in Figure 3.15. The two budget lines correspond to two different prices of Y. When income and the prices of Y and X are I_0, P_{Y_0}, and P_{X_0} respectively, the lower budget line connecting I_0/P_{Y_0} and I_0/P_{X_0} is obtained. The consumer will not maximize utility by selecting bundle A on indifference curve U_0, even though point A satisfies the tangency condition. The consumer maximizes utility by selecting bundle C, a corner solution in which the indifference curve U_2 is reached by specializing in good X. The tangency at point A actually defines utility minimization, because the consumer cannot reach a lower indifference curve while spending his or her entire income.

Now suppose the price of Y falls to P_{Y_1}, with income and the price of X fixed. The budget line rotates upward around C; the consumer selects bundle D in order to reach indifference curve

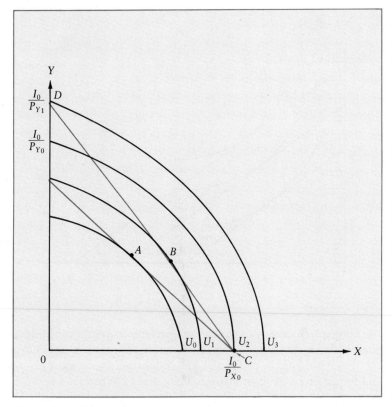

Figure 3.15
Concave Indifference Map

Concavity means that (1) a tangency minimizes utility, (2) a consumer always picks corner solutions, specializing in one good, and (3) small price changes can result in complete switches in commodity specialization.

U_3 rather than the interior tangency at point B on indifference curve U_1.

Concave indifference curves have two implications for consumer behavior that are inconsistent with even casual observation: (1) specialization in consumption, meaning that a consumer purchases only one good in a two-good world, and (2) complete switches in such specialization, as when the consumer switches from consuming all X to all Y when relative prices change, as in Figure 3.15. Because most consumers do not specialize in their consumption, it is reasonable to infer that indifference curves are not concave. You should show yourself that linear indifference curves also make specialization in consumption and complete switching likely and therefore carry the same limitations as concave indifference curves.

The Income-Consumption Curve and the Engel Curve

Now that you understand consumer optimization, you are ready to see what testable hypotheses can be generated from consumer theory. The two main implications discussed in this chapter are the effect of income changes and the effect of price changes on the purchase of goods. This section covers the effect of income changes.

Figure 3.16
The Income-Consumption Curve for a Normal Good

The ICC is composed of the various commodity bundles that the consumer buys when income changes, holding relative prices constant. The ICC is positively sloped for a normal good.

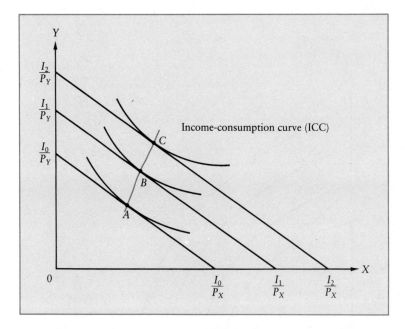

Figure 3.16 displays a consumer's preference map, three budget lines, and three tangency points: A, B, and C. The three budget lines are drawn holding the prices of Y and X constant (hence their ratio) and for different levels of income: I_0, I_1, and I_2. When income is I_0, the consumer maximizes utility by selecting commodity bundle A. When income rises to I_1, the budget line shifts parallel to the right, and the consumer relocates expenditures to point B, which represents larger purchases of both X and Y than before. A further increase in income, to I_2, moves expenditures to point C.

In Figure 3.16, the line through the tangency points A, B, and C is the **income-consumption curve** (ICC). The income-consumption curve records the different bundles of Y and X that the consumer will buy if money income changes but the prices of goods Y and X remain constant. If the price changes, a different ICC is traced out.

The income-consumption curve in Figure 3.16 slopes upward and to the right, implying that higher incomes increase the units purchased of both X and Y. Goods that display this characteristic are called **normal goods.** Of course, the ICC need not look like Figure 3.16. If, as in Figure 3.17, the two goods are steaks and chicken necks, the income-consumption curve may be negatively sloped. An increase in income reduces the quantity of chicken necks purchased. Goods that are less likely to be purchased at higher incomes, such as chicken necks, are called **inferior goods.** The ICC is negatively sloped for inferior goods.

Note that, because the model requires consumers to spend all their income, both goods in a two-good model cannot be inferior;

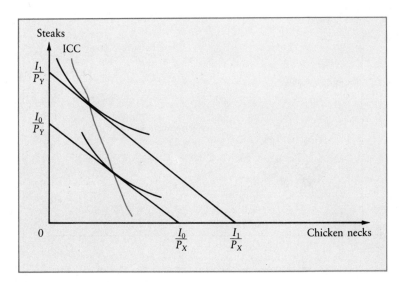

Figure 3.17
**The Income-Consumption Curve
for an Inferior Good**
The ICC is negatively sloped for an
inferior good, such as chicken necks.

if income increases and quantities purchased of both goods fall at constant prices, the budget line would not be reached. Note also that inferiority can only apply to part of the range of income. If the good were inferior at all income levels, it would never be consumed in the first place.

The income-consumption curve is related to the **Engel curve,** named after the nineteenth-century German statistician Christian Engel, who pioneered the study of the relationships between income and family expenditures. Consider the income-consumption curve in Figure 3.18a. For the constant price ratio P_Y/P_X, the consumer purchases X_1 units of X when income is I_1, X_2 when income rises to I_2, and X_3 when income rises to I_3. The Engel curve (see Figure 3.18b) traces out the units of X that the consumer purchases at different levels of income, per unit of time, when the prices of goods X and Y remain constant. The Engel curve shifts when either the price ratio changes or the indifference map shifts due to a change in consumer preferences. For an inferior good, the income-consumption curve will be negatively sloped and the Engel curve will also be negatively sloped.

The Price-Consumption Curve and the Demand Curve

One important use of the theory of consumer optimization is to underpin the theory of demand. Accordingly, this section uses indifference analysis to derive the individual's demand curve.

Figure 3.19a contains an indifference map and three budget lines, each drawn for a different price of X $(P_{X_3} > P_{X_2} > P_{X_1})$, constant income, and a constant price of Y. Point A is the consumer optimum when $P_X = P_{X_1}$. If the price of X increases to P_{X_2}, the budget line rotates to the left and A is no longer optimal. Rather, B is the best the consumer can do; he or she must move to a lower

Figure 3.18
The Engel Curve

(a) The income-consumption curve shows units purchased at different income levels. (b) The Engel curve is derived from the ICC; it records the quantities demanded of good X at various income levels, holding relative prices constant.

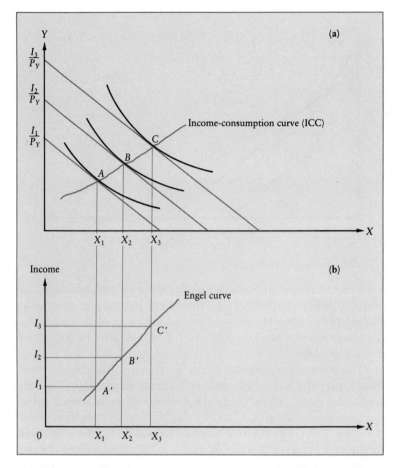

indifference curve, U_1, because the increase in price reduces the choice set. Nevertheless, given the new constraints, B is the new optimum position. Similarly, a further increase in the price of X to P_{X3} generates a new optimum at point C.

In Figure 3.19a, a colored line is drawn through the constrained optimum positions A, B, and C (and all others not shown). This colored line, called the **price-consumption curve (PCC)** or the **offer curve**, records the different combinations of X and Y that the consumer will buy at different prices of X while holding income and the price of Y fixed.

Using the price-consumption curve in Figure 3.19a, we can now derive a traditional demand curve, which records the quantities of X that the consumer will buy at different prices, with income, the price of Y, and all other nonprice determinants held constant. When the price of X is P_{X_1}, point A is the consumer optimum, and the consumer will purchase X_3 units of X. This combination of X_3 and P_{X_1}, is plotted as point A' in Figure 3.19b. At the higher P_{X_2}, B is the consumer optimum, and the consumer will buy only X_2 units of X. This combination is plotted as B' in panel b. Point C' is similarly

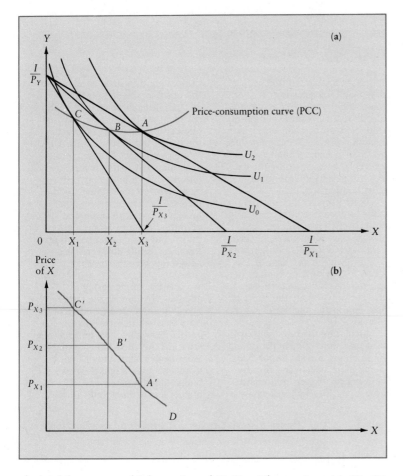

Figure 3.19
The Demand Curve and the Price-Consumption Curve

(a) The price-consumption curve shows the different combinations of goods X and Y that will be purchased at different prices of X, holding income and the price of Y fixed. (b) The demand curve is derived from the PCC. It records the quantities demanded of good X at various prices of X, holding income and all other shift parameters constant.

derived for an even higher price of X, P_{X_3}. Thus points A', B', C', and all others not shown are quantities of X demanded at different prices, where all other significant impacts on demand, such as income, the price of Y, and consumer preferences, are held constant. The collection of such points forms the demand curve, labeled D in Figure 3.19b.

So far, we have drawn budget lines and indifference curves in two-commodity space, placing a single good Y on the vertical axis. To make the analysis more general, we can place on the vertical axis a composite of all the goods other than X that are available to a consumer. This composite good is called the **numeraire** because the prices of X are stated in terms of the units of the numeraire needed to buy one unit of X. Accordingly, the vertical intercept of the budget line represents the units of the numeraire that the consumer could obtain if he or she did not purchase any X. But this value is simply the consumer's money income, so we can use income as the numeraire. Units of income are measured in dollars, and the price of one unit of income (one dollar) is simply one dollar. Therefore, the vertical intercept of the budget line is income, I.

Cash Grants versus In-Kind Gifts versus Subsidies

APPLIED MICRO THEORY

3.1

The purpose of the following example is twofold: (1) to exercise your mind (and pencil and ruler) in the use of the theoretical apparatus of consumer theory and (2) to quickly bridge the gap from theory to application in important policy issues.

Pete and John are brothers who are identical in every respect except in their appreciation of baseball. The boys' only source of income is their allowance of $0A$ dollars per week. In Figure A, the budget line AB defines their money income/baseball ticket commodity space. Income, the numeraire, is measured on the vertical axis and represents all other goods except baseball tickets. The relative slopes of the indifference curves in Figure A reveal that Pete has a stronger preference for baseball than does John. Initially, Pete reaches the

highest attainable indifference curve, U_0^{Pete}, by selecting commodity bundle P. In contrast, John chooses a corner solution at A; he buys no baseball tickets at prevailing prices. (We cannot infer that John is happier than Pete, or vice versa, because utility theory does not permit interpersonal utility comparisons.)

Now suppose their father wants to encourage the boys to see more baseball games. He may (1) increase their allowances, (2) give them baseball tickets outright, or (3) subsidize the purchase of tickets by paying a percentage of the price of each ticket the boys buy. Let's investigate the effect of these options on the boys' behavior.

Increasing the boys' weekly allowance shifts the budget line to CD in Figure B. Pete responds by buying more tickets and thereby achieving the higher indifference curve U_1^{Pete}. (Baseball tickets are a

normal good to Pete, as shown by the positively sloped income-consumption curve ICC^{Pete}.) John spends none of the increased allowance on tickets and reaches the higher indifference curve U_1^{John} at another corner solution, point C. (John's ICC curve is the vertical line AC.) Both boys may properly be grateful to their father for the increase in money income that increased their choice set and permitted them to attain higher utility. But their father may think John's gratitude insincere because he did not buy any baseball tickets.

Instead of increasing allowances, suppose the father takes the direct route and gives the boys baseball tickets. Figures C and D show the effect on each boy separately. If their father prohibits them from selling any of the tickets he gives them, the new budget line becomes AEF. The budget line shifts parallel to the

Figure A Individual Demand Curves for Baseball Tickets

The boys' initial purchases of baseball tickets do not reflect their father's wishes.

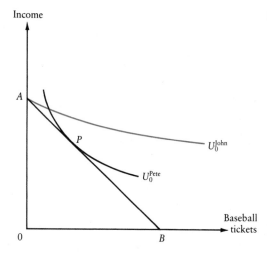

Figure B Cash Grants to Encourage Consumption

The effect of cash grants: Pete increases baseball game attendance, John does not.

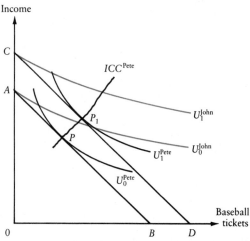

Figure C In-Kind Gifts to Encourage Consumption

Giving tickets outright shifts the budget line to *AEF*. Pete moves to *E* but would go to *K* if allowed to sell part of the gift.

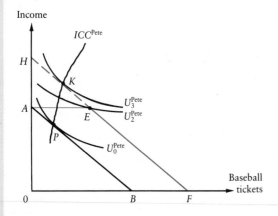

Figure D In-Kind Gifts to Encourage Consumption

John goes to *E* because of the gift. If allowed to sell the tickets, John would sell them all and choose another corner solution, *H*.

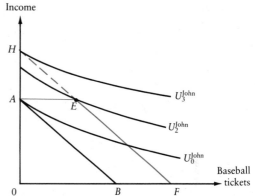

right by the number of tickets given, *AE*. To operate on the dashed segment *EH*, Pete and John would have to sell some of the tickets.

In Figure C, Pete moves to *E* on indifference curve U_2^{Pete}. In Figure D, John moves to point *E* because he has the same income as before and some tickets as well. John uses the tickets because they do not cost him anything.

Note that point *E* is not a consumer optimum for either boy. Both boys could sell some of the gift tickets and improve their utility. If the tickets were given with no strings attached, Pete (Figure C) would move to *K* on indifference curve U_3^{Pete} (moving along ICC^{Pete}), and John (Figure D) would sell all his tickets in order to reach indifference curve U_3^{John} at the corner solution *H*. Whenever the boys value the marginal ticket less than the market price of the ticket, they can improve their utility by selling. Thus their father learns the hard way that gratitude is a marginal concept.

Finally, assume that the father subsidizes the purchase of tickets

("You pay half and I'll pay half"). The subsidy reduces the unit price of tickets to the boys, thereby rotating the budget line around point *A* to *AM* in Figure E. Pete moves along his price-consumption curve to *N* on indifference curve

U_4^{Pete} because, until *N* is reached, the value of the marginal ticket exceeds the market price. John remains at the corner solution *A* because the value he places on the marginal ticket is still less than the

Continued on page 52

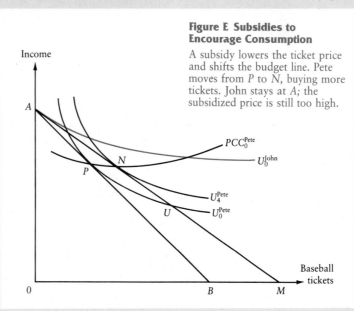

Figure E Subsidies to Encourage Consumption

A subsidy lowers the ticket price and shifts the budget line. Pete moves from *P* to *N*, buying more tickets. John stays at *A*; the subsidized price is still too high.

subsidized price. Thus John's behavior seems to reveal his ingratitude for his father's "generous" offer. In fact, the subsidy is just not large enough to affect John's decision at the margin. A larger subsidy could indeed alter the relationship between the marginal rate of substitution and relative prices, causing John to buy tickets. Could John correctly say to his father, "I'll show more gratitude if you'll increase the subsidy"?

Some general conclusions are in order to gather up the loose ends:

1. Direct cash payments impose fewer limitations on the choice set than in-kind gifts do and permit the broadest utility improvement for consumers. However, direct cash payments are ineffective in increasing the use of goods among consumers who have relatively weak preferences for such goods.

2. Subsidies work much like direct cash payments for consumers with relatively strong preferences for the subsidized good. But among consumers with weak preferences, the subsidy may only weakly encourage consumption. Furthermore, the level of the required subsidy may be very high.

3. In-kind gifts of commodities can induce consumption of those commodities even among consumers with relatively weak preferences. But restrictions on the resale of such gifts—which are necessary to assure that the gift commodity is used by the recipient—may constrain the consumer to a preference level inferior to what could be achieved if the gift were given "with no strings attached." The availability of higher utility through resale explains why many recipients of such in-kind welfare commodities

as food and refrigerators illegally resell the gifts.

Baseball tickets may create burning disputes within a family but are relatively unimportant as a public-policy issue. However, the same concepts can be extended to many similar cases of vast importance. For example, do employees prefer health insurance fringe benefits (in-kind payments) or simply higher money incomes? Should the poor be encouraged to attend college through tuition subsidies, direct cash payments, or education "vouchers," a cash payment that can be used only to pay tuition? Should government agencies assist the poor through negative income taxes (cash payments), food (gifts in kind), or food stamps (subsidies on expenditures)? The theory of consumer behavior provides a framework for organizing thoughts about these enormously important public-policy issues.

The Market Demand Curve

We have seen how a single consumer's demand curve can be derived from constrained optimization using either cardinal or ordinal consumer theory. However, we are seldom interested in individual demand as an end result. Thus we need a theoretical technique for moving from the individual demand curve to the aggregation of all such demands within a particular industry or market. This aggregation is called the **market demand curve**.

The key to aggregating individual demand curves into a market demand curve is to remember that individual demand curves are used—not individual indifference curves. Having derived all the individual demand curves from the indifference maps of each consumer, one could arrive at the market (industry) demand curve by **horizontal summation** of the individual curves. In Figure 3.20 the demand curves d_1 and d_2 represent demand for the only two consumers in a particular market. Each point on the market demand curve D is the result of a horizontal sum of individual quantities demanded at a given price. Thus, added horizontally, $A = a_1 + a_2$ at price P_1 and $B = b_1 + b_2$ at price P_2. Plotting all points such as A and B defines the market demand curve, labeled $\Sigma_h d_i$.[4]

The functional form of the demand curve is

$$Q_d = f(P, \overline{P}^s, \overline{P}^c, \overline{I}, \overline{N}, \overline{\ldots}) \qquad (3.11)$$

4. Remember that the symbol Σ, the Greek letter sigma, means "addemallup." The symbol Σ_h means "addemallup horizontally."

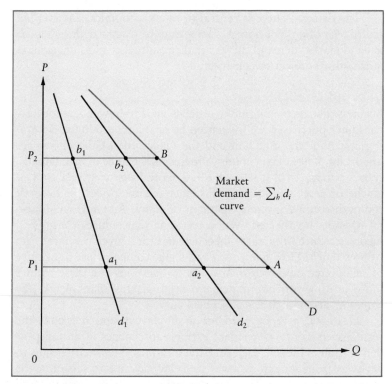

Figure 3.20
The Market Demand Curve
The market demand curve is the horizontal summation of consumers' individual demand curves.

This equation applies to individual as well as market demand curves, except that N, the number of consumers, is only relevant to the market curve. If all shift parameters—such as P^s, P^c, I, and N—are fixed, the demand curve is determined by changing the movement parameter—product price—and tracing out the two-dimensional relationship between price (P) and quantity demanded (Q_d). Changes in the shift parameters displace the demand curve. An increase in income shifts the demand to the right for a normal good and to the left for an inferior good. An increase in the number of consumers shifts the demand curve to the right. Increases in the price of substitutes and complements shift the demand curve to the right and left, respectively. Also, a change in consumer preferences, as when the consumer's indifference map shifts, causes a displacement in the demand curve. Chapter 2 discussed these shifts intuitively. We can now verify those assertions with indifference-curve analysis.

Note too that, if we select income instead of product price as the movement parameter, we derive an Engel curve, a two-dimensional relationship between income (I) and quantity demanded (Q_d). Engel curves are also derived directly from individual indifference curves and aggregated into a market Engel curve by horizontal summation of the individual quantities demanded at each level of income. Changes in the product price—hence relative prices—shift the Engel curve, as do changes in preferences.

The demand curve is central to microeconomics, and we will return to it often. For now it is important to recognize that individual and market demand curves are the result when consumers maximize utility subject to constraints.

Demand Elasticities

Business managers and public officials need to have a feel for how consumer purchases are influenced by changing economic circumstances. Both the direction and the magnitude of the effects are important. If a sporting goods shop lowers the price of racquetballs, *ceteris paribus,* will it sell just a few more balls or attract an avalanche of new customers? Will higher relative prices for hospital rooms discourage just a few patients or many? And how will hospital revenues be affected? Will a recession that reduces consumers' incomes reduce or increase their demand for a given product? And by how much? How many sales will a glue company lose if the price of cellophane tape drops? Answers to questions like these require more information about demand relationships than merely the slopes of demand curves and Engel curves.

Elasticity, a fancy term for a simple concept, measures the responsiveness of a dependent variable to changes in an independent variable. Indeed, each time the meaning of *elasticity* begins to get away from you, an easy way to reel it back in is to substitute the word *responsiveness.* The most general definition of elasticity (ε) is

$$\varepsilon = \frac{\%\Delta \text{ dependent variable}}{\%\Delta \text{ independent variable}}\bigg|_{(x,\, y,\, z,\, \ldots)} \qquad (3.12)$$

Remember that the notation $A|_{(x,\, y,\, z,\, \ldots)}$ means A is calculated holding the terms $(x, y, z, \ldots)$ fixed. Hence, elasticity focuses solely on the percentage changes in the dependent variable arising from a percentage change in *one* independent variable, *ceteris paribus*— that is, holding all other possible influences fixed.

Now let's turn to specific demand elasticities. Consider the following demand equation for good X:

$$X \quad = \quad f(P, \qquad I, \qquad P_Y, \qquad \ldots) \qquad (3.13)$$

price elasticity $= \varepsilon_{XP}$

income elasticity $= \varepsilon_{XI}$

cross-price elasticity $= \varepsilon_{XP_Y}$

any other demand elasticity, such as advertising

The dependent variable, X, is influenced by many independent variables. An elasticity can be calculated for each separate factor, *ceteris paribus.* Hence

$$\text{Price elasticity} = \varepsilon_{XP} = \frac{\%\Delta X}{\%\Delta P}\bigg|_{(I,\ P_Y,\ \ldots)} \qquad (3.14)$$

$$\text{Income elasticity} = \varepsilon_{XI} = \frac{\%\Delta X}{\%\Delta I}\bigg|_{(P,\ P_Y,\ \ldots)} \qquad (3.15)$$

$$\text{Cross-price elasticity} = \varepsilon_{XP_Y} = \frac{\%\Delta X}{\%\Delta P_Y}\bigg|_{(P,\ I,\ \ldots)} \qquad (3.16)$$

Four points regarding elasticity require clarification. First, every measure of elasticity is the ratio of percentage changes, with the dependent variable in the numerator and the independent variable in the denominator. A percentage change is the absolute change in a variable's value divided by the base value; hence, elasticity can be expressed as follows, using price elasticity of demand as a specific example:

$$\varepsilon_{XP} = \frac{\%\Delta X}{\%\Delta P} = \frac{\dfrac{\Delta X}{X}}{\dfrac{\Delta P}{P}} = \frac{\Delta X}{\Delta P}\cdot\frac{P}{X} \qquad (3.17)$$

In the last form, elasticity is the product of two terms: $\Delta X/\Delta P$, the inverse of the slope of the demand curve, and P/X, the ratio of bases. This formulation will prove useful as we proceed. All other elasticities take the same general form: the product of a slope term and a ratio of bases.

The second point about elasticity is that slope alone cannot be used to estimate responsiveness. For example, the most straightforward expression of responsiveness of quantity demanded to price changes would appear to be the slope of the demand curve, $\Delta P/\Delta X$, or its inverse, $\Delta X/\Delta P$. However, slope has the major defect that its value depends on the units by which X and P are measured. If price is measured in dollars in Figure 3.21, the slope of the demand curve between points A and B is -0.1; but if price is measured in cents, the slope is -10. Thus slope may vary due to arbitrary choices of the units of measure, without any change in actual responsiveness. Because slope is such a confusing measure of such response, economists use elasticity instead, which measures percentage changes rather than absolute changes.

Equation 3.17 emphasizes the point that elasticity and slope are not equivalent, although they are related. The term $\Delta X/\Delta P$, the inverse of slope, is one component of the elasticity formula. Multiplying the inverse of the slope by P/X produces a measure of responsiveness that is unaffected by arbitrary unit choices. Because elasticity compares percentage changes of X and P, it does not matter which units are selected; the elasticity value is unaffected by arbitrary selection of unit measurements. You can use Figure 3.21

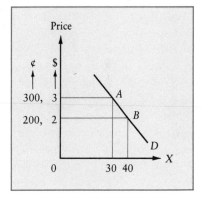

Figure 3.21
Slope versus Elasticity

The demand curve's slope changes when an arbitrary decision is made to measure price in cents instead of dollars. The elasticity does not vary with such changes because all calculations are percentage changes rather than absolute changes.

to verify the last sentence. Compute the price elasticity of demand between *A* and *B* for both price measures. You will find that the slopes differ; the elasticities do not.

The third point about elasticity is that the signs of the various elasticity coefficients are important. The price elasticity coefficient, ε_{XP}, is negative, because price changes cause changes in the opposite direction of the quantity demanded. Even so, absolute values are frequently used for convenience. The income elasticity coefficient, ε_{XI}, is positive for normal goods and negative for inferior goods. The cross-price elasticity coefficient, ε_{XP_Y}, is positive when *Y* is a substitute for *X* and negative when *Y* is a complement.

Fourth, we can, at least conceptually, define an elasticity between any dependent and independent variable, such as the elasticity of housing starts with respect to increases in mortgage interest rates, the elasticity of car accidents with respect to higher travel speeds, or the elasticity of pimples with respect to additional consumption of chocolate bars. But our current topic is product demand, so we have focused on the various demand elasticities. Later, the same concept is used to estimate supply relationships, degrees of input substitutability, supply and demand responses, and so forth.

Study Equation 3.17, the formula for price elasticity of demand, to make sure you understand that it is a ratio of percentage changes. Then, before you proceed to the next section, write out the elasticity formulas for housing starts, car accidents, and pimples, as well as the cross-price and income demand elasticities, using the form in Equation 3.17.

Total Revenue and Price Elasticity of Demand

Firms' **total revenue (TR)** is identical to consumers' **total expenditures (TE)**. Both equal the number of units purchased times the price per unit; they are opposite sides of the same transaction.

$$\text{TR} = \text{TE} = P \cdot X \tag{3.18}$$

How is total revenue influenced by a price reduction? If *X* (quantity purchased) remained constant, a lower price would reduce total revenue. But demand theory teaches us that a lower price will raise *X*, tending to raise total revenue. Every price change moves the quantity sold in the opposite direction. Whether total revenue rises, falls, or stays the same when the price changes depends on how responsive *X* is to *P*. Thus, we must know the price elasticity of demand in order to estimate the effect of a price change on total revenue. The absolute value of the price elasticity of demand is

$$|\varepsilon_{XP}| = \frac{\%\Delta X}{\%\Delta P} \tag{3.19}$$

Table 3.2
Total Revenue and Price Elasticity of Demand

If $|\varepsilon_{XP}|$	Demand Is	A Percentage Change in P	A Change in P
> 1	Price elastic	Causes a greater-than-proportional change in X	Changes TR in the opposite direction
< 1	Price inelastic	Causes a less-than-proportional change in X	Changes TR in the same direction
$= 1$	Unit elastic	Causes a proportional change in X	Does not change TR

Suppose that a 1% price reduction causes a 20% increase in the quantity sold. $|\varepsilon_{XP}|$ is greater than 1 because the numerator exceeds the denominator. Total revenue rises because the upward pull on revenue due to sales expansion dominates the downward pull due to the lower price. In this case, quantity sold is quite responsive to price changes. Demand is considered **price elastic** if a price change leads to a change in total revenue of the opposite direction. $|\varepsilon_{XP}| > 1$ because the price change causes a greater than proportional change in the quantity demanded.

If a 20% reduction in price generates only a 1% increase in the units sold, total revenue falls. The downward pull on revenue due to the lower price per unit is now relatively stronger than the upward pull from selling more X. $|\varepsilon_{XP}| < 1$, and the quantity sold is not very responsive to price changes. Demand is considered **price inelastic** if a price change leads to a change in total revenue of the same direction. $|\varepsilon_{XP}| < 1$ because the price change causes a less than proportional change in the quantity demanded.

Finally, suppose a 1% reduction in price causes a 1% increase in the quantity sold. In this case, total revenue remains the same, and $|\varepsilon_{XP}| = 1$. Demand is considered **unit elastic** if a price change leaves total revenue unchanged. $|\varepsilon_{XP}| = 1$ because the price change and the resulting change in the quantity demanded are proportional.

Table 3.2 summarizes all three of these relationships.

Marginal Revenue and Price Elasticity of Demand

We have just seen, intuitively, how price changes, total revenue changes, and price elasticity of demand are related. Now we must look at these relationships formally, relying on a simple but useful formula. As you read through the four steps that follow, pay special attention to the interpretation of revenue changes.

STEP 1: THE CHANGE IN REVENUE   Look at Figure 3.22 and consider the move from A to B along the demand curve. It indicates that price must be lowered in order to sell more goods. Total revenue at each point is price times quantity:

Figure 3.22
Change in Total Revenue
Total revenue is $P \cdot X$ at A and $(P + \Delta P)(X + \Delta X)$ at B. The change in total revenue when price falls by ΔP is this: $\Delta R = (P + \Delta P)(X + \Delta X) - PX = \Delta X(P + \Delta P) + (\Delta P \cdot X)$. The sign of ΔR depends on the relative size of the revenue *gain* from selling extra units at the lower price, $\Delta X(P + \Delta P)$, and the *loss* from lowering the price on units previously selling at a higher price, $\Delta P \cdot X$.

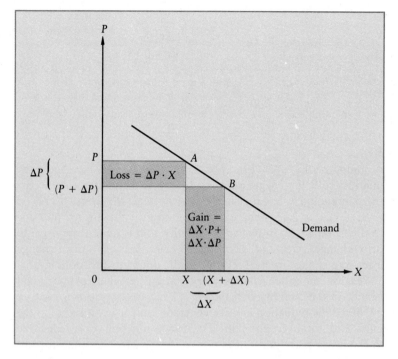

$$\text{Total revenue at } A = R_A = P \cdot X \qquad (3.20)$$

$$\text{Total revenue at } B = R_B = (P + \Delta P)(X + \Delta X)$$

where

$$\Delta P < 0 \quad \text{and} \quad \Delta X > 0$$

The change in total revenue from A to B can be stated as

$$\Delta R = \underset{\text{revenue at } B}{(P + \Delta P)(X + \Delta X)} - \underset{\text{revenue at } A}{(P \cdot X)} \qquad (3.21)$$

Expanding and simplifying Equation 3.21 yields

$$\Delta R = (\Delta P \cdot X) + (\Delta X \cdot P) + (\Delta X \cdot \Delta P) \qquad (3.22)$$
$$= \Delta X(P + \Delta P) + (\Delta P \cdot X)$$

The change in total revenue, ΔR, is the result of two forces, illustrated by the shaded rectangles in Figure 3.22. The term $\Delta X(P + \Delta P)$ is the gain in revenue from selling ΔX new units of output at the lower price $(P + \Delta P)$; the term $\Delta P \cdot X$ is the loss in revenue from lowering the price by ΔP on X units that previously sold at the higher price. Whether ΔR is positive, negative, or zero depends on the relative sizes of gain and loss terms. For example,

$$P = \$30, \quad (P + \Delta P) = \$25, \quad \Delta P = -\$5 \qquad (3.23)$$

$$X = 20 \text{ units}, \quad (X + \Delta X) = 30 \text{ units}, \quad \Delta X = 10 \text{ units}$$

$$\Delta R = \underset{\substack{\text{total revenue} \\ \text{at lower} \\ \text{price}}}{(\$25 \cdot 30)} - \underset{\substack{\text{total revenue} \\ \text{at higher} \\ \text{price}}}{(\$30 \cdot 20)} = \$150$$

The change in revenue, $\Delta R = \$150$, breaks down as follows:

$$\Delta R = \Delta X (P + \Delta P) + (\Delta P \cdot X) \qquad (3.24)$$

$$\Delta R = \underset{\substack{\text{gain in} \\ \text{revenue} \\ \text{from} \\ \text{selling} \\ \text{extra units}}}{10(\$25)} + \underset{\substack{\text{loss in} \\ \text{revenue from} \\ \text{lowering price} \\ \text{on units} \\ \text{previously sold} \\ \text{at higher prices}}}{(-\$5) \cdot 20} = \$150 > 0$$

Because a price cut increases total revenue by $150, demand is price elastic: Gains are greater than losses.

STEP 2: SIMPLIFICATION   We can simplify terms somewhat by selecting a small enough move along the demand curve so that the term $\Delta X \cdot \Delta P$ in Equation 3.22, the product of two arbitrarily small numbers, can be ignored. Thus,

$$\Delta R = \underset{\text{gain}}{(\Delta X \cdot P)} + \underset{\text{loss}}{(\Delta P \cdot X)} \qquad (3.25)$$

This equation for ΔR has the same interpretation as Equation 3.22, except that it has been simplified to take into account small, continuous movements in price and quantity. The revenue gain and loss rectangles in Figure 3.22 also have the same interpretation. Revenue rises by $\Delta X \cdot P$ because ΔX new units of X are sold when the price falls to P; but revenue falls by $\Delta P \cdot X$ because the price reduction, which is necessary to capture extra sales, involves a price cut ΔP on X units that previously sold at higher prices. For example,

$P = \$100 =$ lower price needed to increase sales

$X = 500 \text{ units} =$ initial units sold per time period at higher price

$\Delta P = -\$1 =$ price reduction

$\Delta X = 3 \text{ units} =$ extra units sold when price falls

$$\Delta R = \underset{\text{gain}}{(\Delta X \cdot P)} + \underset{\text{loss}}{(\Delta P \cdot X)}$$

$$\Delta R = 3(\$100) + (-\$1)500 = -\$200 < 0$$

Because a price cut reduces total revenue by $200, demand is price inelastic: Losses are greater than gains.

STEP 3: DERIVATION OF MARGINAL REVENUE   The term ΔR is the total change in total revenues. If we divide Equation 3.25 by ΔX, we obtain

$$\frac{\Delta R}{\Delta X} = \underset{\text{gain}}{P} + \underset{\text{loss}}{X\frac{\Delta P}{\Delta X}} \tag{3.26}$$

The term $\Delta R/\Delta X$ is **marginal revenue (MR),** or the change in total revenue, ΔR, resulting from a change in the units of X sold, ΔX. In other words, marginal revenue is the change in total revenue per unit increase in X. Equation 3.26 expresses marginal revenue as the net result of a gain and a loss, as before, but now per unit of X. P is the gain in revenue from selling one more unit; $X \cdot (\Delta P/\Delta X)$ is the loss in revenue from selling X units per time period at lower prices than before. For example,

$$P = \$40 = \text{new, lower price needed to expand sales}$$

$$X = 70 \text{ units} = \text{units previously sold at higher price}$$

$$\Delta P = -\$2 = \text{price reduction}$$

$$\Delta X = 1$$

$$\text{MR} = \frac{\Delta R}{\Delta X} = P + X\frac{\Delta P}{\Delta X}$$

$$\text{MR} = \$40 + \$70\,\frac{-\$2}{1} = -\$100 < 0$$

Because the MR is negative, the price cut reduces total revenue: Demand is price inelastic.

STEP 4: THE RELATIONSHIP OF MARGINAL REVENUE, PRICE, AND ELASTICITY With a definition of marginal revenue in place, we can relate it rigorously to price elasticity of demand. Dividing Equation 3.26 by price gives us

$$\frac{\text{MR}}{P} = \frac{P}{P} + \frac{X}{P} \cdot \frac{\Delta P}{\Delta X} = (1 + \frac{1}{\varepsilon}) \tag{3.27}$$

because $(X/P) \cdot (\Delta P/\Delta X)$ is the inverse of the price elasticity of demand, ε. Now multiply each side by P:

$$\text{MR} = P(1 + \frac{1}{\varepsilon}) \tag{3.28}$$

As you can see, marginal revenue depends on the price elasticity of demand. Marginal revenue is zero when ε is -1, positive when $\varepsilon < -1$, and negative when $\varepsilon > 1$. Recall, however, that price elasticity is frequently expressed as an absolute value. Table 3.3 includes both conventions in a summary of the relationships between elasticity and marginal revenue.

Table 3.3
Marginal Revenue and Price Elasticity of Demand

Demand Is	When ε	And When $|\varepsilon|$	Implying MR $= \Delta TR/\Delta X$
Perfectly elastic	$= \infty$	$= \infty$	> 0
Elastic	< -1	> 1	> 0
Unit elastic	$= -1$	$= 1$	$= 0$
Inelastic	> -1	< 1	< 0
Perfectly inelastic	$= 0$	$= 0$	$= -\infty$

The Price-Consumption Curve and Price Elasticity of Demand

Elastic, inelastic, and unit elastic demand responses can be visualized quickly by checking the slope of the price-consumption curve. Figure 3.23 measures X on the horizontal axis and the consumer's money income—the numeraire—on the vertical axis. Let M stand for the money income spent on all goods except X. The budget line becomes $I = M + (P_X \cdot X)$, because whatever is not spent on X is spent on other goods. Rearranging the budget equation to standard linear form yields $M = I - P_X X$. The vertical intercept is money income, I, and the absolute value of the slope is the price of X, P_X. The consumer's total expenditures on X—which equal sellers' total revenue—is the distance between I and M on the vertical axis. In

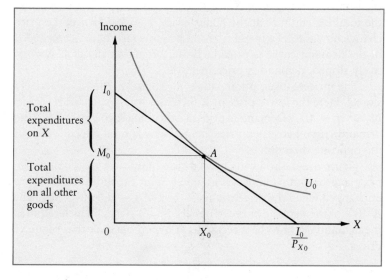

Figure 3.23
The Numeraire and Indifference Analysis

The numeraire is money income spent on all goods except X. For commodity bundle A, M_0 dollars of income are spent on other goods. Because total income is I_0, total expenditures on X_0 units of X is the residual $I_0 - M_0$.

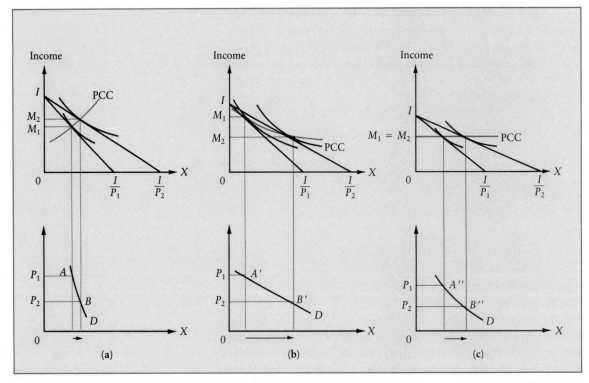

Figure 3.24
Price Elasticity and the Slope of the PCC

(a) Demand is price inelastic when the PCC is positively sloped because a reduction in price reduces total expenditures: $(I - M_1) > (I - M_2)$.
(b) Demand is price elastic when the PCC is negatively sloped because a reduction in price increases total expenditures: $(I - M_1) < (I - M_2)$.
(c) Demand is unit elastic when the PCC is horizontal because a reduction in price does not change total expenditures: $(I - M_1) = (I - M_2)$.

Figure 3.23, the consumer's optimum commodity bundle is point A, purchasing X_0 units of X. I_0 is total income, of which M_0 is spent on all goods but X; $I_0 - M_0$ is spent on X.

Now refer to Figure 3.24a. Reducing the price of X from P_1 to P_2 produces a positively sloped price-consumption curve and a corresponding move along segment AB of the demand curve. Note that the total expenditure on X at the lower price, $I - M_2$, is less than the total expenditure at the higher price, $I - M_1$. Hence, the price change moves total expenditures in the same direction: Segment AB of the demand curve is price inelastic. Whenever the PCC is positively sloped, demand is price inelastic.

The price-consumption curve in Figure 3.24b is negatively sloped. Here the lower price of X increases total expenditures: $(I - M_2) > (I - M_1)$. Demand is price elastic along segment $A'B'$ of the demand curve because a price change moves total expenditures in the opposite direction.

Figure 3.24c shows the special case of unit elasticity. Since the price-consumption curve is horizontal, total expenditures on X are unchanged when the price changes: $(I - M_2) = (I - M_1)$. Segment $A''B''$ of the demand curve in panel c is unit elastic, which requires the demand curve to be a rectangular hyperbola over that range of prices.

Table 3.4
The Price-Consumption Curve and Price Elasticity of Demand

When the PCC Is	Demand Is	And Changes in Price
Positively sloped	Price inelastic	Change revenue in the same direction
Negatively sloped	Price elastic	Change revenue in the opposite direction
Horizontal	Unit elastic	Do not change revenue

Although we have worked in this section with price decreases, the same rules apply to price increases. The slope of the PCC shows the relative price elasticity of demand, as Table 3.4 summarizes.

Computations: Arc versus Point Elasticity

Let's turn now to the specifics of elasticity computations. Consider the demand curve in Figure 3.25. It is usually meaningless to talk about the elasticity of the entire demand schedule.[5] Rather, elasticity is usually measured along a small "arc" of the schedule, such as between points A and B. This practice is referred to as the **arc elasticity** determination. We can make the arc as small as we please. At the extreme, when the arc shrinks to a single point, we measure **point elasticity.** Arc elasticity estimates responsiveness between two points; point elasticity refers to responsiveness close to a single point.

ARC ELASTICITY   Let's begin by computing arc elasticity between points A and B in Figure 3.25. The formula is

$$\varepsilon = \frac{\Delta X/X}{\Delta P/P} = \frac{\Delta X}{\Delta P} \cdot \frac{P}{X} \qquad (3.29)$$

The percentage change of price is the absolute price change, ΔP, divided by the base price, P. Moving from A to B and using $P = 2$ as the base, the percentage change in price is $\Delta P/P = -1/2$. Similarly, $\Delta X/X = 20/50$. Thus $\varepsilon = (2/5)/(-1/2) = -4/5$.

However, if we move from B to A, using the original values as bases, $\varepsilon = (-20/70)/(1/1) = -2/7$. The responsiveness of X to price increases and decreases is the same between A and B. The elasticity coefficients differ because different bases are used in computing percentage changes. This problem is solved by selecting a base that is neither the beginning nor ending base but is the average of the two.

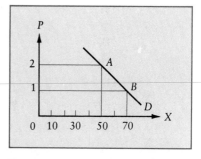

Figure 3.25
Arc Elasticity

Price elasticity along arc AB equals $-1/2$ when average price and quantity bases are used in calculating the percentages.

5. Exceptions include the special cases of demand data that are "fitted" empirically to an exponential demand curve and demand curves that are unit elastic throughout their full range.

The average base, or **midpoint base,** is calculated for X as $(X_1 + X_2)/2$ and for P as $(P_1 + P_2)/2$. Thus arc elasticity may be expressed, using the midpoint base approach, as

$$\varepsilon = \frac{\Delta X}{\Delta P} \cdot \frac{(P_1 + P_2)/2}{(X_1 + X_2)/2} \qquad (3.30)$$

Using this formula, price elasticity is the same regardless of the direction of movement on the demand curve. Arc elasticity is a measure of average elasticity between A and B. Before you proceed, verify for yourself that the arc elasticity coefficient between A and B is $\varepsilon = -1/2$ when the midpoint bases are employed.

POINT ELASTICITY   What is the point elasticity of demand at point A in Figure 3.26? There is no need to calculate average bases now, because we are not moving along the demand curve as in the previous discussion of arc elasticity. Thus the elasticity formula can be applied directly. Recall that $|\varepsilon| = (\Delta X/\Delta P) \cdot (P/X)$ has two terms: the inverse of the slope of the demand curve, $\Delta X/\Delta P$, and the ratio of bases, P/X. In Figure 3.26 the inverse of the slope, in absolute value, is 10. The ratio of bases at A is 4/20. Thus $|\varepsilon| = 10 \cdot (4/20) = 2$. Demand is therefore price elastic at A.

A simple visual test can be used to check point elasticity. For example, the inverse of the slope of the demand curve in Figure 3.26 is DL/AD, and the ratio of bases is $AD/0D$. Hence elasticity, in absolute terms, is

$$|\varepsilon| = \frac{\Delta X}{\Delta P} \cdot \frac{P}{X} = \frac{DL}{AD} \cdot \frac{AD}{0D} = \frac{DL}{0D} \qquad (3.31)$$

Figure 3.26
Point Elasticity

For the linear demand curve shown here, price elasticity of demand at point A is this: $|\varepsilon| = 2 = DL/0D = 0M/MS = AL/SA$.

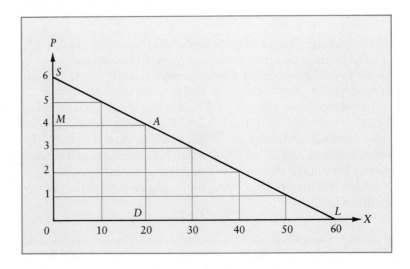

The term $DL/0D$ is a ratio of line segments. It is greater than unity because $DL > 0D$. Therefore, demand is elastic at point A.

Through the magic of similar right triangles, this visual test can also be applied to line segments on the vertical axis or on the demand curve itself. Thus, at point A,

$$|\varepsilon| = \underset{\substack{\text{using} \\ \text{horizontal} \\ \text{axis}}}{\frac{DL}{0D}} = \underset{\substack{\text{using} \\ \text{vertical} \\ \text{axis}}}{\frac{0M}{MS}} = \underset{\substack{\text{using} \\ \text{demand} \\ \text{curve}}}{\frac{AL}{SA}} \quad (3.32)$$

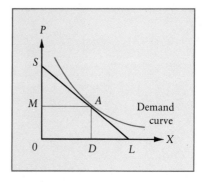

Figure 3.27
Point Elasticity When the Demand Curve Is Nonlinear

The point elasticity at A equals the following: $|\varepsilon| = DL/0D = 0M/MS = AL/SA$. A tangent is drawn to point A to evaluate the inverse slope at A, one of the terms in the elasticity formula.

If the demand curve is nonlinear, as in Figure 3.27, the procedure needs only one modification. The slope at point A is determined by drawing a tangent to the demand curve at point A and computing the slope of the tangent. The slope at A is AD/DL, hence its inverse is DL/AD. Now we can proceed as before:

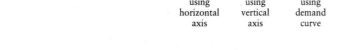

$$|\varepsilon| = \frac{\Delta X}{\Delta P} \cdot \frac{P}{X} = \frac{DL}{AD} \cdot \frac{AD}{0D} = \underset{\substack{\text{using} \\ \text{horizontal} \\ \text{axis}}}{\frac{DL}{0D}} = \underset{\substack{\text{using} \\ \text{vertical} \\ \text{axis}}}{\frac{0M}{MS}} = \underset{\substack{\text{using} \\ \text{demand} \\ \text{curve}}}{\frac{AL}{SA}} \quad (3.33)$$

These ratios are all less than 1. Therefore, demand at point A is price inelastic.

Now consider the straight-line demand curve in Figure 3.28. Using the technique just described, we can determine that unit elasticity occurs only at the middle point, B, because only there is the ratio BC/AB equal to 1. Any point between A and B is price elastic, and any point between B and C is price inelastic.

Demand is most price elastic at the top of the demand curve; it becomes less elastic as price is lowered. Recall that $|\varepsilon| = (\Delta X/\Delta P) \cdot (P/X)$. The term denoting the inverse slope is constant because the demand curve is linear. Elasticity differs at different points on the demand curve only because the bases that are used to calculate percentage changes vary. A movement down the demand curve lowers P and raises X, thereby reducing P/X and $|\varepsilon|$. Price elasticity falls in absolute value as price falls along a linear demand curve.

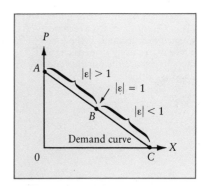

Figure 3.28
Price Elasticity of a Linear Demand Curve

Price elasticity of demand is unity at B, elastic along range AB, and inelastic along range BC.

Determinants of Price Elasticity of Demand
Empirical demand studies are somewhat rare, because they are expensive to produce in time and money. Thus managers and public officials must develop a feel for the price elasticities of goods and services that will enable them to make decisions in the absence of

econometric studies. Here is a rough guide to the major determinants of price elasticity:

1. *Availability of substitute goods:* Demand tends to be more price elastic the greater the presence of alternative goods. When a product's price rises, consumers may select an alternative. Substitution, a key concept in economics, is perhaps the most important determinant of price elasticity.

2. *Time that consumers have to adjust to price changes:* Demand is less elastic in the short run than in the long run, because consumers need time to seek out substitutes when prices change. For example, if heating prices rise, turning down the thermostat may be the only possible short-run adjustment. In the long run, the consumer might consider moving to Ecuador.

3. *Price proximity of substitutes:* Price elasticity tends to be higher the closer in price the available substitutes are. Physical substitutes may exist, but substitution is not feasible if their prices are too high. For example, jogging and a Hawaii vacation may be alternative means of relaxing, but they are not economic substitutes for most people because of the disparity in cost.

4. *Price of the good in relation to the consumer's budget:* Salt, straight pins, and shaving cream take a trivial amount of the typical consumer's total budget. Theoretically, price increases for such products should not discourage much consumption. However, pickled kumquats are probably relatively elastic despite their low burden on budgets. Therefore, this rule of thumb is relatively untrustworthy.

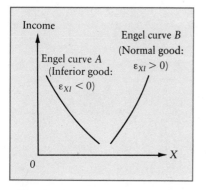

Figure 3.29
Engel Curves and Income Elasticity of Demand

A negatively sloped Engel curve (curve A) pertains to an inferior good, which also exhibits a negative income elasticity of demand. If the Engel curve is positively sloped (curve B), income elasticity is positive and the good is normal.

Income, Cross-Price, and Other Demand Elasticities

Elasticity is relevant for every independent variable influencing the purchase of X. For example, income elasticity of demand, ε_{XI}, measures the percentage change in purchases of X due to a percentage change in consumer income, *ceteris paribus*.

$$\varepsilon_{XI} = \frac{\%\Delta X}{\%\Delta I} = \frac{\Delta X}{\Delta I} \cdot \frac{I}{X} \qquad (3.34)$$

Just as price elasticity of demand differs from the slope of the demand curve, so income elasticity differs from the slope of the Engel curve. (Two Engel curves are shown in Figure 3.29.) Because income elasticity is the product of a slope term, $\Delta X/\Delta I$, and a ratio of bases, I/X, the income elasticity coefficients will have different signs. In Figure 3.29, curve A has a negative slope, and curve B is positively sloped. Specifically, $\varepsilon_{XI} < 0$ for curve A, and $\varepsilon_{XI} > 0$ for curve B. The income elasticity is negative for inferior goods, such as margarine, and positive for normal goods, such as restaurant meals.[6] For either case, the larger the elasticity coefficient in absolute value, the more responsive purchasers are to changes in income.

Income elasticities are important to businesses in estimating sales for their products at various stages in the economy's business cycle. Firms expecting recession and falling incomes may add product lines regarded as income inferior in order to protect themselves during downturns. Chapter 4 will show the important role that income elasticities play in various applications of consumer theory.

Cross-price elasticity of demand, ε_{XP_Y}, measures the responsiveness of sales of X to changes in the price of another good, Y:

$$\varepsilon_{XP_Y} = \frac{\% \Delta X}{\% \Delta P_Y} = \frac{\Delta X}{\Delta P_X} \cdot \frac{P_Y}{X} \qquad (3.35)$$

Figure 3.30 shows two possible relationships between good X (television sets) and the prices of other products. Let's say that good Y is an Atari-type video game played at home on a TV screen. A higher price for such games would reduce TV sales, as shown in curve A. Accordingly, the cross-price elasticity of demand would be negative. If, on the other hand, good Y is movies shown exclusively in theaters, more TV sets should be purchased when movie prices go up, *ceteris paribus*. Cross-price elasticity between movies and TV should be positive. Note that negative cross-price elasticities identify goods that are complements, whereas positive elasticities indicate that goods are substitutes. As always, the greater the absolute values of the coefficient, the higher the elasticity.

Note that cross-price elasticity is an asymmetrical measure of substitutability and complementarity between goods, because it deals only with good X and the price of Y. There is no reason to expect sales of good Y to respond equally to a change in the price of X. A change in the price of video games may influence TV sales more (or less) than a change in the price of TV sets changes sales of video games. Of course, cross-price elasticities would be near zero for products only remotely related to each other, such as dog licenses and creamed spinach.

Demand elasticities can be calculated for all independent influences on demand, such as advertising, population, age composition of the buying public, level of literacy in the population, and so forth. Understanding elasticity is a prerequisite to professional business management and essential in public policymaking.

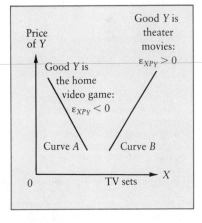

Figure 3.30
Cross-Price Elasticity of Demand

If X and Y are complements, the curve is negatively sloped and the cross-price elasticity is negative. For substitutes, the curve is positively sloped and the cross-price elasticity is positive.

6. Margarine has an income elasticity of -0.2, as reported by H. Wold and L. Jureen, *Demand Analysis* (New York: Wiley, 1953). Restaurant meals have an income elasticity of $+1.4$, as reported by Houthakker and Taylor, *Consumer Demand in the United States: Analysis and Projections* (Cambridge, Mass.: Harvard University Press, 1970).

Price Elasticity of Gas and Oil

APPLIED
MICRO
THEORY

3.2

The oil crisis of the mid-1970s provides an example of the usefulness of the elasticity concept in economic analysis. As fuel supplies shrunk, the upward pressure on gasoline prices was immense. However, many people in responsible places argued against permitting gasoline prices to rise in response to market forces for two reasons. First, there is virtually no substitute for gasoline in our present automobiles. Thus people cannot cut back their consumption of gasoline in response to higher prices. Second, higher gasoline prices must increase consumer expenditures on gasoline.

Let's study these arguments by referring to the accompanying figure, which displays an indifference map in panel a, and three gasoline demand curves in panel b. Money income is the numeraire. With the price of gas at its initial value P_0, the consumer selects commodity bundle A on indifference curve U_4. G_0 gallons of gas are bought at price P_0. Now let price rise to P_1. In the very shortest of runs, before the consumer has time to seek out any substitutes for the higher-priced gas, bundle B will be selected. The same G_0 gallons of gas are purchased at the higher price. The corresponding momentary short-run demand curve in panel b is labeled D_M. It is totally inelastic due to the complete absence of substitution during the limited time period.

Substitution increases in the long run as the consumer consolidates shopping trips, uses mass transit, forms car pools, replaces worn-out large-engine cars with gas-efficient compacts, and even changes residence to be closer to bus and rail terminals or closer to work. Given enough time, the consumer

Short-Run versus Long-Run Price Elasticity of Demand

When gasoline prices rise, the consumer moves from A to B when time is too short to adjust at all. Gradually, the consumer adjusts expenditures along the steeper budget line toward C and ultimately to E. Demand curves are more elastic in the long run than in the short run.

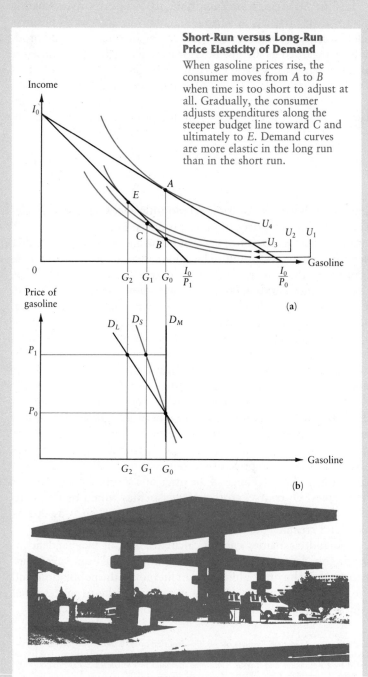

(a)

(b)

can adjust to bundle E on indifference curve U_3. The full long-run demand adjustment to gas price P_1 reduces consumption to G_2; the long-run demand curve is D_L.

However, the move from bundle B to E is gradual. The consumer may make an intermediate adjustment by selecting bundle C on the way to long-run equilibrium at E. Curve D_S is a short-run demand curve that lies between the two extremes of making no substitutions (curve D_M) and completing all adjustments (curve D_L). Demand elasticity increases in the long run as greater substitutability comes into play.

The actual elasticity coefficients of short-run versus long-run demand are empirical questions, the computations of which should play a central role in the current debate concerning gasoline price controls. Theoretically at least, it is possible for gas price increases to reduce consumers' total expenditures on gasoline—if the price increase generates sufficient long-run alternatives.* Thus the usual arguments in favor of gas price controls ignore the role of substitution in consumer decision-making (as well as the other side effects of price controls, which are discussed in Chapter 2).

*Professor Louis Philips has estimated long- and short-run consumer demand price elasticities for gasoline and oil. He reports a short-run price elasticity of −0.11 and a long-run price elasticity of −0.68; demand is therefore price inelastic in both the short and long run but much less inelastic in the long run. According to these figures, total consumer expenditures on gasoline and oil will increase in both the short and long run. See Louis Philips, "A Dynamic Version of the Linear Expenditure Model," *Review of Economics and Statisitics* 54 (1972): 450–488.

A similar analysis applies to natural gas. Houthakker and Taylor report that the price elasticity for residential natural gas consumption is 0.15 in the short run and 10.74 in the long run. Obviously there is much greater substitutability for natural gas than for gasoline! See H. S. Houthakker and Lester D. Taylor, *Consumer Demand in the United States: Analysis and Projections*, 2nd ed. (Cambridge, Mass: Harvard University Press, 1970).

Elasticity of Public Transportation: Transit Fares and Frequency

APPLIED MICRO THEORY

3.3

The demand for transit rides is a function of the money price (the fare) and the "time price." Riders are sensitive to increases in both of these prices. In the case of buses, the time price is a function of bus frequency; it enters peoples' decisions in two ways:

1. *Frequency delay:* Many people are only vaguely aware of bus schedules. Many buses do not adhere to schedules due to traffic congestion or incompetence. Thus riders will find that their waiting time is a function of how frequently a bus arrives at their stop (the more buses, the smaller the delay).

2. *Schedule delay:* When buses do adhere strictly to a schedule, bus frequency is still important. Even though there is very little waiting at the stop, people must still plan their work, leisure, and shopping trips to coincide with the transit schedule. The greater the bus frequency, the smaller the interference with one's daily schedule and the lower the opportunity cost of taking the bus.

For these two reasons, $R = f(P, B)$. That is, ridership (R) is a function of the bus fare (P) and the number of buses (B), which is a proxy for bus frequency.

Professor James P. Moody, in a study of the Milwaukee County Transit System, discovered that ridership with respect to money price (fare) is inelastic ($\varepsilon_P = -0.558$), whereas ridership is roughly unit elastic with respect to bus frequency ($\varepsilon_B = -1.04$).* This means that the reduction in fares favored by many ardent proponents of public transit would reduce revenue and perhaps, in this age of taxpayer revolt, cut down on the frequency of buses, which is far more important to riders than price is.

*James P. Moody, "Supply and Demand for Urban Bus Travel: Theoretical Revision and Empirical Estimation," Department of Economics, University of Wisconsin, Milwaukee, April 1974. (Mimeographed.) Keep in mind that it is an error to generalize from one city to another—or even one part of a city to another. These elasticities depend on population density, rider income, weather, and so on.

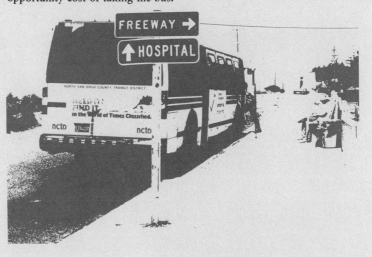

Job Training and Wage Elasticity of Labor Demand

APPLIED
MICRO
THEORY

3.4

Wage elasticity of labor demand is important in selecting suitable industries for government job-training programs. In fact, it is crucial that job training be applied to jobs with relatively high wage elasticities of demand.

Job training increases the labor supply, as illustrated by the shift from supply curve S_0 to S_1 in the accompanying figure. At each wage, the horizontal distance between S_0 and S_1 represents the newly trained workers. Job training reduces the wage from w_0 to w_1 and increases the number of available jobs from L_0 to L_1. If wage elasticity of demand is relatively low, as illustrated here, few new jobs are produced through job training, but the wages of existing employees are cut substantially. New workers $\overline{L_1L_2}$ are hired, but only $\overline{L_1L_0}$ new jobs are created. $\overline{L_0L_2}$ represents the significant number of workers who voluntarily leave the industry due to the lower wage.

The higher the wage elasticity of labor demand, the less the wage reduction induced by a given job-training program, the greater the creation of new jobs, and the less the wage-induced voluntary exit of existing workers.

Job training shifts the labor supply curve from S_0 to S_1, thus reducing wages from w_0 to w_1 and increasing the number of workers hired from L_0 to L_1. $\overline{L_1L_0}$ represents new jobs and $\overline{L_1L_2}$ is newly trained workers, so $\overline{L_0L_2}$ is the number of initial workers who leave the industry due to the lower wage. The higher the wage elasticity of labor demand, the more the new jobs that are created and the less the voluntary exit that occurs.

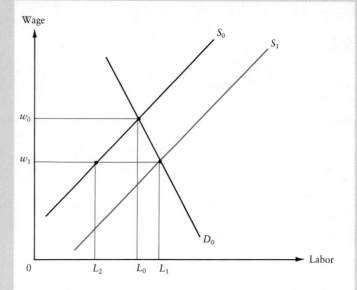

Using Industry Demand Elasticities at the Firm Level

APPLIED
MICRO
THEORY

3.5

Say that, as owner of a firm producing electronic components, you receive a steady stream of market reports containing demand elasticities with respect to price, income, population, and so forth. The latest report indicates that the price elasticity of demand (ϵ_{XP}) is -0.1 and that the population elasticity of demand ($\epsilon_{X,\ POP}$) is 1.0. How can you use these figures in the internal management decisions of your firm?

Demand theory helps you proceed cautiously and intelligently by alerting you to a simple truth: Industry statistics cannot be used directly at the firm level. Even though industry price elasticity of demand is -0.1, your firm cannot increase its price 10% and experience a mere 1% reduction in units sold. If all firms in the industry were to raise prices 10%, the number of units sold would fall collectively by 1%. However, if your industry is extremely competitive, your firm's price elasticity of demand will be vastly more elastic than the overall industry's because of the abundant substitutes that your customers have to choose from. A price increase may well lower your firm's revenue, the industry elasticity of -0.1 notwithstanding. As you can see, industry elasticity figures must be used with extreme caution by individual firms.

Next consider the unit population elasticity. An increase in population of 10% increases the quantity of components demanded by 10% at each price. The population increase shifts the demand curve to the right. How much does product price rise? Because ΔX is 10%, ΔP must be 100%, or ten times 10%, because of the -0.1 price elasticity. However, the price would rise by 100% only if the supply curve had zero price elasticity of supply. The shortage of electronic components arising from the increased population must be eliminated solely by price adjustments if the supply curve is vertical and stationary. If the higher prices attract new competition and also a higher rate of sales from firms already in the industry, the supply of components will increase and price rises will be moderate. Depending on the speed of supply adjustment, there may be very little price rise at all.

Beware of careless and indiscriminate use of industrywide demand studies by single firms. The degree of industry competition and the size of the firm relative to the industry must be taken into account. Consumer analysis, the theoretical basis for elasticity calculations, directs us toward prudent interpretations and inferences.

Summary

Cardinal utility is a logical but empirically empty concept for studying consumer behavior. It requires the measurement of marginal utility in "utils" of satisfaction. Diminishing marginal utility is the underpinning of the cardinal demand curve.

Ordinal utility theory does not rely on measuring utility. It is rooted in three simple consumer axioms: (1) the ordering of bundles, (2) the transitivity of choices, and (3) nonsatiation in consumption. These axioms are used to derive the consumer's indifference map, a statement of the individual's preferences.

The key idea presented in this chapter is constrained optimization, the process by which individuals select commodity bundles that produce maximum utility, given their money income and product price constraints. Constrained optimization is an important component of economic analysis because it assumes both utility maximization and limitations on utility resulting from scarcity. Every point on a consumer's demand curve or Engel curve is derived from constrained utility-maximizing behavior.

It is remarkable that such common-sense consumer axioms can provide such a robust, relevant framework for organizing thoughts. In this chapter, the model was used to show how money payments, gifts-in-kind, and subsidies influence purchases among consumers whose preferences vary. This rudimentary form of analyzing consumer behav-

Key Terms

ior is most helpful in organizing thoughts about public issues, but the extensions that come in Chapter 4 will add a great many useful applications.

Elasticity is a fundamental concept in all sciences. It is the percentage change in a dependent variable divided by a percentage change in an independent variable, *ceteris paribus*. One can measure the elasticity of demand with respect to (1) the price of the good in question (say gasoline), (2) the price of alternatives (small cars use less gasoline), or (3) the money incomes of consumers (gasoline buyers). These elasticities are called, respectively, price elasticity of demand, cross-price elasticity of demand, and income elasticity of demand.

Demand elasticity is the solution to a measurement problem. It provides a way to estimate the responsiveness of the quantity demanded to changes in the independent variables that influence sales. Elasticity calculations are not influenced by arbitrary changes in unit measurements, such as switching from dollars to cents or single units sold to dozens sold, because all computations are percentage changes.

This chapter has presented elasticity in the context of consumer theory. We will encounter it often in the remaining chapters as a method of linking independent and dependent variables and of measuring their responsiveness.

Problems

1. "Blacks spend too much money on clothing and not enough on housing." Assuming that blacks and whites have equal access to both goods and using utility theory, show that this statement is equivalent to a quibbling about preferences.

2. Suppose that blacks are restricted to cheap, low-quality housing but have the same preferences as whites. Reanalyze the statement in the first problem using indifference curves and budget lines.

3. "I don't care how much you charge for water. I will never reduce my consumption below X gallons per day."
   a. Draw the indifference curves corresponding to this statement.
   b. Are you skeptical about the statement?

4. "I believe the only way to drink beer is with an egg and in a chilled glass stein." Draw the indifference curves corresponding to this statement.

5. "My car needs four tires and a spare. Therefore, my demand curve for tires is vertical." Criticize this statement.

6. It is often stated that in many tribal societies the consumption patterns are based on tradition, not relative prices. How did the tradition get started?

7. Suppose that a demand curve is vertical over a given range of prices.
   a. Draw the corresponding indifference map and budget lines.
   b. Draw the income-consumption curve. Is the good normal or inferior?

8. Suppose that that when the price of X rises, the consumption of Y is unchanged.
   a. Draw the corresponding indifference map and budget lines.
   b. Draw the income-consumption curve. Is X an inferior or normal

good? Is Y an inferior or normal good?

9. Draw indifference maps for the following special cases. Show the general shape of each indifference curve (MRS) and the direction of utility improvement in going from one indifference curve to another.
   a. Both products are economic "goods."
   b. The horizontal axis measures a "good," the vertical axis measures a "bad."
   c. Both products are "bads."

10. Economists prefer ordinal utility to cardinal utility in part because utility cannot be measured cardinally. Yet indifference curves cannot be measured either! So why the preference for ordinal utility?

11. Suppose that all products, including good X, are characterized by constant marginal utility. Construct a demand curve for X.

12. Refer to Applied Micro Theory 3.1 and analyze this situation: Should workers prefer health insurance fringe benefits or higher money incomes? How would tax considerations influence your answer? (Fringe benefits are untaxed.)

13. Use indifference-curve analysis to extend the usual analysis of in-kind transfers versus cash transfers to the case of an ex-husband providing child support. Suppose that the court awards the ex-wife the house, the car, the TV, $200 per month for herself, and $200 per month for each child. Suppose that the father wants the kids (but not the ex-wife) to live better than that. Would he give money to the kids, or would he give them goods?

14. This chapter demonstrated how the following expression was derived: $\Delta R/\Delta X = MR = P(1 + 1/\varepsilon)$. Using similar algebra, show that $\Delta R/\Delta P = X(1 + \varepsilon)$. Draw a table similar to Table 3.3 demonstrating the relationship between price elasticity of demand and the total revenue changes caused by price changes.

15. State, show graphically, and explain the condition for consumer optimization when the consumer faces this budget constraint: $\$75,000 = \$5Y + \$3X$.

16. "If the PCC is positively sloped, the price elasticity of demand for good A is a negative fraction between -1 and 0." Is this statement true or false? Support your answer.

17. Use the formula for price elasticity of demand to prove these statements:
   a. A linear demand curve cannot have constant elasticity.
   b. A demand curve with unit elasticity over its entire range cannot be linear.

18. Suppose that the government wants to encourage college education among a group of people who place only a little value on it. Which policy would most likely encourage the most education?
   a. Cash grants with no strings attached
   b. Education vouchers, money that can be used only to pay tuition
   c. Tuition subsidies, in which the government reduces the price of tuition to the student by paying a given percentage.
   (Hint: See the baseball example in Applied Micro Theory 3.1.)

19. If indifference curves are concave rather than convex, the condition $|MRS| = |P_X/P_Y|$ gives a curious result. What is it?

20. What does it mean if an indifference curve between goods X and Y
    a. Becomes parallel to the vertical axis?
    b. Is positively sloped and has higher-order indifference curves to its right?
21. Suppose that marginal revenue, $\Delta R/\Delta X$, is $6, that income elasticity is 0.8, that point elasticity is -2, that cross-price elasticity is 3, and that arc elasticity is -1.8. Find the product price.
22. a. Why is price elasticity of demand considered a more useful measure than the slope of the demand curve?
    b. Why is the income elasticity of demand more useful than the slope of the Engel curve?
23. If the price elasticity of demand for houses in Denver is 0.8 and you are told that the price of houses has *decreased* by 10%, by how much has the quantity of houses sold *increased*?
24. Suppose that at a particular gas station the price of gasoline increases from 36¢ per gallon to 38¢ per gallon and that the quantity of gasoline sold falls from 1000 gallons per day to 900 gallons per day. What is the price elasticity of demand for gasoline in this range of consumption? Why do we say "in this range of consumption"?
25. Show that, when a consumer is satiated with a good, indifference curves are positively sloped in some portions. Is satiation an important problem for a person with a limited income?
26. "I vigorously opposed building a Burrito Bandito fast-food restaurant where the little old park used to be, but now that it's here I have several meals there per month." Show that this statement does not necessarily imply a change in preferences.
27. "The price of gasoline has nothing to do with peoples' driving habits. The American people simply have to drive." Comment, using indifference curves.
28. Given the hypothetical data in Table 3.5 for price, income, and quantity demanded, calculate price elasticities and income elasticities of demand. Are your calculations arc or point elasticities? What demand curves can you sketch? What Engle curves?
29. Draw an indifference map for a good that is inferior at low prices but normal at high prices.

Table 3.5
Quantity Demanded Given Hypothetical Prices and Incomes

	Income	
Price	$10,000 per Year	$20,000 per Year
$0.50	1000 units	1500 units
1.00	900	1100
1.50	800	900

Suggested Readings

Baumol, William J. *Economic Theory and Operations Analysis*. 4th ed. Englewood Cliffs, N.J.: Prentice-Hall, 1977, chap. 9.

Henderson, J. M., and Quandt, R. E. *Microeconomic Theory: A Mathematical Approach*. Rev. ed. New York: McGraw-Hill, 1961, chap. 2.

Hicks, J. R. *Value and Capital*. Oxford, England: Clarendon Press, 1939, chap. 1.

Samuelson, Paul A. *Foundations of Economic Analysis*. New York: Atheneum, 1965, chaps. 2, 5.

Vickrey, William S. *Microstatics*. New York: Harcourt Brace Jovanovich, 1964, chap. 2.

Extensions and Applications of Demand Theory

The study of competitive markets requires an understanding of both demand and supply, and we will turn our attention to the supply side of the market shortly. However, the theory of demand by itself is so extraordinarily useful in organizing thoughts and public-policy decisionmaking that this chapter is devoted to various extensions and applications of demand theory. For example, demand theory will be used to point out the possible error in building highways where traffic counts are highest, in planning television network offerings on the basis of Nielsen ratings, and in determining university curriculum offerings solely on the basis of student enrollments. We will also study price indexes in order to compare living standards in different years when relative prices are changing. These examples and many more show how demand theory can be used to understand many of the world's puzzles and to suggest policy initiatives.

The core theoretical concept in demand theory, and our first topic, is the division of consumer behavior between income and substitution effects. This separation has important applications in public-policy choices and underpins the theory of consumer surplus, as well as the construction of price indexes, which are themselves powerful analytical tools.

Income and Substitution Effects

When the price of good X rises, *ceteris paribus,* the consumer is affected in two principal ways. First, the consumer's real income (purchasing power) is reduced, because the higher price reduces the amount of commodities that can be purchased. This is the **income effect of a price change.** In addition, the price increase makes good X a relatively poorer bargain compared to its substitutes, so the consumer substitutes other goods for X. This is the **substitution effect of a price change.** The sum of these two effects is the **total effect of a price change.**

The total effect of a price change is shown in Figure 4.1, which measures money income as the numeraire, on the vertical axis. When the price of X is P_0, the consumer selects combination A on indifference curve U_0 and purchases X_0 units of X. If the price of X

Figure 4.1
Total Effect of a Price Change

The total effect of a price increase is the movement from A to C along the PCC. The quantity demanded falls from X_0 to X_1.

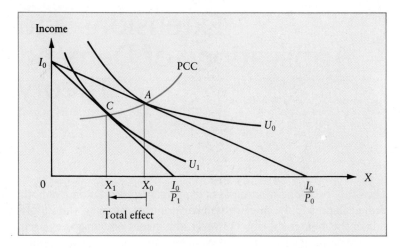

rises to P_1, the individual chooses combination C on indifference curve U_1 and buys X_1 units of X. The total effect of the price increase on the quantity of X demanded is the distance $X_0 - X_1$. The effect shows up in movement along the price-consumption curve from A to C.

Compensating Variations in Income

Given a price increase, how much of the total decrease in quantity demanded results from the reduction in purchasing power (income effect) and how much from the consumer's desire to substitute other goods for X when X is relatively more expensive than before (substitution effect)? The technique is to identify the substitution effect first, by eliminating the income effect. Then we add back the income effect in order to observe the total effect of a price increase.

In Figure 4.2, an increase in the price of X from P_0 to P_1 forces the consumer to cut purchases of X from X_0 to X_1, lowering utility from U_0 to U_1. This is the total effect. The income effect is eliminated—and hence the substitution effect isolated—by holding real income constant, that is, by keeping the consumer on the same indifference curve. One way to keep utility constant when the price of X rises is to increase the consumer's money income. How much money income would the consumer need so that, by a suitable purchase of goods at the new prices, he or she could stay on the original indifference curve? The answer to this imposing question is found by shifting up the new budget line until it becomes tangent to the initial indifference curve, U_0, at B. An increase in money income equal to $I_1 - I_0$ would compensate for the higher price of X and permit the consumer to maintain the initial utility level, U_0. This income increase is called the **compensating variation in income**.

If money income could be increased by $I_1 - I_0$ when the price of X rises, the reduction in real income and standard of living could be avoided. The consumer could purchase $\hat{X}$ units of X. In other

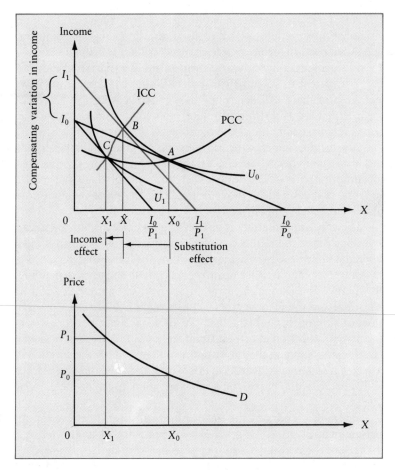

Figure 4.2
Income and Substitution Effects Using Compensating Variations in Income

The total effect on quantity demanded of a price increase is the move from A to C along the PCC. The substitution effect, A to B along U_0, is always negative. The income effect, B to C along the ICC, is positive for normal goods. These reinforcing effects produce a negatively sloped demand curve.

words, the consumer would cut purchases of X from X_0 to $\hat{X}$ when the price of X rises, even if the income-reducing effect of the price increase could be eliminated. The substitution effect in Figure 4.2 is $X_0 - \hat{X}$; it is the reduction in the quantity of X purchased traceable solely to the change in relative prices. The substitution effect is measured by the movement from A to B along the original indifference curve.

The compensating variation in income, $I_1 - I_0$, is merely a conceptual device used to estimate the consumer's response to price changes, holding utility constant. Of course, consumers are not actually compensated for the loss in purchasing power when the price of X changes. In actuality, purchasing power is reduced when price rises. Because the compensating variation in income is never actually given to the consumer, it is in fact a measure of the loss of purchasing power due to the price increase. The income effect is the reduction in X purchased due only to this reduction in money income, or $\hat{X} - X_1$; it is the movement from B to C along the income-consumption curve.

This is a difficult concept, so let's summarize carefully. Income and substitution effects allow us to study the change in quantity demanded resulting from a price change "as if" it takes place in two steps. By making a hypothetical compensating variation in income that is sufficient to keep the consumer's utility constant at the new relative prices, we can determine how much X is cut because it is more expensive (substitution effect) and how much because the price increase has reduced the consumer's income (income effect). The substitution effect is the movement along the original indifference curve, and the income effect is the movement along the income-consumption curve. The total effect, the sum of these two components, is measured by movements along the price-consumption curve. Table 4.1 summarizes.

The substitution effect is always negative because of the negative slope of the indifference curve; quantity demanded always falls when the price of X rises while utility remains fixed. In contrast, the income effect can be either positive, neutral, or negative, depending on whether X is normal, neutral, or inferior. In Figure 4.2, good X is normal and the income effect is positive, as can be seen from the upward-sloping ICC. Note that the income effect reinforces the negative substitution effect; expenditures on X fall for both reasons. The demand curve in the lower panel of Figure 4.2 is the combined effect of a negative substitution effect and a positive income effect. Thus the demand curve for a normal good must be negatively sloped.

Figure 4.3 separates the income and substitution effects of an income-neutral good—a good whose purchase is unaffected by changes in the consumer's money income—and derives the associated demand curve. Here the ICC is vertical, implying that the compensating variation in income, $I_1 - I_0$, does not change the quantity of X purchased. The income effect of the price change is therefore zero, and the reduction in purchases from X_0 to X_1 (or the

Table 4.1
Income and Substitution Effects
(Using Compensating Variation in Income)

Effect	Definition	Read	Geometry
Substitution effect	$\left.\dfrac{\Delta X}{\Delta P}\right\|_{\bar{u}}$	Change in the quantity of X purchased due solely to a change in price, holding utility constant	Measured along the original indifference curve
Income effect	$\left.\dfrac{\Delta X}{\Delta I}\right\|_{\bar{p}}$	Change in the quantity of X purchased due solely to a change in money income, holding price fixed at the new level	Measured along the ICC
Total effect	$SE + IE$	Total change in the quantity of X purchased from both sources	Measured along the PCC

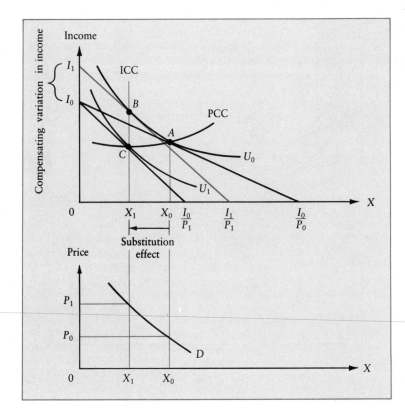

Figure 4.3
**The Demand Curve for an
Income-Neutral Good**

The substitution effect, A to B along U_0, is negative. The income effect, B to C along the vertical ICC, is zero for an income-neutral good. The demand curve is negatively sloped.

move from A to C) is due entirely to the substitution effect. Nevertheless, the demand curve is negatively sloped, because the substitution effect is always negative.

It is easy to suppose—incorrectly—that the demand curve for an inferior good is positively sloped. Figure 4.4 shows why this need not be so. The income effect is the changes in purchases of X arising from the fact that the price increase in effect reduces the consumer's money income by the compensating variation in income. Good X in Figure 4.4 is inferior because the income-consumption curve is negatively sloped. The income effect, the movement along the ICC from B to C, is negative because a reduction in money income increases purchases of X from $\hat{X}$ to X_1. However, the increase in X demanded due to the negative income effect, B to C, is more than offset by the decrease in X demanded due to the substitution effect, A to B. Hence, the total effect of the price increase—the sum of the income and substitution effects—is A to C. On balance, the price increase reduces quantity demanded, and the demand curve is negatively sloped even though the good is inferior.

In contrast, the demand curve for the inferior good X in Figure 4.5, called a **Giffen good,** is positively sloped because the very negative income effect B to C is larger than the substitution effect A to B. Here the price increase leads to an increase in the quantity

Figure 4.4
The Demand Curve for an Inferior Good

The demand curve for an inferior good is negatively sloped because the negative substitution effect, A to B along U_0, is larger than the partially offsetting negative income effect, B to C along the ICC.

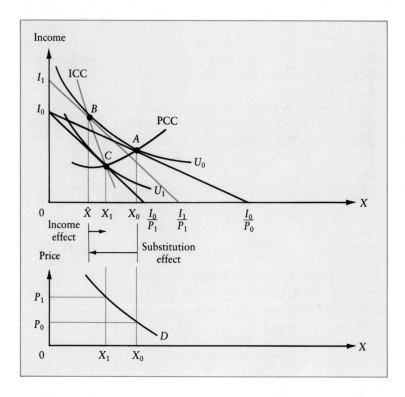

Figure 4.5
The Demand Curve for a Giffen Good

The demand curve for a Giffen good is positively sloped because the negative income effect, B to C, is larger than the negative substitution effect, A to B.

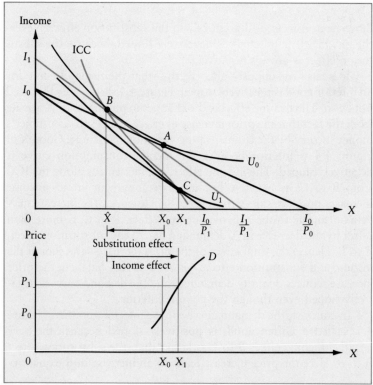

of X demanded; the demand curve is positively sloped. Analysis of the indifference curve demonstrates that upward-sloping demand curves are logical possibilities. However, they are seldom, if ever, observed in empirical studies. As a result, the law of demand is not a law deduced from the modern theory of consumer behavior but a generalization based on the almost complete lack of empirical evidence of positively sloped demand curves. The famous Giffen good, a supposed exception to the law of demand, has created far more interest among economic historians trying to identify Mr. Giffen, the unverified discoverer of the phenomenon, than among research economists claiming evidence of upward-sloping demand curves.

Equivalent versus Compensating Variations in Income

In the previous section we separated the income effect of a price increase from the substitution effect by estimating the compensating variation in income, which is the increase in money income needed to keep the consumer on the original indifference curve when paying the higher price for X. The compensating variation isolates the income effect by shifting the new budget line tangent to the original indifference curve.

There is another way we might have proceeded. Consider the increase in the price of X in Figure 4.6 and the resulting total movement from A to C. Instead of using the compensating variation in income, we can measure the depressing effect of a price increase on purchasing power by asking this question: If the consumer were allowed to pay the original price of X, how much money income would have to be taken away in order to reduce utility to the equivalent level that the price increase actually causes? This income decrease—called the **equivalent variation in income**—is found by establishing a new, lower budget line parallel to the original one until it is tangent to the new indifference curve, U_1. If money income

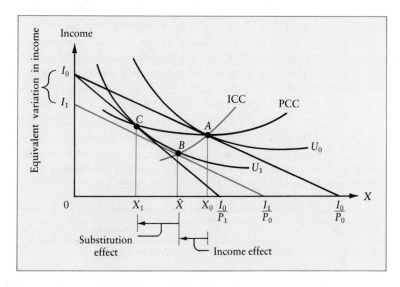

Figure 4.6
Income and Substitution Effects Using Equivalent Variations in Income

The equivalent variation in income, $I_0 - I_1$, is measured against the new indifference curve using the original price ratio. The income effect is A to B along the ICC; the substitution effect is B to C along U_1.

Table 4.2

Compensating and Equivalent Variations in Income

Variation in Income	Meaning	Measured Against	Using
Compensating	Variation in income at new prices necessary to attain the original indifference curve	Original indifference curve	New price ratio
Equivalent	Variation in income at original prices necessary to attain the new indifference curve	New indifference curve	Original price ratio

could be reduced by $I_0 - I_1$ (the equivalent variation), the consumer would reach the new, lower indifference curve U_1 by selecting bundle B at the original price.

The equivalent variation is thus an alternative estimate of the reduced purchasing power caused by an increase in the price of X. The income effect is A to B along the ICC; the consumer cuts purchases of X from X_0 to $\hat{X}$ because purchasing power is reduced. The substitution effect is B to C along the new indifference curve; purchases of X fall from $\hat{X}$ to X_1, because X has become relatively more expensive compared to the substitutes. For the case in Figure 4.6, X is a normal good. The positive income effect reinforces the negative substitution effect, and the demand curve (not drawn) is negatively sloped.

Learning these two different measurements of income and substitution effects is easy once you understand the inevitability of there being two measures. When a commodity price changes, we must always deal with two utility levels (indifference curves) and two price ratios. We always move from an original indifference curve at original prices to a new indifference curve at new prices. Thus we always have a choice in measuring the income effect of a price change. One choice is to identify the change in quantity demanded that would result solely by changing the consumer's money income just enough to allow the attainment of the original indifference curve at the new prices. This method uses compensating variation in income; the compensating income variation is measured against the original indifference curve using the new prices. Or we can measure the change in quantity demanded that would result solely by changing the consumer's money income just enough to allow the attainment of the new indifference curve at the original prices. This method uses equivalent variation in income; the equivalent income variation is measured against the new indifference curve using original prices. These rules are summarized in Table 4.2.[1]

1. In discussing alternate ways of separating income effects from substitution effects—using compensating or equivalent variations in income—we considered price increases only. However, the same rules apply for price decreases. We still must choose between measuring income variations (and the resulting income effects on quantity demanded) against the new indifference curve at original prices or against the original indifference curve at new prices.

Cash versus Housing Subsidies

APPLIED
MICRO
THEORY

4.1

In this age of high taxes and skepticism about the ability of government to provide any service efficiently, some economists have suggested that public housing subsidies for the poor be replaced by cash grants. Recipients of such grants would use the cash, plus their own income, to buy anything they wanted, including rental housing. The question that arises is, of course, how large the subsidy would have to be to compensate for the loss of subsidized housing.

The problem is illustrated in the accompanying figure. Square feet of housing is measured along the horizontal axis; money spent on other goods is measured along the vertical axis. The typical recipient is in initial equilibrium at point A, paying subsidized rent R_0. Without the subsidy, this person would be in equilibrium at point B, paying rent R_1. Therefore, the equivalent variation in income of the public housing program is the cash grant that allows the recipient to achieve equilibrium at point C along budget line $\mathscr{L}$.

The PCC is drawn as a horizontal line and the ICC as a straight line emanating from the origin. These lines reflect empirical studies showing that income and price elasticity of demand for housing are both unitary.[*]

It is clear from the graph that the poor are quite likely to spend cash grants on alternatives to housing if the equivalent variation in income is substituted for public provision of housing. The principles of income and substitution effects demonstrate

how important it is not to judge the success of such a program by the resulting housing quality alone. With cash grants, the poor will certainly live in housing that is smaller than subsidized housing—but by choice. Properly designed, the cash-grant program will compensate with sufficient income.

How can policymakers measure the income compensation necessary to allow increased spending on substitute goods in exchange for the decreased living space? Professor Joseph De Salvo used an algebraic equation to represent indifference curves with the property of unitary income and price elasticity.[†] Because this

"Cobb-Douglas" function allows approximate cardinal measurement of the recipients' indifference curves, De Salvo's methodology permits estimates of the desired equivalent variation in income.

Professor Jack Adams recently applied the De Salvo technique in the Little Rock, Arkansas market and estimated the equivalent variation to be $125 per month per household (estimates vary somewhat by family size, race, and income).[‡] According to this estimate, the average recipient household in Little Rock would therefore suffer no loss in real income if its public housing subsidy was replaced by a cash grant of $125 per month.

[†]Joseph S. De Salvo, "A Methodology for Evaluating Housing Programs," *Journal of Regional Science* 11 (August 1971): 173–185.

[‡]Jack E. Adams, "The Welfare Efficiency of Moving Families into Public Housing in Little Rock, Arkansas," *Land Economics* 58 (May 1982): 217–224.

[*]For a discussion of such empirical estimates, see John M. Quigley, "What Have We Learned about Urban Housing Markets?" in *Current Issues in Urban Economics*, ed. Peter Mieszkowski and Mahlon Straszheim (Baltimore: Johns Hopkins University Press, 1979).

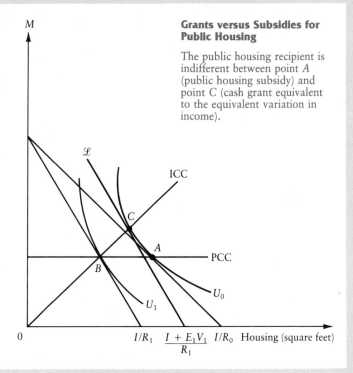

Grants versus Subsidies for Public Housing

The public housing recipient is indifferent between point A (public housing subsidy) and point C (cash grant equivalent to the equivalent variation in income).

The Slutsky Approach to Income and Substitution Effects

The compensating and equivalent variants in income were developed by the British economist J. R. Hicks.[2] They are brilliant theoretical tools that economists use frequently, but they are difficult to measure concretely because they involve tangencies with indifference curves whose exact positions are unknown. Although the general indifference curve properties of slope and convexity are known, specific positions are not. Therefore, we must now investigate another method of separating income and substitution effects. The **Slutsky approach,** for which we are indebted to the Russian economist Eugen Slutsky, does not require such information about indifference curves.[3]

Figure 4.7 shows the original consumer optimum or indifference curve, U_0, when money income is I_0 and the price of X is P_0. Now let the price of X rise to P_1, *ceteris paribus.* The new budget line is tangent to indifference curve U_1 at point C. The total effect, as always, is movement from A to C along the price-consumption curve.

Now let's make a compensating variation in income that differs from the Hicks method and is more pertinent to empirical analysis. Instead of adjusting the consumer's money income so as to achieve the same (unmeasurable) indifference curve, let's adjust money income enough to permit the purchase of the original bundle of goods at point A. The colored budget line, used to separate the income from the substitution effect, must reflect the higher price of X,

Figure 4.7
Slutsky Income and Substitution Effects

The compensating variation in income, $I_1 - I_0$, is an adjustment in money income after prices rise to allow the purchase of the original commodity bundle A. The substitution effect is A to B; the income effect is B to C along the ICC.

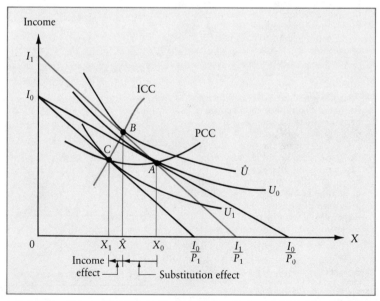

2. J. R. Hicks, *Value and Capital: An Inquiry into Some Fundamental Principles of Economic Theory* (London: Oxford University Press, 1965), pp. 26–37.

3. Eugen Slutsky, "On the Theory of the Budget of the Consumer," *Giornale degli Economisti* 51 (1915): 1–26. Reprinted in *Readings in Price Theory,* ed. George J. Stigler and Kenneth E. Boulding (Homewood, Ill.: Irwin, 1952), pp. 27–56.

which is P_1, and the hypothetical compensating variation in income that would give the consumer enough income to purchase the original bundle A at higher prices. Accordingly, the colored budget line must intersect A and be parallel to the new budget line. Slutsky's compensating variation in income is $I_1 - I_0$; bundle A could be purchased at the higher prices if the consumer were given $I_1 - I_0$ extra money income to compensate for the price increase. But even though bundle A is available, it will not be selected, because B is the preferred bundle. Thus the movement from A to B—or from X_0 to $\hat{X}$—reflects the substitution effect. It is the reduction in purchases of X due solely to a change in relative prices, holding "apparent" real income—the ability to purchase the same commodity bundle—constant. Unlike the Hicksian substitution effect, the Slutsky substitution effect is not a movement along a single indifference curve. Rather, utility rises from U_0 to $\hat{U}$ when the consumer moves from bundle A to bundle B.

The Slutsky compensating variation in income, $I_1 - I_0$, measures the loss in purchasing power due to a price increase. The income effect is the movement from B to C along the income-consumption curve, or from $\hat{X}$ to X_1.

Just as the Hicks method employs compensating and equivalent variations in income, so can the Slutsky approach. Anchoring the budget line to the original commodity bundle at the new price ratio measures compensating variations in income; anchoring the budget line to the new commodity bundle at the original prices produces the equivalent variation in income. Logically, the distinction between compensating and equivalent variations is the same for both the Hicks and Slutsky methods.

This has been a comprehensive treatment of the various methods of measuring income and substitution effects because all play a useful role in modeling consumer behavior. The applicability of income and substitution effects and the need for several methods will become increasingly clear in this chapter.

Income-Compensated Demand Curves

The demand curve developed intuitively in Chapter 2 and derived formally in Chapter 3 is of the form $X = f(P, P^s, P^c, I, \ldots)$. The shift parameter income (I) refers to money income. As the commodity price changes, *ceteris paribus*, the budget line rotates, different indifference curves are attained, and the price-consumption curve is traced out. The demand curve is derived from the price-consumption curve. Thus a movement along this **ordinary demand curve** holds money income constant but involves different levels of real income (utility).

The decision to hold money income constant along the demand curve corresponds to a frequent real-life occurrence: Relative prices change while money incomes stay the same. As we have already seen, this view of the demand curve is useful for studying many

Subsidies and Income Adjustments

APPLIED
MICRO
THEORY

4.2

Income and substitution effects give us insights into government policies that change relative prices via taxes or subsidies, alter consumers' spendable income via income tax surcharges or rebates, or a combination of methods. The following example is directly transferable to many similar choices that governments face.

Agnes's father wants her to deepen her appreciation of the fine arts by going to the opera more often. Agnes's preferences for opera are shown in Figure A. Her only income, I_0, is an allowance she receives from her father. She selects commodity bundle A and buys T_0 opera tickets per season at the original ticket price. How can her father encourage her to attend the opera more often? (We'll ignore gifts-in-kind, a possibility explored in Applied Micro Theory 3.1.)

Policy 1

Agnes's father could provide a subsidy that reimburses Agnes a stipulated percentage of the price of each ticket she buys. ("Kids always fall for this one.") *Result:* The ticket price falls, rotating the budget line to the right. Agnes chooses bundle C, buying T_1 tickets at the lower price and increasing utility from U_0 to U_1. The movement from A to C along the PCC is the total effect of the subsidy.

Policy 2

Agnes's father could give her a subsidy and an allowance reduction sufficient to keep Agnes's utility constant. ("I want to promote opera attendance without spoiling the child.") *Result:* A Hicksian compensating variation (reduction) in income of $I_0 - \hat{I}$ holds Agnes's utility constant at the lower opera price.

She increases opera attendance from T_0 to $\hat{T}$ by decreasing movie attendance and roller skating in response to the change in relative prices. This is the Hicksian substitution effect A to B along indifference curve U_0. The income effect, B to C along the ICC, is eliminated by the allowance reduction.

Policy 3

Agnes's father might choose to give her a subsidy and an allowance reduction sufficient to permit Agnes to buy the original commodity bundle A. ("This is as close as I can come to keeping Agnes at her original utility level.") *Result:* A Slutsky compensating variation (reduction) in income of $I_0 - \tilde{I}$ provides enough income for Agnes to buy the original bundle A at the lower ticket price, because the budget line intersects point A.

But Agnes increases utility to $\tilde{U}$ by increasing opera attendance from T_0 to $\tilde{T}$. This is the Slutsky substitution effect A to $\tilde{B}$. The income effect, $\tilde{B}$ to C along the ICC, is eliminated by the cut in allowance. Agnes should be grateful that her father cannot measure the Hicksian variation; her utility rises when the Slutsky method is used.

Policy 4

Agnes's father could give her no subsidy. Instead, he could give Agnes enough allowance to allow her to reach the same indifference curve that the subsidy would have permitted. ("Agnes drives me crazy with her incessant requests for cash reimbursements under the subsidy. This way I give her one check a year.") *Result:* Refer now to Figure B. Income must rise by $\hat{I} - I_0$ to yield a tangency at B on

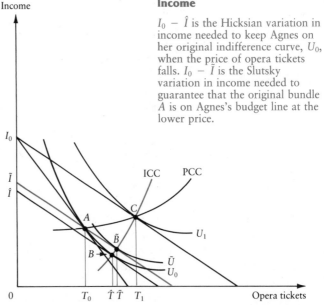

Figure A
Compensating Variations in Income

$I_0 - \hat{I}$ is the Hicksian variation in income needed to keep Agnes on her original indifference curve, U_0, when the price of opera tickets falls. $I_0 - \tilde{I}$ is the Slutsky variation in income needed to guarantee that the original bundle A is on Agnes's budget line at the lower price.

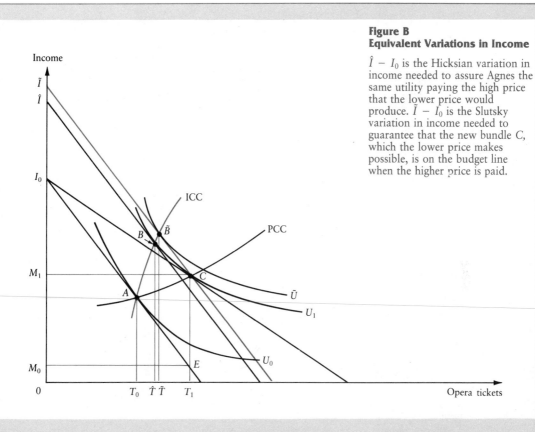

Figure B
Equivalent Variations in Income

$\hat{I} - I_0$ is the Hicksian variation in income needed to assure Agnes the same utility paying the high price that the lower price would produce. $\tilde{I} - I_0$ is the Slutsky variation in income needed to guarantee that the new bundle C, which the lower price makes possible, is on the budget line when the higher price is paid.

indifference curve U_1. Relative prices are unchanged, so only the income effect A to B along the ICC comes into play. Agnes increases ticket purchases from T_0 to $\hat{T}$. This policy takes the form of a Hicksian equivalent variation in income.

Policy 5

Again, Agnes's father could give her no subsidy but instead increase Agnes's allowance enough to allow her to buy the same commodity bundle she would buy if the subsidy were given. ("I prefer policy 4, but who can tell where Agnes's indifference curve is?") *Result:* An increase in income of $\tilde{I} - I_0$, holding relative prices constant, shifts the presubsidy budget line upward and parallel, to an intersection at bundle C. This method is the Slutsky equivalent variation in income. Agnes buys $\tilde{T}$

tickets and increases utility to $\tilde{U}$. In effect, this policy increases Agnes's income by an amount equal to the cost of the subsidy program, if it had been instituted.

The dollars received under policy 5 equal line segment CE, calculated as follows. Agnes buys T_1 tickets at the subsidized price. If she had purchased T_1 tickets at the presubsidy price, total ticket expenditures would have been $I_0 - M_0$, or line segment I_0M_0. When she buys T_1 tickets at the lower, subsidized price, total expenditures are only $I_0 - M_1$, or I_0M_1. The difference is the total cost of the subsidy, M_1M_0 or CE.

An increase in income of CE, holding relative prices constant, shifts the presubsidy budget line upward and parallel by the amount CE, or $\tilde{I} - I_0$. The resulting budget line must intersect point C. Even when her father's

total cost for an income policy equals the cost for a subsidy program, Agnes, if she has a say, should choose the income policy. Under an income policy, she can increase utility to $\tilde{U}$ by buying $\tilde{T}$ tickets. The income effect is A to $\tilde{B}$ along the ICC.

This example employs all of the methods for separating income from substitution effects. Limiting ourselves to only one or two of these alternatives limits the questions we can explore using demand theory. The Hicksian adjustments help organize thoughts at a theoretical level. But in practice, we must use the Slutsky variations, because we can then anchor the budget line to an observed market bundle. Agnes's father knows her commodity bundle; he doesn't know the position of her indifference curves.

Rising Energy Prices and Aid to Poor Families

APPLIED
MICRO
THEORY

4.3

Prices of energy resources, notably gasoline and home-heating fuel, have risen steadily in recent years. Higher prices encourage conservation of these nonrenewable resources; yet families on fixed incomes find high fuel costs especially onerous. Conservation has been considered so important that some have even proposed levying a stiff excise tax on gasoline to raise its price even further and then offsetting the impact of higher prices with income tax relief to poor families. Consumer theory helps sort out the likely impact of such a policy.

In the figure, a low-income family selects commodity bundle A on indifferences curve U_0 when the price of gas is P_0. An excise tax on gasoline that raises the price of gas to P_1 forces the family to the inferior indifference curve U_1, which is tangent to their budget line at C. Demand is price inelastic between prices P_0 and P_1, as demonstrated by the upward-sloping price-consumption curve; the family spends more of its fixed income on gas after the price increase.

Suppose that the government wants to give poor families enough purchasing power through income tax relief or direct cash payments to allow them to keep the original commodity bundle A, even at the higher prices. The budget line needed to accomplish this goal must have a slope reflecting the higher gas prices and intersect point A. One way to do this is to provide a cash grant equal to $I_1 - I_0$, the Slutsky compensating variation in income, which will hold the family's apparent real income constant.

A combined excise tax/income tax reduction policy decomposes into pure income and substitution effects. At the higher price, P_1, the

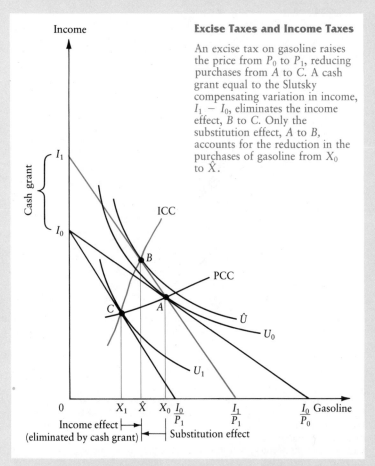

Excise Taxes and Income Taxes

An excise tax on gasoline raises the price from P_0 to P_1, reducing purchases from A to C. A cash grant equal to the Slutsky compensating variation in income, $I_1 - I_0$, eliminates the income effect, B to C. Only the substitution effect, A to B, accounts for the reduction in the purchases of gasoline from X_0 to $\hat{X}$.

family reduces gas consumption from X_0 to $\hat{X}$ by seeking out substitutes such as mass transit, car pooling, and walking. Therefore, A to B is the substitution effect. The government eliminates the income effect (B to C) of the price increase—the further reduction of gas consumption from $\hat{X}$ to X_1—by giving a cash grant.

In summary, a cash-grant policy achieves the following: (1) the family is free to use its new income to purchase alternatives to gasoline; (2) the cash gift permits the family to achieve its original level of utility, at minimum, and

probably to improve it somewhat; and (3) the family has an incentive to participate in gas conservation (that is, the policy does not attempt to override the market pricing signals completely). This example also illustrates the notion that price controls are not needed to maintain the standard of living of poor families during periods of rising prices if the government is willing to make cash grants to boost the real purchasing power of the poor. This is comforting in view of the long list of negative impacts of price controls provided in Chapter 2.

economic problems, including the effect of price changes on firms' total revenue. But for certain analytical purposes it is important to hold real income (utility) constant instead. When commodity price increases, we can hold real income constant by making Hicksian compensating variations in money income. In this way we force the budget line to hug the original indifference curve as prices change and, by doing so, eliminate the income effect, leaving only the substitution effect. The demand curve that holds real income constant by making suitable compensating variations in money income is called the **income-compensated demand curve.**

The distinction between the ordinary demand curve (money income constant) and the income-compensated demand curve (real income constant) is depicted in Figure 4.8. When the price of X is P_0, the consumer selects bundle A and buys X_0 units of X. This choice is plotted in the lower panel of Figure 4.8 as point A'. When the price of X rises to P_1, the consumer moves to bundle C, thereby consuming X_1 units of X. This point is plotted at C'. Thus the ordinary demand curve, $A'C'$, is derived from movement along the price-consumption curve. But if we hold real income constant by

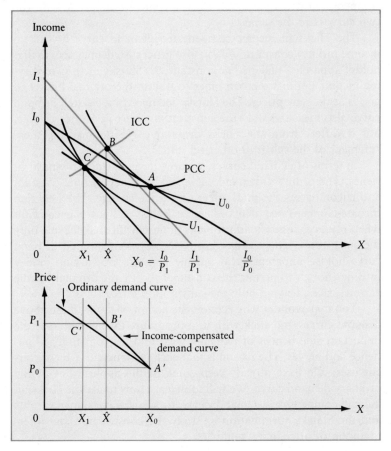

Figure 4.8
Ordinary versus Income-Compensated Demand Curves

The income-compensated demand curve measures only the substitution effect of a price change by eliminating the income effect via compensating variations in income. It holds real income (utility) constant. For a price increase of a normal good, it lies above the ordinary demand curve.

making a compensating variation in money income equal to $I_1 - I_0$, the consumer moves from A to B, which is the pure substitution effect. The consumer purchases X units of X at price P_1 when the income effect is removed. This demand point is plotted as B'. The income-compensated demand curve is therefore $A'B'$ in Figure 4.8; it lies above the ordinary demand curve for price increases.

It is the income effect that makes the difference between ordinary and income-compensated demand curves. Figure 4.8 illustrates one case—a normal good whose price has risen. Yet the relative positions of these two demand curves depend on whether the price has increased or decreased and whether the good is normal or inferior. For example, the income-compensated demand curve lies below the ordinary demand curve for price increases when the good is inferior. You should practice deriving these demand curves under various conditions.

Some goods are income neutral; changes in money income do not affect quantities purchased. In such cases the ICC is vertical, the income effect is zero, and the movement along the price-consumption curve traces out both the ordinary and the income-compensated demand curve. When income effects are absent, the two curves are the same.

The Hicksian income-compensated demand curve holds real income (utility) constant. We can also generate a demand curve that holds "apparent" real income constant; the Slutsky method of varying income permits the consumer to obtain the original basket of goods at the new prices. The Slutsky income-compensated demand curve also measures only the substitution effect of a price change, but it differs from the Hicks demand curve because the measurement of the substitution effect differs.

In terms of demand curves, we now have an embarrassment of riches. The ordinary demand curve holds money income constant and encompasses the total effect of a price change. The Hicksian income-compensated demand curve holds real income constant when prices change via adjustments in money income, leaving only the substitution effect. The Slutsky income-compensated demand curve holds "apparent" real income constant by varying money income enough to permit the consumer to buy the original bundle at new prices, leaving only the substitution effect.

You may wonder why economists do not pick one of the above demand curves and stick with it, a procedure that would have the important side benefit of reducing wear and tear on students' patience and nerves. The reason is that each demand curve has different uses. We have already seen some of the applications of the ordinary demand curve. We will soon learn how to use the Hicksian income-compensated demand curve to analyze consumer surplus and the Slutsky formulation to study the construction and interpretation of price-index numbers.

Consumer Surplus

We can be sure that exchanges between buyers and sellers in free markets are beneficial to both parties, because such exchanges are voluntary and would not be made otherwise. However, decisionmaking in the public sector is not quite so straightforward. Governments typically provide goods (such as highways) and services (such as postal service) to consumers who do not pay directly for their full cost. Although the costs of public goods can be measured, we cannot be sure that the benefits of public projects justify the costs, because these goods are not exchanged in markets. **Consumer surplus,** a demand-related concept, measures consumer benefits and is useful—among other applications—in evaluating the merits of proposed public projects. Consumer surplus is the difference between the amount of money that the consumer is willing to pay for a given quantity of a good and the amount that the consumer actually pays.[4]

You have no doubt purchased goods for much less than the maximum you would have been willing to pay. For example, a 25¢ pocket comb or a $10 phonograph needle may be so important to your grooming or listening pleasure that you would be willing to pay much higher prices, even though market conditions do not require you to. The classic example of this phenomenon is a man who, when buying a crowbar to pry open a treasure chest, remarks to himself that if necessary he would have been willing to pay twice the price.[5] The difference between what you would pay and what you do pay is your consumer surplus.

Consumer Surplus and Indifference Analysis

We will now study how the area under the demand curve is used to estimate consumer surplus. But the first question is, Should we use the ordinary demand curve (money income constant) or an income-compensated demand curve (real income constant)? We must take care to use the correct curve in order to avoid errors in estimating consumer surplus. Indifference analysis helps us select the correct demand concept. For measurements of consumer surplus, the correct concept is the Hicksian income-compensated demand curve.

Figure 4.9 uses indifference analysis in the upper panel to derive demand curves in the lower panel for good X, whose income effect is zero. Consumer income is I_0. The original price, P_0, is too high to induce any purchases of X, so the consumer selects the corner solution A on indifference curve U_0. When price falls to P_1, the consumer chooses bundle C on indifference curve U_1. Drawing on

4. This definition is quite faithful to those of the two earliest investigators of consumer surplus, J. Dupuit and Alfred Marshall. See J. Dupuit, "De la Mesure de l'Utilité des Travaux Publics," *Annales des Ponts et Cheussées* 8 (1844); and Alfred Marshall, *Principles of Economics,* 9th ed. (London: Macmillan, 1961), p. 124.

5. George J. Stigler, *The Theory of Price,* 3rd ed. (New York: Macmillan, 1966), p. 78.

Figure 4.9
Consumer Surplus for an Income-Neutral Good

Consumer surplus is the area below the income-compensated demand curve and above the price line. If income effects are zero, the ordinary and income-compensated demand curves are the same. No error results from using the ordinary demand curve to measure consumer surplus.

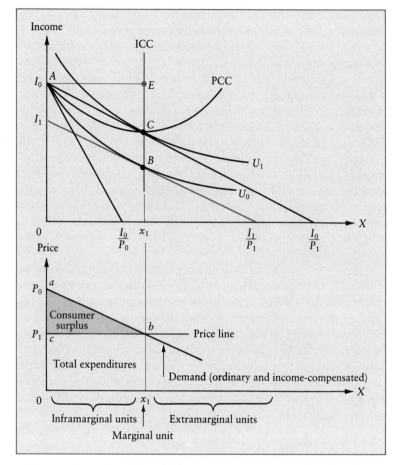

previous analysis, the substitution effect of the price decrease is the movement from A to B along the original indifference curve, U_0, and the income effect is the movement from B to C along the income-consumption curve. However, the ICC is vertical due to the assumption of a zero income effect. Accordingly, the ordinary demand curve in the lower panel is the same as the income-compensated demand curve. The consumer buys x_1 units at price P_1 regardless of whether money income is held constant or real income is fixed by a compensating variation in income, $I_0 - I_1$.

Now measure consumer surplus in the upper panel when x_1 units of X are purchased. The total value of x_1 units equals the maximum amount of other goods (the numeraire, money income) that the consumer would give up to obtain x_1 units. The consumer could give up EB income in exchange for x_1 units of X and stay on the original indifference curve. Hence, the total benefit is EB. The actual money income paid for x_1 units of X is only EC because, for each inframarginal unit purchased at a uniform price, the buyer would be willing to pay more than price P_1. The difference between the amount the individual would be willing to pay (EB) and the amount actually paid (EC) is the consumer surplus (CB).

The income-compensated demand curve is the relevant concept underlying consumer surplus. Here is why: Consumer surplus measures the difference between the buyer's marginal willingness to pay for successive units of a good and the price actually paid. But the marginal willingness to give up income to obtain an extra unit of X is the marginal rate of substitution, that is, the slope of the indifference curve. Hence, we can move along the original indifference curve to calculate the maximum that the consumer is willing to pay for successive units purchased one at a time. But we must also stay on the original indifference curve in constructing the income-compensated demand curve. In effect, the compensating variation in income keeps the consumer on the same indifference curve when prices fall by extracting the consumer surplus. If a price reduction allows buyers to purchase units at a price less than their marginal rate of substitution—that is, less than their marginal willingness to pay—a surplus arises, and total utility increases. Extracting this consumer surplus by a compensating variation in income keeps utility constant. Hence, the only demand concept corresponding to the definition of consumer surplus is the income-compensated demand curve. As in Figure 4.9, consumer surplus and the compensating variation in income are equal: $CB = I_0 - I_1$.

Each point on the income-compensated demand curve measures the maximum price that a consumer would pay for successive units of the good when purchased one at a time. The consumer will pay no more than the **marginal benefit** of each unit. Hence, the demand curve may be called a marginal benefit curve. The sum of the marginal benefits received for all units of consumption, the **total benefit**, is measured by the area under the demand curve.

Consider Figure 4.10, which shows an income-compensated demand curve. The marginal benefit of unit x_2 is the height of the line $\mathcal{L}$ drawn to the demand curve at that quantity demanded. The unit x_2 occupies a small distance along the horizontal axis. Therefore, line $\mathcal{L}$ has a width equal to the x_2 unit of X and a height equal to the marginal benefit of x_2. Line $\mathcal{L}$ thus has a geometric area equal to (height $= MB_2$) $\cdot$ (width $=$ one unit of X). The same is true for all units of output. They all have marginal benefits measured by the area of a narrow line like $\mathcal{L}$. Adding up all the areas of these lines fills the area beneath the demand curve. Because the area of each line is a marginal benefit and the sum of these marginal benefits equals total benefits, the area beneath the income-compensated demand curve equals total benefit.

In Figure 4.9, the total consumer benefit of consuming x_1 units of X is the area beneath the demand curve up to x_1, or the trapezoid $0abx_1$. This area is the sum of marginal benefits, that is, the sum of the expenditures that consumers are willing to make on x_1 units of

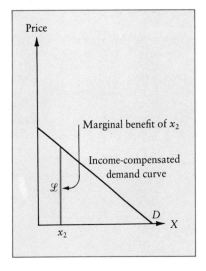

Figure 4.10
Consumer Surplus

The marginal benefit of unit x_2 equals the area of line $\mathcal{L}$. Line $\mathcal{L}$ is one unit wide and has a height equal to the marginal benefit of x_2. All units of output have a similar line; adding the area of all such lines yields the area beneath the income-compensated demand curve, which is equal to total benefit.

X purchased one at a time. Thus it measures total consumer benefit. But the total benefit is not equal to consumer surplus, because the commodity price is positive. At price p_1 consumers pay $0cbx_1$ in order to purchase x_1 units of X. Consumer surplus equals the triangle p_1ab, the difference between the amount consumers are willing to pay ($0abx_1$) and the amount actually paid ($0cbx_1$). Thus consumer surplus is the area below the demand curve and above the price line. Only when the price is zero is consumer surplus equivalent to total value and equal to the full area below the demand curve.

Figure 4.9 shows the relevant measurements in two forms: as lengths of vertical line segments in the upper panel and as corresponding areas in the lower panel.

Total benefit of $x_1 = EB = 0abx_1$ (4.1)

Total expenditure on $x_1 = EC = 0cbx_1$ (4.2)

Consumer surplus for x_1 (vertical line segments) $= EB - EC$ (4.3)
$= CB$

Consumer surplus for x_1 (areas) $= 0abx_1 - 0cbx_1 = abc$ (4.4)

Alfred Marshall, the famed British economist and principal architect of supply and demand curves, noted that consumer surplus can be estimated by the area under the ordinary demand curve only when the income effect of a price change is negligible.[6] This is because the ordinary demand curve and the income-compensated demand curve are the same when income effects are zero, as we have just seen. However, the greater the income effect of a price change, the larger the bias resulting from measuring consumer surplus with ordinary demand curves.

Figure 4.11 illustrates how, when price falls from P_0 to P_1, the consumer expands purchases from 0 to x_2 when both income and substitution effects are taken into account. The ordinary demand curve is the line segment ac in the lower panel. If the income effect is eliminated by a compensating variation in income, $I_0 - I_1$, and if the good is normal, the consumer expands purchases from 0 to only x_1. This more modest response is due entirely to the substitution effect A to B along indifference curve U_0. The resulting income-compensated demand curve, which eliminates income effects by compensating variations in income sufficient to extract consumer surplus, is line segment ab in the lower panel. The two demand curves differ when there are income effects.

When the consumer buys x_1 units of X, the relevant measures are as follows:

6. See Marshall, *Principles of Economics*, books 3 and 4, for his exposition of supply and demand and p. 842 for a discussion of the relationship between a zero income effect (constant marginal utility of money) and consumer surplus.

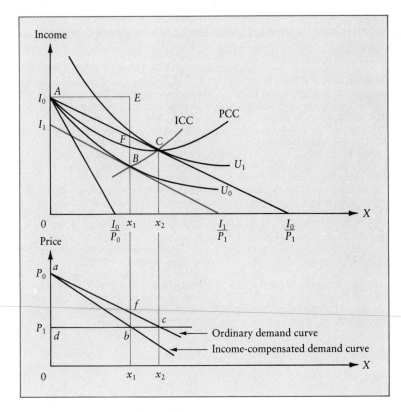

Figure 4.11
Consumer Surplus for a Normal Good

For a price decrease of a normal good, the ordinary demand curve is above the income-compensated demand curve. Using the ordinary demand curve to measure the consumer surplus of buying x_1 units exaggerates the correct measure, *abd*, by the area *acb*.

$$\text{Total benefit of } x_1 = EB = 0abx_1 \tag{4.5}$$

$$\text{Total expenditures on } x_1 = EF = 0dbx_1 \tag{4.6}$$

$$\text{Consumer surplus for } x_1 = FB = I_0 - I_1 = abd \tag{4.7}$$

Consumer surplus will be overstated by the area *acb* if the ordinary demand curve is employed. This bias worsens the greater the income effect of the product is. If the income effect is negligible, the error in estimate is likewise negligible.

Limitations of Consumer Surplus

Consumer surplus is by no means a perfect decisionmaking tool. The need to use the income-compensated demand curve instead of the ordinary demand curve is an important limitation, because the former requires information about the consumer's indifference map—information that we do not have—whereas the ordinary demand curve can often be estimated from actual consumer price-quantity information. However, this difficulty can often be overcome in specific applications. First, estimating consumer surplus from an ordinary demand curve can be useful. Such a measure overstates the true consumer surplus for a normal good; so if that measure is less than the required tax to provide a public good, we

Consumer Surplus and Bridge Building

APPLIED
MICRO
THEORY

4.4

Suppose that the government wants to evaluate the desirability of financing a new bridge partly by a lump-sum tax on each taxpayer and partly by user charges. Let's assume that all taxpayers' preferences are similar enough to be represented by the single indifference map in the accompanying figure. Let's also assume that bridge travel is an income-neutral good: Changes in money income do not affect the quantity demanded of bridge travel. Thus indifference curves are vertically parallel.

The consumer cannot spend any income on bridge travel before the bridge is built. Thus the individual initially uses his or her money income, I_0, to reach indifference curve U_2 at the corner position I_0. The financing arrangements of the bridge have two effects on the individual's budget line. If the charge per trip is P_1 (ignore the tax for now), the budget line becomes I_0L. The consumer could reach indifference curve U_3 by purchasing X_1 bridge trips. However, the effect of the lump-sum tax is to shift the budget line down by the amount of the tax, T (even if the consumer does not use the bridge, spendable income falls by the amount of the tax). With budget line EF the consumer reaches the highest available utility level, U_1, by selecting combination A and purchasing X_1 bridge trips.

The figure shows that the bridge is not worthwhile. The most income that the consumer could give up and stay on the same indifference curve by suitable purchases of bridge trips is $I_0 - I_1$, the compensating variation in income. This amount, equal to BC, is the consumer surplus of purchasing X_1 bridge trips at a price of P_1. But the government extracts more money from the individual through the lump-sum tax, T, than it bestows in consumer surplus. The result is a move to the lower indifference curve U_1 at combination A; the bridge is not desirable. Consumer surplus must be at least as large as the tax to justify the bridge.

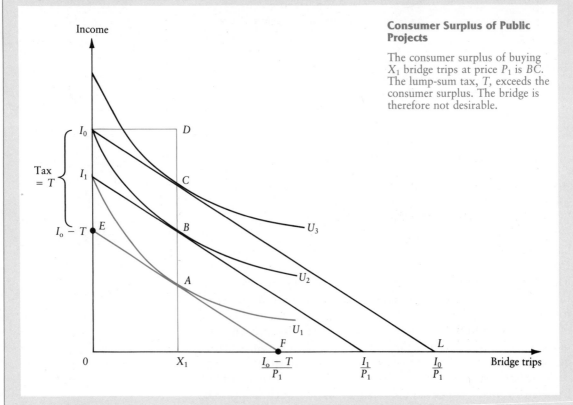

Consumer Surplus of Public Projects

The consumer surplus of buying X_1 bridge trips at price P_1 is BC. The lump-sum tax, T, exceeds the consumer surplus. The bridge is therefore not desirable.

Consumer Surplus and the Traffic Engineer

APPLIED MICRO THEORY

4.5

How can consumer theory, demand, and consumer surplus be applied to highway construction? It is a common practice for local authorities to decide on the location of new highway construction based on traffic counts, the logic being that the most heavily traveled roadways must yield the greatest benefit to drivers. Let's examine this assertion by studying the figure here, which contains three demand curves for travel: P_1A, P_2B, and P_3A. For ease, let's assume that income effects are negligible; then we can use the ordinary demand curve to estimate consumer surplus.

Consider point A, which represents a particular traffic count per unit of time. The traffic count itself is a poor estimate of consumer benefit, because the traffic count A is simply the quantity of travel demanded at zero price. If the price of travel were to rise, consumers would seek out substitute modes of travel, thereby reducing their quantities demanded at higher prices. The demand curve P_1A is relatively more price elastic than the demand curve P_3A; more substitutes exist for travel in the case of the former than for the latter. If the demand curve is P_1A, the consumer surplus derived from travel at zero price is $0P_1A$, the area beneath the demand curve P_1A. But if demand is less elastic, as in demand curve P_3A, the corresponding consumer surplus is the larger area $0P_3A$. In short, traffic counts alone cannot be used to estimate total consumer benefits of particular travel routes.

But it gets worse. Suppose that traffic counts along two alternative arteries yield points A and B in the figure. The area beneath demand curve P_2B is visibly larger than the area beneath demand curve P_1A; in

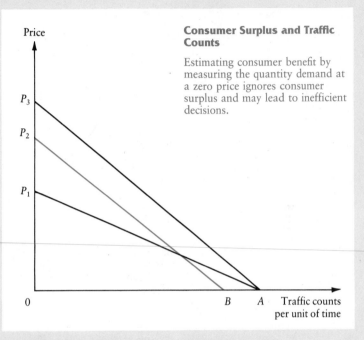

Consumer Surplus and Traffic Counts

Estimating consumer benefit by measuring the quantity demand at a zero price ignores consumer surplus and may lead to inefficient decisions.

this example the consumer surplus is greater for the road with the lower traffic count because of differences in the elasticities of demand for the two roads. Thus the road that will maximize traffic count is the wrong one to build!

Life is replete with similar examples. Television networks generally air programs that score highest in the Nielsen ratings in order to attract advertiser financing. But these ratings are just a measure of quantity demanded at zero price. The demand for educational programming may be much less price elastic than the demand for "Dallas" and its clones, even though the audience for the former is smaller than for the latter. Thus although educational programming may bestow more consumer surplus than alternative network offerings, the audience for the former may not amass the minimum share of

the market needed to get the programs aired.

University enrollment funding works the same way. When university administrators decide which programs to finance based solely on enrollment figures, they ignore the possibility that the programs with smaller total enrollments may possess the larger consumer surplus.

In conclusion, it is unavoidable that goods similar to highways and television programming will frequently be provided at a zero money price. These goods are costly, yet the important willingness-to-pay information needed to estimate consumer surplus is absent when the price is zero. The typical expedient of judging consumer benefit by measuring the quantity demanded at a zero price ignores consumer surplus and is therefore almost automatically inefficient.

The Value of Scarce but Free Parking Spaces

APPLIED
MICRO
THEORY

4.6

In the accompanying figure, the line DE represents drivers' demand curve for parking spaces. If we assume that income effects are negligible, the curve is suitably close to our definition of the income-compensated demand curve. Drivers are depicted along the horizontal axis in declining order of their marginal benefits from parking, the first driver deriving $0D$ marginal benefit and the last driver, at point E, being indifferent between parking and not parking. Thus the demand curve DE is a marginal benefit curve for parking.

Say there are $0E$ drivers but only $0A$ parking spaces. When there is no charge for parking, it is tempting to measure the total benefit as the entire area beneath the demand curve, $0DE$. However, the size of this area overstates benefits, because not all drivers will find parking, and those who do look all have an equal chance, regardless of the marginal benefit derived.

Assume that all drivers have an equal chance to find a space. When parking is free, $0E$ drivers will

search but only $0A$ drivers will find spaces. The chance of finding parking is therefore $0A/0E$ and equal for all drivers. By construction in the figure, $0A = 0E/2$. There are twice as many drivers as parking spaces, so the probability of finding a space is $0A/0E = 1/2$. Therefore, each driver's marginal benefit is suppressed by the probability $0A/0E = 1/2$ of finding a space. The first driver's marginal benefit, $0D$, is cut in half, to $0F$. Driver A's benefit falls from AB to AG. To construct the probabilistic marginal benefit curve containing all points like F and G, first draw line AF parallel to demand curve DE. Now construct the straight line FE. At any point on the horizontal axis, the vertical distance to line FE is $0A/0E$ times the distance to the demand curve. In our example, each driver's marginal benefit is halved, because the probability of finding a space is $1/2$. Driver A's benefit of parking is AB if assured a space. This benefit is reduced to AG if the driver is uncertain about finding a space.

The area $0FE$ beneath the probabilistic marginal benefit line measures the total benefit derived

by the $0E$ drivers when there is no charge for parking. This area equals the drivers' consumer surplus. If a price $0F$ is charged, all drivers desiring a space at that price will find one. The total benefit of $0A$ spaces found with certainty by drivers willing to pay price $0F$ is $0DBA$, which can be broken down as expenditures ($0FBA$) and consumer surplus (FDB). Note these two conclusions:

1. $0DBA > 0FE$: The parking spaces have a greater total value to drivers when market-clearing prices are charged.

2. $FDB < 0FE$: Charging for spaces reduces the consumer surplus of drivers.

These conclusions suggest that a fee for parking can improve the allocation of resources and increase the total benefit of parking spaces. At the same time, vocal drivers will express their regret over fees because of their effect on the consumer surplus.[*]

[*]William Holahan is grateful to William Vickrey for drawing this diagram on a napkin in a sandwich shop in 1974.

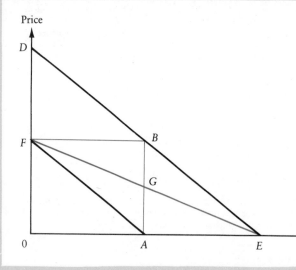

Price

D · F · B · G · 0 · A · E

Drivers and parking spaces

Consumer Surplus and Parking Spaces

If parking is scarce and no price is charged, consumer surplus is $0FE$, the area under the probabilistic marginal benefit curve. If price $0F$ is charged, the total benefit of $0A$ spaces rises to $0DBA$, and consumer surplus falls to $FDB < 0FE$. Imposing parking fees increases benefit but reduces consumer surplus.

Specific Performance versus Money Payments

APPLIED
MICRO
THEORY

4.7

Generally, the law of contracts does not obligate people to do specifically what is promised in a contract. Instead, it gives them the choice of performing their part of the contractual agreement or of breaching the contract but paying money damages. However, in some rare circumstances, most commonly in real estate transactions, parties are required to perform specifically whatever is called for in the contract. The theory of consumers' surplus can be used to show that "specific performance" can be an important part of contract law when the goods being exchanged are relatively unique and are exchanged so infrequently that it is difficult to estimate their value using market prices.

Consider two goods, one commonly available and one unique: a Gideon Bible and a Gutenberg Bible. Suppose that *A* contracts to deliver a Gideon Bible to *B* in one month in exchange for $15 paid today. We can be confident that $15 is a competitive price because a variety of similar Bibles are readily available at bookstores and churches and to be had (albeit with some fall from grace) at virtually every hotel and motel. Furthermore, *B* obtains no consumer surplus from obtaining one particular Gideon Bible over another. The $15 purchase price is an accurate measure of the value of *that* Bible (but, note well, not of having *a* Bible versus having *no* Bible at all). If *A* fails to provide the Bible to *B*, the assessment of damages is straightforward: Award *B* damages equal to $15, which can be used to replace the Gideon Bible that *A* failed to deliver.

Now consider the sale of a Gutenberg Bible—a rare treasure. Suppose that *A* contracts to deliver to *B* a Gutenberg Bible for $50,000 but later reneges. The damages from this breach of contract cannot be estimated from the contract price. The buyer's willingness to pay is very likely above the agreed-on price, resulting in an expected consumer surplus from the purchase. Neither can prices be used to estimate *B*'s damages from breach of contract, because the infrequent market exchange of Gutenberg Bibles limits our ability to observe the willingness to pay of similarly situated individuals. Thus neither the contract price nor market prices are useful measures of damages. One way to avoid these intractible measurement problems is by requiring *specific performance* of contract terms: requiring *A* to deliver the Gutenberg Bible to *B*.*

*See Kronman, *Specific Performance*, 45 U. CHI. L. REV. 351–375 (1978) for more on specific performance.

would know that the project is unwarranted, even using an exaggerated consumer surplus. Second, many public projects require a very small amount of real income per capita. A project cost of $1 million can be fully financed with a property tax levy of $1 per capita in a community of 1 million people or with much less per year if the project is financed through bonds. Ignoring such small income effects by the use of the ordinary demand curve may introduce negligible errors in the estimate of consumer surplus. Finally, the statistical error involved in measuring demand curves themselves probably exceeds the error involved in selecting one demand definition over the other. In conclusion, consumer surplus is an imperfect but helpful device in judging the appropriateness of public projects that, due to their nature, are provided to taxpayers at prices that do not pay the cost of the service.

Price Index Numbers

Still another policy application of the theory of consumer behavior is the construction of **price indexes,** which are numbers used to compare living standards in different years. If only one consumer good existed, such as hamburgers, consumers could know unambiguously whether their standard of living rose or fell between years simply by comparing the price change in hamburgers to their income. If income rose more than the price of hamburgers, the standard of living would have increased—and vice versa. But in a multigood world the problem is more difficult, because as relative prices change, consumers seek substitutes. Although prices have risen in recent years, we cannot deduce the impact of higher movie prices on living standards generally, because people have selected substitutes, including cable television and home video cassette machines.

Substitution is a prevalent consumer activity; thus a standard-of-living index must take it into account. Otherwise, any success that the economy has in creating substitutes would not be counted as improvements. And because substitution shows up so clearly in indifference curves, economists use them in the construction and interpretation of index numbers. Using the theory of consumer behavior as a building block, economists have developed some indexes that allow consumers to compare their standard of living over time as prices, money income, and bundles of goods purchased change. One important advantage of indifference-curve analysis is its ability to demonstrate the inherent ambiguity of price index numbers. We will analyze these ambiguities in detail as we proceed.

The True Price Index

Figure 4.12 contains a single indifference curve, U_1. The vertical axis measures income as the numeraire good. The tangency point Q_1 represents the consumer's optimal combination of goods for the prices prevailing in year 1 and for the consumer's actual money income in year 1, denoted I_1. Say that the relative price of good X rises in year 2. How much additional money income would the consumer need to maintain the same indifference curve at the higher year 2 prices? The answer is given by the Hicksian compensating variation in income, equal to $I_2^T - I_1$ in Figure 4.12. The movement from Q_1 to Q_2 is the reduction in the quantity of X demanded due solely to the higher relative price of X in year 2. It is also the substitution effect, because we have eliminated the income effect of the price change by a compensating variation in money income equal to $I_2^T - I_1$.

The consumer's actual money income in year 1, denoted as I_1, is written as follows for the case of two goods, X and Y:

$$I_1 = P_{X_1}X_1 + P_{Y_1}Y_1 = \Sigma P_1 q_1 \qquad (4.8)$$

The term P_1 refers to the prices of all goods in year 1, and q_1 refers to the quantities of all goods purchased in year 1. Thus $\Sigma P_1 q_1$ is the sum of the consumer's expenditures on all goods in year 1. Equation 4.8 defines the individual's money income in year 1; it is, therefore, the equation for the year 1 budget line.

The minimum money income required in year 2 to achieve indifference curve U_1 is

$$I_2^T = P_{X_2}X_2 + P_{Y_2}Y_2 = \Sigma P_2 q_2 \qquad (4.9)$$

This is the equation for the colored income-compensated budget line for year 2. The superscript T is used because I_2^T is an income level used to calculate the true price index; it is not the consumer's actual year 2 income.

The **true price index,** τ, is the ratio of the income needed in year 2 to achieve year 1's indifference curve (I_2^T) to the consumer's actual income in year 1 (I_1):

$$\frac{I_2^T}{I_1} = \frac{\Sigma P_2 q_2}{\Sigma P_1 q_1} = \tau \qquad (4.10)$$

This is a "true" price index because it entails no ambiguities in assessing consumer utility changes from year to year. If such an index could be constructed, consumers could easily compare the ratio of their actual money incomes in the two years to the true price index. Let I_2 denote the consumer's actual income in year 2. If $I_2/I_1 > \tau$, the consumer is unambiguously better off in year 2, because he or she has more income in year 2 than the minimum necessary to keep utility constant. If $I_2/I_1 < \tau$, utility is lower in year 2, and if $I_2/I_1 = \tau$, utility is the same in both years.

The difficulty with the true price index is that it uses a Hicksian compensating variation in income, which, as we have already seen, is intractible empirically. We have no way of knowing whether an observation like Q_2 in Figure 4.12 is on the same indifference curve as Q_1, because we cannot measure indifference curves. Thus it is impossible empirically to categorize any point like Q_2 as superior, inferior, or indifferent to Q_1. Theoretically, the true price index would be ideal for comparing utility in different periods because it would yield unambiguous results. But it is of no practical use because of empirical limitations in making Hicksian compensating

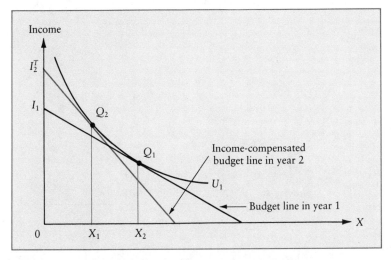

Figure 4.12
The True Price Index

The ratio between the income needed in year 2 to achieve year 1's indifference curve and the consumer's actual year 1 income is I_2^T/I_1.

variations in income. If we can't use the ideal index, what indexes can we construct that are suitably close to the ideal?

The Laspeyres Price Index

Let's begin our search for a usable index with reference to Figure 4.13, which displays an initial optimum at point Q_1, the tangency between the indifference curve U_1 and the budget line for year 1. Assume that the relative price of X rises in year 2. In constructing the true price index, we made a compensating variation in money income to measure the money income needed to reach the same indifference curve at year 2 prices. Because we cannot measure such a variation statistically given the current state of the art, let's make an income variation we can measure and interpret.

Specifically, let's measure the money income needed for the consumer to buy the same commodity bundle in year 2 that was purchased in year 1. If we construct a budget line that intersects commodity combination Q_1 and has a slope reflecting relative prices in year 2, the corresponding money income $I_2^L = \Sigma P_2 q_1$ is certainly sufficient to buy bundle Q_1 at year 2 prices. The distance $I_2^L - I_1$ is a compensating variation in income that allows the purchase of year 1's commodity bundle. It is in fact a Slutsky compensating variation in income, holding "apparent" real income constant. The superscript L is used because I_2^L is an income level used to calculate this particular price index; it is not the consumer's actual year 2 income. If the consumer's actual income in year 2, denoted I_2, is at least I_2^L in Figure 4.13—that is, at least sufficient to buy year 1's bundle—he or she is better off in year 2. Although indifference curve U_1 is available by purchasing bundle Q_1, substitution allows the consumer to reach the higher indifference curve U_2 at combination Q_2.

Using summation notation, the consumer's actual income in year 1 is

$$I_1 = \Sigma P_1 q_1 \qquad (4.11)$$

Figure 4.13
The Laspeyres Price Index

The ratio between the income needed to buy the year 1 bundle at year 2 prices and the actual year 1 income is I_2^L / I_1.

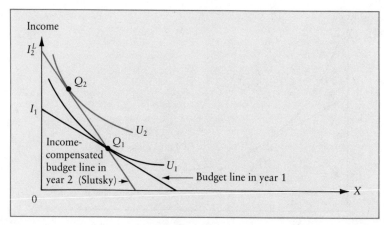

This is the equation for the year 1 budget line. The amount of income that would permit the consumer to buy the year 1 bundle at year 2 prices is

$$I_2^L = \Sigma P_2 q_1 \tag{4.12}$$

This is the equation of the colored, income-compensated budget line intersecting point Q_1 in Figure 4.13. The ratio of the income needed to buy the year 1 bundle at year 2 prices (I_2^L) to the actual year 1 income (I_1) is the **Laspeyres price index,** named after Etienne Laspeyres, a nineteenth-century Italian statistician.

$$\text{Laspeyres price index} = \mathscr{L} = \frac{I_2^L}{I_1} = \frac{\Sigma P_2 q_1}{\Sigma P_1 q_1} \tag{4.13}$$

Consumers need only compare the ratio of their actual income in the two years to the Laspeyres price index to measure changes in their welfare over the two years. Let the consumer's actual year 2 money income equal

$$I_2 = \Sigma P_2 \cdot q_2 \tag{4.14}$$

The individual is better off in year 2 if the actual year 2 money income I_2 equals or exceeds the money income needed to allow purchase of the year 1 bundle at year 2 prices, I_2^L. In symbols, the consumer is better off in year 2 when

$$I_2 \geq I_2^L, \text{ implying } \Sigma P_2 \cdot q_2 \geq \Sigma P_2 \cdot q_1 \tag{4.15}$$

Dividing both sides of Equation 4.15 by the consumer's income in year 1, $\Sigma P_1 q_1$, yields

$$\frac{\Sigma P_2 q_2}{\Sigma P_1 q_1} \geq \frac{\Sigma P_2 q_1}{\Sigma P_1 q_1} = \mathscr{L} \tag{4.16}$$

By substituting the more abbreviated terms, Equation 4.16 becomes

$$\frac{I_2}{I_1} \geq \frac{I_2^L}{I_1} = \mathscr{L} \tag{4.17}$$

Equation 4.17 states that consumers are better off in year 2 when the ratio of their actual money income equals or exceeds the Laspeyres price index. Equation 4.17 may be rewritten as

$$\frac{I_2}{\mathscr{L}} \geq I_1 \tag{4.18}$$

Consumers are better off in year 2 if their actual year 2 income, corrected (divided) by the Laspeyres price index, equals or exceeds their income in year 1. In this form, year 2 incomes are constantly inflated or deflated by the price index $\mathscr{L}$, making incomes in different periods commensurate for purposes of comparing welfare over time. Thus, the consumer is better off in year 2 if his or her actual money income rises faster than the Laspeyres price index.

Conclusion: If the ratio of the consumer's actual incomes in year 2 and year 1 exceeds the Laspeyres price index, the consumer's standard of living is higher in year 2. *Warning:* If the actual income ratio for the two years is less than the Laspeyres index, we cannot conclude that the standard of living has fallen in year 2.

Figure 4.14 displays the income measures needed to calculate the true index (τ) and the Laspeyres index ($\mathscr{L}$):

$$\tau = \frac{I_2^T}{I_1} \tag{4.19}$$

$$\mathscr{L} = \frac{I_2^L}{I_1} \tag{4.20}$$

By definition, $\mathscr{L} > \tau$, because the Slutsky compensating variation in income used to compute $\mathscr{L}$ is larger than the Hicksian compensating variation used to compute τ. Therefore, an individual consumer might be better off in year 2 even when the ratio of the consumer's money incomes in the two years is less than the Laspeyres price index. Suppose that the consumer's actual year 2 income is $\hat{I}_2$, an amount insufficient to purchase year 1 bundle Q_1. Nevertheless,

Figure 4.14
Ambiguity in the Laspeyres Index

If $I_2/I_1 \geq \mathscr{L}$, the consumer is unambiguously better off in year 2. But if $I_2/I_1 < \mathscr{L}$, the consumer isn't necessarily worse off in year 2. If the actual income ratio is $\hat{I}_2/I_1$, then $I_2/I_1 < \mathscr{L}$, but the consumer is still better off in year 2. The index yields ambiguous inferences when $I_2/I_1 < \mathscr{L}$.

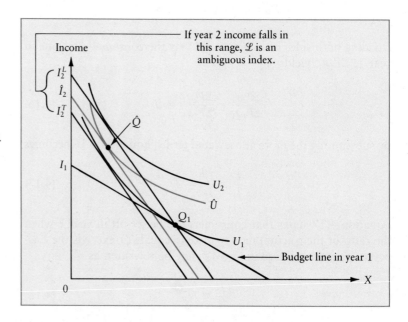

substitution allows the consumer to improve utility to indifference curve $\hat{U}$ by selecting bundle $\hat{Q}$.

In technical language, $I_2/I_1 \geq \mathcal{L}$ is termed a **sufficient condition** for improving the standard of living in year 2, but it is not a **necessary condition.** There is the possibility that $I_2/I_1 < \mathcal{L}$ also leaves the consumer better off in year 2. These ambiguities arise from the necessity of using an imperfect price index.

The Paasche Price Index

The Laspeyres price index is a ratio of incomes needed in different years to purchase year 1's commodity bundle. We could just as well construct a price index that uses year 2 quantities. Such a price index, called the **Paasche price index** ($\mathcal{P}$), is named after Hermann Paasche, a French statistician. It is defined as follows:

$$\text{Paasche price index} = \mathcal{P} = \frac{I_2}{I_1^P} = \frac{\Sigma P_2 q_2}{\Sigma P_1 q_2} \qquad (4.21)$$

The Paasche price index is the ratio of the consumer's money income used to purchase the year 2 bundle at year 2 prices (I_2) to the money income necessary for the consumer to have purchased the year 2 commodity bundle at prices prevailing in year 1 (I_1^P). The Paasche index allows us to make similar inferences about changes in standards of living that we made using the Laspeyres index except that we employ the year 2 commodity bundle as the point of comparison.

To illustrate the Paasche index, Figure 4.15 displays a consumer optimum at combination Q_2, where the year 2 budget line is tangent

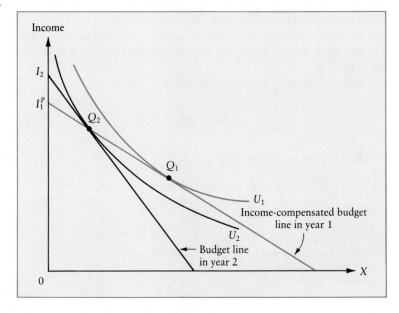

Figure 4.15
The Paasche Index

The ratio between income used to purchase the year 2 bundle at year 2 prices and the income necessary for the consumer to have purchased the year 2 commodity bundle at prices prevailing in year 1 is $\mathcal{P} = I_2/I_1^P$. It yields ambiguous results when $I_2/I_1 > \mathcal{P}$.

to indifference curve U_2. (We can assume that the relative price of X rises from year 1 to year 2.) As before, it would be nice to be able to make a Hicksian compensating variation in income in order to measure the maximum money income needed to keep the consumer on the same indifference curve at the lower year 1 prices. But such a calculation requires the measurement of indifference curves, which we cannot do. So once again we make a Slutsky income variation that we can measure and interpret. This time we measure the maximum money income needed for the consumer to have purchased the same commodity bundle in year 1 that is purchased in year 2. A budget line that intersects commodity bundle Q_2 and has a slope reflecting relative prices in year 1 corresponds to an amount of money income $I_1^P = \Sigma P_1 q_2$, which is sufficient to have allowed the consumer to buy bundle Q_2 at year 1 prices. Thus if income is lower in year 1 by $I_2 - I_1^P$, the Slutsky compensating variation in income, the consumer could have purchased the year 2 bundle at year 1 prices. The superscript P is used because I_1^P is an income level used to calculate the Paasche price index; it is not the consumer's actual year 1 income.

In order to use the Paasche price index to make inferences regarding relative well-being in two years, we must compare the person's actual income in year 1 (I_1) with the money income needed to purchase year 2 goods in year 1 (I_1^P). If the consumer's actual income equals or exceeds I_1^P, we may infer that the individual is better off in year 1. In Figure 4.15, a consumer with actual year 1 income equal to I_1^P had enough income to buy bundle Q_2 but instead selected combination Q_1, because the substitution of X for other goods allowed the consumer to attain the preferred indifference curve U_1. The fact that commodity bundle Q_2 was available in year 1 but was passed up in favor of commodity bundle Q_1 is evidence that Q_1 is on a higher indifference curve than Q_2. Thus we may infer that the consumer with at least I_1^P actual income in year 1 is better off in year 1.

The consumer is better off in year 1 when

$$I_1 \geq I_1^P, \text{ implying } \Sigma P_1 q_1 \geq \Sigma P_1 q_2 \qquad (4.22)$$

Dividing Equation 4.22 by $\Sigma P_2 q_2$ yields

$$\frac{\Sigma P_1 q_1}{\Sigma P_2 q_2} \geq \frac{\Sigma P_1 q_2}{\Sigma P_2 q_2} = \frac{1}{\mathcal{P}} \qquad (4.23)$$

Inverting Equation 4.23, we get

$$\frac{\Sigma P_2 q_2}{\Sigma P_1 q_1} \leq \frac{\Sigma P_2 q_2}{\Sigma P_1 q_2} = \mathcal{P} \qquad (4.24)$$

Price Indexes and Shifting Consumer Preferences

APPLIED
MICRO
THEORY

4.8

Price indexes are valid only when consumer behavior obeys the consumer axioms and when preferences are not shifting from period to period. Curious results are produced when preferences are shifting or inconsistent, regardless of which price index is used.

To illustrate, suppose that a consumer has actual money incomes of I_1 in year 1 and I_2 in year 2. These two budget lines are drawn with solid lines in the accompanying figure; we can assume that the price of X is higher in year 2 than in year 1. Let Q_1 represent the bundle chosen in year 1. The Laspeyres price index is determined by finding the income needed in year 2 to buy year 1's bundle, Q_1. Following established procedures, the income needed to buy bundle Q_1 at year 2 prices is I_2^L. The Laspeyres index is $\mathcal{L} = I_2^L/I_1$. The consumer's actual income ratio I_2/I_1 exceeds $\mathcal{L}$, so the consumer is better off in year 2. He or she has more than enough income in year 2 to buy year 1's goods.

Now let Q_2 be the commodity bundle selected in year 2. The consumer needs income of at least I_1^P in year 1 to purchase year 2 goods at year 1 prices. The Paasche price index is $\mathcal{P} = I_2/I_1^0$, and because the consumer's actual income ratio (I_2/I_1) is less than $\mathcal{P}$, the consumer is better off in year 1. He or she has more than enough income in year 1 to buy year 2's goods.

This may all seem fine, but something is dreadfully wrong. For the consumer in the figure, the following conditions exist:

$$\mathcal{P} > \frac{I_2}{I_1} > \mathcal{L}$$

These inequalities imply that the consumer is better off in both years! When the actual income ratio of the consumer's income is greater than the Laspeyres index

and less than the Paasche index, we are either dealing with a consumer whose preferences violate the conventional consumer axioms or with one whose preferences have shifted. Thus, as in the case of the middle-aged, happily married family man who suddenly runs off with a younger woman, it is impossible to measure changes in standard of living using merely economic data. Shifting or inconsistent preferences, illustrated by the intersecting indifference curves in the figure, make it impossible to measure utility changes.

The table included here summarizes the inferences that we can make about changes in living standards by using price index numbers.

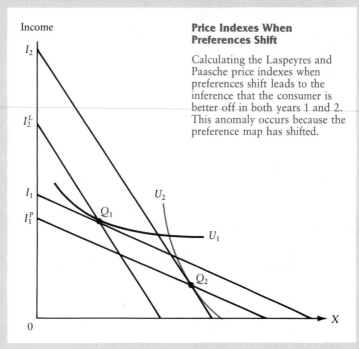

Income

Price Indexes When Preferences Shift

Calculating the Laspeyres and Paasche price indexes when preferences shift leads to the inference that the consumer is better off in both years 1 and 2. This anomaly occurs because the preference map has shifted.

Summary of Living Standard Inferences Using Laspeyres and Paasche Price Indexes

When Income Condition Is	Living Standard Is
$\dfrac{I_2}{I_1} \geq \mathcal{L}$	Higher in year 2
$\dfrac{I_2}{I_1} \geq \mathcal{P}$	Higher in year 1
$\mathcal{P} < \dfrac{I_2}{I_1} < \mathcal{L}$	Ambiguous
$\mathcal{P} \geq \dfrac{I_2}{I_1} \geq \mathcal{L}$	Preferences violate consumer axioms

Social Security Benefits and the Consumer Price Index

APPLIED
MICRO
THEORY

4.9

Inflation is particularly hard on people with fixed incomes. In recent years, the real purchasing power of Social Security benefits has been protected by adjusting them to account for changes in the consumer price index (CPI). The consumer price index is a Laspeyres price index based on a market basket of goods and services purchased in a base year by an urban family of four. The base quantities are revised infrequently because it is expensive to do so. With these facts as background, we can see how Social Security payments to retirees rise faster than inflation when the benefit adjustments are based on the CPI.

Consider a retired couple and a typical urban family of four. They differ in their consumption patterns but especially in their expenses for housing. The figure included here shows a black indifference curve, U_u, for the urban family and a colored indifference curve, U_R, for the retirees. Housing is measured on the horizontal axis, and the numeraire, money income, on the vertical axis. Let's postulate equal money incomes and prices for both families, as illustrated by budget line AB. The retirees select bundle R_1, and the urban family chooses bundle F_1.

For simplicity, let's assume that

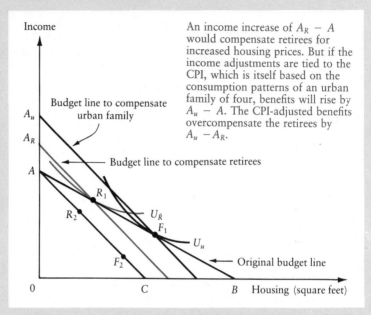

only the price of housing rises. The budget line rotates to AC. Say that the retirees and urban family adjust to R_2 and F_2, respectively. (The inferior indifference curves have been left out of the figure to reduce clutter.) The income increase required to compensate the urban family of four is $A_u - A$, which equals the Slutsky compensating variation in income needed to assure that the urban family can buy the commodity bundle F_1 at the higher housing prices. The consumer price index—a Laspeyres index—is A_u/A.

An income increase of $A_R - A$ would compensate retirees for increased housing prices. But if the income adjustments are tied to the CPI, which is itself based on the consumption patterns of an urban family of four, benefits will rise by $A_u - A$. The CPI-adjusted benefits overcompensate the retirees by $A_u - A_R$.

The income increase required to compensate the retirees is only $A_R - A$, found by rotating the budget line through R_1. Since the retirees' Social Security benefits are adjusted by the CPI based on the urban family's consumption pattern, the retirees will be overcompensated by the amount $A_u - A_R$. The CPI exaggerates the impact of inflation on the retirees because they have considerably different preferences from the urban family for goods that loom large in the CPI, such as housing, food, and transportation.

Substituting compact notation gives us

$$\frac{I_2}{I_1} \leq \mathcal{P} \text{ or } \frac{I_2}{\mathcal{P}} \leq I_1 \qquad (4.25)$$

Consumers are better off in year 1 if their actual year 2 income, corrected (divided) by the Paasche index, is less than their year 1 income. Stated differently, the consumer is worse off in year 2 if his or her actual money income rises slower than the Paasche price index.

Conclusion: If the ratio of the consumer's actual incomes in year 2 and year 1 is equal to or less than the Paasche price index, the individual is better off in year 1. This is the sufficient condition for being better off in year 1. *Warning:* If an individual's actual income ratio exceeds the Paasche price index, the person is not necessarily worse off in year 1. Thus Equation 4.25 is a sufficient but not a necessary condition for the consumer to be better off in year 1. The graphic proof is up to you. Using Figure 4.15, draw a budget line parallel to and below the colored budget line that becomes tangent to an indifference curve higher than U_2. Such a consumer is better off in year 1, even though $I_2/I_1 > \mathscr{P}$. As with the Laspeyres index, the inherent ambiguity in the Paasche index arises from the necessity of employing an imperfect index of consumer well-being.

Summary

The central theme of this chapter is the separation of income effects from substitution effects, which allows us to study the change in quantity demanded resulting from a price change "as if" it takes place in two separate steps. Generally, these effects are divided, either by making compensating or equivalent variations in income when prices change. Compensating variations in income are made in order to hold the consumer's real income (Hicks) or apparent real income (Slutsky) constant at original levels when prices change. Equivalent variations adjust income enough to allow the same level of real income (Hicks) or apparent real income (Slutsky) that the price change would achieve without any compensation. Each of these measures can be used in the course of applying consumer theory to policymaking. Each method results in its own income-compensated demand curve.

Indifference analysis is applied to two major problems in consumer theory: consumer surplus and price index numbers. Consumer surplus is a measure of the net benefit that consumers receive from the consumption of a given quantity of output at a given price. Price measures the benefit of the marginal unit of consumption, whereas consumer surplus measures the net benefit of all inframarginal units. Consumer surplus is especially important in evaluating the net benefits that consumers receive from the consumption of goods they do not pay for in market transactions.

Price indexes give an approximate relative measure of welfare levels under differing price and income sets. In comparing welfare in different periods characterized by changing relative prices and changing money incomes, it is important to break up the effects of the price changes and income changes "as if" they are sequential and not simultaneous. This separation is accomplished by differentiating between income and substitution effects. The Laspeyres and Paasche price indexes allow certain comparisons of utility in different periods, but neither is a perfect index. The true price index theoretically produces unambiguous utility comparisons, but it requires data that are impossible to determine accurately. Thus consumer theory helps interpret the meaning of the various indexes currently in vogue and shows why they can be ambiguous instruments for inferring welfare changes over time.

Key Terms

compensating variation in income 76
consumer surplus 91
equivalent variation in income 81
extramarginal units 92
Giffen good 79
Income-compensated demand curve 89
income effect of a price change 75
inframarginal units 92
Laspeyres price index 103
marginal benefit 93
marginal unit 92
necessary condition 105
ordinary demand curve 85
Paasche price index 105
price indexes 99
Slutsky approach 84
substitution effect of a price change 75
sufficient condition 105
total benefit (total value) 93
total effect of a price change 75
true price index 101

Problems

1. Your city council has a choice of building a museum or an equally expensive symphony hall. A council member says, "More people will attend the museum than the symphony. Let's build the museum." What do you tell the council member?

2. In one diagram, derive from a consumer's indifference map
   a. An ordinary demand curve.
   b. A Hicksian income-compensated demand curve.
   c. A Slutsky income-compensated demand curve.
   Summarize the uses of each.

3. Refer to the figure accompanying Applied Micro Theory 4.9. Is housing price elastic or inelastic for the urban family? For the retirees? Can you tell whether housing is a normal or an inferior good? If not, what information would you need?

4. Assuming that the good is a normal good,
   a. Draw the Hicksian income and substitution effects for a price *decrease* using a compensating variation in income.
   b. On the same diagram, draw the Hicksian income and substitution effects for a price *increase* using an equivalent variation in income.
   c. How many different budget lines did you need in part *b* compared to part *a*? Explain why.

5. Assume the following: $I_{1982} = \$50,000$ and $I^L_{1983} = \$75,000$.
   a. Interpret these figures.
   b. Calculate the Laspeyres price index.
   c. Explain to your roommate its meaning.
   d. What is the minimum income that this consumer must have in year 2 to be assured of being better off in year 2?
   e. Distinguish between sufficient conditions and necessary conditions for welfare improvement over time.

6. a. What does it mean if the Paasche price index is 1? If the Laspeyres price index is 1?
   b. When will the Laspeyres index exceed 1? When will the Paasche index exceed 1?
   c. Can either index be less than 1 for an observed price increase from year 1 to year 2? Must both exceed 1 if prices have risen?

7. a. Why is it necessary to weigh a price index with the commodity bundle in a particular year?
   b. What practical advantages does a Laspeyres index have over a Paasche index? And vice versa?
   c. The major price indexes in current use are the CPI, the producer price index (PPI), and the gross national product (GNP) deflator. Are they Laspeyres or Paasche indexes?

8. How does consumer surplus differ in the following cases?
   a. Mr. Smith buys a Picasso painting from Ms. Jones.
   b. When the price of crankcase oil is 95¢ per quart, 1000 consumers purchase 420,000 quarts.

9. a. Draw a demand curve and price line at random. Which units are inframarginal, which marginal, and which extramarginal?

b. Draw an indifference curve–budget line tangency pertaining to your demand curve. Show why some units are inframarginal by comparing the slopes of indifference curves and budget lines.

c. Relate inframarginality and consumer surplus.

10. Present the diagrams and verbal argument for the derivation of ordinary versus income-compensated demand curves for a price increase for a normal good and for an inferior good. Do the same for a price decrease. (Hint: This may bore you. However, do it once and you will probably never forget the technique. You will certainly never forget the experience. Reread "Income-Compensated Demand Curves" before attempting this problem.)

11. Use consumer theory to show the effects of

a. An excise tax on pornography.

b. The equilibrium consumption of cigarettes due to an excise tax in conjunction with income tax reductions sufficient to maintain real income; sufficient to maintain initial commodity bundles.

12. a. Draw a consumer's indifference map for symphony tickets using money income as the numeraire.

b. Show the initial commodity bundle that the consumer selects for the original income level and price of tickets.

c. What is the price of the numeraire?

d. Show total expenditures on tickets and on all other goods.

e. Show the effect of the city government's lowering ticket prices to encourage patronage. Draw the new tangency so that demand is price elastic.

f. One council member wants to levy an income tax on city residents to keep total utility of patrons constant before and after the price reduction. Can such a mixed policy succeed in enlarging symphony audiences? Does it matter whether symphony attendance is normal or inferior?

g. Name the type of income variation implied by part *f*.

h. If the income tax were levied so as to allow the consumer to buy the original commodity bundle, would the consumer's utility be improved or worsened compared to the income tax policy in part *f*? Why or why not?

13. Construct an indifference map and an initial budget line for a consumer's food purchases using income as the numeraire.

a. Show how a sales tax on food influences prices and equilibrium commodity bundles.

b. How much total sales tax does the family pay? (Hint: See Applied Micro Theory 4.3.)

c. Is the consumer more likely to prefer a sales tax or an income tax of the same size?

d. If the government wants the consumer to have the same total utility whether it imposes a sales tax or an income tax, which tax would raise the most revenue?

e. How do Hicks and Slutsky enter into this problem?

14. Refer again to the baseball application, Applied Micro Theory 3.1. This analysis preceded the discussion of income and substitution effects. In light pencil (to preserve your book's resale value) trace out the income and substitution effects of the father's various strategies.

15. "The true price index requires a Hicksian compensating variation in income, whereas the Laspeyres price index uses a Slutsky variation." Demonstrate this statement graphically and discuss its implications.

16. "Consumer surplus is related to the area below the income-compensated demand curve. However, in no case can we observe it empirically, because we cannot measure indifference curves. Thus consumer surplus is of little value as a decisionmaking tool." Criticize this statement.

17. William Jones spends more money on goods this year than last. All prices have increased, some more than others. His income has also increased.
    a. Propose a method to ascertain whether he is better or worse off now.
    b. Is your method foolproof, or does it give ambiguous results?

18. A rotor is a component of an automobile's electrical system, without which your $20,000 car will not start. A rotor currently costs about $1. Estimate your consumer surplus.

19. a. How is price elasticity of demand related to consumer surplus, if at all?
    b. How is income elasticity of demand related to consumer surplus, if at all?

20. Write a 200-word paragraph relating these concepts: compensating variations in income, consumer surplus, income-compensated demand curves.

21. "Slutsky is more empirically relevant because we can always anchor the budget line at the old commodity bundle and give it the slope of the new price ratio. Therefore, for people whose income is compensated in the Laspeyres sense, we can measure their Slutsky demand curve. For people who are not compensated at all, we can observe their ordinary demand curve. In no case can we find points on the Hicksian demand curve." Critique this statement.

22. Suppose that you are given a budget of $500,000 to calculate the consumer surplus of a proposed water development project.
    a. What information would you need?
    b. How much of your budget would you devote to deriving an income-compensated demand curve for water?
    c. What kinds of simplifying assumptions are you most likely to make?

23. Suppose that you are part of an urban family of seventeen. Does the CPI overstate or understate the effect of inflation on your purchasing power?

24. You own a car that gets 10 miles per gallon. Gasoline prices double to $2 per gallon. Your car is comfortable but expensive to operate. There are small cars on the market for $6000 that get 30 miles per gallon. The trade-in value for your car is only $500, even though it is in very good condition. Should you sell? Does your decision depend on how many miles you drive per year? Will your miles driven per year be the same for each car? (Discuss both income and substitution effects in your answer.)

25. Suppose that the demand curve for a bridge is

$$q = a - bp \qquad\qquad (4.26)$$

where

q = trips per day

p = toll

a, b = positive numbers

Once the bridge is built, the cost to cross it is zero. But to build it costs C. What toll will pay it off? What toll will maximize the net benefits of the bridge?

26. There seems to be an ethic that people follow while they wait in lines to buy gasoline during shortages induced by price controls: Everyone waits the same amount of time—first come, first served. Is this equitable?

27. Use the theory of consumer surplus to solve the water-diamond paradox, the observation that water is more beneficial than diamonds yet sells for a lower price. (Hint: Distinguish between total benefit and the marginal benefit of the last unit purchased.)

28. Refer to the figure accompanying Applied Micro Theory 4.6. Prove that the conclusions derived (total value rises but consumer surplus falls when a clearing price is charged for scarce parking spaces) are valid when the probability of finding parking is greater than 50%; when it's less than 50%.

29. You studied in Applied Micro Theory 4.5 that television financed by advertising can lead to an inefficient array of programs. How is this likelihood changed by an increase in the number of channels?

30. Suppose the "flat tax" is adopted, providing a constant Federal income tax rate of, say, 20% but elimination of deductions for home mortgage interest.

    a. Using indifference curve and budget line analysis, draw the diagram for a person who consumes more housing as a result of the tax change.

    b. Draw another diagram for the person who consumes less as a result of the tax change.

    c. Would you expect the response to such a change to depend on the person's pretax income? In what way?

Suggested Readings

Friedman, Milton. *Price Theory: A Provisional Text.* Chicago: Aldine, 1962, chaps. 2–3.

Hicks, J. R. *Value and Capital.* Oxford, England: Clarendon Press, 1939, chap. 2.

Samuelson, Paul A. *Foundations of Economic Analysis.* New York: Atheneum, 1965, pp. 195–201.

Slutsky, Eugen E. "On the Theory of the Budget of the Consumer." *Giornale degli Economisti* 51 (1915): 1–26. Reprinted in George J. Stigler and Kenneth E. Boulding, *A.E.R. Readings in Price Theory,* vol. 6, pp. 27–56. Homewood, Ill.: Irwin, 1952.

Vickrey, William S. *Microstatics.* New York: Harcourt Brace Jovanovich, 1964, chap .2.

Willig, R. "Consumers' Surplus without Apology." *American Economic Review* 66 (1976): 589–597.

Production

> firms respond to profit
> incentives

Demand theory helps us understand important principles of consumer behavior that can be applied to many problems pertaining to market forces, public policy, and disturbances in consumer expenditures and satisfactions. Another fundamental part of microeconomic theory, known as the **theory of the firm,** treats producer behavior and supply decisions. The theory of the firm underlies models for various decisions made by business firms, including the quantities of output to produce, the mix of productive inputs to use, the prices to charge for products, and the selection of industries.

Be forewarned: The development of supply analysis is a lengthy procedure. For example, predicting a firm's supply decisions presupposes knowledge about the firm's production costs. But costs depend in part on the technical relationships between inputs and final outputs. Accordingly, a theory of competitive firm behavior must be developed in steps: production (Chapter 5)→costs (Chapter 6)→supply (Chapter 7).

As you embark on this journey, two comments may help you. First, production theory—the material in this chapter—is the main building block in the theory of the firm. When the cost and supply discussions in later chapters begin to elude you, return to this chapter and use it as a lifeline. Cost curves and supply curves, which we will encounter throughout the book, do not merely materialize as though pulled from a magician's hat. Nor are they bastards without recognized parentage. In fact, production curves are the progenitors of cost curves.

Second, it is helpful to distinguish between engineering problems and economic problems. Production theory is a description of engineering relationships between inputs and final outputs. It assumes knowledge of engineering solutions, using current technology, applied to the problem of squeezing the maximum output from a given mix of inputs. Having a technician determine the alternatives for combining inputs to produce 5000 television sets is an engineering problem. Deciding whether to produce 5000 sets or 3000 sets, whether to use mostly labor or mechanization, whether to operate the plant 8 hours per day or around the clock, or whether to sell off the physical equipment and abandon the television industry—these are economic decisions that go beyond the mere

physical relation of inputs and output. This chapter focuses on the typical engineering production processes of firms. It lays the foundation for the economic choices to be studied in virtually every remaining chapter.

Firms' Objectives and Constraints

In order to study the theory of the firm, we must seek a model that explains and predicts business firms' behavior. A firm is a business organization that hires factors of production, combines the factors in a production process to create output, and sells the resulting output. The firm organizes its production and sales activities so as to achieve certain objectives. Some possible objectives are to maximize profit, maximize output, or maximize the entrepreneur's utility.

Nearly all economic models of buisness behavior rest on the assumption that firms' actions are forever motivated by a search for maximum profit. This assumption undeniably ignores many additional goals that firms may hold. Still, it is a useful simplification for several reasons. First, profit maximization is a reasonable first approximation of business motivation, because if satisfactory profit levels are not maintained, stockholders will withdraw their financial capital from the firm. Second, models built on the axiom of profit maximization have generated verifiable predictions about business behavior. Finally, nobody has proposed any alternative business objectives that offer the explanatory and predictive power of profit maximization. This assumption is, in short, the best economists have.

No aspect of American business has come under stronger attack in recent years than what some critics refer to as "obscene" profits. Even businesspeople object to having their behavior linked to such greedy motivations.[1] This attitude is unfortunate, because it reveals ignorance about the true economic role of profit in a market economy. The theory of the firm emphasizes the importance of the profit motive, in terms of both business decisionmaking and social control.

Just as consumers maximize their utility, subject to income and price constraints, so too the firm faces constraints in its maximization decisions. Constraints on the firm might include the following:

1. Bureaucratic constraints
   a. Price controls

---

1. See George J. Stigler, *The Theory of Price,* 3rd ed. (New York: Macmillan, 1966), p. 177 for a summary of the results of a pertinent field study. Businesspeople were asked when profit maximization had motivated their decisions. "They indignantly rejected the suggestion. . . . But when the question was reformulated as: would a higher or lower price of the product yield larger profits?, the answer was, usually; no."

b. Antitrust regulation
c. Rate-of-return regulation
d. Taxation

2. Market constraints
   a. Prices of labor, capital, raw materials, and other inputs
   b. Demand for the firm's product
   c. Degree of competition

3. Technological constraints: the production function—the ways that labor, capital, raw materials, and other inputs can be combined to produce useful final goods

We will have abundant opportunities to consider all of these constraints to the firm's behavior in later chapters. In this chapter we will limit ourselves to the technological constraints inherent in the transformation of inputs into final output.

The Production Function

Firms combine inputs to produce final goods. The **production function** represents our knowledge of the amount of final output that can be produced from specific combinations of inputs. The production function is expressed as

$$Q = f(a_1, a_2, a_3, \ldots, a_n) \tag{5.1}$$

where

$$Q = \text{physical units of final output produced}$$
$$a_1, \ldots a_n = \text{firms' productive inputs}$$

The simplest production function imaginable would involve one input and one output, such as a singer performing *a capella;* the input is the singer and the output is the song. At the other extreme are firms that use many inputs in the production of multiple outputs, such as a farmer employing land, capital equipment, labor, fertilizer, and advanced technology to produce a wide variety of agricultural and dairy products. In this chapter we will take the middle ground between these two extremes and define a production function in which the firm uses only two inputs to produce a single output. This compromise allows the principal ideas of production theory to be expressed graphically within the limits imposed by two-dimensional paper. It also permits us to grasp the important concepts inherent in all production analysis, which can then be extended conceptually (although not always geometrically) to the more complex multiinput and multioutput cases.

Our simple production function is written as follows:

$$Q = f(L, K) \tag{5.2}$$

where

Q = physical units of final output produced
L = units of labor (for simplicity, the work force is assumed to be homogeneous unless otherwise noted)
K = units of capital equipment (also assumed homogeneous unless otherwise noted)

The apparent oversimplification of the two-input, one-output production function may be rationalized somewhat by regarding the **labor inputs** and **capital inputs** as broad surrogate groupings into which all inputs may be categorized. Thus labor represents all **variable inputs** of production—those factors that, like labor, can easily be added to or deleted from a production process in a relatively short period of time. Likewise, capital represents all **fixed inputs** not so easily varied, such as land, buildings, accesses, improvements, machinery, and equipment. Of course, labor is sometimes less variable than capital. For example, tenured professors last longer than some buildings. Still, the distinction between labor and capital allows us to study general propositions of production theory when some inputs can be varied and others cannot.

Each value of the production function represents the maximum output that can be obtained from a given combination of labor and capital inputs. This idea presupposes that the engineers have provided a table of labor, capital, and output combinations. However, graphing such a production function becomes a problem, because the three vairables—Q, L, and K—require three axes and therefore three dimensions. Because a piece of paper limits us to two dimensions, we must assign a fixed value to one of the variables and trace out a production curve from the remaining two, *ceteris paribus*. And because capital (K) is fixed in the short run, it is natural to hold its value constant and see how different quantities of labor affect the production of final output.

A production process that is probably familiar to you lies through the golden arches of a McDonald's hamburger emporium. You have seen the incredibly clean capital equipment (K)—the griddles, counter space, cash registers, tables and chairs, floor space, and refrigerators. You have also seen the workers (L), impeccably dressed and trained to the profit-maximizing level of cheerfulness and efficiency. And you have no doubt enjoyed McDonald's final output (Q)—a sandwich served in record time. By drawing on your acquaintance with McDonald's and your intuition, we can develop many of the basic principles of production.

Suppose that a particular franchise hires only one worker. This worker would be required to perform all the tasks involved in the business, such as cleaning, unwrapping raw food, ordering from wholesalers, cooking, wrapping cooked food in paper, taking orders, serving, making change, and filling out the bank deposit slip. Let's say the worker can produce 10 hamburgers per hour under these conditions. If a second worker is hired, the owner could presumably assign the new worker to exactly the same set of tasks and thereby double the output to 20 hamburgers per hour. Instead, he or she will most likely divide the tasks so that each worker can specialize—perhaps one doing all the cooking while the other waits on customers. Such a division of labor will allow the franchise to produce more than 20 hamburgers per hour, perhaps 30 hamburgers.

This example illustrates a basic point in production theory: The division of labor raises workers' average productivity in the early stages of production. In our example, an employee working alone produces 10 hamburgers, whereas the two employees produce an average of 15 hamburgers by dividing up the tasks. The division of labor has clearly increased the labor force's average output.

The average product of labor cannot rise indefinitely through hiring additional workers and specializing their tasks, however, because of the fixity of capital. As more workers are hired at our McDonald's, it becomes increasingly difficult to find counter space to wrap sandwiches, walking space to fill orders, and punching space to operate the cash registers. In the extreme, the labor force could become so immobilized by the presence of so many workers in such a limited work space that they could not move. Hence there are two important countervailing forces in production: efficiencies resulting from the division of tasks versus constraints ultimately imposed by the fixity of capital.

Product Curves

We can now become more rigorous about these ideas. Let capital be fixed at $\overline{K}$. The production function associated with this level of capital is expressed as

$$Q = f(L, \overline{K}) \tag{5.3}$$

Using this notation, suppose the engineers have told us that

$$Q = f(1, \overline{K}) = 10$$
$$Q = f(2, \overline{K}) = 30$$
$$Q = f(3, \overline{K}) = 40$$
$$Q = f(4, \overline{K}) = 44$$

These data points have been plotted two-dimensionally in Figure 5.1. Data points A, B, C, and D are joined with straight lines. The curve, an illustration of the production function holding capital fixed, is called a **total product curve.** It shifts with increases or decreases in capital, because the relationship between labor input and final output changes if workers have a different endowment of capital at their disposal.

Figure 5.1
The Total Product Curve

The amount of output produced by various quantities of labor, limited by a fixed amount of capital, can be represented with a total product curve.

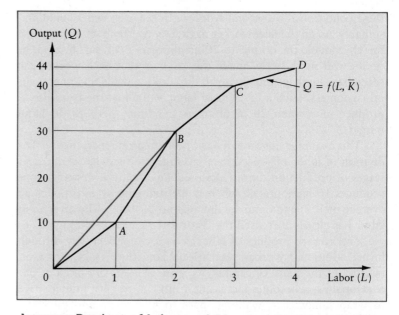

Average Product of Labor and Marginal Product of Labor

The total product curve relates total output to total labor input. All such "total" curves in economics—total output, total utility, total revenue, and so forth—are associated with corresponding average and marginal curves that arrange the data in a useful manner. You can greatly ease the burden of learning the theory of the firm by mastering the total-average-marginal relationships in the context of production theory. Having done so, the analogous relationships for cost and revenue curves—to be encountered later—will seem like old friends.

The **average product of labor** (AP_L) is defined as the average units of output that each worker produces, or[2]

$$AP_L = \frac{Q}{L}\bigg|_K \qquad (5.4)$$

The first and second columns of Table 5.1 use the figures for labor and total output that were used to draw the total product curve in Figure 5.1. The third column of Table 5.1 records the AP_L associated with each size of the labor force. As the labor input increases (holding capital fixed), the average product of labor rises for a time and then falls. As you can see in this case, specialization of labor and capital fixity are countervailing forces.

A convenient geometric method for measuring AP_L from a total product curve is to draw a ray from the origin to any point on the

2. The notation $A|_{(x, y, z, \ldots)}$ has already been used to denote that the value of A is determined for fixed values of $(x, y, z, \ldots)$. Thus K is held constant.

Table 5.1
Total, Average, and Marginal Products of Labor

Labor (L)	Output (Q)	$AP_L = \dfrac{Q}{L}\Big\|_K$	$MP_L = \dfrac{\Delta Q}{\Delta L}\Big\|_K$
1	10	10	10
2	30	15	20
3	40	13.3	10
4	44	11	4

curve and to evaluate the slope of the ray. Recall that slope equals rise/run. The slope of ray $0B$ in Figure 5.1 is $\Delta Q/\Delta L = 30/2 = 15$. Thus $AP_L = 15$ at point B. The AP_L at points A, C, and D can be evaluated similarly. The slope of the ray from the origin always produces the ratio Q/L, which defines the AP_L.

The AP_L tells us, on average, how much output each worker produces. A related measure of labor's productivity tells us how much extra output one extra worker adds. This value is important to those who contemplate hiring more workers; it is a marginal, rather than average, productivity concept.

The **marginal product of labor, MP_L,** is defined as

$$MP_L = \frac{\Delta Q}{\Delta L}\Big|_K \qquad\qquad (5.5)$$

The marginal product of labor is the change in output resulting from a one-unit change in the variable labor input, holding capital fixed. Keep in mind that the computation of "averages" involves the ratio of total output and total labor used, whereas the computation of "marginals" involves the ratio of small changes in these total output and labor values.

The fourth column of Table 5.1 lists the marginal product of labor for the values in the preceding example. The MP_L rises in the initial stages of production; then starting with the third worker, it begins to diminish. We will study this result in detail shortly. For now, simply note that the efficiencies inherent in dividing tasks increase labor's marginal product until the congestion on the fixed factor (capital) introduces enough inefficiencies to force the marginal product to decline. In principle, both the AP_L and the MP_L rise and later fall for the same reasons: division of tasks and capital fixity.

All marginal concepts are defined as changes in the value of a dependent variable in response to changes in the value of an independent variable. Such changes are measured by movements along the relevant graphs. To measure the marginal product of labor, we must therefore consider a move along the total product curve, as between points A and B in Figure 5.1. The slope of the line AB is

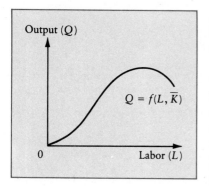

Figure 5.2
A Smooth Total Product Curve

The curve is smooth when the labor force and the final output are continuously divisible.

$\Delta Q / \Delta L = 20/1 = 20$; between points A and B, the MP_L is therefore 20. The MP_L along other sections of the total product curve is calculated in the same way.

As an exercise, measure the AP_L and the MP_L values from the total product curve in Figure 5.1 and compare your answers to the figures in Table 5.1. The AP_L is the slope of a ray from the origin to each point on the curve; the MP_L is the slope of the total product curve itself between data points. Logically, the measurement of MP_L requires at least a small move along the total product curve that will produce the changes in labor and output called for by the definition $MP_L = \Delta Q / \Delta L$. No movement is required to measure $AP_L = Q/L$, because total values (as opposed to changes in totals) are used.

Smoothing the Total Product Curve

The total product curve in Figure 5.1 is made up of several straight-line segments of different slopes. This is because we considered discrete adjustments in labor and output. For most purposes, a continuous, smooth total product curve is more convenient. Such smoothing is a valid first approximation in light of two facts. First, labor is a flow variable, measured per unit of time. The firm cannot hire $1\frac{1}{2}$ workers, but it can hire 3 workers for 2 hours, or $1\frac{1}{2}$ workers per hour. Second, labor is infinitely divisible if measured in hours of labor services rather than in numbers of workers. Figure 5.2 shows a smooth total product curve, which assumes that the labor force and the resulting output are all continuously divisible.

We can now generate the average and marginal product curves that correspond to the smooth total product curve. Only the method of measuring the marginal product is affected by changing discrete data points to the smooth curve.

Consider the AP_L curve first. The upper panel of Figure 5.3 contains a smooth total product curve, from which the average product of labor curve in the lower panel is derived. As before, the AP_L at any rate of production equals the slope of a ray drawn from the origin to the given point on the total product curve. In the upper panel, rays are drawn to points A through E. Each point on the AP_L curve in the lower panel is plotted at a height equal to the slope of the corresponding ray above.

As the labor force expands from zero to L_1, the AP_L rises; ray $0A$ is flatter than $0B$, which in turn is flatter than $0C$. Ray $0C$ is tangent to the total product curve at C; the AP_L achieves its maximum value at C, when L_1 workers are hired. The AP_L falls when labor is expanded beyond L_1, because the slope of ray $0D$ exceeds that of $0E$. Hence, the AP_L curve is an inverted U-shaped curve. It demonstrates graphically that the production efficiencies inherent in specialization of the labor force are eventually offset by the congestion resulting from capital limitations.

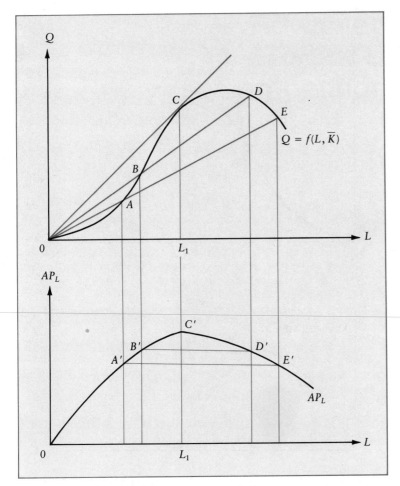

Figure 5.3
Deriving the Average Product of Labor Curve

AP_L is the slope of a ray from the origin to any point on the total product curve. The AP_L rises as labor is expanded to L_1, then diminishes with further labor expansion. The slope of the ray that is tangent to the total product curve at C is the maximum value of AP_L at C'.

The economic meaning of the marginal product of labor is captured by the mathematical definition of the slope of the total product curve: slope $= MP_L = \Delta Q / \Delta L$. For a discontinuous total product curve, MP_L is the slope of each linear segment of the curve (see Figure 5.1). Although a smooth total product curve calls for a slightly more sophisticated technique to accommodate the curve's constantly changing slope, the essence is unchanged: The slope of the total product curve equals MP_L.

Figure 5.4 shows how the MP_L curve (lower panel) is related to the total product curve (upper panel). The total product curve is divided into three segments: $0A$, AB, and the segment beyond B. The corresponding segments on the MP_L curve are $0A'$, $A'B'$, and the segment beyond B'.

Consider segment $0A$. Each tangent has a positive slope, so the MP_L is positive. Also, the tangents' slopes rise as point A is approached. Thus, MP_L increases when the labor force is expanded to

Figure 5.4
Deriving the Marginal Product of Labor Curve

MP_L is the slope of a tangent drawn to any point on the total product curve. The MP_L rises along segment $0A$, is at its maximum at point A (the inflection point), diminishes along segment AB, is zero at B, and is negative beyond B, as seen by the slopes of the tangents. The lower panel shows these results explicitly in the MP_L curve.

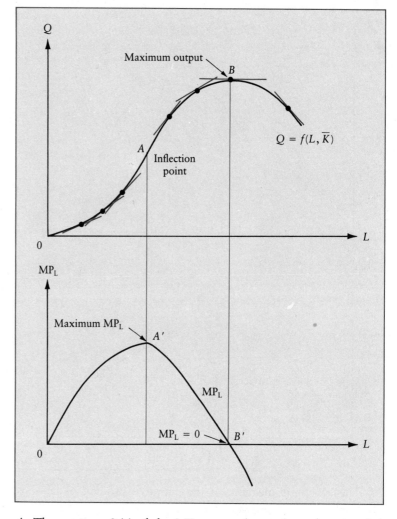

A. The segment $0A'$ of the MP_L curve shows these same results: positive and increasing MP_L.

It is impossible to draw a tangent to point A in the upper panel because it is an **inflection point,** the place where the curve ceases rising at an increasing rate and begins rising at a decreasing rate. The inflection point A identifies the maximum MP_L, denoted A' in the lower panel.

To evaluate slope at any point on a nonlinear total product curve, and hence to measure MP_L, draw a tangent to the given point and measure the slope of the tangent. Because the slope of the tangent is constant and the given point lies on the tangent, the slope of the tangent determines the slope of the total product curve at the given point—and hence the marginal product of labor. The slope measures how much output rises when labor is increased a small amount, precisely the definition of MP_L.

Throughout segment AB in Figure 5.4, each tangent is positively sloped, but the slopes get flatter as point B is approached. Hence MP_L diminishes as more labor is hired between A and B. The corresponding segment $A'B'$ of the MP_L curve therefore diminishes as the labor force expands. Congestion on the fixed factor (capital) is in evidence.

The slope of the tangent drawn to the total product curve's maximum at point B is zero; hence MP_L is zero at B'. Because more labor reduces total output beyond B, the tangents are negatively sloped. Thus the MP_L is also negative, as shown to the right of B' in the lower panel of Figure 5.4.

To summarize:

The MP_L is positive up to B, equals zero at B, and is negative beyond B.

The MP_L increases up to A, the inflection point, and diminishes beyond A.

The MP_L curve, derived from the total product curve in Figure 5.4, is an inverted U-shaped curve.

Fitting Average Product and Marginal Product Curves Together

Now that we know how to derive the AP_L and MP_L curves from a total product curve, we still must learn how to fit the average and marginal curves together properly. All average and marginal measures follow a rule of arithmetic, which can be described in the following three-part rule applied to production theory:

Whenever $MP_L > AP_L$, the AP_L must be rising.

Whenever $MP_L < AP_L$, the AP_L must be falling.

Whenever $MP_L = AP_L$, the AP_L is neither rising nor falling but is at its maximum.

Think of the arithmetic of the average-marginal relationship in a less technical context first. Suppose a mother has two children whose average weight at birth is 7 pounds. If her third child (the marginal child) weighs 50 pounds at birth, the average birth weight must rise (when marginal weight is greater than average weight, the average weight rises). If the third baby weighs only 2 pounds, the average weight falls. If the new baby weighs exactly 7 pounds, the average and marginal weights are equal and the average weight is unchanged.

Now apply the idea to the average and marginal products of labor, where the three-part rule has its graphic counterpart in Figure 5.5.

1. $MP_L > AP_L$ up to point C. Because each worker's marginal product exceeds labor's existing average product, the average product must rise.

Verify this result using the tangent-ray test. Between the origin and point C, the tangent drawn to any point has a steeper slope than a ray drawn from the origin to the same point. Hence, $MP_L > AP_L$ at every point on the curve up to (but not including) point C.

2. $MP_L = AP_L$ at point C. The marginal product of the last worker at C equals the average product of labor. Hence AP_L neither rises nor falls but stays the same—and thereby achieves its maximum value. MP_L intersects AP_L at the latter's maximum.

Applying the tangent-ray test to point C, $MP_L = AP_L$ because the tangent and the ray from the origin are the same line and hence have equal slopes.

3. $MP_L < AP_L$ beyond point C. The average product of labor declines because each worker hired causes an increase in total out-

Figure 5.5
Fitting the AP_L and MP_L Curves Together

The AP_L curve rises throughout segment 0C in the upper panel because $MP_L > AP_L$. The AP_L achieves its maximum at A because $MP_L = AP_L$. The AP_L declines beyond C, because $MP_L < AP_L$. These results are shown explicitly in the lower panel.

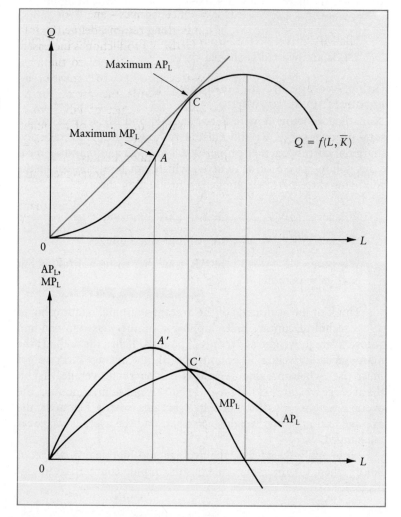

put smaller than the existing average product of labor. The average must therefore decline.

Using the tangent-ray test, tangents drawn to points to the right of A are successively flatter. Thus $MP_L < AP_L$ beyond C, and AP_L must fall.

These results are illustrated in the lower panel.

To summarize the story told by Figure 5.5:

1. $MP_L > AP_L$ up to C', hence AP_L rises.

2. $MP_L = AP_L$ at C', hence AP_L is constant.

3. $MP_L < AP_L$ beyond C', hence AP_L declines.

The Law of Diminishing Returns

The most frequently invoked "law" of economics—and perhaps the least understood—is the **law of diminishing returns,** defined as follows: When the intensity of a fixed factor of production is increased by adding more and more units of a variable factor to the production process, the resulting increases in total output must eventually get smaller and smaller. In other words, the law of diminishing returns asserts that the marginal product of labor must eventually diminish due to the inevitable congestion of the fixed factor of production as variable inputs are expanded. This law is frequently called the **law of variable proportions,** because labor and capital are combined in different proportions whenever the labor force changes and capital is fixed.

Diminishing returns to labor inputs, or the diminishing marginal product of labor, begin at points A and A' in Figure 5.5. If more workers are hired, the resulting increases in output will rise at an ever-decreasing rate, as seen in the decreasing slope of the total product curve beyond A. Diminishing returns show up directly in the negative slope of the MP_L curve to the right of A'. Diminishing returns—falling MP_L—occur for the same reason that AP_L falls eventually. Indeed, we could just as well define returns in average rather than marginal terms. Note in the lower panel that the AP_L begins to fall at point C', whereas the MP_L begins to fall sooner, at point A'. Diminishing marginal returns begin sooner than diminishing average returns because $MP_L > AP_L$ between A' and C'. Although the MP_L is falling between A' and C', it still exceeds the AP_L, which forces the AP_L to rise at the same time the MP_L falls. Thus the exact point at which diminishing returns begin will vary with the arbitrary choice of defining "returns" in marginal or average terms. But either way, diminishing returns occur because of capital fixity. In short, the average and marginal productivity of labor both fall whenever the congestion of labor on the fixed factor more than offsets the efficiencies created by labor specialization.

The Three Stages of Production

Given the "sideways" and elongated S-shape of the smooth total product curve, can we use it to say anything about the ranges in which a firm is most likely to produce? The answer is yes. The total product curve (or the AP_L and MP_L curves) can be divided into three stages, and one stage alone can be identified as an efficient stage of production.

The three **stages of production** are illustrated in Figure 5.6. Stage I is characterized by a rising AP_L, stage II by a diminishing but positive AP_L and MP_L, and stage III by a negative MP_L. Stages I and III are manifestly inefficient; by implication, stage II is the only efficient zone of production.

The key to understanding the distinction between stages is to recognize that a firm uses two inputs, labor and capital, and that production is inefficient whenever these inputs are combined in proportions that hinder production. Stage III is inefficient because it entails a negative MP_L. If production temporarily falls into stage III, the firm can increase output by reducing the size of the work force. By reducing labor inputs, costs fall and output and revenue rise. When the MP_L is no longer negative, production moves into the more efficient stage II. Stage III is clearly inefficient; MP_L is negative because the fixed capital inputs are overloaded.

Whereas stage III features too much labor for the available capital, stage I is inefficient because of too little labor being employed. In stage I, the AP_L rises when the labor force expands. Because of a small labor force relative to the firm's fixed capital, there is little if any congestion on the fixed factor. As a result, the productivity gains achieved by specializing the tasks of the increasing work force increase the workers' average productivity. But by remaining in stage I, a firm fails to fully exploit these gains. A firm would be inefficient if it stopped hiring workers in the midst of productivity improvements.

The profit-maximizing firm should hire enough workers to be out of stage I but few enough to avoid stage III. By a process of elimination, stage II is the only range of production for which labor and capital are not combined in inefficient proportions. Production theory by itself cannot determine the exact quantity of inputs to hire or output to produce within stage II, because these decisions depend on the prices of inputs and output. We will study these decisions in future chapters. Still, we can rule out stages I and III merely by understanding the way that variable inputs influence the production of physical output.

Note that the only efficient stage of production, stage II, exhibits diminishing marginal (and average) returns throughout its entire range. The lesson is clear: Far from avoiding diminishing returns, profit-maximizing firms should seek them out!

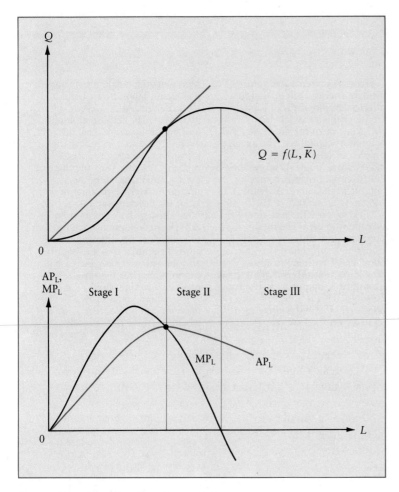

Long-Run Production Functions

Up to now we have been involved in short-run production analysis. The **short run** is the period of time in which the firm's capital stock is fixed. (The short-run total product curve with capital fixed is the major building block in the construction of short-run cost curves in Chapter 6.) Given such fixity of capital, we were able to define the average and marginal product of labor, become acquainted with the concept of diminishing returns, and identify stages of efficient and inefficient production.

We can now discuss production characterized by variations in both labor and capital inputs. Indeed, the **long run** is defined as that period of time in which all factors are infinitely variable.

The Total Product Curve Approach

Consider the rudimentary production function $Q = f(L, K)$. For the short-run production analysis, we assigned a constant value to the

The Inefficiency of Stage I in the Long Run

APPLIED
MICRO
THEORY

5.1

We have already seen why a profit-maximizing firm will not knowingly operate in stage I of production in the short run, when it is not possible to alter capital. Here we will see why a firm will not operate in stage I in the long run, when capital is variable. In particular, stage I operations are undesirable if the production function exhibits **constant returns to scale**, or when a proportionate increase in all inputs increases output by the same proportion. For example, doubling both labor and capital inputs results in a doubling of output under constant returns to scale.

Figure A presents two total product curves, each related to a different employment of capital. Consider the curve labeled $f(L, K_1)$, drawn for the fixed amount of capital K_1. The average product of labor reaches a maximum at point A, where the ray from the origin becomes tangent to the curve. At point A, $AP_L = Q/L = 20/2 = 10$.

Now suppose the firm doubles its capital to $2K_1$. The total product curve shifts to $f(L, 2K_1)$. Under constant returns to scale, a doubling of both inputs also doubles output. Thus if labor goes from 2 to 4, output must rise from 20 to 40. This is a move from point A on the initial curve to point A' on the new one. Point A'

represents the maximum average product of labor after capital and labor double. At A', $AP_L = Q/L = 40/4 = 10$. Because all inputs and output have doubled, all average products, including the maximum average products, remain constant. Thus the slope of the ray $0AA'$ measures the maximum average product of labor for different capital intensities, such as points A and A'. The maximum average product of labor does not change under constant returns to scale, because all total values simply increase in proportion. Thus the ray $0AA'$ must be a straight line.

For capital equal to K_1, maximum output occurs at B, where the slope of the total

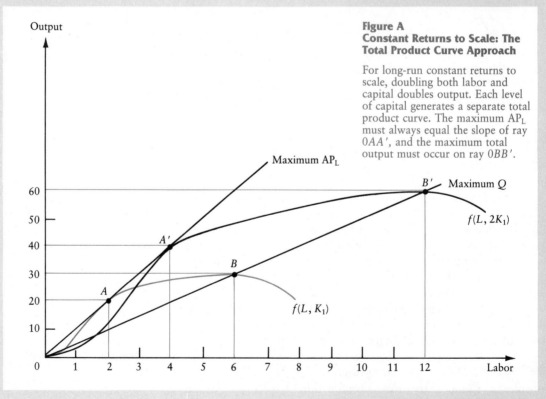

Output

**Figure A
Constant Returns to Scale: The
Total Product Curve Approach**

For long-run constant returns to scale, doubling both labor and capital doubles output. Each level of capital generates a separate total product curve. The maximum AP_L must always equal the slope of ray $0AA'$, and the maximum total output must occur on ray $0BB'$.

Maximum AP_L

B' Maximum Q

$f(L, 2K_1)$

A'

B

A

$f(L, K_1)$

Labor

product curve is zero. At point B, maximum output is 30 and is achieved by hiring 6 units of labor. When capital doubles, maximum output must also double when labor doubles. Thus, increasing labor from 6 to 12 increases output from 30 to 60. This is a move from point B to point B'. The ray $0BB'$ connects all points that represent maximum output. Because inputs and output change proportionately under constant returns to scale, this ray must also be a straight line.

With these properties as background, it can be shown that the firm will not operate in the long run in stage I under constant returns to scale because stage I entails a negative marginal product of capital. Figure B illustrates. Consider point A, which lies in stage I of curve $f(L, K_2)$. Using the properties of constant returns to scale, we can construct another curve $f(L, K_1)$, $K_1 < K_2$, that becomes tangent to the maximum AP_L ray at A', vertically above A. A move from A to A' increases output by decreasing capital. Thus the marginal product of capital, $MP_K = \Delta Q/\Delta K$, is negative at point A. Repeat the argument starting at B. Another total product curve can be drawn that becomes tangent to the maximum AP_L ray at B', implying less capital than K_2 yet more output. (For convenience, this curve is not drawn.) Thus MP_K is negative at point B. As one moves closer to point C, the increase in output that can be obtained by reducing capital gets smaller and smaller; the negative marginal product of capital approaches ever closer to zero. Exactly at C, no curve can be drawn for less capital that will become tangent to the maximum AP_L ray vertically above C. Just at C the marginal product of capital ceases to be negative and becomes zero.

Now consider point D, which lies in stage II. In order to draw a contour tangent to D', more capital must be employed.

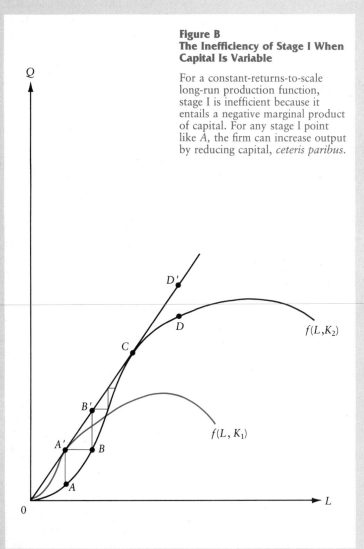

Figure B
The Inefficiency of Stage I When Capital Is Variable

For a constant-returns-to-scale long-run production function, stage I is inefficient because it entails a negative marginal product of capital. For any stage I point like A, the firm can increase output by reducing capital, *ceteris paribus*.

Accordingly, the movement from D to D' increases capital and output; thus the marginal product of capital is positive. Any point such as D in stage II is characterized by positive marginal products of both labor and capital inputs.

Conclusion: All stage I production points, such as A and B, exhibit a negative marginal product of capital. Under constant returns to scale, any such rate of output can be produced with the same labor force but less capital. Stage I is just as inefficient as stage III. Both entail a negative marginal product of an input. Later in this chapter, we will encounter a general proof from the theory of the firm to show what has been explained here intuitively: The competitive firm will never operate in stage I.

firm's employment of capital, then constructed a total product curve that shows how output varies with labor. In the long run, however, capital is continuously variable. Because the amount of output that a given labor force can produce depends on the amount of capital available, each fixed level of capital gives rise to a unique total product curve: Capital is a shift parameter for the total product curve. One method of charting the firm's long-run production function is to illustrate a family of total product curves, each curve dependent on a given amount of capital. This depiction of the production function allows labor, capital, and output to vary in a two-dimensional format. Applied Micro Theory 5.1 employs this method.

The Isoquant Approach

One major theme of microeconomics is the central role of substitution by economic agents. In consumer theory, the terms under which consumers substitute one good for another are conceptualized by the indifference curve. In production theory, firms substitute one input for another, and the graphic device that captures these technical tradeoffs is the **isoquant curve**. *Iso-quant* means "equal-quantity." An isoquant curve connects all labor and capital combinations capable of producing the same quantity of final output. Whereas indifferences curves reflect consumer preferences, isoquant curves express the firm's production technology. A key difference is that isoquant curves are measured cardinally; indifference curves must be expressed ordinally.

Isoquant curves are an alternative to the family of total product curves as a graphic exhibit of the firm's long-run production function. Both visual displays—the family of total product curves and isoquant curves—contain the same technical production information about the relationship between inputs and output. It is helpful to understand both methods of displaying the production function because both will be used in explaining the theory of the firm and its implications for social welfare.

The curve labeled Q_0 in Figure 5.7 is an isoquant curve. It incorporates all labor and capital combinations capable of producing Q_0 units of output using the best available technology. It assumes that labor can be substituted for capital in production without changing total output. The curve is smooth because we have assumed that all inputs are infinitely divisible and adaptable.

Isoquant curves are derived from the production function $Q = f(L, K)$, in which output is held constant while labor and capital vary. Engineers tell us the alternative ways labor and capital can be combined to produce a stipulated rate of output. Output is a shift parameter for the isoquant curve; there is a different isoquant for each level of output.

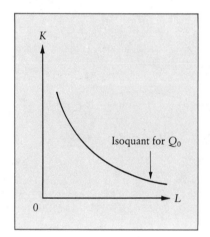

Figure 5.7
The Isoquant Curve

An isoquant curve shows the many labor-capital combinations that result in the same total output.

Isoquant curves possess characteristics similar to indifference curves:

1. Isoquant curves are negatively sloped in the efficient ranges of production.

2. Isoquant curves are everywhere dense.

3. Isoquant curves are nonintersecting.

4. Isoquant curves are convex from the origin.

These properties are discussed more fully in the sections that follow.

PROPERTY I: ISOQUANT CURVES ARE NEGATIVELY SLOPED IN THE EFFICIENT RANGES   The first step in understanding isoquant curves is to define their slope, which is called the **marginal rate of technical substitution (MRTS)**. The MRTS, the production equivalent of the marginal rate of substitution (MRS) from consumer theory, is the rate at which labor can be substituted for capital in the production process without changing the rate of output.

$$\text{MRTS} = \frac{\Delta K}{\Delta L}\bigg|_Q \qquad (5.6)$$

Figure 5.8 shows two isoquant curves. The curve on the left depicts the labor-capital combinations needed to produce Q_0 units of output, and the curve on the right is for Q_1 units of output, where $Q_1 - Q_0$ is a very small change in output. Suppose that the movement from point A to point C on isoquant Q_0 is very small. What

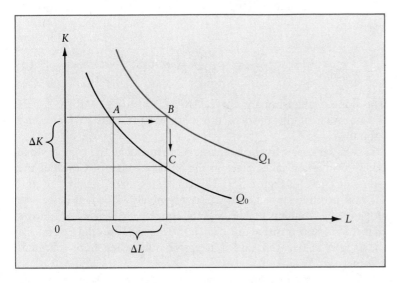

Figure 5.8
The Marginal Rate of Technical Substitution

The MRTS is the slope of the isoquant curve: MRTS = $\Delta K/\Delta L$ = $-\text{MP}_L/\text{MP}_K$.

is the slope of the curve between A and C, and what is its significance?

The move from A to C can be studied "as if" it occurred in two steps: Step 1 is the move from A to B, and step 2 is the move from B to C. For step 1, capital is constant and labor increases by ΔL. The resulting increase in output is $\Delta Q = Q_1 - Q_0$. The change in output, ΔQ, equals the number of new workers hired, ΔL, times the marginal product of these workers, MP_L. Thus

$$\Delta Q = Q_1 - Q_0 = MP_L \cdot \Delta L \qquad (5.7)$$

In step 2, the move from B to C, output falls by $Q_0 - Q_1$, because capital is reduced by ΔK while holding the labor force constant. Output falls by the reduction in capital, ΔK, times the marginal product of capital, MP_K:

$$\Delta Q = Q_0 - Q_1 = MP_K \cdot \Delta K \qquad (5.8)$$

Let's summarize these steps:

	movement	change in output	
step 1	A to B	$(Q_1 - Q_0) = MP_L \cdot \Delta L, (\Delta L > 0)$	(5.9)
step 2	B to C	$(Q_0 - Q_1) = MP_K \cdot \Delta K, (\Delta K < 0)$	
steps 1 plus 2	A to C $\Delta Q =$	0 $= MP_L \cdot \Delta L + MP_K \cdot \Delta K$	

When steps 1 and 2 are added (moving from A to C), the change in output equals zero. Hence, the increase in output due to hiring more labor, $MP_L \cdot \Delta L$, must equal the reduction in output from a smaller employment of capital, $MP_K \cdot \Delta K$. Solving Equation 5.9 for $\Delta K/\Delta L$ produces

$$\frac{\Delta K}{\Delta L} = -\frac{MP_L}{MP_K} = MRTS \qquad (5.10)$$

The slope of the isoquant curve, $\Delta K/\Delta L$, called the MRTS, equals the negative of the ratio of the marginal products of labor and capital.

Now let's see why the isoquant curve must have a negative slope when production takes place in the efficient stage II. Consider the isoquant curve in Figure 5.9. The curve has three ranges: $\overline{AB}$ and $\overline{CD}$ are positive sloped, and $\overline{BC}$ is negatively sloped. Because the slope of the isoquant, or the MRTS, equals $-MP_L/MP_K$, it follows that the slope is positive only when the marginal product of one of the factors is negative and is negative only when both marginal products are positive.

Consider a movement up the positively sloped segment of the

Figure 5.9
Isoquants Are Negatively Sloped

$MRTS = -MP_L/MP_K$ is negative and production is efficient only when the MP_L and MP_K are both positive, as along segment $\overline{BC}$. Along segment $\overline{AB}$, the MRTS ≥ 0 because $MP_K < 0$. For segment $\overline{CD}$, the MRTS > 0 because $MP_L < 0$.

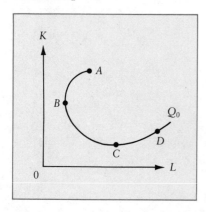

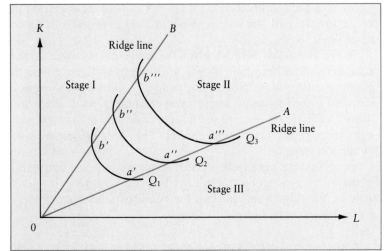

Figure 5.10
Ridge Lines

Ridge lines separate the efficient and inefficient ranges of the isoquant map. Each point on ridge line $0A$ entails zero MP_L, and any point to the southeast lies in stage III, where $MP_L < 0$. The $MP_K = 0$ along ridge line $0B$, and points to the northwest lie in stage I, where $MP_K < 0$. The space between the ridge lines is the efficient stage II: $MP_L > 0$ and $MP_K > 0$.

isoquant from C to D. Both inputs are increased, yet production is constant at Q_0, implying that the marginal product of one of the inputs is negative. The same is true for a move from B toward A. The marginal product of one of the factors must be negative, because both inputs have increased without changing total output. If both inputs were increased and both exhibited positive marginal products, output would rise. This does not happen along a positively sloped isoquant. Upward-sloping isoquants are inefficient, because both inputs can be reduced without reducing output.

A moment's reflection reveals that segment $\overline{CD}$ in Figure 5.9 exhibits a negative MP_L and that segment $\overline{BA}$ shows a negative MP_K. The slope at point C is $\Delta K/\Delta L = -MP_L/MP_K = 0$. The slope is zero at C because the numerator, or MP_L, is zero. If labor is expanded beyond C, MP_L is negative. Thus range $\overline{CD}$ is production stage III, for which $MP_L < 0$.

Similarly, the slope at point B is $\Delta K/\Delta L = -MP_L/MP_K = \infty$. The slope is infinite only when the denominator, MP_K, is zero. If capital rises above B, its MP_K becomes negative. Thus range $\overline{BA}$ is production stage I, for which $MP_K < 0$.

Having eliminated the upward-sloping portions of the isoquant as inefficient, it follows that efficiency pertains only to the negatively sloped segment, $\overline{BC}$. Any movement along a downward-sloping isoquant represents more of one input and less of the other, producing a constant output. Such a result requires positive marginal products for both factors, or production stage II.

A convenient method of identifying the efficient stage of production (stage II) is the use of **ridge lines**. A ridge line separates the negatively sloped portions of isoquant curves from the positively sloped portions. In Figure 5.10, lines $0A$ and $0B$ are ridge lines. Line $0A$ intersects all isoquants at their zero slope, such as points a', a'', and a'''. Production along any of the positively sloped isoquant segments to the southeast of ridge line $0A$ constitutes operation in production stage III, the formal name for a negative marginal product of labor.

Ridge line $0B$ is formed when the isoquants intersect at the other extreme, where their slopes are infinite and just about to become positive, as at points b', b'', and b'''. Operation along any positively sloped isoquant segments to the northwest of ridge line $0B$ also indicates production inefficiency, this time in the form of a negative marginal product of capital. This area corresponds to production stage I.

In summary, negatively sloped isoquants indicate efficiency. Furthermore, production stages have their counterparts in isoquant analysis; the ridge lines establish the boundaries between efficient and inefficient stages of production.

PROPERTY 2: ISOQUANT CURVES ARE EVERYWHERE DENSE   Every point in capital-labor input space is intersected by an isoquant curve. A single isoquant curve refers solely to a given output level. The selection of other levels of output would produce additional isoquant curves. Three of the infinite number of isoquants are drawn in Figure 5.11. The isoquants lying farther to the northeast, in the direction of the arrow, represent larger levels of output, because both inputs are increased and both exhibit positive marginal products. Thus $Q_3 > Q_2 > Q_1$. The family of all such isoquant curves is called the **isoquant map,** just as the family of consumer indifference curves is the indifference map. The isoquant map is a visual image of the firm's long-run production function.

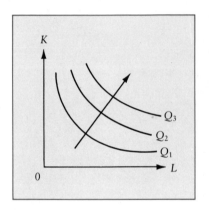

Figure 5.11
The Isoquant Map

Each isoquant curve pertains to one rate of output. Three of the infinite isoquant curves making up the isoquant map are illustrated here. Output rises in the direction of the arrow: $Q_3 > Q_2 > Q_1$.

PROPERTY 3: ISOQUANT CURVES ARE NONINTERSECTING   The nonintersection property of isoquants is closely related to the corresponding property of indifference curves. Intersecting isoquants involve a logical contradiction. Consider the two intersecting isoquants Q_1 and Q_2 in Figure 5.12. Input combinations A and C are on isoquant Q_2; combinations A and B are on isoquant Q_1. Combinations B and C, both equivalent to A, should therefore be equivalent to each other and be on the same isoquant curve. But they are not. Combination C produces more than B because C lies to the northeast of B. Intersecting isoquants can be ruled out because of these logical contradictions.

PROPERTY 4: ISOQUANT CURVES ARE CONVEX FROM THE ORIGIN   The marginal rate of technical substitution, MRTS $= \Delta K / \Delta L = -MP_L/MP_K$, is the slope of the isoquant curve. The isoquant is convex when the slope becomes smaller in absolute value as labor is substituted for capital. Thus the convexity property is frequently called the **diminishing marginal rate of technical substitution.**

Convex isoquants arise when labor and capital are imperfect

substitutes in production. Consider two movements along the convex isoquant in Figure 5.13: the move A to B and then the move D to E. The MRTS along each segment is $(\Delta K/\Delta L)|_{Q_0}$, the rate at which the firm can substitute labor for capital while holding output fixed. Figure 5.13 is constructed so that the two increases in labor are equal: $CB = FE$. And yet the MRTS between A and B is greater than between D and E.

Starting at A, expanding the labor force by $\Delta L_1 = CB$ permits a relatively large reduction in capital, $\Delta K_1 = AC$. Thus MRTS = AC/CB between A and B. However, the rate of exchange between labor and capital is smaller between D and E. Starting at D and increasing by $\Delta L_2 = FE$ (the same increase in the amount of labor as before), the firm can still reduce its use of capital, but the reduction, $\Delta K_2 = DF$, is less than before. The MRTS = DF/FE between D and E. Convexity implies a diminishing MRTS as labor is expanded.

So long as inputs are not perfect substitutes, labor cannot be substituted for capital at a constant rate, because capital becomes increasingly scarce relative to labor. The law of variable proportions informs us that the inputs' marginal products change when their proportions vary. The slope of a convex isoquant falls in absolute value as labor is expanded, because the marginal products of inputs change.

Each time labor is substituted for capital, the input proportions vary; more labor is combined with less capital. When the labor force increases, MP_L falls, even when capital is fixed. But here capital is falling, giving additional force to the falling MP_L. Similarly, reducing capital increases the MP_K. Hence, the absolute value of the slope of the isoquant must fall as labor is substituted for capital, because

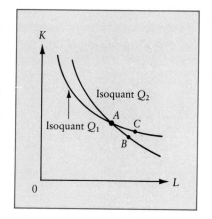

Figure 5.12
Isoquants Cannot Intersect

Because input combinations C and B are both comparable to A, they should lie on the same isoquant. Yet they do not, because of the contradiction created by the intersection of isoquants.

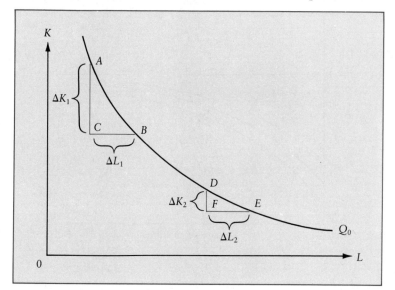

Figure 5.13
The Convexity Property of Isoquants

Convexity means that the MRTS falls in absolute value as labor is substituted for capital along an isoquant. MRTS = $\Delta K_1/\Delta L_1$ between A and B and falls to MRTS = $\Delta K_2/\Delta L_2$ between D and E. When inputs are imperfect substitutes, MP_L falls and MP_K rises when labor is substituted for capital, causing $|MRTS| = |MP_L/MP_K|$ to fall.

Producing Accident Prevention

APPLIED MICRO THEORY

5.2

Production theory is a powerful organizer of thought, even when production does not entail physical output. For example, suppose the element being produced is the probability of achieving a desirable result. Then it is useful to represent production function as $P = f(X, Y)$, where P is the probability of the occurrence of a desirable event (or the avoidance of an undesirable one) and X and Y are inputs that can be used in variable proportions to influence the probability.*

Most of the usual properties of production theory follow. But rather than generate all of the direct analogies, let's take a concrete example.† Suppose we are producing the probability of "avoiding an accident" under the following conditions. A train runs near a field of flax. An accident occurs when a spark from a passing train ignites the flax. Once ignited, the entire field burns.

The probability of avoiding this awful event, measured as 1 − number of fires/total trips, is a function of, among other things, the speed of the train and the distance from the track to the first parallel row of flax. The greater the speed of the train, the higher the boiler temperature and the hotter the sparks when emitted—and hence the longer they will survive. The greater the distance between tracks and flax, the less likely it is that an emitted spark will reach the flax "live."

*John Brown was the first to use the analogy between production theory and accident prevention in the analysis of accident law (torts). See John Prather Brown, "Toward an Economic Theory of Liability," *Journal of Legal Studies* 2 (1973): 323.

†Richard A. Posner, "A Theory of Negligence," *Journal of Legal Studies* 1 (1972): 29.

The production function in this situation is therefore

$$P = f(X, Y)$$

where

P = probability of avoiding accident

  = $1 - \dfrac{\text{number of fires}}{\text{train trips}}$

X = distance between railroad track and field of flax

$Y = \dfrac{1}{\text{speed of train}}$

Working with probabilities instead of output forces us to realize that—unlike usual production processes, in which ever-greater quantities of inputs increase output—the highest possible probability is 1. Nevertheless, the short-run law of diminishing returns still holds, as well as the law of variable proportions and the long-run principle of the diminishing marginal rate of substitution.

Figure A shows three total product curves for which the probability of avoiding an accident rises as X, the distance between the train and the field, increases. The lowest curve holds the train speed at 100 miles per hour. The slope of the curve is the MP_X, or

Figure A
Producing a Probability of Accident Avoidance

The probability production function, $P = f(X, Y)$, represents the probability of avoiding a fire, P, which depends on the distance between the train track and the flax field, X, and the inverse of train speed, Y. The maximum probability is 1. Three probability total product curves are drawn, with X measured explicitly and Y serving as a shift parameter. The lower the train speed, the higher the total probability curve.

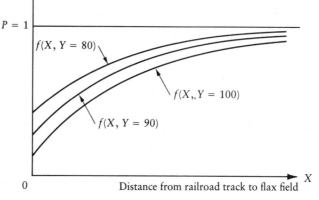

P
Probability of avoiding an accident

$P = 1$

$f(X, Y = 80)$

$f(X, Y = 100)$

$f(X, Y = 90)$

0   Distance from railroad track to flax field X

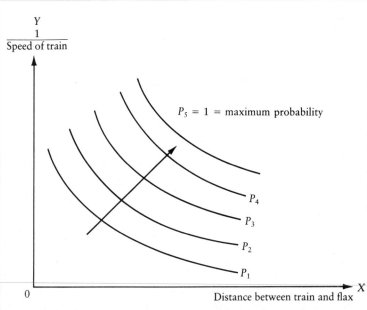

$\dfrac{Y}{\text{Speed of train}}$

$P_5 = 1 = $ maximum probability

P_4

P_3

P_2

P_1

0

Distance between train and flax

X

Figure B
Isoprobability Map

Here the probability production function is displayed using the isoquant technique. The inverse of train speed, Y, and the distance between the train track and the flax, X, is measured on the axes. For each probability ≤ 1, there exists a unique isoprobability curve that measures the various combinations of X and Y capable of achieving a given probability of avoiding an accident. $P_5 = 1$ is the highest probability, regardless of the amount of caution taken.

the increase in the probability of accident avoidance due to an increase in the distance between train and field: $MP_X = \Delta P / \Delta X$. This curve approaches unity, the maximum value of the probability. If the train reduces its speed to 90 mph, and again to 80 mph, the probability of avoiding a fire increases for any given distance X. In the terminology of production theory, the inverse of train speed, Y, is a shift parameter for the total product curve, as Figure A shows.

Figure B presents the same ideas with an isoquant map, or more precisely, an isoprobability map. The inverse of the speed of the train, Y, is measured on the vertical axis, where higher values represent lower speed. The distance between train and flax fields, X, is measured on the horizontal axis. Each isoprobability curve represents a given probability of accident avoidance. The probability rises in the direction of the arrow up to a maximum of unity. Thus the area below the isoquant labeled $P_5 = 1$ is everywhere dense. Isoquants cannot exist above $P_5 = 1$,

because the probability cannot exceed 1. The marginal rate of technical substitution, the slope of the isoprobability curve, now represents how much the train must slow down where flax is planted closer to the train tracks in order to hold the probability of avoiding an accident constant: $MRTS = \Delta Y / \Delta X$.

Inherent in this theory is the recognition that it is impossible to assign causes for this sort of production. Just as production theory implies that neither capital nor labor alone produces output, so several interrelated factors are at work in producing an accident. And just as in standard production theory, these factors are in variable proportions. For example, the avoidance of mining accidents depends on the strength of mineshaft beams, the strength of detonations, and worker precautions. Similarly, the avoidance of airline accidents depends on the number of planes in the air, the number of air traffic controllers who are working, the average number of hours that the controllers have worked (in a

demanding job like theirs, error is related to fatigue), and the sophistication of the electronic equipment. As the relative prices of these factors change, the efficient mix for each level of accident avoidance probability shifts.

Because lives are at stake in matters like these, the principles of price theory become vitally important in determining policy. When a probability of 1 is too expensive, the policymaker must focus on the "best" probability. In a search for the best or most efficient probability, resources must not be wasted; the policymaker must try to equate the marginal product per dollar spent on each resource that helps determine accident avoidance.

We will learn more about this problem when we turn to the costs of producing accident avoidance. As usual, production theory alone, in either its product curve or isoquant version, cannot tell us which levels of inputs or output to choose. Production theory can only help us think in multiple dimensions about the problem at hand. That's all—but it's a lot!

|slope| = |MP$_L$/MP$_K$| and because the numerator falls and the denominator increases.

If inputs are perfect substitutes in production, labor can be exchanged for capital at a constant rate, regardless of the relative scarcities of the factors. In this case, the MRTS is constant and the isoquant is linear, as shown in Figure 5.14a. Note that the output Q_0 can be produced using corner solutions entailing all capital, K_0, or all labor, L_0, a feature that is rare among production functions.

Another extreme case is a production function with fixed proportions. In this case, the isoquants are right angles, as shown in Figure 5.14b. Input combination A is the only one capable of producing Q_0 units of output. Moving to B is pointless, because extra labor has a marginal product of zero so long as capital is fixed. Point C is equally senseless, because extra capital adds nothing to output if labor is not increased also. Expanding output to Q_1 requires a proportional increase in both inputs, to combination D. Whereas linear isoquants suggest perfect substitutability, right-angle isoquants reveal that no substitution between inputs is feasible at the margin.

Linear and right-angle isoquant curves are limiting cases. For most production functions, labor and capital are imperfect substitutes and isoquants are convex.

Returns to Scale: Constant, Increasing, and Decreasing

In studying the properties of long-run production functions, economists have found it useful to ask this question: If all inputs are increased by the same proportion, will output rise proportionately, less than proportionately, or more than proportionately? For example, if all inputs double, output must respond in one of three ways: exactly double, less than double, or more than double. The way that

Figure 5.14
Linear and Fixed-Proportion Isoquants

(a) Linear isoquants indicate that factors are perfect substitutes.
(b) Right-angle isoquants reveal that factors must be used in fixed proportions; hence they are not substitutes at the margin.

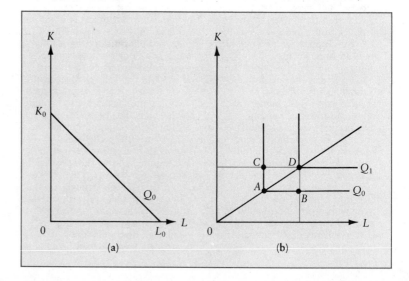

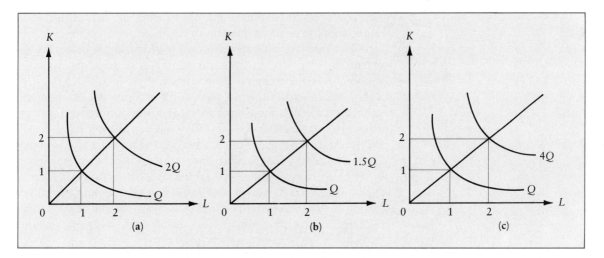

output responds to proportionate, scaled expansions in inputs identifies the production function's characteristic "returns to scale."

As we learned in Applied Micro Theory 5.1, a production function displays constant returns to scale if a doubling of all inputs exactly doubles output.[3] For example, look at Figure 5.15a:

$$f(2L, 2K) = 2 \cdot f(L, K) \qquad (5.11)$$
$$f(2, 2) = 2 \cdot f(1, 1)$$

For **decreasing returns to scale,** a doubling of all inputs results in a less-than-doubled output. This case is shown in Figure 5.15b:

$$f(2L, 2K) < 2 \cdot f(L, K) \qquad (5.12)$$
$$f(2, 2) < 2 \cdot f(1, 1)$$

Under **increasing returns to scale,** shown in Figure 5.15c, a doubling of all inputs more than doubles output.

$$f(2L, 2K) > 2 \cdot f(L, K) \qquad (5.13)$$
$$f(2, 2) > 2 \cdot f(1, 1)$$

The concept of constant returns to scale is an appealing beginning point because it incorporates the reasonable presumption that an entrepreneur can duplicate the production process—with double the quantities of all factors—and derive twice the output as before. If 1 carpenter, 1 hammer, 40 nails, 10 boards, and 20 square feet of elbow room can produce 1 doghouse per day, then 2 carpenters, 2 hammers, 80 nails, 20 boards, and 40 square feet of elbow room should produce 2 doghouses per day, if all inputs are homogeneous.

Figure 5.15
Returns to Scale

(a) With constant returns to scale, doubling all inputs exactly doubles output. (b) With decreasing returns to scale, doubling all inputs less than doubles output. (c) With increasing returns to scale, doubling all inputs more than doubles output.

3. Doublings are used for ease. Any proportionate increase in inputs is adequate for checking returns to scale.

If all inputs could be cloned and put to work in identical fashion, output should rise in proportion to the increase in factors.

What then are the explanations for increasing and decreasing returns to scale? Increasing returns may arise from the specialization of labor and capital that occurs with an increase in the size of the firm. In small firms, workers and machinery are of necessity generalists, whereas these inputs can become specialized as the firm grows. The single employee of a mom-and-pop grocery store stocks shelves, cuts meat, checks out customers, and trims lettuce. In large chains these tasks are specialized, thereby raising the physical productivity of labor. Similar specialization is open to capital. In a small store, a single two-wheel dolly may be the only means of hauling case goods, regardless of the size and weight of the loads, but larger stores have dollies of various sizes, including forklift trucks, that are scaled to specific needs.

Increasing returns to scale may also occur because of arithmetic. For example, doubling the dimensions of a cube more than doubles the volume in cubic feet. The volume of a cube that is 2 feet by 2 feet by 2 feet is 8 cubic feet. Doubling the dimensions to 4 feet by 4 feet by 4 feet increases the volume to 64 cubic feet. Likewise, doubling the diameter of a sewage or water pipe more than doubles the flow capacity of the pipe, resulting in increasing returns to scale.

Decreasing returns to scale may arise when it is impossible to expand all inputs proportionately, even though every effort is made to do so. Suppose an insurance company doubles all labor and capital inputs, including the sales force, fleet cars, order pools, and computer facilities to process policies. When a firm is just starting to grow, such an expansion may more than double output, for reasons already mentioned. In addition, the ability of the owner to manage and coordinate its inputs will be affected. If the management function itself improves with size, increasing returns to scale are fortified. But if management loses its effectiveness in training, supervising, and coordinating all components of an increasingly complex firm, decreasing returns to scale could result. This is quite apart from the practical matter of finding homogeneous inputs. As a firm expands, it hires workers who require training and whose productivity is lower than that of current workers.

Returns to scale are defined as the empirical relationship between output and inputs when all inputs are homogeneous and expanded proportionately. Curiously, most examples of increasing and decreasing returns to scale involve either inputs that are not homogeneous or input expansions that fail to increase all factors proportionately, such as management skills, weather, good will, and other intangibles.

Economists often use **homogeneous production functions** in empirical and theoretical work, the essential characteristic of which is a linear expansion path. A production function is homogeneous to degree j if a proportional increase in all inputs equal to λ increases output by the jth power of λ:

$$f(\lambda L, \lambda K) = \lambda^j f(L, K) \qquad (5.14)$$

A special class of homogeneity occurs when a doubling of all inputs doubles output. In this case, $\lambda = 2$, the increase in output is $\lambda^j = 2^1$, and the production function is **linear homogeneous** or **homogeneous to degree 1**. A production function demonstrating constant returns to scale is linearly homogeneous, and in addition to having a linear expansion path, it displays equidistant isoquants. Such homogeneous production functions are used by economists in studying the behavior of firms, not because they are believed to be the most realistic, but because their underlying assumptions have convenient analytical properties.[4]

In Chapter 6 we will see how returns to scale influence the firm's long-run cost curves. There is no doubt about the importance of returns to scale, in spite of the difficulty in defining the concept. It has implications for the optimal size of firms, the tendency for industries to become monopolized, the ability of small firms to compete with large ones, and many other problems in private market and government decisionmaking.

Summary

Every issue on the supply side of output markets (and hence on the demand side of input markets) involves the technical ability to combine the factors of production with the alteration of raw materials for the production of final goods. Every remaining chapter in this book is keyed to the concepts of production analysis presented in this chapter.

In drawing two-dimensional graphs of relationships that exhibit more than two dimensions, we must always fix the values of all but two variables. In our simple production function, three variables are important: output, labor and capital. To draw the production function in two dimensions, we must select one of these values as a shift parameter. By holding capital constant, we can construct the total product curve, the slope of which is the marginal product of labor. By holding output constant, we produce an isoquant curve, the slope of which is the marginal rate of technical substitution. These are alternate methods of solving the problem of drawing in two dimensions a production function that is really multidimensional. You should be well acquainted with both conventions, because they both have important functions and applications.

An essential concept for both short-run and long-run production functions is the distinction between the diminishing marginal product and returns to scale. The diminishing marginal product of labor derives from the eventual restraint on production imposed by the fixity of

Key Terms

average product of labor (AP_L) 120
capital inputs 118
constant returns to scale 130
decreasing returns to scale 141
diminishing marginal rate of technical
    substitution 136
fixed inputs 118
homogeneous production
    functions 142
increasing returns to scale 141
inflection point 124
isoquant curve 132
isoquant map 136
labor inputs 118
long run 129
law of diminishing returns 127
law of variable proportions 127
linear homogeneous (homogeneous to
    degree 1) 143
marginal product of labor (MP_L) 121
marginal rate of technical substitution
    (MRTS) 133
production function 117
ridge lines 135
short run 129
stages of production 128
theory of the firm 115
total product curve 119
variable inputs 118

4. See Eugene Silberberg, *The Structure of Economics: A Mathematical Analysis* (New York: McGraw-Hill, 1978), pp. 89, 300–303, for an advanced discussion of homogeneous production functions.

capital. In contrast, returns to scale result when both capital and labor inputs increase proportionally. The diminishing marginal product involves a change in the proportions of the factors that are used as labor changes against a backdrop of fixed capital; returns to scale keep the ratio of input use constant by considering scaled changes in inputs in order to measure their effect on output. The former is displayed by the total product curve, the latter by the spacing of the isoquant map. The theoretical uses and policy implications of these production concepts will unfold in future chapters.

Problems

1. Indifference curves and isoquant curves are somewhat analogous. Why is the analogy not perfect?
2. The chancellor of a small midwestern university stated in a speech, "In the past decade we have doubled the number of classrooms and doubled the number of professors but the number of students has increased only 50 percent. Therefore we should expand no more because we have reached diminishing returns." Comment.
3. Noted physicists have shown that huge satellites with photovoltaic cells can transmit electricity via laser beams to the earth that is equivalent to 10 percent of the sun's energy that falls on the cells. The efficiency of ground-based photovoltaic cells is only 5 percent.
   a. Would the ground-based cells ever be more efficient than the satellite cells?
   b. How are you defining *efficiency* in your answer to part *a?*
   c. What do you say to a physicist who insists that the satellite cells are always more efficient?
4. Real-life examples of stage III production are exceedingly rare because it is so easy to spot and also so easy to eliminate. Can you cite examples of stage III production? Is it more common in the public than in the private sector?
5. Early kidney patients needing dialysis treatment paid about $50,000 a year for the service. New techniques, learned with the cooperation of these early patients, have lowered the price of kidney dialysis to about $12,000 a year. Consider these early patients as a factor of production. Should these people have paid for dialysis as consumers or been paid as factors of production?
6. The probability of an automobile accident is a function of drivers' caution levels. Let there be two drivers, driver *A* and driver *B*. Let *P(A, B)* be the probability of avoiding an accident.
   a. Draw isoprobability curves analogous to the production isoquant curves discussed in this chapter.
   b. Draw probability total product curves analogous to those discussed in this chapter.
   c. In production theory we can always increase output by expanding all inputs. But we can never produce an accident avoidance probability greater than 1, no matter how cautious drivers *A* and *B* become. How does this fact affect the shape of your isoprobability map and your probability total product curves?

  d. Caution is costly; it requires time, effort, and resources. Explain why drivers do not take complete caution, even when mature and sober. (Do physicians eliminate all risks in surgery? Why or why not?)

7. Consider college education to be a form of production:
   a. List all fixed and variable factors in the production of college education.
   b. Are tenured faculty members fixed or variable inputs?
   c. Are untenured faculty members fixed or variable inputs?
   d. If buildings and tenured professors are fixed factors and taxpayers demand a reduction in costs, can costs be reduced without reducing efficiency?

8. Consider the economics of pothole repair. Let the output be the number of potholes repaired and the inputs be a truck, asphalt, shovels, and workers. It has been noted (by Republicans) that one worker often fills potholes while two workers rest on their shovels.
   a. Does this observation imply production in stage III, which is characterized by a redundancy of labor and excessive labor costs? (Hint: What if some streets have many potholes and others have only a few?)
   b. Asphalt is partly a petroleum distillate that emits a gas in hot weather. Prolonged exposure to this gas makes strong men weak. Discuss "resting on the shovel" as a factor of production.
   c. Presidents of the United States have played golf, sailed, played the piano, and played touch football. Is such leisure a factor of production?

9. Show that, for production functions involving constant returns to scale, the ridge lines are straight lines.

10. Draw the isoquants when the factors of production are perfect substitutes; perfect complements. Using these as limiting cases, draw the isoquants when factors are highly substitutable; poor substitutes.

11. Draw an isoquant curve. How does it shift if the quality of the product is increased? The quantity?

12. Draw a total product curve for the quantity of capital K_0. Now send all the workers to a training program so they become more productive. Redraw the total product curve.

13. Table 5.2 contains production data for a given capital stock. Compute the corresponding MP_L and AP_L values and check to see whether the following conditions hold true: (1) MP_L begins to fall before AP_L falls; (2) $MP_L = AP_L$ at the minimum of AP_L; (3) Q is maximized at the level of labor utilization for which $MP_L = 0$; (4) Q diminishes when MP_L is negative. (Hint: These conditions will only be approximate because of the use of discrete data. The postulated properties hold exactly only when the data are continuous and the curves are smooth.)

14. Suppose the short-run total product curve is linear. Derive the corresponding MP_L and AP_L curves. How might you explain such production responses?

15. Use what you have learned about isoquants to draw the following graphs:

Table 5.2
Figuring Average and Marginal Products of Labor

Labor (L)	Output (Q)	AP_L	MP_L
1	2		
2	5		
3	9		
4	12		
5	14		
6	15		
7	15		
8	14		
9	12		
10	9		

a. Draw an isoquant map that exhibits increasing, constant, and decreasing returns to scale over different ranges of production.
b. Draw and interpret an isoquant that is concave from the origin.
c. Draw an isoquant map whose isoquants are nearly but not totally vertical. Interpret the meaning of the implied MRTS.
d. Draw an isoquant curve that is negatively sloped, is convex from the origin, and intersects both the labor and capital axes. Are the inputs perfect substitutes, considering that the same output can be produced using either all capital or all labor?

16. As a certain firm expands its labor force with capital fixed, output rises first at an increasing rate, then at a constant rate. Draw the total product curve and the MP_L and AP_L curves of this curious production function.

Suggested Readings

Henderson, J. M., and Quandt, R.E. *Microeconomic Theory: A Mathematical Approach.* 3rd ed. New York: McGraw-Hill, 1980, chap. 4.

Levenson, A. M., and Solow, Babette S. "Returns to Scale and the Spacing of Isoquants." *American Economic Review* 56 (1966): 501–505.

Stigler, George J. "The Division of Labor Is Limited by the Extent of the Market." *Journal of Political Economy* 59 (1951): 185–193.

Stigler, George J. *The Theory of Price.* New York: Macmillan, 1966, chap. 6.

Tangri, Om P. "Omissions in the Treatment of the Law of Variable Proportions." *American Economic Review* 61 (1966): 484–493.

Vickrey, William S. *Microstatics.* New York: Harcourt Brace Jovanovich, 1964, chap. 4.

The Costs of Production

A primitive Eskimo tribe is said to have devised a diabolical method of torture and eventual execution. The victim was seated on a large block of ice, beneath which was positioned a sharp spear. As the ice melted, the victim was slowly impaled. In similar fashion, you confront two ice blocks: production theory (Chapter 5) and the conversion of production curves into cost curves (this chapter). Only after these two ice blocks are melted away by the heat of your study will you begin to get the point of all the curve bending you have endured. Do not dispair. The analysis and applications of this chapter will reveal how useful production-cost analysis can be in guiding decisions.

This chapter transforms production concepts into their cost equivalents. Here dollar signs are attached to the labor and capital inputs that a firm employs, and cost curves are formulated. (So far only the physical relationship between inputs and output has been discussed.) Cost curves will assist you in almost every microeconomic problem you will ever confront, right up to your Ph.D. qualifying examinations. Cost curves are powerful analytical tools when properly understood.

The Meaning of Costs

Economists and accountants define *costs* differently. Both definitions are correct, because they are used for vastly different purposes. Accountants follow conventions that yield profit statements that are used as a basis for tax computations. In contrast, economists employ a definition of *costs* that helps model decisions about what to produce and how much to produce and whether to enter or exit an industry.

To see how accounting costs and economic costs differ, let's use two inputs—labor and capital. Suppose a firm incurs $10,000 of labor costs per year. Furthermore, assume that the firm owns machines that cost $20,000 when purchased five years ago. What are the current costs of production?

Accountants include the $10,000 labor expense in current costs. Current capital costs are more difficult to determine but would include a portion of the original purchase price ($20,000) by reference to a depreciation formula. For example, if the machines are depreciated evenly over a 10-year period, the annual capital cost would be $2000 per year for 10 years and then would fall to zero. Thus the **accounting cost** would be $12,000 for the current year (labor expense plus one year's capital depreciation).

The economist proceeds differently. **Economic cost** means opportunity cost—the value of forgone options. What are the forgone alternatives in the previous example? The wages of labor are determined broadly by the alternative uses of labor. Thus the economist includes the $10,000 labor cost as a surrogate for the value of the labor in alternative employment. The economist and the accountant treat labor costs the same way.

But what about capital costs? Economists measure capital costs as the value of the machines in alternative uses. Suppose the machines could be rented out to other firms for $40,000 per year. The economist measures the capital costs at $40,000—the forgone value of the machines in alternative uses. Note that the historical capital cost of $20,000 is irrelevant to the economist. It is a **sunk cost** and does not represent a measure of the opportunity cost of the machines. For example, the accountant's capital cost of the machine falls to zero once the machines are fully depreciated, whereas the economist's capital cost continues to reflect the forgone rental value of the machine.

Economists are interested in still another cost component—the **entrepreneurial opportunity cost.** Entrepreneurs must earn a profit at least as great as they could earn in their next best alternative employments. Thus a profit equal to the entrepreneur's next-best alternative—the entrepreneurial opportunity cost—is a necessary cost of keeping the entrepreneur in the current activity.

Let's summarize our results. In our simple example, the accountant records the current expenses of hiring labor and the current year's share of the historical costs after allowing for depreciation. The economist measures the value of the labor, capital, and entrepreneurial services in their alternative uses. These are vastly different measures. Economic costs exceed accounting costs because they include the value of the entrepreneur in alternative employments. Hence the owner of a bicycle repair shop that reports accounting profits of $20,000 is actually earning negative economic profits if he or she is worth $25,000 to Schwinn as a bicycle mechanic.

One final concept is important to our discussion of economic costs: The cost of capital is $r \cdot K$, where K measures the units of capital equipment employed per time period and r is the per-period price of renting a unit of capital. The variable r is referred to as the

implicit rental rate of capital or **rental rate of capital.** If the firm
rents its capital equipment, r is the per-unit rental rate; it measures
explicitly the market value of capital. If the firm owns its capital,
then r measures the forgone rental value of the capital, an implicit
opportunity cost to the firm. Either way, the value of capital in
alternative uses is measured by r, the rental rate of capital.

This chapter develops the cost curves of the labor and capital
inputs; entrepreneurial opportunity costs are added in Chapter 7.
Accounting costs differ from economic costs, so it follows that
accounting profits will also differ from economic profits. We will
study this distinction in detail in Chapter 7. Meanwhile, train yourself to include all opportunity costs and ignore all sunk (historical)
costs in considering decisions in the current period. The economist's
definition of cost is one of economic theory's outstanding contributions to human knowledge.

Total Costs in the Short Run

You are by now accustomed to regarding the short run as the
analytic period in which at least one factor of production cannot be
varied. It is natural to treat capital as the fixed factor. When capital
is fixed, the firm experiences diminishing marginal returns. Now
let's study the firm's costs of production in the presence of such
short-run capital fixities.

Figure 6.1a contains a short-run total product curve that, for
convenience, ignores the negatively sloped portion that corresponds
to the inefficient production stage III. To develop the desired cost
concept, it is convenient to redraw the product curve with output
(Q) on the horizontal axis and labor (L) on the vertical axis. There
are at least two ways to visualize the effect of such a switch:

1. Trace the total product curve on thin paper, turn the paper
   over, hold it up to a light and position the axes so output is
   measured on the horizontal axis.

2. Imagine grasping the vertial axis (Q) from beneath with the
   thumb and forefinger of your right hand and the horizontal axis
   (L) with your left and then exchanging the position of the axes.

Either method results in a total product curve with the slope illustrated in Figure 6.1b. Panels a and b both illustrate the same relationship between input and output. The curve's change in appear-
ance is due solely to the exchange of axes.

Next suppose that the firm must pay $1 for each unit of labor
service it hires. The total product curve in panel b is transformed
into a cost curve in panel c by multiplying the units of labor on the
horizontal axis by the per-unit cost of labor, or the wage rate (w).
For example, point A in panel b tells us that producing 30 units of

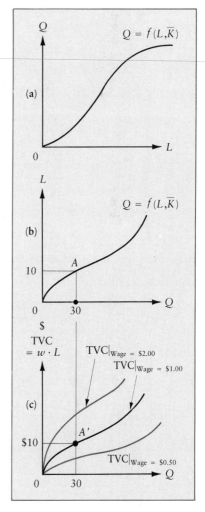

Figure 6.1
Total Variable Cost Curve

(a) The total product curve is $Q = f(L, \overline{K})$. (b) This panel shows the same
curve as in Figure 6.1a but with the
labor and output axes reversed. (c) All
three TVC curves shown here depend
on a given wage rate. The TVC curve
is derived by multiplying the labor
force by the wage at each output.

output requires 10 workers. This is a production statement. In contrast, point A' in panel c tells us that 30 units of output require a labor cost outlay of $10 ($w \cdot L = \$1 \cdot 10$).

The cost curve in Figure 6.1c is called the **total variable cost (TVC)** curve because it traces out the relationship between output (Q) and the cost of hiring the variable resources necessary for such production. The TVC may be expressed formally as

$$TVC = w \cdot L \qquad (6.1)$$

where

w = wage rate
L = units of labor

There are four things you should note carefully about the TVC curve. First, its shape is determined by the total product curve. Thus the concept of diminishing marginal productivity reappears in the TVC curve. Second, a shift in the total product curve shifts the TVC curve. Third, it is drawn for a unique wage rate. When the wage rate is exactly $1, as in our example, the total product curve in panel b and the TVC curve in panel c will appear the same. (But remember, the vertical axis of the total product curve is units of labor, whereas the vertical axis of the TVC curve is dollar costs.) Two other TVC curves are drawn in Figure 6.1c. A reduction in wage rates shifts the TVC curve downward and flattens it. Increasing wage rates have the opposite effect. But regardless of the position of the TVC, its tendency to rise at a decreasing rate at first and later at an increasing rate reflects its dependence on the production characteristics of increasing and diminishing marginal productivity. (We will learn more about this production-cost duality later.) Finally, the TVC curve emanates from the origin because all variable costs may be eliminated in the short run by reducing to zero both output and the hiring of the variable resource.

Let's return to the matter of fixed costs for a moment. They have two essential characteristics: (1) They cannot be avoided in the short run, and (2) they do not change as a result of expansions or contractions in output. Firms often have such fixed expenses as property tax liabilities, lease payments, monthly bank loan obligations, and management service contracts, which are independent of the firms' rates of output and cannot be avoided in the short run. Because fixed costs are independent of the firm's output, the **total fixed cost (TFC)** curve is a horizontal line, as shown in Figure 6.2.

Recall that *capital* is a generic term representing all fixed factors. Thus TFC is defined as

$$TFC = r \cdot \overline{K} \qquad (6.2)$$

where

Figure 6.2
Total Fixed Cost Curve

Total fixed costs do not vary with change in output. Hence, the TFC curve is horizontal.

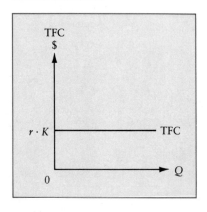

$\overline{K}$ = units of capital input (the bar is drawn over K to represent its short-run fixity)

r = the per-unit rental rate of capital

The variable r is not the interest rate but rather, the rental rate of capital, because the rate at which capital may be rented is a proxy for its market price.[1] Although capital is often owned outright, the price at which it could be rented is still a good guide to its market value in a given time period. For this reason, r is also called the implicit rental rate of capital.

Now we can define the **short-run total cost (TC)**. TC is simply the sum of the variable and fixed cost components, as illustrated in Figure 6.3. The TVC curve emanates from the origin, whereas the TFC curve is a horizontal line. The short-run total cost curve is derived by vertical summation, that is, by adding the two cost components at every level of output. The TC in Figure 6.3 exceeds the TVC by exactly $100—the amount of fixed costs. For example, when output is zero, TC = TFC. At all other outputs, such as Q_1 and Q_2, TC is plotted by adding the $100 of fixed costs to the variable costs. The only difference between TC and TVC is the vertical displacement of TC due to the addition of fixed costs. Although the positions of the two curves are different, their slopes are the same.

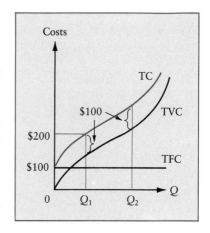

Figure 6.3
Short-Run Total Cost Curve

The total cost curve is the sum of total variable and total fixed costs. The TC curve lies above the TVC curve by the amount of total fixed costs. These curves have identical slopes.

Short-Run Cost Curves

You know by now that every total magnitude must have its average counterpart. We can now derive the average cost curves that correspond to the three total cost curves presented in the previous section.

The Average Variable Cost Curve

The **average variable cost (AVC)** is defined as

$$\text{AVC} = \frac{\text{TVC}}{Q} = \frac{w \cdot L}{Q} \tag{6.3}$$

The AVC is the cost of obtaining the variable factors of production per unit of final output. This value is derived by dividing the TVC by Q, the units of final output produced. The AVC is the slope of a ray drawn from the origin to an arbitrary point on the TVC curve. In Figure 6.4*a*, three such rays are drawn to points A, B, and C of the TVC curve. The slopes of these rays measure the AVC for each level of output. (Refer to the derivation of AP_L in Chapter 5 if the reason for this statement escapes you.) The slope of the ray $0A$ is

---

1. See Chapter 12 for an extensive discussion of the relationship between the rental rate of capital, the interest rate, and the price of capital.

Figure 6.4
Average Variable Cost Curve

(a) The TVC curve can be used to derive the AVC curve. (b) The AVC curve is the slope of a ray from the origin to any point on the TVC curve. The AVC declines up to output Q_2, then rises. It has a U-shaped curve.

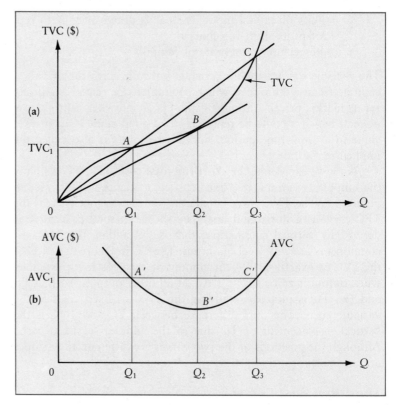

TVC_1/Q_1, which equals AVC at point A. The value $AVC_1 = TVC_1/Q_1$ is plotted as point A' on the AVC curve in panel b. All other points on the AVC curve are derived similarly.

The slope of ray $0A$ exceeds that of $0B$ and equals the slope of $0C$. The ray $0B$ is tangent to the TVC curve and is thus the flattest ray that can be drawn to the TVC curve. Because the slopes of the rays define AVC, we can conclude that the AVC falls up to output Q_2 and rises thereafter. The AVC is a U-shaped curve that reaches its minimum at the level of output at which a ray from the origin becomes tangent to the TVC curve.

The Average Fixed Cost Curve

The **average fixed cost (AFC)** is defined as

$$AFC = \frac{TFC}{Q} = \frac{r \cdot \overline{K}}{Q} \qquad (6.4)$$

Let's use the same familiar technique to derive the AFC curve from the TFC curve. Because the TFC curve is a horizontal line, the slopes of the rays drawn to the curve at larger quantities of output will fall continuously. Thus the AFC curve continues to fall and approaches the horizontal axis asymptotically, as seen in Figure 6.5.

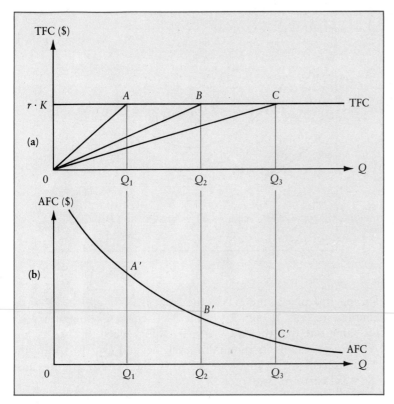

Figure 6.5
Average Fixed Cost Curve

(a) The TFC curve is horizontal. (b) Using the ray technique to measure AFC, we can see that it declines throughout. Therefore, the slopes of the rays decline continuously. The AFC curve is a rectangular hyperbola.

The AFC curve is a rectangular hyperbola, because the product of the AFC and Q always equals the constant TFC. A continuously falling AFC reflects the effect of spreading overhead over larger units of output.

The Short-Run Average Total Cost Curve

The short-run **average total cost** (ATC) is defined as

$$\text{ATC} = \frac{\text{TC}}{Q} = \frac{\text{TVC} + \text{TFC}}{Q} = \text{AVC} + \text{AFC} \qquad (6.5)$$

We now have two ways to proceed; like "good morning" and "buenos dias," they amount to the same thing. First, we can vertically add the two average cost components (AVC and AFC) at each level of output to derive the ATC curve. As illustrated in Figure 6.6, this procedure involves adding the U-shaped AVC curve and the negatively sloped AFC curve, drawn in color for convenience. For small levels of output, both the AVC and AFC are falling; thus the ATC must also fall. The AVC reaches its minimum at Q_1; but because the AFC still falls, the ATC must continue to fall beyond the output at which AVC attains its minimum value. Between output levels Q_1 and Q_2, the AFC is falling faster than the AVC is rising.

Figure 6.6
Average Total Cost Curve

The average total cost (ATC) curve is the vertical sum of the AVC and AFC curves. The ATC achieves its minimum at Q_2; the AVC is minimized at the smaller output, Q_1. The vertical distance between the ATC and AVC curves is the AFC.

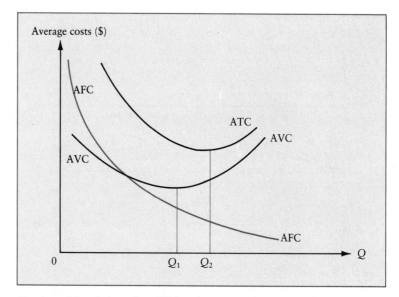

During this phase, the ATC—the sum of AVC and AFC—must continue to fall. At output Q_2, the AVC curve is rising at exactly the same rate that the AFC curve is falling; when this occurs, the ATC curve attains its minimum level. Beyond Q_2, the rise in the AVC exceeds the decrease in the AFC; the net effect is to cause the ATC curve to rise.

Thus the ATC curve is U-shaped, lies above the AVC by the amount of AFC (which gets continually smaller), and achieves its minimum at a larger level of output than does the AVC curve. That is, the minimum of the ATC curve occurs to the right of the minimum of the AVC curve.

From the construction of the ATC curve in Figure 6.6 it should be clear that the vertical distance between ATC and AVC is AFC. This fact has two implications:

The ATC and AVC curves get closer together as output increases, because AFC gets smaller with larger output.

AFC shows up twice in Figure 6.6; once in the hyperbolic AFC curve itself and again as the difference between ATC and AVC. It is often convenient to eliminate this redundancy by dropping the explicit representation of the AFC curve. No information is lost, and the diagram becomes less cluttered. Thus, the standard depiction of the firm's short-run average cost curves includes only the two U-shaped ATC and AVC curves.

Rather than summing the average fixed and variable cost components to derive ATC, we could have used a second method—deriving it directly from the TC curve. As an exercise, you should construct rays to the TC curve in Figure 6.3, derive the ATC curve, and prove that (1) the ATC is a U-shaped curve, (2) it lies above the AVC curve, (3) its minimum point occurs to the right of the minimum of the AVC curve, and (4) the vertical distance between AVC and ATC diminishes at larger levels of output and equals AFC.

The Short-Run Marginal Cost Curve

Just as each total curve has a corresponding average curve, so does it also have a corresponding marginal curve. **Short-run marginal cost (SMC)** is defined as the change in total cost resulting from a small increase in output, holding capital fixed.

$$SMC = \frac{\Delta TC}{\Delta Q}\bigg|_{\overline{K}} \qquad (6.6)$$

Because total cost has a variable and a fixed component and the fixed component is independent of the rate of output, any change in total cost due to a change in production must arise from a change in the variable cost component. Accordingly,

$$SMC = \frac{\Delta TC}{\Delta Q} = \frac{\Delta TVC}{\Delta Q} \qquad (6.7)$$

As usual in economic theory, the definition of the marginal concept is equivalent to the mathematical definition of slope. Thus marginal cost is the slope of the corresponding total cost. And although there are three total-cost curves (TC, TVC, and TFC), there is only one relevant marginal cost curve. The TFC curve is horizontal; the slope is always zero. This is another way of saying that changes in output do not change total fixed costs. Also recall that the TC curve possesses the same slope as the TVC curve and lies above it by the amount of total fixed costs. Because the slopes of the TVC and TC curves are identical, marginal cost may be derived by evaluating the slope of either curve. There is only one SMC curve to be concerned with; it is the slope of both the TVC and TC curves.

We have seen in other contexts that the slope of a curvilinear function is measured geometrically by constructing tangents to different points of the total curve and measuring the slopes of these tangents. Figure 6.7 shows how to use this method to derive the SMC curve. Tangents are drawn to points *A*, *B*, *C*, *D*, and *E* of the TVC curve in panel *a*. The slope of the tangent at *A* exceeds the slope of the tangent at *B*. These marginal cost values are plotted as *A'* and *B'* in panel *b*; SMC is falling in this range of output. The slope of the TVC curve (which equals SMC) continues to fall up to the inflection point *C*. Beyond *C* the slopes of the tangents increase, as illustrated by the tangents drawn to points *D* and *E*. No tangent can be drawn to the inflection point because the curve is changing

Figure 6.7
Short-Run Marginal Cost Curve

(a) The slopes of tangents drawn to the TVC curve decline to the inflection point C, then rise. (b) The SMC curve reflects the slope of the TVC curve. Hence, the SMC declines up to output Q_3, then rises.

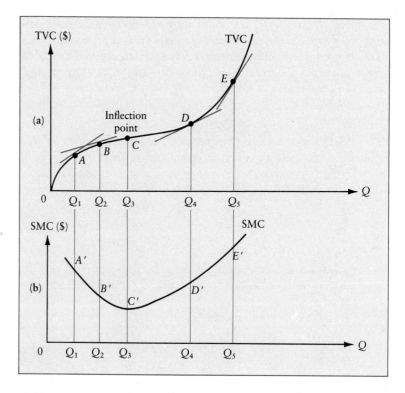

Figure 6.8
Combining the AVC and SMC Curves

(a) The TVC curve can be used to derive the SMC curve, as well as the AVC curve. (b) When SMC < AVC between 0 and Q_2, the AVC curve falls. When SMC = AVC at Q_2, the AVC achieves its minimum value. When SMC > AVC beyond Q_2, the AVC curve rises.

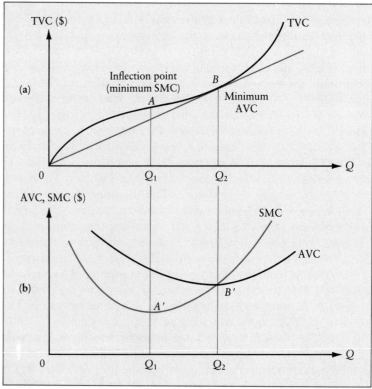

direction at that level of output. Thus the SMC curve falls up to the inflection point and rises thereafter; short-run marginal cost is a U-shaped curve. The SMC curve plays an important role in the firm's decisions, because it measures the cost changes that result from output changes.

Fitting Average and Marginal Cost Curves Together

By now you should be comfortable with the idea that average and marginal curves derived from any total curve must not only show the proper relationship to the total curve but also to each other. Using AVC and SMC to illustrate, the rules of arithmetic governing average and marginal costs are as follows:

When SMC < AVC, AVC must fall as output increases.

When SMC > AVC, AVC must rise as output increases.

When SMC = AVC, AVC neither rises nor falls but remains at its minimum value for small changes in output.

The same three-part rule applies to the relationship between SMC and ATC. This is a matter of arithmetic; averages are influenced by marginal observations. For example, no student ever raised a test-score average by scoring lower than the average on the next (marginal) exam. To raise (lower) an average, the marginal observation must exceed (be less than) the present average.

Figure 6.8 shows the graphic relationship between TVC, AVC and SMC. The SMC curve is the slope of the TVC curve and is a U-shaped curve that attains its minimum at the inflection point of TVC (point *A* in Figure 6.8*a*). The AVC is represented by a U-shaped curve that reaches its minimum at the output at which the ray from the origin becomes tangent to the TVC curve (point *B*). You should satisfy yourself that, for any point on the TVC curve up to point *B,* the marginal cost (the slope of the TVC curve) is less than the average variable cost (the slope of the ray from the origin to the TVC curve). And because SMC < AVC, AVC falls up to point *B.* To the right of *B,* SMC > AVC (the slope of the TVC curve > the slope of the rays to the TVC curve), and the AVC rises. Just at *B,* the slope of the TVC curve and the slope of the ray are the same. Thus, SMC = AVC at point *B.* The SMC curve must therefore intersect the AVC curve from below at precisely the minimum AVC.

These average and marginal curves are drawn in Figure 6.8*b.* You should forswear all other activities in life until you are able to derive the average and marginal curves from the total curve.

We have only one more simple step to take before leaving this discussion of short-run cost relationships: connecting SMC and ATC, just as we have done with SMC and AVC. The relationships are identical; the marginal cost will be below ATC when ATC is falling, will intersect the ATC curve from below at exactly the minimum ATC, and will be above ATC when ATC is rising.

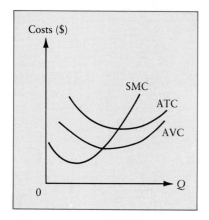

Figure 6.9
The Family of Short-Run Average and Marginal Cost Curves

The ATC, AVC, and SMC curves are shown here explicitly. The AFC curve is implied by the vertical distance between the ATC and AVC curves. Hence, four cost relationships are illustrated, not just three.

Figure 6.9 presents the complete set of short-run marginal and average cost curves associated with the employment of labor and capital resources. Because the AFC curve appears as the vertical distance between the ATC curve and its variable component, AVC, Figure 6.9 actually shows four cost relationships, not just the obvious three.

Production-Cost Duality

The main focus of this chapter is the dependency of costs on production. We have already seen that the TVC curve (and therefore the TC, AVC, ATC, and SMC curves also) derives its slope from the total product curve and the underlying property of diminishing marginal productivity. This section merely emphasizes this dual nature of production and costs.

Short-run marginal cost has been defined as

$$\text{SMC} = \frac{\Delta \text{TVC}}{\Delta Q} \qquad (6.8)$$

Because $\text{TVC} = w \cdot L$, we can write

$$\text{SMC} = \frac{\Delta \text{TVC}}{\Delta Q} = \frac{w \cdot \Delta L}{\Delta Q} \qquad (6.9)$$

For a given wage rate, the marginal cost can change only if the quantity of labor hired changes. The term $\Delta L / \Delta Q$ in Equation 6.9 is the inverse of the marginal product of labor; $\Delta L / \Delta Q = 1/(\Delta Q / \Delta L) = 1/\text{MP}_L$. Thus Equation 6.9 may be rewritten as

$$\text{SMC} = \frac{\Delta \text{TVC}}{\Delta Q} = \frac{w}{\text{MP}_L} \qquad (6.10)$$

Now the production-cost duality is explicit. The wage rate, w, is the change in labor cost from hiring an additional unit of labor, and the MP_L is the additional output from using an extra unit of labor. Thus marginal cost, the ratio of the wage rate and the marginal product of labor, measures the change in labor costs resulting from an increase in production.

Equation 6.10 illustrates how production affects costs. When the MP_L is rising (as it may at low levels of Q), SMC must be falling, because the denominator in Equation 6.10 is rising. Conversely, SMC will rise when the MP_L falls; falling marginal productivity is reflected in rising marginal cost. Note also that the level of labor that maximizes the marginal product of labor determines the level of output for which marginal cost is minimized. Thus the SMC is a mirror image of the MP_L. The SMC curve reflects the productivity

Progressive Income Taxation and Marginal Reasoning

APPLIED
MICRO
THEORY

6.1

There is considerable confusion about the income tax rates under a progressive tax structure. Marginal reasoning can be helpful in analyzing many tax issues, including these two: (1) If an income increase pushes one into a higher tax bracket, can the higher tax rate actually reduce the individual's after-tax take-home pay? (Many people use this argument as a reason to limit their work effort and, no doubt, to underreport earned income.) (2) Can an income tax be fashioned that is both progressive and capable of encouraging higher-income groups to work harder?

The figure illustrates a total tax curve, for which total income tax payments, T, are a rising function of the level of taxable income, Y. No tax is paid on income less than $0A$ because of exemptions, exclusions, deductibles, and so forth.

The tax rate can be stated in both marginal and average terms. The **average tax rate**, t_a, is the percentage of total taxable income paid in taxes. Thus $t_a = T/Y$. The **marginal tax rate**, t_m, is the tax levied on the last dollar of taxable income. Hence $t_m = \Delta T/\Delta Y$. Remember that average measurements are always ratios of total magnitudes and that marginal measurements always refer to changes in total magnitudes. The same is true of average and marginal tax rates.

The figure presents a simple way to identify these tax rates. The slope of the total tax curve measures the marginal tax rate, whereas the slope of a ray drawn from the origin to the total tax curve measures the average tax rate. The figure depicts a constant *marginal* tax rate (the total tax curve is linear) and an increasing *average* tax rate (ray $0C$ is steeper than ray $0B$). The arithmetic rule governing average-marginal

relationships is therefore satisfied: t_a increases with income because $t_m > t_a$ at all levels of taxable income.

Can earning more taxable income reduce take-home pay under a progressive tax structure? Under the constant tax structure in the figure, a higher taxable income would increase the tax liability and the average tax rate, t_a. The important thing, however, is the marginal tax rate, t_m. As long as the trajectory of the total tax curve is flatter than the 45-degree line, t_m is less than 1 and each new dollar of taxable income is taxed at less than 100%. Thus more taxable income must leave more after-tax take-home pay.

But what if the marginal tax rate is not constant but rises with income, as in the case of the U.S. income tax? The same analysis applies. If t_m rises, the total tax curve rises at an increasing rate. But as long as t_m is less than 1, the
Continued on page 160

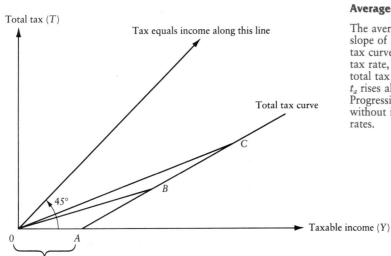

Total tax (T)

Tax equals income along this line

Total tax curve

C

B

45°

0   A

Deductible income

Taxable income (Y)

Average and Marginal Tax Rates

The average tax rate, t_a, is the slope of rays drawn to the total tax curve: $t_a = T/Y$. The marginal tax rate, t_m, is the slope of the total tax curve: $t_m = \Delta T/\Delta Y$. Thus t_a rises although t_m is constant. Progressivity can be achieved without increasing marginal tax rates.

higher rates cannot lower after-tax income. Such a result would require a marginal tax rate greater than 1!*

Now let's turn to the second issue—the degree to which a

*If taxpayers are moved into higher average (and marginal) brackets merely by inflation, such "bracket creep" can rob real income. Suppose that the increase in nominal taxable income is just offset by inflation, so that the worker's real income is unchanged. By moving into a higher tax bracket, the worker pays a higher average tax rate on the same real income. Hence inflation bites twice; it erodes the purchasing power of nominal income and increases the tax liability on the same real income.

progressive tax discourages work. We may begin by defining progressivity. An income tax is progressive when higher-income groups pay a larger percentage of their income in taxes than do lower-income groups. Thus progressivity requires a rising t_a, but not a rising t_m. (The figure depicts progressivity with a constant t_m.) Therefore, if a sense of "fairness" calls for progressive taxation and hence increasing average tax rates, this social goal can be accomplished without the rising marginal rates that produce work disincentives for higher-income groups.

This is an important lesson in

marginal reasoning. "Flat-tax" advocates, such as President Ronald Reagan, use just such logic in promulgating a reduction in marginal tax rates for upper-income taxpayers.† Theirs is not an argument for eliminating the progressive income tax. Instead, they seek to preserve progressivity and promote positive work incentives for upper-income groups through lower and constant (flat) marginal tax rates.

†For an explanation of the "flat tax," see "Economics Commentary," *Business Week*, 19 July 1982, p. 130; and Susan Lee, "Rating the Flat-Rate Tax," *Wall Street Journal*, 30 June 1982.

of variable factors as incorporated in the MP_L curve.

An equivalent duality may be shown between the AVC curve and the AP_L curve:

$$\text{AVC} = \frac{\text{TVC}}{Q} = \frac{w \cdot L}{Q} \tag{6.11}$$

The term L/Q is the inverse of AP_L: $L/Q = 1/(Q/L) = 1/AP_L$. By substitution,

$$\text{AVC} = \frac{\text{TVC}}{Q} = \frac{w}{AP_L} \tag{6.12}$$

For a constant wage, the AVC depends uniquely on AP_L. In short, the total product curve and its associated average and marginal productivities underpin all the short-run cost curves—except the TFC and AFC curves. Understanding the duality of production and costs can help you remember the unusually large number of production and cost curves presented so far.

Long-Run Costs

Up to now we have been content to hold capital fixed for the purpose of developing short-run cost curves. When we relax capital fixity, we move from short-run to long-run analysis. There are essentially two ways to investigate long-run costs. The first way is to consider the long run as a planning horizon in which the firm is free to select different quantities of the fixed factor. In this view, the long run is merely a series of short runs, and we can use the short-run cost schedules to develop long-run cost schedules in a straightforward manner. Or we can use the isoquant map introduced in

Chapter 5, which is a more explicit representation of long-run production when all inputs are variable. This section presents the first method. Later we will use the isoquant method to advance our understanding of long-run costs.

Short-Run Scales of Plant and Long-Run Costs

The long run may be regarded as a planning horizon for the firm in which different combinations of labor and capital inputs may be contemplated. To simplify, suppose the firm is considering just three **scales of plant.** Each scale of plant (plant size) is determined by the amount of the capital input. Because the quantity of capital is a parameter to the total product curve and because a given total product curve translates into a unique set of short-run cost curves, the assumption of three alternative levels of capital gives rise to the three TC curves and corresponding ATC curves depicted in Figure 6.10 $(K_3 > K_2 > K_1)$. Thus TC_1 (and ATC_1) is the cost curve associated with the smallest scale of plant; TC_2 is the next largest; and TC_3 is the largest. Which scale of plant the firm builds depends on the expected rate of output. If the firm wishes to produce in the range from 0 to Q_1, it can accomplish such production at least cost by the smallest scale of plant, TC_1. Output in the range Q_1 to Q_2 is produced at least cost by increasing the capital input so as to achieve

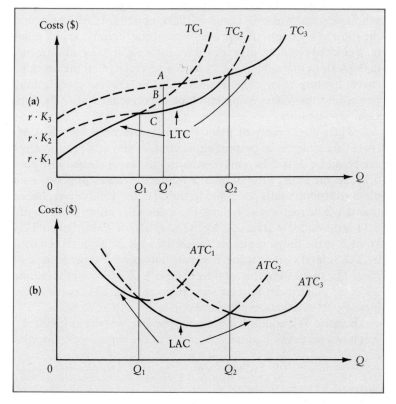

Figure 6.10
Long-Run Total and Average Cost Curves

(a) The LTC curve is composed of the least-cost segments of three short-run scales of plant: TC_1, TC_2, and TC_3.
(b) The LAC curve is composed of the least-cost segments of three short-run scales of plant: ATC_1, ATC_2, and ATC_3. Long-run cost curves, total or average, imply least-cost production when all inputs are variable.

the scale of plant TC_2. Any rate of output larger than Q_2 should be produced with the largest scale of plant, TC_3.

The **long-run total cost** (**LTC**) is the total cost of producing a given output when the scale of plant is adjusted to achieve production at least cost. Long-run cost curves allow for all appropriate cost-minimizing adjustments in the combination of factors to be made. In Figure 6.10a, the LTC curve is composed of the scalloped, solid segments of the individual TC curves, because these are the least-cost segments. The colored segments of the TC curves are irrelevant to the LTC curve because any output on a colored segment can be produced cheaper by adopting a different scale of plant. For example, output Q' may be produced at a total cost of $Q'A$ using the largest scale of plant and $Q'B$ using the smallest. But the least-cost method of producing Q' is to adopt the intermediate scale of plant TC_2 and reduce total cost to $Q'C$. Points A and B are not part of the LTC curve because they do not represent least-cost methods of producing output Q'.

The three short-run ATC curves in Figure 6.10b are the average counterparts to the TC curves above. Each ATC curve is also referred to as a scale of plant. The **long-run average cost** (**LAC**) is the average cost of producing a given output when the scale of plant is adjusted to achieve production at the lowest average cost. (Of course, lowest total cost implies lowest average cost.) The scalloped, solid segments of the ATC curves make up the LAC curve. Again, the colored segments are not cost-minimizing, because at any point on a colored segment, average costs can be reduced by adjustments in the scale of plant. The LAC curve has several names: the envelope curve, because it envelops the several ATC curves; the planning curve; and the **Viner-Wong envelope curve,** named after its principal investigators.[2]

When the number of plant sizes is small, the LTC and LAC curves are scalloped. For most applications, many scale adjustments are possible; thus these curves smooth out, as illustrated in Figure 6.11. At the limit, with an infinite number of scales of plant, each plant contributes only one point to the LTC and LAC curves, rather than a whole segment as before. For example, output Q_1 in Figure 6.11 is produced at least cost by the adoption of scale of plant TC_1. Point A is the only output for which the scale of plant represented by TC_1 is least cost; it is therefore the only contribution of scale of plant TC_1 to the long-run total cost curve (LTC). Each of the infinite scales of plant contributes a similar point. The LTC curve is the locus of all such cost-minimizing points.

Because TC_1 equals LTC at only one level of output (point A), it follows that ATC_1 equals LAC only at the same level of output

2. Jacob Viner, "Cost Curves and Supply Curves," *Zeitschrift für Nationalökonomie* 3 (1931): 23–46. Reprinted in George J. Stigler and Kenneth E. Boulding, eds., *Readings in Price Theory* (Homewood, Ill.: Irwin, 1952), pp. 199–232.

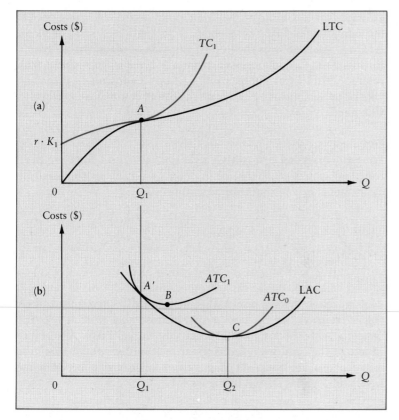

Figure 6.11
Viner-Wong Envelope Curve (LAC)

(a) If inputs are infinitely divisible, the LTC and LAC curves are smooth. Each scale of plant contributes a single point to the LTC and LAC curves. (b) The LAC curve is an envelope of all cost-minimizing scales of plant. ATC_0 is the "optimum" scale of plant because it results in overall minimization of average costs.

(point A'). ATC_1 is the least-cost scale of plant only for output level Q_1. Each ATC curve is tangent to the LAC curve, and that tangency defines the least-cost scale of plant for producing that given output.

Except in one special case, the cost-minimizing tangency of an ATC curve with the Viner-Wong envelope curve does not occur at the minimum point of the ATC curve. For example, ATC_1 in Figure 6.11 is minimized at B; but the firm would not operate scale of plant ATC_1 at B because a cheaper scale of plant is available. A tangency between the LAC curve and any ATC curve means that the slopes are equal at that point. When the LAC curve is negatively sloped, as it is up to output Q_2 in Figure 6.11, any tangency must occur along the negatively sloped portion of the ATC as well.[3] For outputs exceeding Q_2, tangencies must occur along the positively sloped portion of both the LAC and the ATC curves. The LAC = ATC

---

3. Viner attempted to draw tangencies between a negatively sloped LAC curve and the minimum points of several short-run ATC curves, where slopes are zero. This is an impossible task, as he graciously and humorously acknowledged in his refusal to correct the error so "future teachers and students may share the pleasure of many of their predecessors of pointing out that if I had known what an 'envelope' was I would not have given my excellent draftsman the technically impossible and economically inappropriate assignment of drawing an LAC curve which would pass through the lowest cost points of all the ATC curves and yet not rise above any ATC curve at any point." See Viner, "Cost Curves," pp. 215, 227.

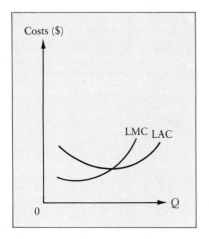

Costs ($)

LMC LAC

0   Q

Figure 6.12
Combining the LAC and LMC Curves

The average-marginal rules of arithmetic also apply to long-run costs.

tangency can occur at the minimum point of an ATC curve only at the minimum of LAC, or point C. This particular scale of plant, ATC_0, is referred to as the "optimum scale of plant" because only for this plant is minimum short-run average cost compatible with total long-run cost minimization. The optimum scale of plant will take on special meaning in our discussion of competitive markets in Chapter 7.

Deriving Long-Run Marginal Cost

Long-run marginal cost (**LMC**) is the change in total long-run costs resulting from a small change in output when all cost-minimizing adjustments in all inputs are accomplished.

$$LMC = \frac{\Delta LTC}{\Delta Q} \qquad (6.13)$$

Figure 6.11 contains the long-run total cost curve, LTC. You should be able to derive the corresponding LMC curve in the same way we have derived the MP_L and the SMC curves from their respective total curves. You should also be able to fit it together properly with the long-run average cost curve, LAC. Any elaboration of the total-average-marginal relationship would surely be monotonous at this point. The proper relationship between the LAC and LMC is shown in Figure 6.12.

Combining Short- and Long-Run Marginal Cost Curves

To complete our picture of cost curves, we must learn how the SMC and LMC curves fit together. Refer back to Figure 6.11a, which contains a short-run and a long-run total cost curve. SMC equals the slope of TC_1, and LMC equals the slope of LTC. The slopes of TC_1 and LTC are equal only at the tangency point A. Thus LMC = SMC_1 at the level of output for which the scale of plant TC_1 is the least-cost method of production. For outputs less than Q_1, LMC > SMC_1 (the slope of the LTC curve is greater than the slope of TC_1); and for outputs greater than Q_1, SMC_1 > LMC. The equality of SMC_1 and LMC at output Q_1 may be interpreted to mean that, for a very small adjustment in output around Q_1, costs will change by the same amount, whether the firm expands output along TC_1 by varying labor or chooses a slightly larger scale of plant.

If LMC > SMC_1, it is cheaper for the firm to expand output by increasing the variable factors and holding capital fixed. This is shown in Figure 6.13, which contains a tangency at point T between LTC and TC_1. Suppose the firm is currently producing output Q_1, where LMC > SMC_1 (the slope of the LTC curve at A is greater than the slope of TC_1 at B). The least-cost method of expanding output to Q_2 is to move along TC_1 by hiring more labor and holding capital fixed. This increases total costs by the amount BC. Changing the scale of plant and thereby moving along the LTC curve from A to

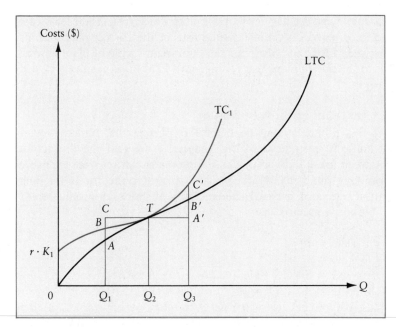

Figure 6.13
The Least-Cost Method of Expanding Output

If LMC > SMC, as between Q_1 and Q_2, output is increased at least cost by holding the scale of plant constant and moving along TC_1. If LMC < SMC, as between Q_2 and Q_3, least-cost production occurs by increasing the scale of plant and moving along the LTC curve.

T increases total costs by $AC > BC$. The short-run adjustment is less costly whenever LMC > SMC. For small output changes around output Q_2, both options yield the same marginal cost, because LMC = SMC at output Q_2. In adjusting output from Q_2 to Q_3, LMC < SMC_1. The less costly method now is to increase the scale of plant, move along the LTC curve from T to B', and incur an increase in total costs of $A'B'$. To produce Q_3 with the scale of plant TC_1 would increase costs by $A'C' > A'B'$. Adjustments in the scale of plant are preferred whenever LMC < SMC.

The relationship between LMC and SMC_1 is illustrated in Figure 6.14 for the scale of plant represented by ATC_1. Note that SMC_1 = LMC at point A, the same level of output at which ATC_1 = LAC

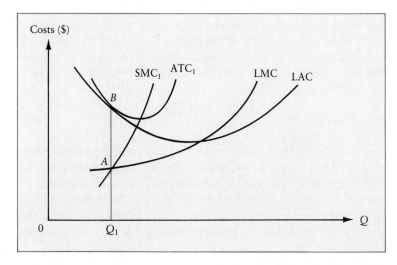

Figure 6.14
Combining the SMC and LMC Curves

Each SMC curve intersects the LMC curve at the same output for which the scale of plant ATC is tangent to the LAC: SMC_1 intersects the LMC curve at A. ATC_1 is tangent to the LAC curve at B. Both pertain to output Q_1.

(point B) and the only level of output at which ATC_1 is the least-cost scale of plant. As an exercise, construct the correct relationships between LMC and SMC for the "optimum" scale of plant as well as for a scale of plant that is tangent to LAC in its positively sloped region.

Cost Definitions: A Summary

At this point, it may be helpful to review the numerous cost definitions introduced in this chapter. Note that the distinction between fixed and variable costs become irrelevant once we move into long-run analysis; all costs are variable to the firm in the long run. Fixed costs are characteristic only of short-run production.

Short-run costs:

$$\text{TVC} = w \cdot L$$
$$\text{TFC} = r \cdot \overline{K}$$
$$\text{TC} = \text{TVC} + \text{TFC} = (w \cdot L) + (r \cdot \overline{K})$$
$$\text{AVC} = \text{TVC}/Q = (w \cdot L)/Q = w/\text{AP}_L$$
$$\text{AFC} = \text{TFC}/Q = (r \cdot \overline{K})/Q = r/\text{AP}_K$$
$$\text{ATC} = \text{TC}/Q = (\text{TVC} + \text{TFC})/Q = \text{AVC} + \text{AFC}$$
$$\text{SMC} = \Delta\text{TC}/\Delta Q = \Delta\text{TVC}/\Delta Q = (w \cdot \Delta L)/\Delta Q = w/\text{MP}_L$$

Long-run costs:

$$\text{LTC} = (w \cdot L) + (r \cdot K)$$
$$\text{LAC} = [(w \cdot L) + (r \cdot K)]/Q$$
$$\text{LMC} = \Delta\text{LTC}/\Delta Q$$

The Isoquants and Isocosts

We can now reinforce and expand the analysis of long-run costs by developing cost curves directly from the isoquant analysis presented in Chapter 5. Recall that an isoquant shows all labor and capital combinations capable of producing a given quantity of output. When many output levels are considered, the resulting family of isoquant curves is called an isoquant map. The isoquant map illustrates the firm's technical production possibilities when all factors are variable.

The Isocost Line

In the long run, a firm can alter the size of its labor force and its capital stock. To maximize profit, its managers must get the greatest possible production from a given budget by combining labor and capital inputs in the correct proportions. Naturally, the ratio of labor to capital will depend in part on the respective prices of wages (w) and the rental rate of capital (r). Thus factor prices limit the quantity of inputs that a firm can purchase for a given expenditure.

The total cost of production is

$$C = wL + rK \qquad (6.14)$$

If we know the total outlay of the firm, C, and the values of w and r, we can construct the necessary constraint on production. This constraint, pictured in Figure 6.15, is called an **isocost line;** it is the production equivalent of the consumer's budget line. An isocost ("equal-cost") line illustrates for given factor prices the different combinations of factors that can be purchased for any given cost outlay. Suppose a firm spends C_1 dollars on inputs. If the firm uses its entire cost outlay to purchase capital, C_1/r units of capital can be purchased. Thus C_1/r is the vertical intercept of the isocost line. If only labor is purchased, C_1/w units of labor are available, which is the horizontal intercept. The isocost line is constructed by connecting the two intercepts with a straight line. This line represents the rate at which the firm can exchange purchases of capital for labor. Each isocost line represents a given outlay. If the cost outlay increases to C_2, given factor prices, the isocost line shifts parallel to the right, as Figure 6.15 shows.

The linear equation for the isocost line is easily derived by rearranging the total cost equation, $C = wL + rK$. Solving for K yields

$$K = \frac{C}{r} - \left(\frac{w}{r}\right)L \qquad (6.15)$$

In this form, C/r is the vertical intercept of the isocost line and the slope is $-w/r$. Thus the rate at which the two factors can be exchanged without changing total outlay is determined by the ratio of factor prices.

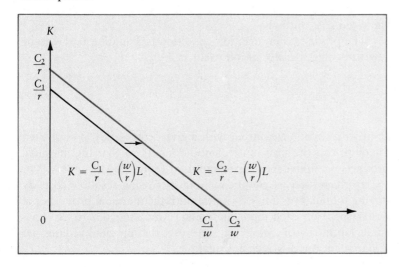

Figure 6.15
The Isocost Line

An isocost line shows the different combinations of factors that the firm can purchase for a given cost with given factor prices. The linear equation is $K = C/r - (w/r)L$. The vertical intercept is C/r, and the slope is $-(w/r)$.

Producer Optimization:
Choosing Efficient Factor Combinations

Now let's combine the isoquant map with the isocost constraint to describe **producer optimization,** the condition prevailing when firms combine labor and capital in efficient combinations. Recall from Chapter 5 that the slope of the isoquant, called the marginal rate of technical substitution (MRTS), defines the technical rate at which labor and capital can be substituted in order to maintain a constant output. Recall further that the MRTS equals the negative of the ratio of marginal products of factors. Thus $|\text{MRTS}| = (\text{MP}_L/\text{MP}_K)$.

Figure 6.16 contains an isoquant map and a linear isocost line. The maximum output the firm can produce with a cost outlay of C_0 at given factor prices is determined by the tangency of the isocost line with the highest attainable isoquant curve, Q_2. At the tangency, point A, the firm employes K_0 units of capital and L_0 units of labor. Also at the tangency, the slope of the isoquant in absolute value $(\text{MP}_L/\text{MP}_K)$ equals the slope of the isocost in absolute value (w/r). In other words, the condition for producer optimization is

$$\frac{\text{MP}_L}{\text{MP}_K} = \frac{w}{r} \tag{6.16}$$

Any adjustment in factor combinations at tangency point A pushes production along the isocost line, which inevitably generates intersections with lower isoquants. For example, points B and D represent reduced producer optimization; without spending another penny on resources, the firm could increase its total output from Q_1 to Q_2 by adjusting its factor combination to A. Once the tangency is achieved, no further changes in factor proportions can increase total output. Thus producer optimization requires the firm to allocate costs so that the ratio of marginal products equals the ratio of factor prices. When this is done, the firm maximizes its output for the given cost outlay.

The producer optimization condition in Equation 6.15 can be rewritten algebraically as follows:

$$\frac{\text{MP}_L}{w} = \frac{\text{MP}_K}{r} \tag{6.17}$$

In order to maximize output with a given cost outlay at stipulated factor prices, the firm must combine inputs so that the marginal products per dollar spent on all inputs are equal. If $\text{MP}_L/w > \text{MP}_K/r$, the firm can increase output without increasing resource costs by buying more labor and less capital until the marginal products per dollar spent on each input are equal. Note the similarity to consumer optimization, which requires that the marginal utilities per dollar spent on all goods be equal.

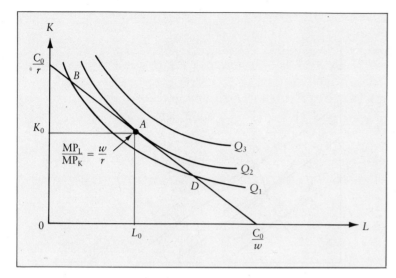

Figure 6.16
Producer (Least-Cost) Optimization

Producer optimization is achieved when $MP_L/MP_K = w/r$, as at point A. Points B and D are not efficient. Output can rise from Q_1 to Q_2 with no additional cost by adjusting to the correct factor combination at A.

We have encountered producer optimization as though the firm's objective is to produce the maximum output for a given cost outlay. This is output maximization subject to a cost constraint. We could also seek the least costly means of producing a given output, a method known as cost minimization subject to an output constraint. Either way, producer optimization requires inputs to be combined so that the ratio of their marginal products equals the ratio of their prices. Any other circumstance will not achieve either output maximization (constrained by costs) or cost minimization (constrained by output).

The Expansion Path

The direct link between isoquant-isocost analysis and long-run cost curves is the **expansion path (EP)**. As you may recall, long-run cost is the cost of producing a given output when all cost-minimizing factor adjustments are made. These adjustments have been described in terms of adjustments in the scale of plant. Now they can be described in isoquant-isocost language.

Suppose the firm is considering output levels of Q_1, Q_2 and Q_3, where $Q_1 < Q_2 < Q_3$. The isoquants representing these output levels are illustrated in Figure 6.17a. The tangencies of the three isocost lines with the isoquants representing these three output levels identify the least-cost methods of producing outputs. For given factor prices, output must be produced so the ratio of factor prices equals the ratio of the factors' marginal products. For output Q_1 a cost outlay of C_1 is required, for Q_2 an outlay of C_2 is necessary, and so on. As output rises, employment of labor and capital inputs must rise; as long as factor prices are constant, the factor combinations must be adjusted to keep the ratio of their marginal products constant.

Figure 6.17
The Expansion Path and Long-Run Costs

(a) The expansion path (EP) shows all least-cost factor combinations for all possible output levels, given factor prices. (b) The LTC curve may be derived from the expansion path. (c) The LMC and LAC curves are derived from the LTC curve. Each expansion path underpins a given set of LTC, LMC, and LAC curves.

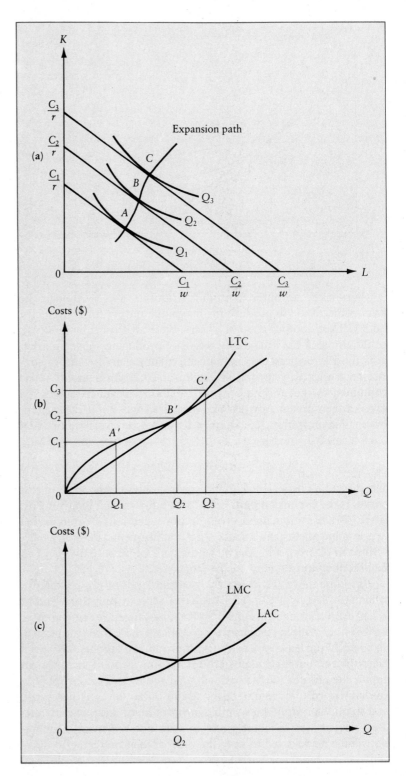

The expansion path shows all least-cost factor combinations for all possible output levels, given factor prices. It shows the factor combinations that the firm will select as it expands (or contracts) output. For given factor prices, least-cost producer optimization requires that the factor combination be adjusted to keep the ratio of marginal products constant and equal to the ratio of factor prices. The expansion path reflects the factor adjustments made necessary by expanding (or contracting) output, hence its name. The expansion path is analogous to the income-consumption curve in consumer theory.

THE EXPANSION PATH AND LONG-RUN COST CURVES   The long-run total cost curve (LTC) relates the lowest total cost of producing alternative levels of output when the factor prices are given and when all factors are variable. This same information is contained indirectly in the expansion path diagram. We can derive the LTC from the information contained in the expansion path. For example, the output Q_1 can be produced with an expenditure outlay of C_1 if labor and capital are hired in the ratio defined by the tangency at A on the expansion path. Thus the combination (C_1, Q_1) is one point on the long-run total cost curve, plotted as point A' in Figure 6.17b. Similarly, output Q_2 can be produced with a minimum cost outlay of C_2 if the factor combination dictated by point B on the expansion path is achieved. Thus the cost-output combination (C_2, Q_2) is another point on the LTC curve, plotted as B' in Figure 6.17b. Point C' is derived in the same way for output Q_3. The collection of such least-cost points is the LTC curve, as shown in Figure 6.17b. From the LTC curve, the corresponding LAC and LMC curves in Figure 6.17c are easily derived, using methods you are already familiar with.

ADJUSTING FACTOR COMBINATIONS IN RESPONSE TO HIGHER WAGES We can use the expansion path to show that, for any given level of output, the firm will reduce its use of an increasingly costly factor of production in the long run but not in the short run. Say that the firm in Figure 6.18 is producing Q_0 at a total cost of C_0 and uses the cost-minimizing input combination A for factor prices $w = w_0$ and $r = r_0$. Point A lies on the expansion path EP (w_0, r_0).

Now let the wage rate rise from w_0 to w_1. For the constant cost outlay C_0, the isocost line rotates around point C_0/r_0. This new isocost line is drawn in color; its slope reflects the new ratio of factor prices. The firm would have to reduce output to Q_1 in the long run if it continued to spend the same cost outlay, C_0. However, the firm is not constrained to output Q_1. In fact, there is nothing in isoquant-isocost theory that tells us what level of output the firm will produce! This decision is a matter of profit maximization; costs alone are insufficient in selecting the best level of output for the firm. It is

Figure 6.18
Adjusting Factor Combinations When Relative Factor Prices Change

For the initial factor price ratio w_0/r_0, the firm produces Q_0 units of output at least cost (C_0) using input combination A. When wages rise relative to rental rates of capital, the same output is produced with combination D when all long-run factor adjustments are implemented. In the long run, any given output is produced with less of a factor that becomes relatively more expensive.

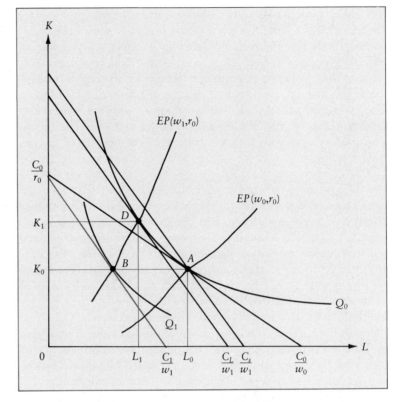

therefore pointless for us to speculate about the level of output the firm will select until we study its profit-maximizing output behavior, a subject begun in Chapter 7. A more fruitful approach is to determine the input combinations and the required cost outlay that the firm will select for a given level of output. This is all that is implied by the least-cost optimizing behavior of firms.

In the short run, the firm will produce output Q_0 with the same factor combination as before, combination A. Capital is fixed at K_0 in the short run, and L_0 is the least amount of labor that, in combination with K_0, can produce output Q_0. To measure the total cost of producing output Q_0 with the same factor combinations (K_0, L_0), draw an isocost line through A with the slope of the colored isocost line. This higher isocost line reflects the higher ratio of labor to capital prices after wages rise. A total outlay of C_s is required to buy the same resources after wage rates rise.

In the long run, when the firm can adjust its use of capital, output Q_0 can be produced at a total cost less than C_s. The factor combination at A is not cost-minimizing for factor prices w_1 and r_0, because the ratio of marginal products at A (slope of isoquant) is less than the ratio of factor prices in absolute value (slope of isocost line). If the firm adjusts its factor combination to D, using K_1 capital and L_1 labor, Q_0 can be produced for the lower total cost outlay C_L.

Rate-of-Return Regulation and Factor Utilization

APPLIED
MICRO
THEORY

6.2

Regulatory commissions limit, among other things, the profit that public utilities can earn. One common means of controlling profits is by **rate-of-return regulation,** in which the maximum allowable profit is calculated as a percentage of invested capital. Such regulation induces the firm to select an inefficient combination of inputs in its production process, according to the famous **Averch-Johnson effect.*** We can use isoquant-isocost analysis to study this remarkable hypothesis.

The accompanying figure contains the standard isoquant-isocost-expansion path apparatus. Let the wage rate equal w_1 and the rental rate of capital equal r_1. If w_1 and r_1 are market-determined factor prices that reflect true opportunity costs of the resources, output Q_0 is produced at least opportunity cost with the factor combination A. Similarly, any other rate of output would be produced efficiently with a factor mix along the expansion path EP (w_1, r_1), because the ratio of marginal products equals the ratio of factor prices everywhere on the expansion path.

Now let the regulatory commission set a profit limit equal to some percentage return on invested capital. Because profits are regulated as a percentage return on capital (and not as a limit on total profits), the firm can gain total profit by increasing the size of the capital stock on which the rate of return is based. In effect, the firm can consider the cost of purchasing

capital to be less than r_1; extra capital expansion increases allowed profit. Thus rate-of-return regulation drives a wedge between the true opportunity cost of capital and what the firm perceives as the lower price of capital. This perceived price is what the firm uses in decisionmaking. If r_2 is the rental rate of capital that the firm perceives, $r_2 < r_1$, then the isocost line rises in slope and output Q_0 will be produced with the inefficient factor combination B.

Indeed, any rate of output will be produced with input mixes along the inefficient expansion path EP (w_1, r_2). Firms will produce any rate of output with a capital stock that is too large from society's point of view. Because public utilities are naturally large, and because rate-of-return regulation tends to enlarge the scale of plant even more, this public policy has an impact on capital markets that cannot be ignored by the general business community.

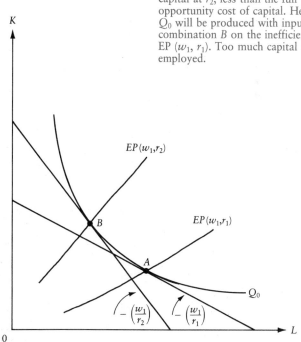

Rate-of-Return Regulation Fosters Inefficiency

When the unregulated factor price ratio is w_1/r_1, output Q_0 is produced with input combination A, a point on EP (w_1, r_1). Rate-of-return regulation causes firms to evaluate the rental rate of capital at r_2, less than the full opportunity cost of capital. Hence, Q_0 will be produced with input combination B on the inefficient EP (w_1, r_1). Too much capital is employed.

*H. Averch and L. L. Johnson, "Behavior of the Firm under Regulatory Constraint," *American Economic Review* 52 (1962): 1053–1069. For a graphic treatment of their theory, see J. L. Stein and G. H. Borts, "Behavior of the Firm under Regulatory Constraint," *American Economic Review* 62 (1972): 964–970.

Note that point D lies on the expansion path EP (w_1, r_0). Every output level will be produced with more capital and less labor at factor prices w_2 and r_1 than at prices w_1 and r_1. Thus the long-run adjustment to wage rates rising faster than the rental rate of capital is to reduce the use of labor, the increasingly expensive resource.

The Marginal Rule for Optimizing Objectives

A man brings his Rolls Royce to a screeching halt in front of Chicago's O'Hare airport, runs to concourse B, gate 13, boards WTA flight 263 for Trinidad, and never sees his car again. How can we explain this behavior? Apparently the expected marginal benefit of the decision to abandon the automobile is greater than the expected marginal cost. Maybe the police are after him. Perhaps he is rushing to a tryst in Trinidad with a movie queen. Whatever the facts may be, the decision is rational if the marginal benefit exceeds the marginal cost of the decision. Most of us decide against abandoning our cars at airports for the opposite reason: Marginal cost is greater than marginal benefit. Comparing these marginal values can tell us whether certain courses of action are prudent or foolish. Even when we cannot measure marginal benefits and costs precisely, we can still improve our decisionmaking by using these marginal ideas to get a feel for the choice at hand.

Profit-maximizing output decisions for firms also require information about marginal costs and marginal benefits of production. The marginal benefit is called marginal revenue (MR), the addition to total revenue of expanding sales by one unit. If a firm can sell any amount of output it desires at the same price, its marginal revenue equals price and is depicted as a horizontal line, as in Figure 6.19a. Figure 6.19a also shows the firm's long-run marginal cost curve (LMC), which measures the addition to total cost of expanding sales by one unit at a time.

Now we have the firm's marginal revenue and marginal cost curves in the same diagram. How much output should the firm produce to maximize profit? The logic (if not the measurement) of the decision is simple. Profits rise whenever an extra unit of production adds more to revenues than to costs. Conversely, profits fall if an extra unit of output adds more to costs than to revenues. Because profits rise when MR > LMC and begin to fall as soon as LMC > MR, it follows that profits are maximized when production is driven to the point where marginal revenue equals marginal cost. Hence the profit-maximizing rule is

$$\text{MR} = \text{LMC} \tag{6.18}$$

The MR = LMC profit-maximizing rule is achieved at output Q_1 in Figure 6.19a. Profit will fall if output is either expanded or contracted from Q_1. If output falls, the extra cost savings (LMC) is

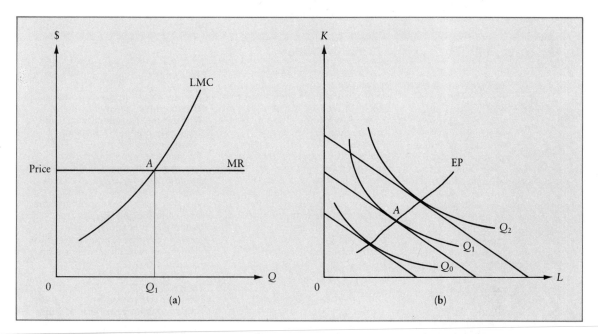

Figure 6.19
Profit Maximization and Producer Optimization

(a) The firm maximizes profit by equating MR and LMC at point A and producing output Q_1. (b) Output Q_1 is produced at least cost by using input combination A'.

less than the extra revenue forgone (MR). If output rises above Q_1, the extra costs incurred (LMC) exceed the additional revenue obtained (MR). Q_1 is the firm's best rate of production because it is the only output for which marginal revenue equals marginal cost.

Note the relationship between the LMC curve in Figure 6.19a and the isoquant map in Figure 6.19b. Once the firm's profit-maximizing rate of output, Q_1, is established, the isoquant-isocost analysis determines the factor combinations needed to produce output Q_1 at the best total cost. Point A on the LMC curve in Figure 6.19a corresponds to point A' on the expansion path in Figure 6.19b; production-cost analysis by itself is too weak to set the firm's rate of output and hence its factor combinations. The marginal revenue—in conjunction with marginal cost—is needed to determine the best rate of output.

Returns to Scale and Long-Run Cost Curves

For ease, the long-run total cost curves have been drawn with the same general shape as the short-run total cost curves. Although the concept of eventual diminishing returns makes it necessary for the short-run TC curve to possess this general shape, no such principle underlies the shape of the LTC curve. The shape of the LTC curve is dictated by the scale characteristics of the firm's production function. If the production function exhibits constant returns to scale, the LTC curve is linear; if increasing returns are present, the LTC curve rises at a decreasing rate; a decreasing returns-to-scale production function causes LTC to rise at an increasing rate. A production function can have a range of each.

Farm Acreage Restrictions and Factor Utilization

6.3

Acreage restrictions have long been used to enhance farm incomes. Limiting farmers to a maximum acreage reduces the total supply of agricultural commodities, raises farm prices, and if demand is price inelastic, expands farm revenues. But the impact of such policies goes far beyond price alone.

Figures A and B illustrate the inefficiencies caused by acreage restrictions. Figure A shows the firm's production function in isoquant form. With land measured on the vertical axis and all other inputs on the horizontal, the expansion path indicates the least-cost input combinations for alternative rates of agricultural production. This firm, however, faces an acreage restriction. At most, it can plant L_R acres of land. As long as output is not greater than Q_0, the restriction is non-binding; inputs can be combined efficiently anywhere along segment JR of the expansion path. But the constraint becomes binding for output rates greater than Q_0. The horizontal line RR' depicts the input combinations that will be required to produce output rates in excess of Q_0 when L_R units of land is the firm's maximum plantable acreage. Note that any rate of production greater than Q_0 is achieved with factor combinations off the efficient expansion path. This means that the land will be used too intensively as labor, machinery, fertilizer, pesticides, and so forth are used to boost yields.

Figure B shows the firm's marginal cost curves. The LMC curve is the long-run marginal cost of production when the firm is free to combine inputs efficiently as output changes. Let price P_1 be the original industry price before acreage restriction is imposed. The firm equates LMC and P_1 at point A by producing output Q_1. The LAC curve has been omitted to

prevent clutter, but the total cost of producing Q_1 is indicated by the height of the isocost curve ZZ' in Figure A when the efficient input combination A' is selected.

Acreage restrictions, by encouraging inefficient use of the factors of production, increases marginal cost to the level of the curve labeled MC_R. At the same time, if acreage restrictions are imposed on all farmers, the industry supply of some crops will decrease and prices will increase to, say, P_2.

The farmer now equates MC_R

and P_2 at point B by cutting production to Q_2. But is this output cut accomplished by moving to the efficient input combination C' in Figure A? Not at all. Instead, combination B' is selected. The acreage restriction induces the substitution of inputs whose uses are not controlled.

Input combination B' in Figure A is of course a technically feasible way of producing Q_2. But it is economically wasteful at the prevailing factor prices. In fact, as this figure is drawn, the smaller output

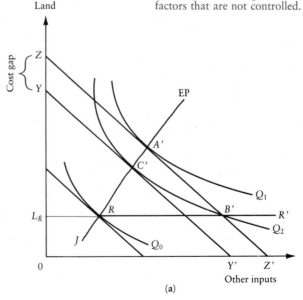

Figure A
Isoquant-Isocost-Expansion Path Analysis of Acreage Restrictions

Without acreage restrictions, output Q_1 is produced with factor combination A', and Q_2 is produced with combination C'. If acreage is restricted to L_R, output Q_2 is produced with the inefficient input combination B' at too great a cost by substituting nonland factors that are not controlled.

(a)

Figure B
Cost Analysis of Acreage Restrictions

When price is P_1, the firm produces Q_1. ($P_1 = $ LMC at Q_1.) Acreage restrictions increase marginal cost to MC_R due to inefficiencies. If industry price rises to P_2, the firm reduces output to Q_2 and employs an inefficient input mix.

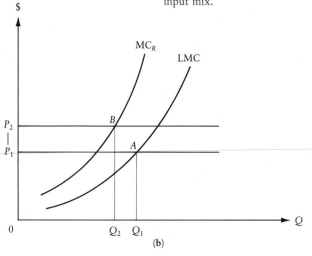

(b)

(Q_2) requires the same cost outlay as the larger output (Q_1). Inefficient use of factors is the cause.

Note that the government is not able to reliably cut farm output by cutting land use. Output will fall below unregulated levels, to be sure, but not in proportion to the cut in land. Farmers partially offset the intent of the government policy by substituting productive resources that are not restricted. Also, output Q_2 becomes too costly. This can be seen in Figure A and Figure B. In Figure A, the vertical gap between isocost ZZ' (the actual cost of Q_2 using the inefficient input mix B') and isocost YY' (the cost of Q_2 using the efficient input mix C') measures the excessive cost of producing Q_2 due solely to acreage restrictions. In Figure A, $MC_R > $ LMC for output Q_2. This inequality is another reflection of the economic waste attributable to restrictions.

In addition to stressing the importance of the agricultural issue, this exercise also emphasizes the link between isoquant curves and cost curves. Both are important analytical tools. Isoquants illustrate factor utilization; cost curves focus our attention directly on the costs of production.

Tort Liability Rules

APPLIED MICRO THEORY

6.4

Tort law is the branch of law that allocates resources following "unintentional harms."* Because such harms are probabilistic, we can study them using the probability production theory presented in Chapter 5. If you've assimilated that analysis, you may be skeptical of the term *unintentional:* Acci-

*Economists have been studying tort rules using production/cost theory since publication of the seminal article: John P. Brown, "Toward an Economic Theory of Liability," *Journal of Legal Studies* 2 (1973): 323.

dents are probabilistic, and the probability of accidents is influenced by the employment of the factors of production in variable proportions. There is generally more that could be done to reduce the probability of accidents. Harm occurs because people do not take greater care, usually because to do so is too expensive relative to the expected benefits.

The economic analysis of torts focuses on the incentives created prior to accidents by tort rules that allocate liability after the accident occurs. The parties to an accident, both victim and injurer, are cast as people who know the conse-

quences of increasing or decreasing their precaution efforts. The purpose of our analysis here is to discover which tort rules best induce efficient combinations of precautions and the efficient probability of accident avoidance.

Choosing efficient precaution combinations is analogous to an entrepreneur selecting efficient combinations of capital and labor along an expansion path. Say that inputs X and Y are used to influence the probability of accident avoidance, P. Using these variables, the isoprobability map presented in Chapter 5 is repeated

Continued on page 178

in Figure A. Adding the isocost lines allows us to formulate an expansion path, which is the connection of all efficient combinations of accident-avoiding inputs.

Suppose first that one individual owns both accident-avoiding inputs (X and Y) and also stands to suffer the costs and enjoy the benefits of avoiding harm. This individual could select any input combinations on the expansion path that would equate the per-dollar marginal probability of the factors. He or she could also choose the cost-minimizing input combination for a given probability.

Similarly, this individual could select the optimum probability of accident avoidance. The LMC curve in Figure B corresponds to

the expansion path in Figure A. Increasing the probability of accident avoidance by moving along the LMC is accomplished by maintaining efficient input combinations. The incentive is to equate the marginal cost and marginal benefit of accident avoidance. The solution under sole ownership of inputs is depicted at point A in Figure B: The efficient probability of accident avoidance is $\hat{P}$, where the LMC equals marginal benefit. This requires caution levels $\hat{X}$ and $\hat{Y}$ in Figure A. Generally, an individual will not try to prevent all accidents, because to do so is too costly compared to the benefits.

In contrast, if the owner cannot vary the precaution level of one of the inputs, he or she will be operating off the expansion path

and off the LMC curve. Instead, he or she will operate on a cost curve depicting inefficient factor combinations, such as SMC. (The analogy to the standard short-run marginal cost is direct.) The sole owner now selects probability $\bar{P}$ by equating SMC and MB at B. For the sole owner, efficiency depends on control over inputs.

The problem of allocating liability, which is addressed by tort law, arises when more than one individual owns the means of avoiding accidents. The rules of tort law are most efficient when they mimic the incentives of the solution for single owners. The three rules we will analyze here are

1. Strict liability.
2. Negligence with contributory negligence.

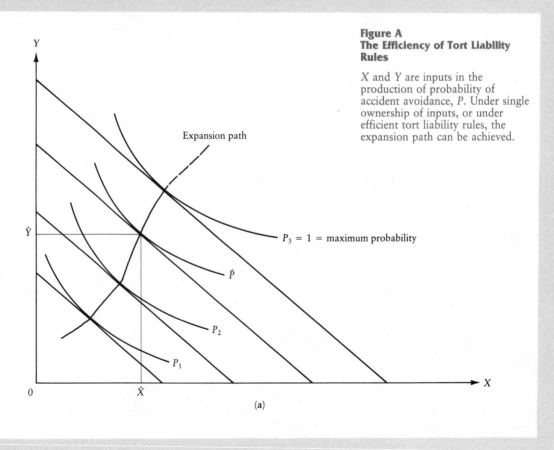

Figure A
The Efficiency of Tort Liability Rules

X and Y are inputs in the production of probability of accident avoidance, P. Under single ownership of inputs, or under efficient tort liability rules, the expansion path can be achieved.

Expansion path

$P_3 = 1 =$ maximum probability

$\hat{P}$

P_2

P_1

$\hat{Y}$

0 $\hat{X}$

Y

X

(a)

Figure B
The Efficiency of Tort Liability Rules

The cost curve LMC represents least-cost production of accident avoidance. The SMC curve applies to inefficient input combinations. At A, the LMC equals marginal benefit; hence $\hat{P}$ is efficient. In Figure A, $\hat{P}$ requires equilibrium input values $\hat{X}$ and $\hat{Y}$.

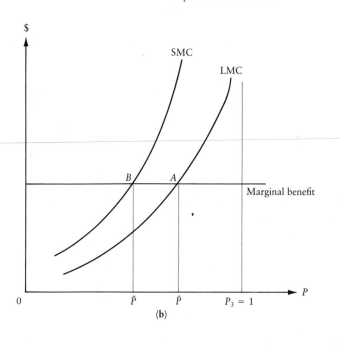

(b)

(injurer) would respond by slowing down and overinvesting in spark arresters, and still there would be too many fires.

Negligence with Contributory Negligence

Under this rule the injurer is liable if he or she is negligent and the victim is not. Otherwise, the injurer is not liable. This rule is efficient if juries hold both parties to a standard of negligence equivalent to the efficiency standard. The injurer has strong incentives to be efficient, because taking sufficient caution absolves the injurer in all cases. The victim also has incentives to meet the efficiency standard: Nonnegligence automatically shifts liability to the negligent injurer and is cost-minimizing when the injurer is nonnegligent. Hence, this rule leads to efficient levels of caution, namely $\hat{X}$, $\hat{Y}$, and $\hat{P}$ in Figure A.

Strict Liability with Contributory Negligence

Under this rule, the injurer is liable whenever the victim is nonnegligent. The victim therefore has incentives to shift liability to the injurer by being nonnegligent; the injurer minimizes costs by being nonnegligent. This rule achieves the efficient combination of precaution, $\hat{X}$ and $\hat{Y}$, and hence the optimum probability of accident avoidance, $\hat{P}$.

It is important to note that the increase in accidents under inefficient tort rules generally causes prices to rise. The prices of the victim's goods increase (in our example, due to a reduction in the supply of flax), as do the prices of the injurer's goods (due to increased costs resulting from traveling too slowly and resulting from the flax farmer's failure to coordinate accident prevention). Society has a stake in the efficiency of liability rules for accidents, because the results of liability cases are incorporated into market prices and living standards.

3. Strict liability with contributory negligence.

To analyze the efficiency of these rules, we will use the example of a train traveling through a flax field, which was introduced in Applied Micro Theory 5.2. Our underlying assumption is that all parties to an accident—the injurer and the victim—know that, should an accident occur, a judge will instruct the jury to apply the given rule and will provide the jury with a standard of precaution.

Strict Liability

Under the rule of strict liability, the injurer is always liable to the victim for damages. The victim will underproduce caution, forcing the injurer to operate on the inefficient cost curve, SMC, in Figure B. This course of action results in too low a probability of accident avoidance, $\tilde{P}$, hence too many accidents and too great an effort by the injurer to prevent accidents.

In the railroad example, the farmer (victim) would grow crops too close to the tracks, the train

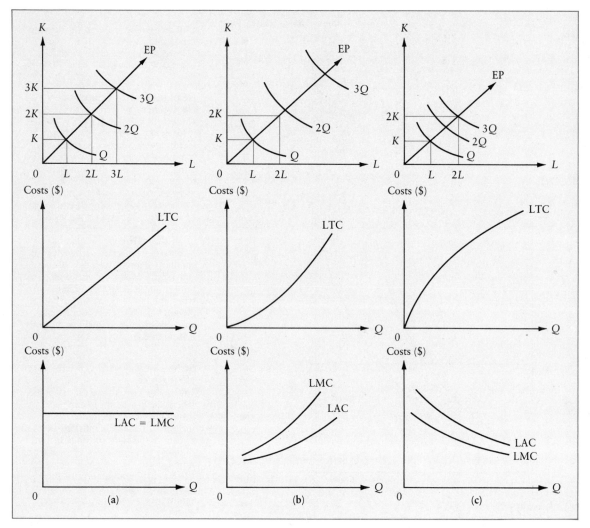

Figure 6.20
Returns to Scale and Cost Curves

(a) For a constant-returns-to-scale production function, the LTC curve is linear and LAC = LMC (constant). (b) For decreasing returns to scale, the LTC rises at an increasing rate, LMC > LAC, and the LAC rises. (c) For increasing returns to scale, the LTC rises at a decreasing rate, LMC < LAC, and the LAC falls.

Figure 6.20 illustrates these relationships with three isoquant maps, each of which is assumed to have a linear expansion path. Movement along a linear expansion path means that labor and capital are being changed proportionately. You may recall from Chapter 5 that this is the method used to investigate returns to scale.

The top panel in Figure 6.20a illustrates a constant-returns-to-scale production function. Increases in inputs yield exactly proportionate increases in output: Output Q requires L labor and K capital, output 2Q requires 2L labor and 2K capital, and so forth. With input prices constant, the EP curve rises at a constant rate. The marginal cost of producing an additional unit of output is always the same under these conditions. The resulting linear LTC, and horizontal LAC and LMC curves are shown in the middle and lower panels of Figure 6.20a.

Figure 6.20*b* depicts a decreasing-returns-to-scale production function. Increases in inputs yield less-than-proportionate increases in output. Accordingly, the LTC curve rises at an increasing rate (the middle panel); the corresponding LAC and LMC curves are shown in the lower panel.

Increasing returns to scale is illustrated in Figure 6.20*c*. Be certain you understand the generation of the corresponding LTC, LAC, and LMC curves.

Of course, a single production function may indicate constant, increasing, or decreasing returns to scale in different ranges of production. If increasing returns to scale occur for small output levels and decreasing returns to scale appear for larger outputs, the resulting LTC curve will look very much like the short-run curves. But be sure you see the driving forces behind the two curves: Increasing and eventually diminishing returns in the presence of capital fixity underlie the short-run TC curve; the various returns to scale when all factors are variable underlie the LTC curve. Short-run diminishing returns occur so universally that the phenomenon has nearly approached the status of a "law." In contrast, no such generality occurs in the case of long-run returns to scale, which must be analyzed empirically.

Summary

We should not leave this chapter without reviewing some important cautions about production-cost analysis. First, there is an apparent similarity between isoquant analysis in production-cost theory and indifference analysis in consumer theory. Economists say "apparent" similarity because the differences are subtle. Yet they are important. The mechanics of the two approaches are very similar in the definition and interpretation of slopes, tangency conditions, optimization conditions, and so forth. Both sets of tools emphasize the importance of substitution in economics and develop the important concept of constrained optimization. Let's examine the differences.

Indifference curves require ordinal measurement, whereas isoquants can be measured cardinally with sufficient engineering information. A more important difference is one you may already have discovered when, to your infinite relief, you did not find a discussion of income and substitution effects in this chapter. The reason that price changes in production factors are not divided into substitution and income (or more properly, expenditure) effects has to do with the difference in the constraints faced by the firm and the consumer: The consumer faces a budget constraint, but the firm can adjust its expenditures.

Recall from the discussion of a wage-rate increase accompanying Figure 6.18 that we did not analyze the move from output Q_0 at point A to Q_1 at point B in response to an increase in wages. Technically, we could have parceled out the total effect of the wage increase between substitution and income effect, as we did in the chapters on consumer theory. But we didn't even analyze the move to a lower isoquant,

Key Terms

accounting cost 148
average fixed cost (AFC) 152
average tax rate 159
average total cost (ATC) 153
average variable cost (AVC) 151
Averch-Johnson effect 173
economic cost 148
entrepreneurial opportunity cost 148
expansion path (EP) 169
implicit rental rate of capital (rental rate of capital) 149
isocost line 165
long-run average cost (LAC) 162
long-run marginal cost (LMC) 164
long-run total cost (LTC) 162
marginal tax rate 159
producer optimization 168
rate-of-return regulation 173
scales of plant 161
short-run marginal cost (SMC) 155
short-run total cost (TC) 151
sunk cost 148
total fixed cost (TFC) 150
total variable cost (TVC) 150
Viner-Wong envelope curve 162

because cost analysis alone is insufficient to tell us anything about the firm's optimal output level.

The firm's optimization process with regard to cost is to produce a given output at least cost or, what amounts to the same thing, to achieve a maximum output for a given cost outlay. Thus when factor prices change, the firm is free to let its isocost line jump around a bit in order to measure the least cost associated with the production of a given output.

The problem is that what we have called producer optimization is only a first step to full optimization. We cannot tell from the firm's least-cost optimization procedure outline here which of the infinite levels of output it will choose to produce. This output decision is the result of the firm's final optimization decision and involves considerations of profit maximization. Production and cost analysis merely establishes two prior optimization conditions: (1) The production function must be optimized in the sense that the maximum rate of output is obtained from a given combination of inputs, and (2) the cost function must be optimized in the sense that each point on the total cost curves (long- and short-run) must represent the minimum total cost of producing a given output.

In short, everything in Chapters 5 and 6 pertains to deriving points on the cost curves. Because income and substitution effects do not help us derive cost curves, they are excess baggage in production-cost analysis.

It is difficult to overstate the importance of the production-cost analysis you have just completed. Market analysis involves the study of the supply and demand for goods and services. As you will soon see, production and cost underpin the supply of final goods as well as the demand for factors of production. You should gain a growing respect for the importance and power of these cost concepts as they are integrated into the theory and application of firm behavior.

Three related sets of tools have emerged in Chapters 5 and 6: Total product curves, isoquants-isocosts, and cost curves. This chapter has shown that cost curves may be generated either from the short-run total product curves or from the isoquant-isocost apparatus. There are good reasons for this dual approach. First, you will find that different authors have their own preferences, and you should be acquainted with both sets of language. But more important is the different emphasis these approaches lend to problem solving. Total product curves and isoquants stress the firm's technology and efficient input combinations. Cost curves, on the other hand, focus attention on output-supply decisions. For these reasons, both techniques are useful analytical tools for organizing decisions. A solid foundation in production-cost analysis, perhaps painfully achieved, can aid you time and again in solving economic problems.

Problems

1. Why can't we tell the shape of the long-run average cost curve from the law of diminishing returns? We can for the short run average cost curve.

2. Consider a U-shaped long-run average cost curve. What does such a curve imply about the isoquant map?

3. a. Assume a U-shaped LAC curve. At what level of output would a firm choose a scale of plant that is (1) underutilized; (2) overutilized; (3) properly utilized?
   b. How would you define "properly utilized"?
   c. Assuming a horizontal LAC curve, at what level of output would a firm choose a scale of plant that is (1) underutilized; (2) overutilized; (3) properly utilized?
   d. What does a horizontal LAC curve imply about the isoquant map?

4. Explain the relationship among ATC, SMC, LAC, and LMC at a given level of output.

5. a. What is the average cost of trips across a bridge? What is the marginal cost?
   b. What is the average cost of jogging through a park? What is the marginal cost? Does it matter which park?
   c. What is the shape of the marginal cost curve as a function of total output and as a function of the rate of output? (Hint: Does production and cost theory make any sense if output is not measured in flow terms?)

6. a. Show that, as prices of inputs rise, the LMC and LAC curves shift upward proportionally but not in parallel fashion.
   b. Show that this response from LMC and LAC curves means that the penalty for choosing the wrong scale of plant for a given rate of output is more severe the higher factor prices are.

7. Suppose you are the owner of a firm producing jelly beans at the average costs per box indicated in Table 6.1. Initially you produce 200 boxes of jelly beans per time period. Then the President calls you long distance and places an order for a box, requiring you to increase your output to 201 boxes. He offers you $350 for the box. Should you produce it?

8. Let Q = units of output, L = units of labor, w = wage rate per worker per time period = $1, TFC = $10. Capital is fixed. Using these data, fill in the blank spaces in Table 6.2. Check for the following properties: (1) U-shaped average and marginal cost

Table 6.1
Jelly Bean Production

Units of Output	Average Cost
200	$200
201	201
202	202

Table 6.2
Computing Costs

Output (Q)	Labor (L)	TVC	TFC	TC	AVC	ATC	SMC
1	11						
2	19						
3	24						
4	32						
5	46						
6	64						
7	88						
8	119						
9	158						
10	206						

curves; (2) an SMC curve that intersects both the AVC and ATC curves from below at their minimum points; (3) an AVC that attains a minimum at a smaller level of output than the ATC. (Hint: Some of these conditions will be satisfied only approximately due to the discrete nature of the data.)

9. Prove that a constant average tax rate beyond some income level Y_1 requires either no deductible or a regressive marginal tax rate.

10. This chapter defines an average tax rate, t_a, and a marginal tax rate, t_m.
    a. Use these terms to define a progressive income tax structure.
    b. If t_m is positive but diminishing, will extra taxable income result in a lower total tax liability? A lower average tax rate? A regressive tax structure?

11. Show graphically that lower-income groups pay a higher average tax rate on the same income if they have fewer exemptions and deductibles.

12. Prove that a *ceteris paribus* doubling of the wage rate
    a. Shifts the AVC curve upward proportionally and not in parallel fashion.
    b. Does not change the rate of output at which the AVC is minimized.
    c. Shifts the ATC upward and causes it to achieve its minimum at a larger rate of output.
    d. Shifts the SMC upward.

13. Prove that a *ceteris paribus* doubling of the implicit rental rate of capital
    a. Does not shift the AVC or SMC curves.
    b. Shifts the ATC curve upward and increases the rate of output for which the ATC is minimized.

14. Derive the short-run TVC, TC, AVC, ATC, and MC curves under these assumptions:
    a. Production exhibits a constant marginal productivity of labor.
    b. Production exhibits a diminishing marginal productivity of labor.
    c. Production exhibits an increasing marginal productivity of labor.
    d. All costs are fixed.
    e. All costs are variable.

Suggested Readings

Brumberg, Richard E. "Ceteris Paribus for Supply Curves." *Economic Journal* 63 (1953): 462–467.

Friedman, Milton. *Price Theory: A Provisional Text*. Chicago: Aldine, 1963, chaps. 5, 6.

Stigler, George. *The Theory of Price*. New York: Macmillan, 1966, chaps. 6, 7, 8, 9.

Viner, Jacob. "Cost Curves and Supply Curves." *Zeitschrift für Nationalökonomie* 3 (1931): 23–46.

Walters, A. A. "Production and Cost Functions." *Econometrica* 31 (1963): 1–66.

Competition

In Chapters 5 and 6 we saw that the firm's costs are rooted in its production technology. Those chapters distinguished between short- and long-run production adjustments, showed the relationship between the short- and long-run cost curves, and described the theoretical apparatus by which firms choose the optimal combination of labor and capital inputs in the production of a given quantity of output.

Production-cost analysis is the first step in understanding the economic behavior of firms. A firm is an institution that combines inputs to produce final output and sells that output to consumers. Raw materials do not spontaneously combine to produce the great variety of outputs that consumers desire, and consumers cannot economically produce for themselves all the goods they actually consume. Thus the firm acts as an intermediary between consumers and raw materials. Firms also play an important role in capturing the efficiencies that result from specialization and division of tasks; these efficiencies would be lost if all consumers were self-sufficient.

It is important to distinguish between the words *firm* and *plant*. A firm is a decisionmaker that stands to win or lose from the consequences of its economic decisions. The firm is the entrepreneur that takes the financial risks inherent in production and sales in return for the expectation of profit—the residual of revenues over costs. In contrast, the plant is the place of production and sales of the firm's output. A plant is a factor of production that combines with all other factors in the production and sale of goods and services. A firm may have many plants, a few, or perhaps only one. Plants may have differing sizes and productivities. These plant decisions are some of the many decisions the entrepreneur must make.

This chapter is principally concerned with the following three decisions of firms: (1) the level of output that maximizes profits in the short run (capital stock fixed), (2) the level of output that maximizes profits in the long run (capital stock variable), and (3) the decision to enter or exit an industry. We will concentrate on competitive firms—to be defined shortly—and study the price and output of both the competitive firm and the industry to which it belongs.

A full understanding of competitive equilibrium requires a careful definition of the terms *cost* and *profit*. **Profit (π)**, the central focus of this chapter, is the difference between total revenue and total cost.[1] In other words,

$$\pi = \text{TR} - \text{TC} \tag{7.1}$$

Total revenue, a concept discussed in the demand chapters, is merely price times quantity; it is easily handled in modeling the competitive firm. Total cost is the subject we began to study in Chapter 6. To evaluate the firm's profit, can't we just perform the algebraic subtraction called for in Equation 7.1 and call it a day? No, we cannot, and here's the reason. The costs defined in Chapter 6 are only the costs of acquiring the variable and fixed resources. But if entrepreneurs have valuable alternatives to their present occupations, the highest-valued forgone alternative is also a cost of producing in their current industries. This alternative cost is what economists call *entrepreneurial opportunity cost*. Failure to include all production costs—resource costs and entrepreneurial opportunity costs—introduces error in the calculation of economic profit, flaws internal management decisionmaking, and more important to us, limits our understanding of the economic consequences of firm behavior, particularly the decision to enter or leave an industry.

Perfect Competition versus Pure Competition

This chapter is about competitive firms and industries. In a competitive industry, each firm's output is so small relative to the industry output that the firm cannot affect industry price by expansion or contraction of its own output. For example, say there are 1000 firms in a competitive industry, each producing 1000 units of output. Each firm contributes a share of the total industry output equal to 1/1000, or 0.001. If one firm increases its output by 10 percent, to 1100 units, a large expansion for that one firm, it increases its share of the total industry output to only 0.0011. Such a miniscule increase does not noticeably change the location of the industry supply and demand curves, the intersection of which determines price. Accordingly, the competitive firm is a **price taker;** it cannot affect the market price of its output. Competitive price is set at the industry level, and each firm takes price as a parameter. Price-taking behavior is often called **parametric pricing.**

1. An immigrant businessman was visited one Christmas by his oldest son, an accountant. The son noticed that his father's accounts receivable were placed in a shoebox under the counter, that cash went into his father's pockets, that bills were paid haphazardly, and that there was no inventory control, no double-entry accounting, not even a systematic way of filling out the bank deposit slip. The son criticized his father's management techniques and asked whether he even knew if he was making a profit. The father answered in broken English: "Son, when I came to this country, all I had was the pants I wore off the boat. Now I have a home that's paid for, three children graduated from college, a summer cottage, two cars, and a fat bank account. Take all that and subtract the pants, and that's my profit." In this chapter we move toward a more precise, if less charming, definition of profit.

Competitive equilibrium involves the decentralized coordination of many firms and consumers and can be very hard to explain. In order to facilitate the exposition of competition, many authors over the years have presented a paradigm case called **perfect competition**. Starting from the assumption of parametric pricing, perfect competition further assumes that all firms are identical in all dimensions, including production functions and technologies, costs, management skills, location, and entrepreneurial opportunities. In addition, resources are assumed to be freely mobile in the economy, which permits identical firms to freely enter and exit the industry. The paradigm model of perfect competition is a fruitful method for exploring many important short-run and long-run aspects of the competitive mechanism. It is the model employed in this chapter.

As useful as the model of perfect competition is, excessive concentration on it has led to confusion about several aspects of competition, including the definition and economic significance of profit, the question of how output is distributed to the factors of production in competitive markets, the entry and exit decision, and how such a simplistic theory can guide the decisions of real firms and government policymakers. **Pure competition** is a less restrictive model; the only assumptions retained from perfect competition are parametric pricing and free entry and exit. This definition of pure competition corresponds to that of Paul Samuelson.[2] In pure competition, firms are allowed to differ in entrepreneurial skills and opportunities, location, production techniques, and the like. Thus pure competition emphasizes parametric pricing without requiring firms to be identical in anything except price. Parametric pricing is the key to pure competition and the key to applying its concepts to the real world of nonidentical firms.

This chapter is confined to the paradigm case of perfect competition (identical firms and parametric pricing). Chapter 8 extends the analysis to pure competition (nonidentical firms and parametric pricing). There is much to be gained by studying both models, because there is a lesson to be learned from each. Nevertheless, the key to each model is parametric pricing.

The Competitive Firm's Revenue Curves

The competitive firm's revenue curves reflect the fact that every competitive firm is a price taker. Each firm accepts industry price as a parameter and adjusts its output accordingly. Price-taking behavior by competitive firms results in a linear **total revenue curve** and a perfectly elastic demand curve at the price set at the industry level. Figure 7.1 illustrates these revenue curves. In panel c, the industry supply and demand curves set the equilibrium price P_1. The demand curve that the firm faces is the horizontal, perfectly elastic curve in

2. Paul A. Samuelson, *Foundations of Economic Analysis* (New York: Atheneum, 1965), p. 82.

Figure 7.1
Revenue Curves in Competition

(a) In competition, total revenue is linear. (b) The horizontal price line is the firm's MR and AR curve. (c) Price is set at P_1 by market forces.

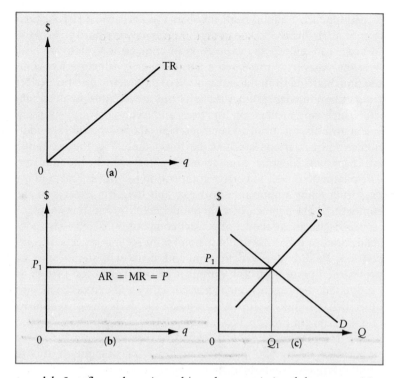

panel b. It reflects the price-taking characteristic of the competitive firm. The firm can sell as much output as it wishes without affecting industry price P_1. If the firm raises its price above P_1, it will lose all its customers (they can buy elsewhere). There is no need to lower its price below P_1 because the firm can sell all its relatively small output at the industry price P_1. Thus the competitive firm faces the infinitely elastic (horizontal) demand curve at height P_1. Price is fixed for the firm, so each unit sold adds a constant amount to the firm's total revenue. The total revenue curve (TR) is linear, as depicted in panel a.

Revenue curves obey the arithmetic rules that govern the total-marginal-average relationships. Total revenue is price times quantity, or TR = $P \cdot q$.[3] You may recall from Chapter 3 that marginal revenue is the change in total revenue resulting from a change in output sold. Marginal revenue may be written as

$$MR = \frac{\Delta TR}{\Delta q} = P + q \frac{\Delta P}{\Delta q} \qquad (7.2)$$

Equation 7.2 has a straightforward interpretation. Generally, lower prices are necessary to sell more output. Marginal revenue is the sum of the two terms in Equation 7.2. The firm gains an amount of

---

3. The lowercase q denotes the output of any single firm; the uppercase Q represents industry output.

revenue equal to the price of the last (marginal) unit sold. This is the first term, P. The firm loses an amount of revenue equal to the price reduction on all inframarginal units of output that previously sold at higher prices. This is the second term $q \cdot (\Delta P / \Delta q)$. Recall that $\Delta P / \Delta q$ is the slope of the demand curve; to sell more output requires a movement down a demand curve, which in turn requires a reduction in the price of inframarginal units that previously sold for a higher price. Marginal revenue is the algebraic sum of these two effects: the price of the marginal unit sold less the price reduction on inframarginal units.

In competition, we make the special assumption that the firm is a price taker and accordingly need not reduce price to sell additional units of output. This is the meaning of the perfectly elastic demand curve the firm faces, for which the slope $\Delta P / \Delta q$ is zero. Thus marginal revenue for the competitive firm contains only the first term in Equation 7.2, or

$$\text{MR} = \frac{\Delta \text{TR}}{\Delta q} = P \qquad (7.3)$$

For the competitive firm, marginal revenue equals price, which is set by industry supply and demand curves and is a parameter to the firm. In such circumstances, the total revenue curve is linear, and its slope equals price.

We can define the firm's **average revenue (AR)** as

$$\text{AR} \equiv \frac{\text{TR}}{q} \equiv \frac{P \cdot q}{q} \equiv P \qquad (7.4)$$

Average revenue is identically equal to price. Thus the competitive firm faces a perfectly elastic demand curve, the value of which equals marginal revenue, average revenue, and price.

With the revenue curves in hand, we are prepared to combine the costs and revenues of a competitive firm to study profit-maximizing conditions and their implications for short- and long-run competitive equilibrium.

Short-Run Competitive Equilibrium

To proceed in an orderly fashion, we must begin our analysis of perfect competition by assuming that firms' owners are useless in any other economic activity. Because the entrepreneurial opportunity cost of production in their present occupations is therefore zero, the only costs these firms incur are the labor and capital costs studied in Chapter 6. This naive assumption provides an "engine" for investigating the rudiments of short-run competitive behavior. Later, we can add entrepreneurial opportunity cost to our analysis of the firm's entry/exit decision.

Figure 7.2
Costs, Revenues, and Profit

(a) This firm's total revenue and total cost curves show that it is a price taker. (b) Profit is the vertical distance between TR and TC at each output. (c) Combining the data in panels *a* and *b* with these average and marginal costs and revenues, we can clearly see that profit maximization occurs at output q_3.

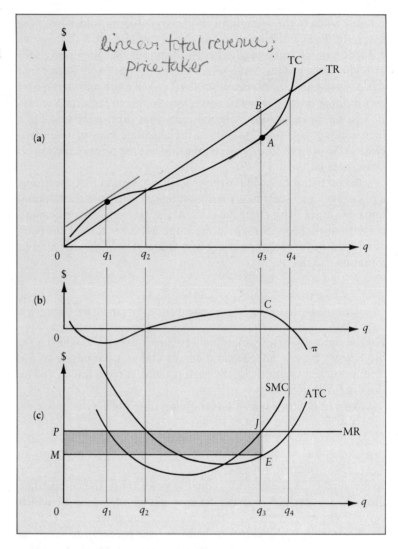

Short-Run Profit Maximization

Figure 7.2 shows the revenue, cost, and profit curves of one of many identical firms in a competitive industry. In panel *a*, the linear total revenue curve tells us that the firm is a price taker. Profit is defined as the residual of revenues over costs, or

$$\pi = TR - TC \qquad (7.5)$$

Profit may be positive, negative, or zero and is represented in Figure 7.2*a* by the vertical distance between the total revenue and total cost curves. This vertical distance is maximized by producing output q_3. The profit residual *AB* is the largest available to the firm, given its cost and revenue constraints.

Figure 7.2*b* explicitly shows the firm's **total profit curve.** Each point on the total profit curve is plotted at a height equal to the difference between total revenue and total cost. Thus, profit is zero at q_2 and q_4, where total revenue equals total cost. The total profit curve reaches its maximum at output q_3: The maximum profit AB in panel *a* equals q_3C in panel *b*.

The profit-maximizing condition is easily stated in language that incorporates the marginal concepts defined previously. Profits rise whenever the production of an extra unit of output adds more to revenue than it adds to cost. In other words, profits rise when MR > SMC. Conversely, profits fall when additional output adds more to costs than to revenue, that is, when SMC > MR. Therefore, the profit-maximizing rule is to continue production until the marginal revenue and marginal cost are equal, or

$$MR = SMC \qquad (7.6)$$

This is the short-run profit-maximizing condition. Because every marginal magnitude equals the slope of its respective total curve, the slope of the TR curve is the MR value and the slope of the TC curve is the SMC value. Therefore, marginal cost equals marginal revenue at output q_3 in Figure 7.2. (The slope of the TR curve at B in Figure 7.2*a* is equal to the slope of the TC curve at A.) If the firm lowers output to, say, q_2, profit falls, because MR > SMC at q_2: The firm is not fully exploiting its profit potential. Conversely, if the firm tries to increase profit by increasing output to q_4, it will fail because excessive production has caused marginal cost to rise above marginal revenue. Profits are at a maximum only when marginal revenue equals marginal cost, which occurs only at output q_3 in Figure 7.2. The total profit curve in panel *b* confirms the fact that q_3 is the profit-maximizing rate of output.

The short-run profit-maximizing condition, MR = SMC, appears more explicitly in Figure 7.2*c*. The firm equates marginal revenue and marginal cost at point J by producing output q_3. Total profit can be illustrated using the average cost curve. The average total cost at q_3 equals q_3E and is transformed into total cost as follows:

$$TC = ATC \cdot q = q_3E \cdot Oq_3 = OMEq_3 \qquad (7.7)$$

Similarly,

$$TR = AR \cdot q = q_3J \cdot Oq_3 = OPJq_3 \qquad (7.8)$$

Also,

$$\pi = TR - TC = OPJq_3 - OMEq_3 = MPJE \qquad (7.9)$$

Figure 7.3
Short-Run Loss Minimization

A firm should produce at a loss in the short run when ATC > P ≥ AVC. The loss is P_1BMJ, which is less than the total fixed cost $ABML$, the loss from shutting down.

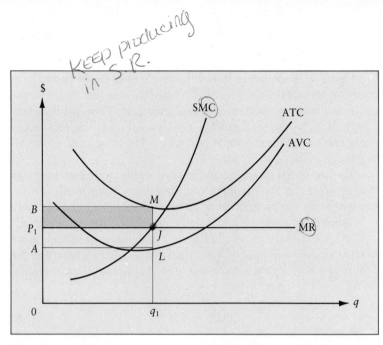

[Handwritten annotations:]

KEEP producing in S.R.

price (everywhere) below ATC (P is too low)

— negative profits
Total fixed cost = ABML

which is greater than the loss incurred by producing q₁

~ incurs smaller loss by producing than by completely shutting down

MR = SMC for loss too. provided the firm decides to stay in business in the SR

The total profit, *MPJE*, is depicted as the shaded rectangular area in Figure 7.2c. The vertical distances AB in panel a and q_3C in panel b are the equivalents of the profit area $MPJE$ in panel c.[4]

There is one qualification to the short-run profit-maximizing rule, MR = SMC. Note that the rule is satisfied at two levels of output in Figure 7.2: q_1 and q_3. But at q_3, P < ATC; hence a loss is incurred. The firm should therefore expand output to q_3. The marginal cost curve must cut the marginal revenue curve from below, as at point J.

Short-Run Loss Minimization and the Shutdown Decision

A competitive firm's short-run cost and revenue curves are depicted in Figure 7.3. Marginal revenue equals short-run marginal cost at point J. However, the price is too low to permit positive profits because it is everywhere below average total cost (ATC). By equating marginal revenue and marginal cost, the firm incurs negative profits equal to P_1BMJ, the shaded area. Is there any other output level that would make the firm's losses smaller than P_1BMJ? No. If the firm produces at all, it should produce q_1; losses get larger with any other output owing to the same logic described for positive profits. For example, if the firm produces one less unit, marginal cost is less than marginal revenue: The firm gives up more revenue (MR) than it saves in costs (SMC), and its loss will be larger. Thus the profit-maximizing rule MR = SMC, where the marginal cost curve cuts the marginal revenue curve from below, is also the rule for **loss minimization**, providing the firm decides to stay in business in the short run.

4. Remember that vertical distances in a graph with totals measured on the ordinate translate into areas on graphs with averages measured on the ordinate.

Shut down (handwritten)

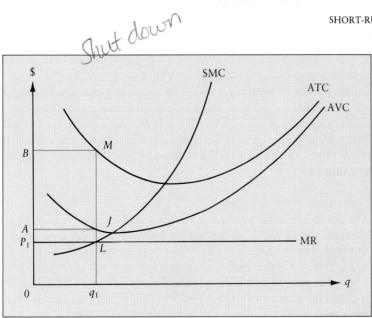

Figure 7.4
Short-Run Loss Minimization

This firm should shut down in the short run, because P < AVC. The loss is P_1BML if the firm operates but only $ABMJ$ if it shuts down.

Price lower than AVC ∴ Shutdown (handwritten)

But the firm in Figure 7.3 is incurring a loss, so should it not shut down? Not necessarily. This decision must be made by comparing the loss incurred at output q_1 with the loss that would be incurred at zero output. If the firm shuts down, it eliminates its sales revenues as well as its total variable costs. Accordingly, its total loss will be the fixed cost. In Figure 7.3, the total fixed cost is $ABML$, which is greater than the loss incurred by producing q_1 units of output, P_1BMJ. Thus the firm incurs a smaller loss by producing q_1 units than by completely shutting down.

We must conclude that a firm producing at a loss should continue to do so in the short run if price exceeds average variable cost. If $P > AVC$, as in Figure 7.3, then TR > TVC. Total revenue is sufficient to pay all variable costs $OALq_1$ and to pay AP_1JL toward the fixed costs of $ABML$. Only if total revenue exceeds total variable cost can losses be minimized by continued production.

firm producing at a loss should continue to do so in the S.R. if price exceeds AVC (handwritten)

Consider Figure 7.4, where price is below the average variable cost. If the firm selects output q_1 by equating MR and SMC at point L, it incurs a loss (P_1BML) greater than the fixed cost ($ABMJ$). This firm should shut down in the short run, because its total revenue does not pay the total variable cost. A firm need never lose more than its fixed costs.

This discussion of the shutdown decision applies strictly to the short run, in which the firm has fixed costs that must be paid even if the firm stops operating. Naturally, a firm that is forced to operate at a loss to minimize short-run losses will make every effort to eliminate the fixed costs. This may require renegotiating leases, paying off bank loans, selling or depreciating capital equipment, or even initiating bankruptcy proceedings. But these are long-run adjustments. As long as firms have fixed-cost obligations, operating at a loss is cost-minimizing when TR ≥ TVC.

S.R → firm has fixed costs that must be paid even if the firm stops operating (handwritten)

As long as firms have fixed-cost obligations, operating @ a loss is cost-minimizing when TR≥TVC (handwritten)

A complete statement of the firm's short-run profit-maximizing and loss-minimizing conditions may now be given: The firm maximizes profits or minimizes losses by producing the rate of output for which MR = SMC if the SMC curve intersects the MR curve from below and if TR ≥ TVC. If the SMC curve intersects the MR curve from above, profits are minimized instead of maximized. If TR < TVC, the firm should shut down. These statements make up the **shutdown rule.**

Short-Run Firm Supply

The short-run rule outlined in the previous section permits us to generate the firm's short-run supply curve. Figure 7.5 displays the firm's short-run cost curves and four possible prices, $P_4 > P_3 > P_2 > P_1$. Price P_1 is the lowest price that brings forth any output; for any lower price, TR < TVC and the firm shuts down. Thus price P_1 is called the **shutdown price.** Similarly, point A, the minimum average variable cost, is referred to as the **shutdown point.** At the shutdown point, the firm can either shut down or produce because the loss will equal the total fixed cost for either decision. For any price less than P_1, it will surely shut down, and for any price greater than P_1, it will produce. If price is P_2, the firm produces q_2 units of output

Figure 7.5
The Firm's Short-Run Supply Curve

The short-run supply curve is the SMC curve above point A, which is the minimum AVC. For $P < P_1$, the firm closes. For $P > P_1$, the firm produces where P = SMC.

P_1 = Shutdown price

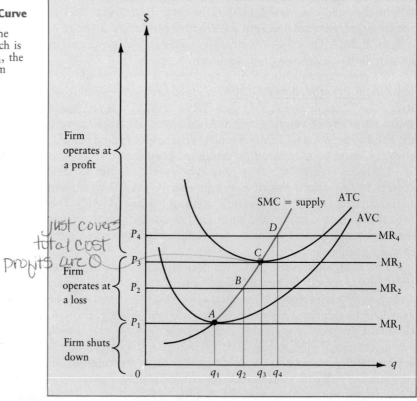

and incurs a loss. When price is P_3, total revenue just covers total cost at output q_3, and profits are zero. (This last sentence will be clarified several times in this chapter.) Any price greater than P_3, such as P_4, where the firm produces q_4 units of output, yields positive profits.

Points A, B, C, and D on the marginal cost curve in Figure 7.5 are derived from profit-maximizing rules and represent the amounts of output that the firm wants to sell at various prices, for given input prices, capital inputs, and technology. In other words, the short-run marginal cost curve above the minimum average variable cost is the firm's **short-run supply curve.** The portion of the marginal cost curve below the shutdown point, drawn in black in Figure 7.5, does not establish supply points, because output is zero for any price less than the minimum average variable cost. The upward-sloping short-run supply curve, developed intuitively in Chapter 2, is now revealed to be the result of profit-maximizing decisions of firms facing diminishing marginal returns in production.

The Inefficiency of Stage I Production

APPLIED MICRO THEORY

7.1

Chapter 5 shows intuitively that firms will not operate in production stage I. We can now prove this assertion. Stage I is the region of rising average product of labor, diagrammed in the adjacent figure. We know from production-cost duality that AP_L and AVC are related as follows:

$$AVC = \frac{w}{AP_L}$$

Thus when AP_L is at a maximum, as it is at the beginning of stage II, the AVC curve is at a minimum. For the firm to produce, price must equal or exceed the average variable cost; otherwise the firm will shut down. Notice in the figure that no output below Q_0 will be produced, because price is wholly below the AVC for these outputs. *Stage I corresponds to the shutdown region.* Thus the conclusion that competitive firms will not operate in stage I follows directly from the loss-minimizing behavior of firms. Producing in stage I violates the shutdown rule.

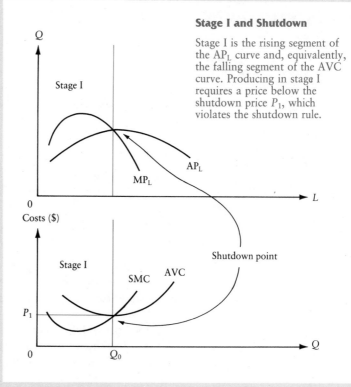

Stage I and Shutdown

Stage I is the rising segment of the AP_L curve and, equivalently, the falling segment of the AVC curve. Producing in stage I requires a price below the shutdown price P_1, which violates the shutdown rule.

Shutdown and Labor Fringe Benefits

APPLIED
MICRO
THEORY

7.2

Payments for labor are seldom as simple as a straight hourly wage. Typically, payments include a fringe benefit package with such items as contributions to unemployment insurance, various forms of insurance coverage, and free parking privileges.* Many

Earl Dotter / American Labor

of these benefits are negotiated so that the employer has a continuing obligation to pay them even if the plant shuts down—at least for a time. Therefore, such payments tend to shift the cost structure in favor of keeping the plant open,

*Total fringe benefits rose dramatically from 17.8% of total compensation in 1959 to 27.2% in 1977. The portion of fringe benefits that represents relatively fixed costs—life, accident, and health insurance and pension contributions— rose from 5.1% to 9.4%. See U.S. Chamber of Commerce, "Data for All Employees in Larger Manufacturing Firms," *Fringe Benefits and Employee Benefits*, 1959, 1977.

Fringe Benefits and Shutdown

If the fixed-cost components of fringe benefits rise by the same amount that wage payments fall, the AVC curve shifts downward, lowering the shutdown point from A to B. Labor's risk of layoff is thereby reduced.

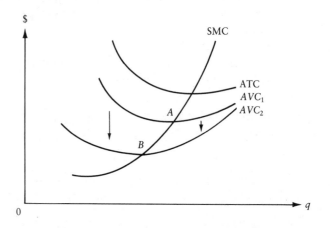

because these components of workers' compensation are fixed costs to the firm.

The accompanying figure illustrates. Suppose initially that the firm's average variable costs are AVC_1. If labor succeeds in negotiating a compensation package that reduces wage payments and increases the fixed-cost forms of fringe benefits by the same amount, AVC_1 will fall to AVC_2;

the ATC curve will be stationary. The firm's total costs are the same, but the shutdown point has fallen from A to B. Hence, workers have a vested interest in receiving part of their compensation in fringe benefits. There are, of course, obvious income tax advantages. But in addition, the more fixed labor costs there are, the lower the shutdown point and the lower labor's risk of layoff.

Short-Run Industry Supply

We have seen that the firm's short-run supply curve is the portion of its short-run marginal cost curve above the minimum average variable cost. The industry **short-run supply curve** might be thought of as the horizontal sum of such firm supply curves, $\Sigma_h \text{SMC}$, just as industry demand is the horizontal sum of individual demand curves. However, as price rises and all firms expand their output by obtaining additional variable factors of production, the combined expansion of industry output could put upward pressure on the prices of

[handwritten margin note:] Short R. Supply curve horizontal Summation

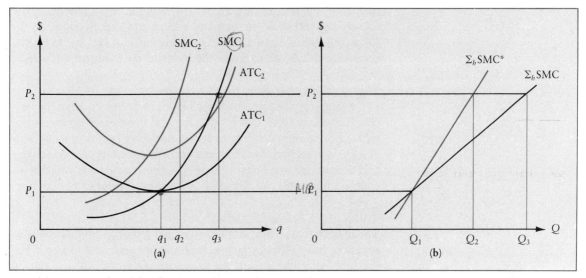

Figure 7.6
The Short-Run Industry Supply Curve

variable inputs. If so, the firm's average and marginal cost curves shift upward, and each firm expands output by less than the amount suggested by the original marginal cost.

Figure 7.6 shows this effect. The rise in price from P_1 to P_2 causes the firm (panel a) to increase output from q_1 to q_3, a movement along SMC_1. This output adjustment occurs as long as the wage rate is fixed. The curve $\Sigma_h SMC$ (panel b) is the horizontal summation of all firms' output responses when the wage is constant. For price P_1, industry supply is Q_1, and for price P_2, it rises to Q_3. If wages do not change as a result of industrywide expansion, then the curve $\Sigma_h SMC$ is the correct short-run industry supply curve.

However, if the simultaneous expansion of output by all firms bids up the price of labor, the ATC and SMC curves shift upward, as illustrated by the colored curves ATC_2 and SMC_2. Each firm produces only q_2 when price is P_2, rather than q_3, the amount that each firm would have produced if wages hadn't risen. The firm's output expands only to q_2 when price rises to P_2 because output is set by the new curve, SMC_2, once wages have risen. These smaller increases in firm output sum to an output of only Q_2 at the industry level. Thus the curve $\Sigma_h SMC^*$ is the industry short-run supply curve when the horizontal summation of firms' supply curves is corrected for the effect of factor price increases. The $\Sigma_h SMC^*$ curve is less price elastic than the uncorrected $\Sigma_h SMC$ curve.

A less likely circumstance is that the industry expansion may cause factor prices to fall, due perhaps to the ability of a larger industry to buy in quantity discounts or to share expensive inputs, thereby acquiring them at lower per-unit cost. If this occurs, the corrected short-run industry supply curve $\Sigma_h SMC^*$ will be more elastic than the horizontal sum of marginal costs. Of course, if the short-run industry expansion of output does not cause input prices

(a) The firm responds to an increase in price with movement along SMC_1.
(b) The industry supply curve ($\Sigma_h SMC^*$) is less elastic than the horizontal sum of firms' supply curves ($\Sigma_h SMC$) if industry expansion increases the wage rate.

to change, the horizontal sum of firm marginal costs, $\Sigma_h SMC$, is the correct derivation of the industry's short-run supply curve. In the following discussions, little if any substance is lost by using the uncorrected $\Sigma_h SMC$ curve as the industry short-run supply curve.

The Firm's Long-Run Supply Adjustments

In the long run, the firm makes two kinds of decisions. First, the firm can vary all its factors of production and thereby adjust its output and factor combinations in order to maximize profits in its present occupation. Second, the firm can choose between its present activity and alternative activities; that is, the firm can decide whether to enter another industry (by exiting the present one) or to stay put.

Choosing a Scale of Plant

The first method a firm can use to adjust long-run production is to select the most efficient factor combinations and scale of plant. For the time being, let's continue to ignore the entry/exit decision by assuming that entrepreneurs are unfit to work in any other activity or industry.

Figure 7.7 exhibits the cost curves associated with two short-run scales of plant: ATC_1 is for capital K_1 and ATC_2 for capital K_2; $K_2 > K_1$. The long-run average cost curve, LAC (The Viner-Wong

Handwritten margin note:
Profit Max
LR.
$P = LMC = SMC_2$

Figure 7.7
Long-Run Profit Maximization

For the scale of plant ATC_1, the firm maximizes short-run profits by producing q_1. In the long run, the scale of plant is increased to ATC_2 and q_2 is produced, where the long-run profit-maximizing condition holds: $P = LMC = SMC_2$.

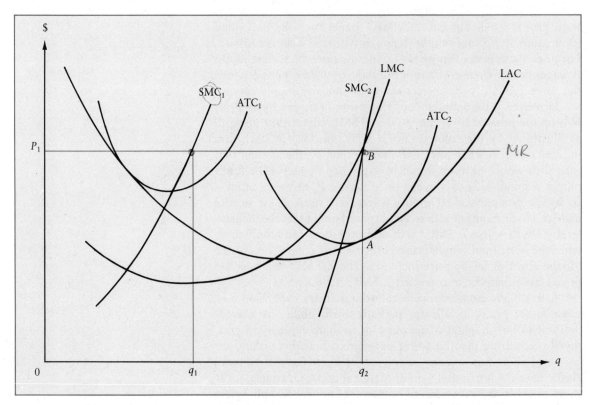

envelope curve), is also presented in Figure 7.7. If the firm has selected the scale of plant K_1 and hence the cost curve ATC_1, it will equate price P_1 and SMC_1, thereby maximizing short-run profits by producing q_1 units of output. The scale of plant is not variable in the short run, so the firm cannot earn higher profits than those resulting from output q_1. Yet long-run profits are not maximized at q_1, because $P_1 > LMC$ at q_1. If P_1 is regarded as permanent, the firm will take steps to enlarge its output to q_2, because $P_1 = LMC$ at q_2. Output q_2 could not be produced with scale of plant K_1 without enormous losses, because it entails excessive congestion of the variable factor on the fixed factor; short-run marginal cost SMC_1 greatly exceeds price at output q_2. However, the firm can move to output q_2 and increase its total profit by adopting a larger quantity of capital; that is, output may be expanded by increasing the use of all inputs, capital and labor. Thus the profit-maximizing long-run adjustment for the firm for any given price is to equate price with long-run marginal cost, as at output q_2. Because long-run profit maximization subsumes short-run optimization for the scale of plant chosen, the profit-maximizing condition for price P_1 in Figure 7.7 is

$$P_1 = LMC = SMC_2 \qquad (7.10)$$

Output q_2 is being produced at lowest unit cost with the scale of plant K_2, as shown by the tangency between ATC_2 and LAC at point A. And $P_1 = LMC$ at q_2, so the firm can make no further profit-increasing adjustment in its factor combinations or its output level.

Point B equates price and long-run marginal cost and tells us how much output the firm will produce at price P_1 when sufficient time is allowed for the firm to exploit all profit possibilities by adjusting its scale of plant as well as its labor. If price rises above P_1, the firm has long-run profit impulses to increase its output further. It can increase output by additional enlargement of its scale of plant, moving further up the stationary LMC curve until the $P = LMC$ condition is restored at the higher price. The firm's **long-run supply curve** is therefore its long-run marginal cost curve above the minimum long-run average cost (LAC). The reason for this qualification will become clear in the next section. For now, note that prices below the minimum long-run average cost will cause negative profits, which will induce the firm to leave the industry, releasing its labor and selling or scrapping its capital. Thus prices below the minimum LAC do not generate long-run supply in the present industry when all adjustments are allowed for.

The Entry/Exit Decision

One of the firm's long-run decisions is selecting a scale of plant. The other long-run decision that firms must make is whether (and when) to enter or exit an industry. The **entry/exit decision** is extremely important from the standpoint of any individual firm and is the driving force in a competitive industry's move toward long-run equilibrium.

In order to streamline the presentation of certain components of perfect competition, this chapter has thus far included only the firm's explicit costs of obtaining resources. But because owners have valuable economic alternatives, staying in a given industry entails opportunity costs. These costs must be taken into account in choosing the most profitable industries to participate in.

THE OWNER'S OPPORTUNITY COST Owners invest funds in their businesses, funds that could have been used elsewhere. The forgone returns on invested capital are an important component of the owner's opportunity cost. When ownership takes the form of holding corporate stock, the opportunity cost is the market rate of return on other financial investments. In addition, however, many owners devote time and energy to the day-to-day operations of their businesses. The forgone value of the time spent running the firm is another component of opportunity cost. Thus **entrepreneurial opportunity cost** equals the forgone value of invested capital as well as the forgone value of the owners' time.

Our graphic model of the firm's costs will be complete once we have added the owner's opportunity cost to the labor and capital costs. Entrepreneurial opportunity cost enters our cost calculations as a fixed cost, because the owner's forgone options in other industries are the same regardless of the firm's rate of production in its present industry.

Figure 7.8 illustrates the effect on short- and long-run cost curves of including the owner's opportunity cost as a component of fixed cost. In both cases, the average cost curves shift upward, just as they would with the addition of any fixed cost. In the short run, depicted in Figure 7.8*a,* a change in a fixed cost does not alter the marginal cost of output expansion. Hence the ATC curve merely slides up along a stationary short-run marginal cost curve. (Remember that fixed costs do not change decisions at the margin.) As for the long run, shown in Figure 7.8*b,* introducing the owner's opportunity cost shifts the LAC upward. The LAC curve is an envelope of all short-run ATC curves. But we now have a new set of ATC curves, each of which has shifted upward. An envelope of these new short-run scales of plant, which include opportunity cost as a fixed cost, can be constructed just as before. The new envelope curve, LAC, lies above the old one and reaches its minimum at a larger level of output. We know this is so because the addition of the fixed cost does not shift the long-run marginal cost curve (LMC). Thus the new envelope curve must slide up the LMC curve, just as the short-run ATC curve slides up the SMC curve when opportunity

Figure 7.8
Entrepreneurial Opportunity Cost

The opportunity cost enters the cost curves as a fixed cost. The ATC and LAC curves shift up, but the SMC and LMC curves do not change when opportunity costs are added. (a) These are short-run costs. (b) Long-run costs are presented in this panel.

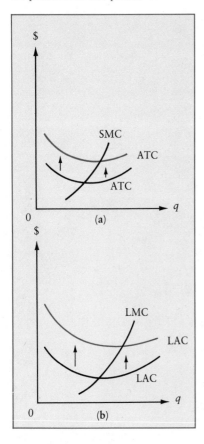

costs are included. It is important to realize that every short-run ATC curve and long-run LAC curve includes the opportunity cost of the owner.

ECONOMIC PROFIT   **Economic profit** is the money that the firm has left over when it uses its revenues to pay all costs, including the owner's opportunity cost.

$$\text{Economic profit} = \qquad\qquad (7.11)$$
$$\text{total revenue} - \text{explicit costs} - \text{entrepreneurial opportunity costs}$$

Economic profit can be positive, negative, or zero, and each of these values carries significance for the entry/exit decision.

To investigate the entry/exit decisions of firms, let's first consider the behavior of one firm in isolation from its industry. Figure 7.9 shows the long-run costs of a competitive, price-taking firm. The short-run average and marginal costs are suppressed to avoid clutter. When price is P_3, the firm maximizes long-run profits by choosing the scale of plant and level of output that equates price and long-run marginal cost. This occurs at output q_3, where $\text{LMC}(q_3) = P_3$. At q_3, $\text{LAC}(q_3) < P_3$. Thus the firm earns positive economic profits, because the difference between total revenue and all the firm's costs, including the owner's opportunity cost, is positive. Positive economic profit means that the owner has net revenue left over after paying explicit and opportunity costs; that is, the owner earns more with his or her resources in this industry than in the best forgone industry. Earnings exceed the owner's opportunity costs when economic profits are positive.

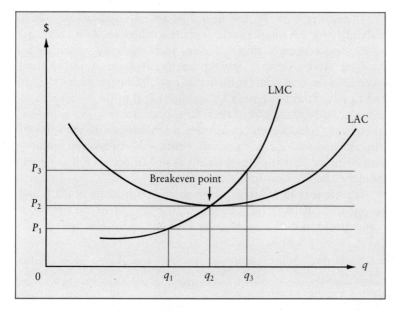

Figure 7.9
The Entry/Exit Decision

If $P > \text{LAC}$, as at q_3, the economic profit is positive and the owner is in the correct industry. If $P = \text{LAC}$, as at q_2, the economic profit is zero and the owner just breaks even by exactly covering opportunity costs. If $P < \text{LAC}$, as at q_1, the economic profit is negative and the firm exits the industry in the long run.

P = LAC Breakeven pt.

P < LAC exits

Are Patents Necessary?

APPLIED
MICRO
THEORY

7.3

The competitive mechanism and cost analysis provide a useful foundation for the study of patents. Research and new-product development are expensive, time-consuming, and—because they may not result in a useful product—inherently risky. Moreover, once the new invention is on the market, rival firms can easily break it down and scrutinize its inner workings. The fruits of inventive activity, whether a new design, a secret formula, or a novel application, can be laid bare for rival engineers to examine. Compared to the inventing firm, which "starts from scratch," the rival firm faces lower costs. We can use competitive theory to investigate the economic consequences of such piracy.

Without some form of patent protection, the price of the invention would be driven down to just production costs; price would not include a return to the inventor. Knowing this in ad-vance, the inventor would be greatly deterred from engaging in inventive activity in the first place. And firms would surely be reluctant to pay high salaries to creative people if their inventions could be reproduced at lower cost by rival firms. Competition would stifle creativity and would cer-tainly lose its claim to be a stimulus of efficiency. Clearly, government must provide an incentive to invent. But how? Let's discuss three possibilities: grants, prizes, and patents.

Grants are paid in advance as a way of encouraging creative effort. But success can never be guaran-teed. Past success is often used as a guide to the future, a practice that does not encourage the budding young genius or the elderly tinkerer. Grants are ineffective incentives because there is no direct link between the payment and the ultimate value of the invention.

Prizes solve the problem inherent in grants because they allow an assessment of the worth of the invention after it is accom-plished. Awarding a prize to the inventor targets the incentive and rewards success. The drawback is that prizes are typically awarded in predetermined categories. Another limitation is the size of the prize. Presumably, it should bear some relation to the value of the contribution. But this is rarely the case. In fact, the dollar value of prizes is usually announced in advance.

The use of patents skirts all these problems. Patents reward inventive activity by providing for a period of monopoly control over the invention. The "prize" here is in proportion to the value of the achievement, as measured by the profit earned during the life of the patent. Furthermore, and most important, the nature of the achievement need not be known in advance in order to offer a prize. With the patent, both the size of the prize and the nature of the achievement are determined after the fact, but the incentives are in place beforehand.

If price falls to P_2, the firm adjusts its output to q_2, where $LMC(q_2) = P_2$. A smaller scale of plant is called for. At q_2, $LAC(q_2) = P_2$, and economic profit is zero. Here we must take care to interpret *zero economic profit* properly: It means that the total revenue of the firm is just sufficient to pay all labor and capital costs and to pay the entrepreneur an amount equal to his or her oppor-tunity cost. Nothing is left after these costs are paid; thus the en-trepreneur "breaks even" by earning a return equal to the value of forgone options. Zero economic profit—the **breakeven point**—simply means that the entrepreneur is poised between the current industry and the next-best alternative.[5]

If price should fall to P_1, the firm adjusts its scale of plant and output to $LMC(q_1) = P_1$. However, the firm earns negative eco-nomic profit at output q_1 because $LAC(q_1) > P_1$. The firm should

5. During the 1960 Presidential campaign, candidate John F. Kennedy quipped about the farmer who "hoped to break even this year because he really needed the money." This was a clever political barb. Yet in economic terms, a breakeven entrepreneur is making money in an amount just equal to the best available alternative.

exit this industry. Negative economic profit means that, after the explicit costs are paid, there is not enough revenue left to pay the owner an amount as large as could be earned in an alternative employment. In the event of negative economic profit, the owner should find another industry that offers higher profits. The firm should exit its current industry at price P_1 or, more generally, at any price below P_2. In Figure 7.9, P_2 is the breakeven price, and the minimum LAC is called the breakeven point. Exit is called for whenever the industry price falls below the minimum LAC.

Long-Run Industry Supply

We have seen that the firm will maximize long-run profits by selecting the scale of plant and producing the output that equates industry price and long-run marginal cost (LMC). We have also seen that the firm will exit the industry when industry price is less than the minimum of LAC; under these circumstances the entrepreneur earns higher accounting profits elsewhere. However, this information is not enough to allow us to conclude that the industry's **long-run supply curve** is the horizontal sum of the firm's long-run marginal cost curves above minimum LAC. That curve, Σ_hLMC, is illustrated in Figure 7.10. (The term Σ_h is a reminder that the summation is horizontal.) No industry output is produced at a price less than minimum LAC; instead firms exit. Symmetrically, no industry output is produced at a price greater than minimum LAC in the long run because firms will enter, produce more output, and force price down to minimum LAC. Because all firms are assumed to exhibit identical resource and opportunity costs, the breakeven price P is the same for all firms. We can conclude that the long-run supply curve is the horizontal S_{LR} curve.

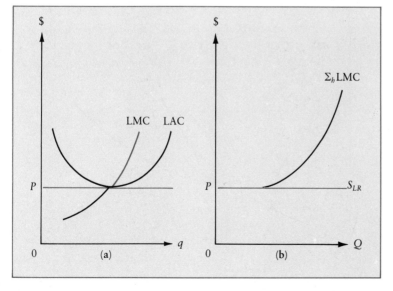

Figure 7.10
The Long-Run Industry Supply Curve

(a) A firm's long-run cost curves are presented here. (b) Industry supply is not the horizontal sum of firms' LMC curves, or Σ_hLMC, above the minimum LAC.

Long-Run Competitive Equilibrium

Equilibrium in the short run is established when industry supply equals industry demand and each firm in the industry is maximizing profits with its prevailing scale of plant. However, **long-run competitive equilibrium** is not such a simple matter. It requires that sufficient time pass to permit all firms in the industry to adjust their scales of plant in order to set long-run marginal cost equal to price and to permit firms either to enter or to exit the industry until there is no further incentive for entry or exit.

The scale-of-plant adjustment is complete when $P = $ LMC for firms. Entry and exit will occur whenever economic profits do not equal zero. If economic profits are positive, firms in this industry are earning higher accounting profits than they could earn in any alternative industry. Entrepreneurs from these other industries will enter the industry in search of these positive economic profits. If economic profits are negative, owners can earn higher accounting profits in other industries, resulting in exit. The incentive to enter or exit is fully eliminated when the economic profit for all firms is zero, or $P = $ LAC. For these two conditions to be satisfied simultaneously, the "optimal" scale of plant must be selected by each firm, as illustrated by ATC_0 in Figure 7.11. Each firm is operating its optimal scale of plant at the minimum of its long-run cost schedule, LAC. The long-run equilibrium conditions can be met only at the minimum of the LAC curve, because only there does LMC = LAC. Full long-run equilibrium occurs when all firms earn zero economic profit. The equation for long-run competitive equilibrium:

$$P = \text{LMC} = \text{minimum LAC} \qquad (7.12)$$

Figure 7.11
Long-Run Equilibrium

In perfect competition, all firms earn zero economic profit in long-run equilibrium and all operate at the minimum of both the LAC and the optimum scale of plant, ATC_0.

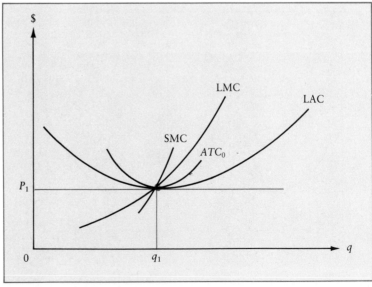

The "Reasonableness" of Collusive Prices

APPLIED
MICRO
THEORY

7.4

In the early days of antitrust enforcement, firms caught in the act of price fixing often argued that the prices they were charging under the agreement were reasonable because their rate of return on investment was no higher than a normal or "fair" rate.* But the Trenton Potteries

*The great railroad trusts of the late nineteenth century often argued that, due to high fixed costs, competition would result in losses. Competing railroads would try to cover only short-run costs. This reasoning could apply to any industry populated by shortsighted firms. See United States v. Trans-Missouri Freight Association, 166 U.S. 290, 17 Sup. Ct. 540, 41 L. Ed. 1007 (1897).

case, in which the reasonableness of prices was declared to be inadmissible evidence, established price fixing as a "per se" violation of law.†

Using the figure included here, we can easily counter the reasonableness argument with economic theory. The left-hand panel shows the cost curves of a typical firm; the industry demand curve is represented in the right-hand panel. Suppose the market-clearing noncollusive price is P_1. This is obviously not a long-run equilibrium price, because it does not generate a market rate of return.

†United States v. Trenton Potteries Company, 273 U.S. 392, 47 Sup. Ct. 377, 71 L. Ed. 700 (1927).

For the long-run market-clearing price P_0 to be achieved, some exit from the industry must occur. If, instead, the firms agree to help one another remain in business, the industry will continue with excess capacity. Even though the collusive price P_2 generates only a fair rate of return ($P_2 = AC$), the consumer is hurt because $P_2 > P_0 > P_1$. Without collusion, the competitive price would begin at P_1 and drive excess capacity out of the industry, a desirable result from society's viewpoint. Although the price does rise during this adjustment, it is always less than P_2. Hence prices are always lower than collusive prices, which should be the ultimate goal of antitrust activity.

Collusive Prices and Rate of Return

Collusive prices are not "reasonable" if they yield only the normal rate of return on investment. Collusive price P_2 yields a normal return higher than the noncollusive price, P_0, which also yields a normal return.

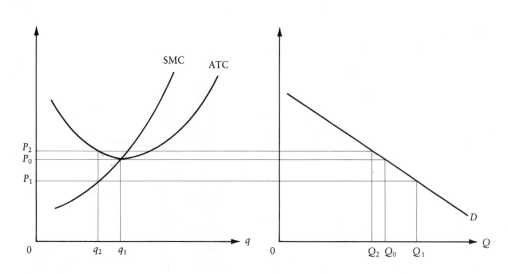

Because price is a proxy for the value that consumers place on the marginal unit of output, price measures the marginal benefit of output to society. Marginal cost measures the societal resources that must be sacrificed in the production of an additional unit. The $P =$ LMC equilibrium condition implies that the marginal cost of production equals the marginal benefit. Consequently, society's welfare is maximized by increasing output in the competitive industry whenever the marginal benefit (P) exceeds the marginal cost (LMC). Resources are allocatd efficiently by competitive markets. No resources that are more valued in this industry are used elsewhere, and vice versa.

The $P =$ minimum LAC condition implies that the optimal scale of plant is selected. Moreover, prices cannot remain higher than the amount necessary to permit firms to earn zero economic profits, or to earn just what they could earn in their next-best alternatives. Thus in the long run, firms respond to consumers' desires by producing goods and charging the lowest price that is compatible with resource and opportunity costs.

Before leaving this section, we must understand that the zero economic profit for all firms in long-run equilibrium is a result of the assumption that all firms are identical, a tenet of perfect competition. This long-run equilibrium condition will be amended in Chapter 8, which introduces pure competition.

Long-Run Adjustments to an Increase in Demand

So far, we have assumed that all firms have identical production function, resource costs, and opportunity costs. Now we will study the response of a competitive industry to an increase in demand. This exercise will reinforce the definition of long-run competitive equilibrium provided previously.

It is convenient to divide the response to demand increases into two parts: increased output by existing firms and the entry of new firms. Figure 7.12b illustrates an original industry demand curve, D; an original short-run supply curve, $\Sigma_h SMC$; and the resulting equilibrium price P_0. Panel a displays the behavior of one of the identical competitive firms in initial long-run zero-profit equilibrium, where $P =$ LMC $=$ minimum LAC. The short-run marginal cost corresponding to the "optimal" scale of plant is denoted $SMC(K_0)$, and its short-run average total cost curve (ATC) is omitted for convenience. The industry initially produces Q_0 units of output; each firm's contribution, measured on a smaller scale, is q_0 units; $\Sigma q_0 = Q_0$.

Now let industry demand increase to D_1. Price initially rises to P_2, causing the firm to adjust output along its short-run marginal cost curve to q_1 units. We can assume that this industry output expansion does not affect the price of resources or the position of the firm's cost curves. Output q_1 is only temporary. Because $P_2 >$

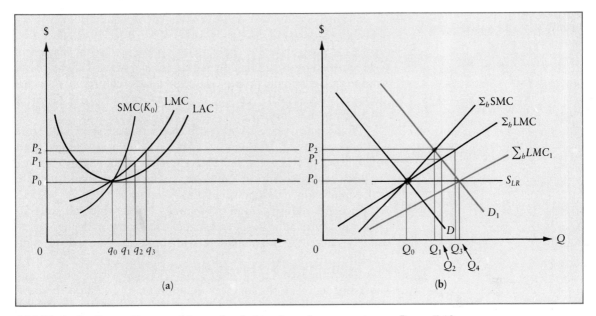

(a)   (b)

LMC(q_1), the firm will expand its scale of plant in order to produce q_3 units and maximize long-run profits. Such long-run output adjustments move the firm along its LMC curve and the industry along the curve Σ_hLMC. Clearly Σ_hLMC is more elastic than Σ_hSMC; but when all firms produce q_3 units, the industry output $\Sigma q_3 = Q_3$ exceeds the quantity demanded at price P_2. This surplus is eliminated by a price reduction to P_1. Firms maximize long-run profits at price P_1 by cutting output to q_2 through suitable reductions in their scales of plant.

The market clears at price P_1, and at that price each firm is maximizing long-run profit with the condition $P_1 = $ LMC(q_2). This appears to be an equilibrium position. However, note that $P_1 > $ LAC(q_2); economic profits are positive, and firms are earning higher profits than they forgo in their best alternative. For this reason the seeming equilibrium at P_1 and q_2 cannot be sustained; positive economic profits attract the entry of competing firms. As new firms enter, they add their supplies to existing supplies. The Σ_hLMC curve begins to shift to the right to reflect the supply of the new firms. As new firms enter, prices are forced down, gradually and simultaneously causing each firm to reduce its capital stock and to experience falling economic profits. Entry will continue to increase industry supply Σ_hLMC, reduce price, and squeeze out economic profit until all economic profit is eliminated, at which time entry will stop. Economic profits return to zero when $P = $ minimum LAC for each firm. Thus new entry will continue until the industry marginal cost curve Σ_hLMC reaches Σ_hLMC$_1$, reducing price to P_0.

At price P_0 all economic profits are eliminated, the incentive to enter the industry is totally exploited, and the output adjustments

Figure 7.12

Firm and Industry Response to an Increase in Demand

(a) The firm's response to an increase in demand is to expand output in the short run by hiring labor and to expand further in the long run by increasing the scale of plant. (b) An increase in industry demand from D to D_1 raises the price to P_2. Eventually, positive economic profits attract entry, which reduces price. In equilibrium, the firm is left with zero economic profit, having earned positive profits during the adjustment period.

Figure 7.13
Time Trends and Adjustments to Demand Increases

(a) Price rises initially, then falls due to entry. (b) Capital is fixed until time period t_1, then rises as scales of plant are increased. Entry reduces price and eventually capital. (c) Firm output rises initially, then falls as entry reduces price and profit. (d) Industry output rises, in part from expansion of the initial firms' output and in part from entry.

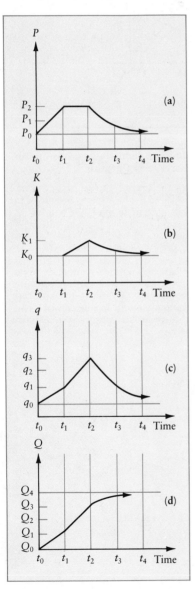

have run their course. Long-run competitive equilibrium is reestablished. Industry output rises to Q_4 when price P_0 is reachieved (price has risen and fallen again in the interim). Note that each firm has returned to its original output q_0, to its optimal scale of plant, and to zero economic profit. The original firms contribute the same industry output as before, Q_0, leaving the output $Q_4 - Q_0$ to be supplied by new firms.

Two kinds of industry long-run cost curves are shown in Figure 7.12. The curves $\Sigma_h \text{LMC}$ and $\Sigma_h \text{LMC}_1$ are the vertical summations of all firms' LMC curves. These curves measure the supply response to price changes before and after the competitive market adjusts to full equilibrium. The long-run industry supply curve S_{LR} is the locus of price and industry output combinations for which all scale-of-plant and entry adjustments are made. Each point on the horizontal supply curve S_{LR} is compatible with long-run competitive equilibrium.

The time trend graphs in Figure 7.13 summarize the essential adjustments from one long-run equilibrium to another. The horizontal axes all measure time; the vertical axes measure price (P), firm purchase of capital (K), firm output (q), and industry output (Q).

Time period t_0 represents the variables in initial equilibria at P_0, K_0, q_0, and Q_0. At time period t_1, demand increases and price rises from P_0 to P_2. The firm sets $P_2 = \text{SMC}$ without altering the scale of plant K_0. Firm output rises from q_0 to q_1, while industry output rises to Q_1.

In the next round of adjustment to time period t_2, firms expand capital to K_1 in order to set $P_2 = \text{LMC}(q_2)$. Firm output rises to q_3 and industry output rises to Q_3. By time period t_3, the effect of the increased capital expansion in the previous period begins to lower prices, causing firms to reduce capital stocks and output in order to reduce LMC to the lower price. In addition, entry starts to reduce prices, erode profits, and induce additional sell-off or depreciation of capital. By time period t_4 the process of adjustment is complete. Price has returned to its original level $P_0 = $ minimum LAC, the buildup of capital stock by existing firms in order to capture initial profits has all been sold off or depreciated, and each firm has returned to its optimal scale of plant K_0. The new industry output $Q_4 - Q_0$ is produced by the entry of new firms.

The speed and ease of entry into an industry affects the nature of time trends like these. If high entry costs cause entry to be slow, existing firms may increase capital quickly in order to capture the profits at the initially elevated prices and later sell capital gradually as entry dictates. Or the speed of entry may be so fast that existing firms do not have time to adjust their scales of plant at all. In this case, entry would be the primary mode of returning the industry to competitive equilibrium.

Price Controls and Competitive Adjustments

APPLIED
MICRO
THEORY

7.5

Price controls are often imposed when fear of runaway prices runs high. (Controlling profits of firms experiencing rapid growth in prices is another motive for instituting controls.) Figure A compares the time trend of the prices that policymakers fear with the more likely time trend that analysis of long-run competitive equilibrium suggests: Entry will eventually cause prices to moderate.

It is useful to know what impact government-established price controls will have on the long-run adjustment process and on firms' profits during the transition. Beginning with the original equilibrium price P_0 in Figure B, let demand rise to D_1 and, accordingly, equilibrium price to P_1. If price is allowed to rise to P_1, the resulting profits attract entry, supply rises to S_1, and the adjustment process will proceed normally over time, as de-

Figure A
Price Trajectories When Demand Increases

The rising price trajectory is feared, although prices will probably taper off and fall. The initial high prices tend to attract competition.

picted by the black time trend line in the right-hand panel of Figure B. However, if a price ceiling is set at P_C, the entry adjustment process is slowed down; prices will tend to follow the colored trend line instead. Let's study the implications of disturbing the long-run adjustment process by imposing price controls.

The horizontal axis in the right-hand panel of Figure B divides time into four zones: $\overline{T_0T_A}$, $\overline{T_AT_B}$, $\overline{T_BT_C}$, and $\overline{T_CT_D}$.

1. $\overline{T_0T_A}$: In this zone, the market price is allowed to rise in response to the demand shift.

2. $\overline{T_AT_B}$: Now the controlled price, P_C, is below the price that would prevail without controls. Shortages emerge during this time period.

3. $\overline{T_BT_C}$: During this period, the equilibrium price that would have prevailed but for the

Continued on page 210

Figure B
Price Controls and Long-Run Adjustments

Price controls slow entry yet keep prices and profits above the free-market levels during time period T_BT_C.

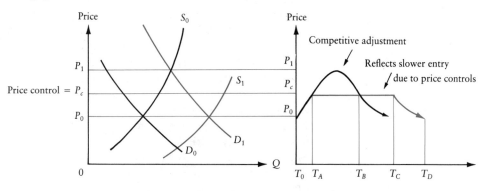

controls, falls below the control price. Shortages persist.

4. T_C: Entry, albeit slowed by the controls, is finally great enough to bring the market price below the price ceiling, P_C.

5. $\overline{T_C T_D}$: Entry continues until price falls low enough to assure firms a fair rate of return. When economic profits are eliminated, entry stops and long-run equilibrium is achieved.

Thus, in respect to price controls, we see that

1. It cannot be said that price controls keep *costs* down, because the transaction costs resulting from the shortage exceed the price that the market would have produced.

2. It cannot be said that price controls keep *prices* down, because (as Figure B indicates) there are some periods in which the controlled price is above the market price that would prevail without controls.

3. It cannot be said that price controls prevent capitalists from obtaining unfair profits, because during period $\overline{T_B T_C}$, prices and profits are higher under controls than they would be in a free market.

Price controls not only distort economic relationships in the short run, as discussed in Chapter 2, but also inhibit the transfer of resources among industries in the long run and thereby distort the best allocation of productive resources. Of course, price controls are often defended on the grounds that many industries are not competitive and will not adjust according to the analysis presented here. However, very few industries are so monopolized that profit incentives do not attract competitors. And whatever tendency these industries may have to adjust is greatly hampered by price controls. Perhaps the resources used to implement and enforce price controls in such industries could be more usefully employed in eliminating barriers to entry and other structural and legal hindrances to competition.

Constant-Cost, Increasing-Cost, and Decreasing-Cost Industries

When output expansion occurs throughout an industry, the prices of the factors of production may or may not be affected. If the industry is small relative to the factor markets, industry output can increase without bidding up the price of the inputs. Such an industry is called a **constant-cost industry**. If the industry is relatively large compared to the resource markets, industry expansion will drive factor prices up. This is an **increasing-cost industry**. The possibility also exists that industry expansion may actually reduce factor prices. Perhaps firms cannot afford the costs of electronic data processing until industry expansion brings together a critical mass of firms to share time on a jointly purchased computer. Such circumstances typify a **decreasing-cost industry**.

Constant-, increasing-, and decreasing-cost industries are defined according to whether the long-run industry supply curve, S_{LR}, is horizontal, positively sloped, or negatively sloped, respectively. How does the zero long-run profit resulting from perfect competition show up in the slope of the long-run industry supply curve S_{LR}? Starting with the constant-cost industry, Figure 7.14*a* shows a representative firm with zero profits in long-run equilibrium at industry price P_0. Say that demand rises to D_1, which raises the industry price to P_1. The firm increases output to q_1 by suitable adjustments in its scale of plant. Positive economic profits of AP_1BC appear, which attract new entrants. In a constant-cost industry, the expansion of existing firms and the entry of new firms do not raise factor prices. Thus the cost curves do not shift due to

---

Handwritten margin notes:

Constant cost
Small relative to factor mkts, industry output can ↑ w/out bidding up P of inputs.

Increasing cost
Large industry compared to resource mkts, industry expansion will drive up factor prices

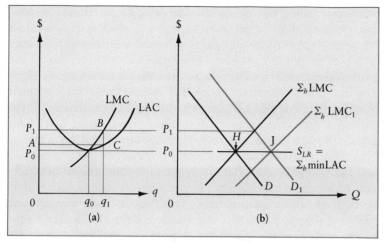

Figure 7.14
Constant-Cost Industry

(a) This firm has zero profits and is in long-run equilibrium at industry price P_0. (b) Starting at H, an increase in demand attracts new firms and a new equilibrium at J for a constant-cost industry. The long-run supply curve, S_{LR}, is horizontal.

industry expansion. Entry shifts the supply curve $\Sigma_h \text{LMC}$ to the right, causing output prices to sag. As prices fall, firms cut back production, and their economic profits fall. Entry will continue until economic profits are pushed to zero in all firms: As long as the cost curves are not shifting in this process, entry will not stop until price returns to its initial level, which requires the supply curve to shift to $\Sigma_h \text{LMC}_1$. The initial industry equilibrium occurs at point H. The increase in demand caused industry expansion and entry, but the new long-run equilibrium occurs at point J, the same price as before and a larger industry output. The collection of all long-run equilibrium points like H and J makes up the industry long-run supply curve, S_{LR}. In perfect competition, S_{LR} must be horizontal for a constant-cost industry. All points on the S_{LR} curve represent the horizontal summation of the output of the firms at minimum LAC. For this reason, the curve is labeled $S_{LR} = \Sigma_h \text{minLAC}$.

Figure 7.15 repeats the analysis for an increasing-cost industry.

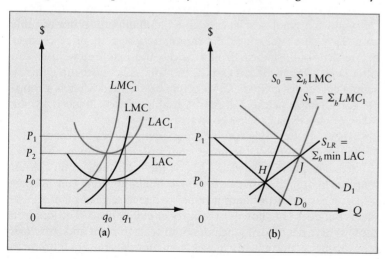

Figure 7.15
Increasing-Cost Industry

(a) The entry of other firms increases firm costs in an increasing-cost industry. (b) Zero profit equilibrium is achieved at J, a higher price than at H. The long-run supply curve, S_{LR}, is positively sloped.

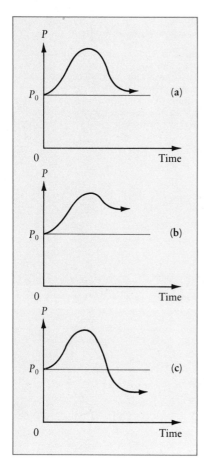

Figure 7.16
Price Time Trends for Perfect Competition in Response to an Increase in Demand

(a) This panel depicts a constant-cost industry. (b) This is an increasing-cost industry. (c) A decreasing-cost industry is shown here.

The initial industry price is P_0, and all firms are in zero-profit long-run equilibrium. Let demand increase to D_1, which increases industry price to P_1, encourages existing firms to expand output, and produces the positive economic profits that attract entry. So far the story is the same. However, in an increasing-cost industry expansion results in higher factor prices. If all factor prices change proportionally, the LAC and LMC curves shift up proportionally. These shifts are shown in Figure 7.15 as the colored curves LAC_1 and LMC_1. Now the long-run industry equilibrium will be achieved before the product price returns to its original level. Only points H and J are supply points that satisfy the zero economic profit condition of long-run equilibrium. The positive economic profits that result from the demand-induced price increase are now pinched from both ends; prices fall and resource costs rise. Positive economic profits are eliminated before price can return to its original level, because rising costs are now helping to reduce profits. Thus the long-run industry supply curve, S_{LR}, is positively sloped. Each point on the S_{LR} curve is still the horizontal sum of firms' minimum LAC curves.

The case of the decreasing-cost industry is yours to work through as an exercise. You should show that the long-run industry supply curve, S_{LR}, is negatively sloped in perfect competition. Note that nearly everyone believes decreasing-cost industries to be at least as rare as the dodo bird.

Figure 7.16 summarizes this discussion by illustrating the time trends of prices that result from an increase in demand in the different classes of industries. Remember, these time trend lines are the product of the assumptions of perfect competition.

Price Elasticity of Supply

Three kinds of industry supply curves are shown in Figure 7.17. The short-run supply curve is the horizontal summation of the firm's short-run marginal cost curves above minimum average variable cost. This curve measures the output response to price changes before firms adjust their capital stocks and before new firms can enter or existing firms can exit the industry. The short-run industry supply curve, designated $\Sigma_h SMC$, may be adjusted when appropriate for changes in the prices of variable factors induced by the industrywide expansion or contraction of output.

There are two long-run industry supply curves in Figure 7.17, each bearing on the two long-run competitive adjustments we have studied. The curve labeled $\Sigma_h LMC$ is the horizontal sum of firms' long-run marginal cost curves above minimum long-run average cost; it measures firms' output response due to scale of plant adjustments but does not allow for the entry or exit of firms. The long-run supply curve denoted S_{LR} includes both scale of plant and entry/exit adjustments as the industry moves from one long-run equilibrium to another.

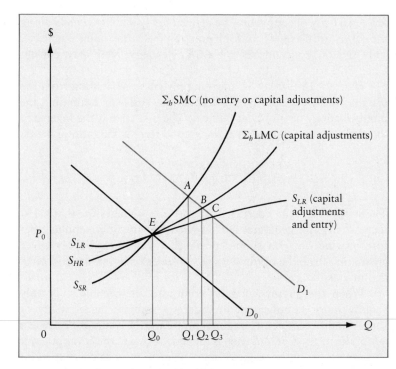

$

Σ_hSMC (no entry or capital adjustments)

Σ_hLMC (capital adjustments)

A

B

C

S_{LR} (capital adjustments and entry)

E

P_0

S_{LR}

S_{HR}

S_{SR}

D_1

D_0

Q

0 Q_0 Q_1 Q_2 Q_3

Figure 7.17
Price Elasticity of Supply

Starting at E, let demand rise. In the short run, output rises along Σ_hSMC to Q_1. Via capital adjustments, output rises along Σ_hLMC to Q_2. When full entry is permitted, zero profit equilibrium is attained; output rises along the S_{LR} curve to Q_3. Long-run supply curves are more price elastic than short-run curves.

In Figure 7.17, the initial equilibrium price is P_0. If demand rises to D_1, price is bid up to Q_1A in the short run, and firms increase output to Q_1 by hiring more variable inputs. This short-run supply response is the move from E to A along Σ_hSMC.

The long-run scale-of-plant adjustments made in response to higher prices are captured in the move from E to B along the long-run supply curve Σ_hLMC. These scale adjustments lead to an industry output of Q_2 and a price of Q_2B. When sufficient entry reestablishes zero-profit long-run equilibrium, output will have risen to Q_3 at price Q_3C. The movement along the S_{LR} curve from E to C incorporates all long-run supply adjustments—scale of plant and entry—as the industry responds to the demand increase.

In short, the price elasticity of supply is greater in the long run than in the short run, as the supply curves in Figure 7.17 reveal. This fact corresponds perfectly to the discussion of supply in Chapter 2, which emphasized that supply responses depend largely on the substitutes available to firms. Longer time periods allow firms to seek out more substitutes in production technology, including the expansion of capital. Of course, firm entry adds even more to industry output in response to rising prices.

Formally, **price elasticity of supply**, ε^s, is the percentage change in quantity supplied resulting from a percentage change in price, *ceteris paribus*.

$$\varepsilon^s = \frac{\%\Delta Q_s}{\%\Delta P} = \frac{\Delta Q_s}{\Delta P} \cdot \frac{P}{Q_s} \qquad (7.13)$$

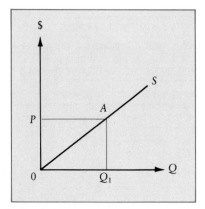

Figure 7.18
Price Elasticity of Supply

Any linear supply curve emanating from the origin is unit price elastic regardless of its slope.

Figure 7.19
Point Price Elasticity of Supply

Point price elasticity of supply is 1 at A, where a tangent intersects the origin. At B, elasticity is less than 1, and at C, elasticity exceeds 1.

Price elasticity of supply may be defined for a small movement along the curve (arc elasticity) or for a point on the curve (point elasticity). This section concentrates on point elasticity; you may consult Chapter 3 for the method of measuring arc elasticity.

Figure 7.18 displays a linear supply curve emanating from the origin. We can use Equation 7.12 as the basis for evaluating the point elasticity of supply at point A. The first term is the inverse of the slope of the supply curve; the second term is the ratio of bases:

$$\varepsilon^s(A) = \frac{0Q}{0P} \cdot \frac{0P}{0Q} = 1 \qquad (7.14)$$

The supply elasticity coefficient at A is unity, suggesting that a 1% increase in price generates a 1% increase in quantity supplied. Before moving on, you should prove that any linear supply curve emanating from the origin with any slope (except infinite and zero) is unit elastic.

When the supply curve is nonlinear, the technique is only slightly more complicated. In order to evaluate the elasticity of supply at different points on the supply curve in Figure 7.19, we can adopt the method of tangents. A tangent drawn to the curve at point A emanates from the origin. Using our method of calculating point elasticity, it follows that supply is unit elastic at point A. The elasticity at point B is

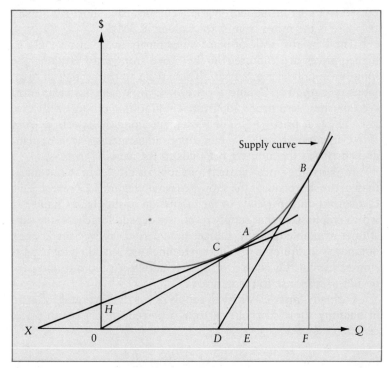

$$\varepsilon^s(B) = \frac{\Delta Q^s}{\Delta P} \cdot \frac{P}{Q} = \frac{DF}{BF} \cdot \frac{BF}{0F} = \frac{DF}{0F} < 1 \qquad (7.15)$$

Consequently, supply at point B is price inelastic; a 1% increase in price causes an increase in quantity supplied of less than 1%. For point C:

$$\varepsilon^s(C) = \frac{\Delta Q^s}{\Delta P} \cdot \frac{P}{Q} = \frac{XD}{CD} \cdot \frac{CD}{0D} = \frac{XD}{0D} > 1 \qquad (7.16)$$

Supply is price elastic at C.

The use of tangents provides a simple visual method for distinguishing between elasticity differences along a nonlinear supply curve. Supply is unit elastic at the point where the tangent intersects the origin. For higher price-quantity points, the tangent intersects the horizontal axis; supply is therefore price inelastic. At price-quantity points below unit elasticity, the tangent intersects the vertical axis, as at point H in Figure 7.19; supply in that case is price elastic.

Distinguishing among Labor, Capital, and the Entrepreneur

The theory of production and costs begins with some striking over-simplifications, including the following:

Resources are of two distinct types: labor (variable) and capital (fixed).

Labor is homogeneous.

Capital is homogeneous.

Labor and capital are the resources devoted to production. The entrepreneur, in contrast, is the risk taker and decisionmaker whose compensation takes the form of profit, a residual of revenues over costs.

These simplifying assumptions allow economists to separate issues and derive many useful relationships, such as the shapes of production functions and cost curves, the technical tradeoffs among inputs, diminishing returns, returns to scale, shutdown rules, and entry/exit considerations. These are more than mere mechanical exercises and sources of unjust enrichment for purveyors of geometry. Rather, the ability to think rigorously about tradeoffs, relative fixities, and short-run versus long-run effects is enhanced by seeing the analysis illustrated on paper. But paper is two-dimensional and hence can only start the process of thinking about multidimensional tradeoffs.

At this point it is necessary, albeit disheartening, to declare these beginning assumptions a fiction. Labor is not homogeneous, nor is capital. Moreoever, the distinction between labor and capital is artificial. Labor is not always completely variable nor capital completely fixed. Relative fixities overlap, in that some workers have greater fixity than some equipment.

The distinction between the entrepreneur and the labor and capital inputs is also artificial. The human capital embodied in the entrepreneur is akin to equipment, just as the specific skills of labor are (see Chapter 12). And the entrepreneur's effort, at least for an owner-operated business, is in part a form of labor. Separating labor, capital, and entrepreneurship is not the simple procedure implied by the model.

Entrepreneur is the time-honored term for risk taker and decisionmaker. In the simplest of firms, these roles do often coincide. However, the more complex and sophisticated the financial structure of the firm, the looser is the link between ownership (and the implied assumption of risk) and decisionmaking responsibility. This latter role need not be played by investors-stockholders-entrepreneurs, and microeconomic theory should not be so narrowly focused as to imply that it is. The cost curves, the competitive mechanism, and other constructions can be used to study modern, sophisticated firms in which the investors-entrepreneurs are disparate and far removed from any decisionmaking authority. As long as the LAC curve includes the investors' opportunity costs, it will be living up to its main job of organizing the long-run entry/exit decision.

To summarize, the entrepreneur is often a composite of labor, capital, risk bearer, and decisionmaker. At other times, the entrepreneur is the source of invested capital and little else. In either case, entrepreneurs must receive a monetary and/or psychic payment at least as great as their evaluation of the next-best opportunity for the application of the same skills, time, invested capital, and risk factors. Every LAC curve, properly constructed, will include a "fair rate of return" to the entrepreneur as a cost of doing business.

In studying the entry/exit mechanism in competition, we have focused on an entrepreneur whose main job is to search for the industry that will yield the greatest accounting profit. Some textbooks have attributed much more complex roles to the entrepreneur. So will this one later. But for now, it's sufficient to understand the rules governing entry into and exit from industries.

Summary

The key to competition is parametric pricing: Each competitive firm's supply is so small relative to industry supply that the firm cannot affect industry price by its own expansion or contraction of output.

This chapter presents the model of perfect competition, which assumes that firms are identical in all regards, including their production functions, resource costs, and entrepreneurial opportunity costs. All firms earn zero economic profit in long-run equilibrium. Perfect competition is a means of studying certain components of firm decisions and industry consequences that do not require more complex assumptions. In the following chapter, the oversimplifications of perfect competition are corrected somewhat by studying pure competition, in which the differences in firms' cost structures are taken into account.

One central theme of this chapter is profit maximization, which lies at the heart of the short-run shutdown decision and the long-run exit decision. Profit maximization occurs when the firm equates marginal revenue and marginal cost. In the short run, $P \geq$ AVC must also be satisfied; otherwise, the firm shuts down. In the long run, $P \geq$ LAC is required; if not, the entrepreneur earns negative economic profit and will exit the industry in the long run. Both decisions are implications of the assumption that firms are profit-maximizing agents.

Throughout this chapter, the relationship between the firm and the industry has been explored, in both the short run and long run. Industry supply curves are, subject to some caveats, the horizontal summation of firm supply curves. Firms adjust to market shocks and inevitably move toward zero economic profit in long-run equilibrium.

This chapter sets the stage for Chapter 8, which broadens the scope of competitive analysis by studying price competition (in nonidentical firms), multiproduct firms, and intertemporal supply choices.

Key Terms

Problems

1. You run a hamburger palace that is open from 11 A.M. to midnight. You are considering adding a breakfast menu that would require the same griddle space, seating area, cash register space, and so forth. What costs are relevant to your decision? What costs are irrelevant?

2. You run a large midwestern university. Many of the students are from other states that have their own large universities. Most state schools are losing enrollments because the baby-boom bulge is ending. The losses in enrollment result in reduced funding. A popular idea among state legislators is to recoup some of the lost revenue by raising the tuition to out-of-state students. Analyze such a policy, paying attention to marginal costs of extra students and the elasticity of demand.

3. You own and rent out a cabin in northern Wisconsin. It is booked solid from late May to the middle of September, after which bookings depend on the weather. Suppose you can anticipate demand accurately once you get the weather forecast. What cost components would you consider in your decision to stay open?

4. Former Secretary of Health, Education, and Welfare Joseph Califano quit smoking and would like to encourage others to do likewise. One of his proposals to discourage smoking is for the government to end the price-support program for tobacco. The American Tobacco Institute has chided Califano, saying "if you eliminate the price support for tobacco, the farmers will not cooperate with acreage restrictions and will plant more acres and increase the supply of tobacco, thus driving down the price of cigarettes and *encouraging smoking*." Surely Califano expects a different result. Which do you expect?

5. Due to rising prices for feed grains, the price of meat rose sharply in 1973. Various consumer groups, aided by access to TV and newspaper coverage, organized a meat boycott. Consumption dropped about 10% at the prevailing prices. Ranching is in fact competitive, so the boycott caused some ranchers to reduce their herd size and others to "sell out" (exit for good). Exit in any industry involves the sale or scrap of capital, but in ranching a major portion of capital is cattle. So exit drove prices down in the short run. Use microeconomic theory to trace the effect of the boycott over time on the price of meat and the size of herds. Can such a boycott succeed? In the long run? In the short run? What happens when the boycott is called off?

6. Construct time trend lines for price that illustrate the long-run adjustment process in perfect competition arising from a decrease in demand in a constant-cost industry; a decreasing-cost industry; an increasing-cost industry.

7. Does the ancient term *entrepreneur* have any equivalent in the modern corporation? What—or who—is an entrepreneur?

8. a. Prove that a change in the rental rate of capital, r, shifts the expansion path, whereas a change in the entrepreneur's opportunity cost will not.

   b. How do these two changes affect the firm's LMC and LAC curves?

9. a. Suggest reasons why predatory pricing ("price wars") is suicidal in competitive markets.

   b. Why is advertising suicidal in competitive markets?

10. Devise a list of ten industries that you regard as competitive. What do you mean by competitive?

11. a. Use the theory of the firm to analyze the most important determinants of price elasticity of supply.

   b. What is a firm's short-run price elasticity of supply if production exhibits a constant marginal product of the variable input and if fixed costs are zero? If fixed costs are $100? If fixed costs are $1000?

12. Suppose you own a movie theater. What factors help you decide the hours you should operate? How many days a week should you show films? What factors help you decide whether or not to sell the theater or to renovate it and open a skating rink in its place?

Suggested Readings

Coase, R. H. "The Nature of the Firm." *Economica* 4 (1937): 386–405.

Ellis, H. S., and Fellner, W. "External Economies and Diseconomies." *American Economic Review* 33 (1943): 493–511.

Knight, F. H. "Some Fallacies in the Interpretation of Social Cost." *Quarterly Journal of Economics* 38 (1924): 582–606.

Samuelson, Paul A. *Foundations of Economic Analysis.* New York: Atheneum, 1965, chap. 4.

Stigler, George. *The Theory of Price.* New York: Macmillan, 1966, chap. 6.

Advanced Topics in Competition

The standard model of competitive markets presented in Chapter 7 is a powerful mechanism for organizing thoughts about the decisions of competitive firms and their effects on the allocation of resources. This chapter extends the model to encompass three topics that the simpler model is not designed to handle:

Nonidentical firms (pure competition).

Multiproduct firms.

Multiperiod (intertemporal) decisions.

The rudimentary model, of identical firms producing a single product in a single time period, can easily be modified to include industries whose firms are disparate, which produce a variety of products, and whose decisions span time periods.

Pure Competition

Firms are not identical. However, the model of identical firms (perfect competition) can easily be adjusted to incorporate the more general case of nonidentical firms (pure competition). Pure competition becomes vastly more relevant to policymaking by drawing a significant distinction that perfect competition does not: among marginal, inframarginal, and extramarginal firms.

Suppose that firms are identical in every regard except the opportunity costs of the entrepreneurs. Under this assumption, the long-run competitive equilibrium condition set out in Chapter 7 must be amended. When entrepreneurs have differing opportunity costs, it is not true that all firms earn zero economic profit in the long run. It may seem to you that we have merely set up a straw man and will now knock it over. But the zero-profit issue runs deeper than this. The notion that long-run competitive equilibrium must produce zero economic profits for all firms is important because of

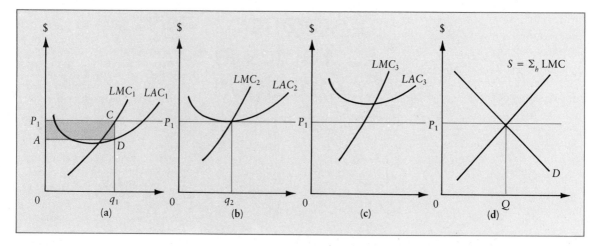

Figure 8.1
Long-Run Equilibrium, Pure Competition

(a) Firm 1 is an inframarginal firm.
(b) Firm 2 is a marginal firm. Note that it alone has zero economic profit. (c) Firm 3 is an extramarginal firm. (d) All three firms take industry price as a parameter.

its implications for economic efficiency, because economists and lawyers commonly hold it to be true, and because it leads to the incorrect conclusion that when positive economic profits exist, competition is absent.

Figure 8.1 illustrates long-run competitive equilibrium when firms still have identical production functions and resource costs but when owners possess varying entrepreneurial opportunity costs. The cost curves of three firms are depicted in panels a, b, and c. The labor and capital costs of all three firms are identical, because of their identical production functions and their lack of control over per-unit input prices (w and r). So the difference in the positions of the LAC curves is due solely to different opportunity costs. The owner of the firm in panel a has few alternatives and hence low opportunity costs. The LAC curve in panel b is higher than the one in panel a, reflecting the higher opportunity costs of forgone alternatives. The LAC curve in panel c is highest of all, an indication of still greater opportunity costs. (Entrepreneurial opportunity costs are a fixed cost, so they do not affect the firms' marginal cost curves.) Figure 8.1 shows that firms can have different cost structures even when they face identical production functions and input prices.

Panel d in Figure 8.1 displays the industry supply and demand curves; their intersection establishes industry price, P_1. Firm 1 (in panel a) produces q_1 units of output and earns the positive economic profit AP_1CD; firm 2 produces q_2 units of output ($q_1 = q_2$) but earns zero economic profit; firm 3 would earn negative economic profit by producing in this industry and therefore seeks higher profits elsewhere.

Any firm that, like firm 1, earns positive economic profits in long-run equilibrium is an **inframarginal firm.** Firm 2 earns zero economic profit; it is earning just enough accounting profit to keep producing in the present industry. Such a firm is called a **marginal**

firm. Firm 3 does not produce in the industry at price P_1 because of the negative economic profits that would result. This kind of firm is an **extramarginal firm.**

You may ask why the presence of positive economic profits for firm 1 would not invite more firms to enter the industry, shift the industry supply curve to the right, reduce industry price, and continue to squeeze economic profits until all remaining firms earn zero profits in equilibrium, as in perfect competition. In moving to industry price P_1, these are exactly the adjustments that occur. But at price P_1, all entry and exit have ceased. Only firms that have lower opportunity costs than firm 2 (lower LAC curves) could profitably enter the industry at price P_1. When all such inframarginal firms have entered, there are no more firms that have entry prices below P_1. Also, all extramarginal firms—those earning negative economic profits at price P_1—have exited. The industry supply curve $S = \Sigma_h \text{LMC}$ will not be shifted by further entry or exit. Thus price P_1 is the long-run equilibrium price, the industry is in long-run equilibrium, and inframarginal firms earn positive economic profits. Only the marginal firms earn zero economic profits.

We can now restate the conditions for long-run competitive equilibrium more accurately, if somewhat more loosely: It occurs when no firms are entering or exiting the industry at the prevailing industry price. The marginal firms—those just willing to remain in the industry rather than produce elsewhere—earn zero economic profit; the inframarginal firms earn positive long-run economic profits due to lower costs (in the present example, lower entrepreneurial opportunity costs). The commonly held view that long-run economic profit is zero for all firms applies only to the special case of perfect competition, in which all enterpreneurs have identical production functions, resource costs, and opportunity costs. When firms have different costs, they have different entry and exit prices. Thus the industry's long-run equilibrium can coexist with positive economic profits for the inframarginal, low-cost firms.

Inframarginal firms earn positive economic profit, that is, a return in excess of available alternatives. Although we have started with an example in which firms' costs differed solely because of different opportunity costs, inframarginal profits may result from any source of cost differences, such as efficient management, access to superior resources, locational advantages, better production technologies, and newer physical plants. Relatively low-cost, inframarginal firms can produce along the positively sloped segment of their LAC curves. The higher-cost, marginal firms operate at a minimum LAC and earn zero economic profit. Inframarginal profits are perfectly compatible with competition. The key is that each firm is small relative to industry output. Understanding this point is essential to both theory and policy.

A Potpourri of Marginal, Inframarginal, and Extramarginal Concepts

APPLIED
MICRO
THEORY

8.1

The distinction among marginal, inframarginal, and extramarginal is a powerful concept incorporating succinct, compact language.
Consider the demand curve in Figure A. At price P the consumer purchases Q_1 units. The Q_1th unit is the "marginal unit," because only for that unit is the marginal benefit to the consumer equal to the price paid. All units up to the Q_1th unit are inframarginal, because the marginal benefit to the consumer exceeds the price actually paid. All units in excess of Q_1 units are extramarginal, because the price P exceeds the marginal benefit for all such units. Note that the marginal, inframarginal, and extramarginal concepts are directly tied to a given price.
Figure B continues the example with a supply curve. At price P,

the Q_2th unit is the marginal unit, because only for the Q_2th unit does the price charged exactly cover the firm's marginal cost of production. Units previous to Q_2 are inframarginal ($P > MC$), and all units in excess of Q_2 are extramarginal ($P < MC$). Again the distinction is only relevant with respect to a given price.
Figure C shows a similar distinction in consumer theory. Given the indifference curve U_0 and the relative prices implied by the slope of the budget line, the consumer selects X_1 units of X. The X_1th unit of X is the marginal unit, because only there is MRS = P_X/P_Y. All units up to X_1 are inframarginal, because MRS > P_X/P_Y, and hence the consumer can buy these units of X at a price less than he or she would have been willing to pay. Conversely, units of X in excess of X_1 are extramarginal and will not be purchased at prevailing

prices, because MRS < P_X/P_Y. As always, these terms are tied to given prices.
Finally, the terms can be attached to price-taking firms as well as to production units. In Figure D price is set at the industry level. Firms that earn a normal return equal to their entrepreneurial opportunity costs are marginal firms; lower-cost firms that earn profits in excess of opportunity costs are inframarginal firms. Extramarginal firms have costs too high to allow entry at the prevailing price.
These examples illustrate that the terms *marginal, inframarginal,* and *extramarginal* can be used in all cases involving optimization by economic agents at a given price. Furthermore, the concepts add content to the analysis of competition.

Figure A
The Demand Curve

Inframarginal units are those worth more to consumers than the price. Consumers break even on the marginal unit.

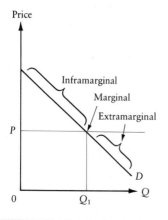

Figure B
The Supply Curve

Inframarginal units are those that cost less to produce than the price. Extramarginal units cost more than the price and are therefore not produced. Suppliers break even on the marginal unit.

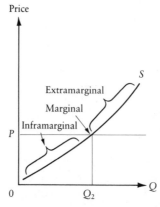

Figure C
Consumer Optimization

The marginal rate of substitution exceeds the price ratio for inframarginal units, equals the price ratio for the marginal unit, and falls below the price ratio for extramarginal units.

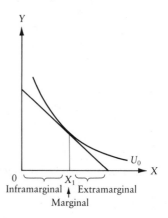

Figure D
Firms in Long-Run Equilibrium

The inframarginal firm is profitable at price P; the marginal firm breaks even; the extramarginal firm does not enter the industry, because average costs, including all opportunity costs, exceed P for all levels of output.

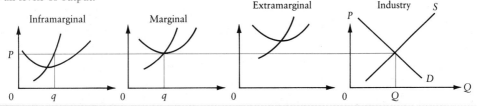

Risk in Marginal and Inframarginal Farms

APPLIED MICRO THEORY

8.2

Farming is a risky business because the weather largely determines the quantity and quality of the farmer's crops and because the demand for farm output is price inelastic. How can farmers deal with the risk they face?

Consider each crop to be a risky asset. As with any earning asset, the riskiness can be reduced by spreading the risk. There are many nonfarm examples of spreading the risk. For example, we do not know in advance which house will burn down, which car will crash, or which life will be shortened. But we can pool these risks so that everyone who does not suffer a calamity can make a small contribution toward a large payment to those who do. Insurance therefore is one way of reducing risk by spreading it over many participants.

A second way to spread risk is diversification. Business firms diversify their product lines so that losses on unfortunate investments can be outweighed by gains on others. A loss is less likely to force an entrepreneur out of business and workers out of jobs if the firm has a well-diversified product line. The same is true for financial investments. Risk spreading is the application of the principle of not putting all the eggs in the same basket.

Risk spreading is essential in the farming industry. There are at least three ways a farmer can spread risk: (1) plant a diversified portfolio of crops, (2) use futures markets, and (3) use the loan markets. We have already seen how diversification spreads risk. The futures market works like this: The farmer sells the risk to a company that can pool such a risk. For example, Continental Grain Corporation can buy a diversified portfolio of farm crops in advance (while the crops are still growing) and take the risk on the harvest-time price. The buyer of crop futures spreads risk by buying diversified crops and in the process reduces the risk to each farmer who sells crops in advance. In the third method, access to loan markets allows risk to be spread over good and bad years. Loans may be taken out in bad years and repaid in good years.

The farmer with small landholdings has risk disadvantages that the large-scale farmer or corporation farm does not have. When it comes to diversification, for example, farmers have an incentive to plant large acreages for each crop in order to capture economies of scale. A farmer who does not have much land cannot achieve this goal and crop diversification too. The futures market can also be of great importance in spreading risk, but it is more expensive for the small-scale farmer than for the large-scale farmer. The costs of gathering information prior to a transaction and of bargaining are proportionally less for large sales than for small. Finally, loan markets may offer high interest rates and the danger of foreclosure after several bad years in succession. A large-scale farmer has lower costs due to economies of scale and less risk as a result of greater diversification and greater participation in futures markets; this type of farmer is thus a better loan prospect and can get lower interest rates.

It seems that in farming the word is "Get big or get out." Risk-spreading advantages allow larger farms to be comfortably inframarginal while the small-scale farmer struggles to break even.*

*This is reflected in the fact that the number of farms in the United States fell from 5,388,000 in 1960 to 2,730,000 in 1970, while average size rose from 215.5 acres to 389.5 acres. Data from U.S. Department of Commerce, *Census of Agriculture, 1960* and *Census of Agriculture, 1970*.

Hunting for Monopolies

One major activity of the government is the regulation of monopoly profits. Indeed, a principal item in President Jimmy Carter's energy bill was identification and control of the monopoly profits of energy-producing firms. The analysis of inframarginal competitive long-run profits shows that the presence of positive economic profits—a greater than normal return—is not a valid test for the existence of monopoly. Still, this is the usual test applied by political subcommittees in search of monopolies.

To identify an inframarginal competitive firm as a monopolist solely on the evidence of positive economic profits and then to tax away the profits or otherwise regulate the firm as a monopolist is both bad economics and bad politics. Yet the model of perfect competition—typically the only

competitive model presented—promotes such misguided policies by its theorem of zero long-run economic profits for all firms. Excessive reliance on this model has important consequences for public policy and hence for the regulatory environment of competitive firms.

California's Proposition 13 and Apartment Rental Rates

Recently, a California state law referendum limiting property taxes to 1% of market value passed by a 2-to-1 vote. This remarkable public support was due in part to the votes of apartment dwellers, who were told that their landlords' tax savings would be passed on to them. After all, the rental housing market is quite competitive. In competitive markets, are cost reductions not passed on to customers in the form of lower prices?

Applying the theory of pure competition, we can see that the promise made to California renters cannot be kept at all in the short run and not completely in the long run either. Recall that price is determined by industry supply and demand at the minimum of the marginal firms' LAC curves. The inframarginal firm (apartment house) earns positive economic profit due to such factors as prime location or better management. These profits are reflected in the property value of the inframarginal apartment house. For the marginal, zero-profit firms, property value is

strictly the book value of the apartment; it includes no economic profit. Therefore, the property value of the inframarginal apartment house is greater than that of the marginal apartment house, and hence any percentage decrease in property taxes will be bigger in absolute terms for the inframarginal than for the marginal landlord.

Now let's use competitive theory to see how much of a rent reduction will follow a tax reduction. The initial industry price is set at P_1 by supply and demand, as shown in the lower right-hand

panel of the figure. The other panels show three types of apartment-owning firms before the passage of Proposition 13: inframarginal firm 1, marginal firm 2, and extramarginal firm 3. Now let Proposition 13 pass and property taxes be reduced. In the short run, property taxes are fixed costs. Reducing property taxes shifts the LAC curves down without affecting the firms' marginal cost curves or the industry supply curve, $\Sigma_h LMC$. Note that the profitable inframarginal apartments receive a larger tax reduction than the less-profitable apartments. The remarkable result is that there will be no impact on rental rates in the short run!

In the long run, previously extramarginal firms like firm 3 will enter the industry, shifting the industry supply curve to $\Sigma_h LMC_1$. Entry reduces price to P_2, but by virtue of the higher costs of the entering firms, entry cannot bring price into line with firm 2's costs and certainly not with firm 1's costs. Although there is long-run entry, it bears little relation to the size of the cost reductions of the inframarginal firms. Rent

The Effect of Proposition 13 on Rental Rates

Initially, inframarginal apartment-owning firm 1 owns property with a higher value than that owned by marginal apartment-owning firm 2. Proposition 13 results in greater tax earnings for firm 1 than for firm 2 and invites the entry of previously extramarginal firm 3. Short-run rental rates are unaffected. Long-run rental rates fall only to the minimum of LAC_3.

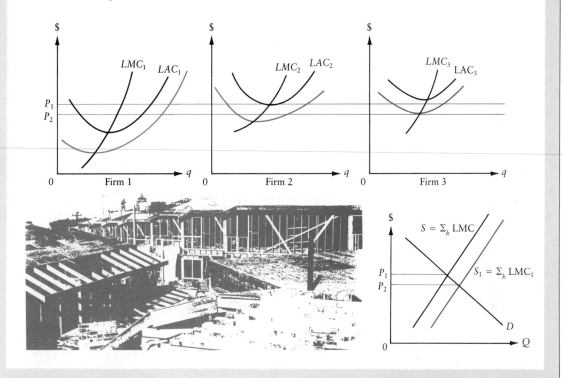

reductions depend only on the number of previously extra-marginal firms that can enter under the new tax formula.

To summarize, property tax reductions will produce no rent relief in the short run and some reduction only in the long run. With a percentage reduction, property taxes will be reduced more on the more profitable apartments, which have greater property value. But this rental rate reduction will be smaller than the property tax reduction. The competitive market will not pass through the cost savings. Instead,

any rental rate reduction will be due to the entry of new higher-cost or poorly located apartments that could not survive under the previous tax rates.*

*There is considerable debate about whether the property tax on dwellings is a tax on profits and hence not passed on to the consumer or largely shifted to the consumer in the long run, much like an excise tax. Our analysis indicates that it is a combination of both once the industry supply responds fully to the tax reduction. For a detailed theoretical treatment of this issue, see Peter Mieszkowski, "The Property Tax: An Excise Tax or a Profits Tax?" *Journal of Public Economics* 1 (1972): 73–96.

This analysis changes if demand shifts outward or if there is inflation. If there is inflation, the entry of new firms will reduce rental rates in real terms but not in nominal terms. If, as recent data indicate, people continue to move to warmer climes, California will experience an increase in the demand for housing. If this development shifts the demand curve by more than the entry of new firms shifts the supply curve, rental rates will go up, not down. This reinforces our point: Rental rates have little to do with taxes on inframarginal apartments.

The Distribution of Economic Profit

We have concluded earlier that all competitive firms earn zero economic profit in long-run equilibrium only when firms have identical production functions, resource costs, and entrepreneurial opportunity costs. Much economic analysis of competitive markets is carried on with this naive view of competition. However, a more sophisticated argument also purports to show why all competitive firms earn zero long-run economic profits. We must analyze this argument in some detail because of the misunderstanding it has caused and because of the inherent danger in the concept.

Figure 8.2 exhibits the long-run cost curves of a competitive firm. The LAC curve, as always, is the envelope of the firm's short-run ATC curves and includes the labor and capital costs and the entrepreneurial opportunity costs. (Ignore the curve labeled LAC^* for now.) Let the industry long-run equilibrium price equal P_1. The firm maximizes long-run profit by selecting the scale of plant and output consistent with $P_1 = \text{LMC}(q_1)$. The firm earns economic profits of AP_1BC in long-run equilibrium; this is an inframarginal firm.

The economic profit of the inframarginal firm is called by various names, including **inframarginal profit, economic rent,** and **inframarginal rent**. It is important to understand the intellectual heritage of the term *rent*. It was used originally to describe the

Figure 8.2
The Inframarginal Firm's LAC and Rent-Inclusive _LAC*_

Tautologically, all firms operate at the minimum LAC^*, because it is price-determined.

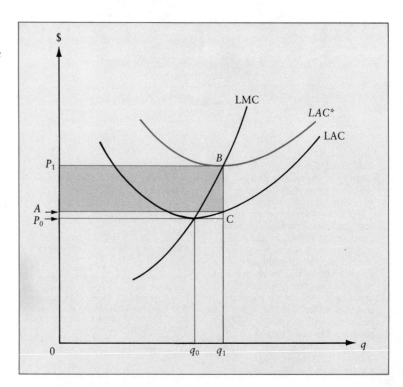

surplus paid to the owners of land, a surplus that accrued due to land's being in scarce supply. The term has now been broadened to include the surplus resulting from any scarce factor of production. Economic (inframarginal) rent is therefore the surplus of a specialized resource's earnings over what the resource could earn in its most valuable forgone use; this difference equals the definition of *economic profit* provided in Chapter 7. (Note that *economic rent* is unrelated to *contractual rent,* a sum of money that a renter pays to a landlord.)

In Figure 8.2 the inframarginal rent AP_1BC arises because the firm has cost advantages over the higher-cost, marginal firms. The inframarginal firm may have a location advantage, a newer and more efficient physical plant, more efficient management, or simply lower opportunity costs. If these special advantages were to vanish or to become generally available to all firms, the inframarginal rent would disappear. Rent (and economic profit) is a surplus bestowed by a valuable resource in short supply.

Some scholars have attempted to preserve the theorem of zero economic profit by proving that these inframarginal rents must vanish in the long run. They argue that the owners of the superior resources that the entrepreneur uses will be able to raise their asking prices and scoop up the entrepreneur's inframarginal rents, returning the entrepreneur's long-run profits to zero. Let's examine this assertion by considering alternative ownership of one specialized resource, land.

Suppose a valuable land parcel in Chicago's high-rent district endows the owner of an apartment building with inframarginal rent. Assume further that the building owner does not own the land parcel responsible for the surplus but leases it from a landlord. The lease price of the superior land parcel can increase by enough to extract the surplus from the entrepreneur and give it to the resource's owner, the landlord, without encouraging the building owner to abandon the building. In Figure 8.2, if the rent AP_1BC is paid to the landlord, another cost curve can be drawn that adds the rent to the LAC curve. This is the **rent-inclusive long-run average cost LAC^* curve.** At price P_1 the firm operates at the minimum of the LAC^* curve and earns zero economic profits when rent is included in the firm's long-run costs.

Let's assume now that the entrepreneur owns the land, which is the specialized resource responsible for the economic rent. The rent AP_1BC is now paid to the entrepreneur rather than to a landlord. Yet if we wish, we can still force the analysis into the zero-profit mold by recognizing that the entrepreneur always has the option of selling the land parcel. How much could the land parcel responsible for the rent AP_1BC be sold for? What is the least the entrepreneur would accept and the most a prospective purchaser would offer for the land parcel? This sale price must equal the inframarginal rent AP_1BC, which is the expected economic profit arising solely from the land parcel. The forgone option of selling the land parcel is an "opportunity cost" of the entrepreneur equal to the inframarginal rent AP_1BC. If the forgone opportunity to sell the land parcel is added to the firm's other costs, which are measured by the LAC curve, the rent-inclusive LAC^* curve is attained. The firm still operates at the minimum of the LAC^* curve and earns zero profits when rent is included as a cost.

Note that it doesn't matter whether the rent is actually paid to a landlord or accrues to the entrepreneur. These considerations only determine how the profit is distributed, not whether it exists. Either way, including the rent as a cost always forces the firm to produce at the minimum of its rent-inclusive LAC^* curve. Rent-inclusive profits equal to zero is a tautology and does not only apply to competitive firms. Imagine the spectacle of Howard Hughes's attorneys arguing before a tax court or regulatory agency that the economic profits of the Hughes Corporation were zero because of the high opportunity cost of selling the firm!

If the prediction of zero economic profit, based on the resource owner's ability to scoop out the entrepreneur's rent, is to be perfectly general, it should also apply when the entrepreneur possesses the superior resource. But here we see that it does not. The entrepreneur, by virtue of ownership of the land parcel, earns a profit greater than that available to him or her in the most valuable forgone industry.

Many theorists find significance in the fact that, in the tendency toward zero long-run profit in competition, no factor is paid more than its opportunity cost. However, this certainly is not the case; the argument is self-contradictory. When the landlord owns the land, the very process that bids up the lease price of the land parcel until firm profits are zero also bids up the return on the land parcel above the return it could earn in its next-best use. If the entrepreneur owns the land, this surplus is the profit of the firm and is larger than the entrepreneur could earn in the most valuable forgone industry. To repeat a point made earlier, the key is the existence of rents, not their distribution. Inframarginal rent, a surplus paid to a specialized factor, is consistent with a price-taking model of competition and will not be completely dissipated by entry of new firms unless all firms are identical. But if all firms are identical, as in the perfectly competitive case, there can be no specialized factors.

Inframarginal Profit: A Price-Determined Cost

The model of pure competition illustrates that inframarginal firms can earn positive economic profits in long-run equilibrium. It is sometimes argued that profits are positive because all relevant costs are not included. Specifically, it is said, the owner always has the option of selling the firm. The sale price of the firm would equal the inframarginal rent. As long as the owner does not sell, the forgone option to sell is an opportunity cost. If the forgone opportunity cost of selling the firm is added to the firm's other costs, already captured in the LAC courve, the rent-inclusive LAC^* curve is attained. It would appear that a firm earns a zero profit at price P_1 if the opportunity cost of selling the firm is counted as a cost.

Although it is useful, the LAC^* has the potential to lead to incorrect analysis of the entry and exit decision. Let's see why. Managers and economists are interested in cost curves principally to help them understand the determination of industry price and profit-maximizing output and entry/exit decisions. The LAC and LMC curves are relevant to these decisions; the LAC^* curve is not. The reason is that rent is a **price-determined cost,** whereas all other costs we have studied are **price-determining costs.** We have already seen how labor, capital, and the owner's opportunity costs help to determine prices. If wages rise as owners develop more valuable alternatives in other industries, the industry supply curve shifts to the left and price rises.

In contrast, economic rent is price-determined, not price-determining. Economic rent rises whenever price increases, *ceteris paribus*. In Figure 8.2, the firm produces q_0 at price P_0 and earns a zero economic profit. If price rises to P_1, the firm expands output to q_1, and economic profit AP_1BC appears. This rent results from the higher product price; it is therefore price-determined. If price falls, economic rent falls too. But the change in economic rent plays no role in determining price.

A price-determined cost does not affect profit-maximizing decisions about production or entry/exit. At price P_1 the firm produces q_1 units, because $P_1 = \text{LMC}(q_1)$. The firm's revenue exceeds the return on the next-best alternative, because $P_1 > \text{LAC}(q_1)$; its profits are higher in this industry than anywhere else. Now suppose that we include rent in the firm's cost curve, increasing average costs to LAC^* and giving the illusion that the firm earns zero economic profit. Will the firm change its output? No; $P_1 = \text{LMC}(q_1)$ just as before. Will the firm exit the industry? No; $P_1 > \text{LAC}(q_1)$. There is still no alternative that would provide higher profits. Finally, LAC^* always equals price; therefore, it hides the tautology in the argument that all firms operate at zero long-run profits. Thus rent should not be included in the firm's costs if we are trying to model the firm's entry/exit decisions.

Calling economic rent a price-determined cost is perhaps the most difficult concept presented in this book up to now. But its importance is commensurate with its difficulty. Applied Micro Theory 8.5 gives you practice in using the concept.

Taxi Medallions

APPLIED
MICRO
THEORY

8.5

We can use the theory of pure competition to understand the taxi industry. In most large cities there are enough taxicabs to force each one to be a price taker. However, there is also usually a restriction on entry, because taxi owners are required to register their cabs. The ostensible purpose of taxi registration is to screen drivers so that corrupt, antisocial, and potentially dangerous men and women do not get licensed. (The passenger can't gather accurate information by asking the driver, "Are you incompetent, a nut, on parole, or a pervert?") It has long been argued that such quality control is best handled at the licensing stage. A successful applicant is required to purchase a taxi medallion, the medallion serving as evidence to customers of legitimate registration.

Aside from the safety aspects of taxi licensing, the medallions have been used to limit the supply of taxis and drive up fares. The following comparative static analysis helps us see who gains and who loses from taxi regulation. Assume that the initial industry supply and demand curves shown in the accompanying figure determine the long-run equilibrium price P_0. The firm in the left-hand panel is a marginal firm earning zero economic profits in long-run equilibrium. The firm produces q_0 units of output (taxi rides) and operates at the minimum LAC. The taxi owner has a taxi medallion, acquired at zero cost from the regulatory agency, but assume, for simplicity, that it can be sold in the open market to anyone presenting a valid registration form.

Now let demand increase over time from D_0 to D_1 while the number of medallions that the

regulatory agency issues remains fixed. The industry price rises to P_1, and the firm responds by increasing trips sold to q_1. The increase in demand and price gives the medallion owner a rent of AP_1BC. The price-determined rent results from the limited supply of licensed taxi drivers. The customers pay a higher price.

Now suppose the medallion is sold on the open market to a person approved by the regulatory agency. How much will the medallion sell for? Its price will equal the present value of the expected economic profits that the medallion makes possible, the economic rent AP_1BC. Note, however, that the new owner's LAC curve does not rise to LAC^*, because he or she must pay the lump sum AP_1BC for the medallion. The new owner's correct average cost curve is the same as the old owner's.

The old owner could have

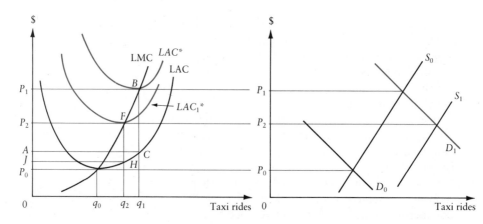

The Effect of Taxi Regulation on Production and Exit Decisions

Entry restrictions due to limits on the number of medallions in the taxicab market result in economic rent as demand increases. The rent-inclusive LAC^* curve rises and falls with price.

constructed a rent-inclusive LAC^* curve by including the rent as an opportunity cost of sale. The new owner would have discovered that the rent had actually been extracted, and so the new owner's rent-inclusive cost curve is also LAC^*. But the costs of the commonly available capital (cab) and labor (hours roaming the streets) resources are unchanged, as are the entrepreneurial opportunity costs. If the new owner's opportunity cost is roughly the same as the initial owner's, the LAC curve is the same for both.

Say that the regulatory agency increases the supply of medallions, so that the supply of taxi service increases to S_1 (see the right-hand panel). Price falls to P_2. The firm reduces rides to q_2. The rent-inclusive LAC^* curve shifts down to LAC^*_1. The rent from the medallion was originally AP_1BC, a lump sum that the new owner paid. But the rent has now fallen to JP_2FH, due to the reduction in the commodity price. The new owner has suffered a reduction in

the asset value of the medallion. Does the cabbie lose money as a result of the loss in rent? Yes, because the total payments (including labor and capital costs, entrepreneurial opportunity costs, and the loan payment on the medallion purchase) exceed total revenue: $P_2 < LAC^*(q_2)$. Does the cabbie exit the industry? If you regard the firm as operating at zero economic profit at point B on the LAC^* curve, it would seem any price below P_1 would generate negative economic profits and cause the owner to exit. But wait: $P_2 > LAC(q_2)$. The lower price P_2 still exceeds the per-unit cost of labor, capital, and entrepreneurial opportunity. Thus economic profits are positive—and the taxi industry is still the best of the cabbie's alternatives. To be sure, he or she is worse off because the medallion has lost value, but this is a sunk cost (not a fixed cost). If the cabbie exits the taxi industry, he or she will still have to pay the loan on the medallion purchase. The loss in the medallion's value

does not affect the decision to exit the taxi industry. That loss is now a cost to the owner's life, not to the selection of a particular industry. It is therefore a sunk cost and not an appropriate inclusion in the firm's average cost curve for the purpose of making an entry/exit decision.

As long as price stays above P_0, the new cabbie should stay in the taxi industry (and regret the loss in value of the medallion at every stop sign), because the opportunities are worse elsewhere. If the price falls below P_0, exit is called for. The cabbie should enter the next-best industry, say truck driving (and continue to regret the loss in value of the medallion at every stop sign).

Note carefully that the cabbie's production and exit decisions are not related to the firm's economic rent or its loss of rent. The rent-inclusive LAC^* curves move about with changes in price and are not relevant in the cabbie's profit-maximizing output and exit decisions.

Academic Entry and Exit

APPLIED
MICRO
THEORY

8.6

The concept of pure competition provides useful insights into academic markets. Consider each professor a firm producing a roughly homogeneous composite of university services, including classroom instruction, research, and public service. If the market for professors is competitive, the price they charge for services is set by supply and demand forces and is uniform for all. Hence, market price is P_0 in the lower right-hand panel of the figure shown here.

The other three panels depict the cost curves of three professors. Assume that the only important cost difference among professors is the opportunity costs of forgone alternatives, and remember that

Continued on page 232

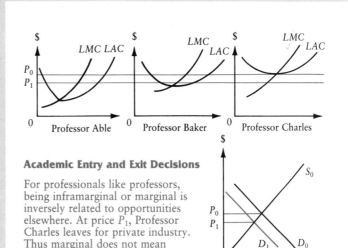

Academic Entry and Exit Decisions

For professionals like professors, being inframarginal or marginal is inversely related to opportunities elsewhere. At price P_1, Professor Charles leaves for private industry. Thus marginal does not mean "worst"; in fact, it may mean "best."

these opportunity costs are contained in the cost curves. Professor Able's LAC curve is low because he has few if any alternatives. Professor Baker has better alternatives in nonacademic positions, which is reflected in a higher LAC curve. Professor Charles has even more valuable alternatives and hence a higher LAC curve.

At the initial price P_0, Professor Charles is marginal; her profit as a professor equals the best forgone option. Professors Able and Baker, however, are inframarginal. Supply and demand forces provide them with a return in excess of their opportunity costs. The market price, in combination with low opportunity costs, bestows economic rent on Professors Able and Baker.

Now let the demand for professors fall to D_1 *ceteris paribus*, which reduces price to P_1. Professor Charles is immediately

extramarginal; she exits the academic market in the long run. Note carefully that Professor Charles is not extramarginal because she is less efficient. Quite the contrary. Professor Charles leaves first because she has skills that are valuable in business and/or government. *Extramarginal* doesn't always mean "inefficient." It just means that costs (including opportunity costs) are too high to allow participation in the industry at the current price.

The exit of extramarginal professors who have academic opportunities reduces industry supply and brings price up somewhat. Long-run equilibrium (not drawn in the figure) is reestablished when the only remaining professors are those who cover their opportunity costs. But Professors Able and Baker never once think of exiting. Falling prices have reduced their economic rent,

to be sure, but the paucity of alternatives keeps them in place.

The pure competition model of nonidentical firms provides insight into the dynamics of entry and exit. In the model of perfect competition, in which firms are identical, all firms would become extramarginal when prices fell and, logically, all should exit. On the other hand, pure competition emphasizes an orderly and predictable exit mechanism, starting with the highest-cost, most extramarginal firms and proceeding downward. The model also shows why some industries take so long to die in the face of falling demand. The decision to exit depends on better alternatives elsewhere. If industries are made up of firms whose owner's alternatives are limited, falling demands and prices merely reduce economic rents without triggering exit, thereby producing a relatively sustained death rattle.

Constant-Cost, Increasing-Cost, and Decreasing-Cost Industries

When competitive analysis allows for nonidentical firms and inframarginal profit, the connection between the various kinds of industries and the slopes of the long-run supply curves is severed. Figure 8.3 shows that the S_{LR} curve for a constant-cost industry in pure competition is positively sloped, not horizontal as in the case of perfect competition. Suppose the industry supply and demand curves set price at P_1 in initial long-run equilibrium. At price P_1, firm 1 in panel *a* is inframarginal (earns positive economic profits), firm 2 in panel *b* is marginal (earns zero economic profits), and firm 3 in panel *c* is extramarginal (does not produce in the industry due to the negative economic profits that would result). The marginal firm 2 is the highest-cost firm that can remain in the industry at price P_1.

Now let industry demand increase to D_1, forcing price up to P_3. Firms 1 and 2 expand output along their marginal cost curves; firm 3, previously an extramarginal firm, enters the industry. This entry shifts the $\Sigma_h LMC$ supply curve to the right, to $\Sigma_h LMC_1$. Because it takes place in a constant-cost industry, this expansion and entry will not change the factor prices; thus the cost curves do not shift. Note that the $\Sigma_h LMC_1$ supply curve cannot shift enough to bring price back to P_1 and allow the S_{LR} curve to be horizontal. Extramarginal firms, like firm 3, have higher average costs than the highest average cost of firms previously in the industry. Thus entry will have

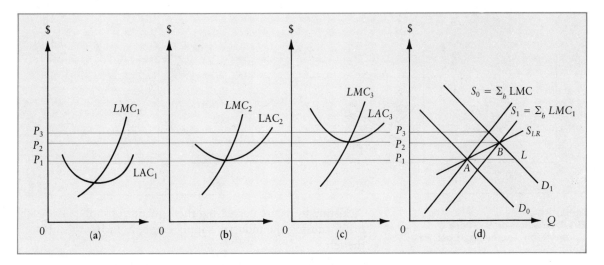

Figure 8.3
The Derivation of S_{LR}: Pure Competition, Constant-Cost Industry

(a) Firm 1 is inframarginal. (b) Firm 2 is marginal at P_1, inframarginal at $P > P_1$. (c) Firm 3 is extramarginal at P_1, marginal at P_2. (d) The entry of extramarginal firms in response to an outward shift of the demand curve causes the long-run supply curve, S_{LR}, to be positively sloped in a constant-cost industry.

squeezed all economic profit from these higher-cost firms when price reaches P_2. Note that firm 3 is a marginal firm at price P_2, and firm 2 is inframarginal. The supply curve will not shift far enough to intersect the demand curve D_1 at point L, as the perfect competition theory suggests. The entry of higher-cost, previously extramarginal firms will shut off entry before the original price P_1 is reattained. When all economic profit is squeezed from the highest-cost firms entering the industry, entry stops and the industry returns to long-run equilibrium.

The long-run supply curve, S_{LR}, is not horizontal in Figure 8.3. The S_{LR} curve is the combination of all points, such as A and B in Figure 8.4d, that satisfy long-run competitive equilibrium. This curve must have a positive slope even in a constant-cost industry due to the entry of previously extramarginal firms. Also, the S_{LR} curve in pure competition is no longer the horizontal sum of firms' minimum LAC points, as in perfect competition. Instead, the S_{LR} curve at any price-quantity combination has a height equal to the minimum LAC of the firms that are marginal at that price. Inframarginal firms have a minimum LAC less than price, and hence we cannot horizontally sum the minimum LAC points to get a meaningful construction.

The increasing-cost case is not so straightforward as the constant-cost case. Figure 8.4 shows an initial industry long-run equilibrium at point A, an initial price of P_0, and the cost curves of three firms, as before. Now let demand rise to D_1. Price increases to P_1, leading to expansion and entry. But for an increasing-cost industry, industry expansion increases factor prices. Suppose that prices for labor and capital rise proportionally, which increases the LMC and LAC curves proportionally. These shifts are shown by the colored curves in Figure 8.4. The final position of the supply curve, $\Sigma_h LMC_1$, is the balance of two forces:

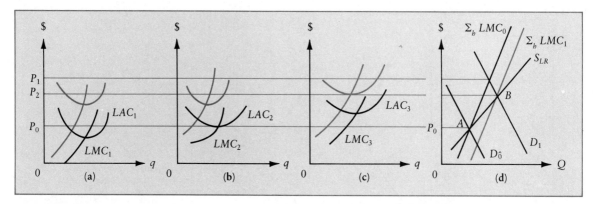

Figure 8.4
**The Derivation of S_{LR}: Pure
Competition, Increasing-Cost
Industry**

(a) Firm 1 is inframarginal. (b) Firm
2 is marginal at P_0, inframarginal at
$P > P_0$. (c) Firm 3 is extramarginal
at P_0, marginal at P_2. (d) In the
increasing-cost industry, expansion
causes input prices, and therefore
cost curves, to rise. The S_{LR} curve is
positively sloped—due to both the
entry of previously extramarginal
firms and higher costs for previously
existing firms.

Existing firms are decreasing their quantities supplied at each
price, causing the industry supply curve, Σ_hLMC, to shift to
the left.

Previously extramarginal firms are entering the industry due to
the higher price, shifting the Σ_hLMC curve to the right.

The shape of the long-run supply curve, S_{LR}, will depend on the
relative strength of these two forces. If the entry effect on the
Σ_hLMC curve is stronger than the effect of the factor price increases, the S_{LR} curve will look like the one in Figure 8.4. This result
harmonizes with our expectations that the elasticity of supply increases with the length of time available to seek production substitutes. Still, if the entry effect is not very strong, it is possible for the
S_{LR} curve to appear as it does in Figure 8.5, passing through points

Figure 8.5
A Possible Shape of the S_{LR} Curve

It is possible for the S_{LR} curve to be
more elastic than Σ_hLMC, as shown
here.

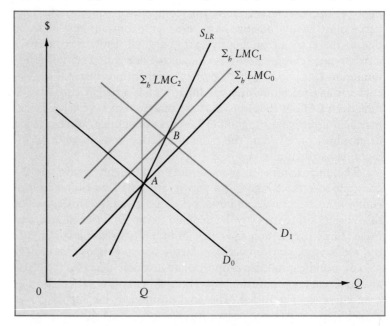

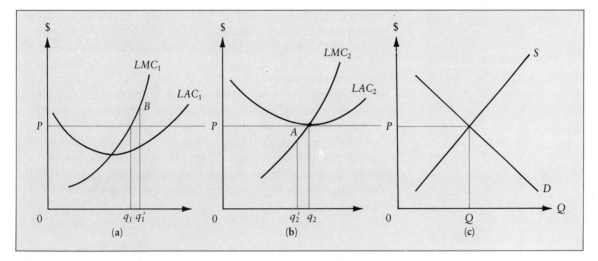

Figure 8.6
The Equal Marginal Cost Principle

(a) Firm 1 produces q_1·where LMC_1 = P. (b) Firm 2 produces q_2 where LMC_2 = P. (c) To produce a given output Q at minimum cost, firms 1 and 2 must equate their marginal costs. Parametric price-taking competitors do this noncollusively by each setting $LMC = P$.

A and B and less elastic than $\Sigma_h LMC_0$. This is a counterintuitive result but nevertheless a possibility. We know S_{LR} must be less elastic for an increasing-cost industry than for a constant-cost industry, because the firm cost curves are rising. We also know that the $\Sigma_h LMC$ curve cannot shift as far as $\Sigma_h LMC_2$ in Figure 8.5 because this would imply a vertical S_{LR} curve, with the implication that no industry expansion would occur at all—the very expansion that is presumed to give rise to increasing factor prices. Any position between these two extremes is possible.

Once again, the rare case of a decreasing-cost industry is yours to work out as an exercise. Show that the S_{LR} may be, but is not necessarily, negatively sloped when inframarginal rents are allowed in a full analysis of competitive markets.

The Equal Marginal Cost Principle of Efficiency

It is tempting to suppose that, when all firms are not operating at zero profit, the industry output is not produced at least cost. That is, doesn't the presence of inframarginal firms imply inefficiency?

The industry output in long-run competitive equilibrium will be produced at lowest possible total cost even though all firms do not operate at the minimum point of their long-run cost curve. Least-cost production is achieved for any output level when all firms produce at the same long-run marginal cost.

$$LMC_1 = LMC_2 = \cdots = LMC_n \qquad (8.1)$$

When the last unit of output in each firm is produced at identical marginal cost, there can be no cost savings from rearranging the production among firms. In Figure 8.6, firms 1 and 2 (panels a and b) produce outputs of q_1 and q_2, respectively, at identical marginal cost: $LMC_1(q_1) = LMC_2(q_2)$. Shifting one unit of production from firm 2 (high average costs) to firm 1 (low average costs) does not reduce total cost but increases it. The reduction in output from q_2 to q_2' in firm 2 yields a reduction in total cost equal to the marginal cost $q_2'A$. The increase in output from q_1 to q_1' in firm 1 adds to the total cost the marginal cost $q_1'B$. Because $q_1'B > q_2'A$, the output rearrangement increases total cost. Thus output is produced at least total cost when all firms produce at equal marginal cost regardless of the position of their average costs.

The **equal marginal cost principle** expressed in Equation 8.1 applies to any level of output. The additional requirement that the equal marginal costs also equal commodity price assures that the equilibrium amount of industry output will be produced.

$$LMC_1 = LMC_2 = \cdots = LMC_n = \cdots = P \qquad (8.2)$$

Joint Production

The competitive models set forth so far deal with firms that produce a single output. This simplification is extremely useful for approaching the ideas of competitive efficiency, profit maximization, the short-run shutdown decision, entry and exit, fair rates of return (zero economic profit), and so forth. Now we can extend our analysis to encompass firms that produce and sell multiple products, a more typical case. Even firms selling a single output face the potential of adding product lines.

The model presented in this section lends richness to the study of microeconomics; it does not contradict but rather extends previous analyses into concrete areas of actual problem solving. This extension is quite easily managed and intuitively appealing, and the extra analytical power it provides is well worth the effort.

Industry-Level Joint Production

When goods are produced jointly—as with beef and hides, mutton and wool, oil and natural gas—we encounter a problem that is fundamentally different from any problem accompanying the single-product models studied so far. The analytical tool that captures this difference is **vertical summation**.

Figure 8.7 illustrates vertical summation of demand curves, using beef and hides as an example. The curve labeled D_b is the demand curve for steers by beef users, and curve D_h is the demand curve for steers by hide users. Our goal is to construct an aggregate demand curve for steers, a curve that shows the maximum price that can be obtained for each steer. Horizontal summation of the two demand curves is not correct here because, unlike our previous demand analysis, each steer contributes to the benefits of both classes of users. Rather than horizontally summing the number of steers demanded at each price, we must sum vertically the amounts of money that all users are willing to pay for each additional steer. This is the essence of vertical summation.

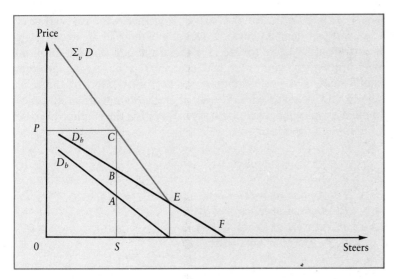

Figure 8.7
Vertical Summation of Demand Curves

To aggregate demand curves of jointly produced goods, vertical summation is required. Here the demand for steers is the vertical summation of the demands for the components, beef and hides.

To illustrate the technique in Figure 8.7, say that beef users are willing to pay SA for the Sth steer and that hide users are willing to pay SB for the same Sth steer. Because the two demands are for different uses of the same steer, the total price that will be offered for the Sth steer by both classes of users is $OP = SA + SB = SC$. Point C is the vertical summation of points A and B for the Sth steer.

Similar vertical summation for all other quantities of steers produces the aggregate demand curve labeled $\Sigma_v D$. (The subscript v is carried with the summation sign to signify vertical summation.) In Figure 8.7, the aggregate demand curve for steers, $\Sigma_v D$, has a kink at point E, the level of output at which the beef users' demand vanishes. Line segment EF is a component of both the hide users' demand curve and the aggregate demand curve $\Sigma_v D$.

Figure 8.8 illustrates market equilibrium for joint production.

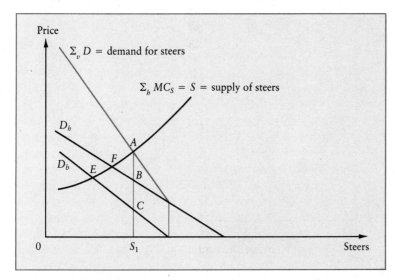

Figure 8.8
Market Equilibrium in Joint Production

Supply and demand are equated at price $\overline{S_1 A}$, the sum of the price of beef, $\overline{S_1 C}$, and the price of hides, $\overline{S_1 B}$.

The beef and hide demand curves, together with the vertically summed steer demand curve, $\Sigma_v D$, are like those in Figure 8.7. The industry supply curve for steers is the horizontal summation of all steer-producing firms' marginal cost curves, or $\Sigma_h MC_s$. Market equilibrium is achieved at point A, the intersection of the steer supply and demand curves. Note that the competitive efficiency implied by marginal cost pricing is achieved at the equilibrium rate of industry output S_1:

$$P_b + P_h = P_s = MC_s \qquad (8.3)$$

where

$$
\begin{aligned}
P_b &= \text{price of beef} = S_1 C \\
P_h &= \text{price of hides} = S_1 B \\
P_s &= \text{price of steers} = S_1 A \\
MC_s &= \text{marginal cost of steers} = S_1 A
\end{aligned}
$$

Firm-Level Joint Production

Now let's study the competitive firm's joint product equilibrium. Figure 8.9 shows the industry supply and demand curves for steers in panel b and the corresponding curves for the firm in panel a. Market forces will establish these industry prices: price of steers = P_s; price of beef = P_b; price of hides = P_h. All three prices are taken as parameters by each competitive firm. Hence the competitive firm-relevant demand curves for beef, hides, and steers are the perfectly elastic price lines P_b, P_h, and P_s. Note that the firm's demand curve for steers, P_s, is the vertical summation of the beef and hide demand curves. Profit maximization is achieved when the firm produces the rate of steer output for which $P_s = MC_s$, as at point A. The firm sells $\hat{S}$ steers and receives a total price of P_s for each steer, paid partly by beef customers and partly by hide customers.

Figure 8.9
Firm and Industry Equilibrium in Joint Production

(a) The competitive steer producer takes P_b and P_h as parameters and sets their sum equal to marginal cost: $P_b + P_h = P_s = MC_S$. (b) Market forces establish industry prices P_h and P_b, the price parameters for each firm in the industry.

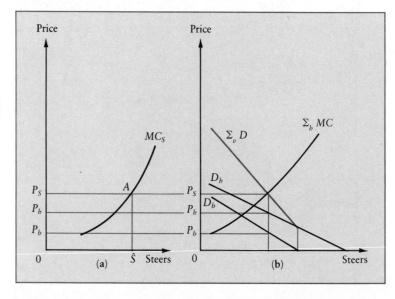

Defining the Term *Subsidy*

APPLIED
MICRO
THEORY

8.7

In our beef and hide example of joint production, the price of beef is lower than it would be in the absence of the demand for hides. In Figure 8.8, the price of beef is S_1C. However, save for the demand for hides, beef prices would be set at the higher level consistent with point E, the intersection of the beef demand curve and the steer supply curve. Do hide users therefore subsidize beef eaters? Or do beef eaters subsidize hide users? After all, the price of hides in Figure 8.8 is S_1B, lower than the price at point F that would prevail

if there were no demand for beef. In fact, neither subsidizes the other; they affect each other's prices symbiotically. The presence of both demand components keeps both prices lower than could otherwise be achieved.

A rigorous definition of *subsidy* will clarify the issue. A subsidy occurs when one economic agent allows another to purchase goods at a price less than marginal cost. In our example, firms equate the price of steers and the marginal cost of producing steers: $P_{steers} = P_{beef} + P_{hides} = MC_{steers}$. But users don't buy the steer; they buy beef or hides! The firm's marginal cost of beef is the marginal cost of the

steer less the proceeds for the hide, or

$$MC_{beef} = MC_{steer} - P_{hides} = P_{beef}$$

Similarly, the marginal cost of hides can be expressed as follows:

$$MC_{hides} = MC_{steer} - P_{beef} = P_{hides}$$

Because the market has no trouble allocating goods according to these rules, $P_{beef} = MC_{beef}$ and $P_{hides} = MC_{hides}$. Hence there is no subsidy.*

*Chapter 14 shows that the question of subsidies is especially nettlesome when dealing with collective goods that the market cannot allocate efficiently but that are jointly produced nonetheless.

Allocating the Costs of Jointly Produced Goods

APPLIED
MICRO
THEORY

8.8

Suppose you own a cattle ranch that earns a normal economic profit. You raise steers and sell the jointly produced beef and hides to separate users. You want to know how much of your total cost should be attributed to beef and how much to hides. Unfortunately, any such cost allocation is impossible. The costs of joint production, fixed or variable, cannot be attributed to either product. Furthermore, the prices of the joint products cannot be used meaningfully to allocate costs.

The figure included here depicts your firm at zero-profit equilibrium in the left-hand panel and the steer industry in the right-hand panel. The price of steers, P_s, is set by the intersection of the industry supply and demand curves for steers at point E. Industry output is $\hat{S}_{ind.}$. Beef and hide prices are demand-determined, because they depend on the height of the respective demand curves at output $\hat{S}_{ind.}$. Your firm, being competitive,

Continued on page 240

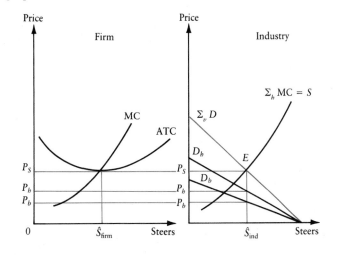

Joint-Cost Allocation

In economic logic, it is impossible to attribute joint costs uniquely among joint products. The necessary accounting rules of thumb are usually based on the demand-determined price proportions.

takes all prices as parameters and, by assumption, earns zero economic profit by raising and selling $\hat{S}_{firm}$ steers.

Initially, the price of hides is greater than the price of beef. But these prices do not reflect costs. We cannot conclude that the average cost of hides exceeds the average cost of beef for two reasons: (1) beef and hides are produced jointly, not separately, and (2) prices reflect only the height of the component demand curves. Suppose we interchange the demand curves for beef and hides in the right-hand panel. The vertically summed demand curve is unchanged, which means that the number of steers and hence the amount of beef and the number of hides are all unchanged. Therefore, neither variable nor fixed costs change. The prices of beef and hides bear no relation to the average variable cost and average fixed cost, except that the totals must be equal in the case of a zero-profit firm. Any allocation of costs is arbitrary and lacks a logical basis. Accountants must make cost allocations for tax purposes, of course, but this example demonstrates how crude and unscientific such allocations must be.

Judicial Use of Multiproduct Pricing Theory

APPLIED MICRO THEORY

8.9

The fact that fixed costs cannot be allocated precisely is of immense importance in the internal accounting of firms and in the judicial examination of those accounts when firms are defendants in antitrust suits accused of predatory business practices. In such cases, firms are typically accused of lowering the price on one product to drive rivals out of business while subsidizing this predation with profits on other products. Areeda and Turner have proposed a defense in which firms accused of such predatory pricing must show that the prices of their products are above the average variable cost, not the average cost.* As we saw in Applied Micro Theory 8.8, even this calculation is troublesome to an economist, because even average variable costs cannot be allocated precisely for joint products. However, the Areeda-

Turner rule is a great improvement over the practice of fully allocating costs.

A recent case in the telephone industry provides a useful illustration of the Areeda-Turner rule. In this case, Northeastern Telephone Company sued Ma Bell and, in particular, its affiliate, Southern New England Telephone Company. Northeastern Telephone accused them of predatory pricing

of equipment.† What concerns us is judicial appreciation of the complexity of multiproduct firms; no more eloquent statement exists than that of Circuit Judge Kaufman in this case:

Northeastern's argument in favor of a fully distributed cost test is based on a misunderstanding of the economic notion of subsidization. Northeastern seems to believe that whenever a product's price fails to cover fully distributed costs, the enterprise must subsidize that product's revenues with revenues earned elsewhere. But when the price of an item exceeds the costs directly attributable to its production, that is, when price exceeds marginal or average variable costs, no subsidy is necessary. On the contrary, any surplus can be used to defray the firm's nonallocable expenses.

†Northeastern Telephone Company v. American Telephone and Telegraph Company, _____ F. 2d _____ (2nd Cir. 1981). (The blank lines in this citation indicate that the decision has been handed down but that its place in the 2nd Circuit Reporter was not set at the time of this writing.)

*Areeda and Turner, "Predatory Pricing and Related Practices under Section 2 of the Sherman Act," *Harvard Law Review* 88 (1975): 697.

Price Controls and Jointly Produced Goods

APPLIED
MICRO
THEORY

8.10

At several points in previous chapters we have examined the impact of price controls. Now we can extend the analysis to joint production. Oil and natural gas are often jointly produced. How does a price control on natural gas affect both the natural gas industry and the oil industry?

The accompanying figure exhibits the standard joint-product analytics before and after imposition of the price control on natural gas. The horizontal axis measures the number of wells drilled. (Wells are similar to steers in the previous example. Each well contains the jointly produced oil and natural gas.) The demand curve for wells ($\Sigma_v D$) is the vertical summation of the demand curves for oil (D_{oil}) and natural gas (D_{ng}). The industry supply curve for wells is labeled $\Sigma_h MC = S$. The market clears at point E; $\hat{W}$ wells will be drilled in equilibrium, and the prices of natural gas and oil are $\hat{W}A$ and $\hat{W}B$ respectively.

When a price ceiling equal to $0H$ is imposed on natural gas, the effective demand curve for natural gas becomes the colored horizontal line, and the vertically summed demand curve becomes the colored curve. The price control on natural gas distorts the vertical summation of demand and thus the markets for both natural gas and the jointly produced good, oil.

The price control forces a reduction in wells from $\hat{W}$ to W_1 and a concomitant reduction in the production of both natural gas and oil. Note that the price of oil rises from $\hat{W}B$ to W_1F, whereas the (money) price of natural gas falls from $\hat{W}A$ to the controlled price $0H$. The diagram reveals that there is no shortage of oil; buyers cut their quantity of oil demanded in response to the higher price. There is, however, a shortage of natural gas. At the controlled price, buyers

Price Controls on Joint Products

Price controls on one product affect the market for jointly produced goods. Here a control on natural gas results in an increase in the price of oil.

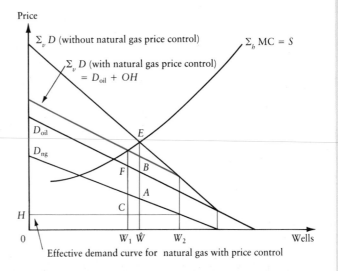

want to buy the output of W_2 wells, which is more natural gas than is available from the W_1 wells operating under the control price $0H$.

It must be emphasized that the price control distorts both markets, even though technically no shortage exists in the oil industry. Although oil shortages are avoided by price adjustments, the market

cannot avoid the ultimate economic distortion of producing an inefficient rate of output. Price controls in one market (natural gas) can create waste, not only in its own industry but in related markets (oil) as well—even when the related markets are not themselves subject to the price restraints.

Intertemporal Supply

So far, we have studied the choices of firms as if decisions take place in a single time period. However, firms must often choose between supplying output in the current period at current prices or in a future period at future prices. Firms also purchase in the current period capital assets whose returns accrue in future periods. **Intertemporal analysis** extends the principles of economics to decisions that span multiple time periods.

The first step in studying intertemporal choices is to see how flows of costs and benefits occurring in different periods can be made comparable.

Compounding and Future Value

Given the choice of receiving $1 today or a year from today, which would you choose? Naturally you would take the dollar now, because you can invest it at the current interest rate and end up with more than $1 by next year. Thus, sums of money cannot be compared intertemporally without first making the sums commensurable: $1(today) \neq $1(next year).

Let P_0 represent a sum of money that you possess now. How much is the P_0 worth 1 year from today? If you invest P_0 at the rate of interest i, the sum P_0 will grow in value by next year to P_1:

$$P_1 = P_0 + P_0 i = P_0(1 + i) \tag{8.4}$$

The value P_1, next year's value of P_0 invested at interest rate i, equals the original principal (P_0) plus the interest earned on the principal $(P_0 i)$. Thus $1000 invested at 5% interest grows to $1050 in one year: $P_1 = $1000(1 + 0.05) = 1050. The process whereby money sums increase over time is called **compounding**.

What is the compound value of P_0 in 2 years if both the principal and the interest earned in the first year continue to earn interest in year 2? P_2 equals $P_1 = P_0(1 + i)$ plus the interest on P_1 in year 2, or $P_1 i = P_0(1 + i)i$. Thus,

$$P_2 = P_1 + P_1 i = P_0(1 + i) + P_0(1 + i)i \tag{8.5}$$

Factoring $P_0(1 + i)$ yields

$$P_2 = P_0(1 + i)(1 + i) = P_0(1 + i)^2 \tag{8.6}$$

Generalizing, the compound value of P_0 after n years, P_n, is

$$P_n = P_0(1 + i)^n \tag{8.7}$$

This formula allows us to compute the future compound value of any sum of money invested in the current period when principal and accumulating interest payments continue to earn interest for n

years. This formula is for simple compounding, meaning that interest is computed only once per year. More complex—yet conceptually similar—formulas are required if interest is compounded semiannually, monthly, daily, or continuously.

Discounting and Present Value

We can reverse the logic of the compounding analysis and ask how much a future sum of money (P_n) is worth today (P_0). For example, how much money must be invested today in order to end up with the sum P_1 by next year? The answer is derived by solving Equation 8.4 for P_0:

$$P_0 = \frac{P_1}{1 + i} \qquad (8.8)$$

If you want to have $1050 a year from now, you must invest $1000 today at an interest rate of 5%, because $1050/(1 + 0.05) = \$1000$. This process of finding today's value of a future sum is called **discounting**. The sum P_0 is called the **present value**, or the **discounted value** of the future sum P_1.

The present value of any future sum is computed with the following formula, derived by solving Equation 8.7 for P_0:

$$P_0 = \frac{P_n}{(1 + i)^n} \qquad (8.9)$$

The present value of the sum P_n to be received n years hence is P_n divided by the discount factor, $(1 + i)^n$.

The Entry/Exit Concept Expanded: Geographic and Intertemporal Resource Allocation

Up to now, we have concentrated on how the entry and exit of competitive firms allocate resources among industries. The general principle is that firms produce in the most profitable industries. Here we discover that this unifying concept can be applied to geographic areas and different time periods. Competitive entrepreneurs will select the most profitable geographic markets to sell in. Many owners also have the option of selling their output in the present period or in a future period. The basic principle of entry and exit applies to switching supplies among industries, geographic areas, and time periods.

GEOGRAPHIC ALLOCATION   Consider a product being sold in two geographic markets by competitive firms. If we assume zero transportation costs, there can be no price difference between the two markets in equilibrium. If prices differ, there are profit incentives to shift supplies from the lower-priced market to the higher-priced one, until the price differential that induces the shifts is eliminated. In fact, such responses make it difficult to think of the two markets as separate. If transportation costs are positive and there are no barriers to entry, equilibrium prices in different geographic areas can differ only by the transportation costs.

INTERTEMPORAL ALLOCATION   Intertemporal supply choices are especially interesting for firms selling exhaustible, storable resources, such as oil, natural gas, and coal. Selling a ton of coal today forecloses the opportunity of selling it in any other period, when it may bring a higher price. Entrepreneurs selling storable resources have an asset that they can choose to sell in the most profitable time period, taking into account the growth path of selling prices and storage costs over time.

To see how prices of exhaustible resources compare in different time periods, consider the substitutability of two different stores of value: a financial asset (bond) and a ton of coal. The financial asset must rise in value over time in order to induce people to hold it. Similarly, the ton of coal must rise in value to induce storage.

Suppose the stores of value for bonds and coal rise at different rates. Entrepreneurs holding the asset with the slower rate of increase will sell some of it and buy some of the faster-rising asset. These switches bring the relative rates of value increase closer together. The process stops when the two rates are equal. Thus the equilibrium price of exhaustible assets like coal must rise at the same rate as financial assets. This is the famous **Hotelling principle** of intertemporal resource allocation: Profit-maximizing entrepreneurship in competitive markets forces the prices of exhaustible resources to rise at the rate of interest, net of costs.[1]

Let's examine the intertemporal entry/exit mechanism more closely, assuming that the storage costs of holding coal in the ground are negligible. Suppose that coal can be sold in period 1 or period 2. Period 2's price, P_2, must equal period 1's price, P_1, plus interest earned on P_1 between the current period and the next period, $P_1 \cdot i$. In symbols,

$$P_2 = P_1 + P_1 \cdot i = P_1(1 + i) \qquad (8.10)$$

or

$$P_1 = \frac{P_2}{1 + i} \qquad (8.11)$$

The price in period 2 equals period 1's price, which requires that P_2 exceed P_1 by the rate of interest.

Suppose that $P_1 < P_2/(1 + i)$ temporarily. The present value of

1. Harold Hotelling, "The Economics of Exhaustible Resources," *Journal of Political Economy* 39 (1931): 137–175.

Intertemporal Supply and Price Controls

APPLIED
MICRO
THEORY

8.11

Suppose that price controls are imposed on natural gas. We have seen how controls misallocate resources and retard long-run equilibrium adjustments between industries. We will now discover how price controls distort the intertemporal consumption of natural gas.

Surprisingly, controls may actually increase supplies of natural gas in the short run. At any given time, natural gas is both stored and extracted. Price controls curtail investments in future extraction but give owners a greater incentive to deplete present stocks sooner (unless they believe that the controlled price will be lifted soon). If price controls are such that $P_1 = P_2$ and if costs are negligible, then $P_1 > P_2/(1 + i)$. It is more profitable to sell natural gas stocks in the current period and invest in something other than resource storage and extraction than to store and sell natural gas later at the same price. This fact increases the supply of natural gas in the current period and may even drive the price below the controlled price. Thus there may be no apparent shortages or upward pressure on prices soon after the imposition of controls. But stored gas is being depleted and exploration curtailed. Eventually, the industry will suffer severe shortages of stored reserves and a shortage of invested capital and equipment for producing more when the stored gas is depleted. Furthermore, the shortage will hit consumers more suddenly than if prices rose gradually. Consumers have little incentive to insulate, install solar panels, or relocate to smaller houses while prices are artificially low. When the shortage of natural gas occurs suddenly, all the markets for these substitutes have to adjust suddenly. Sudden adjustments are more expensive than gradual adjustments.

Thus the initial reaction to price controls—an increase in supply—may seem very desirable, but it may mask the true long-run impacts. An inherent danger in our political system is that politicians, seeking reelection in the short run, may have incentives to concentrate on the apparent short-run benefits of controls and ignore the inevitable long-run shortages.

The counterpart of this argument occurs during periods of decontrol. When prices are again market-determined after a period of price controls, suppliers store their gas supplies in expectation of higher prices caused by limited investment in exploration and storage. In short, the supply of gas in the current period may not be very elastic with respect to higher prices.

Members of Congress and Presidents have often assailed profiteering companies for storing gas while waiting for prices to rise and have interpreted such behavior as evidence of monopoly. But this is a natural response to price controls, and we should expect competitive firms to respond in this way. Storage of natural resources is neither a necessary nor a sufficient test for monopoly power. Competitive firms will also sell natural gas in the most profitable time period. If public policy raises the expectation that the present value of future prices exceeds current prices, price-taking competitors will store resources while prices rise.

price in period 2 is greater than the price in period 1, and so it is profitable for the individual firm to store more gas until period 2. However, the industry effect of many individual firm decisions to stop selling gas in the present period by storing for the future reduces the current period supplies, increases future period supplies, and pushes the present value of the different period prices toward equality. These intertemporal adjusments continue until the price in period 1 equals the present value of the price in period 2; $P_1 = P_2/(1 + i)$.

Conversely, if $P_1 > P_2/(1 + i)$, firms have a profit incentive to sell more gas in the current period, but the increases in period 1 supplies and decreases in period 2 supplies force the different prices closer together—until $P_1 = P_2/(1 + i)$ once again. In this way, the competitive market assures that nonreproducible resources will be stored for future use and sold in the current period in an orderly way.

Contracts and Intertemporal Efficiency

APPLIED
MICRO
THEORY

8.12

For many results in microeconomics, exchange can be treated as simultaneous, with no delay between agreements and their performance. In fact, many actions of economic agents are separated in time, and the theory would be of limited usefulness if it did not apply to intertemporal bargaining.

The simple purchase of a magazine may appear to be a simultaneous exchange of money and printed paper. But it may be days later that the buyer discovers that pages are missing. More complicated transactions, such as the exchange of labor services, equipment purchases, and the building of skyscrapers, require a great deal of time between agreement and performance. During such periods, there is the potential for any party to regret the deal—as a result of, among other things, changes in relative prices. These risks may make people reluctant to enter the agreement in the first place.

Contracts facilitate such intertemporal agreements. State enforcement of contract terms allows parties to rely on agreements prior to completion of their performance. However, courts do not generally require parties to carry out the terms of their agreements. But if people unilaterally renege, they must pay damages to restore the value of the contract to the injured party. Consequently, contracts permit longer-term arrangements when they are in the parties' mutual interest. Thus the role of contracts is to provide incentives for careful writing and efficiency in entering into agreements and to allow people to trust long-term agreements. This role is a requirement for efficient allocation of intertemporal resources.

Suppose a new firm wants to produce a higher-cost, higher-quality television set. If the firm provides a guarantee, durability claims can be enforced by contract, and the higher-quality TV set can compete with low-priced sets. In similar fashion, contracts allow mail-order houses to compete with local stores by making claims by new firms more believable and reliable. In general, state enforcement of contracts facilitates sequential exchange; without contracts, exchange would be more simultaneous and hence less efficient.*

*For further discussion of the intertemporal effects of contract enforcement, see Anthony T. Kronman and Richard A. Posner, *The Economics of Contract Law* (Boston: Little Brown, 1979), especially chapter 2.

Beginning in intertemporal long-run equilibrium, where $P_1 = P_2/(1 + i)$, let the interest rate rise to i', so that $P_1 > P_2/(1 + i')$. In this situation, firms have an incentive to switch output from the future to the present. This switch continues until the intertemporal supply changes reduce P_1 and increase P_2—until $P_1' = P_2'/(1 + i')$. Because a higher real interest rate implies that consumers place a higher value on current consumption than on future consumption, it is proper that the competitive market allocates a larger portion of the nonrenewable resource to present consumption. In contrast, a lower interest rate would reduce the current consumption rate of the resource and increase storage for the future.

Limitations of the Competitive Model

We have seen that competitive equilibrium induces efficiency in the use of resources, both intratemporally and intertemporally. But competitive equilibrium generates efficiency only when the firm pays the full social cost of its resources. For example, if pollution damages are not incorporated into the firm's costs, competition from "dirty" firms will force "clean" firms to adopt dirty production techniques or to exit the industry. In addition, firms' marginal costs will be understated, a practice that encourages firms to produce too much output and consequently to generate excessive pollution, in both the production and consumption of goods.

Another example of the undesirable results of competitive equilibrium occurs when profitable pornographic movies and magazines attract the entry of competing firms that allow material to get increasingly obscene in order to keep "down" with the competition. Because the full social cost of such material is not paid by producing firms, marginal costs are understated, industry supply is overstated, prices are too low, and an excessive quantity of output is produced as long-run adjustments move the industry to equilibrium.

Many of the problems associated with the incomplete reflection of full societal costs in product prices are solved by property right systems, which are treated in detail in Chapter 14. For now, note that the competitive efficiency discussed in this chapter must be limited to the minimization of private costs.

Summary

This chapter expands the concept of competition in three ways: It distinguishes between perfect and pure competition, introduces the concept of joint production of goods within a firm, and introduces the concept of intertemporal competition.

The key distinction between pure and perfect competition is that firms in pure competition are not identical. The central ingredient of competition, parametric pricing, is the same; although firms in pure competition are not identical, they are too small to affect price. A number of important implications flow from the theory of pure competition. For example, it is possible for economic rent to be earned in a purely competitive industry. Thus firms may be categorized as marginal, inframarginal, or extramarginal. Only the marginal firm breaks even—there is no economic rent. However, economic rent is available to the inframarginal firm, and it is determined by the gap between price and costs. Thus small farms may struggle to survive while larger, more efficient farms prosper, and inframarginal apartment houses may not pass on to renters reductions in property taxes.

The joint production of beef and hides or of oil and natural gas exemplifies a common departure from the model of the single-product firm that we have encountered in previous chapters. In fact, multiple-product firms are common, and single-product firms are rare. However, the analysis required for joint production is a rather simple extension of competitive theory. One powerful implication of joint production is that production costs cannot be divided up and accurately attributed to individual products. A recent antitrust ruling drives home the importance of this theory.

Finally, competition over time affects supply and demand and the entry/exit process as it coordinates the intertemporal allocation of resources. As usual, price controls distort this allocation by removing the incentive to store goods. Government enforcement of contracts is an important element in intertemporal efficiency, because it reduces risk when agreements and the carrying out of agreements are significantly separated in time.

Key Terms

compounding 242
discounting 243
economic rent 226
equal marginal cost principle 236
extramarginal firm 221
Hotelling principle 244
inframarginal firm 220
inframarginal profit 226
inframarginal rent 226
intertemporal analysis 242
marginal firm 220
present value (discounted value) 243
price-determined cost 229
price-determining costs 229
rent-inclusive long-run average cost (LAC^*) 227
vertical summation 236

Problems

1. a. Suppose your backyard well produces both oil and natural gas in fixed proportions. Show how an increase in the price of oil will affect your output of natural gas.

   b. Suppose that the cost of keeping the well operating is $10,000 per year for labor, equipment, and so forth. How much of that cost is attributable to the oil and how much to the gas?

2. Show that, if beef demand rises sufficiently, slaughterhouses will give away hides or pay people to take them away.

3. Reread Applied Micro Theory 8.4 and then analyze the impact of an income tax on apartment income, net of capital and labor costs. What would happen to the supply of apartments and rental rates?

4. Reread Applied Micro Theory 8.5. What happens to the value of a taxicab medallion when the price of gasoline rises?

5. What happens to the current supply of a storable good when a substitute is discovered or developed?

6. Urban areas are expanding into farming areas. As a result, a lot of prime cropland is being sold to developers. Why isn't the less desirable cropland all that is sold to developers?

7. Consider a crop like asparagus, which is harvested only once per year. Draw a diagram with price on the vertical axis and time on the horizontal axis. Then trace your prediction of the time trend of the price of asparagus. Now introduce a technological innovation that allows asparagus to be harvested twice a year. Retrace the time trend. (Hint: Would entry occur?)

8. Suppose the owner of a marginal firm wants to set up a factory on a parcel of land. She doesn't know if the firm will be inframarginal in the future or not, but once the factory is in place, it will be very costly to move. Should she buy the parcel of land or rent it? If you decide that she should rent, describe the rental terms that she should insist on.

9. Suppose the government decides to subsidize the production of a storable good. What will happen to current and future supplies of that good in a competitive market?

10. Suppose the government decides to stockpile a competitively produced storable good. What do you predict will happen to current and future production and total (private plus government) storage of the good?

11. A major increase in property taxes is announced to pay for a new sewer system. Before the announcement, there is a brisk market for homes on your block—homes sell quickly at an average price of $70,000. After the announcement, some homeowners say, "I'm fed up with taxes; I'll sell my $70,000 home, move to exurbia with a septic tank, and avoid those new taxes." For Sale signs remain up for months, and many discouraged would-be sellers give up and stay in the neighborhood. Explain the forces at work in this example.

12. A home is built in 1903 at a cost of $7500. Over time it deteriorates badly and begins to require frequent maintenance of all kinds. In 1975 it sells for $35,000, and in 1978 it is appraised at $65,000.

No major improvements—such as garages, additions, finished basement, or attic—have been made.

a. Show how the appreciation in the value of the home can be explained by an increase in demand. Note that the increase from 1975 to 1978 was far faster than inflation.

b. What supply response would you expect?

c. Under what conditions would the price fall below $65,000? Below $35,000? Below any other price?

d. Explain the impact of a new freeway on the price of this house (1) if it is located near employment centers and (2) if it is out in the boondocks, near the end of the new freeway.

e. What effect does the 1903 price have on your answers?

13. Miller Brewing Company has plants in Milwaukee, Wisconsin; Eden, North Carolina; Forth Worth, Texas; Azusa, California; and Fulton, New York—but none in Arizona or New Mexico, where population is growing. Suppose that the demand for beer grows in Arizona and New Mexico. As a result, suppose that Miller Brewing Company plans an expansion in output.

a. Suppose transportation is costless (or costs very little compared to other production costs). A vice president of Miller suggests producing all the extra output in the plant closest to the expanding market. Is this a good idea? What has to be true of the company's cost curves for this to be a profit-maximizing move?

b. Suppose transportation costs are 2¢ per thousand miles per bottle or can. Restate the equal marginal cost rule in light of these costs.

14. Paul Samuelson noted that some economists use very strange logic to conclude that price equals average costs: "A typical form of the argument is as follows: (1) a firm will equate marginal cost to price; (2) it will also try to minimize its unit costs; (3) at the point of minimum unit cost average cost equals marginal cost; (4) hence, average cost must equal price (average revenue) and profits will be zero."[2] Using the theory of pure competition, demonstrate the failure of logic in the argument he quotes.

15. Suppose Firm A is breaking even. Then entry of lower cost firms results in lower prices. Firm A then faces a price below the break-even price but above AVC. A piece of equipment then breaks down. How should this hapless firm determine whether to repair the machine or to exit the industry?

16. What rule do you use to determine whether a joint product firm is marginal or inframarginal?

17. Is a firm that produces oil a joint product firm because it produces oil in two time periods? (Hint: Can the oil sold in each period be treated as separate products as can beef and hides?)

18. Suppose the government places a price ceiling on oil that is to be removed on January 1, 1987. Discuss the decision to sell oil in the period before and after that date. Now suppose the removal of the control is to be "phased"; every six months the price can be raised

2. Paul A. Samuelson, *Foundations of Economic Analysis* (New York: Atheneum, 1965), p. 83.

5 percent until the control price is above the equilibrium price. Discuss this policy. What do you expect during periods close to the semiannual price jump? How is your answer related to the rate of interest?

19. Suppose you own a complex of apartment buildings in Texas. Your property tax liability is slashed by the passage of Question 7 in a general referendum vote. Your management team advises you to reduce rents in order to allow your tenants to share in the tax reduction. They claim that lowering rents will benefit the public and thereby build good will toward your firm. Do you agree with your management team? (Hint: What will happen if rents are lowered? Are you sure good will is enhanced? What bad will could be engendered? What extra decisions will you face after rents are lowered?)

Suggested Readings

Coase, R. H. "The Nature of the Firm." *Economica* 4 (1937): 386–405.

Henry, William R., and Haynes, W. Warren. *Managerial Economics.* Dallas: Business Publications, 1978, chap. 12.

Samuelson, Paul A. *Foundations of Economic Analysis.* New York: Atheneum, 1965, chap. 4.

Monopoly

We have been studying the consequences of firm behavior under competitive conditions, in which all firms are price takers and thus lack the market power to set industry price or output. We can now turn our attention to the monopolist. The competitive firm cannot influence industry price or output, but the **monopolist,** being the only seller in the industry, must set both price and output. Major economic consequences arise from the monopolist's control over price and output.

We begin our study of the monopolist with the simplest assumptions: The monopolist firm (1) charges the same price to all customers, (2) produces its output in a single plant, and (3) is not regulated by government. These assumptions allow us to explore the essentials of monopoly behavior without undue complexity. Later we can analyze more meaningful monopoly cases, in which the monopoly firm charges different prices to its customers and produces output in multiple plants. (Monopoly regulation is reserved for Chapter 13.) Also, we will study the theory of the cartel, a collection of potentially competing firms that coordinate their market decisions in order to approximate the profit-maximizing behavior of the monopolist. Cartels play an important role in our present domestic and world economy and thus deserve our scrutiny.

An overarching concern is the effect of monopoly on the efficiency of resource allocation. Does monopoly necessarily lead to an inefficient use of scarce resources? Could the resources that the monopolist uses, if used differently, improve the welfare of some people without reducing the welfare of anyone? These are important questions, and we can get revealing answers by using what we know about competitive firms as a benchmark to evaluate the real costs that monopoly inflicts on our economic system.

Explanations for Monopoly

The dictionary tells us that *monopoly* is of Greek derivation and means "single seller." There are many reasons a firm may face no competition in its industry and therefore become a monopoly; six of these reasons deserve special mention here.

First, and most trivial, is the monopoly that exists because industry demand is not sufficient to support more than one producer. For example an American firm producing mustache cups will

9

have few if any competitors due to limited consumer demand.[1]
② Second, firms are given government-awarded patents and copyrights that protect against competition for many years (17 years for most patents and 50 years for song lyrics). Third, a firm may have ③ control over an essential resource or have unique knowledge of a production process, making it difficult for other firms to compete in its industry. However, neither patents nor sole command over resources is a perfect barrier to entry, because competing firms can often produce close substitutes using available resources and without violating patent laws.

④ Fourth, a firm's production function may be characterized by decreasing costs, that is, by a negatively sloped long-run average cost curve. In such cases, the firm can always lower its per-unit production costs by expanding output. If other firms have U-shaped long-run average cost curves, the monopoly firm can eliminate its competitors by increasing its output and placing itself in a more favorable cost position compared to the competition. By eliminating all competitors in this way, the firm becomes the industry's only seller and gains complete control over its price and output. Such firms are called **natural monopolies** or **technological monopolies** because they exist due to the special characteristics of their production functions. The electric power utilities, the telecommunications industry, and municipal sewage systems are typical examples. These industries are inconsistent with long-run competitive equilibrium; because competition cannot be achieved, the government often awards them exclusive production franchises in exchange for the right to regulate and monitor their pricing, output, and quality decisions. Thus government franchise and regulation, the fifth reason for monopoly, is closely related to the presence of natural monopoly.

⑥ Finally, monopoly behavior occurs when otherwise competitive firms choose to coordinate their pricing and output decisions in order to become an effective monopoly. Such collusive arrangements among firms have been popularized most recently by the Organization of Petroleum Exporting Countries (OPEC) cartel.

Let's begin our investigation of monopoly by assuming that the monopolist's cost curves are substantially the same as the competitor's—U-shaped ATC and LAC curves—and thereby concentrate on monopolists' behavior resulting solely from the absence of competition. Chapter 13 gives special attention to the aspects of monopoly that arise from decreasing long-run average costs.

The Simple Monopolist

The essential distinction between a competitive firm and a monopoly firm lies in the demand curves that the two firms face. The

---

1. A mustache cup has a straight piece inside, just below the rim, for holding back a man's mustache while he is drinking.

competitive firm faces a perfectly elastic demand curve, cannot influence price, and therefore adjusts only its output in seeking its profit-maximizing equilibrium. In contrast, the monopolist faces the industry demand curve as the only seller in the industry. The **simple monopolist** must therefore set its price and output within the bounds established by consumer demand.[2]

Although the monopolist sets both price and output, these are not set independently. The industry demand curve in Figure 9.1 illustrates this dependency. If the monopolist sets a price of $5, the most output it can sell at that price is 1 unit. Point A, representing sales of 3 units of output at a price of $5, is outside the bounds set by demand. Thus the typical criticism levied against monopolies—their unbridled ability to sell any quantity of output at any prices—is absurd and ignores the demand constraint that monopolists face.

The profit-maximizing rule for competitive firms was defined in Chapter 7: MR = MC, with MC rising. The monopolist must also equate marginal revenue and marginal cost to maximize profits. However, the monopolist's revenue characteristics differ from the competitor's: Because the monopolist faces the industry demand curve, it must lower its price to sell more output. In monopoly, price cannot equal marginal revenue.

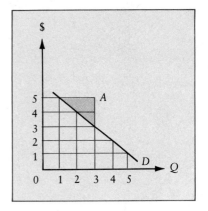

Figure 9.1
The Downward-Sloping Monopoly Demand Curve

Increased sales require a lower price. Point A is not possible.

Price and Marginal Revenue

It is difficult to overstate the importance of the inequality of price and marginal revenue in the theory of monopoly. The rule for the monopolist is $P > MR$. To see why, refer to the formal definition of marginal revenue first given in Chapter 7:

$$MR = P + Q\frac{\Delta P}{\Delta Q} \qquad (9.1)$$

Marginal revenue is the sum of the two terms in Equation 9.1. The increase in total revenue resulting from the sale of an additional unit of output, the first term in Equation 9.1, equals the price at which the marginal unit is sold. The reduction in total revenue resulting from the reduction in the price of all units sold previously at a higher price, the second term in Equation 9.1, is the product of the slope of the demand curve, $\Delta P/\Delta Q$, and the number of inframarginal units to which the price reduction applies, Q.

In competition, price equals marginal revenue because of the special assumption that the firm need not reduce price to sell more output. The slope of the perfectly elastic demand curve that the competitor faces, $\Delta P/\Delta Q$, is zero. Thus the second term in Equation 9.1, $Q \cdot (\Delta P/\Delta Q)$, is zero; marginal revenue for the competitor equals price.

---

2. A simple monopolist faces **arbitrage** for its products, meaning that efforts to sell the product at two different prices will be frustrated by people buying low and undercutting the monopolist's high prices. Thus a simple monopolist charges uniform prices to all customers.

Table 9.1
Revenue Data
Corresponding to the Demand Curve in Figure 9.1

Price	×	Quantity Sold	=	Total Revenue $(P \cdot Q)$	Marginal Revenue $(\Delta TR/\Delta Q)$
5		1		5	5
4		2		8	3
3		3		9	1
2		4		8	−1
1		5		5	−3

For the simple monopolist, the algebraic sum of the two effects in Equation 9.1 is always less than price, except in the trivial case of the first unit sold. Consider Figure 9.1. When the price is $4, the monopolist sells 2 units and has total revenue of $8. To sell an additional unit, the monopolist must lower the price to $3 on all units sold, pushing total revenue to $9. Note that price ($3) exceeds marginal revenue ($1). According to Equation 9.1, marginal revenue is the algebraic sum of $3 (the price received on the last unit sold) and −$2 (the loss in revenue of $1 each on units 1 and 2, which previously sold for $4 instead of $3): $Q \cdot (\Delta P/\Delta Q) = 2 \cdot (-1/1) = -\$2$.

Table 9.1 contains revenue data corresponding to the demand curve in Figure 9.1. You should use Equation 9.1 to verify the marginal revenue figures in the last column of Table 9.1. There is no use reading farther into this chapter until you know why $P > MR$ for the monopolist, a result that shows up directly in Table 9.1 for all units except the first one.

Price, Marginal Revenue, and Price Elasticity of Demand

The discussion of price elasticity of demand in Chapter 3 showed that marginal revenue is related to the price elasticity of demand according to the following formula:

$$MR = P(1 + \frac{1}{\varepsilon}) \qquad (9.2)$$

In this equation, ε refers to the price elasticity of demand. We can now use these relationships to derive the monopolist's family of revenue curves: marginal revenue (MR), average revenue (AR), and total revenue (TR).

Table 9.2 arranges the relationships between P, MR, and ε in a useful manner. The first column shows the possible values for the price elasticity of demand (ε). If we know ε, we can deduce all the other relationships.

Table 9.2
The Effect of the Price Elasticity of Demand (ε)
on the Monopolist's Revenue Curves

When ε	$\text{MR}(\frac{\Delta TR}{\Delta Q})$	$P \equiv \text{AR}$	TR
< -1 (elastic)	> 0	$>$ MR	Rises
$= -1$ (unit elastic)	$= 0$	$>$ MR	Attains its maximum
> -1 (inelastic)	< 0	$>$ MR	Falls
$= -\infty$ (perfectly elastic)	> 0	$=$ MR	Is linear

Consider the demand curve D in Figure 9.2*a*. It will help to recall that price is equal to average revenue: $\text{AR} = \text{TR}/Q = (P \cdot Q)/Q = P$. The demand curve measures the average revenue (or price) that can be charged for different levels of output. Thus the demand curve is the average revenue curve and equals price at every point on the curve.

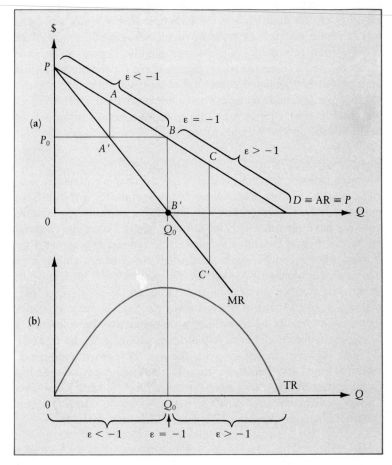

Figure 9.2
The Monopolist's Marginal, Average, and Total Revenue Curves

(a) For a straight-line demand curve, marginal revenue is a straight line with twice the slope. (b) The total revenue curve is a parabola.

The demand curve in Figure 9.2*a* is linear, so price elasticity ranges from elastic to inelastic. At point *A*, $\varepsilon < -1$; thus marginal revenue must be positive and less than price. The marginal revenue value corresponding to the demand point *A* is plotted at point *A'* on the marginal revenue curve. At point *B* on the demand curve, $\varepsilon = -1$, and marginal revenue must be zero (see point *B'*). At point *C*, $\varepsilon > -1$, and the marginal revenue is negative (see point *C'*). The marginal revenue curve lies entirely below the demand (average revenue) curve because $P = AR > MR$ in a simple monopoly. Thus at any point on the demand curve, we know the price and can compute the price elasticity of demand. With this information and Equation 9.2, we can also calculate the marginal revenue.

The marginal revenue curve is the slope of the total revenue curve, so we can work backward to derive the total revenue curve. By definition, if MR is positive, the slope of TR must be positive; if MR is zero, the slope of TR is zero; and if MR is negative, the slope of TR is negative. In Figure 9.2, when the firm lowers price from P to P_0, demand is price elastic. The additional units sold at the lower prices between P and P_0 cause total revenue to rise, as shown in Figure 9.2*b*. At price P_0, $\varepsilon = -1$, marginal revenue is zero, and total revenue is at its maximum. Further price reductions from P_0 to 0 cause total revenue to fall, because demand is price inelastic at prices below P_0. Thus the total revenue curve for the monopolist is an inverted bowl-shaped curve and is uniquely related to the demand and marginal revenue curves.[3] Observe that the total-average-marginal relationships that pertain to other contexts are preserved in the monopolist's revenue curves.

Positioning the Marginal Revenue Curve

The area beneath any marginal curve of a variable equals the total value of the variable. This is an obvious proposition if you have mastered integral calculus and a simple intuitive concept if you have not. We have already used this concept in discussions of cardinal utility theory and consumer surplus. For example, in Chapter 4 we studied the income-compensated demand curve, which is a marginal-willingness-to-pay curve. We saw that the area beneath the income-compensated demand curve equals the consumer's total willingness to pay and, if price is zero, also equals total consumer surplus. The beauty of economics is that once you have learned a concept you need not relearn it in different contexts. Thus, applying the same concept to Figure 9.3*a*, the area beneath the short-run marginal cost curve between output levels *A* and *B* equals the total variable cost of increasing output from *A* to *B*. Similarly, the area under the MR curve in Figure 9.3*b* between outputs *C* and *D* equals the total change in revenue, $\text{TR}(D) - \text{TR}(C)$.

---

3. "Mathephiles" will note that, for a straight-line demand curve, the shape is actually a parabola.

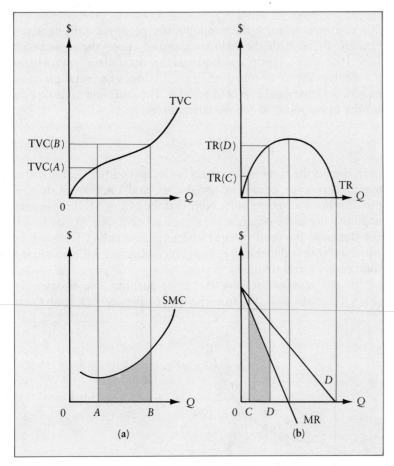

(a)

(b)

Figure 9.3
The Simple Monopolist's Marginal Revenue Curve

The area under any marginal curve measures a total. (a) The area under the SMC curve between outputs A and B equals $TVC(B) - TVC(A)$. (b) The area under the MR curve between outputs C and D equals $TR(D) - TR(C)$.

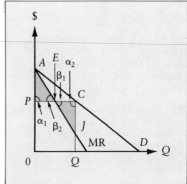

Figure 9.4
Positioning Marginal Revenue

Marginal revenue falls twice as fast as the demand curve. Because triangles PAE and ECJ are congruent, distance $\overline{PE}$ equals $\overline{EC}$.

Now let's use this equality between total values and the area beneath the marginal curve to position the marginal revenue curve when the demand curve is linear. In Figure 9.4, total revenue can be measured in two ways: as price times quantity and as the area beneath the marginal revenue curve. When Q units of output are sold, total revenue equals both areas $0PCQ$ and $0AEJQ$. The area $0PEJQ$ is common to both measures. Thus are areas APE and ECJ must be equal. The angle β_1 equals angle β_2; because angles α_1 and α_2 are right angles, triangles APE and ECJ are congruent. Corresponding sides of congruent triangles are equal in length, so the line segment AP equals segment CJ. Thus when output is Q, the marginal revenue is found by plotting point J below C, so that $AP = CJ$. It follows that the distance PE equals the distance EC; the marginal revenue curve falls exactly twice as fast as the demand curve. This conclusion applies only to linear demand curves but is a convenient device in sketching the monopolist's revenue curves. Caution: Remember that marginal revenue is a function of output. Thus marginal revenue for output Q in Figure 9.4 equals QJ.

Profit-Maximizing Equilibrium of the Simple Monopolist

We can now identify the monopolist's profit-maximizing equilibrium. Faced with the industry demand curve, the monopolist selects the price-quantity combination that maximizes profit. Figure 9.5 displays the profit-maximizing equilibrium using total curves in panel *a* and marginal curves in panel *b*. The profit-maximizing rule for the monopolist, as for the competitor, is

$$MR = MC \qquad\qquad (9.3)$$

In Figure 9.5 the monopolist selects the level of output Q_0, for which marginal revenue equals marginal cost, and simultaneously sets price to clear the market at P_0. Note that the MR = MC intersection at point *e* in panel *b* occurs at the same level of output, Q_0, for which the slopes of the total revenue and total cost curves are equal in panel *a*. Profit is illustrated as the vertical distance *AB* between the total revenue and total cost curves.

If the monopolist sets the price-quantity combination at (P_1, Q_1), profit falls, because the output between Q_0 and Q_1 is

Figure 9.5
Monopoly Profit-Maximization Condition: MR = MC

Any output other than Q_0, where MR = MC, yields a lower profit (proof by contradiction). (a) The profit-maximizing equilibrium can be shown with total curves. (b) It can also be shown with marginal curves.

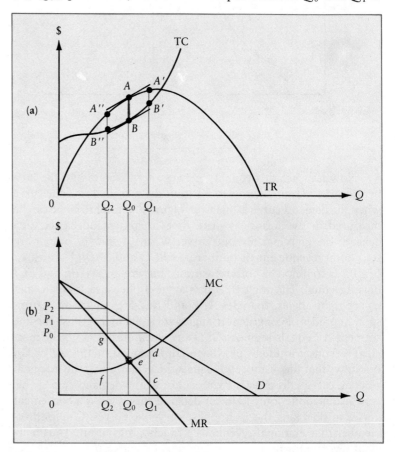

produced and sold at a marginal cost exceeding the marginal revenue. Panel a shows profits falling to $A'B' < AB$. In panel b the additional output $Q_1 - Q_0$ adds costs of Q_0edQ_1 (the area beneath the marginal cost curve) but revenues of only Q_0ecQ_1 (the area beneath the marginal revenue curve). Therefore, increasing output from Q_0 to Q_1 reduces total profit by the area edc. If the price-quantity combination (P_2, Q_2) is selected, profits are reduced to $A''B''$ or equivalently by the area egf, because for the units $Q_0 - Q_2$, MR > MC. Output reductions give up more revenue than is saved in costs. Thus profits are maximized when MR = MC and price is set to clear the market. This profit-maximizing rule is perfectly generalizable to all market structures.

We qualified the MR = MC profit-maximizing condition for competition by requiring that the marginal cost curve cut the marginal revenue curve from below. Because the marginal revenue curve is horizontal in competition, requiring the marginal cost curve to cut the marginal revenue curve from below is equivalent to requiring marginal cost to be rising. Monopoly still requires that the marginal cost curve cut the marginal revenue curve from below. But because marginal revenue falls for the monopolist, this condition may be satisfied even with marginal cost falling, as long as marginal cost is falling more slowly than marginal revenue. In Figure 9.6, the MC curve cuts the MR curve from below at point A, satisfying the profit-maximizing condition. At point B, MC cuts MR from above, which is not a profit-maximizing condition. Thus output should be expanded to Q_0.

Figure 9.7 is a more complete representation of monopoly equilibrium. The monopolist sets LMC = MR (point e) by selecting a

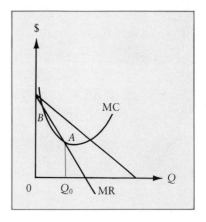

Figure 9.6
Monopoly Profit Maximization

To maximize profits, a monopolist must set MR = MC, and the MC curve must cut the MR curve from below.

Figure 9.7
The Welfare Loss Triangle

Because of underproduction, $P >$ MC. The value lost to the economy is measured by the area efb.

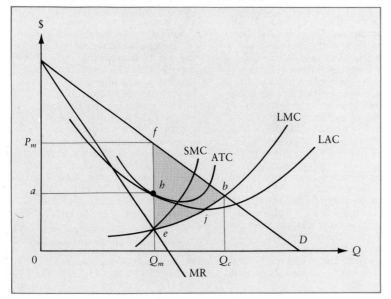

level of capital so that ATC = LAC (point h) and consequently SMC = LMC = MR (point e). The price that clears the market when Q_m is produced is P_m, determined by point f on the demand curve. Thus Figure 9.7 helps organize our thoughts on several variables at once: output (Q), price (P), capital (K), labor (L), revenue (R), cost (C), and profit (π).

It is essential to the existence of monopoly that the profits aP_mfh in Figure 9.7 not be dissipated by entering firms. $P > \text{LAC}(Q_m)$ and positive economic profits can exist in long-run equilibrium.

Properties of Monopoly Equilibrium

We have seen that long-run profit maximization requires the monopolist to equate short- and long-run marginal cost, as at point e in Figure 9.7. The condition SMC = LMC implies that the firm has selected the correct combination of inputs for the production of the selected output. The short-run ATC curve is tangent to the long-run LAC curve at output level Q_m, and the input efficiency condition $MP_L/MP_K = w/r$, described in Chapter 7, is achieved. There is no way to reduce the cost of producing this level of output by rearranging capital and labor inputs.

The long-run competitive equilibrium condition $P = \text{LMC}$ is not satisfied in monopoly. Because profits are maximized in monop-

Tie-in Sales and Reciprocity

APPLIED MICRO THEORY 9.1

A tie-in sale is the sale of one good contingent on the sale of another. A reciprocity agreement binds sellers and buyers to the purchase of each others' products. Both of these devices have been used by firms for mutual gains in efficiency. And both of these sales arrangements have been fought successfully under the antitrust laws on the theory that they allow monopolists to extend their monopoly in one product into another market. The microeconomic analysis of this section disputes this contention.

Suppose a firm had a monopoly in widgets (the economist's all-purpose good) at a monopoly price of P_0 (refer back to Figure 9.5). Suppose further that the widget monopolist also sold gadgets in a competitive market at the market price of $10 apiece. An attempt to tie the sale of widgets to the sale of gadgets cannot increase the profit from the profit level of independent sales. There is a willingness-to-pay or demand curve for widgets and a profit-maximizing price. The tie-in can only change the composition of payments. For example, in the tie-in sale the monopolist could raise the price of gadgets to, say, $2 above the competitive price— but only by compensating the buyer with a lower price of widgets equal to $P_0 - \$2$. There is no possibility of selling the combination for a higher total price without a reduction in profit, because the monopoly is not transferred from widgets to gadgets. The gadget market is still competitive, and widgets are still monopolized. The monopoly power in widgets can only be exercised once.

Similarly, monopoly power does not increase when the monopolist engages in reciprocal buying. Suppose the widget manufacturer will buy brackets for use in producing widgets only if the bracket producer purchases some widgets. The widget monopolist cannot, by such a reciprocity requirement, increase its monopoly power by obtaining better terms for brackets. Monopoly power can only be exercised once and is restrained by the demand curve. The profit-maximizing price does not change due to reciprocity.*

*For an extensive discussion of tie-in sales and reciprocity, see Robert Bork, *The Antitrust Paradox* (New York: Basic Books, 1978), see chap. 19.

oly when MR = LMC and $P > $ MR, price must exceed LMC, as shown in Figure 9.7. This condition implies that the monopolist produces too little output. Recall that price measures the additional benefit of the last unit purchased by consumers. Recall also that long-run marginal cost is the marginal benefit forgone in the next-best use of the capital and labor diverted to the production of one more unit of the monopolist's output. Therefore, the condition $P > $ LMC implies that the marginal benefit of producing one more unit of the monopolist's good is greater than the value of the forgone uses of the resouces that would be drawn from elsewhere in the economy to produce the additional unit. Because $P > $ MR for the simple monopolist, production stops before all the efficiency gains implied by $P > $ LMC are exploited, and therefore monopoly causes too few resources to be withdrawn from other activities and used to produce the monopolist's product. In short, the monopolist misdirects the economy's resources by producing too little output.

A convenient measure of the welfare loss associated with monopoly presents itself in Figure 9.7. If output increased to Q_c, where $P = $ LMC at point b, all the welfare gains generated by producing output whenever $P > $ LMC would be exhausted. (Because this is the competitive equilibrium condition, the output is denoted Q_c.) The total benefit of increasing output from Q_m to Q_c is the area beneath the demand curve $(Q)_m fbQ_c$. The total cost of using capital and labor resources to increase output from Q_m to Q_c—the opportunity cost of the resources—is the area beneath the LMC curve, $Q_m ebQ_c$. The net benefit of such output expansion—total benefit minus total cost—is the shaded area efb. Because monopoly prevents output from increasing from Q_m to Q_c, the area efb measures the monopoly-induced loss in welfare; it is referred to as the **welfare loss triangle.** It is often said that the monopolist produces too little and charges too much. This is true, as you can see from Figure 9.7: $Q_m < Q_c$ and $P_m > P_c$. But these are not independent problems; both arise because $P > $ MR in monopoly, and both contribute to the welfare loss attributed to monopoly and measured by the welfare loss triangle.

There are other sources of inefficiency inherent in simple monopoly. The complete barrier to entry necessary for the existence of monopoly means that price may exceed average cost in the long run. There is no market mechanism to push the firm to the optimal scale of plant and hence to the minimum long-run average total cost, such as point j in Figure 9.7. Of course, inframarginal competitive firms also do not operate with optimal scales of plant, as we saw in Chapter 8.

In addition, the $P > LAC(Q_m)$ condition makes long-run profits available for use in ways that perpetuate the inefficiencies of the monopoly. For example, some tempting uses of monopoly profits include buying up firms that produce substitute products, buying up resources essential to competitors, lobbying for legislative protection of the monopoly, and bribing politicians. Any or all of these uses of monopoly profits can lead to even greater inefficiencies.

In summary, monopoly equilibrium MR = LMC implies the following:

SMC = LMC: efficient input combination for the output produced.

P > LMC: welfare losses caused by too little production.

P > LAC: positive long-run economic profits.

P > minimum LAC: optimal scale of plant not adopted.

Vertical Integration: Monopolistic or Risk-Spreading Device?

APPLIED MICRO THEORY

9.2

Individuals have the option of renting or purchasing such items as cars, houses, clothing, and bicycles. So why is it that we rent a car very infrequently, usually when we are far from home, or rent clothing only for a wedding or a wake? Why do so many people own instead of rent their dwelling? And why do those who rent prefer long-term leases (using daily leases only in motels and hotels)?

The answer is that it is desirable to make long-term arrangements as a substitute for frequent market activities. Long-term contracts and outright purchase reduce the risk of a home, car, or bicycle not being available when desired. Also, the sheer numbers of transactions—and hence transaction costs—are reduced. Information-gathering costs are also reduced. A variety of cost reductions take place from outright ownership or long-term contracting.

There is a direct application of these observations to **vertical integration**. Typically, there are several stages of production between raw materials and finished goods. A firm is vertically integrated when it owns the means of production in two or more successive stages. For example, an oil company could own all of the following:

1. Exploratory vessels.
2. Drilling equipment.
3. Wells.
4. Tankers.
5. Pipelines.
6. Refineries.
7. Distribution trucks.
8. Storage tanks.
9. Gas stations.

Firms like this are called major oil companies. Alternatively, an oil company could own just the last four and rely on other companies to provide crude oil to its

refineries, as do the "independent" companies. Or a company could just own a few gas stations.

What are the advantages of vertical integration—owning several stages of production? A chief benefit is the certainty of supply, which allows for more efficient use of capacity at the various production stages. Idle refineries and tankers are costly, and the certainty of supply arising from vertical integration reduces this cost. The same is true for pipelines, which are fixed capacity-in-place and are most economically used at high volumes of flow. Owning several stages of production therefore substitutes for frequent market transactions and cuts costs by spreading risk and diminishing the number of transactions and the information required to make the transactions.

Vertical integration may be a procompetitive, not an anticompetitive, tactic. Competition is a process in which economic agents, acting in their own interests, seek technological and organizational improvements to reduce costs and raise profits. These cost reductions are passed on to consumers if many independent firms compete. The competitive paradigm is closely mimicked when many vertically integrated firms compete.

The Nonexistence of the Monopoly Supply Curve

Under competition, the marginal cost curve is the firm's supply curve and an important building block of industry supply and long-run equilibrium. Although much of competitive analysis carries over into monopoly, this phenomenon does not. The marginal cost curve of the monopolist is not the monopolist's supply curve. Indeed, no curve establishes a unique relationship between price and output supplied for a monopolist—the monopoly supply curve does not exist.

Figure 9.8 shows that the monopolist's marginal cost curve is not a supply schedule. When the demand and marginal revenue curves are D_1 and MR_1, marginal revenue and marginal cost intersect at point A; the firm maximizes profits by selling output Q_0 at price P_1. However, if demand and marginal revenue are D_2 and MR_2, the optimal output is still Q_0 but the price is P_2. Point A on the marginal cost curve, which equates marginal revenue and thereby determines output Q_0, is consistent with many different prices, each determined by the demand curve. Accordingly, the marginal cost curve is not the monopolist's supply curve. The monopolist does not have a supply curve as it is conventionally defined; there is no unique relationship between price and quantity supplied.

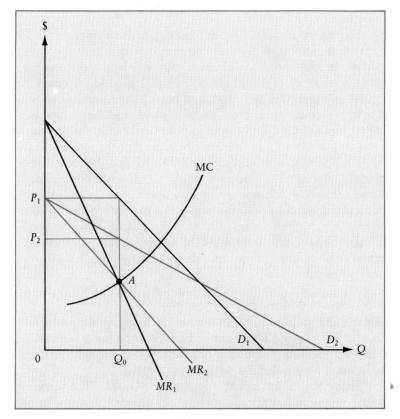

Figure 9.8
The Nonexistence of the Monopoly Supply Curve

There can be no two-dimensional relationship between price and quantity in a monopoly, because the market-clearing price depends on the demand curve.

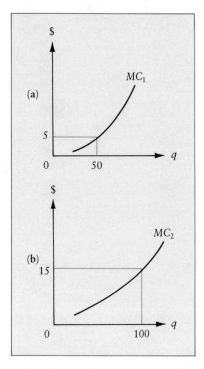

Figure 9.9
The Equal Marginal Cost Principle

To maximize profits, the multiplant monopolist must minimize costs for the output selected—by expanding and contracting output in the various plants until marginal costs are equal. (a) Plant 1, which has a low marginal cost, should be expanded. (b) Plant 2, which has a high marginal cost, should be contracted.

The Multiplant Monopolist

Up to now, we have assumed that the monopolist operates only one plant. A more realistic case is for the monopolist to own many plants. Because the competitive equilibrium is also a multiplant equilibrium, albeit with many owners, we have a useful basis for comparing competition and monopoly. In fact, the only meaningful comparison of monopoly and competition must be between competition at the industry level and **multiplant monopoly.**

The Equal Marginal Cost Principle

The key building block in the model of multiplant monopoly is cost minimization. A monopolist wants to produce any given rate of output at minimum total cost; to do otherwise would involve forgone profit. Chapter 8 demonstrated that a given output is produced at lowest total cost when all firms produce at identical marginal cost. This is the equal marginal cost principle. The same cost-minimizing principle applies to the multiplant monopolist. The monopolist minimizes the total cost of a given rate of output by allocating production among several plants, so that the marginal cost of production is equal in all plants, or

$$MC_1 = MC_2 = \ldots = MC_n \qquad (9.4)$$

To prove that marginal costs must be equal in all plants in order to minimize total costs, assume that marginal costs are not equal in two of the monopolist's n plants. Figure 9.9 depicts the marginal cost curves of plant 1 and plant 2. Plant 1 produces 50 units of output at a marginal cost of $5, and plant 2 produces 100 units at a marginal cost of $15. If the monopolist expands output in plant 1 by 1 unit and contracts output in plant 2 by 1 unit, the combined total output of 150 units remains the same, but the total cost falls by $10. The total cost in plant 1 rises by $5, and the total cost in plant 2 falls by $15. The monopolist, who owns both plants, is better off by $10. More generally, any time that the marginal costs in all plants are not equal, the monopolist can reduce the total cost of producing a given output by transferring output from plants with a high marginal cost to those with a low marginal cost. When the marginal costs in all plants are equal, the monopolist's total costs are minimized.

A Multiplant Monopolist's Marginal Cost Curve

We can use the equal marginal cost rule to derive the multiplant monopolist's marginal cost curve. Each point on the marginal cost curve represents a distribution of production that equals marginal costs in all plants: $MC_1 = MC_2 = \ldots = MC_n$.

Figure 9.10 illustrates this important principle. The marginal cost curves of two of the many plants are shown in panels a and b,

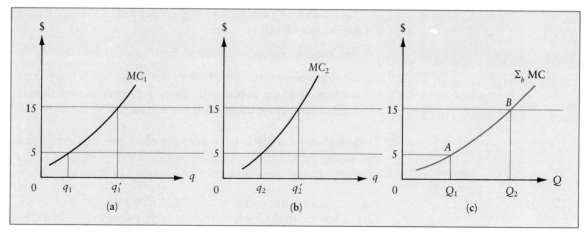

Figure 9.10
The Multiplant Marginal Cost Curve

(a) Plant 1 has marginal cost curve MC_1. (b) Plant 2 has marginal cost curve MC_2. (c) The horizontal summation of marginal costs is the multiplant monopolist's MC curve, when and only when the equal marginal cost rule is followed.

and the monopolist's marginal cost curve is shown in panel c. For the firm to produce a total output of $0Q_1$ at least cost, it must allocate production among the many plants, so that marginal costs are equal in all plants. Suppose the equal marginal cost rule is satisfied in Figure 9.10. The output $0Q_1$ is the sum of the outputs $0q_1$ in plant 1, $0q_2$ in plant 2, and the individual outputs of all other plants not shown in Figure 9.10. Point A is the horizontal sum of the various plants' output when and only when the equal marginal cost rule is satisfied. Point B, another point on the monopolist's marginal cost curve, is the horizontal sum of the output of the individual plants when all plants produce their part of the total output Q_2 and when the marginal cost is $15 in all plants.

Points A, B, and all other similarly derived points make up the multiplant monopolist's marginal cost curve; in Figure 9.10c it is labeled $\Sigma_h MC$.[4] Note carefully that the marginal cost curve $\Sigma_h MC$ has meaning only if each level of output satisfies the equal marginal cost rule: $MC_1 = MC_2 = \ldots = MC_n$. Of course, the equal marginal cost rule derives from underlying economic forces related to profit maximization; the monopolist has a profit incentive to follow the equal marginal cost rule.

Profit-Maximizing Equilibrium and the Multiplant Monopolist

In order to compare competitive and monopoly equilibrium, we must make the following assumptions:

The monopolist buys up all firms in a competitive industry and effectively blocks any further entry.

---

4. Remember that the symbol Σ, the Greek letter sigma, means summation. The symbol Σ_h means the summation of horizontal distances. Horizontal summation was used previously in deriving the industry demand curve and the industry short-run and long-run marginal cost curves in competitive industries.

Each previously competitive firm is operated as a separate plant by the monopoly.

The production functions of all firms (plants) are identical.

The entrepreneurial opportunity costs of the competitive firms' owners equal the opportunity costs of the managerial skills needed to operate the monopolist's plants.

These assumptions allow us to keep the plant cost curves the same and study the effect of monopoly ownership in a perfectly competitive industry containing the same number of plants.

PERFECT COMPETITION VERSUS MULTIPLANT MONOPOLY   Figure 9.11 gets us started in the analysis of monopoly ownership of N_c plants, which could form N_c independent firms in perfect competition. Under competition, the intersection at point A of the industry supply curve (Σ_h LMC) and the industry demand curve (D) establishes the competitive price P_c and output Q_c. Each identical price-taking firm produces output q_c and earns zero long-run profits by adopting the optimal scale of plant and producing at the minimum of its long-run average cost curve, LAC (see Figure 9.11a).

When the industry is monopolized and all previously competitive firms are under the same ownership, the monopolist changes the equilibrium price-quantity combination in the aggregate as well as for each plant. The monopolist's profit-maximizing

Figure 9.11
Perfect Competition versus Multiplant Monopoly

(a) In competition, each plant produces q_c; but in monopoly, each produces q_m. (b) Using the same number of plants, the monopolist will cut total output from Q_c to Q_m and the output in each plant from q_c to q_m. Price will rise from P_c to P_m.

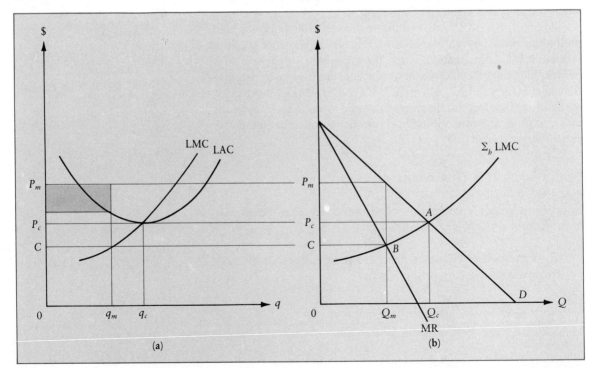

rule is MR = Σ_hLMC, which occurs at point B. The monopolist reduces total output to Q_m and increases price to P_m. It is the monopolist's ability to restrict output and raise prices that generates monopoly profits.

The monopolist will operate each plant at the output level for which the monopolist's marginal revenue equals the plant's long-run marginal cost. Marginal revenue at output Q_m is $0C$; accordingly, the plant illustrated in panel a equates MR and LMC and produces q_m units of output. Each plant earns an economic profit equal to the shaded area by reducing its scale of plant and operating at an output rate below the minimum LAC. The monopolist's total economic profits are the sum of the economic profits earned in each plant.

Figure 9.11 does not present the complete long-run profit-maximizing adjustment of the multiplant monopolist. In final equilibrium there are further adjustments in the scales of plant and plant closings. Specifically, the multiplant monopolist closes down many of the plants and operates the others at their optimum scales of plant. As it makes these adjustments, the monopolist selects aggregate output (Q), price (P), output in each plant (q_i), capital (K), labor (L), and the number of plants (N). The full power of the cost curves can be seen in the final equilibrium. Now let's follow the steps that the monopolist takes.

In Figure 9.12 the curve Σ_hLMC is the horizontal summation of marginal costs of the original number of plants, N_c. If the monopo-

Figure 9.12
Perfect Competition versus Multiplant Monopoly

(a) Plants that are absorbed by a monopolist reach equilibrium at point j. (b) After the closing of excess plants, the monopolist will produce $q_{m0} = q_c$ in each of the plants it operates and set MR = $\Sigma_h LMC_2$ = S_{LR} and $P = P_{m0}$.

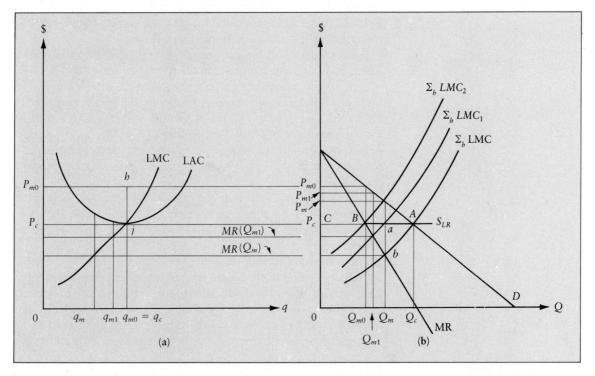

list chose to operate all N_c plants, it would select the total output Q_m, where MR = Σ_hLMC. Assuming that all plants are identical (an assumption that is abandoned in the following section), each plant produces $Q_m/N_c = q_m$ units of output, and marginal costs are equal in all plants. Note, however, that none of the plants now operate at minimum long-run average cost. There is an advantage to closing some plants altogether and shifting their production to the remaining plants, because this rearrangement reduces the long-run average costs of production for the same output rate. The profit-maximizing number of plants for the given output Q_m is achieved when all producing plants operate at minimum long-run average cost and produce output q_c (see Figure 9.12).

But this still is not the final equilibrium. When the monopolist closes plants, the curve Σ_hLMC shifts to the left, as shown by the shift to $\Sigma_h LMC_1$ in Figure 9.12. Reading off $\Sigma_h LMC_1$, we see that $\Sigma_h LMC_1(Q_m) >$ MR(Q_m), or $Q_m a > Q_m b$. Thus output Q_m is no longer the profit-maximizing output. Instead, Q_{m1} should be produced, because $\Sigma_h LMC_1(Q_{m1}) =$ MR(Q_{m1}).

We now face the same adjustments with output Q_{m1} that were just described for output Q_m. The monopolist should close entire plants down and push their output toward the remaining plants, thereby permitting the remaining plants to adopt the scale of operation that yields the lowest average cost. For any given output, profit maximization requires that all firms produce at minimum average cost, which the multiplant monopolist can achieve by suitable closings of superfluous plants. But these closings again shift the Σ_hLMC curve upward, again changing the correct output level of the firm and requiring additional plant closings.

After many such adjustments, the final equilibrium is found where LMC = minimum LAC in the remaining plants and Σ_hLMC = MR. These two conditions, both required for equilibrium, eliminate any further profit increase resulting from plant closings. In Figure 9.12, equilibrium occurs at point B, where $\Sigma_h LMC_2 =$ MR. Each of the remaining N_m plants produces $Q_{m0}/N_m = q_{m0} = q_c$ units of output at minimum long-run average cost. Each plant earns a total economic profit of $P_c P_{m0} hj$ (in panel a), and total monopoly profit is $P_c P_{m0} hj \cdot N_m$.

Note in Figure 9.12 that the monopolist moves from point A (the competitive equilibrium) to point B (the multiplant monopolist's equilibrium) by closing down entire plants. There is a convenient interpretation for this movement. The horizontal line AB is equal to the long-run supply curve of the competitive industry S_{LR}. Its height is equal to the height of the competitive firm's minimum LAC curves. When demand rises or falls, the competitive long-run equilibrium moves horizontally along the curve S_{LR} by entry or exit of competitive firms. The long-run supply curve S_{LR} is therefore the "marginal cost of entry or exit," or in the language of the multiplant monopolist, the **marginal cost of plant openings or closings.** The monopolist moves along the curve S_{LR} and continues to close plants whenever $S_{LR} >$ MR; at such points the firm saves more in total costs from a plant closing than it sacrifices in total revenue from the lost production. When $S_{LR} =$ MR, as at point B in Figure 9.12, the optimal number of plant closings has been accomplished; all remaining plants operate at minimum LAC. Thus the monopolist's profits are maximized at B. Because S_{LR} is horizontal in the case of perfect competition, output must fall enough to drive marginal revenue up to the competitive price P_c.

If the demand curve is linear, we can be more specific about the number of plant closings. Because the demand and marginal revenue curves in Figure 9.12 are linear, then the distances CB and BA are equal. The output of the multiplant monopolist is exactly half the competitive output; and because each remaining plant operates at the competitive level, it follows that the monopolist will use only half the competitive number of plants.

PURE COMPETITION VERSUS MULTIPLANT MONOPOLY   This section can be relatively brief, because the tone of the analysis has been set in the discussion of multiplant monopoly using perfectly competitive assumptions. Now let's permit some of the original competitive firms (and later the monopolist's plants) to earn inframarginal rents, as discussed in Chapter 8. Does the presence of inframarginal firms change the results?

Figure 9.13 shows the equilibrium of the multiplant monopolist in the presence of inframarginal plants. Competitive equilibrium occurs at point A in panel d, where $P = \Sigma_h$LMC = minimum LAC of the marginal firms. At this point, the monopolist begins to close plants, reduce output, and increase price in order to maximize profits. The highest-cost plants, initially the marginally competitive firms like the plant in panel c, will be closed first; plant closings will

Figure 9.13
Long-Run Equilibrium of the Multiplant Monopolist with Inframarginal Plants

(a) Firm 1 is inframarginal in competition and in monopoly. (b) Firm 2 is inframarginal in competition, marginal in monopoly. (c) Firm 3 is marginal in competition, extramarginal (and thus not operated) in monopoly. (d) The aggregate output of the multiplant monopolist is therefore Q_m, where $S_{LR} =$ MR.

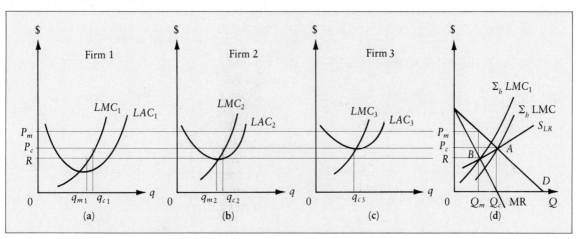

Taxing the Multiplant Monopolist

APPLIED
MICRO
THEORY

9.3

Monopoly profits are of great concern to many people. Professor John Kenneth Galbraith, in discussing the market power of monopolists over price and profit, tells us, "In the English language only a few words—fraud, defalcation, subversion, and sodomy—have a greater connotation of nonviolent wickedness."* One proposed method to control monopoly is to tax away the profits. Will the monopolist absorb the losses of a lump-sum tax, or can the firm shift these tax costs to customers by further reductions in output and increases in product price?

For simplicity, assume that all plants are identical. Each of N plants produces $q_n = Q_n/N$ units of output at a minimum LAC, as shown in Figure A. Commodity price is P_n, and the initial pretax profit is $abcd \cdot N$. In Figure B, the monopolist maximizes profits by producing output Q_n, where $MR(Q_n) = \Sigma_h LMC(N \text{ plants}) = S_{LR}$.

*John Kenneth Galbraith, *The New Industrial State* (New York: Signet Books, 1967), p. 190.

Assume that half the monopoly profits are taxed away in a lump sum. The tax, a fixed cost to the firm, shifts the average cost curve up to (LAC + tax). The new (LAC + tax) curve must intersect point f, which is half the distance between points d and c. This assures that exactly half the profit is taxed away. Should the monopolist continue to operate each plant at the optimum scale of plant and maintain output Q_n and price P_n by holding the number of plants constant at N? Or should output be raised to q_m in each plant in order to operate at the minimum of the (LAC + tax) curve, total output be cut to Q_m and the number of plants reduced to M, and price be raised to P_m?

The profits resulting from these two strategies are as follows:

$$\pi(Q_n) = ebcf \cdot N = \tfrac{1}{2}(abcd) \cdot N$$
$$\pi(Q_m) = gkih \cdot M$$

The untaxed monopolist always had the option to produce $Q_m = q_m \cdot M$ and to earn profit $nkij \cdot M$ on each of M plants [point B, where $\Sigma_h LMC(M \text{ plants}) = MR(Q_m)$]. The monopolist chose instead to produce $Q_n = q_n \cdot N$

[point A, where $\Sigma_h LMC(N \text{ plants}) = MR(Q_n) = S_{LR}$]. This implies that

$$abcd \cdot N > gkih \cdot M$$

But by construction,

$$nkij \cdot M > gkih \cdot M$$

Hence

$$\pi(Q_n) = \tfrac{1}{2}(abcd) \cdot N > gkih \cdot M$$
$$= \pi(Q_m)$$

The monopolist will therefore continue to produce the same output, Q_n, after taxes, use the same number of plants, N, and charge the same price, P_n. The monopolist will absorb the tax and not pass it on to consumers in the form of further output restrictions, plant closings, or price increases.

This result is perfectly generalizable to the case of inframarginal plants. Lump-sum taxes on the monopolist's profits do not affect the monopolist's profit-maximizing rate of output or the commodity price. Remarkably, taxes in proportion to profits also do not change price, output, the number of plants, or the output in each plant. Can you prove this?

Figure A
Taxing the Multiplant Monopolist

Exactly half of each plant's profits is taxed away.

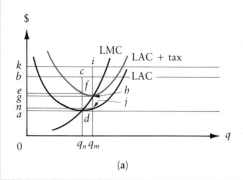

(a)

Figure B
Taxing the Multiplant Monopolist

For the monopolist, a tax on profits does not affect output, price, or the number of plants.

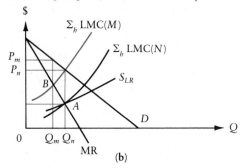

(b)

continue in descending order of cost, until output falls to Q_m, where S_{LR} = MR. The plant closings move the monopolist along S_{LR}, the marginal cost curve of plant closings. At point B the optimal number of plant closings is achieved, because S_{LR} = MR.

Remember that the height of the S_{LR} curve equals the height of the minimum point of the highest-cost plant's LAC curve. In equilibrium at point B, firm 2 (panel b) is the "marginal" plant, operating its optimum scale of plant where MR = LMC_2. Firm 1 (in panel a) continues to be inframarginal in long-run equilibrium, whereas firm 3 (in panel c)—and all other plants with a minimum LAC greater than marginal revenue ($0R$)—is closed down.

Note that in the case of perfect competition the monopolist reduced output only by closing entire plants and allowing the remaining firms to produce at the competitive rate of output. In the case of pure competition, where there are inframarginal plants, output falls for two reasons: (1) entire plant closings of high-cost plants and (2) reductions in the output of inframarginal plants. In Figure 9.13, plants 1 and 2 both reduce their scales of plant and their output because $MR(Q_m) < P_c$.

Cartels

It is natural to follow a discussion of multiplant monopoly with a section on cartels, because a cartel is a group of potentially competitive firms that coordinates its output and pricing decisions in order to reduce industry output below competitive levels and to raise prices and profits. A cartel acts insofar as possible like a multiplant monopolist. The collusive, price-fixing behavior of cartels in the United States is subject to prosecution by the Justice Department under the Sherman Antitrust Act of 1890. Paradoxically, the U.S. government sponsors some forms of cartelization, as when agricultural prices are raised above competitive levels by crop-restriction programs. Cartels to not have the legal or moral stigma in many foreign countries that they have in the United States. One of these international cartels—OPEC—is unique in its influence in international politics and economics.

Major economic difficulties arise in the organization and perpetuation of a cartel. The cartel's long-run profit-maximizing equilibrium is the same as the multiplant monopolist's. Achieving that equilibrium is hard for the monopolist; the cartel faces the added complication that it does not have the single ownership of all plants that accommodates the adjustments. As with multiplant monopoly, cartel profit maximization—compared to competitive equilibrium—requires that (1) each producing firm be given an output quota smaller than its competitive rate of output and (2) many firms be closed down.

Just as the multiplant monopolist operates fewer than the competitive number of plants, so does the cartel aim to reduce output by closing down the highest-cost firms. But are these entrepreneurs willing to exit? Exiting firms must be paid a suitable exit fee out of the expected cartel profits. The remaining firms may be reluctant to make these payments out of fear that the cartel will break down and eliminate the profits. The choice of which firms to close and the reluctance to pay for their exit creates organizational difficulty for the cartel right from the beginning.

If the cartel is successfully organized, the next obstacle is its inherent instability. Consider Figure 9.14, which displays the equilibrium of the cartel and the cost curves of one participant firm. The cartel's optimal output is Q_m; the inframarginal firm that produced q_c under competitive equilibrium is given a quota of q_m by the cartel. (The individual firm must produce where cartel MR = LMC of the firm at point A.)

The firm's profits are higher under the cartel quota than under competitive conditions; otherwise the firm would not join the cartel. So why is the cartel inherently unstable? Because at q_m the cartel price P_m exceeds long-run marginal cost by the distance AC. The seller, happy to have the cartel profits, can increase profits even more by expanding output to q_{cheat}, where the cartel price equals long-run marginal cost. The seller has a profit incentive to exceed the cartel output quota, particularly if it is felt that such cheating will not be detected. But what is sauce for the goose is sauce for the gander. If enough members exceed production quotas in response to these latent profit impulses, the cartel will break down. Cheating is more likely the greater the number of sellers, the smaller the output

Figure 9.14
The Inherent Instability of Cartels

(a) At q_m, the cartel price at C is greater than the LMC at A. Because P_m is greater than the LMC, the firm has an incentive to cheat. (b) The competitive price, P_c, is established where Σ_h LMC (competition) crosses D and S_{LR} at Q_c. Cartel price is established with less plant capacity where Σ_h LMC (cartel), MR, and S_{LR} intersect at Q_m, forcing price above competitive levels.

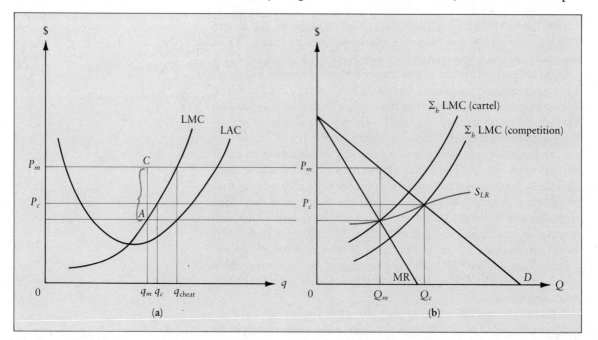

(a)   (b)

of each firm compared to total cartel output, the more heterogeneous the product, and the easier it is to distribute the product under alternative brand names.

The greater the number of sellers, the less significant the effect of one firm's cheating on market price, because the firm views itself as a price taker. Cheating is also more difficult to detect when each firm represents a small portion of the total market. Thus small firms are more likely to cheat and less likely to get caught.

When products are heterogeneous, quality can be improved without incorporating the increased cost into the price. When price exceeds long-run marginal cost, a firm has an incentive to increase output, even if it means shaving the price a bit to attract customers.

Resale Price Maintenance: Evidence of Cartels?

APPLIED
MICRO
THEORY

9.4

Resale price maintenance is a device that a manufacturer uses to place a floor under the price its retailers may charge at the point of sale. It is now illegal in most cases on the grounds that it restrains price competition among dealers—or worse, that it is a device used to aid a collusive dealer cartel. But there is one nagging argument in defense of resale price maintenance—the point-of-sale service defense. In a nutshell, this defense concerns the incentive that retailers have to provide information—expert explanation or showroom display and demonstration—when that information can be gained from one dealer but the product can be purchased from a second dealer with no payment to the dealer who provided the information.

Providing information about a product is expensive; the second dealer can provide the product without information at lower cost than the first dealer and hence charge a lower price to attract customers away from the first dealer. In this way, the second dealer acts as a "free rider," a concept discussed in more detail and in many contexts in Chapter 14. In turn, the first dealer has an incentive to cut expenses by cutting the information services,

which bring no return. In this circumstance, the information is a collective good, and each dealer has an incentive to provide an inefficiently small amount of it. So the product is provided with too little information at a dealer price that is too low. For any price set at the factory gate, the manufacturer wants the dealers to maximize sales. But this sort of competition among dealers produces less than maximum sales, because the free-rider problem leads to too little point-of-sale information.

Resale price maintenance provides a remedy for the free-rider problem. Dealers who underprovide information cannot offer a

price below that offered by dealers who provide the efficient level of information.

This defense of resale price maintenance is quite plausible. But as economists and lawyers point out, there are other institutional arrangements designed to prevent free riding.* The simplest is for the dealer to charge for presale services or for the manufacturer to provide information through general media advertising. Furthermore, not all dealers' services are so completely substitutable that free riding is feasible.

This issue is unresolved at the theoretical level. As a matter of law, however, the beneficent incentives of the competitive market to keep consumer prices down are apparently considered a stronger force than whatever inefficiencies are caused by free riding. The point-of-sale service defense has been roundly rejected, and resale price maintenance has been used as evidence of a cartel.

*Robert H. Bork, "The Rule of Reason and the Per Se Concept: Price Fixing and Market Division," *Yale Law Journal* 75 (1966): 373; Ward S. Bowman, "The Prerequisites and Effects of Resale Price Maintenance," *University of Chicago Law Review* 22 (1966): 825; Richard A Posner, *Antitrust Law: An Economic Perspective* (Chicago: University of Chicago Press, 1976), especially pp. 67–68; and Lester G. Telser, "Why Should Manufacturers Want Fair Trade?" *Journal of Law and Economics* 3 (1962): 86.

Inventory Profits versus Created Shortages

APPLIED
MICRO
THEORY

9.5

The oil crises of the 1970s have allowed consumers to take note of two simultaneous events: shortages in the supplies of oil products and rising profits among U.S. oil companies. Many observers believe that this evidence implies that oil companies have created the shortages in order to jack up profits. Here we encounter an example of companies' profits rising when they expand domestic production.

Consider the accompanying figure, which exhibits the cost curves of a marginal oil producer earning a normal return at price P_1 by producing Q_1 units of output. Suppose the OPEC cartel votes to increase world prices to P_2. The domestic firm, facing price P_2, will increase output to Q_2, which increases the firm's profit from zero to AP_2BC. This profit is an **inventory profit**; it arises because the value of the firm's inventories rises through forces external to the firm's decisions. It is similar to the capital gain that homeowners receive when the demand for housing increases and housing prices appreciate.

In the long run these inventory profits will fall, because the firm's extraction costs rise as depletion

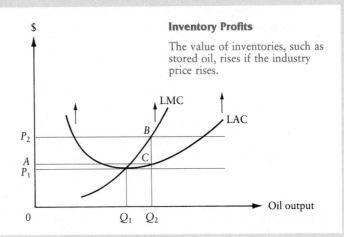

Inventory Profits

The value of inventories, such as stored oil, rises if the industry price rises.

takes place. The arrows in the figure indicate rising costs due to depletion. Thus domestic firms' profits will rise whenever the OPEC cartel raises prices and then will tend to fall as depletion costs rise in the long run. Here we see a case where prices and profits rise among firms that have no control over the world shortages. Indeed, these firms actually increase output during the period of rising profits.

Even though domestic oil producers may not be involved directly in OPEC cartel pricing and output decisions, they may nevertheless be reluctant to participate in weakening the cartel. In fact, we can see why oil producers in Scotland pray for OPEC price increases. Of course, the entry of new firms in response to OPEC price increases is risky because of the rising costs as depletion occurs. If the government taxes the inventory profits of well owners, there will be less incentive for domestic exploration and production, and the goal of domestic energy independence will be retarded. Similarly, if gambling winnings are taxed without allowing losses to be written off, there will be fewer poker players.

A similar response is to raise the quality a bit or to improve financing and payment terms and guarantees without raising the price. Both price reductions and quality improvements lead to increased sales and higher profits. To solve these problems, cartels often require complex pricing schemes and market-sharing agreements.

When the products of the cartel members are marketed under a variety of brand names, an immense problem of detection is created; it is very difficult to know which producers are cheating.

So if you ever work for the Justice Department's Antitrust Division and your office has limited funds for the investigation and prosecution of price-fixing cases, note carefully these forces of instability in cartels lest you prosecute cartels that collapse of their own weight before your case is closed.

Aside from instability and cheating, another cartel problem is the establishment of the right price and quantity. This is particularly troublesome in the extractive industries, where different firms—or countries—have vastly different reserves and hence different time horizons. The longer the firm's time horizon, the greater the threat that the cartel monopoly price will induce technical change or the discovery of new sources of output. Hence members with longer time horizons will perceive greater elasticity of demand and argue for a lower price than the members with shorter time horizons. This explains why Saudi Arabia, with immense known oil reserves and a long time horizon, usually argues for lower OPEC price increases than the other member countries.

This discussion of cartels would not be complete without mention of one strategy available to firms that must deal with cartels. Firms and countries that purchase goods from cartels can prey on their inherent instability by adopting secret bidding. Periodically, the purchaser can accept bids from individual cartel members that are sealed to prevent producers from finding out the other bids. Nor should the winning bid be announced after the decision. This practice gives each cartel member an extra incentive to cheat. As distrust grows, the cartel is pushed closer toward breakdown.

Price Discrimination by Market Separation: Different Prices for Different Customers

Up to now, we have analyzed simple monopoly, in which the monopolist charges uniform prices to all customers. Under arbitrage, any attempt to sell a commodity at two different prices will be frustrated by customers buying at the low price and undercutting the monopolist in the high-price market. However, casual observation shows that firms with monopoly power often sell their output at different prices: Movie houses have adult and child tickets; universities charge different tuition rates to the in-state and out-of-state students; barbers set differential prices according to age; doctors charge wealthy patients more than poor patients for similar health care; some firms sell in foreign markets at lower prices than in domestic markets, even though transportation costs are higher. Such products are not subject to arbitrage. A customer cannot very well view a movie and then resell it; an education or an appendectomy is not subject to resale.

Price discrimination is the practice of selling the same good in different markets at prices that are out of proportion to differences in marginal cost. The mere observation of price differentials is not sufficient to identify price discrimination, because marginal cost differences may account for price differences, as when transportation costs are higher for one market than for another. Price discrimination occurs only when cost differences cannot explain the differentials in price charged in different markets.

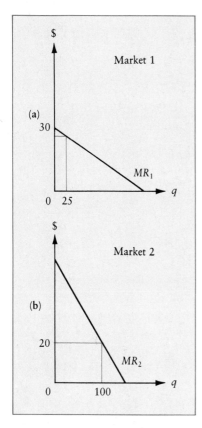

Figure 9.15
The Equal Marginal Revenue Principle

To maximize the revenue from a given amount of output, the monopolist must equate the marginal revenues from various markets. (a) Market 1 has a higher marginal revenue than market 2. (b) Sales should be shifted from market 2 to market 1.

The Equal Marginal Revenue Principle

Previous discussions of competition and multiplant monopoly described the equal marginal cost principle and demonstrated that the total cost of producing a given quantity of output is minimized by allocating production among plants or firms so that the marginal costs in all plants are equal. A companion concept is the **equal marginal revenue principle.** If the monopolist is able to sell its output in different markets with differing demand, marginal revenue, and price elasticity, it should distribute its sales of a given output so that the marginal revenue is equal in all markets. If marginal revenues are unequal, total revenue can be increased by switching the sale of output from the market of low marginal revenue to one of higher marginal revenue.

Figure 9.15 demonstrates the equal marginal revenue rule. Suppose a monopolist initially sells 25 units in market 1 and 100 units in market 2. The monopolist sells a total of 125 units. But the marginal revenue in market 1 ($30) exceeds the marginal revenue in market 2 ($20). If the monopolist transfers 1 unit of sales from market 2 to market 1, the combined output remains the same, but there is a revenue increase of $10. Revenue falls by $20 in market 2 but rises by $30 in market 1.

By transferring sales from the market with low marginal revenue to the market with high marginal revenue, the firm gains total revenue for a given output equal to the difference in marginal revenues. All such gains are exhausted when sales have been divided so that marginal revenues are equal in both markets. The same principle is involved as in the equal marginal cost principle.

The Simple Monopolist Selling in Two Markets

The equal marginal revenue principle assures that a given output is sold at maximum total revenue. But the monopolist must still decide how much total output to sell and what prices to charge. In order to understand the behavior of a discriminating monopolist, which can separate markets and sell at different prices, we must understand the behavior of the simple monopolist, which may also serve different markets but cannot discriminate because of arbitrage.

Say that the simple monopolist sells in two markets; the demand and marginal revenue curves of these two markets are illustrated in Figure 9.16a and 9.16b. The simple monopolist derives the aggregate demand of the two markets (Figure 9.16c) by horizontally summing the individual demand curves, a procedure that we are familiar with. The horizontal summation of the demand curves D_1 and D_2 produces the curve labeled $\Sigma_h D$ in panel c. This aggregate demand curve is made up of two segments, AB and BC. The segment AB corresponds to the demand curve in market 1, because at prices above P_i market 2 does not contribute any quantities demanded. For prices below P_i, both markets contribute quantities

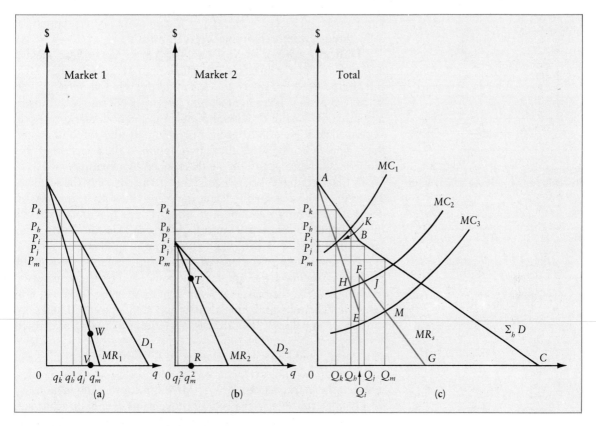

demanded. The segment BC of the aggregate demand curve, $\Sigma_h D$, reflects the horizontal addition of the demand curve D_2 to curve D_1.

The next step is to derive the simple monopolist's marginal revenue curve, MR_s. But we can't simply perform a horizontal summation of the individual markets' marginal revenue curves. Instead, marginal revenue must be linked properly to the demand curve. As shown in Figure 9.16, the marginal revenue lies below the demand curve at every output level. For linear demand curves, the marginal revenue curve falls twice as fast as the demand curve.

Now, however, the demand curve is kinked. Thus we must construct a marginal revenue segment for each demand segment. Proceeding as usual, the marginal revenue segment AE corresponds to the demand segment AB; the marginal revenue segment FG corresponds to the demand segment BC. Thus the simple monopolist's marginal revenue curve is $AEFG$, or the two segments AE and FG. The discontinuity at output Q_i corresponds to the kink at point B on the demand curve.

The behavior of the simple monopolist selling in two markets subject to arbitrage depends on the position of the marginal cost curve. If the MC curve cuts only segment AE of the firm's marginal revenue curve, the monopolist should sell only in the stronger mar-

Figure 9.16
The Simple Monopolist Selling in Two Markets

(a) Market 1 demands quantity q_m^1 at price P_m. (b) Market 2 demands quantity q_m^2 at the same price. (c) The marginal revenue curve for the aggregate market consists of segments AE and FG, not the horizontal summation of MR_1 and MR_2.

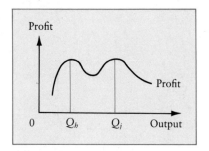

Figure 9.17
Possible Multiple Profit-Maximizing Outputs

When a simple monopolist serves two markets, the profit-maximizing condition MC = MR may occur at two output levels.

ket. For MC_1 in Figure 9.16, $MC_1 = MR_s$ at point K; the monopolist sells output Q_k entirely in market 1 at price P_k.

Difficulty arises if the marginal cost curve cuts both segments, AE and FG, of the marginal revenue curve MR_s. Note that MC_2 intersects MR_s at points H and J. Should the firm sell output Q_h at price P_h only in market 1, or should the larger output Q_j be chosen and price reduced to P_j, allowing some sales in both markets? Both options determine a local profit maximum, as illustrated in Figure 9.17. The choice between these two options—the selection of the global maximum—can only be determined by experimentation.

If the marginal cost curve in Figure 9.16c cuts only the segment FG of the firm's marginal revenue curve, as when MC_3 cuts MR_s at point M, the simple monopolist will produce Q_m units and sell output in both markets at a uniform price of P_m. Specifically q_m^1 units are sold in market 1, and q_m^2 units are sold in market 2.

Before moving to the case of price discrimination, you should note that, whenever the simple monopolist charges the same price in both markets, the marginal revenue in these markets differs. For example, when the firm equates MC_3 and MR_s at point M and sells output Q_m at price P_m in both markets, output q_m^1 is sold in market 1 and q_m^2 is sold in market 2. But $MR_1(q_m^1) = VW < MR_2(q_m^2) = RT$. Output Q_m could be sold at a larger profit if the monopolist could separate the two markets, charge different prices, and switch sales between the markets until $MR_1 = MR_2$. But for the simple monopolist facing arbitrage, such profit improvements cannot be achieved.

The Simple Monopolist versus the Discriminating Monopolist

The key distinction between simple and discriminating monopolists lies in the derivation of their marginal revenue curves. When the monopolist's price is taken from the aggregate demand curve, $\Sigma_h D$, the only meaningful construction of marginal revenue is to tie MR directly to $\Sigma_h D$, as in the case of the simple monopolist. However, the discriminating monopolist does not select a price from the aggregate demand curve; instead, it equates marginal revenues in all markets and selects prices in the individual markets from the individual curves D_1 and D_2. Thus we need a different method of calculating the discriminating firm's aggregate marginal revenue curve. Because the price discriminator always allocates sales so as to equate marginal revenue in all markets, a convenient derivation presents itself: Horizontally sum the marginal revenue curves MR_1 and MR_2 to derive the aggregate marginal revenue curve labeled $\Sigma_h MR$. A movement along the $\Sigma_h MR$ curve means that output and sales are always expanded by selling each incremental unit in the market yielding the highest marginal revenue. This procedure keeps marginal revenue equal in both markets.

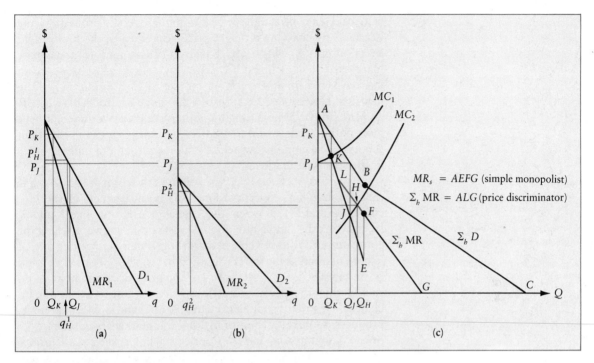

Figure 9.18 illustrates the aggregate marginal revenue curve, $\Sigma_h MR$, which is also made up of two disjointed line segments, AL and LG. The price discriminator's marginal revenue curve coincides with the simple monopolist's marginal revenue curve, MR_s, everywhere except between points L and F. For outputs between these points, the simple monopolist moves along the MR_s segment LE, producing only in market 1. In contrast, the price discriminator finds it profitable to sell in both markets and to equate marginal revenue in both markets by suitable price differentials.

We can now compare the behavior of the simple monopolist to that of the price discriminator. Not surprisingly, the comparison depends on the position of the marginal cost curve. There are four basic positions for marginal cost, as illustrated in Figures 9.18 and 9.19. (The comparison causes such clutter in the diagrams that two figures are used.) In Figure 9.18c, when the marginal cost curve cuts the segment AL of either MR_s or $\Sigma_h MR$, both monopolists behave the same. For MC_1 in Figure 9.18c, $MC_1 = MR_s = \Sigma_h MR$ at point K; both monopolists produce output Q_K and sell all the output in market 1 at price P_K. Even though the two markets are separable, it does not pay the monopolist to lower the price in market 2 enough to bring the weaker market into service.

Next suppose that the marginal cost curve intersects segment LE of MR_s and segment LF of $\Sigma_h MR$, as when MC_2 in Figure 9.18c intersects points J and H. The simple monopolist would choose output Q_J, would sell only in market 1, and would charge a uniform

Figure 9.18
Comparing Simple and Price-Discriminating Monopolists

(a) When MC = MC_1, only market 1 is served; Q_K units are sold. If MC = MC_2, the simple monopolist sells Q_J in market 1. The discriminating monopolist serves both markets; q_H^1 at P_H^1. (b) Market 2 is served only by the discriminating monopolist when MC = MC_2; q_H^2 units are sold at P_H^2. (c) If MC = MC_1, the simple monopolist and the price discriminator will both produce the same output, Q_K. If MC = MC_2, the simple monopolist charges P_J and sells in only one market; the price discriminator produces Q_H and sells in both markets.

price of P_J. In contrast, the price discriminator could profitably serve market 2 by charging different prices. Specifically, the firm should select output Q_H, where MC_2 equals $\Sigma_h MR$ at point H, and equate marginal revenues in both markets by selling q_H^1 at price P_H^1 in market 1 and q_H^2 at price P_H^2 in market 2. *Conclusion:* When the marginal cost curve cuts $\Sigma_h MR$ in the range LF (for which $\Sigma_h MR = MR_s$), the discriminating monopolist sells in two markets, sells more output, charges different prices, and earns a greater profit than the simple monopolist, which sells all its output at a uniform price in the strongest market.

Now turn to Figure 9.19 to continue the comparison. Assume that the marginal cost curve intersects both segments of the MR_s curve, LE and FG, as when MC_3 intersects MR_s at points X and Y. In this case, the simple monopolist must choose between selling the entire output Q_X at price P_X in the stronger market or selling output in both markets at the lower price P_Y; that is, sell q_{YS}^1 in market 1 and q_{YS}^2 in market 2, for a total of Q_Y. The price discriminator has no such ambiguity, because $\Sigma_h MR$ is ALG; segment LE is not included. The price discriminator equates MC_3 and $\Sigma_h MR$ at point Y, produces output Q_Y, equates MR in both markets by selling q_{YD}^1 at price P_{YD}^1 in market 1 and q_{YD}^2 at price P_{YD}^2 in market 2. *Conclusion:* Price discrimination solves the problem of price and output ambigu-

Figure 9.19
Comparing Simple and Price-Discriminating Monopolists

(a) Price and quantity in market 1 follow the same demand and MR curves presented in Figure 9.18. (b) Market 2 has its own set of demand and MR curves, with a different combination of prices and quantities. (c) If $MC = MC_3$, there is once again output ambiguity for the simple monopolist. The price discriminator earns a greater profit and produces Q_Y. If $MC = MC_4$, both produce Q_R.

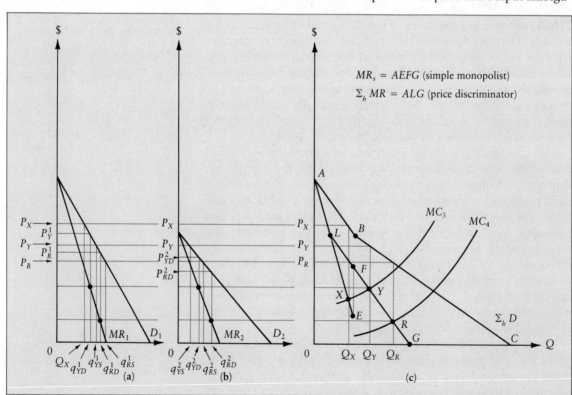

Table 9.3
Comparison of the Simple and the Discriminating Monopolist

When the MC curve intersects only segment AL, where $MR_s = \Sigma_h MR$, the simple and discriminating monopolists produce the same output, charge the same price, and sell in only the stronger market.

When the MC curve intersects both MR_s in segment LE and $\Sigma_h MR$ in segment LF, the simple monopolist sells only in the stronger market at uniform prices. The discriminating monopolist produces more output than the simple monopolist, sells in two markets at different prices, and earns a higher profit.

When the MC curve intersects both segments of the MR_s curve, LE and FG, the simple monopolist must choose between selling in one or both markets. Both choices produce local profit maximums. The global maximum is determined by experience. The discriminating monopolist selects the larger output and sells in both markets at different prices. Profits exceed those of the simple monopolist.

When the MC curve intersects only segment FG, where $MR_s = \Sigma_h MR$, both simple and discriminating monopolists select the same output. The latter sells at different prices in the two markets and earns higher profits than the single-priced monopolist does.

ity faced by the simple monopolist. The price discriminator maximizes profit by operating along the $\Sigma_h MR$ curve.

Finally, marginal cost may intersect marginal revenue at a point for which $\Sigma_h MR = MR_s$ (segment FG), as when MC_4 intersects $MR_s = \Sigma_h MR$ at point R. In this case, the optimal output is the same for both types of monopoly. However, the simple monopolist sells all output at price P_R, selling q_{RS}^1 units in market 1 and q_{RS}^2 units in market 2. The discriminating monopolist can increase profits by reducing the units sold in market 1 to q_{RD}^1 units at the higher price P_{RD}^1 and by increasing sales in market 2 to q_{RD}^2 units at the lower price P_{RD}^2. These prices equate the marginal revenues in the two markets and maximize the total profit of output Q_R. *Conclusion:* When the MC curve intersects only segment FG of the marginal revenue curve, total output is the same for both types of monopoly, but prices and individual market sales differ.

Most textbook analyses merely show that the price discriminator can increase profits of a given level of output by equating marginal revenue in all markets. It is usually thought that the output of the simple and price-discriminating monopolist is always the same. But we have seen that price discrimination often leads to a different total output for the simple monopolist as well as differential prices in each market. These conclusions are summarized in Table 9.3, which is directly related to Figures 9.18 and 9.19.

The price discrimination described here is feasible only if the price elasticities of demand differ in the different markets. Recall the relationship between price, marginal revenue, and elasticity described in Equation 9.2:

$$MR = P\left(1 + \frac{1}{\varepsilon}\right) \tag{9.2}$$

The equal marginal revenue principle, necessary for profit maximization under price discrimination, requires that

$$MR_1 = P_1\left(1 + \frac{1}{\varepsilon_1}\right) = P_2\left(1 + \frac{1}{\varepsilon_2}\right) = MR_2 \qquad (9.5)$$

Equation 9.5 may be rewritten as

$$\frac{P_1}{P_2} = \frac{\left(1 + \dfrac{1}{\varepsilon_2}\right)}{\left(1 + \dfrac{1}{\varepsilon_1}\right)} \qquad (9.6)$$

In the special case of price elasticities being the same in each market ($\varepsilon_1 = \varepsilon_2$), marginal revenues must be the same in both markets, as must prices. The equal marginal revenue rule is satisfied when the prices in both markets are the same. Separating markets and charging differential prices in markets with identical price elasticities of demand can only reduce profits.

In summary, price discrimination requires that the monopolist's product not be subject to arbitrage and that demand elasticities differ among markets. Medical services, movie tickets, and many similar markets appear to satisfy these criteria. However, policing the arbitrage that price discrimination induces is costly, and firms will not bother to separate markets and charge different prices when the benefits of price discrimination are less than the costs incurred in preventing arbitrage.

Perfect Price Discrimination: Different Prices in the Same Market

Figure 9.20
Perfect Price Discrimination

All consumer surplus is extracted from the market when the monopolist has the power to exercise perfect price discrimination.

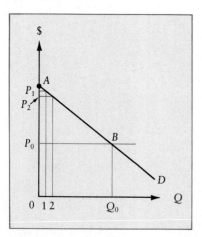

The previous discussion of price discrimination was limited to the case of market separation—selling the same commodity in different markets at different prices. In some cases, a monopolist may even be able to charge the same customer different prices for different quantities of the good. Although such market power is rare, the implications of such monopoly behavior are interesting and important to study. This sort of monopoly power is called **perfect price discrimination.**

Refer to the demand curve in Figure 9.20. For simplicity, assume that income effects are negligible, so that the ordinary and income-compensated demand curves correspond. If a uniform price of P_0 is charged, the consumer derives a consumer surplus of P_0AB; the total value of Q_0 units of output ($0ABQ_0$) exceeds the total cost ($0P_0BQ_0$). But if the consumer is forced to pay P_1 for the first unit, P_2 for the second, and so forth, the consumer surplus vanishes. When prices and output units are infinitesimally small, such a pricing policy extracts all consumer surplus.

Another pricing procedure, much simpler to administer, amounts to the same thing. A monopolist can make a consumer an "all or nothing, take it or leave it" offer. For example, in Figure 9.20, the monopolist might offer the consumer Q_0 units at a total price equal to the area $0ABQ_0$ (or maybe just a little less to sweeten the deal). If the consumer accepts, the end result is the same as if the consumer purchased units one at a time at continuously falling prices; all consumer surplus is extracted from consumers and ends up in the monopolist's profits.

In the typical case of the simple, nondiscriminating monopolist, a price reduction causes price to be lowered on all units previously sold at a higher price. We have seen previously in this chapter that under these circumstances price exceeds marginal revenue and that the area below the marginal revenue curve equals total revenue. But under perfect price discrimination, in which the monopolist lowers price on the marginal unit but not on the inframarginal units, the demand curve itself defines the marginal revenue from an extra unit sold. For the perfect price discriminator, price equals marginal revenue, as it does in competition. Thus both price and marginal revenue are measured by the demand curve. The demand curve—the marginal-willingness-to-pay curve—is the marginal revenue curve for the perfect price discriminator. The area beneath the demand curve measures the monopolist's total revenue and the consumers' total benefit, which are equal under perfect price discrimination.

In Figure 9.21, let the demand curve D equal the horizontal summation of all the individual consumers' demand curves. (Assume that the individual demand curves are identical.) If the monopolist is not a perfect price discriminator, output Q_1 is produced, because LMC = MR at Q_1; the marginal revenue curve measures the additional revenue resulting from the sale of an extra unit of output when uniform prices are charged. If the monopolist is able

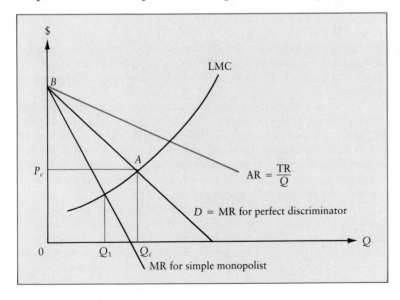

Figure 9.21
Perfect Price Discrimination

The demand curve, D, is also the marginal revenue curve, MR. Average revenue, AR, has half the slope of D. The competitive level of output is profit-maximizing.

to extract the entire consumer surplus from consumers by perfect price discrimination, the relevant marginal revenue curve is the demand curve itself. The fact that prices on previous units are not lowered under perfect price discrimination makes the usual MR schedule irrelevant to decisionmaking. Accordingly, the monopolist will maximize profit by expanding output to Q_c, where LMC equals price at point A. The monopolist will charge price P_c for the last unit sold and higher prices for previous units.

Note that output Q_c is the optimal competitive output. Paradoxically, when monopolists can completely exploit their market power by extracting all consumer surplus through perfect price discrimination, the usual output-reducing evil of monopoly does not exist. Perfect discriminators do not sell too little output; rather they produce the competitive optimum rate of output but at higher prices for all but the marginal unit.

Note too that the perfect price discriminator's demand curve is no longer the average revenue curve. Total revenue no longer equals price times quantity when uniform prices are not charged. Instead, total revenue equals an amount greater than price times quantity. In Figure 9.21, total revenue for output Q_c is not $0P_cAQ_c$ but rather the larger amount $0BAQ_c$, the area beneath the demand curve. Thus the average revenue, defined as AR = TR/Q, must exceed P_c, the price charged for the last unit sold; the average revenue curve must lie above the demand curve. These relationships are shown in Figure 9.21.

Key Terms

arbitrage 253
cartel 251
equal marginal revenue principle 276
inventory profit 274
marginal cost of plant openings or closings 269
monopolist 251
multiplant monopoly 264
natural monopolies (technological monopolies) 252
perfect price discrimination 282
price discrimination 275
resale price maintenance 273
simple monopolist 253
vertical integration 262
welfare loss triangle 261

Summary

We have studied many manifestations of monopoly power in this chapter, including simple monopoly, multiplant monopoly, various forms of monopoly price discrimination, cartel behavior, and monopoly profit. Several of the following chapters are closely related to this one, particularly Chapter 10 (on imperfect competition) and Chapter 13 (on decreasing-cost industries and the regulation of utilities and natural monopolies). For now, you should feel comfortable with the monopoly model and understand why economists deplore monopoly structure as inefficient.

The core analytical concept in monopoly is the relationship between price and marginal revenue. For the simple monopolist $P > $ MR, because to sell an extra (marginal) unit of output, the firm must lower price on all inframarginal units as well. In contrast, $P = $ MR for the perfect price-discriminating monopolist, which extracts buyers' full consumer surplus by dropping the price on marginal units without lowering the price of inframarginal units.

The multiplant monopoly model provides a useful means for comparing the efficiency with which competitive firms and monopolists allocate resources. Cartel analysis is a natural extension of the analysis of multiplant monopoly, the chief difference being the lack of single ownership and decisionmaking power in cartels. Speaking analytically, there is a smooth progression from competition (many firms working independently) to multiplant monopoly (single ownership of many plants) to cartel (many firms under separate ownership coordinating price and production decisions in order to produce monopoly profits).

Problems

1. Suppose that a multiplant monopolist is also a price discriminator. Draw a multipaneled diagram to demonstrate equilibrium.
2. Many textbooks compare competition and monopoly using one plant by equating marginal cost and marginal revenue to depict monopoly equilibrium and by equating average cost and demand to depict competitive equilibrium. Why is this wrong?
3. In this chapter's discussion of the naive case of identical firms, it was shown that the monopolist will operate half as many plants as under competition when there is a linear demand curve. What if the demand curve is convex? Concave?
4. Show that a tax on accounting profits will be passed on to the consumer in a competitive market but absorbed by the monopolist.
5. Suppose that you had 75% of a market and that several other firms shared the other 25% equally. Under what circumstances would this be a stable equilibrium? (Hint: Think inframarginal.)
6. A grocer has 10 feet of shelf space to devote to two cereals: Wheaties and Cheerios. He is restocked by the distributor once a week. The grocer knows nothing about revenue or cost curves, but he has learned to adjust his order so as to have only two boxes of each cereal when the distributor restocks his shelves. The two cereals are priced the same.
   a. Can you show that an equal marginal revenue principle is being satisfied?
   b. How did the grocer decide to devote 10 feet of shelf space to cereals in the first place?
   c. Derive a general rule for the determination of space to all products in the store. Translate this into a rule of thumb for the grocer. What economic forces would lead him to discover the rule by himself? (Hint: What would happen if he did not follow the rule?)
7. "Many oil firms are holding oil off the market, waiting for oil prices to go up. This is evidence of monopoly power." Comment on this statement. (Hint: Look up *evidence* in the dictionary. Would competitive firms hold oil off the market?)
8. Why is mail delivered to your house by a monopoly while food, which is sold in competitive stores, is seldom delivered?
9. Show that the multiplant monopolist will shut down a plant if $P > AVC > MR$.
10. Suppose that a firm allocates specific territories to its dealers. Is this evidence of a monopolistic practice? (Hint: Reread Applied Micro Theory 9.4.)
11. Suppose that a simple monopolist faces a demand curve and total cost curve that trace the data shown in Table 9.4. What is the profit-maximizing price and quantity?

Table 9.4
Sample Demand and Total Cost Data for a Simple Monopolist

Quantity	Price	Total Cost
0	1.00	20
1	0.95	21
2	0.90	22
3	0.85	23
4	0.80	24
5	0.75	25
6	0.70	28
7	0.65	32
8	0.60	38
9	0.55	50
10	0.50	80

12. "All other things being equal, it is more feasible for a cartel member to cheat on the agreement when there are few buyers than when the buyers are numerous." Analyze this statement.

Suggested Readings

Hicks, J. R. "The Theory of Monopoly." *Econometrica* 3 (1935): 1–20.

Lerner, Abba P. "The Concept of Monopoly and the Measurement of Monopoly Power." *Review of Economic Studies* 1 (1934): 157–175.

Machlup, F. "Monopoly and Competition: A Classification of Market Position." *American Economic Review* 27 (1937): 445–451.

Machlup, F. *The Political Economy of Monopoly.* Baltimore: Johns Hopkins Press, 1952.

Patinkin, Don. "Multiple-Plant Firms, Cartels, and Imperfect Competition." *Quarterly Journal of Economics* (1947): 173–205.

Stigler, George. *The Theory of Price.* 3rd ed. New York: Macmillan, 1966, chap. 13.

Vickrey, William S. *Microstatics.* New York: Harcourt Brace Jovanovich, 1964, chap. 7.

Duopoly, Oligopoly, and Monopolistic Competition

The magnitude of the economic hardships endured during the depression years of the 1930s caused the free world's economic intelligentsia to take stock of itself. The cause for alarm was the apparent unsuitability of the profession's main engine of analysis—the competitive model. The contradictions between the predictions of the competitive model and the observed facts during the 1930s were set out in bold relief. One such contradiction pertained to the macro economy. The competitive model predicted that labor (or any other) market surpluses would be self-eliminating in the long run through wage and price adjustments. But the Great Depression made it clear that unemployment was not so easily disposed of. This disparity between theory and fact motivated Britain's Lord John Maynard Keynes to formulate an alternative theory of the macro economy, a theory capable of explaining the root causes of unemployment and of providing relevant policy options.[1] Keynes's reformulation took on such far-reaching intellectual, theoretical, philosophical, and political dimensions that it has justifiably been called the "Keynesian revolution." The impact on world affairs of Keynes's ideas about macroeconomic theory and countercyclical economic policy can scarcely be overstated.

At the same time the seeds of the Keynesian revolution were germinating, other troubled winds were blowing over economic theory. In brief, the competitive and monopoly models left us with extra behavior these models could not explain, such as product differentiation, advertising strategy, price wars, price leadership, tacit and open collusion, strategic behavior among competitors, and excess capacity of firms. Such behavior could readily be observed in the economy. Additional theory was clearly required to improve understanding of the workings of the market.

Thus was born the study of **imperfect competition,** a catchall term comprising all the models that purport to analyze the middle ground between the two polar models of competition (many sellers)

---

1. See John Maynard Keynes, *The General Theory of Employment, Interest, and Money* (New York: Harcourt Brace Jovanovich, 1964), in which the theory was first set down.

and monopoly (one seller). Models of imperfect competition take into account the fact that nearly every firm possesses some monopoly power over its product. The pure monopoly model was already well in place by the 1930s, and so it was a natural transition to adapt certain aspects of monopoly behavior whenever firms' demand curves displayed the least bit of price elasticity. Among other things, these new models explained why a firm may exhibit excess capacity, something the competitive model seemingly could not do. Remember that perfect competition requires all entrepreneurs to adopt the optimum scale of plant and thereby produce up to capacity in the long run. Joan Robinson, a giant figure in the analysis of imperfectly competitive markets, reminisced about the felt need for new models during the depression years:

> Here we were, in 1930, in a deep slump, and this is what we were being asked to believe. Under perfect competition, any plant that was working at all must be working up to capacity. . . . [But] in the world around us, more or less all plants were working part time.[2]

In this climate, the search for more compelling explanations of observed market behavior began. To be perfectly honest, the initial burst of enthusiasm about the potential usefulness of models of imperfect competition was tempered by the fact that many of the methods proved to be intractable from both a methodological and empirical point of view. As we are soon to see, the linkages from demand and costs to price and output are much less precise here than we have come to expect in the competitive and monopoly models. Thus if we expect too much from the models of imperfect competition, we are sure to be disappointed. Even so, the intellectual world of imperfect competition is quite rich and useful in many areas where the competitive model simply does not apply. That there is much room for improvement is beyond dispute. Still, a study of competing firms under less than perfectly competitive conditions is well worth the effort.

Models of imperfect competition break down into two groups: (1) duopoly and oligopoly, where the number of firms is small and the emphasis is on the interdependence of rivals' behavior, and (2) monopolistic competition, where the number of firms is quite large and the emphasis is on product differentiation.

Models of Conjectural Variation

Of all the middle ground between pure competition and monopoly, only **duopoly** (two sellers) had been explored extensively prior to the 1930s. Duopoly is a special case of a broader industry structure called **oligopoly**. An oligopolistic industry is made up of more than

---

2. Joan Robinson, *The Economics of Imperfect Competition*, 2nd ed. (New York: St. Martin's, 1969), p. vi.

one firm but of few enough so that the behavior of any one affects market price. For example, the U.S. automobile-manufacturing and copper-producing industries are typical oligopolistic industries. The duopoly models reveal the essential aspects of oligopoly analysis and can be generalized to include the cases of more than two firms. Duopoly models can also be generalized to study two "groups" of firms, such as the cheating and noncheating coalitions of a cartel. So the study of oligopoly takes the form of duopoly analysis for the most part.

Duopoly and oligopoly models can be divided into two groups: models that assume firms act independently and models that assume some degree of collusion. We study the former in this section and turn to models of tacit collusion later. The key to studying non-collusive duopoly lies in the "conjectures" or guesses that each competitor must make about the behavior of the other firm. "If I raise my output, what will my competitor do?" "If I raise my price, what will my competitor do?" The answers to such questions are the basis on which both firms make decisions. Thus the central core of duopoly analysis is interdependence among firms. Gone are the price-taking firms without control over price, and gone also are the monopolists who set price and output with no one looking over their shoulder.

To be more concrete, each firm must base its price and output decisions on its rival's expected reaction to such decisions. In terms of output, each firm must place a value on the following term:

$$\frac{\Delta q_i}{\Delta q_j} \tag{10.1}$$

This term, the **conjectural variation in output,** measures the change in output of the ith firm in response to an output change of the jth firm. Its value represents the conjecture that the jth firm makes about how its own output adjustments will be met by its rival, the ith firm. If $\Delta q_i/\Delta q_j = 0$, the jth firm believes that its rival's output is fixed.

The **conjectural variation in price** is the price analogue of the conjectural variation in output:

$$\frac{\Delta p_i}{\Delta p_j} \tag{10.2}$$

In the duopoly models that follow, the assumptions about these conjectural variations are critical. The Cournot and Stackelberg models deal with the conjectural variations in quantity; the Edgeworth and kinked demand curve models work with price conjectures.

Figure 10.1
The Cournot Reaction Function

(a) Each set of demand and marginal revenue curves is based on a different assumption of firm 2's output. Each point on the reaction function is a rate of output determined by equating MC with the relevant MR curve. (b) Firm 1's reaction function measures the quantity of output that firm 1 will sell based on its conjecture of firm 2's sales.

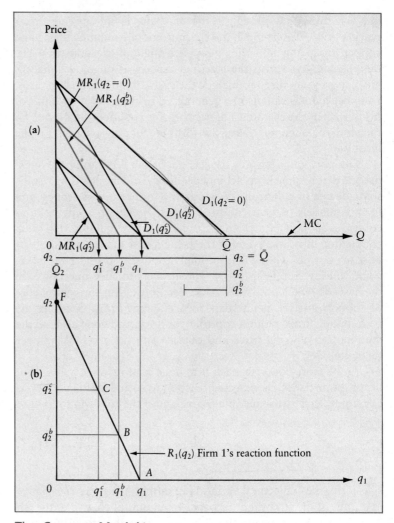

The Cournot Model

As early as 1838, the French mathematical economist Augustin Cournot published the first duopoly model.[3] (That no one paid it the least attention for 45 years may have been due to his strictly mathematical exposition.) Cournot contemplated the following puzzle: Two firms each extract spring water from their wells at zero cost; jointly, they fill the market demand for spring water and in doing so charge the same price. Cournot sought answers to these questions: How much output would each firm sell? What would be the market price? How much profit would the duopolists earn?

The basic Cournot duopoly setup is exhibited in Figure 10.1. Panel *a* contains a collection of demand and marginal revenue curves. Our initial interest is in the curve labeled $D_1(q_2 = 0)$, which

3. Augustin Cournot, *Researches into the Mathematical Principles of the Theory of Wealth*, trans. N. T. Bacon (Homewood, Ill.: Irwin, 1963).

is the total market demand curve that both firms face jointly and that firm 1 would face alone if it were a monopolist. The curve labeled $MR_1(q_2 = 0)$ is the corresponding marginal revenue curve. The marginal cost of production for both firms corresponds with the horizontal axis, because by assumption the spring water is extracted at zero cost.

Cournot's central assumption, that each firm acts as if the rival's output is fixed, makes the term for conjectural variation in output zero for both firms:

$$\left[\frac{\Delta q_2}{\Delta q_1}\right]_{\text{firm 1}} = \left[\frac{\Delta q_1}{\Delta q_2}\right]_{\text{firm 2}} = 0 \qquad (10.3)$$

Each firm sets its output with the conviction that the rival will not change its output in response. In other words, each firm sees itself as a follower, responding to the rival's decisions but not causing the rival to respond in turn.

As an arbitrary beginning point, suppose that firm 1 believes firm 2's output is and will continue to be zero. Firm 1 will behave like a monopolist by producing output q_1, because $MR_1(q_2 = 0) = MC = 0$. If firm 1 faces the aggregate demand curve $D_1(q_2 = 0)$, and therefore marginal revenue $MR_1(q_2 = 0)$, output q_1 maximizes its profits.

Figure 10.1b illustrates an output space; firm 1's output is measured on the horizontal axis, and firm 2's output is measured on the vertical axis. Point A in panel b corresponds to the profit-maximizing output of firm 1 when firm 2 produces zero output.

Next suppose that firm 2 produces q_2^b units of output. Firm 1, a follower, finds a new profit-maximizing output when it perceives that firm 2's output will remain fixed at q_2^b. Firm 1 can no longer regard $D_1(q_2 = 0)$ as its relevant demand curve. Instead, the curve labeled $D_1(q_2^b)$ is relevant. It is derived by horizontally subtracting firm 2's output q_2^b from the total demand curve $D_1(q_2 = 0)$, and it measures the quantity demanded at each price after firm 2's output of q_2^b is sold first. The curve $MR_1(q_2^b)$ is the marginal revenue curve relating to the demand curve $D_1(q_2^b)$. Firm 1's profit-maximizing output now is q_1^b, at which $MR_1(q_2^b) = MC = 0$. In Figure 10.1b, point B corresponds to the best output level for firm 1 when firm 2 sells q_2^b units. By similar adjustments, output q_1^c is optimal for firm 1 when firm 2 sells q_2^c units (point C in panel b) and $q_1 = 0$ is optimal if firm 2 satisfies the largest possible quantity demanded, $\overline{Q}$ (point F).

The curve labeled $R_1(q_2)$ is firm 1's **reaction function,** which connects such points as $A, B, C,$ and F. The reaction function shows the optimal output for firm 1 as a function of firm 2's output. Firm 1 takes the output of firm 2 as a datum and reacts by selecting its best output in response. Firm 1 strives for a position on its reaction

Figure 10.2
Isoprofit Curves and the Reaction Function

Profit is constant along each inverted U-shaped isoprofit curve. Profits increase in shifting to lower curves. The reaction function must intersect each isoprofit curve at its maximum point.

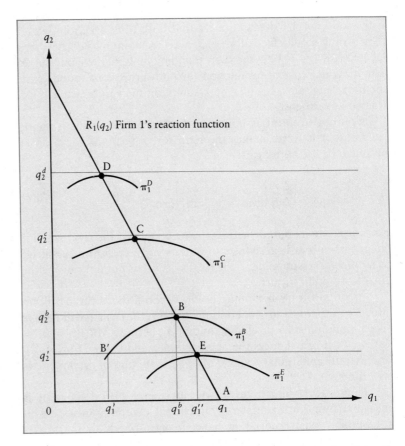

function; precisely which point on the function it strives for depends on firm 2's output level.

Figure 10.2 adds another family of curves to firm 1's reaction function, $R_1(q_2)$. The inverted U-shaped curves are **isoprofit** (equal profit) **curves.** Along a given curve, firm 1's profit remains constant. Consider point B, which shows that output q_1^b maximizes firm 1's profits when firm 2's sales are fixed at q_2^b. Let firm 1's profit at point B equal π_1^B. This same profit level could be earned anywhere along the π_1^B curve. For example, if firm 2 reduces output to q_2', firm 1 could maintain profits of π_1^B by reducing its output to q_1' at point B'. However, the optimal output for firm 1 would then be q_1'' at point E. The isoprofit curve π_1^E represents higher profits than the curve π_1^B.

Isoprofit curves display characteristics similar to indifference curves and isoquant curves, which we are already familiar with. Just as indifference curves are equal-utility surfaces drawn in output space, these isoprofit curves are equal-profit surfaces drawn in output space. Note that the firm's reaction function intersects the maximum point on each isoprofit curve. For any given output of firm 2, firm 1 maximizes profit by selecting an output level for which firm 2's horizontal quantity line becomes tangent to an isoprofit curve.

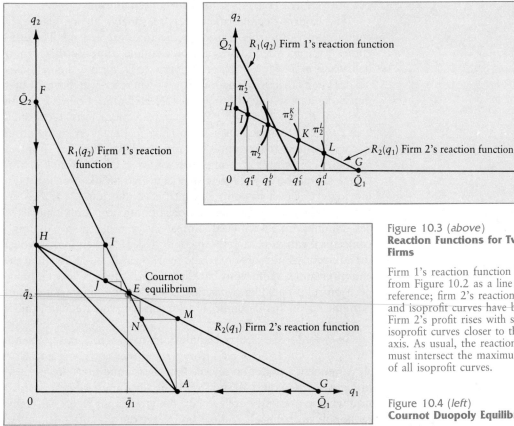

Figure 10.3 (*above*)
Reaction Functions for Two Rival Firms

Firm 1's reaction function is repeated from Figure 10.2 as a line of reference; firm 2's reaction function and isoprofit curves have been added. Firm 2's profit rises with shifts to isoprofit curves closer to the vertical axis. As usual, the reaction function must intersect the maximum points of all isoprofit curves.

Figure 10.4 (*left*)
Cournot Duopoly Equilibrium

Each firm sets its output based on the assumption that its rival's output is fixed. Cournot equilibrium occurs at the intersection of reaction functions, point E here. Firm 1 produces q_1 units, and firm 2 produces q_2 units. Any other output mix will induce firms to adjust their rates of production.

Profits increase by movements down the reaction function, $R_1(q_2)$; lower curves represent higher profits.

In order for the model to be determinate, we need to know firm 2's output. But surely you have guessed that our selection of firm 1 was arbitrary. Firm 2 is also a follower in the Cournot model; it too possesses a reaction function of its own that follows from its assumption that firm 1's output is fixed. In short, the two firms are symmetrical in their costs, demand, and decisions. Firm 2's reaction function, $R_2(q_1)$, is shown in Figure 10.3. (Firm 1's reaction function is included as a point of reference.) Firm 2's isoprofit curves are concave to the vertical axis. The reaction function $R_2(q_1)$ intersects the maximum points of all isoprofit curves, such as H, I, J, K, L, and G. Firm 2's profits rise by movements up the reaction function from G to H.

Figure 10.4 brings the two firms' reaction functions together in order to describe equilibrium. The isoprofit curves are suppressed temporarily for the sake of clarity. The duopolists achieve equilibrium at the intersection of their reaction functions, which is point E. At E each sets its output according to the other's output. Both firms remain at E because their conjectures about their rival's output are verified. Point E is the **Cournot equilibrium**.

The Cournot equilibrium seems reasonable at first glance. In equilibrium, both firms' a priori conjectures are verified. The difficulties arise in disequilibrium. For example, suppose that firm 1 believes firm 2 will sell the entire output, $\underline{Q}$. Firm 1 then chooses point F on its reaction function, $R_1(q_2)$, where $q_1 = 0$. Firm 2 notes that its rival is selling nothing, so it selects point H on its reaction function, $R_2(q_1)$. Now we have a contradiction. Firm 1 expected firm 2 to be at F; instead firm 2 is at H. Firm 1 must revise its output to correspond to the output it sees firm 2 selling. Thus firm 1 moves to point I. Now firm 2's conjecture is proven false. If firm 1 is at I, firm 2 should be at J. Clearly they could go on like this for days, moving ever closer to point E, which is equilibrium. At E the outputs $\overline{q}_1$ and $\overline{q}_2$ satisfy the expectations of both firms simultaneously, and equilibrium is achieved. But at every other point, the zero conjectural variation remains unconfirmed. However, in this model the conjecture is repeated over and over; regardless of how often the entrepreneurs' assumptions backfire, they dutifully follow the same decision rule. Thus the conjecture is confirmed only in static equilibrium, not in the dynamic adjustments by which equilibrium is attained.

In order for the Cournot equilibrium to be stable, it is necessary for $R_1(q_2)$ to intersect $R_2(q_1)$ from above; that is, $F > H$ and $G > A$. A moment's reflection reveals that these conditions are satisfied in Figure 10.4. Points A and H are the maximum outputs of each firm when it presumes itself to be a monopolist. In Figure 10.1, this monopoly output is q_1. Points F and G are the quantities demanded at zero price, equal to $\overline{Q}$ by reference to Figure 10.1. Clearly, $F > H$ and $G > A$. Point E is a stable equilibrium. Starting the adjustments from either side of E will cause E to be attained. If $R_1(q_2)$ intersected $R_2(q_1)$ from below, the equilibrium would be unstable. Any disequilibrium adjustments would move the firms farther away from E.

Note too that a line connecting the monopoly outputs A and H is a constant output equal to the monopoly rate of output. The Cournot equilibrium E represents a total combined output greater than the monopoly output: $E > A \equiv H$.

Figure 10.5 is a complete picture of the Cournot duopoly equilibrium. The 45-degree line clarifies the duopoly model and adds content to the cartel extensions that come later. Any point on the 45-degree line represents an equal market share for both entrepreneurs. In the symmetrical case we are studying, where both firms have the same costs (zero) and both face the same demand curve, the ultimate Cournot equilibrium occurs on the 45-degree line.

A concrete example will help to illustrate. If the horizontal intercept of a particular aggregate demand curve is 24 units, then both firms' reaction curves begin at 24, as shown in Figure 10.5. If

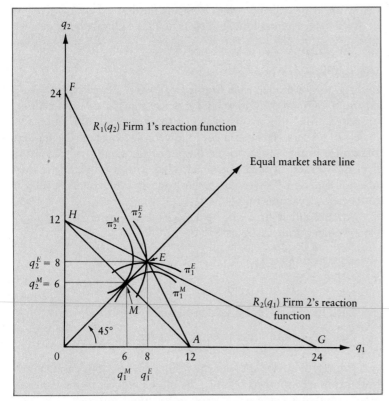

Figure 10.5
Cournot and Monopoly Equilibria Compared

Cournot equilibrium occurs at point E, the intersection of reaction functions. Total output is 16 units. If the rival firms colluded to maximize joint profits, they would move to point M, which reduces output to 12 units but increases the profit of both firms.

the demand curve is linear, the monopoly profit-maximizing output is 12, because the MR curve falls twice as fast as the demand curve. However, the Cournot equilibrium must occur where the reaction functions intersect, in this case at output 8 for each firm. Together the firms sell 16 units of output. Combined duopoly output is thus larger than the monopoly output of 12 units, and profits must be smaller. In Figure 10.5, a symmetrical example, the Cournot solution yields profits of $\pi = \pi_1^E + \pi_2^E$, where $\pi_1^E = \pi_2^E$. But if the firms colluded and behaved like a multiplant monopolist, total profits and both firms' profits could be increased by moving to point M. At M both firms move to higher isoprofit curves, and joint profits are maximized because $\pi_1^M > \pi_1^E$ and $\pi_2^M > \pi_2^E$. At point M each firm sells 6 units. Point M must be on the constant monopoly output line AH. Thus the Cournot equilibrium at E entails a greater output and a smaller combined profit than the monopoly or collusion point M. Also, a competitive market would produce where $P = MC = 0$, selling 24 units of output at zero profit. Thus the Cournot duopolists' output and profits lie between the monopoly and competitive levels. This is a plausible result.

The naivete of Cournot's assumption of zero conjectural variation brings the results of the equilibrium into question. Still, given the assumptions of the model, one thing is clear: The duopolists are better off with collusion than with uncoordinated behavior. This message comes across loud and clear in all the oligopoly models we study.

The Stackelberg Model

In the Cournot model, each firm is a follower. Heinrich von Stackelberg, a German economist and finance minister to Adolf Hitler, proposed a duopoly model in which the firms could be either followers or leaders.[4] If the firm is a follower, the Cournot rule applies: Maximize profit subject to the output of the rival firm. But if the firm is a leader, it need not be satisfied with a point on its own reaction function. As we will see, the leader maximizes profit subject to its rival's reaction function.

Because either firm can be a leader or follower in the Stackelberg model, four cases arise:

Case I: Both firms are followers.

Case II: Firm 1 is a leader, and firm 2 is a follower.

Case III: Firm 2 is a leader, and firm 1 is a follower.

Case IV: Both firms attempt to be leaders.

Figure 10.6 helps sort out the results of these four cases. When both firms are followers (case I), the model reduces to the Cournot equilibrium at E, where the reaction functions intersect.

If firm 1 is a leader while firm 2 is a follower (case II), firm 1 can exploit firm 2's willingness to respond to, but not hope to affect, firm 1's output. By moving to S_1, firm 1 selects the rate of output that maximizes its profits and that keeps firm 2 on its reaction function, $R_2(q_1)$. At S_1, firm 1's profits exceed the profits at the Cournot equilibrium E, and firm 2's profits are reduced.

Case III is the mirror image of case II. Now firm 2 is the leader; by selecting point S_2, it achieves the highest isoprofit curve consistent with firm 1's reaction function, $R_1(q_2)$. By comparison to the Cournot solution, firm 2's profits are greater and firm 1's are smaller. Leading clearly has its advantages.

So far so good. But Stackelberg believed that both firms would seek the profits arising from market leadership (case IV). And here we see another fallacy of composition. Either firm can become a leader if the other firm remains a follower. But a follower may not follow for long. When both attempt to lead simultaneously, there is an attempt to move to point S_u. But at S_u neither firm earns the profit it expected, because these outputs were selected in the conviction that the rival firm was a follower and would merely adjust to its

4. Heinrich von Stackelberg, *The Theory of the Market Economy*, trans. A. T. Peacock (New York: Oxford University Press, 1952).

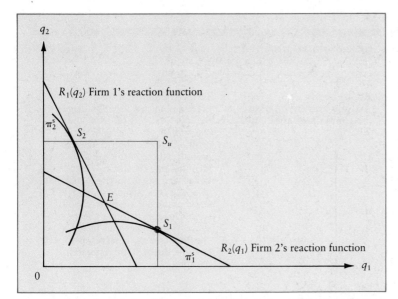

Figure 10.6
Stackelberg Disequilibrium

Cournot equilibrium at point E occurs when both firms are followers. If firm 1 is a leader and firm 2 is a follower, a stable equilibrium is achieved at S_1. If firm 2 is a leader and firm 1 is a follower, equilibrium occurs at S_2. However, if both firms attempt to lead, Stackelberg disequilibrium occurs at S_u.

reaction function. Point S_u is the **Stackelberg disequilibrium.** If dual leadership results in the disequilibrium point S_u, the ultimate outcome cannot be predicted. Many possibilities arise as it becomes clear to both firms that each wishes to dominate the market. Presumably the conditions are ripe for economic warfare, and a stable equilibrium will emerge only when one firm has submitted to the other's leadership or both have become Cournot-type followers. In the presence of this warfare, the firms cannot help but notice the benefits of collusion. Collusive behavior becomes an attractive alternative to the unstable conditions and lower profits that firms encounter in the Stackelberg disequilibrium. A leader may even be willing to make a lump-sum payment to its rival to assure that the rival remains a follower. The size of the payment would be determined by the profits the leader would lose if the rival's behavior launched them into disequilibrium.

In summary, the results of the Cournot and Stackelberg approaches depend on the conjectural variations of each firm regarding the rival's output. The jth firm, a follower, exhibits a conjectural variation of zero: $\Delta q_i / \Delta q_j = 0$. In contrast, a leader such as the ith firm holds that the output of the rival firm will depend on how much the leader produces. Thus

$$\frac{\Delta q_j}{\Delta q_i} = \frac{\Delta R_j(q_i)}{\Delta q_i} \qquad (10.4)$$

The leader, the jth firm, believes that any change in its output will move the rival firm along the rival's own reaction function, $R_j(q_i)$. The results of these duopoly models depend strictly on the assumptions made about the conjectural variation term.

Cartel Stability and the Market Share Maintenance Rule

APPLIED
MICRO
THEORY

10.1

The purpose of collusion is to maximize cartel members' joint profits. The oligopoly methods of maximizing joint profit that are under study here require varying degrees of collusion and cartel behavior. But cartels are inherently unstable; although each firm is better off when the cartel is organized, each also has a profit incentive to weaken the cartel by cheating via unauthorized expansion of output (see Chapter 9). If the cartel is to survive, these cheating incentives must be controlled. One proposed strategy to reduce cartel cheating and increase cartel stability is the **market share maintenance rule.**

In brief, the rule works like this: When cartel cheating in the form of unauthorized output expansion is discovered, all cartel members retaliate by increasing output in proportion to the cheaters' output so as to maintain a constant share of the market. This rule forces the cheaters to share in the total losses in cartel profits arising from the cheating, thereby eliminating the expected gains from cheating. If effective, the rule should inhibit initial cheating or, at worst, encourage cheaters to cooperate in reestablishing the joint profit cartel equilibrium.

Two cases must be distinguished. In both, adoption of the rule stabilizes the cartel by allowing the noncheating members to pose a "credible threat" to the cheaters by communicating the following message: "If you cheat, our retaliations will make us better off and you worse off. Therefore, you are better off not cheating."

Symmetry: Conditions Favor Noncheaters

Figure A illustrates the output space of two groups of firms in a cartel: The horizontal axis measures the cheating coalition's output, and the vertical axis measures the noncheaters' or loyal coalition's output. The curved lines are isoprofit curves. The isoprofit curves are labeled π_c and π_l, the subscripts referring to cheaters and loyalists, respectively. The two coalitions' reaction functions are also included in the diagram. Cartel instability and the stabilizing effect of the market share maintenance rule can thus be shown using the familiar duopoly

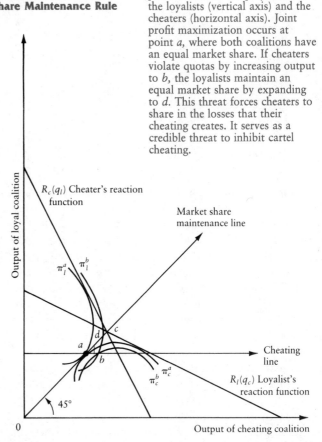

**Figure A
Cartels and the Market Share Maintenance Rule**

$R_c(q_l)$ Cheater's reaction function

Market share maintenance line

Output of loyal coalition

π_l^a π_l^b

d c

a

b

Cheating line

π_c^b π_c^a

$R_l(q_c)$ Loyalist's reaction function

45°

0   Output of cheating coalition

Two coalitions of a cartel are presented in the duopoly format: the loyalists (vertical axis) and the cheaters (horizontal axis). Joint profit maximization occurs at point a, where both coalitions have an equal market share. If cheaters violate quotas by increasing output to b, the loyalists maintain an equal market share by expanding to d. This threat forces cheaters to share in the losses that their cheating creates. It serves as a credible threat to inhibit cartel cheating.

apparatus we have already studied.

Figure A is drawn on the assumption of symmetry among firms; all firms face the same demand and cost conditions. As demonstrated in Figure 10.5, two conditions must hold on the 45-degree line in the symmetrical case: The reaction functions must intersect there, implying an equal market share in Cournot equilibrium, and the joint profit maximization condition—indicated by a tangency of isoprofit functions—must occur on the 45-degree line. In Figure A, the cartel joint profit maximization occurs at point a, and the reaction functions intersect at point c. The 45-degree line is the market share maintenance line. If both cartel coalitions are to maintain the same market share as at point a, a point on the 45-degree line must be attained.

Let the horizontal line labeled "Cheating line" represent the cheaters' unauthorized output increase. Beginning at the cartel equilibrium point a, suppose the cheaters increase output along the cheating line to point b in order to achieve the higher profit curve $\pi_c^b > \pi_c^a$. The loyal coalition should retaliate by increasing output to d on the 45-degree line. Such retaliation reestablishes the previous market share. Note that, by moving from a to b, the cheaters' profits rise and the loyalists' profits fall. But by the retaliatory market maintenance move from b to d, the cheaters are made worse off than at a or b, and the loyalists are better off at d than standing pat at b. For this reason, conditions favor the noncheaters. Herein lies the credible threat: Retaliations designed to maintain market share are always in the direction of increasing loyalists' profits and reducing cheaters' profits. Equivalently, such retaliation allows the loyalists to adjust output in the same direction (if not in the same amount) as Cournot or Stackelberg followers, always moving toward their reaction function. Thus in the symmetrical case, adoption of the market share maintenance rule inhibits cheating and motivates recalcitrant cheaters to cooperate in reachieving cartel equilibrium at point a.

Nonsymmetry: Conditions Favor Cheaters

It is important to note that the previous results do not generalize to the nonsymmetrical case. Figure B illustrates a counterexample—a nonsymmetrical case where retaliations by the loyalists to maintain market share do not increase prof-

Figure B
Cartels and the Market Share Maintenance Rule: Nonsymmetry

If cheaters move from a to g, the loyalists have two choices: Maintain their market share by moving to h, or maximize short-run profit by moving to i.

Moving to i may result in Cournot or Stackelberg equilibrium at point c or s, leaving the cheaters with higher profits. Moving to h reduces the short-run profits of the loyalists but also reduces the profits of the cheaters. Such a credible threat is imperative to the viability of the cartel.

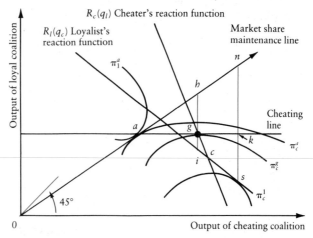

its. Here such retaliations actually reduce the loyalists' profits by moving them away from their reaction function. In this case, conditions favor the cheaters. Even so, the market share maintenance rule is still the best strategy for loyalists who want to stabilize the cartel.

In Figure B the cheaters are assumed to have lower costs than the loyalists. Thus the cheaters' isoprofit curves have less curvature than those of the loyalists. Accordingly, Figure B differs from Figure A in a couple of major ways. First, the market share at the cartel equilibrium point a no longer occurs on the 45-degree line. The lower-cost firms produce more output than their high-cost rivals. Thus the market share maintenance line lies below the 45-degree line. Second, the reaction functions no longer intersect on the 45-degree line or even on the market share maintenance line. Figure B is

drawn with the intersection of the reaction functions inside the cheaters' isoprofit curve π_c^a, the profit earned by the cheaters in cartel joint profit-maximizing equilibrium before any cheating occurs.

If the cheaters expand output along the cheating line from a to g, what should the loyalists do? Note that a retaliation to point h moves the loyalists away from their reaction function. Thus the loyalists' profits fall twice: once when the cheaters weaken the cartel and again when the loyalists attempt to strengthen it by keeping a constant market share. The profit-maximizing retaliation would be for the loyalists to reduce output to i, a point on the loyalists' reaction function. Further actions by both coalitions would induce a Cournot equilibrium at point c, the intersection of the reaction functions. An enterprising cheating

Continued on page 300

coalition might even cheat to point k, a point vertically above point s. Now the loyalists would adjust to point s by moving to their reaction function. Point s is the Stackelberg solution, where the loyalists are followers and the cheaters are leaders.

Here we can see the danger that arises when the loyalists do not follow the market share maintenance rule, even though short-run profits must be sacrificed. If the loyalists react like Cournot or Stackelberg followers, cheating pays off for the cheaters by giving them permanent gains at the same time that the loyalists are worse off. This is no way to punish cheaters! Such incentives can be expected to dissolve the cartel. Loyalists must avoid the Cournot and Stackelberg solutions at c and s.

Now let's examine the benefits of sticking to the market share

maintenance rule even though it means a loss of short-run profit to the loyal coalition. Suppose that the cheaters move to point k. They cannot know in advance whether conditions are favorable or unfavorable for such cheating. That is, they cannot know a priori the position of the loyalists' isoprofit curves and reaction function. If conditions are favorable for cheating, as they are in Figure B, the loyalists must not reveal that fact to the cheaters by moving routinely to the Stackelberg point s. The market share maintenance rule is for the loyalists to adjust output to point n, reducing both coalitions' profits. This strategy leaves the cheaters in the dark. They know their own profits have fallen, but they have no way of discovering whether the loyalists are bluffing. The cheaters may believe that the loyalists' response moves in the direction of profit maximi

zation. Therefore, this strategy eliminates the profits that the cheaters expected and perhaps convinces the cheaters that their rivals' retaliations increase loyalists profits. In this way the cheaters are encouraged to rejoin the cartel equilibrium at point a.

To summarize, strict adherence to the market share maintenance rule tends to stabilize cartels, even when this strategy reduces the loyal coalition's short-run profits. If the strategy saves the cartel, the long-run benefits may outweigh the loss of short-run profits. Thus the rule is a credible threat to potential cheaters in both the symmetrical and nonsymmetrical cases.*

*For a fuller treatment of these issues, see D. K. Osborne, "Cartel Problems," *American Economic Review* 66 (1976): 835–844; and W. L. Holahan, "Cartel Problems: Comment," *American Economic Review* 68 (1978): 942–946.

The Edgeworth Model

Many analysts have preferred to assume that business rivals set prices rather than quantities sold. Professor Francis Edgeworth (father of the Edgeworth box and the indifference curve) produced a duopoly model based on a suggestion by the original critic of Cournot, Joseph Bertrand, who maintained that the firm's first decision variable is price, not quantity of sales. Thus Edgeworth transformed the Cournot assumption about conjectural variations into its price equivalent:

$$\frac{\Delta P_i}{\Delta P_j} = 0 \tag{10.5}$$

Firms set their prices with the conviction that their rival's prices will remain fixed. Under these assumptions, Edgeworth concluded that market price and output will oscillate irregularly with no equilibrium at all. Let's see how Edgeworth derived this remarkable result.[5]

Assume that at each price the duopolists each serve half the quantity demanded. Thus in Figure 10.7, firm 1 faces demand curve D_1 and firm 2 faces demand curve D_2. The two demand curves are drawn as mirror images, a construction that allows the vertical price axis to serve both quadrants. Edgeworth assumed that both firms

5. F. Edgeworth, "L Teoria Para del Monopolio," *Giornale degli Economisti* (1897).

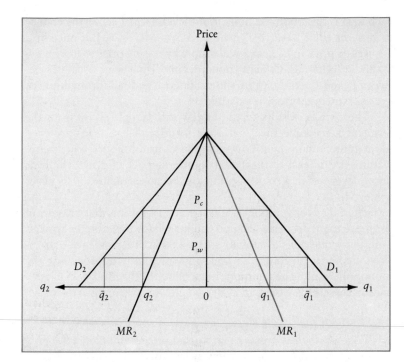

Figure 10.7
The Edgeworth Duopoly Model

Price oscillates between P_c and P_w, and output oscillates between $q_1 + q_2$ and $\bar{q}_1 + \bar{q}_2$. No equilibrium exists.

produce at zero cost but that neither has enough capacity to completely serve its half of the market when price is zero. In Figure 10.7, outputs $\bar{q}_1$ and $\bar{q}_2$ represent these output constraints. As before, the horizontal axes correspond to zero marginal cost.

If the duopolists colluded, they would each set price at P_c and sell q_1 and q_2 units of output. At price P_c, each firm sets MR = MC = 0. However, if the firms act independently, each has an incentive to shave its price. For example, firm 1 has output equal to $\bar{q}_1 - q_1$ that is not sold at price P_c. If these units could be sold, profits would rise. The strategy is clear: Lower price fractionally below firm 2's price of P_c and attract the rival's customers. This strategy makes sense to firm 1, which operates under the zero conjectural variation assumption that firm 2 will not respond in kind. But of course firm 2 will respond. It will lower its price fractionally below firm 1's new price in order to recoup old customers and attract additional ones from firm 1. Such price wars will continue until price P_w is achieved. At price P_w, both firms are selling their entire output. Neither firm can gain by lowering prices below P_w, because they could not serve all the new customers that lower prices would attract.

It might seem that price P_w is the equilibrium price, but it is not. By participating in the price war, both firms have allowed themselves to sell units of output for which marginal revenue is negative. Each price reduction below P_c appears profitable to the firm because it believes that the rival will keep its price fixed. However, the conjecture is wrong 100% of the time. By the time P_w is reached, each firm is disappointed in its profit level. Firm 1 seizes the chance to raise its price back to P_c, where MR = MC = 0. But once firm 1 raises its price to P_c, firm 2 will follow by raising price to just below P_c, and another adjustment round begins. Thus price oscillates between P_c and P_w, and output and profits rise and fall throughout the cycles. No equilibrium is possible.

The curious results of the Edgeworth model follow from the term for zero conjectural variation in price. These firms are even more gullible than the followers in the Cournot model, whose conjectures are at least confirmed in equilibrium. The Edgeworth firms do not even get that small satisfaction, because equilibrium is never achieved.

The Edgeworth model is unsatisfactory for another reason. In the presence of arbitrage, a good cannot sell for two different prices. Still, the model tells a familiar story. The interdependence of decisions makes it profitable to find ways of jointly approaching the monopoly result. The temptation to collude as the firms gain experience in these Edgeworthian cycles would seem virtually irresistible.

The Kinked Demand Curve Model

The Edgeworth view seems to imply that price stability in a duopoly or oligopoly requires some form of collusion. Carried to the extreme, price stability could be considered prima facie evidence of collusion. Almost simultaneously, two studies appeared that demonstrated how price stability in oligopolistic markets may be the natural result of noncollusive, uncoordinated behavior of rival firms.[6] These papers presented a **kinked demand curve.**

The central feature of the kinked demand curve model is that each firm has a term for asymmetrical conjectural variation regarding price changes. Consider a firm selling at a particular price. If the firm lowers its price, it expects competitors to follow the price reduction in order to maintain their customers. Thus for price reductions, the conjectural variation term, $\Delta P_i / \Delta P_j$, equals unity. Price reductions are expected to be matched by the rival firms. But for price increases, the firm does not expect competitors to follow; rival firms will be content to allow the price-raising firm to price itself out of the market. Thus for price increases, $\Delta P_i / \Delta P_j = 0$.

It is this asymmetry that produces the kink in the demand curve. In Figure 10.8, the beginning price = quantity combination is represented by point A. If the firm lowers price, it expects other firms to follow. Thus for prices below P_k, the firm perceives a relatively inelastic demand curve, such as AB. But if price is raised above P_k, the firm anticipates large losses in customers, because it believes that its competitors will not follow the price increase for the express

6. R. L. Hall and C. J. Hitch, "Price Theory and Business Behavior," *Oxford Economic Papers*, no. 2 (1939), pp. 12–45; and Paul M. Sweezy, "Demand under Conditions of Oligopoly," *Journal of Political Economy* 47 (1939): 568–573.

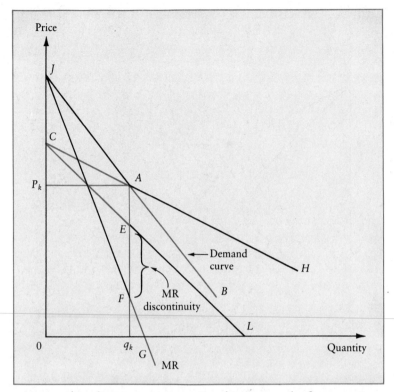

Figure 10.8
The Kinked Demand Curve

The demand curve is *CAB*, with a kink at *A*. Starting at price P_k, the firm perceives that rivals will follow price cuts but not price increases. The marginal revenue curve has two segments, *CE* and *FG*, with a discontinuity of *EF* at output q_k.

purpose of stealing its customers. For this reason, the firm perceives a relatively elastic demand curve for prices above P_k, such as segment *CA*. Thus the firm really faces two demand curves: curve *CA* and another curve *AB*. Another way to express the same thing is to say that the single demand curve *CAB* has a kink at point *A*. And it is this kink that produces the price and output stability so utterly lacking in the Edgeworth model.

The stability implications are most easily seen by deriving the firm's marginal revenue curve. This derivation is a little trickier than usual because, like the demand curve, the MR curve has two segments. For ease in construction, suppose temporarily that the firm faced the demand curve *JAB;* the segment *JA* is merely an imagined extension of the actual demand segment *AB*. The marginal revenue curve corresponding to the demand curve *JAB* is *JFG*. Next make an imagined extension of *CA*, resulting in the demand curve *CAH*. The corresponding marginal revenue curve is *CEL*. Now erase the imagined demand segments, drawn in black in Figure 10.8, and the marginal revenue segments to which they pertain. After the erasures are cleared off, the marginal revenue curve that remains comprises the two segments *CE* and *FG*, as shown in color in Figure 10.8. Note that the marginal revenue curve is discontinuous exactly at the output corresponding to the kink; that is, there is no unique marginal revenue at output q_k. This discontinuity is illustrated by the

Figure 10.9
Kinked Demand and the Stability of Oligopolistic Pricing

When MC_1 is the firm's marginal cost curve, MC_1 intersects the MR discontinuity between E and F. P_k and q_k are the profit-maximizing price and output. If MC_1 rises to MC_2 or falls to MC_3, profit maximization calls for the same price and quantity.

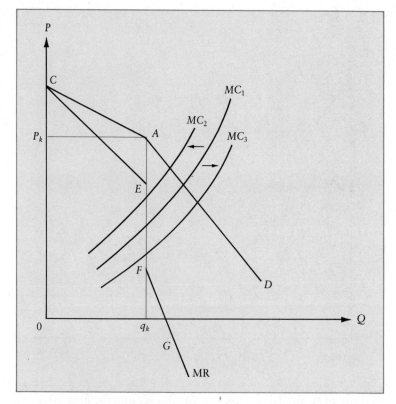

vertical segment EF. The kink in the demand curve at q_k forces a discontinuity in the firm's marginal revenue curve at the same output level.

Figure 10.9 illustrates the stability characteristics of the model. Let the firm's marginal cost curve equal MC_1. The MR = MC profit-maximizing rule is not satisfied, because MR is not defined at output q_k, where the MC curve "intersects" the discontinuity. Still, taking discrete changes in output away from q_k in either direction reveals that q_k is the best output available, because MR > MC at outputs less than q_k and MR < MC at outputs greater than q_k.

Now consider the effect on price and quantity of moderate increases or decreases in the firm's marginal cost, as shown by MC_2 and MC_3. Because all three marginal cost curves intersect the line segment EF, P_k and q_k continue to be the profit-maximizing price and output of the firm. Moderate cost changes do not result in price and output adjustments, as they would in the deterministic models of competition and monopoly. The kink produces unusual price stability.

Figure 10.10 demonstrates a similar price stability when demand shifts. Assume that the firm experiences a marked increase in demand, from D_0 to D_1. If the kink occurs at the same price, P_k, this demand shift would give the firm no incentive to change price,

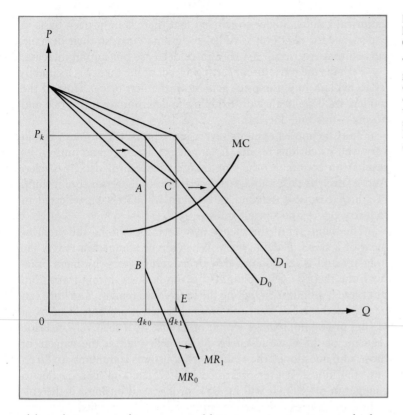

Figure 10.10
Kinked Demand and the Stability of Oligopolistic Pricing

The original demand curve is D_0, giving rise to an MR curve with the discontinuity AB. Shifting the demand curve to D_1 results in the MR curve with discontinuity CE. Moderate shifts in demand may leave price largely unaffected while changing the quantity sold.

although its rate of output would increase in response to higher demand.

The kinked demand curve puts the analysis of oligopoly on a much different footing in comparison to Edgeworth's model. For Edgeworth, noncollusive oligopoly results in unstable price and output patterns, even when costs and demand are stable. With the kinked demand curve, moderate cost and demand shifts can occur without causing firms to alter their prices and output. Somehow both results seem extreme.

The kinked demand curve model enjoyed a pleasant honeymoon; many economists came to regard it as "the" model of oligopoly behavior. The honeymoon was over, however, when Professor George Stigler questioned the theoretical and empirical relevance of the kink.[7] Stigler studied the historical pricing policies and dynamics of seven oligopolies in search of behavioral evidence that price decreases are followed more regularly and quickly than price increases. He was not able to observe any systematic behavior that could be attributed to firms by the theory. On the basis of his

---

7. George J. Stigler, "The Kinky Oligopoly Demand Curve and Rigid Prices," *Journal of Political Economy* 55 (1947): 432–449. Both the Sweezy paper and the Stigler criticism are reprinted in G. J. Stigler and K. E. Boulding, eds., *Readings in Price Theory*, vol. 6 (Homewood, Ill.: Irwin, 1952).

empirical results, Stigler concluded that there is no proven basis in experience for oligopolists to believe a kink exists in their demand curves, that rivals will match a price decrease but not an increase.

Perhaps the most disconcerting aspect of the theory is its inability to explain how the price gets set in the first place. Most of the models we have dealt with explain the determination of price and output—this one does not.

Thus the model exhibits severe limitations. It does not explain very well its curious results. It cannot predict price and output. Its results run counter to the empirical evidence provided by Stigler. And it surely is unsuitable as a description of long-run equilibrium, in which cost and demand shifts must ultimately be reflected in industry prices and output rates.

The main use of the theory may be in describing the predicament of a small, fledgling firm. When a new competitor enters the industry and is unacquainted with its competitors' business practices, the theory may explain its pricing policies during transition. But there is a limit to how long the kink could remain. The kink can be regarded as a hindrance to profits because it prevents firms from raising prices along what would otherwise be a relatively inelastic segment of the demand curve. Stigler marveled at the naivete of those who questioned the ability of the business community to "iron out" the kink if it ever presented itself: "The kink is a barrier to changes in prices that will increase profits, and business is the collection of devices for circumventing barriers to profits. That this barrier should thwart businessmen—especially when it is wholly of their own fabrication—is unbelievable. There are many ways in which it can be circumvented."[8] Let's proceed to a discussion of the various noncollusive and collusive devices that oligopolists use to achieve joint profit maximization.

Models of Joint Profit Maximization

The models requiring firms to evaluate rivals' responses to their price and output decisions—models of conjectural variation—do not provide a complete picture of oligopolistic behavior. In this section, we turn our attention to the ways that diverse firms can coordinate their behavior in order to achieve maximization of profits.

Either by firsthand experience or through their formal training in economics and business administration, entrepreneurs know about the inherent dangers of price wars and noncooperative solutions to price and output decisions. Among competing firms that are too large to be considered price takers, joint profit maximization resulting from coordinated price and output policies becomes an ideal. Adam Smith recognized the potential benefit of collusive be-

8. Stigler, "The Kinky Oligopoly," p. 435.

havior among firms when he noted, "People of the same trade seldom meet together, even for merriment and diversion, but the conversation ends in a conspiracy against the public, or in some contrivance to raise prices."[9] Collusion is illegal in the United States, but even so the steady number of annual prosecutions and convictions under the Sherman Antitrust Act of 1890 bears witness to the attractions of collusion.

If firms are to keep prices high and output correspondingly low in order to achieve the monopoly ideal, a communications system that can glue the oligopolists together must evolve. Price shaving that leads to price wars must be avoided. Excessive prices that attract new competitors also need to be shunned. Thus maximum joint profits require that pricing be an industry matter. Oligopolists must coordinate their pricing decisions via an effective communications network.

The most effective forms of communication are all illegal—the face-to-face meetings, whether in the office or on the golf course, where prices are agreed on and output quotas allocated. Other forms of communication that are not quite so patently illegal have arisen, including various forms of price leadership. In what follows, we can hardly scratch the surface of devices that the business sector has fashioned to avoid the specter of truly competitive market results.

A word of caution is necessary before we begin to explore models of oligopoly profits. Oligopoly profits do not necessarily imply collusion among firms—tacit or express. Theories of "guilt by profitability" view profits as prima facie evidence of deliberate departures from competition rather than as manifestations of hard work, cleverness, foresight, efficiency, and luck. Collusion is seldom the full story in explaining oligopoly profits. There are often alternative, less conspiratorial explanations.

The Chamberlin Model

Professor Edward Chamberlin's duopoly model is a criticism of both the Cournot and Edgeworth solutions.[10] Chamberlin insists that the assumption of zero conjectural variation made by Cournot and Edgeworth is a denial that a firm considers its total influence on price and output, both direct and indirect. In evaluating the assumption of zero conjectural variation, Chamberlin remarks, "When a move by one seller evidently forces the other to make a counter move, he is very stupidly refusing to look further than his nose if he proceeds on the assumption that it will not."[11] Zero conjectural

9. Adam Smith, *An Inquiry into the Nature and Causes of the Wealth of Nations* (New York: Modern Library, 1937).

10. Edward H. Chamberlin, *The Theory of Monopolistic Competition* (1933; reprinted., Cambridge, Mass.: Harvard University Press, 1962), pp. 46–51.

11. Chamberlin, *Monopolistic Competition*, p. 46.

variation allows duopolists to compete as if their actions are independent—an assumption that ignores the essential duopoly characteristic of interdependence.

So Chamberlin assumes that firms consider the total consequences of their pricing and output policies. When they do so, it is clear that Cournot and Edgeworth responses are self-defeating. Thus the joint profit-maximizing solutions implied by the monopoly equilibrium can be achieved by firms without collusion, provided the firms are minimally intelligent and can judge the danger encountered by ignoring the effect of their actions on their competitors. Under these conditions, neither rival will undertake price and quantity adjustments away from the monopoly ideal. Actions are not collusive, yet monopoly results are obtained. Here the partial loss of monopoly profits implied by the Cournot equilibrium and the complete instability of the Edgeworth solution are replaced by an uncoordinated monopoly result.

Chamberlin's criticism of the Cournot and Edgeworth models is no doubt a step in the right direction; firms will find a way to avoid the loss of profits implied by those solutions. However, Chamberlin does not give us a clue as to how the firms interact in order to produce joint profit maximization.

Dominant-Firm Price Leadership

A major component of any communications network among competing oligopolistic firms is the price leader. Price leadership takes two general forms. First, there is the dominant firm structure, in which one firm clearly dominates the market and a collection of price-taking firms operate beneath the umbrella of the major firm. Second, there is barometric price leadership, in which the oligopolistic industry "selects" a firm to act as the initiator of price changes and other firms follow the leader. A barometric price leader may or may not hold a dominant position in the industry.

Dominant-firm price leadership, also called the "leader-follower model," works like this: The dominant firm sets the industry price; the price-taking competitive firms sell their desired outputs at that price. The dominant firm serves the market that remains after the competitors have adjusted their sales to the profit-maximizing levels. Figure 10.11 illustrates the model. The demand curve in Figure 10.11a is the aggregate demand for the industry's output. The curve labeled $S = \Sigma_h \text{MC}$ is the horizontal sum of the competitive firms' marginal cost curves. Thus $S = \Sigma_h \text{MC}$ is the aggregate supply curve of the price-taking competitors. The dominant firm's demand curve (D_d in panel b) is derived by subtracting the quantities supplied by the competitive firms from the aggregate demand curve. Thus the demand curve faced by the dominant firm is AH. At price P_1 the competitive firms serve the entire market, and

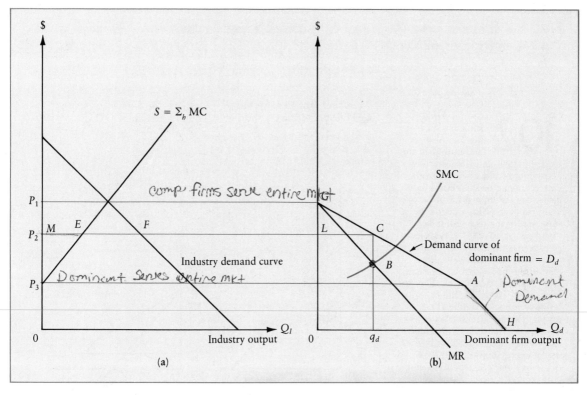

(a)

(b)

at price P_3 the dominant firm serves the entire market. Thus between prices P_1 and P_3 the dominant firm's demand curve, D_d, is this horizontal subtraction:

$$D_d = D - \Sigma_h MC \qquad (10.6)$$

For prices below P_3, the dominant firm faces the aggregate demand curve segment AH.

The marginal revenue curve is related to the demand curve segment GA of the dominant firm. The short-run marginal cost curve, SMC, is that of the dominant firm. The dominant firm maximizes profit by equating MR and MC at B and selects price P_2. At price P_2 the dominant firm sells $0q_d = LC$ units of output. The competing firms sell ME units of output. Changes in the industry demand curve, the competitive supply curve, or the dominant firm's marginal cost curve will cause the price and quantity to change. However, the solutions are strictly determinate here, in sharp contrast to many other oligopoly models. This is the model used in Applied Micro Theory 10.2 to study the OPEC cartel and the advisability of wellhead taxes on domestic oil production. Many retail drug and grocery markets also fit this model, where one major chain often competes with numerous small neighborhood stores.

Figure 10.11
The Leader-Follower Model

(a) $S = \Sigma_h MC$ is the supply curve of the competitive fringe. (b) The leader faces demand equal to the difference between total demand and the supply of the competitive fringe. The leader sets output at B, where marginal cost and marginal revenue are equal, and sets price at P_2, which the followers take as a parameter.

The Tax on Old Oil and the OPEC Cartel

APPLIED
MICRO
THEORY

10.2

The oil industry presents us with two facts: OPEC is a principal force in determining oil price and output in the United States, and domestic U.S. petroleum producers are earning vast economic profits resulting in part from the high price of petroleum products. Many people have suggested that these profits be taxed away, leaving the petroleum producers with a normal return on investment; the goal is to redistribute profits by extracting them from the firms and giving them to consumers. However, this is an unlikely result of wellhead taxes on oil. Taxing domestic oil producers is more likely to strengthen the OPEC cartel's position in the world energy market at the expense of domestic producers and consumers.

Let's use the dominant-firm (leader-follower) model to analyze the pricing and output decisions of the OPEC monopoly cartel (the leader) and non-OPEC producers (the followers). This is a convenient and plausible model, because it considers the OPEC cartel the price-setting leader in the industry and the domestic oil producers as price takers at the price set by the cartel. Cartels can survive with competition if they have monopoly power over the lowest-cost production processes. Then only higher-cost competitors, whose entry cannot entirely wipe out the cartel's profits, can enter. This is true in the oil industry because OPEC oil is produced at a much lower cost than U.S. oil is.

The demand curve labeled D_{US} in Figure A represents the U.S. demand for oil, and the curve labeled S_{US} is the aggregate supply of domestic oil producers. Price P_2 is the lowest price that generates domestic production. The supply schedule S_{US} is anchored at this minimum price. For simplicity,

Figure A
The Dominant-Firm Model of OPEC/U.S. Petroleum Producers

In the left-hand panel, D_{US} is the U.S. demand for oil and S_{US} is the supply provided by U.S. oil

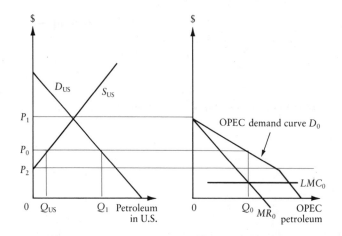

producers. OPEC's demand curve, D_O, is the difference between D_{US} and S_{US}. MR_O is OPEC's marginal revenue curve, derived in conventional fashion from the demand curve D_O.

let's assume that the only foreign source of oil is OPEC. Then the curve D_0 is the demand faced by the leader, OPEC, and is derived as a residual of total U.S. demand and the supply of the followers, the U.S. domestic producers: $D_0 = D_{US} - S_{US}$. Thus OPEC's residual demand curve extends between price P_1, at which all U.S. demand is satisfied by U.S. suppliers, and the lower price P_2, at which U.S. supply vanishes and the entire U.S. demand is met by OPEC producers.

OPEC's marginal revenue, MR_0, is derived from the demand curve D_0. The OPEC marginal cost, LMC_0, is drawn below the minimum price for domestic output to reflect the lower costs of OPEC oil compared to domestic oil. For exposition, LMC_0 is drawn horizontal to the quantity axis, although a positive slope produces the same qualitative results. The cartel

maximizes total cartel profit by producing where $MR_0 = LMC_0$ (at A) and by setting the OPEC price at P_0. At price P_0, OPEC produces Q_0 units for the United States; the additional quantity, $Q_1 - Q_{US}$ is produced by domestic sellers. Neither OPEC nor domestic suppliers can set price without regard to market conditions. They are both confronted by the consequences of the other's decisions.

Let's examine domestic oil supply more closely. In the oil industry, firms face differing costs because of differing well depths, geological structures, distance from distribution facilities, and so forth. For any given price for the final product, there will be marginal wells that just break even, inframarginal wells that earn economic profit, and extramarginal wells that would lose money if brought into production. As firms enter the market, supply increases and price falls. Equilibrium is established when the price is equal to the minimum LAC of the marginal well and no more inframarginal wells are left to enter. The marginal well breaks even, but the inframarginal wells gain rents that cannot be competed away, because there are no more inframarginal wells left that can enter and bring the price down further.

The wellhead tax is an effort to extract domestic producers' inframarginal rents. As we saw in Chapter 9, a tax on monopoly profits does not affect firm pricing and production. However, we lack good information on the oil-extraction costs of different firms, information we would need to institute a perfectly calibrated wellhead tax. As a practical compromise, the wellhead tax could be levied on "old" oil, meaning oil discovered prior to a given year. Such a "hands-on" practical tax could be used to hold the net reward to, say, $6 per barrel of old oil. The idea behind taxing "old" oil is that old oil is low-cost oil from which rents are generated.

What impact will such a tax have on the petroleum market and, in particular, on the behavior of the OPEC cartel and its relatively

competitive domestic rivals in the United States?

Figure B illustrates the effect on the cost curves and supply of the wellhead tax on old oil. The left-hand panel contains the cost curves of firm 1, which produces "old" oil; the center panel shows the cost curves of firm 2, which produces "new" oil; and the right-hand panel shows the industry supply curves, which are, as usual, horizontal summations of producers' marginal cost curves.

When no taxes are levied, the industry long-run supply curve is

the sum of all producers' long-run marginal cost curves, labeled Σ_hLMC(all oil) in the right-hand panel. Now suppose that firm 1 is taxed so that the net return on "old" oil cannot rise above $6 per barrel. Such a firm will expand output when prices rise to $6; this expansion is reflected in segment AB of the curve labeled Σ_hLMC (all oil). There is never an incentive to raise the rate of production above q_1, however, because the returns from doing so will be eliminated by the tax. Thus at prices above $6 per barrel, the slope of the industry supply curve will merely reflect the horizontal sum of the marginal cost curves of firms producing "new," untaxed oil. This curve, labeled Σ_hLMC (tax), rises at the same rate as the Σ_hLMC(new oil) curve, which is the horizontal sum of the marginal cost curves of owners producing new oil. The horizontal distance between Σ_hLMC(new oil) and Σ_hLMC(tax) at prices above $6 reflects the output of the taxed firms, such as q_1 for firm 1. To summarize, the wellhead tax on old oil reduces the domestic supply curve from Σ_hLMC(all oil) to Σ_hLMC(tax).

Continued on page 312

**Figure B
The Effect of an Old-Oil Wellhead Tax on Industry Supply**

Firm 1 (left-hand panel) produces "old" oil. Firm 2 (center panel) produces "new" oil. The industry supply curve (right-hand panel) includes all oil suppliers. Producers of old oil have no incentive to produce more output than q_1, because the tax holds the net return to $6. The quantity AB in the right-hand panel is the fixed sum of all old oil that firms will produce. The total supply is Σ_hLMC(tax).

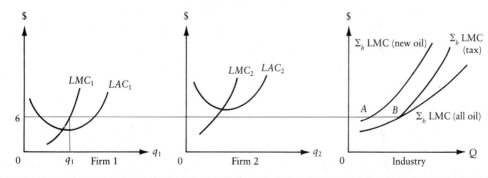

Now consider Figure C. It looks imposing but is actually quite easy to interpret. The black lines are the cost and revenue curves from Figure A. OPEC sets the price P_0, and the United States imports the amount Q_0 from OPEC in order to satisfy the total quantity demanded at price P_0.

What is the effect of the tax on the "old" oil of domestic producers? We have shown that the tax causes the supply curve S_{US} to rotate to the left, from S_{US} to S'_{US}. If the S_{US} curve pivots around P_2, the OPEC demand curve D_0 pivots around point B to D'_0 and becomes relatively more inelastic. And because the demand curves D_0 and D'_0 intersect at B, the marginal revenues of each must pass through point C—half the distance of EC. Also, because MR_0 begins at P_1 and MR'_0 begins at the higher price P_3, the marginal revenue curves must cross at C. As a result of the domestic price control on oil, the OPEC cartel will set marginal cost equal to its new marginal revenue curve, MR'_0. This adjustment requires a reduction in cartel output from Q_0 to Q'_0 and allows an increase in the world oil price from P_0 to P'_0. Thus U.S. domestic wellhead taxes allow the OPEC cartel to exaggerate the very output reductions and price in-

Figure C
The Effect of an Old-Oil Wellhead Tax on Industry Supply

The impact of the tax is a leftward shift of domestic supply, which causes a rightward shift of demand for OPEC oil.

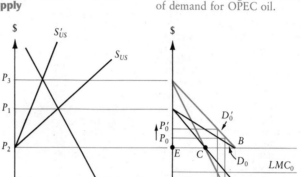

creases that constituted the incentive to organize the cartel in the beginning. The wellhead tax on U.S. producers actually solidifies the cartel and strengthens its economic and political power.

The wellhead tax does extract a portion of the profit from the inframarginal firms as they reduce their output in response to the tax. However, these profits are not eliminated; rather they are ex-

ported to the monopoly OPEC producers. One may not approve of the distribution of income inherent in free-market pricing of oil, but to attempt income redistribution through wellhead taxes in a market dominated by foreign governments can only redistribute income across national borders. Wellhead taxes replace domestic millionaires with foreign millionaires—and raise prices.

Market Definition in the "Cellophane Case"

APPLIED
MICRO
THEORY

10.3

In the famous "Cellophane case," the U.S. Justice Department accused Du Pont, former holder of the patent for Cellophane, of monopolizing the cellophane market.* The evidence of monopoly included Du Pont's share of the cellophane market (70%) and its large returns on investment for a long period of time. Du Pont argued in its defense

*United States v. E. I. Du Pont de Nemours and Company, 351 U.S. 377 (1956).

that Cellophane faced high cross-elasticity of demand due to intense competition from other flexible wrapping materials, including glassine and greaseproof papers, Pliofilm, and Kraft papers. Du Pont's market share fell to 21% when these products were included in the overall market for flexible wrap. Du Pont won the case, but the economic logic of the decision was flawed, as can be demonstrated by an analysis based on the leader-follower model.

Consider the accompanying figure, which shows the leader-follower apparatus. Du Pont is treated as the leader in the flexible

wrap market, and the producers of all other flexible wraps are the followers. Du Pont's demand curve for Cellophane, $D_{cello.}$, is drawn in the right-hand panel as the horizontal difference between the total demand for flexible wrap and the competitors' supply of noncellophane wrap (in the left-hand panel). Du Pont's marginal revenue curve, $MR_{cello.}$, is derived from $D_{cello.}$, as usual. If $MC_{cello.}$ is Du Pont's marginal cost, it maximizes profit by equating $MR_{cello.}$ and $MC_{cello.}$ at A, producing W_0^C units of cellophane, and charging price P_0. Other suppliers—the followers—produce W_0^{ND} units of

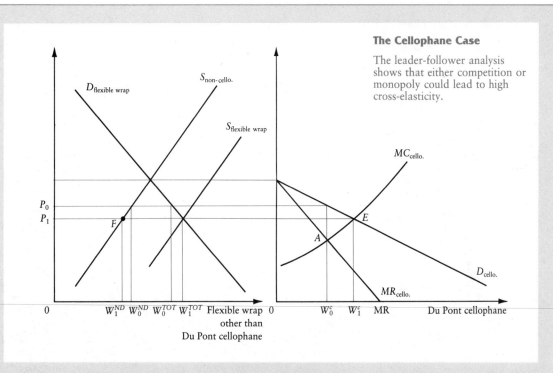

The Cellophane Case

The leader-follower analysis shows that either competition or monopoly could lead to high cross-elasticity.

wrap at price P_0. Total production of flexible wrap at P_0 is W_0^{TOT}.

To see that the decision should not hinge on cross-elasticity, consider the logical counterargument, keeping in mind that antitrust laws are intended to benefit consumers. Du Pont's large profit was the consequence of its many plants being able to produce Cellophane at less cost than other manufacturers could produce flexible wrap and its ability to achieve market power, despite the fringe competition of wrapping manufacturers. Du Pont's small share of the flexible wrap market was not the result of intense competition, as the company argued, but instead derived from the fact that it restrained output in order to raise price. Furthermore, cross-elasticity of demand does not elucidate this situation, because a firm with monopoly power will always price its goods so that demand is elastic. In a leader-follower industry, elasticity must arise from the substitutability of other products.

The question was whether Du Pont should be required to divest itself of plants so that they could compete. If all Du Pont plants were free to act independently, as competitors, the $MC_{cello.}$ curve would have been added horizontally with $S_{non-Du Pont}$ to produce the total flexible-wrap supply curve $S_{flexible wrap}$. In the absence of monopoly power, market forces would have set price at P_1, determined by the intersection of supply and demand at B. At the lower price P_1, the sale of Cellophane would have risen to W_1^C ($P_1 = MC_{cello.}$ at E), and the sale of flexible wrap would have fallen to W_1^{ND} ($P_1 = S_{noncello.}$ at F). Total flexible-wrap sales would have risen to W_1^{TOT}.

The leader-follower model shows that Du Pont's low market share for flexible wrap, rather than resulting from vigorous competition, could have resulted from the output restrictions made possible by its market position. It is just as reasonable to argue that Du Pont had such a small market share and high cross-elasticity precisely because it was exercising market power to the detriment of consumers.

Assessing Industrial Concentration

APPLIED MICRO THEORY

10.4

For assessing mergers, concentration is typically measured by the concentration ratios and by the Herfindahl index. The **n-firm concentration ratios** are merely the share of the market held by the top n firms. Usually four firms or eight firms are considered. The **Herfindahl index** is a bit more subtle in that it is the sum of the squared market shares of the firms ($\sum S_i^2$, where S_i is the share of the ith firm). The Herfindahl index can range from a high of 1 to a low of 1/(number of firms in an industry composed of firms of equal shares). The index reflects the share of the largest firms. For any given concentration ratio, the index will be higher the more unequal the shares are. Thus the Herfindahl index is sensitive to the price leadership problem.

To see how the Herfindahl index reflects price leadership, consider a horizontal merger between the largest firm and another large firm.

The Herfindahl index is large and will grow substantially when the merger is accounted for if the largest firm has a substantial share initially, but is not large and will not grow substantially if the largest firm does not have a substantial share initially. The following numerical example illustrates this principle. Suppose that industry A has fifteen firms, with market shares of one at 11%, four at 10%, nine at 5%, and one at 4%—for a total of 100%. The Herfindahl index is therefore $H = (0.11)^2 + 4(0.10)^2 + 9(0.05)^2 + (0.04)^2 = 0.0762$. If the leading firm merges with the fifth-largest firm, one of the 5% firms, $H = (0.16)^2 + 4(0.10)^2 + 8(0.05)^2 + (0.04)^2 = 0.0872$. Both the initial Herfindahl index and the post-merger Herfindahl index are quite low.

Now consider the more concentrated industry B, which also has fifteen firms. The five largest firms have market shares of 40%, 30%,

Barometric Price Leadership

The dominant-firm model of price leadership is a hybrid of monopoly and competitive analysis. Perhaps more in keeping with this chapter's emphasis on the interdependence of oligopoly firms is **barometric price leadership.** This form of price leadership occurs in industries where instability in pricing policies threatens to erode the firms' joint profits. The barometric firm is the first firm in the industry to make price changes; the rivals, anxious to avoid destructive price competition, follow the lead of the price leader. The price leader may or may not be a dominant force in the market. Regardless, the firm taking the role of price leader must be able to assess accurately the changing demand and cost conditions in the industry and to set its pricing policies accordingly. Barometric price leadership allows firms to respond in an orderly fashion to cost and demand shifts without interpreting competitors' price changes as hostile acts of economic aggression. If a barometric price leader emerges, all firms may benefit.

Unlike competitive, price-taking firms, oligopoly firms are large compared to industry output and must set price. Because of the

10%, 8%, and 5%, and the remaining ten each have a market share of 0.7%—for a total of 100%. In industry B, the Herfindahl index is $H = (0.40)^2 + (0.30)^2 + (0.10)^2 + (0.08)^2 + (0.05)^2 + 10(0.007)^2 = 0.26939$. The value of H clearly indicates that this is a much more concentrated industry than industry A. When the largest firm merges with the fifth-largest firm, which has a 5% share before the merger, $H = (0.45)^2 + (0.30)^2 + (0.10)^2 + (0.08)^2 + 10(0.007)^2 = 0.30939$. The Herfindahl index jumps sub-

stantially when an already-large firm merges. Thus the Herfindahl index is very sensitive to additional concentrations in an already concentrated market.

However, the Herfindahl index is unreliable when assessing mergers between firms that have substantially smaller shares than the leaders in a concentrated industry. Consider the recent merger attempt between Schlitz Brewing Company and Heileman Brewing Company, which was abandoned when the Justice Department sued to block it. In the beer industry in 1981, Anheuser Busch and Miller ac-

counted for 51% of the total sales in the country; Schlitz and Heileman controlled roughly 8% apiece. It was thought that a merger between Schlitz and Heileman "might substantially lessen competition in the beer industry in violation of section 7 of the Clayton Act. . . . it would significantly increase the industry's Herfindahl index by .0118 from .1644 to .1762."*

This reliance on the Herfindahl index is misplaced. The industry has lopsided shares, with Anheuser Busch and Miller way ahead of the pack. The economic theory of cartels indicates that the anticompetitive danger is from express or tacit collusion among these two leaders. Because they are so large, the Herfindahl index is naturally numerically large. Because Schlitz and Heileman are large companies, although quite small relative to the leaders, their merger must make a numerically significant difference. All of this misses the crucial point that the merger would actually loosen the tight oligopoly structure at the top end of the industry.

*Assistant Attorney General W. Baxter to Congressman Henry Reuss, 23 April 1982.

interdependence of firms, the pricing policies of one firm may set off retaliatory pricing by rivals. Hence firms must experiment with their pricing structures in order to arrive at the best prices, taking into account rival response. Experimentation is the key word in oligopoly pricing.

Oligopoly industries often exhibit the following characteristics: (1) long periods of stable prices that are uniform across firms; (2) prices that change quite a bit when they do change; (3) price experimentation that may begin with any one of a number of firms; (4) a lengthy period of stable prices that emerges after a period of price jockeying. The theory of barometric pricing explains this price behavior.

To understand barometric pricing, it is useful to recognize three facts. First, price changes are costly. Often a large sales staff must be coordinated. Furthermore, determining the "right" price is expensive. Second, price changes are risky. If rivals do not match price increases, significant erosion of market share could result. In fact, the price experiment is to see if rivals will match or, through countermoves, "suggest" a different price. Third, firms in the industry face similar cost pressures, particularly for labor, energy, materials, and finance. It is reasonable for one firm to assume that its cost pressures are hurting rivals also.

Figure 10.12 traces the prices of two rival oligopoly firms, for convenience named Solid Citizens, Inc. (the black line) and Rusted Hopes, Ltd. (the colored line). Suppose that both firms begin to feel cost pressure. With equal prices in the time block $\overline{0T_1}$, there is an initial reluctance to raise price because of the inherent costs and risks of doing so. Eventually, however, rising costs lead to price experimentation. At time T_1, Solid Citizens raises its price. Rusted Hopes now faces a choice: Meet Solid Citizens's price or undercut it. If Rusted Hopes calculates that it can earn a fair rate of return at Solid Citizens's new price, it may choose to match the price increase. At time T_2, Rusted Hopes matches Solid Citizens's price. Thus Solid Citizens acts as the barometric price leader, does the initial price experimenting, and invites other firms to follow if they choose.

Say that at time T_3 Solid Citizens raises its price again but that Rusted Hopes sees an opportunity to gain customers and make fuller use of its plant capacity by not matching the new price. At time T_4, Rusted Hopes decides to undercut Solid Citizens's price increase. Solid Citizens suffers customer erosion and revises prices downward at time T_5. As you can see, price experimentation may be risky. Rivals tend to return to a stable, uniform price.

In barometric pricing, price jockeying takes place as firms attempt to find, without collusion, a price that will accomplish two goals: (1) last a long time, so as to avoid the cost and risk of price changes and the loss of customer good will; and (2) earn a fair rate of return for investors, lest managers be replaced.

Figure 10.12
Barometric Pricing over Time

Price changes are expensive, risky experiments for an oligopoly. Therefore, they are large and infrequent. The black lines show time trends of price for Solid Citizens, Inc.; the colored lines show time trends for Rusted Hopes, Ltd. In time blocks $0T_1$, T_2, T_3, and beyond T_5, the prices are equal (although shown here slightly apart).

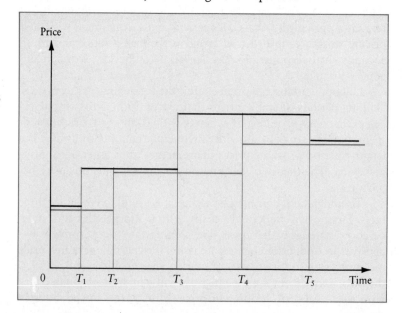

Focal-Point Pricing

APPLIED
MICRO
THEORY

10.5

Focal-point pricing is another form of communication that oligopolists use to avoid the legal risks of overt collusion while gaining some of the treasures such collusion would yield.* The theory of focal-point pricing follows from this general premise: Certain prices communicate information better than other prices. For example, pretend you and your best friend are each shopping

*The basic reference on focal-point pricing is Thomas C. Schelling, *The Strategy of Conflict* (Cambridge, Mass.: Harvard University Press, 1960).

for a new car. You arrive together at the car lot and are each attended by a different sales representative. You select identical cars and options packages. Your sales representative quotes you a price of $6999.99, and your friend gets a quote from the other sales representative of $7035.42. These price quotes are powerful in what they communicate. Your price, $6999.99, says in effect, "I have done everything I can for you to keep the price under $7000. I cannot do much better than this." The price of $7035.42 says, "You can at least bargain me down to $7000."

Oligopolists use the "language

of numbers" to talk to each other in this fashion. For whatever reason, certain price points are standard in the industry: Blue denim pants sell at $14.99, and electric drills sell for $19.99. Price leaders can jump to such focal points in the process of changing prices as a signal to the rest of the industry that they are shooting for a stable price at the new level. The use of focal points in price adjustments is an invitation to industry stability, an expression of "We had to lower prices this far for market-related reasons, but we will not go any farther. Please follow." Maybe love is not the only universal nonverbal language.

Basing-Point Pricing

APPLIED
MICRO
THEORY

10.6

Another problem in oligopolist price discipline arises when rival producers are geographically separated. Then the prices charged to customers contain two components: the mill price and the transportation costs. One common pricing system is FOB pricing (the initials stand for "free on board"), under which all prices quoted are mill prices. The customer pays the transportation costs to the point of delivery.

Holding cost and technology constant for all firms, each customer has an incentive to buy from the closest producer in order to keep transportation costs low. In other words, strict adherence to FOB pricing prevents firms from selling in their rivals' market areas. Indeed, the only way a firm can expand its market area is to engage in price-cutting initiatives. Under these conditions price wars can break out at any moment—the very thing that managers of oligopolist firms are paid to prevent.

Locational advantages among cartel members can be eliminated by calculating transport costs for all firms from a base point. Thus customers are charged "phantom freight" rates.

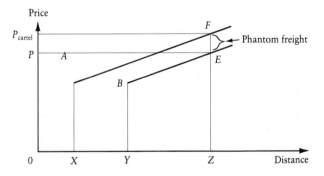

One way to eliminate such geographical price competition is the use of **basing-point pricing**. Under this system, all producers quote the same prices to a given customer, regardless of the distance between the producer and the consumer.

The figure illustrates the system. The horizontal axis measures geographical distance, and the vertical axis measures the price of output. Point A is the basing point; all firms, regardless of location, quote

Continued on page 318

delivered prices as if the goods were shipped from point A. Suppose the mill price is the same for goods produced at X and Y: XA = YB = mill price. The transportation costs rise with distance, along line AF from point A and along BE from point B. Under FOB pricing, the total price charged to a customer at point Z—including the mill price and transportation costs—would depend on the origin of the output. If goods are shipped from X to Z, the price would be ZF; but if they are shipped from Y, the price would be only ZE. Under basing-point pricing, the firm at Y charges the price $0P_{cartel}$ = ZF by including a transportation charge from X (the base point) instead of from the actual origin point, Y. The price gap EF

is called "phantom freight," because it is based on a travel distance from X even though goods actually traveled only from Y. Thus the system allows the customer at Z to buy from sellers at either X or Y at the same price. Oligopoly competition can thus proceed in more familiar and comfortable forms, with emphasis on such nonprice elements as product quality, service agreements and warranties, and promptness of delivery. Price wars are averted, and joint profit maximization can continue in an atmosphere of price stability.

The most celebrated case of phantom freight occurred in the U.S. steel industry when Pittsburgh was selected as the base point. Thus arose the "Pittsburgh-plus"

pricing system of the early twentieth century; all steel prices included a transportation charge from Pittsburgh regardless of actual shipping origin.

Not surprisingly, basing-point pricing is an illegal form of oligopolistic communication. It is a more obvious form of collusion than barometric price leadership and focal-point pricing and has been outlawed for over 30 years. The effects of such pricing seem quite clear: It creates collusion and tends to achieve the higher prices and joint profits for which it was devised.*

*For a comprehensive discussion of basing-point pricing, refer to F. M. Scherer, *Industrial Market Structure and Economic Performance* (Chicago: Rand McNally, 1970), pp. 262–272.

Entry in Oligopoly Industries

Long-run entry is an important feature of all models in which firm interdependence is important. We have studied entry and exit in competitive models. Here we study several implications of entry in oligopoly markets.

Lumpy Entry

The nature of a product usually determines the efficient size of firms necessary to produce it. In oligopoly, firms are large with respect to the aggregate industry output. A would-be entrant must enter with a large amount of new productive capacity. Therefore, that entrant must look not merely at the profits being earned by the firms in the industry but at the postentry profits as well. If a firm's entry would itself depress prices so that postentry profits were negative, entry would be deterred, even if preentry profits were quite high. Naturally, this effect is greatest in industries that are already quite concentrated. The problem does not arise in competition, because each prospective entrant is small and cannot influence industry price by its entry.

Figure 10.13 illustrates the problem of **lumpy entry**. Initially, suppose there are four firms of the same capacity serving the demand curve D, charging the price P_1, and jointly selling an aggregate output of Q_4. Each firm sells a fourth of the industry output, or $Q_4/4$. The LAC and LMC curves represent the typical costs of the firms. At price P_1, all four firms earn a positive economic profit equal to the shaded area.

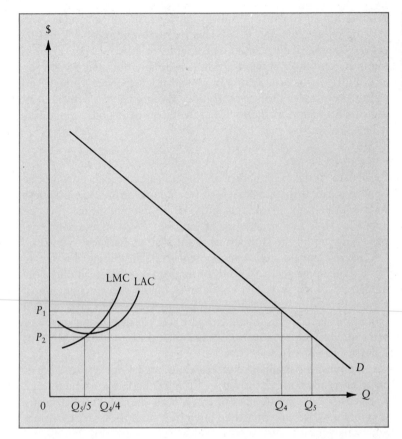

Figure 10.13
Lumpy Entry

Large-scale entry requirements can result in positive economic profits but no entry. Here four firms can produce profitably—but five cannot.

Now suppose that a new firm enters with similar capacity, which is a requirement for producing the good in question. If its entry drives the price down to P_2, the entering firm (and also the original firms) are pushed to a rate of output $Q_5/5$ and, given the cost structure, negative economic profit. Thus the new firm is deterred from entering despite the current positive economic profits.

Starting with four firms, a fifth would represent 20% of postentry capacity, assuming that firms are the same size. With ten firms, the eleventh would make up only 9.1% of postentry capacity and would be less likely to depress the price into the negative economic profit range. In competition, where the number of firms is very large, new entrants need not worry about the effect of their own entry on postentry profits. They are too small to have any impact. Thus lumpy entry is important in oligopoly but not in competition.

Regional Monopoly

Lumpy entry may limit the number of oligopoly firms that positive economic profits can attract to a given industry. Another limiting factor to entry arises from the geographical dispersal of firms. If the product has significant transportation costs, nearby customers will essentially face just one seller. This **regional monopoly** will not be eroded by entry if entry is at all profitable for other reasons, because the most profitable entry location is generally not next door to an existing rival. Hence, again, entry will not wipe out profits. And again, the greater the concentration, the greater the effect. If an industry can support many firms, the effect of regional monopoly is less.

Barriers to Entry

Regardless of the exact nature of oligopolistic interdependence, one thing is clear: If the industry is to retain joint profits suitably close to the monopoly ideal, the entry of competing firms must be avoided. Thus the probability of long-run profit maintenance depends in part on the strength of the industry's **barriers to entry.**

There is considerable confusion over the meaning of *barriers to entry.* One approach is to point to the high fixed costs in oligopoly industries as effective barriers because of the sheer magnitude of capital needed by prospective entrants. It is true that large capital requirements make it difficult to enter. Yet effective management of firms already in the industry does also. Are we to list efficiency as a barrier to entry?

We must distinguish between requirements of entry and barriers to entry. Because of the nature of most oligopoly products, high fixed costs are a requirement of entry, not a barrier. Fixed costs are no more a barrier to entry than any other costs necessary to attract and satisfy customers, such as those for advertising, labor, and entrepreneurial skills. After all, is a factory a barrier to building cars? Is a good voice a barrier to operatic success? If we equate requirement and barrier, the word *barrier* loses its operational meaning.

A barrier to entry exists when a firm is barred from an industry even though it can meet all cost and production requirements. For example, the barring of superior black athletes from professional baseball prior to the 1950s was a true barrier to entry. However, 60-year-old men are not considered to be barred from baseball, because they simply do not meet the industry requirements for entry. If a firm could enter the taxi business in New York City but for the artificial cost of a medallion (see Applied Micro Theory 8.5), it faces a barrier to entry.

In summary, the term *barriers to entry,* to be operational, must refer to artificial barriers that may be imposed by government, the mob, or the oligopoly firms themselves. Examples would include import barriers, licensing restrictions not based on legitimate economic considerations, government-supported cartel protection, discrimination, certain forms of industry predation, and threats.

Competition versus Concentration

APPLIED
MICRO
THEORY

10.7

There is considerable confusion in economic literature and antitrust law about the relationship between the number of firms in an industry and the degree of competition. It is often supposed that an industry becomes less competitive if the number of firms in the industry falls. This is not necessarily true, as the accompanying figure shows. The figure exhibits the cost curves of firms employing different technologies and the industry demand curve served by the firms. MC_1 and AC_1 permit five firms to exist at price P_1. MC_2 and AC_2 depict the costs of firms using a more advanced technology but having greater economies of scale. With MC_2 and AC_2, only three firms can serve the market demand, even though the price is lower. Paradoxically, consumers are better off with fewer firms because of greater output and lower price.

The competitive process can lead to greater industry concentration as firms adopt new technologies: Food retailing, banking, beer brewing, and food processing are industries where this has occurred. For example, the refrigerator car led to

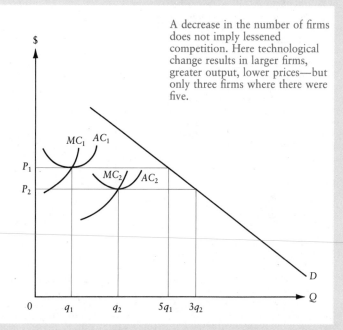

A decrease in the number of firms does not imply lessened competition. Here technological change results in larger firms, greater output, lower prices—but only three firms where there were five.

higher concentration in the meat-packing industry, and the interstate highway system induced greater competition in beer brewing but fewer firms. Modern electronics permits branch banking. And Mom and Pop retired when the automobile made it possible for

consumers to drive to supermarkets. These examples represent vigorous competition, lower prices, improved consumer welfare, and fewer firms. They show that competition and industry concentration are not necessarily antithetical.

Predatory Pricing

APPLIED
MICRO
THEORY

10.8

Predatory pricing is the pejorative term applied to the act of lowering a firm's product price for the purpose of driving a rival firm out of business and then raising the price. The objective is to reduce the price below a rival's average cost long enough to cause the rival to exit the market. Such a practice is often called a "price

war." As with any war, the promise of the rosy "postwar" period must be sufficiently better than the prewar period to pay for the war. Such an outcome cannot occur unless it also benefits consumers.

The following analysis examines two cases. Case 1 concerns firms that have identical costs. It shows that predatory pricing is suicidal for them. Case 2 concerns firms that exhibit considerably different costs. In this case, pricing to cap-

ture economies of scale may drive rivals out of business as an unhappy by-product (for the rival) of a gain in efficiency and lower prices for consumers.

Case 1: Identical Firms
The figure shows the identical cost curves of two firms. The curves of the "predatee" are on the left; those of the predator are on the right. Assume an initial breakeven

Continued on page 322

equilibrium—both firms produce amount q_0. In order to decrease price, the predator must increase output. Suppose this action results in a drop in price to P_1. The predatee loses money, of course, but minimizes those losses by setting MC = P_1 at point b and producing q_1. That is, the predatee responds to the predator by reducing output. This response creates problems for the predator, because preservation of the lower price requires greater aggregate output. Note that, in the left-hand panel, the predatee has cut output by an amount labeled x. The predator must increase output by substantially more than x to keep price below P_0. In so doing, the predator incurs much larger losses than the predatee. The predator must extend production further into the zone of diminishing returns, and hence higher MC, while the predatee cuts back both output and marginal cost. The predatee can cut total costs by the area $abcd$, whereas the predator, required to increase output to q_2 in order to sustain the lower price P_1, experiences an increase in total costs equal to the area $efgh$. Predatory pricing is obviously suicidal among firms with identical costs.

Case 2: Nonidentical Firms
This case is simply stated. One

Suicidal Predatory Pricing

It is suicidal to attempt to drive an identical rival out of business via price cuts. The predator must expand output by more than the predatee contracts output and set marginal cost well above price.

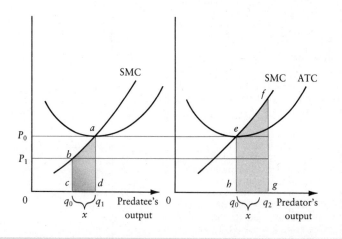

firm adopts a new scale of plant entailing economies of scale that can only be captured if the firm lowers the price to attract customers to buy an increased output. Firms that adopt the new technology and can fit under the demand curve (see Applied Micro Theory 10.7) will survive. Rivals who do not will exit as a by-product of the competition.

Final note: The analysis of predatory pricing presupposes oligopoly: In a competitive market, no firm can drive out a rival by expanding output to reduce price.*

*For a further discussion of predatory pricing, see Phillip Areeda and Donald Turner, "Predatory Pricing and Related Practices under Section II of the Sherman Act," *Harvard Law Review* 88 (1975): 697.

Monopolistic Competition

Somewhere between competition (many sellers with no influence over price) and monopoly (one seller with complete influence over price) lies the uncertain world of imperfect competition. There is no single theory of imperfect competition. Instead, there are numerous approaches to the study of this middle ground. So far in this chapter, we have encountered various models of oligopoly and duopoly, with the emphasis on the interdependence of rivals' market decisions. Now we will study **monopolistic competition**, which stresses the role of product differentiation in otherwise competitive markets.

Consider the soap industry. We know from watching television commercials that the firms in this industry are very aggressive in differentiating their products and in communicating these differences to consumers via elaborate advertising ("Buy our soap with the green dots instead of the soap with the lower-quality blue dots"). Paper products, tobacco, liquor, gasoline, restaurants, automobile sales and service, retail grocery and drug stores, insurance, and toothpaste are representative of the many industries that differentiate products and advertise. Neither the competitive nor the monopoly model explains this behavior. Competitors sell closely substitutable products and hence have no reason to advertise. And the monopolist's product specification and advertising are not rivalrous. Thus the sole use of competitive and monopoly models leaves us with unexplained behavior in important industries. The theory of monopolistic competition is an aid in studying firms' product differentiation and advertising behavior.

Let's begin our study of monopolistic competition with a list of the assumptions of the most prominent model:[12]

> *Product differentiation:* Each producer sells a product that is a close but not perfect substitute for its rivals' product. **Product differentiation** can take many forms: changes in the physical attributes of the good, differences in packaging, changes in location, differences in warranties and service, or merely a fancied difference in the minds of consumers.

> *Product group:* There is assumed to exist an identifiable cluster of firms whose products are quite similar. The collection of such firms constitutes a **product group.** This formulation is an attempt to define an industry among firms whose products are not identical.

> *Competition in the group:* Competition within the group is atomistic; there are many firms, and entry and exit are virtually free—as free as in perfect competition.

> *Uniformity:* All firms in the group are assumed to exhibit identical cost curves and to face identical demand curves for their products.

> *Symmetry:* One firm's adjustment in any of its decision variables (price, product variation, advertising) is distributed evenly over the large number of rivals in the group so that the effects of one firm's decisions on any rival firm are negligible.

These assumptions have met with sharp criticism from the theory's detractors, most notably Professor George Stigler.[13] Stigler is especially critical of the assumption that firms producing differ-

---

12. These assumptions were first outlined by Edward H. Chamberlin, *The Theory of Monopolistic Competition* (Cambridge, Mass.: Harvard University Press, 1933). Joan Robinson published a related work in the same year. See Joan Robinson, *The Economics of Imperfect Competition* (London: Macmillan, 1933).

13. George J. Stigler, *Five Lectures on Economic Problems* (London: Longmans, Green, 1949), chap. 2.

entiated products are identical and of the concept of the product group. It seems that the concept of identical firms is as unnecessary here as it is in the competitive model. The following analysis drops the myth of the identical firm.

But what about the product group? The most straightforward way to collect firms into groups is by the degree of substitutability of their products. Consider the cross-elasticity of demand, θ_{XY}, of products X and Y:

$$\theta_{XY} = \frac{\%\Delta \text{ in good } X}{\%\Delta \text{ in price of good } Y} = \frac{\Delta X}{\Delta P_Y} \cdot \frac{P_Y}{X} \qquad (10.7)$$

The cross-elasticity of demand measures the percentage change in the sales of one good in response to a percentage change in the price of another good. If θ equals zero, the goods are not substitutes, because a change in relative prices does not induce any substitutions. At the other extreme, two goods are perfect substitutes if θ is infinite, because complete substitutions between the goods can occur without any change in relative prices. Thus the larger the cross-elasticity of demand θ, the greater the substitutability of products. The product group is an imprecise way of aggregating firms whose products are reasonably good substitutes.

Stigler rejects the concept of the product group by observing,

> It is perfectly plausible . . . that the group contain only one firm, or, on the contrary, that it include all of the firms in the economy. This latter possibility can readily follow from the asymmetry of substitution relationships among firms: taking any one product as our point of departure, each substitute has in turn its substitutes, so that the adjacent cross-elasticities may not diminish, and even increase, as we move further away from the "base" firm in some technological or geographical sense.[14]

But the product group should not be dismissed so cavalierly. Firms can be grouped together by a reasonable, commonsense evaluation of the substitutability of their products. Even though the grouping cannot be precise, products do fall into broad groups. Detergent and chopsticks are manifestly not in the same group. Detergent and shampoo are also not in the same product group, despite their similarities as cleaning agents, as witnessed by the small number of people who wash their clothes with shampoo. The large number of differentiated detergent and shampoo products separate quite naturally into two distinct product groups. (This is true at current relative prices, but consumers might well wash clothes in shampoo if detergent became too expensive relative to shampoo.) Color television sets and electric typewriters are not

14. Stigler, *Five Lectures*, p. 15.

close substitutes. Although both are electronic devices, you cannot watch the World Series on your typewriter. Similarly, automobiles and horses are no longer in the same product group in the United States; for most uses they are very imperfect substitutes. Yet some ranchers may still consider them substitute modes of transportation in checking fences and riding herd on animals. In such cases, the automobile and horse would be in the same product group, and relative prices would determine whether the cowboy rides the range in a Mustang or on a mustang.

With these introductory remarks in hand, we can begin an analysis of monopolistic competition. The three decision variables available to a profit-maximizing monopolistic competitor that are not open to a competitive firm are changes in price, changes in product, and changes in advertising and sales effort. Because the monopolistically competitive firm has a small degree of monopoly power due to the differentiation of its product, it is a price setter. Reductions in price expand sales by movements along the firm's demand curve. Product differentiation and advertising are ways of increasing the size of the firm's market by shifting the demand curve.

Short-Run Price and Output Equilibrium

Suppose we are able to identify a product group by reference to the substitutability of the firms' products. We assume that these firms differ in the demand curves and cost curves they face. Thus we abandon the fiction of identical firms and focus our analysis on the marginal firm in the group, just as we did in the analysis of pure competition in Chapter 8.

The description of price and output equilibrium employs two demand curves, both of which are displayed in Figure 10.14. The curve labeled d_f is the demand curve the firm faces when its own price reductions occur *ceteris paribus*, that is, with the prices of all substitute products held constant. Because the firm knows it is a small component of a large product group, it can hope its own price adjustments will not be met by similar price changes by rivals. The demand curve d_f is relatively elastic because products in the group are reasonably close substitutes.

The less elastic curve, labeled D_g in Figure 10.14, measures the changes in quantity demanded when the firm's price reduction is accompanied by price cuts of other firms in the group. Curve D_g is a **mutatis mutandis** demand curve, the Latin phrase meaning "the necessary changes having been made." Thus points on D_g measure the quantities the firm can sell when its price reductions occur simultaneously with similar (but not necessarily identical) price cuts by other (but not necessarily all) firms in the group. The subscript g is used as a reminder that D_g is the firm's share of total group demand when other firms in the group reduce their prices at the

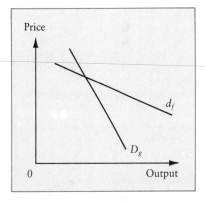

Figure 10.14
The Demand Curves of the Monopolistic Competitor

The *ceteris paribus* demand curve is d_f; D_g is the *mutatis mutandis* demand curve.

same time. The entrepreneur knows the other firms will change their prices if their demand and cost curves call for it. But the firm cannot know the position of its rivals' demand and cost curves and thus cannot know how the position of the D_g curve will change in response to changes in the economy, except vaguely. The ultimate equilibrium must occur at a point on D_g because the firm's sales will depend in part on its rivals' pricing policies. But because D_g is not known to the firm, equilibrium must be found by trial and error.

Now let's trace the move to an equilibrium price and quantity in Figure 10.15. While examining the pricing decision of the firm, we will temporarily ignore the entrepreneur's product and advertising decisions. Advertising is easily omitted by assuming that consumer wants are given and that consumers have perfect knowledge about their substitution possibilities. Advertising is pointless in such a world; it raises costs without increasing firm revenues or consumer benefits. (These assumptions will be relaxed in later sections.)

Let point A in Figure 10.15 be our arbitrary starting point, where price is P_3 and quantity sold is Q_1. Beginning at P_3, the firm attempts to find its profit-maximizing price by trial and error. The

Figure 10.15
Price and Output Adjustment in Monopolistic Competition

The firm must experiment with prices to find D_g.

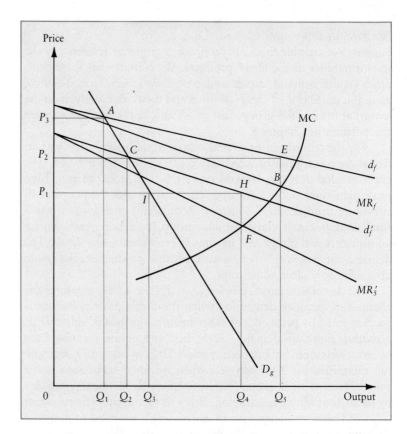

firm may, for example, attempt to maximize profit by finding the optimum position on the demand curve d_f, which passes through A. The curve labeled MR_f is the marginal revenue curve associated with the demand curve d_f. Using this strategy, the firm selects the price and output combination P_2 and Q_5, because $MR_f = MC$ at B. But if other firms face similar incentives because of their demand and cost configurations, they will be reducing their prices too. Thus the firm expects to sell Q_5 units at price P_2 (point E on d_f) but instead sells only Q_2 (point C on D_g). In this way the firm moves from A to C on the demand curve D_g. Point C on the demand curve D_g is only known to the firm after the fact.

But point C does not maximize profits, because price P_2 doesn't produce the anticipated sales of Q_5 units. Additional price changes are required. Beginning now at C (P_2 and Q_2), the firm perceives another curve, d_f, that measures the change in sales resulting from a price change away from P_2, assuming that all rivals' prices are fixed. In other words, there is a d_f curve intersecting each point of the D_g curve. When price falls along D_g, the perceived curve d_f slides down the D_g curve. Beginning at C, the *ceteris paribus* demand curve d_f' is available to the firm for repetitions of the process. The relevant marginal revenue curve, MR_f', corresponds to the demand curve d_f'. The firm now equates MR_f' and MC at F and sells Q_4 units at price P_1. As before, rivals' price reductions limit the firm's sales to Q_3 at price P_1. Point I on demand curve D_g is now revealed to the firm. The firm is led once again to continue its search for the best price along these same lines, always faced with a lack of information about rival responses.

Equilibrium is the final result of this search for a profit-maximizing price. Note in Figure 10.16 that the firm has an incentive to change its price and output whenever the D_g and d_f curves intersect at a different rate of output from which MR_f equals MC. Each time the firm lowers price, the d_f curve slides down the D_g curve. Ultimately, the equilibrium depicted in Figure 10.16 is reached where the d_f curve intersects D_g at point A. Price and output are P_0 and Q_0. Because $MR_f = MC$ at Q_0, the firm finally achieves a price and output combination that maximizes profits. The firm has no further incentive to change its price and output. Thus, when the intersections at points A and B in Figure 10.16 occur at the same output level, firm short-run equilibrium is attained.

The short-run equilibrium described in Figure 10.16 does not contain an average cost curve: Economic profits are not indicated. Clearly, economic profits can be positive, zero, or negative in the short run for monopolistically competitive firms. If profits are negative in the short run, the shutdown analysis of Chapter 7 applies: Revenue must cover variable costs in order to justify producing with short-run losses.

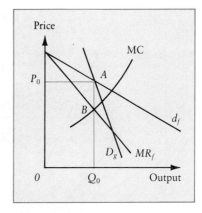

Figure 10.16
Short-Run Price and Output Equilibrium of the Monopolistic Competitor

D_g and d_f intersect at the same output as the MC and MR_f intersection.

Long-Run Price and Output Equilibrium

The long run allows for two kinds of adjustments not permitted in the short run: changes in the firm's scale of plant and entry or exit of firms. Thus long-run equilibrium requires two conditions in addition to those necessary for short-run equilibrium: Each firm must be operating a scale of plant at a rate of output for which the short-run cost curve ATC is tangent to the Viner-Wong envelope curve LAC, and entry or exit must have driven economic profit to zero for the marginal firms, thereby eliminating any further entry or exit. Figure 10.17 illustrates the adjustments to long-run equilibrium. The diagram appears imposing, but with sufficient care we can interpret it easily.

Figure 10.17 depicts the revenue and cost curves of a marginal firm. Specifically, it contains the long-run Viner-Wong envelope curve (LAC), its corresponding long-run marginal cost curve (LMC), two short-run average and marginal cost curves, two D_g demand curves, two d_f curves, and two MR_f curves. Suppose the firm establishes an initial short-run equilibrium at point A, selling

Figure 10.17
Long-Run Price and Output Equilibrium in Monopolistic Competition

Equilibrium occurs at point E: (1) $MR_f = LMC = MC'$ and $D_g' = d_f'$ at Q_m; (2) the firm selects ATC', the least-cost scale of plant; (3) ATC, LAC, and d_f' are tangent, implying zero economic profit for the marginal firm.

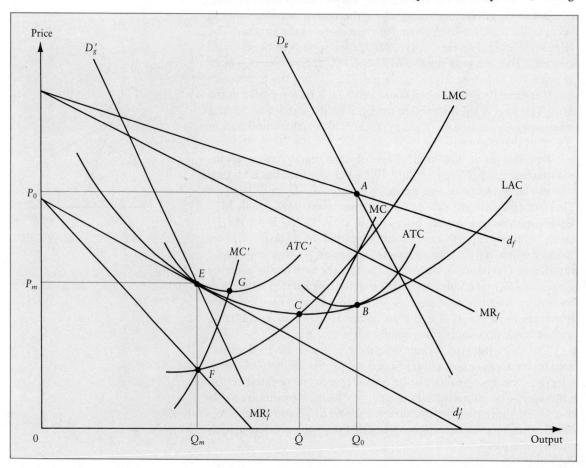

Q_0 units of output at price P_0. The firm is producing Q_0 units with the scale of plant ATC, which is the least-cost scale of plant for the rate of output Q_0. All aspects of long-run equilibrium are satisfied except one: At output Q_0 the firm earns positive economic profits. Positive profits attract new entrants into the product group. And because the demand curve D_g reflects the firm's share of the group market, the entry of new firms shifts D_g to the left by reducing the firm's share of sales. When D_g shifts, the equilibrium at A is disturbed, and forces are set in motion that lead to a genuine long-run equilibrium where entry has reduced the marginal firms' profits to zero and where entry has therefore stopped.

In Figure 10.17 the adjustment to full long-run equilibrium is the movement from A to E. It involves (1) a shifting D_g curve in response to entry, (2) shifting d_f curves as the firm is required to define these demand curves with reference to a shifting D_g curve, and (3) adjustments in the firm's scale of plant. Positive profits continue to attract new firms into the group until the highest-cost firms that can enter profitably have done so and marginal firms earn zero profits. Entry shifts D_g to the left; as the size of the firm's market is reduced, the firm reduces the scale of its plant. Thus leftward shifts in D_g cause the firm to move from point B on the envelope curve LAC toward point E by adopting smaller capital stocks.

The establishment of an equilibrium price and quantity proceeds as outlined in the previous section, except that the long-run cost curves apply. The firm continues to adjust its price, output, and scale of plant until the D_g and d_f demand curves once again intersect at the same output level at which $MR_f = MC = LMC$. These intersections occur at output Q_m at points E and F. For E to be a true long-run equilibrium, D_g must have stopped shifting, which occurs only when economic profits are zero for the marginal firms and entry ceases. Profits are zero at E for the marginal firm in Figure 10.17 because both the LAC and ATC' curves are tangent to the demand curve d_f' at output Q_m. All conditions for long-run equilibrium are attained at point E: (1) $MR_f' = LMC = MC'$ and $D_g' = d_f'$ at the same output Q_m; (2) the firm selects the least-cost scale of plant for output Q_m, ATC'; and (3) economic profits are zero for the marginal firm.

Product Differentiation

We have seen the equilibrium that results when each monopolistically competitive firm sets its own price. In addition to price competition, the firm can attempt to enlarge its market by selling a product that differs from the products of competitors within the group. The economic incentive to differentiate products arises from the fact that consumers' preferences vary so widely. One firm may cater to a price-conscious clientele by offering a "no-frills" product that perhaps sacrifices some quality in order to keep prices low. Another firm serves the quality-conscious customer whose main interest is a high-quality product even if it costs a bit more. Firms are constantly on the lookout for ways to "position" their products in order to gain a larger share of the market and increase profits.

In discussing price and output equilibrium, previous sections assumed that the firm's decisions about product characteristics were already made. However, no useful graphic method exists for reversing this analysis by holding price and quantity constant and adjusting product characteristics, because product quality is multidimensional. But it is clear that product differentiation, as well as entry and exit, shift all the demand and cost curves in Figure 10.17. Curve D_g shifts if the variation in product characteristics is successful in capturing a larger share of market sales. And the cost curves shift when the firm changes its product. Nevertheless, the final equilibrium conditions are the same as before. The firm's incentive is to experiment with various products and to produce the most profitable one. The firm has an incentive to advertise in order to establish and maintain its product in the consumers' minds relative to competing products. Of the many dimensions of product differentiation, advertising is the easiest to study using graphic analysis.

Monopoly Advertising

In studying the firm's price and product differentiation decisions, we ignored the advertising decision temporarily. If consumer wants are given and consumers have perfect knowledge about their substitution possibilities, advertising is superfluous. Now let's relax these assumptions and bring advertising directly into the model. Advertising expenses are the expenditures that the firm makes solely to alter the position of the demand curve.

In analyzing the price-setting firm's advertising decisions, it is helpful to treat the monopoly case first. This allows us to marshal our attention for the advertising decision per se, without the added complexity of rivalrous advertising. (The next section shows how the rivalrous advertising of monopolistic competition differs from the monopoly case.) The quantity of advertising undertaken by the monopolist depends, as expected, on the marginal benefits and marginal costs of advertising. Furthermore, an unregulated monopolist produces inefficient levels of output and (truthful) advertising.[15]

In Figure 10.18, the initial demand and marginal revenue curves of the monopolist are D_1 and MR_1. Assume initially that the monopolist does not advertise. Monopoly profits are maximized by equating MR_1 and LMC_P at point B, selling Q_1 units of output at price P_1. (The LMC_P curve is drawn as a horizontal line merely as a

15. For a treatment of a similar problem in monopoly analysis, see A. M. Spence, "Monopoly, Quality and Regulation," *Bell Journal of Economics and Management Science* 6 (1975): 417–429.

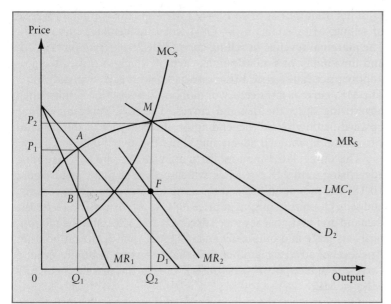

Figure 10.18
Monopoly Advertising Equilibrium

$MR_S = MC_S$ and $MR_2 = LMC_P$ at point M.

matter of convenience. The subscript P is attached to the LMC_P curve as a reminder that the curve measures production costs. Advertising costs are about to be introduced into the monopoly model, and these cost components should be separated.)

Advertising affects both costs and revenues. The curve labeled MC_S in Figure 10.18, the **marginal cost of selling curve,** measures the extra sales expenses needed to find customers for the incremental units of output. The MC_S curve slopes upward as a reflection of the diminishing productivity of hiring, training, and supervising a sales force. It is increasingly more costly to expand the market via advertising.

If the advertising is effective, the firm's demand curve will shift to the right. Thus within the neighborhood of the initial equilibrium at point A, a small increase in advertising allows an extra unit of output to be sold at the current price P_1. In other words, the marginal revenue of selling, MR_S, equals price. Hence the monopolist can gain revenue in two ways in the neighborhood of output Q_1: lower price on the marginal and all inframarginal units, which produces a marginal revenue of Q_1B, or shift the demand curve via advertising and charge the price P_1 for the marginal unit, in turn producing a marginal revenue of $P_1 = Q_1A$. Thus output expansion entails a choice: Either lower price on marginal and inframarginal units or sell at a given price by expanding the demand curve through advertising.

In the neighborhood of output Q_1, $MR_S = P_1 = Q_1A$. But as advertising causes the demand curve to drift rightward, Q_1 no longer maximizes profit. For example, suppose advertising shifts the demand and marginal revenue curves to D_2 and MR_2 in Figure 10.18. The monopolist equates MR_2 and LMC_P at point F and sells

Q_2 units of output at price $P_2 = Q_2M$. Thus the marginal revenue of selling, MR_S, equals $P_2 = Q_2M$ when the demand curve is D_2. The **marginal revenue of selling curve,** MR_S, connects points A, M, and the infinity of similar points, each of which measures the monopoly price (and hence MR_S) associated with each demand curve. The MR_S curve is a trajectory of monopoly prices that results when advertising shifts the demand curves. The MR_S curve may slope upward or downward, depending on the elasticity of the demand curves and how much advertising shifts the demand curve.

The unregulated monopolist maximizes profits by expanding advertising until $MR_S = MC_S$, which occurs at point M in Figure 10.18. The monopolist advertises until demand curve D_2 is attained and sells Q_2 units of output at price $P_2 = Q_2M$. Advertising fixes the demand and marginal revenue curves D_2 and MR_2, and the monopolist sets price and output by equating MR_2 and LMC_P at point F. Any level of advertising other than that necessary to attain demand curve D_2 reduces profits, because it breaks the marginal equality $MR_S = MC_S$.

On the margin, the monopolist spends more on advertising than on production; that is, $MC_S > LMC_P$ in equilibrium. This is necessary because $P > MR$ for the monopolist. Equilibrium occurs when $MR_S = MC_S$ and $MR = LMC_P$ at the same level of output. Because $P = MR_S > MR$, equilibrium can only be achieved when $MC_S > LMC_P$.

Advertising in Monopolistic Competition

The advertising of the monopolistic competitor differs from monopoly advertising due to the presence of rival firms in monopolistic competition. When the firm's rivals increase their advertising, the MR_S and MC_S curves shift. Rivalrous advertising makes it more costly to attract each customer. Hence the MC_S shifts upward due to the advertising of rivals. Rival advertising reduces the firm's market share, *ceteris paribus,* thereby shifting the firm's D_g curve down for each level of advertising undertaken by the firm in question. By construction, the MR_S curve will shift downward when rivals increase their advertising; each unit sold through advertising must be sold at a lower price when rival advertising drops the firm's demand curve D_g. Figure 10.19 shows the effects of expanded advertising of rivals: the MR_S curve shifts down to MR_S'; the MC_S curve shifts up to MC_S'; and the profit-maximizing output and advertising falls from A to A'. Entry and exit also shift these curves.

We are now ready to diagram the final long-run equilibrium of the marginal firm in monopolistic competition with respect to its pricing and advertising decisions. The dynamics involved in the achievement of equilibrium are complex because of the effect of rivals' behavior on the firm's revenue and cost curves. Nevertheless,

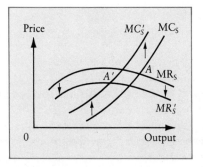

Figure 10.19
The Effect of Rival Advertising on the Firm's MR_S and MC_S Curves

As a rival increases advertising, MR_S falls to MR_S' and MC_S rises to MC_S'.

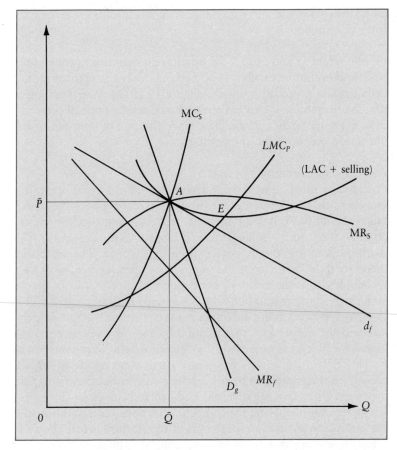

Figure 10.20
Price, Output, and Advertising Long-Run Equilibrium for the Marginal Firm in Monopolistic Competition

$D_g = d_f$ and MR $= LMC_P$ at output $\overline{Q}$. $MR_S = MC_S$ at point $\overline{Q}$. (LAC + selling) is tangent to d_f at $\overline{Q}$.

the comparative static long-run equilibrium can be shown easily.

Figure 10.20 displays the final equilibrium of the marginal firm. At point *A* all dimensions of long-run equilibrium are satisfied. These conditions are the following:

1. $D_g = d_f$ and $MR_f = LMC_P$ at output $\overline{Q}$. This condition assures that $\bar{P}$ and $\overline{Q}$ are equilibrium values.

2. $MR_S = MC_S$. The effects of rivalrous advertising and entry and exit have equated the MR_S and MC_S curves at the equilibrium output $\overline{Q}$. The firm has achieved the profit-maximizing rate of advertising; any more or less advertising would shift the demand curve away from its optimum position and reduce profits.

3. Economic profits are zero for the marginal firm. The (LAC + selling) curve is merely the familiar LAC curve to which the per-unit cost of advertising and selling the equilibrium $\overline{Q}$ units of output had been added. (LAC + selling) is the relevant long-run average cost curve when firms advertise. At point *A*, (LAC + selling) is tangent

to the firm's demand curve d_f. Hence economic profits are zero, and entry or exit stops.

At output $\overline{Q}$ and price $\overline{P}$ the firm has no incentive to change its price and output or to alter its advertising. Only the optimal product variation is not diagramed in Figure 10.20. Because it assumes that the demand and cost curves are based on the optimal product design, Figure 10.20 is a complete representation of long-run equilibrium in monopolistic competition.

The Excess-Capacity Theorem

Perhaps the most controversial aspect of long-run equilibrium in monopolistic competition is the oft-cited **excess-capacity theorem**. Figure 10.20 illustrates the theorem. In zero profit equilibrium at point A, the (LAC + selling) curve is tangent to the demand curve d_f. By assumption, the d_f curve is negatively sloped. The tangency therefore must occur along the negatively sloped segment of (LAC + selling). Thus the firm will not operate its chosen scale of plant at the lowest unit cost or build the "optimum" scale of plant. Excess capacity is defined as the difference between the firm's actual output rate and the output rate that minimizes long-run average cost. In Figure 10.20, excess capacity is the difference between points A and E. This excess capacity is frequently cited as an aspect of waste arising from competition by firms selling similar but differentiated products. Firms face negatively sloped demand curves for their differentiated products, and the competition among firms in the product group forces firms to a zero profit equilibrium before the full range of increasing returns to scale can be exploited. Thus it is argued that monopolistic competition results in higher prices for consumers because the firms cannot produce at minimum average cost. Also, production is spread over too many firms, each forced to produce with idle capacity.

Some writers have argued that the apparent existence of excess capacity is the result of analyzing firm price and output decision-making with a short-run instead of a long-run marginal revenue curve.[16] In this view, monopolistic competitors set prices below the price that would maximize short-run profits as a deterrent to entry. Because the long-run demand and marginal revenue curves are more elastic than their short-run counterparts, the long-run price results in less, and perhaps much less, excess capacity than the model seems to suggest.

The excess-capacity theorem is weak on additional theoretical grounds. Excess capacity is defined in relation to the competitive ideal of minimum average cost. However, the analysis of pure competition in Chapter 8 showed that only the marginal firms adopt the

16. R. F. Harrod, *Economic Essays* (New York: Harcourt Brace Jovanovich, 1952).

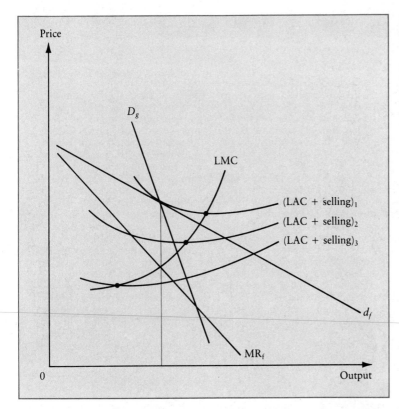

Figure 10.21
Equilibrium for the Nonidentical Firm

$(LAC + selling)_1$ yields zero profit and excess capacity. $(LAC + selling)_2$ yields nonzero profit and excess capacity. $(LAC + selling)_3$ yields nonzero profit and insufficient capacity.

optimal scale of plant. Inframarginal firms operate with "insufficient" capacity, the converse of "excess" capacity. Inframarginal firms in competitive markets operate on the positively sloped segment of their long-run average cost curves and hence do not themselves satisfy the minimum average cost optimum so often ascribed to competition. Unless competitive firms are identical, the benchmark of optimum capacity is not achieved by all firms.

We have assumed throughout this chapter that firms within a product group in monopolistic competition are nonidentical. The three (LAC + selling) curves in Figure 10.21 represent the costs of three firms that face the same demand curve. Long-run equilibrium is attained when entry and exit cease, leaving the highest-cost marginal firms with zero profits. In Figure 10.21, firm 1 is a marginal firm earning zero profits and operating with excess capacity. Firm 2 earns positive profits and also exhibits excess capacity. Firm 3 earns positive economic profits and has "insufficient" capacity.

Thus the excess-capacity theorem is weak. When firms are not identical, optimum capacity is not guaranteed in competition, and excess capacity is not a necessary result in monopolistic competition. Also, some excess capacity may be needed to meet the fluctuating demand for many services, including taxis, airplanes, electricity, elevators, and restrooms.

Trading Stamps, Bingo, and Horse Races

APPLIED MICRO THEORY

10.9

Retail food stores are relatively few in number in a given neighborhood. Generally, the consumers' choices are further limited because the available stores belong to a small number of chains. Food stores provide a service that is physically quite substitutable for the services of rivals. So how can food stores differentiate their products when the food is virtually the same in all stores? The answer, of course, is promotions.

Here is a random sample of common promotions:

1. *Trading and redemption stamps* (such as S & H Green Stamps).
2. *Bingo:* For every $100 of food purchased, you receive a bingo chip. Fill a row, column, or diagonal and you win a cash prize or gift. Many people love these games.
3. *Horse races:* For every $100 of food purchased, you get a ticket linked to a horse that will be in a film of a long-forgotten race televised the following week. If the horse wins, places, or shows, you get a prize. This game is especially exciting, because it is usually rigged so that the horse most people are backing leads the race until the last 20 yards and then falls flat on its nose.

To analyze the effectiveness of promotions like these, start by assuming that no store has a promotional gimmick and that all stores earn a normal rate of return. Then store 1 adopts a gimmick, say redemption stamps. If this ploy is successful, the demand for store 1's product will rise. Store 1 may raise prices, but it can profit without price increases merely by the greater volume of customers its gimmick has attracted away from rivals. Remember: The food is the same, but the gimmick is not!

One by one, other food stores retaliate by adopting gimmicks of their own. Of course, product differentiation calls for gimmick differentiation. The percentage of stores employing gimmicks rises over time. But the profits are squeezed out, because the promotions tend to cancel one another out. Eventually, prices must rise throughout the industry to pay the promotion costs.

What is the best way to differentiate when many stores have promotions? Cancel the promotion and cut prices! Advertise lower prices at exactly the same time the bingo games or races are having their grand finale. The profit incentive underlying the institution and eventual cessation of promotions indicates that the percentage of stores using gimmicks will tend to rise and fall cyclically. From a manager's viewpoint, success depends on knowing when to start and, just as important, when to stop the gimmick.

Summary

Oligopoly is an industrial structure in which there are few enough firms that each must worry about competitors' reactions. In competitive industries, where firms are tied together by parametric pricing, competitors' reactions are not at issue. In monopoly and cartel structures, single or joint decisionmaking makes rival reactions unimportant.

In the various models presented in this chapter, reaction is analyzed in regard to price or quantity. If oligopolists' tacit collusion succeeds in establishing joint profit maximization, oligopoly creates much of the same waste we saw in monopoly. Thus oligopoly is a near relative to monopoly in terms of its potential for misallocating resources. The degree to which price is too high and output too low is, as always, an empirical question. We could expect to find a greater gap between price and marginal cost among oligopolistic industries that have high entry costs and that exhibit effective communication systems—whether overt or tacit.

Oligopoly and cartel behavior is intriguing and puzzling. Comparative statics—so useful a method in the analysis of competitive and pure monopoly—is somewhat less appealing here because of the indeterminacy of certain results. A perfectly determinate and general theory of oligopoly is out of the question, because each industry presents its own problems and characteristics. This chapter has presented several approaches to the analysis of oligopoly behavior. Economists choose the most promising of these tools for the problem at hand. But many problems simply cannot be handled in the abstract. Industry-by-industry case studies are often the most fruitful avenues for oligopoly research.

Monopolistic competition has engendered a body of theory for studying the behavior of firms that compete ·on several levels: price, product differentiation, and advertising. With product differentiation in an industry, the firm faces a negatively sloped demand curve for its product and has some market power over its price. Advertising is a method of communicating product differences to potential customers.

The excess-capacity theorem is invalid once the fiction of identical firms is removed. The marginal firm in monopolistic competition operates with excess capacity, but the inframarginal firms need not do so. Overconcentration on the paradigm case of identical firms led economists to pursue a line of analysis irrelevant in the evaluation of monopolistic competition.

The theory of monopolistic competition is not nearly so well developed as the competitive and monopoly models. Most economists would agree that it is one of the weakest microeconomic models. Still, firms' advertising and product positioning cannot be understood by sole reference to competitive or monopoly models. Therefore, microeconomists may have much to learn from a continuing development of the theory of monopolistic competition.

Key Terms

barometric price leadership 314
barriers to entry 320
basing-point pricing 317
conjectural variation in output 289
conjectural variation in price 289
Cournot equilibrium 294
dominant-firm price leadership 308
duopoly 288
excess-capacity theorem 334
focal-point pricing 317
Herfindahl index 314
imperfect competition 287
isoprofit curves 292
kinked demand curve 302
lumpy entry 318
marginal cost of selling curve 331
marginal revenue of selling curve 332
market share maintenance rule 298
monopolistic competition 322
mutatis mutandis 325
n-firm concentration ratios 314
oligopoly 288
predatory pricing 321
product differentiation 323
product group 323
reaction function 291
regional monopoly 320
Stackelberg disequilibrium 297

Problems

1. Price wars often occur in industries whose firms exhibit high capital costs as a component of total costs. Why should these cost factors make a difference?

2. Suppose that a cartel is being stabilized by a market share maintenance rule, as described in this chapter. Suppose also that one of the parties experiences a technological change resulting in lower costs. How can this firm take advantage of this technological change, and how is it limited by the market share maintenance rule?

3. Discuss the changes that occur in a leader-follower industry when the leader experiences a reduction in costs due to technological change.

4. a. Derive the kinked demand curve and its associated marginal revenue curve when the firm assumes that its price reductions will not be followed by rivals but that its price increases will be.

   b. Under such a case, how does the firm decide which price to charge?

   c. Would you expect such an assumption to be verified by experience?

5. The theory of the kinked demand curve may be flawed, but it does serve the pedagogical role of forcing students to understand that MR is a function of Q. Explain why?

6. Let's give Cournot a little more credit for realism. Instead of assuming that rivals have zero conjectural variation, let's assume that firms just don't know what their rivals will do in response to an output change and that the only way to find out is to experiment. How does this assumption change industry equilibrium and the adjustment process?

7. Use the leader-follower model to show that a tax on U.S. supplies of domestic oil will strengthen OPEC whereas a tax on U.S. consumers will weaken OPEC.

8. Suppose that a multiplant monopolist's high price encourages entry by new firms but that entry is slow because of heavy investment costs. Should the monopolist
   a. Close plants and reduce output in order to keep the price up?
   b. Expand output to lower the price in order to slow down entry?
   c. Buy out the entrants?

9. Why are car manufacturers reluctant to advertise safety features?

10. a. What incentive is there for an individual competitor to provide truthful information about its product?
    b. Compare the equilibrium of the competitive market and the monopoly firm when information is an important variable in the demand function. Show that monopoly output can be larger than competitive output.
    c. Suppose the government provides the efficient level of information in a competitive market. Compare output and price to that of a monopoly equilibrium.

11. A famous aspirin company advertises the highest-quality aspirin and charges a high price. Suppose this high quality derives not from superior chemical compounds but from stock rotation that guarantees freshness. Why would the company not reveal in its advertising the reason for its higher-quality product?

12. a. Distinguish between the marginal revenue associated with a price change and the marginal revenue of advertising.
    b. Distinguish between the marginal cost of production and the marginal cost of advertising.

13. The concept of a product group relates to substitutability in demand. Is substitutability in production irrelevant to the definition of *product group?*

14. One way of collecting firms into product groups is by considering the cross-price elasticity of demand. An alternative way is to measure the loss in market share as one price is raised. Do you see advantages in each?

15. The Federal Trade Commission has charged major cereal manufacturers with producing so many brands of cereal (brand-name proliferation) that shelf space is unavailable to small producers. This situation creates a barrier to entry. Concentrating on the store owner's incentives, develop a counterargument.

16. Is product differentiation desirable to the consumer? Why or why not?

17. Is the automobile industry more competitive now than in 1960? What changes have occurred? What changes in technological innovation do you expect now that you would not have expected in 1960?

18. In 1982, worries over the hemorrhaging federal budget brought forth proposals to tax imported oil. Using a leader-follower diagram, explain the difference between taxing all imported oil and taxing only oil imported from OPEC.

19. Suppose that all cement firms agree to raise the price of cement by $2 per ton on January 1. When January 1 arrives, they all raise the price by $2. Is the economic damage to their customers greater than, less than, or equal to $2?

20. What changes in the production and distribution of beer would you expect due to the construction of the interstate highway system and the development of beer that does not require refrigeration? Would competition lead to an increase or decrease in the number of firms as a result? (Hint: How does your answer depend on demand elasticity?)

21. The following is a quote from the "findings of fact" in the famous "Cellophane case":

    "Cellophane has always been higher-priced than the two largest-selling flexible packaging materials, wax paper and glassine, and this has represented a disadvantage to sales of cellophane."

    Does the fact that cellophane had a higher price per square inch refute the analysis in this chapter? If so, repair it. If not, defend it.

22. Natural gas, which lies below 15,000 feet, is not subject to price controls and sells for about $4 per thousand cubic feet. Meanwhile, oil that lies above 15,000 feet is subject to an $.83 price cap.
    a. Draw the appropriate diagram to illustrate such a regulation.
    b. If the control on "shallow" gas were removed, would the price of gas rise faster or slower than if the controls remain in effect?

23. What would be the effect of the decontrol of natural gas on the OPEC oil price?

24. Suppose two industries, A and B, have identical size composition, five firms, and a Herfindahl index of .2. The demand in industry A is highly elastic, while that in B is inelastic. Which industry should get more attention from the Antitrust Division in the event of a merger attempt?

25. Is predatory pricing more likely to occur in an industry with high capital costs or in one with low capital costs?

Suggested Readings

Bain, J. *Barriers to New Competition.* Cambridge, Mass.: Harvard University Press, 1956.

Bishop, Robert L. "The Theory of Monopolistic Competition after Thirty Years: The Impact on General Theory." *American Economic Review* 54 (1964): 33–43.

Chamberlin, E. H. *The Theory of Monopolistic Competition.* Cambridge, Mass.: Harvard University Press, 1933.

Fellner, W. *Competition among the Few*. New York: Knopf, 1950.

Osborne, D. "Cartel Problems." *American Economic Review* 66 (1976): 835–844.

Patinkin, D. "Multiple-Plant Firms, Cartels and Imperfect Competition." *Quarterly Journal of Economics* 66 (1947): 173–205.

Robinson, J. *The Economics of Imperfect Competition*. London: Macmillan, 1933.

Stigler, George J. "The Kinky Oligopoly Demand Curve and Rigid Prices." *Journal of Political Economy* 55 (1947): 432–449.

Stigler, George J. "Monopolistic Competition in Retrospect." In *Five Lectures on Economic Problems*, pp. 12–24. New York: Macmillan, 1949.

Sweezy, Paul M. "Demand under Conditions of Oligopoly." *Journal of Political Economy* 47 (1939): 568–573.

Triffin, R. *Monopolistic Competition and General Equilibrium Theory*. Cambridge, Mass.: Harvard University Press, 1949.

The Factors of Production: Competition

The link between the firm's output and the resources it employs is the production function. Once the firm chooses its rate of output, its use of inputs is set via the production function. Up to now in our analysis, the roles of input pricing and employment decisions have been suppressed; we have studied only the output decisions of the firm. In order to concentrate on product market considerations, we treated the input side of the firm's decisions in a simple way: (1) We defined a production function in which output depends on input combinations, and (2) we assumed that the firm faces parametric factor prices. The cost curves we constructed were used as a framework for organizing thoughts about the cost (supply) side of market behavior. Now it's time to make input markets our principal concern and to retire the firms' output markets to the background. Just because we've waited this long to study input markets does not mean that factor markets are any less important than product markets. In fact, a first principle of economics is the interdependence of output and input markets.

The interdependence of output and input markets is illustrated by the simple circular flow diagram in Figure 11.1. The activities of the two principal economic agents, consumers and firms, are inevitably intertwined. The colored lines represent the flow of units of input from consumers to firms and units of output from firms to consumers; the black lines represent the dollar equivalents. Thus firms buy inputs and sell output; consumers buy output and sell inputs. Firms cannot buy inputs unless they expect to receive payments for the output these inputs help produce. Likewise, consumers cannot purchase final goods and services from firms without obtaining the means of payment (income) by selling inputs in the factor markets. Thus the input and output markets are interdependent; each market generates the purchasing power that the demand for the other market depends on.

We should note in passing that, for the economy as a whole, output and income are synonymous. The nation's income—the distribution of which is so hotly debated—is nothing other than the

Figure 11.1
Circular Flow in Microeconomics

The interrelatedness of inputs and outputs and of consumers and firms is illustrated by the flows of goods and the money that pays for them.

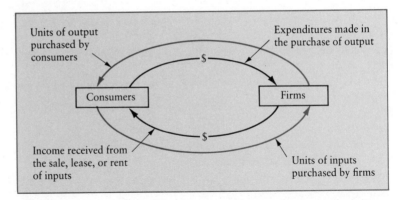

output that the nation produces. Arguments about the distribution of income amount to differences about how society's output should be divided among the nation's population. The equivalence of output and income has been especially important in the development of neo-Keynesian macroeconomic models.

In changing our emphasis to input markets, we will cover much familiar ground. Many results of input analysis are analogous to those already studied in regard to output markets. Watch for these, but note that the analysis is transposed. Product demand curves model consumer behavior, whereas factor demand curves model the behavior of firms. Also, product supply curves reflect firm decisions; input supply curves measure the decisions of consumers as resource owners. With this transposition in mind, the analogies between output and input market analysis are easy to spot.

So far, this book has used labor and capital as broad surrogates for all variable and fixed factors. This chapter continues the convention, although it will become increasingly clear that capital and labor differ more in degree than in kind. For example, capital is regarded as the fixed factor in part because the returns to capital typically accrue to the firm over many periods. But these multiperiod returns have an analogy in labor factors. Expenditures for training and educating human beings are investments that yield multiperiod returns similar to the returns on capital investments. Because investments in human beings imbed a component of capital in workers, such investments can be studied within the framework of capital theory.

This chapter is limited to competitive firms that are price takers in both their input and output markets. The firm can sell (buy) as many units of output (input) as it wishes without affecting the price of output (inputs). As usual, the essential characteristic of competition is parametric pricing, which results when the firm is small in relation to the market for both inputs and output. When firms do not face parametric prices, either in output or input markets, the allocation of inputs is affected in important and interesting ways. The effect of monopoly on the factor markets is the subject of Chapter 12.

Revenue Curves

Our first task is to derive the demand curve for an input. For convenience, we can use labor as the input, but the concepts described here are perfectly generalizable to any other input. The demand for a factor is a **derived demand,** meaning that it is derived from the market demand for the output produced by the input. The demand for elephant trainers (a labor input) depends on there being a market demand for trained elephants (an output); the latter is a precondition for the existence of the former.

The basic building block in factor demand is the **marginal revenue product (MRP)** curve, to be defined shortly. The MRP curve is not the factor demand curve for the firm except in a very limited special case. Still, it is through the MRP curve that the correct firm and industry input demand curves are derived.

Figure 11.2 develops the apparatus necessary to study the demand for labor. Panel *a* contains a total product curve, which should already be familiar from Chapter 5. The curve in panel *b* is a **total revenue product of labor (TRP$_L$)** curve, which indicates the

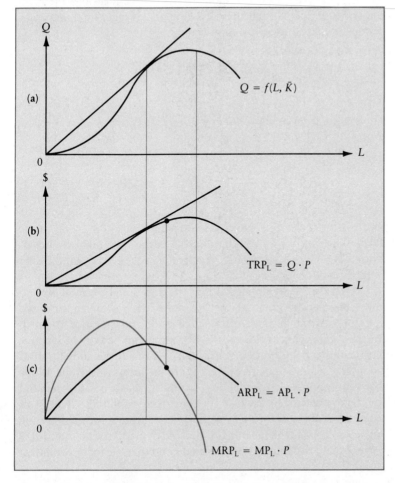

Figure 11.2
Deriving the MRP$_L$ and ARP$_L$ Curves

Several curves are useful in studying the demand for labor: (a) the product curve; (b) the TRP$_L$ curve; and (c) the ARP$_L$ and MRP$_L$ curves. The TRP$_L$ curve is derived from the product curve merely by multiplying $P \cdot Q$. The MRP$_L$ is the slope of the TRP$_L$ curve for various levels of L; the ARP$_L$ measures TRP$_L/L$.

$Q = f(L, \bar{K})$

(a)

$TRP_L = Q \cdot P$

(b)

$ARP_L = AP_L \cdot P$

(c)

$MRP_L = MP_L \cdot P$

total revenue generated from the sale of the output produced by various quantities of labor input. The vertical axis in panel *a* measures output. These units of output for each level of labor use are multiplied by product price and replotted in panel *b* as the TRP_L curve. The vertical axis of the TRP_L curve measures total revenue in dollars. Thus

$$TRP_L = Q \cdot P \tag{11.1}$$

The TRP_L curve must display the same stages of increasing, diminishing, and negative marginal returns to labor that appear in the total product curve, because all quantities of output in panel *a* are merely multiplied by a constant price in deriving the TRP_L curve in panel *b*.

Figure 11.2*c* displays the average and marginal curves that correspond to the TRP_L curve in panel *b*. These derivations and relationships are too familiar now to require any elaboration. The **average revenue product of labor** (**ARP_L**) curve measures the revenue attributable to each unit of labor on average, or the average product of labor times product price:

$$ARP_L = \frac{TRP_L}{L} = \frac{Q}{L} \cdot P = AP_L \cdot P \tag{11.2}$$

The **marginal revenue product of labor** (**MRP_L**) curve measures the change in total revenue resulting from a change in labor, or

$$MRP_L = \frac{\Delta TRP_L}{\Delta L} = \frac{\Delta Q}{\Delta L} \cdot P = MP_L \cdot P \tag{11.3}$$

As always, the marginal curve, MRP_L, is the slope of the total curve, TRP_L. The first term in Equation 11.3 is the marginal product of labor, MP_L. Thus MRP_L equals the product of the marginal product of labor and product price.

Equation 11.3 emphasizes that the additional revenue obtainable from an additional labor input—the MRP_L—depends on two components: the marginal product of labor and the price at which the additional output can be sold. An input can be very productive technically and still not be demanded by firms if the added output cannot be sold at a positive price. Space engineers in the late 1960s were enormously productive in a technical sense, but the demand for their services fell because the American public lost interest in paying for the space program, the final output produced by the engineers. This is the meaning of derived demand for an input; it is derived from the demand for the final good that the input produces.

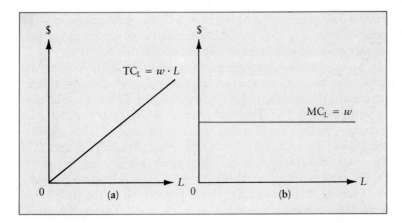

Figure 11.3
Deriving the Marginal Cost of Labor

(a) The total cost of labor (TC_L) is a function of labor. (b) The marginal cost of labor (MC_L), also a function of labor, is merely the wage rate, w, or the slope of the TC_L curve.

Cost Curves

If the firm is a wage taker in the labor market, it can buy any amount of labor without affecting the wage rate. Accordingly, the **total labor cost** (TC_L) equals the number of workers hired times the wage per worker:

$$TC_L = w \cdot L \qquad (11.4)$$

The TC_L curve is drawn in Figure 11.3*a*. It rises at a constant rate because each unit of labor hired adds a constant amount (the wage) to total labor costs.

The **marginal cost of labor** (MC_L) curve, shown in Figure 11.3*b*, is the slope of the TC_L curve; it measures the added cost of employing one more unit of labor. When the firm is a wage taker, the MC_L is a constant, equal to the wage:

$$MC_L = \frac{\Delta TC_L}{\Delta L} = w \qquad (11.5)$$

Note the similarity between the TC_L and the TVC. Both equal $w \cdot L$, but the TC_L is drawn as a function of labor, whereas the TVC is a function of output. Note too the similarity between the standard revenue curves in competition (TR and MR) and the labor cost curves just presented (TC_L and MC_L). Their shapes reflect the assumption of parametric pricing.

Selecting the Profit-Maximizing Level of Labor

In product market analysis, we determined the profit-maximizing level of output for the firm using the following rule: Equate MR and MC, where the MC curve cuts the MR curve from below. Once the correct level of output has been determined, the cost-minimizing combination of inputs can be fixed via the production function. Now we can approach the problem of profit maximization from the perspective of input utilization. When the firm determines the profit-maximizing level and the combination of inputs to employ, its rate of output is then fixed by the production function.

To explore the short-run profit-maximizing input decision, assume that the firm is a wage taker and that it employs a fixed amount of capital. For wage rate w_1 in Figure 11.4a, the total cost of hiring labor is TC_L. The total revenue of hiring labor is TRP_L. To maximize profits, the firm should select the level of labor employment that maximizes the positive difference between TRP_L and TC_L. This vertical distance does not equal profit, because the cost of the capital resource is not included in the TC_L curve. However, adding the fixed capital cost to TC_L would merely shift the TC_L curve upward by a constant amount. Thus the level of labor that maximizes the vertical distance between TRP_L and TC_L would also maximize the distance between TRP_L and a total cost curve that included the fixed cost. For wage rate w_1, the profit-maximizing use of labor is L_1.

Figure 11.4
Choosing the Profit-Maximizing Level of Labor

(a) The maximum distance between the TRP_L and TC_L curves occurs at L_1. (b) The slope of the TC_L curve is w, and the slope of the TRP_L curve is MRP_L. MRP_L equals w at L_1.

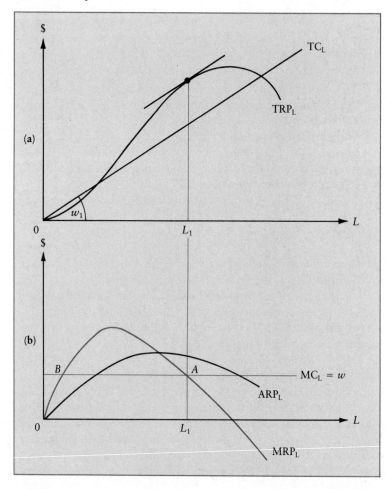

We can now state the input version of the profit-maximizing rule in marginal terms. Profit is maximized where the TRP_L and TC_L achieve the greatest difference. This occurs when the slopes of the TRP_L and TC_L are equal. These slopes, MRP_L and MC_L respectively, are drawn together in Figure 11.4*b*. The **profit-maximizing condition** is therefore

$$MRP_L = MC_L \qquad\qquad (11.6)$$

In Figure 11.4*b*, the profit-maximizing employment of L_1 units of labor is revealed by the equality of MRP_L and MC_L at point *A*. The firm should continue to hire more labor as long as each added worker adds more to revenue (MRP_L) than it adds to costs (MC_L). When $MRP_L = MC_L$, the profit-maximizing rate of labor hiring has been achieved. Any more or less labor would reduce the firm's profits (or increase its losses).

Note that $MRP_L = MC_L$ occurs at points *A* and *B* in Figure 11.4*b*. Point *B* must be ruled out as a profit-maximizing position, however, because movements away from *B* in either direction improve the firm's profit position. Just as the MC curve must cut the MR curve from below in output analysis, so the MRP_L curve must cut the MC_L curve from above in input analysis.

The Firm's Demand Curve for Labor

We can now begin to derive the **firm's demand curve for labor.** Figure 11.5 displays the ARP_L and MRP_L curves of a representative

Figure 11.5
The Firm's Demand for Labor

The MRP_L curve is the firm's demand curve for labor only if changes in the wage rate do not result in MRP_L shifts due to changes in *K*, *P*, or *r*. (a) Demand equals MRP_L below *E*. (b) The wage is set by industry supply and demand.

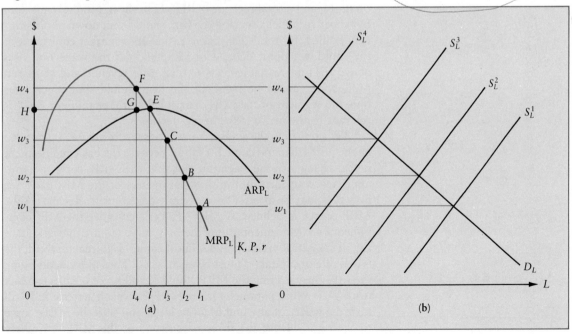

firm in panel *a* and the industry supply and demand curves for labor in panel *b*. The wage rate is determined at the industry level, and the firm uses this wage rate to select its profit-maximizing labor force. Panel *b* shows four possible labor supply curves. When the labor supply curve is S_L^1, the industry wage is w_1. The firm maximizes profit by equating MRP_L and w_1 at point A and hiring l_1 units of labor. If the labor supply shifts to S_L^2, the wage rate rises to w_2, inducing the firm to reduce its labor hiring to l_2, which is depicted by the equality of MRP_L and w_2 at point B. Another shift in the labor supply curve to S_L^3 raises the wage rate to w_3 and causes the firm to move to C on the MRP_L curve.

The points A, B, C, and an infinity of similarly derived points trace out a two-dimensional relationship between the wage rate and the quantity of labor demand by the firm, *ceteris paribus*. But this is the labor demand curve! Because points A, B, C, and all similar profit-maximizing points are on the MRP_L curve, it follows that the MRP_L curve is the firm's demand curve for labor—but only under an extremely limited set of assumptions. The MRP_L is the firm's labor demand curve only if changes in the wage rate do not cause the MRP_L to shift. When a change in the wage rate shifts the MRP_L curve for any reason, it cannot be regarded as the labor demand curve. We will return to this point shortly.

Note that the relevant segment of the MRP_L curve for identifying labor use is the segment below the maximum of the ARP_L curve. Thus if the labor supply curve is S_L^4 and the wage rate is w_4, selecting l_4 units of labor at point F would result in a total labor cost of $0w_4Fl_4$ and a total revenue of $0HGl_4$. In short, total revenue does not cover variable costs, and the firm should shut down in the short run. Point E on the MRP_L curve is the labor market equivalent of the shutdown point defined in Chapter 7. If the wage rate rises above lE, total variable costs exceed total revenue and short-run production cannot be justified; the firm should shut down. Thus only the segment of the MRP_L curve below the maximum ARP_L is relevant to the firm's labor hiring decisions.

Let's return to the assumptions necessary for the MRP_L curve to be the firm's demand curve for labor. Because the basic requirement is that changes in the wage rate not shift the MRP_L curve, a useful approach is to identify the shift parameters of the MRP_L and see how they may be affected by wage rate adjustments. Recall that the MRP_L curve is defined as $MP_L \cdot P$. Let's consider the MP_L component first. Movements along the MP_L curve require that the quantity of capital (K) remain fixed. But if capital is to remain fixed, the rental rate of capital (r) must be unchanged. Thus movements along the MP_L (hence along the MRP_L) hold K and r fixed. Also, product price (P) is a shift parameter in the MRP_L curve; an increase in P will raise the MRP_L of any unit of labor input and shift the MRP_L curve to the right. Hence the three parameters of the MRP_L curve are

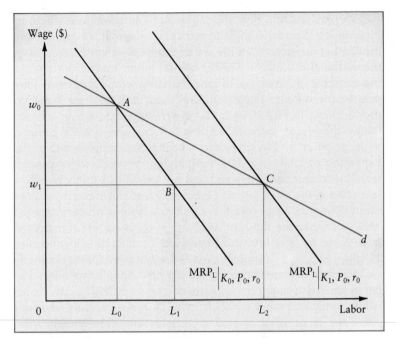

Figure 11.6
The Firm's Demand for Labor When K Varies

Adjustments in K following wage changes cause demand to be more elastic than the MRP_L.

capital (K), product price (P), and the price of capital (r). Symbolically, these parameters can be expressed as follows:

$$MRP_L = MRP_L \big| K, P, r \qquad (11.7)$$

If none of the three parameters is affected by the changes in wage rates, the MRP_L curve will not shift. In fact, the firm can use the stationary MRP_L curve to select the profit-maximizing level of labor at the various wage rates. In this case, the MRP_L curve is the firm's demand curve for labor. However, there are sound reasons for thinking that under most circumstances the three parameters will be affected, in which case the derived labor demand curve is different from the MRP_L curve. Thus the key to conceptualizing the labor demand curve lies in the way wage rate changes shift the MRP_L curve. The next three subsections derive the labor demand curve under various assumptions about these shift parameters.

WHEN CAPITAL IS VARIABLE   In the long run, capital is a variable input. Suppose the initial MRP_L curve is $MRP_L \big|_{K_0, P_0, r_0}$ in Figure 11.6.[1] (The 0 subscripts refer to initial values.) At the initial wage w_0, the firm selects L_0 labor units by equating $MRP_L \big|_{K_0, P_0, r_0}$ and w_0 at point A. Now suppose the wage rate falls to w_1. What will happen to the employment of capital in the long run?

1. The term $MRP_L \big|_{K_0, P_0, r_0}$ is not a fraction. Instead, it is the MRP_L curve for a given set of shift parameters, K_0, P_0, and r_0.

We can assume that the labor and capital inputs are complementary. **Factor complementarity** in stage II of production means that an increase in the use of labor (meat cutters) increases the marginal productivity of the capital input (butcher knives). In this example, the presence of more butchers would reduce the idleness of the butcher knives on hand and increase their marginal productivity. In Figure 11.6, the lower wage rate would initially induce the firm to increase is hiring to L_1, at which $\text{MRP}_L|_{K_0,\, P_0,\, r_0} = w_1$ at point B. But if labor and capital are complementary, the expansion of labor increases the marginal productivity of capital, which increases the firm's demand for capital. In other words, a reduction in the wage rate will eventually lead the firm to hire more capital (because it is complementary to labor), which shifts the MRP_L curve to the right, to $\text{MRP}_L|_{K_1,\, P_0,\, r_0}$, as capital is increased from K_0 to K_1. The firm will then select L_2 units of labor, because $\text{MRP}_L|_{K_1,\, P_0,\, r_0} = w_1$ at point C. Accordingly, A and C are two points on the firm's demand curve for labor when capital is variable. The curve labeled d connects all such points; each MRP_L curve contributes only one point to the d curve. Thus d is the firm's demand curve for labor when capital is variable and complementary to labor. By construction, curve d still holds P and r constant. Of the three MRP_L curve parameters under discussion, only K varies along the demand curve d.

WHEN CAPITAL AND PRODUCT PRICE ARE BOTH VARIABLE   In the previous section, we saw how a lower wage rate shifted the MRP_L curve by inducing an increase in capital employment. Initially the firm may ignore the effect of these changes on product price. However, when all firms increase the employment of both labor and capital inputs when the wage falls, the industry supply of output will increase and the market price of output will fall. But the product price is another shift parameter in the MRP_L curve. Thus the rightward shift in the MRP_L curve arising from expanded capital employment will be partially offset by a lower product price. In Figure 11.7 the MRP_L curves and curve d are repeated as a point of reference. The colored $\text{MRP}_L|_{K_1,\, P_1,\, r_0}$ curve represents the net effect of two shifts: An increase in capital increases the MRP_L curve, and a reduction in product price reduces it. Thus at the wage rate w_1, the firm selects labor use from the $\text{MRP}_L|_{K_1,\, P_1,\, r_0}$ curve, which lies to the left of $\text{MRP}_L|_{K_1,\, P_0,\, r_0}$. Thus E (instead of C) is a point on the labor demand curve at wage rate w_1 when product price and capital are both variable. The connection of points A, E, and other such points, labeled d_T in Figure 11.7, is the firm's labor demand curve when capital and product price are variable. The d_T curve is less elastic than the d curve.

WHEN CAPITAL, PRODUCT PRICE, AND RENTAL RATE OF CAPITAL ARE ALL VARIABLE   In deriving the demand curve d_T, we allowed the demand

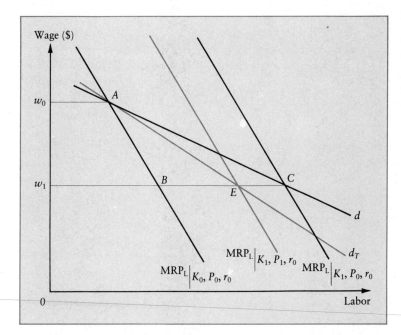

Figure 11.7
The Firm's Demand for Labor When K and P Vary

The increased quantity demanded for L is tempered by the fall in product price.

for capital to rise in response to a wage rate reduction, but so far we have held the rental rate of capital fixed. If the industry supply of capital is not perfectly elastic, the capital demand shift must increase r, the rental rate of capital. If the rental rate of capital ultimately rises in response to a lower wage rate, firms will buy less capital than indicated in previous sections. Thus the MRP_L curves will not shift so far as previously shown. When the effect on the rental rate of capital is included in the analysis, we get a curve connecting all profit-maximizing points that is still less elastic than d_T. This labor demand curve, which takes one point from each MRP_L curve when K, P, and r are all allowed to vary, is shown at d_{TT} in Figure 11.8.

One point about the slope of the demand curve for labor remains to be made. We have seen that the slope depends on the degree to which a wage rate change affects the K, P, and r variables. Because changes in these variables exert differential directional shifts in the firms' MRP_L curves, is it not at least theoretically possible that the net effect of such shifts could actually produce an upward-sloping labor demand curve, much like the Giffen good in product demand? In the case of derived demand for inputs, C. E. Ferguson has shown that the factor demand curve must be negatively sloped.[2] There can be no Giffen case for factor demand curves. We can derive the industry demand curves for labor by horizontal summation of firm demand curves, a procedure we have used in many other applications. No further adjustments are necessary beyond those already made in deriving the various firm demand curves.

2. C. E. Ferguson, *The Neoclassical Theory of Production and Distribution* (Cambridge, England: Cambridge University Press, 1969).

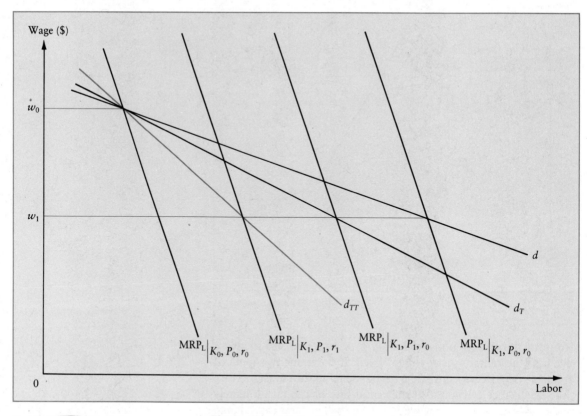

Figure 11.8
The Firm's Demand for Labor When K, P, and r Vary

The increased quantity demanded for L is accompanied by an adjustment in K. This process is tempered by a rise in r.

Elasticity of Substitution

The analysis of input demand is rooted in the theory of production. We can deepen our understanding of the demand for inputs by seeking to comprehend the **elasticity of substitution, (σ)**. Formally, the elasticity of substitution is defined as the percentage change in the capital/labor ratio resulting from a percentage change in the price ratio of labor and capital:

$$\sigma = \frac{\%\Delta(K/L)}{\%\Delta(w/r)} = \frac{\Delta(K/L)/(K/L)}{\Delta(w/r)/(w/r)} \qquad (11.8)$$

Both the numerator and denominator of Equation 11.8 can be visualized as a movement along a given production isoquant.

We can consider the numerator with the help of Figure 11.9. The capital/labor ratio at a given point on the isoquant curve Q_0 is given by the slope of a ray drawn from the origin to the point in question. At point A, the capital/labor ratio is $(K/L)_A = 0K_2/0L_1$, and at B it is $(K/L)_B = 0K_1/0L_2$. Clearly, the K/L ratio must fall as labor is substituted for capital in moving from A to B. For such movements, the percentage change in the K/L ratio is negative; the numerator in Equation 11.8 is negative for movements down an isoquant curve.

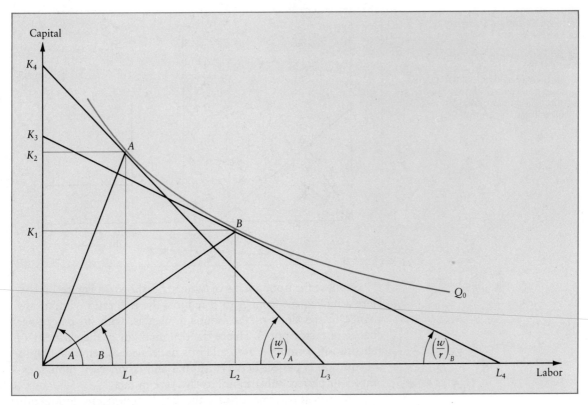

Figure 11.9
The Elasticity of Substitution

The percentage change in the K/L ratio that results from a percentage change in the w/L ratio is the elasticity of substitution.

The denominator of Equation 11.8 measures the percentage change in the ratio of factor prices. Production optimization requires that the firm equate the ratio of factor prices to the marginal rate of technical substitution, $MRTS = MP_L/MP_K$. Thus the denominator can be regarded as either the percentage change in factor price ratios or the percentage change in the MRTS, and the numerator is the percentage change in K/L required to bring about the percentage change in the MRTS. In equilibrium, both the MRTS and the w/r ratios are given by the negative of the slope of the isoquant curve. Thus the absolute value of the slope of the isoquant at point A, where $MRTS_A = (w/r)_A$, equals $0K_4/0L_3$; the slope at point B, where $MRTS_B = (w/r)_B$, equals $0K_3/0L_4$. In moving from A to B, the MRTS has fallen in absolute terms, because the MP_L has fallen and the MP_K has risen. Clearly, the ratio of factor prices, w/r, has fallen. Thus the denominator in Equation 11.8 is also negative. The value of the elasticity coefficient σ is therefore positive. A percentage reduction in w/r (which makes labor relatively cheaper) will call forth a percentage reduction in the K/L ratio (more labor will be employed relative to capital when labor is cheaper and when the same output is produced). Thus the elasticity of substitution measures the ease with which labor and capital can be substituted for each other when their relative prices change.

Figure 11.10
Extreme Cases of Elasticity of Substitution

(a) When isoquants are linear, $\sigma = +\infty$ and inputs are perfect substitutes. (b) When isoquants are right angles, $\sigma = 0$ and no substitution among inputs is possible at the margin.

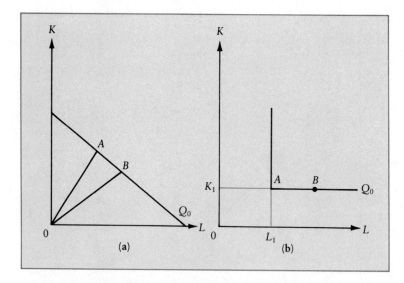

Suppose the isoquant curve is linear, as shown in Figure 11.10a. Here a movement from A to B reduces the K/L ratio without any change in the slope of the isoquant, that is, with no percentage change in factor prices. Hence the denominator in the elasticity of substitution formula is zero and σ is undefined. When σ is infinite, substitution is perfect between capital and labor, even though examples of perfect substitutability are rare in fact.

The other extreme case is the fixed-proportions production function, for which the isoquants are right angles, or L-shaped. In Figure 11.10b, no substitution is possible between capital and labor for the given output Q_0, regardless of factor prices. The firm will always produce Q_0 units of output at point A, for which the K/L ratio is $0K_1/0L_1$. Moving to point B merely increases total costs without adding any output and is therefore pointless. Thus for fixed-proportion production functions, the numerator in the elasticity of substitution formula is zero, and σ equals zero. At the margin, no substitution between capital and labor is possible.

Linear and right-angle isoquant curves are the limiting cases. For most production functions, the isoquant curves are convex, and the elasticity of substitution coefficient is positive but not infinite: $\infty > \sigma > 0$. The concept of the elasticity of substitution will be useful to us as we continue our study of input demand.

Price Elasticity of Labor Demand

The **price elasticity of labor demand** is the percentage change in the quantity of labor demanded resulting from a percentage change in the wage, *ceteris paribus*.

$$\varepsilon_w = \frac{\%\Delta L}{\%\Delta w} = \frac{\Delta L}{\Delta w} \cdot \frac{w}{L} \qquad (11.9)$$

As in product demand, elasticity is often more useful than slope in the analysis of factor demand, because elasticity is independent of arbitrary unit choices. Equation 11.9 is a reminder that all elasticities can be expressed as the product of a slope term and a ratio of bases. The term $\Delta L/\Delta w$ is the inverse of the slope of the labor demand curve. Multiplying $\Delta L/\Delta w$ by w/L puts the elasticity measure in percentage terms. As with product demand, the price elasticity of labor demand is negative, although many scholars prefer the convention of using absolute values.

Among the many determinants of labor demand elasticity, the four that follow deserve special mention.

CHARACTERISTICS OF THE PRODUCTION FUNCTION   Three aspects of the production function affect the price elasticity of labor demand: the steepness of the MP_L curve; the elasticity of substitution, σ, which measures the degree of substitutability between capital and labor; and the degree of complementarity between capital and labor.

First consider the short run, in which capital is fixed and the MRP_L curve is the firm's demand curve for labor. Because $MRP_L = MP_L \cdot P$, the steepness of the MP_L curve determines the elasticity of demand for labor. Thus labor demand elasticity varies inversely with the degree of diminishing returns to labor: The more limiting the capital constraints in the production process, the less elastic the demand for labor.

Now let capital vary. The two basic relationships between capital and labor are substitutability and complementarity. Labor and capital are substitutes along any negatively sloped isoquant curve. The price elasticity of labor demand is positively related to the ease of substitution. But the relative ease of factor substitution is measured by σ, the coefficient of elasticity of substitution, where $\infty > \sigma > 0$. Let wages fall. The greatest substitution of labor for capital for a given rate of output occurs when $\sigma = \infty$ and the least when $\sigma = 0$. Thus the elasticity of labor demand is positively related to the elasticity of substitution.

Labor and capital are substitutes for a given rate of output but can be complementary in the production of higher rates of output. Factor complementarity arises when an increase in the employment of one input increases the marginal product of the other input. We can assume that inputs are complementary without limit, that production always occurs in stage II. To the basic question of whether inputs are substitutes or complements in production, we can answer that they are both: substitutes in the production of a given output and complements in the production of different rates of output. For example, the expanded use of capital in the twentieth century has not replaced the labor force, as many had feared, but rather has been the base for expanding the labor force. Clearly, labor and capital have been complementary inputs in the recent economic experience of industrialized nations.

The price elasticity of demand for labor varies with this degree of complementarity. For example, complementarity causes the difference between demand curves MRP_L and d in Figure 11.6. The stronger the complementarity among inputs, *ceteris paribus,* the greater the price elasticity of factor demand.

PRICE ELASTICITY OF DEMAND OF THE FINAL PRODUCT   The demand for labor is derived from the demand for the product that labor produces. If the price elasticity of demand for the final good is relatively elastic, an increase in wages that shifts to the left the curve for industry supply of output will raise output price slightly while substantially reducing the quantity of output demanded at the higher price. Thus there will be a substantial reduction in the amount of labor needed to produce the lower rate of output. In contrast, if an increase in wages causes a leftward shift in the output supply curve and the output demand curve is price inelastic, quantity demanded falls less than before and the amount of labor demanded also falls less.

ELASTICITY OF THE SUPPLY OF CAPITAL   We are dealing with complementary factors. When the wage rate falls, labor and capital inputs can increase. If the demand for capital increases along a perfectly elastic supply curve, the rental rate of capital does not increase. In such a case, the amount of capital employed is determined entirely by demand. If the supply of capital is less than perfectly elastic, the rental rate of capital rises with shifts in the demand for capital. For a given wage rate, the amount of capital employed, and hence the amount of complementary labor, is greater the more elastic the supply of capital is.

LENGTH OF TIME FOR ADJUSTMENT   The price elasticity of labor demand increases with the time the firm has to adjust its input combinations and to select its profit-maximizing rate of output in response to a change in relative input prices. Given greater time, the firm can make more adjustments to labor's complementary factor, capital (and as we shall see later, to human capital), when wages rise.

Generalizing the Profit-Maximizing Labor Rule

We have concentrated on labor in deriving the profit-maximizing rule for the use of inputs and in deriving the input demand curve. But this rule applies generally to all inputs, not just to labor.

In order to produce a given output at least cost, the firm employs inputs along its expansion path so that

$$\text{MRTS} \equiv \frac{\text{MP}_L}{\text{MP}_K} = \frac{w}{r} \qquad (11.10)$$

Equation 11.10 defines the tangencies between isoquant curves and isocost lines; it can be rearranged to read

$$\frac{w}{\text{MP}_L} = \frac{r}{\text{MP}_K} \qquad (11.11)$$

The denominators in Equation 11.11 represent the added output from employing an extra unit of either input, and the numerators measure the addition to total cost resulting from doing so. Thus both w/MP_L and r/MP_K measure the change in total cost as a result of producing additional output. But these terms define marginal cost, because for labor,

$$\text{MC} = \frac{\Delta \text{TC}}{\Delta Q} = \frac{w \cdot \Delta L}{\Delta Q} = \frac{w}{\Delta Q/\Delta L} = \frac{w}{\text{MP}_L} \qquad (11.12)$$

Thus least-cost employment of factors requires that

$$\frac{w}{\text{MP}_L} = \frac{r}{\text{MP}_K} = \text{MC} \qquad (11.13)$$

The conditions outlined in Equation 11.13 are satisfied everywhere along the firm's expansion path. The correct rate of output, or the correct point of the expansion path, is found by equating marginal cost and marginal revenue. Thus the competitive firm, for which $\text{MR} \equiv P$, maximizes profit by achieving the following conditions:

$$\frac{w}{\text{MP}_L} = \frac{r}{\text{MP}_K} = \text{MC} = P \qquad (11.14)$$

The firm must produce the output level and select the input combination for each factor for which the ratio of the factor price to its marginal product must equal the output price. Thus the following conditions are required for each input:

$$w = \text{MP}_L \cdot P \equiv \text{MRP}_L \qquad (11.15)$$

$$r = \text{MP}_K \cdot P \equiv \text{MRP}_K \qquad (11.16)$$

Each input should be hired up to the point where the MP of the input times the product price equals the input price. But the term $\text{MP} \cdot P$ equals each input's MRP. Thus the profit-maximizing rule for inputs is perfectly general. The derivation of the demand curve for any input can proceed along the same lines as before, because the profit-maximizing rule for input use is the basic underpinning of factor demand.

The Value of Marginal Product Curve

The marginal revenue product (MRP) curve measures the addition to total revenue that results from employing an extra unit of input. The MRP is obtained by multiplying the units of output that an additional unit of input produces (MP of the input) by the amount these units can be sold for. If the firm faces parametric prices in the output market, the MRP_L curve is

$$MRP_L = MP_L \cdot P \qquad (11.17)$$

Each unit of output can be sold for the market price. When the firm is competitive in the output market, the MRP_L is often called the **value of marginal product of labor (VMP_L)**. The VMP_L equals the MRP_L when the firm is a price taker in its output market.

More generally, the MRP_L curve is

$$MRP_L = MP_L \cdot MR \qquad (11.18)$$

The extra output of the firm yields the marginal revenue, which is less than price for imperfect competitors that must reduce price on the marginal and inframarginal units to sell more output. Thus the VMP_L is a special case of the MRP_L curve when the firm is competitive in the output market. This point comes up again in Chapter 12, when we study the input markets of imperfectly competitive firms.

The Labor Supply Curve

Chapter 3 used indifference maps and budget lines to derive demand curves for consumer goods. The same tools can be employed to generate the supply of labor. Our first task in deriving the supply of labor is to define the commodity space. Figure 11.11a measures the consumer's money income in dollars on the vertical axis and hours of leisure time (R) on the horizontal axis.[3] Individuals must divide their total time endowment between working for income and enjoying leisure time. The indifference map in Figure 11.11a expresses the individual's relative preference for income versus leisure; the slope of the indifference curves is the marginal rate of substitution of income for leisure.

The consumer's utility is constrained by the amount of time available for either work or leisure and by the hourly wage rate paid to labor. These constraints are incorporated in the budget lines in

---

3. We cannot use L for leisure because it already stands for labor, but we can use R for recreation to stand for all nonwork time.

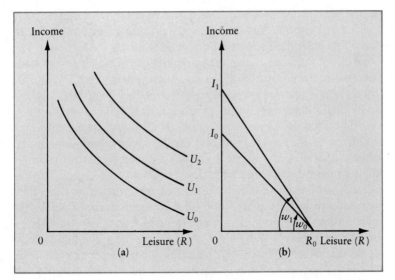

Figure 11.11
The Relationship between Income and Leisure

(a) An indifference map can be drawn in income-leisure space. (b) A worker's budget line is drawn where the wage rate determines the slope.

panel b. Point R_0 represents the consumer's total time endowment per week. The slope of the budget line is the negative of the hourly wage rate, because the wage is the rate at which a leisure hour can be exchanged for income. If the wage rate is $1 per hour, the slope of the budget line, $\Delta I / \Delta R$, is -1 and the vertical income intercept is, say, $100 per week. In more general terms, the budget line $I_0 R_0$ in Figure 11.11b corresponds to the wage rate w_0. A higher wage rate, w_1, rotates the budget line around point B_0 to $I_1 B_0$.

The indifference map and budget lines are combined in Figure 11.12. For wage rate w_0, the individual selects point A on indifference curve U_0. Point A corresponds to $R_0 - R_1$ hours of work. Now

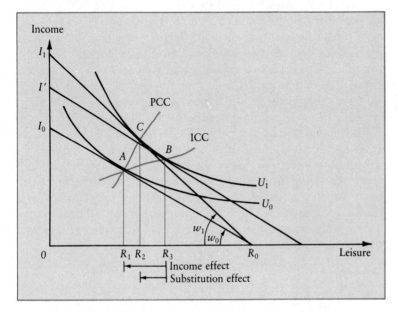

Figure 11.12
Income and Substitution Effects of a Wage Change

As in consumer theory (see Chapter 3), a change in wage (the price of leisure) gives rise to an income effect and a substitution effect and to corresponding ICC and PCC curves.

let the wage rate rise to w_1. This is equivalent to an increase in the price of leisure. The higher wage rate, w_1, rotates the budget line to $I_1 R_0$. The individual selects point C and works $R_0 - R_2$ hours. The total effect on leisure (hence on work effort) resulting from the wage increase is traced out by the price-consumption curve, PCC. This total effect is the move from A to C: The higher wage increased the individual's consumption of leisure and thus reduced work effort.

The total effect on work effort of changing wages is the net result of two countervailing forces: the income and substitution effects. If leisure is a normal good, the income effect is positive; higher money incomes increase the consumption of leisure. The size of the income effect can be measured by making an equivalent variation in income that would allow the consumer to obtain the new indifference curve, U_1, at the original wage rate, w_0. This income variation is $I' - I_0$, which would move the individual to point C on indifference curve U_1. Thus the income effect of the price change is the move from A to B along the income-consumption curve, ICC.

In addition to making the individual richer in income, the increased wage rate increases the relative price of leisure. The move from B to C along indifference curve U_1 is a reduction in leisure due solely to the change in its relative price. The move from B to C is the substitution effect. By construction, the increase in leisure due to the income effect is larger than the reduction in leisure due to the substitution effect. On balance, the higher wage rate increases this individual's consumption of leisure and reduces work effort.

We can use these ideas to construct the individual's labor supply curve. Figure 11.13a shows an indifference map and three budget lines, each representing a different wage rate. The PCC connects all optimizing positions, such as A, B, and C. The PCC is used to trace out the labor supply curve in panel b, where hours of labor are measured along the horizontal axis from right to left. This convention makes it easy to compute hours worked as the difference between total time available, R_0, and the individual's consumption of leisure. For example, for wage rate w_1, leisure is R_1 and hours worked is $L_1 = R_0 - R_1$. For wage rate w_2, hours worked rises to L_2, but for wage rate w_3, work falls to L_3 hours. Increases in the wage rate up to w_2 increase work effort: In this range the negative substitution effect outweighs the positive income effect. But for wages above w_2, the income effect is dominant, resulting in a negatively sloped segment of the individual's labor supply curve. This is the famous "backward-bending" labor supply curve. Higher wages reduce work effort if the income effect of a wage change is greater than the substitution effect.

When wages change, workers can expand or contract work

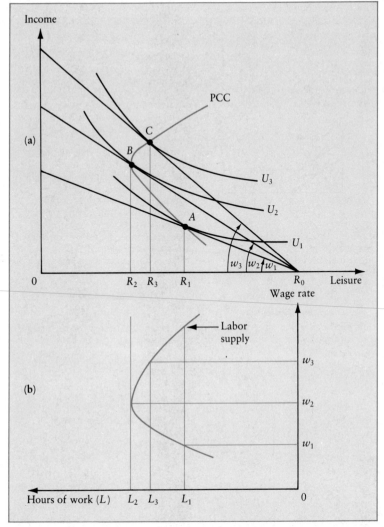

Figure 11.13
The Derivation of Labor Supply

(a) The PCC here connects the optimal income-leisure positions for three individuals. (b) The relative sizes of the income and subsitution effects at different wages can give rise to the backward-bending labor supply curve.

effort by moonlighting, calling in sick, seeking parttime employment, retiring early or late in life, working part of the year or all of it, or lobbying through unions for shorter work weeks and longer vacations. Thus consumer theory models not only the individual's decisions in dividing up a limited budget between different goods and services but also the division of a limited time allotment between work and leisure. Indeed, the labor supply decision determines the consumer's income, which is then allocated to different commodities in the current period by spending and in future periods through saving. Consumer theory illuminates two of consumers' most essential economic decisions: how much to work and how to spend the resulting income.

The Work Incentives of Inheritances versus Earnings

APPLIED MICRO THEORY

11.1

Now that we know something about worker's allocation of time between work and leisure, we shall see how various labor market policies affect the work decision. We know that an increase in hourly earnings pivots the budget constraint. How does an inheritance affect the budget constraint? In Figure A, an inheritance of H_1R_0 shifts the budget line from I_0R_0 to I_1H_1. The consumer receives income equal to the inheritance when he or she does not work at all. And beyond that

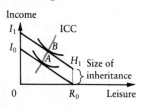

Figure A

An inheritance gives rise to a move along an ICC.

minimum, leisure may be exchanged for income at the same rate as before—the wage rate. Thus the inheritance does not

affect the slope of the budget line, only its position. The income-consumption curve, a line through points A and B, is positively sloped if we assume that income and leisure are both normal goods, which we do.

In Figure B, wage rate w_1 determines the initial budget line I_0R_0. Suppose we wish to provide a stipulated income of I to the consumer, and we are considering two options: (1) increasing the worker's wages or (2) giving the worker an inheritance (a no-strings-attached cash payment). Using wage policy, wage w_2 is needed to induce the worker to point C,

Figure B

An inheritance will lead to less work effort than if the same income is derived from earnings.

Figure C

An inheritance will lead to less work effort than if the same utility is derived from earnings.

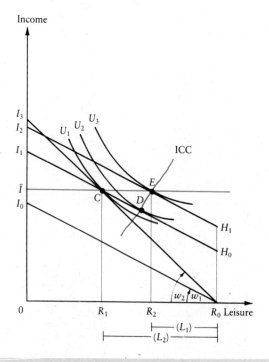

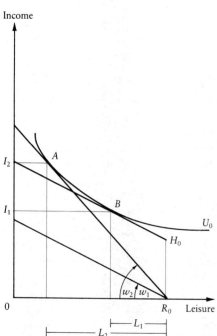

where the new budget line I_3R_0 becomes tangent to indifference curve U_1.

What size of cash inheritance would be needed to provide the same income, $\bar{I}$? An inheritance of H_0R_0, which causes the budget line at the original wage w_1 to pass through point C, is too small. Because the MRS of income for leisure exceeds the wage rate at C, the consumer can reach the higher indifference curve U_2 at point D by

working less than at C and earning less income. The larger inheritance, H_1R_0, is needed to produce the tangency E at the stipulated income level $\bar{I}$.

If a person gets the same income via earnings or inheritances, consumer utility is lower when income is earned (U_1 compared to U_3 for inheritances) and work effort is greater when income is earned (L_2 compared to L_1 for inheritances).

Instead of awarding the same

money income by two policies, suppose the same level of utility is sought. In Figure C, the initial wage rate is w_1 and indifference curve U_0 is sought. The wage rate w_2 produces a tangency at point A, whereas inheritance H_0R_0 generates a tangency at B. Both income and work effort are higher under the earnings policy than under inheritance policy when equal utility is the policy goal.

Social Security and Work Incentives

APPLIED MICRO THEORY

11.2

Consumer theory is useful in investigating Social Security. Social Security benefits are paid to eligible retirees, who may supplement these benefits with private earnings up to a stipulated maximum. If private earnings exceed this maximum, Social Security benefits are withdrawn. Such a policy tends to keep retired workers out of the labor force, you say. But let's take a closer look.

The effect of Social Security on the worker's initial budget line, I_0R_0, is shown in Figure A. Social Security payments of H_0R_0 produce a step-function budget line, I_0ABH_0. Without working, the individual receives income equal to the Social Security benefits H_0R_0. The worker may transform leisure into income and move along the segment H_0B. But when private income exceeds $\bar{I}$, Social Security payments are withdrawn, and the budget line drops to I_0A.

The Social Security system affects work incentives differently, depending on workers' ability to earn private income. The indifference maps and budget lines for two workers are illustrated in the linked panels in Figure B. The budget lines are drawn for a low-wage earner (w_1) on the left and for a high-wage earner (w_2) on the right. For convenience, let's assume that the maximum allowed private earnings, $\bar{I}$, are the same for both workers. Social Security payments

Figure A
The Impact of Social Security Income on the Budget Line

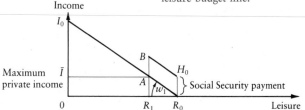

The elimination of benefits once a recipient earns the maximum private income creates a discontinuity in the income-leisure budget line.

Figure B
The Differential Impact of Maximum Income

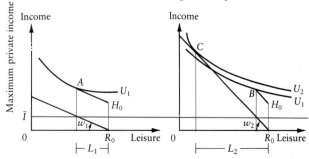

A low-wage earner (left-hand panel) is more likely to be in equilibrium at the maximum income than a high-wage earner (right-hand panel) is.

of H_0R_0 move the low-wage earner to point A on indifference curve U_1. To work more than L_1 hours entails the loss of Social Security payments. And it is not possible for the worker to reach an indifference curve superior to U_1 at

the wage rate w_1; the choice set is too constrained. Thus low-wage earners are induced to limit work, which keeps their income close to the Social Security allotment.

The high-wage earner is in a

Continued on page 364

very different position. This individual quickly reaches the maximum income allowed, due to high hourly wages; indifference curve U_1 is reached at point B. If this worker loses the Social Security payments H_0R_0, the high wage rate quickly expands the choice set. This worker achieves the superior indifference curve U_2 at C by forgoing Social Security payments

and increasing work to L_2 hours.

The Social Security system, as presently administered, provides incentives for the low-wage earner to remain relatively poor and inactive and for the high-wage earner to remain in the work force. In short, a program intended to aid the poor actually erects harsh barriers against them for self-help and industry.

There is one sense in which the poor and the rich are treated equally by Social Security: Both are given incentives to cheat. You should be able to show that, by not reporting private earnings, both workers can eliminate the discontinuity in their budget lines, expanding their choice sets and allowing the attainment of even higher indifference curves.

Guaranteed Incomes and Work Incentives

APPLIED
MICRO
THEORY

11.3

Consumer theory may also be used to investigate the much-discussed guaranteed income, a welfare proposal under which all citizens would be guaranteed a minimum income by right of citizenship. In the figure, income I_g represents the guaranteed income, which exceeds the private income I_1 of the worker in the left-hand panel. This worker may continue to work L_1 hours, earn I_1 private income, and receive a government check of AB dollars to bring him or her up to the guarantee. Although such a strategy improves the consumer's utility from U_1 to U_2, reducing work to zero and accepting a check for the full guarantee, I_g, yields the even higher utility U_3. As long as leisure is a "good"

with positive value, the consumer in the left-hand panel has a clear-cut disincentive to work.

The worker in the center panel initially earns a private income I_2, modestly above the guaranteed level, I_g. Will such a person quit to accept a lower income? Yes, if such a decision increases utility, even though income is reduced. For the preference map shown in the center panel, the worker will accept the guaranteed income and the leisure, because utility is improved from U_1 to U_2. In short, the loss of income is more than offset by the value of the leisure obtained. Thus the oft-repeated assertion by advocates of a guaranteed income that workers earning above the minimum will not experience work disincentives does not hold up under the bright light of consumer theory.

Of course, not all workers with incomes above the guaranteed level will be affected by the policy. In the right-hand panel, the high-wage earner has an income substantially above the floor. Given the indifference map, accepting the guaranteed income and reducing work effort to zero would reduce utility from U_2 to U_1.

The negative work effects of a guaranteed income will be felt among the poor and near poor, those whose incomes are either below or not greatly above the guarantee. The dividing line between the workers who will and will not be affected is an empirical question. Thus the policy involves only negative work incentives—how negative the effect might be cannot be determined in advance.

The Differential Impact of Guaranteed Income

A guaranteed income gives the poor (left-hand panel) a higher income if they drop out of the work force. The near-poor (center panel) trade income for leisure. But the higher-wage earner (right-hand panel) finds such a tradeoff unacceptable.

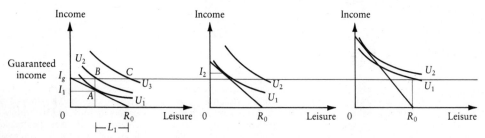

Labor Supply and Overtime Pay

APPLIED
MICRO
THEORY

11.4

Labor supply theory helps us study the impact of overtime pay on work effort. Figure A contains a price-consumption curve that becomes positively sloped at point A. This means that the wage rate w_2 is the highest wage that will induce people to increase their work effort. If wages rise above w_2, work effort falls, because the income effect of the wage increase exceeds the substitution effect. The maximum work hours at any straight wage is max L.

In these circumstances, the employer can induce the worker to work more than at any straight-line wage by offering a suitable overtime package. Consider the budget line I_0R_0, drawn for wage rate w_1. The individual works L_1 hours at this straight-line wage and reaches indifference curve U_1. But by paying overtime wages of w_{OT} for all hours worked over (say) max L hours (point B), the employer induces the worker to work L_{OT} hours. The overtime wage rate w_{OT} changes the slope of the budget line at point B. This new budget line becomes tangent to indifference curve U_2 at point C. Thus the overtime package induces the worker to move to a position such as C and work more than the maximum hours under straight-line wages. (Point C would not be selected at wage rate w_2.) In this case, overtime pay increases work effort, increases income paid to the worker, and reduces the worker's utility.

Furthermore, the employer can use overtime to get more work from employees for the same pay. In Figure B, the PCC traces out the various combinations of income and leisure that consumers will select for alternative straight-line wages. Wage w_2 yields the maximum work effort at A, denoted by max L. Total income paid to workers for this amount of work is

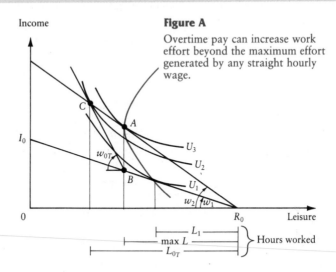

Figure A

Overtime pay can increase work effort beyond the maximum effort generated by any straight hourly wage.

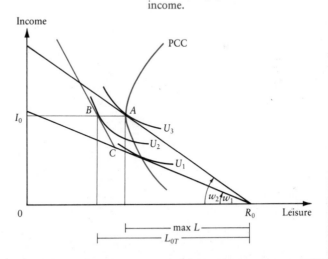

Figure B

Overtime pay increases work effort for any given amount of income.

I_0. But the employer can get the individual to work L_{OT} hours (greater than max L) and earn the same income, I_0, by an overtime package. A straight-line wage of w_1 up to (say) point C, then an overtime rate beyond C, would move the person to point B: The individual works more for the same income that he or she would get working for the straight wage w_2. Overtime pay can increase work effort for any given amount of income earned.

Labor Market Equilibrium

Figure 11.14*b* combines the industry supply and demand curves for labor. The demand curve, D_L, is the horizontal sum of the properly defined firm labor demand curves. The supply curve, S_L, is the horizontal sum of workers' labor supply curves. It is drawn with a positive slope, which requires that the substitution effect of a wage change dominate the income effect. In what follows, nothing is lost by ignoring the possibility of a backward-bending region.

The labor market is in equilibrium at wage w_1 and L_1 units of labor employed. The adjustment process to equilibrium is similar to that in other markets; shortages and surpluses send signals that force the wage toward equilibrium. Wage w_1 is the only wage that coordinates the buyers and sellers of labor.

The competitive firm's labor decisions are shown in Figure 11.14*a*. The firm is a competitive price taker in output markets and in labor input markets, in output because $MRP_L = VMP_L$ and in labor because $MC_L = w$. Profit is maximized by hiring l_1 units of labor, because $MRP_L = MC_L$ at l_1.

Figure 11.14 summarizes the elements of the neoclassical **marginal productivity theory of wages**. This nomenclature is used because, in this analysis, wages are set by market forces and workers receive a wage equal to the value of their marginal product, VMP_L.

Figure 11.14
Labor-Market Wage Determination

(a) The individual firm is a wage taker. (b) The industry wage is determined by supply and demand.

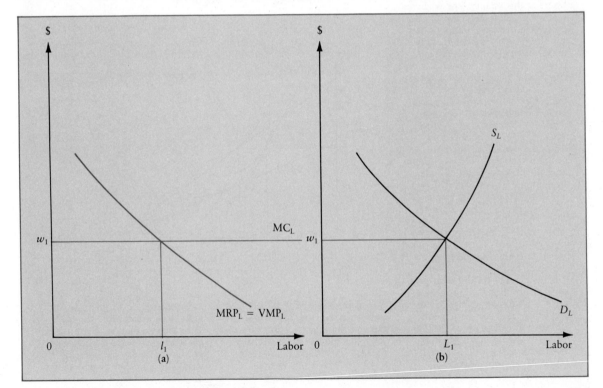

(a)

(b)

Wage Differentials

APPLIED MICRO THEORY

11.5

The marginal productivity theory of wages shows that wage rates are market-determined, just as all other prices of goods and services are. But as it stands, the theory has a major limitation: It fails to explain how the wages of workers doing the same tasks can vary or how the wages of identical workers engaged in different jobs can vary. We need to dig deeper into the supply side of the labor market to understand the existence and function of such **wage differentials.**

We can begin by making three drastic assumptions about the labor force in order to isolate different causes of wage differences:

1. Workers assign no nonpecuniary (nonmonetary) value to any employment. The only benefit derived from work is the wage.
2. Workers are identical in innate talents and acquired skills. The labor force is homogeneous.
3. The labor force is perfectly mobile. Labor can always move to jobs offering the highest wages.

If these three assumptions were to hold simultaneously in all markets, there would be one wage everywhere; the same wage should prevail in every occupation and in every area of the economy. Any disequilibrium differences in wages would be eliminated by labor supply shifts into the high-wage jobs and out of the low-wage jobs.

Now let's relax these assumptions one at a time to gain an understanding of the reason for and purpose of the wage differences observed in the labor force.

No Nonmonetary Value of Work

We can relax this assumption by permitting workers to have preferences for different tasks, independent of the wage received. Say that all workers have the same order of preference for alternative jobs, according to agreeableness, prestige, safety, and ease. The supply of labor will obviously be greater in the more desirable occupations and lower in the less desirable ones. These labor supply shifts produce a lower wage for the desirable jobs compared to the wages paid for undesirable labor. This market-determined difference in wages among different occupations is called an **equalizing wage differential.** Because the pleasant job (perhaps wine taster) assigns a nonwage benefit to the worker and the unpleasant job (mortician) assigns a negative benefit, a wage differential is needed to equalize the net benefit of work between identical workers. Equalizing wage differentials arise as a reflection of the relative marginal unpleasantness of tasks, and they are needed to attract workers into the less desirable occupations.

To illustrate the equalizing differential, consider a firm that operates around the clock, employing three 8-hour shifts. The midnight to 8 A.M. shift (referred to as the third shift or graveyard shift) must pay a wage premium if the labor force is homogeneous in ability and in work preferences. A wage differential is needed to attract workers to the unpleasant third shift. Similarly, oil companies drilling in Alaska pay a premium wage. In the opposite direction, the freedom and fringe benefits of academic life result in very talented people accepting miserable salaries. (The three fringe benefits are June, July, and August.) In this way, the price system allocates workers with identical work preferences to different occupations. It is important to realize that equalizing wage differentials represent labor market

Continued on page 368

equilibrium, not disequilibrium.

When workers exhibit different preferences for jobs, we cannot assert what specific wage rate structure will exist. But some broad generalizations are possible. By and large, wage differentials need not be so large when workers have different work preferences as when they have identical work preferences. Consider the wage differential between university professors and pressured business executives. Presumably, the presence of some people who thrive on pressure (pressure lovers) or who are less adverse to pressure than others (pressure tolerators) allows a smaller differential between the two occupations than if all were equally adverse to pressure.

To summarize, we would expect to observe equilibrium wage rate differentials in an economy of homogeneous workers and perfect labor mobility as a way of equalizing the relative unpleasantness of jobs. Wage differentials allocate labor services among all the necessary tasks of society. Indeed, equal wage rates in such a world would be evidence of disequilibrium.

Homogeneous Ability

Now let's restore the assumption that work has no nonmonetary value and relax the assumption of homogeneous ability. Workers' abilities can vary because of differences in either native abilities or acquired skills.

First consider differences in native skills. Different occupations require different skills. Wages paid to a worker in a given occupation depend in part on the worker's productivity, which in turn depends on the scarcity of the required skills. In occupations where only a few people have the required skills, marginal productivity is high, because skills are scarce. When required skills are mundane and widely available, the relative abundance of skills results in low marginal productivity of labor. Because competitive wages reflect the value of the worker's marginal product, wages will generally be higher for those whose scarce skills

keep marginal productivity high. One word of caution is needed here: Competitive wages equal VMP_L, not MP_L. Highly skilled workers can earn lower wages than low-skilled workers if the physical output produced by the highly skilled workers is not in demand. Few workers can stack marbles 10 feet high without a spill; the marginal physical productivity of those who can is high due to the scarcity of the skill. But there is little demand for the output that these skills produce; accordingly, the VMP_L and the wage are low.

The difference in wage rates that arises from differences in marginal productivities of variously skilled workers is called a **nonequalizing wage differential.** In general, nonequalizing wage differentials are demand-determined in the short run, because the market-determined wages are influenced principally by labor demand (VMP_L) differences. In contrast, equalizing differentials are determined largely by labor supply shifts in the short run.

Wage differentials must also reflect the cost of acquiring skills, at least in the long run. If the supply of doctors is not to diminish over time, wage differentials must allow for the cost of a medical education. And remember, we are analyzing only competitive markets in this chapter. When a labor market cannot make competitive adjustments—as in the market for doctors, where supply is restricted—wage differentials can exceed the cost differentials of acquiring skills.

Nonequalizing wage differentials emerge only if there is a suitable derived demand for the required skills. The postwar baby boom increased the demand for teachers in the 1960s, which in turn temporarily caused the wage rates for teachers to rise above the cost of acquiring the education. However, the high salaries for teachers increased the supply of teachers by entry and caused salaries to level off. Thus nonequalizing wage differentials are demand-determined in the short run but are limited to

cost differentials in the long run if entry is free and labor is mobile.

Perfect Labor Mobility

Labor may be immobile if the labor force does not have knowledge of alternatives or if certain geographical areas are attractive to workers for reasons independent of employment opportunities (some people may like Nevada). Because mobility reduces wage differentials, it follows that labor immobility creates higher wage differentials; the supply of labor cannot follow the high wages so easily.

Labor immobility from South to North has in part accounted for the regional wage differentials in the United States during the first half of the twentieth century. In theory, however, if capital is mobile, it will be attracted to the low-wage areas; as a result, the marginal productivity of labor and its wage rate will rise. Capital mobility tends to shift production to low-wage areas and raise wage rates there.

Minimum-wage laws retard the movement of capital from high-wage to low-wage areas. It is interesting to observe that the original support for minimum-wage legislation in the United States came principally from New England. Presumably, the motivation for federal minimum-wage legislation was to suppress the movement of capital from North to South rather than to serve as a social instrument to help the poor. Indeed strong support from New England suggests that either New England had a disproportionate share of humanitarians or it was reluctant to lose its capital to southern industry.

Minimum wages create unemployment by raising the price of labor and forcing firms to reduce the amount of labor hired at the controlled wage. Minimum wages also suppress capital movements into low-wage areas, although increased capital would increase labor demand and wage rates in poor areas. Thus opposition to minimum wages appears to be the more humanitarian stance.

Selecting the Optimum Quantity of Capital

We have seen in preceding sections that the competitive firm selects the optimum employment of labor by satisfying the following condition:

$$\text{MRP}_L = \text{MP}_L \cdot P = w \qquad (11.19)$$

Conceptually, the same condition is required for the optimum employment of capital, namely

$$\text{MRP}_K = \text{MP}_K \cdot P = r \qquad (11.20)$$

where

r = rental rate of a unit of capital per period

If the firm is a competitive, price-taking buyer of capital, r is a parameter to the firm. Equation 11.20 is the general formulation from which the demand for capital is derived, just as the demand for labor is derived from the profit-maximizing condition in Equation 11.19. Indeed, the analysis of the demand for labor is perfectly generalizable to the demand for capital. The derived demand curves for both labor and capital are negatively sloped with respect to their prices, w and r.[4]

Multiperiod Analysis of the Demand for Capital

Treating labor and capital analogously masks an important characteristic of capital: A capital good is long-lived and generates multiperiod revenue. Indeed, the multiperiod characteristic of capital is one reason we can consider capital to be approximately fixed in the short run. When a firm purchases a unit of capital, such as a machine, it either buys the machine out of retained earnings or borrows the money from a creditor. Either way, the cost of the machine to the firm is P_K, the price of the capital good. The revenues that the machine produces—its MRP_K—must be regarded as a time stream, the present discounted value of which is $\Sigma MRP_{Kt}/(1 + i)^t$, where t stands for time period. (Refer to Chapter 8 for a review of discounting and present value.) In evaluating how much capital to employ in a multiperiod analysis, we must compare the price of the capital good, P_K, with the present value of the time stream of revenue involved. Thus the multiperiod analogue of Equation 11.20 is

$$\frac{\Sigma MRP_{Kt}}{(1 + i)^t} = \frac{\Sigma_{rt}}{(1 + i)^t} = P_K \qquad (11.21)$$

---

4. The proof of this assertion exceeds the scope of this book. See R. R. Russell, "A Graphical Proof of the Impossibility of a Positively Inclined Demand Curve for a Factor of Production," *American Economic Review* 54 (1964): 726–732, for a graphic proof that factor demand curves are negatively sloped; and C. E. Ferguson, *Neoclassical Theory,* chaps. 6 and 9, for a mathematical proof.

The purchase price of the last machine must equal the present value of the stream of revenues attributable to the machine. Note that the purchase price of the machine, P_K, must also equal the present value of the per-period rental payments of the machine $\Sigma_{r_t}/(1 + i)^t$ (or the present value of the multiperiod obligations incurred if the machine is financed).

Price of Capital, Rental Rate of Capital, and Interest Rate

There is often great confusion among the three variables P_K, r, and i. We must be especially clear about the meaning of r, because it has been used throughout the book as the rental rate of a unit of capital per period. P_K, r, and i are not the same thing at all, as is often presumed incorrectly. (Even on the face of it these variables are different, because P_K and r are dollar magnitudes and i is a percentage magnitude).

Suppose a firm purchases a unit of capital (a machine) at price P_K. The machine depreciates steadily for n years, after which it has no further value, either as a productive input or as scrap. The firm can either use the machine itself or rent it to another firm. The amount of money for which the machine can be rented per period equals r, the rental rate of capital.

If the firm decides to rent out its machine, how much rent per period (r) can it charge for the machine? In equilibrium and in perfect capital markets, the rental rate of capital, r, must provide the owner of capital a return equal to the forgone return that could have been earned by using the sum of money P_K to buy an earning asset that yields the market interest rate, i. In other words, r must exactly cover the firm's total cost of owning capital, including opportunity cost. What are these costs of capital? First is the interest opportunity cost. For each period the firm has P_K dollars tied up in a machine, it forgoes the chance to earn the market rate of interest on P_K if invested in an earning asset. The per-period interest opportunity cost equals $i \cdot P_K$. Second, the firm faces a depreciation charge. The firm must set aside a sum of money each period, the compounded value of which will equal the purchase price of the machine by the time it is fully depreciated at the end of the machine's life. This procedure allows the firm to replace the worn-out machine. (This is the equivalent of receiving back the principal when investing in a monetary earning asset.) Let d be the depreciation rate or the proportion of the purchase price of capital, P_K, that must be set aside per time period. The per-period depreciation charge is then $d \cdot P_K$.

The per-period rental rate of capital, r, must cover both the interest opportunity cost and the depreciation cost of owning capital. Thus

$$r = (i \cdot P_K) + (d \cdot P_K) = (i + d)P_K \qquad (11.22)$$

From Equation 11.22 it is clear that the variables r, P_K, and i are not equal; instead they are interrelated. A change in the interest rate or the purchase price of capital will change r, the rental rate of capital. If we assume that the machine is infinitely long-lived, then $d = 0$. In this case, Equation 11.22 reduces to

$$i = \frac{r}{P_K} \qquad (11.23)$$

Because the machine never wears out, it yields a perpetual annual return to the firm, r/P_K, equal to the rate of interest. This is equivalent to the return on a financial perpetuity. If the machine wears out the same year it is purchased, then $\alpha = 1$ and Equation 11.22 reduces to

$$r = P_K \qquad (11.24)$$

But this is equivalent to a single-period analysis. Thus the rental rate of capital equals the purchase price of a capital good only in the extremely atypical case of short-lived, single-period capital.

Three points of special importance must be made here. First, labor and capital are commensurable in our analysis. The wage rate, w, is the price of the labor services provided by one unit of labor per time period. Similarly, the rental rate of capital, r, is the price of the capital services provided by one unit of capital per period. The demand for labor and capital is for the flow of services provided by these inputs. The respective prices of obtaining these service flows per period are w and r.

Second, the per-period rental rate of capital is r, whether the firm rents its capital inputs or purchases them outright. If the firm rents capital, r is an explicit payment per unit of capital rented. If the firm buys and uses its own units of capital, it forgoes the opportunity to rent them out to other firms at r dollars per period. In the latter case, r is an implicit opportunity cost. Either way, r is the cost of obtaining the services of a unit of capital per time period. The rental rate does not depend on the ownership of capital.

Finally, the multiperiod profit-maximizing condition contained in Equation 11.21 introduces a subtle but important distinction by comparison to the single-period condition in Equation 11.20. For capital to be profitable, the present value of the MRP_K time stream must equal or exceed the purchase price of the capital good. Even though $r < MRP_K$ in any given period, the capital good is profitable if the present value of the MRP_K flows equals or exceeds the present value of the per-period rent payments (which equal P_K).

In this way a distinction is drawn between variable and fixed factors. A variable factor whose returns are generated largely in the same period as the employment of the factor will be hired only if the

MRP of the factor equals or exceeds the price of the factor in each period. In contrast, a fixed factor such as capital will be hired when the present discounted value of the MRP_K equals or exceeds the price of capital, even though $MRP_K < r_t$ in some periods.

Investing in Human Capital

Up to now we have assumed that labor is variable in the short run because it exerts its influence on the firm's revenues in the present period and that capital is fixed in the short run because it affects the firm's revenues primarily in future periods. Using this distinction, we were able to analyze the labor market in the context of a single-period model. Only in studying the optimal employment of capital was it necessary to introduce a **multiperiod analysis,** in which the revenues and costs of the marginal input were compared in terms of the present discounted values of their respective time streams.

However, a moment's reflection reveals that certain aspects of the labor input exhibit characteristics similar to capital. A firm can give special training to its work force and increase the profits attributable to labor in future periods. In other words, investment in a piece of capital equipment and investment in the training, education, and productivity of the labor force are both undertaken in order to increase future profits. And surely the training received in a university or vocational school is desired, partially if not entirely, for the future returns such an education promises. Consider dentists who wish to increase their time stream of profits. They can purchase higher-speed drills, go back to school for refresher courses, or train technicians to help in "four-handed dentistry." All three investments are made to increase future profits. The drill is an investment in physical capital. The training (either for the dentist or the technician) is an investment in **human capital.** Training adds a component of capital to the human being. There are, of course, important differences between the drill and training and between capital and human capital. Barring acts of God, incredibly inept handling, or theft, the drill cannot suddenly "die" or "change jobs," as can human capital. Thus human capital is subject to "instantaneous" depreciation, with the death, disability, or job switch of the worker. Still, the analogy between investing in capital and in human capital is sufficiently close that economists have employed capital theory to study the optimal investment in human beings.[5]

When the returns to an investment in the training of people occur in future periods, we must employ a multiperiod analogue of the single-period profit-maximizing equation we have used up to now in selecting the optimum quantity of labor. The single-period

5. This section and the following Applied Micro Theories rely heavily on Gary S. Becker, "Investment in Human Capital: A Theoretical Analysis," *Journal of Political Economy* 70 (1962): 9–49; and Walter Y. Oi, "Labor as a Quasi-Fixed Factor," *Journal of Political Economy,* 70 (1962): 538–555.

analysis of labor markets hides the explanation of some important observed phenomena that are related to skill acquisition and training. Such phenomena include (1) the stability of labor employment in economic downturns despite sticky wage rates, (2) the uneven incidence of unemployment, (3) the persistence of differential labor turnover rates and quit rates in different industries, and (4) discriminatory policies in the hiring and firing of labor. The elementary neoclassical labor market model presented up to now is unable to explain these phenomena, because labor is regarded as homogeneous in such models and because the human capital aspects of investment are ignored. What can we learn about labor markets by studying hiring and training in a multiperiod analysis?

The multiperiod analogue of the single-period formula for optimal labor employment is akin to the formula for capital goods:

$$\frac{\Sigma MRP_t}{(1 + i)^t} = \frac{\Sigma w_t}{(1 + i)^t} \tag{11.25}$$

for the last worker hired. (All references to costs and revenues in this section are related to labor. Thus the subscript L denoting labor will be dropped to avoid clutter.) In Equation 11.25, the equality of the last worker's costs and revenues is expressed in terms of the present value of their respective time streams. If $MRP_t = w_t$ in each time period, then their present discounted values will also be equal. In contrast, the discounted values of revenues and costs can be equal without equality between MRP_t and w_t in each (or in any) period. The firm may take losses on its human capital investment in some periods as long as the present value of the revenues equals or exceeds the present value of wage costs.

Human Capital and General Training

Training a worker is only one of several ways to invest in human capital. (Other methods might include providing exercise programs and regular medical checkups and distributing nutrition information.) During the period of employment, typical employees increase their productivity, by either learning by doing or formal training programs. Thus workers' MRPs increase with training. If the skills they acquire are general enough to be marketable to other firms, the competitive forces in the labor market will bid up their wages until the $MRP_t = w_t$ in each time period. The newly acquired skills increase the MRP of the work force in all firms, not just in the firm providing the training. Because such **general training** involves the equality of MRP_t and w_t in each period, the present discounted values of MRP and w must also be equal. When training is general, the wage rate rises to equality with the higher MRP attributable to the training, because in a competitive labor market the workers shift jobs according to wage offers.

The firm has nothing to gain by providing general training to its work force, because the cost of training cannot be recouped by paying the workers a wage less than the MRP in future periods. The rational firm will therefore not provide any general training at its own expense. Examples of general training are typing and clerical skills, machinist skills, and medical and legal training.

It is useful to have a profit-maximizing equation in which training appears explicitly. Consider this equation:

$$MRP_0 + \sum_{t=1}^{n} \frac{MRP_t}{(1 + i)^t} = w_0 + T_0 + \sum_{t=1}^{n} \frac{w_t}{(1 + i)^t} \quad \text{(11.26)}$$

where

T_0 = training costs, incurred entirely in period 0
MRP_0 = MRP during training period 0
w_0 = wage paid during training period 0
t = time periods, where $t = 0, 1, 2, \ldots n$

The present value of the MRP in all periods equals the present value of all wage and training costs in all periods. If training is general, $MRP_t = w_t$ in each period after the training is completed. Hence

$$\sum_{t=1}^{n} \frac{MRP_t}{(1 + i)^t} = \sum_{t=1}^{n} \frac{w_t}{(1 + i)^t} \quad \text{(11.27)}$$

which implies that $MRP_0 - T_0 = w_0$ and that $MRP_0 > w_0$.

Generally trained workers must "pay" for their own training by accepting a wage during the training period that is less than MRP_0 by the amount of training costs incurred by the firm. Is this exploitation of the worker? No! The wage rate $w_0 < MRP_0$ is the value of the employment to the firm net of training costs for training that enhances the worker's future wage rates. Because the firm stands to gain nothing from this investment in human capital, the trainee pays for the training in the form of depressed wage rates. Also, general training often takes place outside the firm, as in secretarial or engineering schools.

If the worker's MRP_0 during training is negative, as might be the case for a barber or hairdresser, the training must take place in a school. The wage in period 0 would be $w_0 = MRP_0 - T_0 < -T_0 < 0$ when $MRP_0 < 0$. To be trained on the job, such a costly trainee would have to pay the firm. Better to go to barber school and pay

6. There is no analogy between the investment in general training and the collateral a bank requires when investing in physical capital. Hence a person without physical assets finds it hard if not impossible to finance an education through loans negotiated in an unregulated market. In contrast, a person with, say, a house can mortgage it to pay for an education. This inequality has led to government-guaranteed educational loans for the needy.

only the training costs than be trained on the job and pay training costs and the lost revenue that haircuts engender.[6]

Human Capital and Specific Training

Specific training occurs when received skills are not readily marketable to other firms. Thus specific training raises the MRP_t without raising the w_t, because the skills acquired in specific training are useful only to the firm providing the training and thus do not increase the marginal product of labor at the industry level, where wages are determined. Specific training includes trade secrets that are not (legally) marketable, specialized knowledge of a firm's workers,[7] and certain skills taught in the military, such as repairing missiles and shooting M-16 rifles. These skills are specific in that they cannot be transferred to other firms.

Because specific training is not marketable, the firm can increase workers' MRP without bidding up their wage to equal the higher MRP. Thus it is important to realize that the persistence of $MRP_t > w_t$ is not sufficient evidence of imperfect labor markets when specific training occurs. In the presence of specific training, the competitive market will not equate MRP_t and w_t, as suggested by the single-period neoclassical marginal productivity theory of wages. Specific training drives a wedge between MRP_t and w_t. Also, the firm can tolerate $MRP_t < w_t$ in some time periods as long as the present discounted value of the revenues equals or exceeds the present value of the wage costs.

The firm must pay the costs of specific training because the training adds to worker productivity without increasing wages; therefore, it is not a return to the worker. To illustrate, Equation 11.26 may be rewritten as

$$MRP_0 - w_0 - T_0 = \sum_{t=1}^{n} \frac{w_t}{(1+i)^t} - \sum_{t=1}^{n} \frac{MRP_t}{(1+i)^t} \quad \textbf{(11.28)}$$

But because the worker is unwilling to invest in specific training, $MRP_0 = w_0$ in the initial period. Thus

$$T_0 = \sum_{t+1}^{n} \frac{MRP_t}{(1+i)^t} - \sum_{t=1}^{n} \frac{w_t}{(1+i)^t} \quad \textbf{(11.29)}$$

Equation 11.29 states that the firm pays the training costs, which equal the difference between the present values of revenues and costs of labor.

7. The ability to get along with, organize, and motivate workers is marketable and can be gained and demonstrated by successful experience. But knowledge of specific people and their abilities is not marketable.

Economic Downturns and General versus Specific Training

APPLIED
MICRO
THEORY

11.6

The firm breaks even on generally trained workers in each period, as we have seen: $MRP_t = w_t$. Now suppose there is a reduction in the demand for the firm's product, which in turn reduces the price of output and hence the MRP of labor. When the MRP falls off a bit, the rational firm lays off some workers who have only general training. Whether the downturn proves to be short or long term, the firm can easily replace such workers when market conditions improve with other workers who have similar skills. Typically, the rule followed is "last hired, first fired," because the newest employees generally have accumulated the least specific training and hence are the most variable as a factor of production.

Let t_r refer to a time period in which the MRP for the labor input falls. Initially MRP > w for specifically trained workers. Even though MRP_{tr} is off some, it may nevertheless still exceed w_{tr}, in which event the worker will be retained. But suppose $MRP_{tr} < w_{tr}$. Under a single-period analysis, labor would be laid off. But the firm may still expect

$$\sum_{t=t_r+1}^{n} \frac{MRP_t}{(1+i)^t} > \sum_{t=t_r+1}^{n} \frac{w_t}{(1+i)^t}$$

If so, workers with specific training are retained, because the present value of MRP exceeds the present value of wage costs after the recession lets up. In this case, the worker is retained even though $MRP_{tr} < w_{tr}$, just as a piece of physical capital that is already paid for and still promises future net profits would be retained.

Specifically trained labor resembles capital as a factor of production. The capital value of the

Bob Glasheen / Photophile

training is already paid for, and a temporary downturn in demand that generates losses in some periods will not cause layoffs (as happens with generally trained workers) so long as the present value of the revenues equals or exceeds the present value of wage costs. Of course, whenever the time stream of costs exceeds the time stream of revenues, specifically trained workers will also be laid off. Even though the firm has invested training in the worker, there is no use throwing good money after bad. The training is a sunk cost and is not considered in the decision to lay off a worker whose employment diminishes the present value of the firm's profits.

The firm is also more reluctant to lay off workers with specific rather than general training because the former may take another job. As a result, the firm would lose its human capital investment. Thus workers with specific training improve their chances of keeping

their jobs during a recession by making it abundantly clear that they will seek alternative employment if laid off. The firm is thereby given an extra incentive to keep the worker and to avoid the total depreciation of its training investment. This is especially true if the downturn is expected to be of short duration or if it is merely a reduction in the demand for a particular product. If the recession affects the entire economy, there is less likelihood that laid-off workers will find work in other firms. If the firm believes workers will not seek or cannot find alternative employment, its reluctance to lay them off during a recession is diminished.

In conclusion, human capital analysis permits some broad generalization in four areas. First, schooling is generally undertaken at an early age to spread the benefits over a longer period. (However, education requires sufficient maturity, so it cannot be undertaken too early.) Second, firms will not provide specific training to employees who they think will not be around long. (Until recently, women were considered to be in this category.) Such employees tend to receive only general training and must pay for it themselves in lower wages during training. Third, the slogan "equal pay for equal work" must be interpreted in light of multiperiod analysis to mean "an equal time stream of payments for an equal time stream of MRP." It is analytically incorrect to debate the equal pay issue with reference to wage differentials in a given period. The time streams of revenues and costs of workers must be considered. Finally, workers with specific training are paid a wage less than their actual MRP but more than the competitive MRP. This strategy reduces labor quit rates and preserves the firm's investment in human capital.

The Distribution of Income in Perfectly Competitive Factor Markets

The elementary marginal productivity theory of factor pricing elucidates two broad functions of the price system: (1) Inputs are allocated to industries for which the value to society of marginal products is greatest; and (2) income (output) is distributed to the owners of factors on the basis of the value of marginal products of the factors. In this section we investigate the implications of this theory for the distribution of income.[8]

Suppose the production function for the whole economy is

$$Q = f(L, K) \tag{11.30}$$

Labor and capital are both homogeneous; all firms face parametric prices for labor and capital. The total payment to labor is $w \cdot L$, and the total payment to capital (including, for simplicity, the payment to the entrepreneur) is $r \cdot K$. Output and income are equal, so the value of output must equal the value of incomes paid to the factors. Thus

$$P \cdot Q = P \cdot f(L, K) = wL + rK \tag{11.31}$$

Figure 11.15 is a graphic depiction of the distribution of income. The area beneath the VMP_L curve equals the value of the total product produced by labor. Initially suppose that the relevant curve is VMP_L^1. When the competitive wage rate is w_1, profit-maximizing behavior leads to the employment of L_1 units of labor. The area $0ABL_1$ equals the total value of output in the economy. The VMP_L of the last worker, L_1, is $L_1B = w_1$, but the VMP_L of all inframarginal workers is greater. The sum of the VMPs of all workers measures the value of the economy's total output, $0ABL_1$. Total labor income thus equals $w_1L_1 = 0w_1BL_1$. In our two-factor model, capital receives as income the residual of total income over the income payments to labor. Thus capital receives $r \cdot K$, or area ABw_1.

Although Figure 11.15 treats capital as a residual, we are not facing a Marxian theory of surplus value. We could just as easily derive the payment to capital first by equating VMP_K and r and deriving the labor income as a residual. In fact, the prices and

---

8. Historically, theories of income distribution have been used to advance various moral positions. Karl Marx used his theory of surplus value to show how capitalism "exploits" labor. John Bates Clark, the father of the marginal productivity theory, regarded the implications of the theory an ethical utopia. Our analysis is positive rather than normative. For Clark's analysis, see John Bates Clark, *The Distribution of Wealth* (New York: Macmillan, 1900).

Figure 11.15
Income Payments to Inputs

Payments to labor and capital must sum to the total value of output produced.

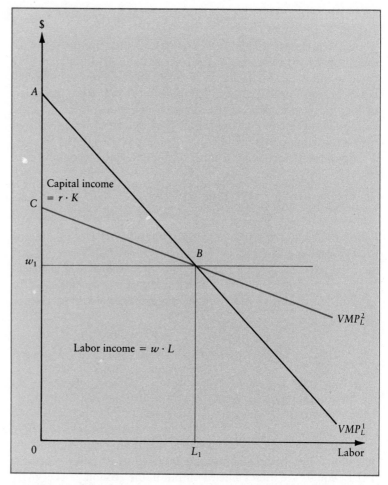

quantities of both factors are market-determined and are conveniently illustrated in the wage-labor space in Figure 11.15.

It is important to realize the difference between the total payment to a factor and the VMP of the factor at the margin. The VMP_L^2 curve in Figure 11.20 is constructed to emphasize this essential point. If the value of the marginal product of labor curve is VMP_L^1, total labor income equals $0w_1BL_1$ and capital's income is the residual ABw_1. If VMP_L^2 applies, labor's income is still $0w_1BL_1$, but capital's income falls to CBw_1. Even though the inframarginal units of labor are less productive than before, the total payment to labor is the same, because the wage and employment is determined by the value of marginal product of the last worker. The productivity of the inframarginal workers is less than before, because they are combined with less-productive complementary capital inputs. Accordingly, total production falls to $0CBL_1$, and capital's share falls to CBw_1.

The Product Exhaustion Theorem and the Adding-Up Controversy

APPLIED
MICRO
THEORY

11.7

The **product exhaustion theorem** can be stated simply: In competition, the value of output is fully distributed to each factor of production because each factor is paid its value of marginal product.* The debate over whether the product exhaustion theorem is valid has come to be called the **adding-up controversy** because the sum of factor payments may or may not equal the value of output produced when all factors are paid the value of their marginal product. Many authors conclude that the marginal productivity theory of income distribution—the competitive model of input markets—is invalid if the product exhaustion theorem does not hold.

We can use the distinction between perfect and pure competition (presented in Chapter 8) to show that the adding-up controversy is a red herring. The product exhaustion theorem is true for perfect competition but false for pure competition. Once the concept of the inframarginal firm is understood, it is easy to see why the nonvalidity of the product exhaustion theorem should never have been regarded as evidence of internal contradiction in the competitive model.

In perfect competition there is no economic profit in the long run. Each factor of production, including the entrepreneur, is paid an amount just equal to that factor's best opportunity forgone. We can write the accounting identity between output and the associated factor income payments as follows:

$$P \cdot Q = wL + rK + eE$$

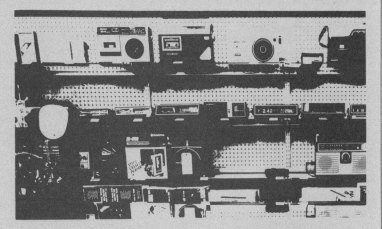

where $P \cdot Q$ is the value of total output; w, r, and e are the per-unit payments to the factors (including e, the per-unit payment to the entrepreneur); and L, K, and E are the units of inputs (including E, the effort level of entrepreneurs). Now multiply wL by $1 = MP_L/MP_L$; rK by $1 = MP_K/MP_K$; and eE by $1 = MP_E/MP_E$. The result, with some rearranging is

$$P \cdot Q = \left(\frac{w}{MP_L}\right) \cdot MP_L \cdot L +$$
$$\left(\frac{r}{MP_K}\right) \cdot MP_K \cdot K + \frac{e}{MP_E} \cdot MP_E \cdot E$$

Because each factor is paid a competitive return equal to its marginal product, we know that

$$MC = \frac{w}{MP_L} = \frac{r}{MP_K} = \frac{e}{MP_E} = P$$

Marginal cost equals the ratio of each factor's price to marginal

product and also equals product price. Thus

$$P \cdot Q = (P \cdot MP_L \cdot L) + (P \cdot MP_K \cdot K) + (P \cdot MP_E \cdot E)$$

This latter equation is the product exhaustion equation for perfect competition. It states that the value of the output equals the sum of the products of factors' VMP times factor usage. When labor, capital, and entrepreneurial resources are paid the value of their marginal product, the sum of these factor payments equals the value of the output produced.

In perfect competition, the output value of every firm is exhausted in payments to all factors, including the owner of the firm. But in pure competition, only the output value of the marginal firms is exhausted. The return to a specialized factor is not determined by

Continued on page 380

*The fount of wisdom on the product exhaustion theorem is Paul A. Samuelson, *Foundations of Economic Analysis* (New York: Atheneum, 1965), pp. 83–84.

the value of marginal product forgone on a competitive market for inframarginal firms. Instead, inframarginal rents are price-determined; that is, they rise and fall with product price. Put another way, price exceeds input market-determined costs for the inframarginal firm. So if some input, say the entrepreneur, is specialized, a rent component, R, will be added to the market-determined return to that factor. The payment to such an entrepreneur is $P \cdot MP_E + R$.

Now the accounting identity between output and income is

$$P \cdot Q = P \cdot MP_L \cdot L +$$
$$P \cdot MP_K \cdot K + (P \cdot MP_E + R) \cdot E$$

Now the value of the product is not exhausted by merely paying each factor its VMP. The product exhaustion theorem is invalid for pure competition in which certain factors receive payments in excess of opportunity costs.

In summary, whether or not product is exhausted by paying all factors, the value of their marginal product is merely a reflection of the form of the competitive model being considered. Indeed, the result

is tautological: If no factor earns a payment in excess of the market-determined opportunity costs for that factor, total revenue equals total cost; product is exhausted by factors earning VMP. If some factor is unique, its payment will not be set by market-determined opportunity costs for the factor, total revenue will exceed total market-determined costs for the factor, and product will not be exhausted by factors being paid VMP. Product exhaustion is not a test of the validity of the competitive model but rather a reflection of the particular form of competition being analyzed.

The Adding-Up Controversy and Constant Returns to Scale

11.8

Sole focus on perfect competition is in part responsible for the emphasis that economists have given to the adding-up controversy and, inadvertently, for much of the criticism of the competitive model in general. In broad terms, the reasoning has gone like this:

1. In (perfect) competition, total revenue must equal total cost (including entrepreneurial opportunity cost).

2. Distribution of the output to all inputs, including the entre-

preneur, must exactly exhaust the product, because there can be no residual (by assumption).

3. The kind of production function that assures that product is exactly exhausted by paying the factors VMP is a constant returns to scale (CRS) production function.

4. Conclusion: Perfect competition requires that firms operate with CRS production functions. This conclusion has left the competitive model wide open for criticism on at least three essential points:

1. A CRS production function for the firm would result in a horizontal long-run marginal cost curve, and no unique equilibrium would be possible.

2. If more traditional, U-shaped long-run average and marginal cost curves are used to produce a unique equilibrium, the CRS production function necessary for the adding-up property is inappropriate.

3. Empirical estimation of production functions that contradict constant returns to scale casts doubt over the usefulness of competition in modeling such firms and industries.

The key to untangling the apparent contradiction between the need for a rising long-run marginal cost curve to assure a unique equilibrium and a horizontal long-run marginal cost to guarantee product exhaustion is that the CRS production function is necessary for the industry, not the firm. But much more important, the discussion of adding up and the need for CRS production functions becomes irrelevant once the model of pure competition is employed. This is another advantage of pure competition over the perfectly competitive model.

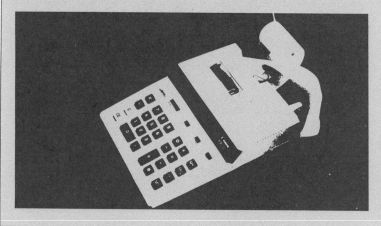

Relative Factor Shares, Elasticity of Substitution, and Public Policy

APPLIED MICRO THEORY

11.9

We can use the marginal productivity theory to investigate another aspect of income distribution: How are the **relative factor shares** of labor and capital determined, and how are these relative shares affected by public policy? The share of income paid to labor is $(w \cdot L)/(P \cdot Q)$, and the share paid to capital is $(r \cdot K)/(P \cdot Q)$. By forming a ratio of these factor shares, we can derive the relative shares of labor and capital:

$$\frac{w \cdot L}{P \cdot Q} \Big/ \frac{r \cdot K}{P \cdot Q} = \left(\frac{w}{r}\right)\left(\frac{L}{K}\right)$$

You may recall that the elasticity of substitution, σ, measures the relative ease of substituting labor for capital and vice versa (see Equation 11.8). One important question is how a change in the relative prices of inputs will affect the relative shares of income paid to the labor and capital inputs. Suppose w rises and r is fixed. Then w/r rises and firms substitute capital for labor. The effect of such substitution on the relative factor shares of income depends on the value of the elasticity of substitution, σ. Specifically, an increase in the w/r ratio will increase, decrease, or leave unchanged the relative share of labor to capital, depending on whether the elasticity of substitution, σ, is less than, greater than, or equal to unity. Let's take a concrete example. If

w/r rises by 1%, K/L will also rise by 1% if $\sigma = 1$. But a 1% rise in K/L is equivalent to a 1% fall in the inverse of K/L, which is L/K. Now look at the previous equation, the ratio of factor shares. When $\sigma = 1$, the rise in w/r is exactly offset by the proportional fall in L/K. Hence, the ratio of factor shares is unchanged.

If $\sigma < 1$, the substitution of capital for labor is more difficult. The percentage increase in w/r is greater than the percentage increase in K/L that can be accom-

plished by switching to the relatively cheaper capital input. In terms of the equation, w/r will rise more than L/K will fall. In such a case, the ratio of factor shares must rise, with labor receiving a larger share of income after the wage increase than before. By similar logic, $\sigma > 1$ will cause an increase in w/r to result in a greater than proportional switch out of labor and into capital, producing a reduction in the relative share of income paid to labor. Thus we see here what we have seen so many other times throughout the book.

Assertions about the impact of changes in one variable on another often require information about the relevant elasticities involved. The importance of elasticity in the analysis of cause and effect cannot be overemphasized. The table summarizes the relationship between changes in w/r, the elasticity of substitution, σ, and changes in the relative income shares of labor and capital.

The public-policy application of these relationships is self-evident. When government imposes minimum-wage legislation, it effectively raises the factor price ratio w/r. Presumably, minimum wages are sought as a way to increase the share of income paid to labor. But if $\sigma > 1$, which suggests very easy substitution of capital for labor, the policy will end up reducing labor's share of income, as the table reveals.

Controlling the return to capital is often discussed as a way of reducing the share of income paid to owners of capital and alleviating the "monopoly power" of the owners of capital. Thus w/r will rise if r is regulated while w is allowed to rise. But if $\sigma > 1$, the relative cheapness of capital will cause a greater than proportional substitution of capital for labor and capital's share of income will actually rise, not fall. Accordingly, elasticity is more than an entrapment for economics students; it aids in the formulation of public policy and alerts us to pitfalls inherent in certain naive policy initiatives.

Relationship among Changes in w/r, the Elasticity of Substitution, and Factor Shares of Income

When σ	An Increase in w/r Will
< 1	Increase $(w \cdot L)/(r \cdot K)$, the share of income paid to labor relative to capital
> 1	Reduce $(w \cdot L)/(r \cdot K)$, the share of income paid to labor relative to capital
$= 1$	Leave unchanged $(w \cdot L)/(r \cdot K)$, the share of income paid to labor relative to capital

Key Terms

adding-up controversy 379
average revenue product of labor
   (ARP_L) 344
derived demand 343
elasticity of substitution (σ) 352
equalizing wage differential 367
factor complementarity 350
firm's demand curve for labor 347
general training 373
human capital 372
marginal cost of labor 345
marginal productivity theory of
   wages 366
marginal revenue product (MRP) 343
marginal revenue product of labor
   (MRP_L) 344
multiperiod analysis 372
nonequalizing wage differential 368
price elasticity of labor demand 354
product exhaustion theorem 379
profit-maximizing condition 347
relative factor shares 381
specific training 375
total labor cost 345
total revenue product of labor
   (TRP_L) 343
value of marginal product of labor
   (VMP_L) 358
wage differentials 367

Summary

Every competitive firm faces the product market in which it sells its output and the inputs markets in which it purchases productive resources. Our analysis of competition began in Chapter 7, where the product market decisions of the firm received prominent consideration and factor markets played a passive, although important, role. Here we continued our study of competition, this time giving special attention to the input markets.

The two cornerstones of this chapter are marginal revenue product, which is the foundation of factor demand analysis, and ordinal consumer theory, which underlies factor supply. Factor demand rsults from the optimization decisions of firms, and factor supply curves result from the optimization decisions of resource owners.

This chapter employed multiperiod analysis to explain the investment in physical and human capital. It distinguished between general and specific training and outlined the types of training likely to be paid for by the employer and by the employee.

The chapter concluded by examining various implications of the competitive model for the distribution of income. The adding-up controversy—a major criticism of the perfectly competitive model—was shown to be irrelevant when inframarginal firms are allowed in an analysis of pure competition.

Problems

1. Why do we tax capital gains but not human capital gains?
2. Medical schools typically prefer applicants in their 20s rather than over 35. Does this necessarily constitute age discrimination?
3. Suppose that the probability of success in medical school, P, is a function of past environment, E, and MCAT scores, S: $P = f(E, S)$. Make an economic argument for requiring people with intellectual home environments to achieve a higher MCAT score than students from intellectually sterile home environments. Suppose such a practice were called discriminatory. Develop the counterargument that to use scores alone would be discriminatory.
4. Explain why research and teaching are complementary factors in the production of education.
5. Explain why a firm will provide executive training programs but not secretarial training programs.
6. Suppose that labor is heterogeneous, not homogeneous. Will the demand for labor still slope downward? Why or why not?
7. What is the output of a university? Are the professors factors of production, or are they entrepreneurs?
8. "Minimum-wage laws protect highly skilled workers from the competition of low-skilled workers." How can this statement be true if the mere existence of unemployed workers brings down all wages?
9. "Unionized workers do not enjoy higher income than non-unionized workers because investors are less willing to invest in enterprises that are union shops. Thus productivity in union shops falls to the nonunionized level." Is the theory of this chapter consistent with this statement?

10. "Open immigration into the United States would benefit the average American and the migrant." Comment.

11. "There are only a fixed number of jobs to go around." Comment.

12. "If the supply curve of labor bends backward above some wage, then it is possible for the demand curve to lie everywhere above the supply curve; hence no equilibrium." Comment.

13. a. Why must the MRP_L curve intersect the wage line from above for profit maximization?
    b. $TVC = w \cdot L$, and $TC_L = w \cdot L$. Why then is the TVC curve not linear, as the TC_L curve is?
    c. What are the principal shift parameters?

14. List as many analogies as you can between output and input analysis.

15. What is the effect of the minimum wage on the supply of illegal aliens in the United States? If the minimum wages were abolished, would the number of jobs for legal workers increase or decrease? (What elasticity information do you need to answer this question?) If the minimum wage were mandated to cover all workers, legal and illegal, what would happen to the number of jobs for legal workers?

16. "Jobs are moving to the Sun Belt." What is the cause of such movement? What equilibrating forces would you expect to put an end to such movement. Which of the equilibrium equations presented in this chapter would you expect to hold in the long run?

17. Some unions bargain for more overtime while others bargain for less. Explain.

18. Use the theory of specific human capital to explain why firms and universities offer early retirement benefits. Treat the human capital of the early retiree and the younger replacement.

19. University tenure systems provide lifetime job security upon promotion to the tenured faculty. Explain why this is needed to protect the integrity of research. What would happen to university salaries if tenure were abolished.

20. When product price falls below ATC in a firm, why not cut wages to make labor absorb part of the loss.

21. In Applied Micro Theory 11.2, an analysis of the impact of Social Security benefits on work incentives is considered. Suppose that the facts are changed and that above some level one must pay income taxes on the benefits, rather than relinquish them. Show how this would change the analysis.

22. Use an income-leisure diagram to illustrate the policy of reducing an income guarantee while reducing the income tax for low-income persons.

23. Illustrate on an income-leisure diagram the work incentives of a lump-sum payment for work upon completion of a certain number of work hours. Are there any advantages for the employer in such a plan? Compare the amount that needs to be paid and the hours that can be coaxed out of workers under this pay plan versus straight hourly wages.

24. The latest rage is the microcomputer, which can be used in the home without much formal education in computing. Usually com-

puter stores provide a great deal of in-store explanation and advice. Why not dispense with these services and the associated costs and charge a lower price? Is the expertise specific training or general training?

Suggested Readings

Becker, Gary. "Investment in Human Capital: A Theoretical Analysis." *Journal of Political Economy* 70 (1962): 9–49.

Clark, John Bates. *The Distribution of Wealth.* New York: Macmillan, 1968.

Hicks, J. *The Theory of Wages.* New York: Macmillan, 1932.

Hirshleifer, J. "An Exposition of the Equilibrium of the Firm: Symmetry between Product and Factor Analysis." *Economica* 24 (1962): 263–268.

Marshall, A. *Principles of Economics,* book V. London: Macmillan, 1922, chap. 6.

Stigler, George. *The Theory of Price.* New York: Macmillan, 1966, chaps. 14 and 16.

The Factors
of Production:
Imperfect Competition

Chapter 11 set forth the profit-maximizing rules of input use and output production for firms that are competitive in both selling output and purchasing inputs. This chapter shows how these rules are modified by the introduction of monopoly in input and output markets and explains the effect of such monopoly power on resource allocation. Monopoly can take many forms, all of which affect input use and resource allocation. Finally, this chapter shows that there are inputs so unique that their supply curves are perfectly inelastic (Muhammed Ali, Henry Kissinger, or Kareem Abdul Jabbar, for example). How are the factor payments to these unique resources determined?

Profit Maximization and Market Structure

For this section, we can assume that labor is the only variable input of firms. Thus each firm faces two markets simultaneously: the product market and the labor market. Each firm is either competitive or monopolistic in each market and thus falls into one of these four categories:

Competitor in labor and output markets.

Competitor in labor market, monopolist in output market.

Monopolist in labor market, competitor in output market.

Monopolist in labor and output markets.

These four permutations provide a handy structure for studying the profit-maximizing rules of firms under different market conditions. *Monopolist* is used here to stand for any type of market structure that is not competitive, that is, not characterized by price-taking behavior.

12

Competitor in Labor and Output Markets

In selecting the best use of the labor input, every firm follows this general rule:

$$MRP_L = MC_L \qquad (12.1)$$

But $MRP_L = VMP_L$ and $MC_L = w$ when the firm is competitive in output and labor markets. Thus, Equation 12.1 becomes

$$VMP_L = MP_L \cdot P = w \qquad (12.2)$$

This competitive firm hires labor until the VMP_L equals the wage. Note carefully that Equation 12.2 is written in labor input language. But we know from Chapter 7 that, when the firm can buy any desired amount of labor services at the market-determined wage, marginal cost equals the ratio of the wage to the marginal product of labor:

$$MC = \frac{w}{MP_L} \qquad (12.3)$$

Solving Equation 12.3 for w and substituting into Equation 12.2 yields

$$MC = P \qquad (12.4)$$

Equation 12.4, the profit-maximizing condition for output, is written in output language. It is clear that Equations 12.2 and 12.4 are equivalent profit-maximizing conditions; the one is implied by and derived from the other. The link between these equivalent rules is the production-cost duality statement contained in Equation 12.3.

Figure 12.1 illustrates graphically the duality of the profit-maximizing conditions expressed in Equations 12.2 and 12.4. The

Figure 12.1
Profit Maximization for a Competitor in the Labor and Product Markets

(a) In the labor market, $VMP_L = w$.
(b) In the product market, $MC = P$.

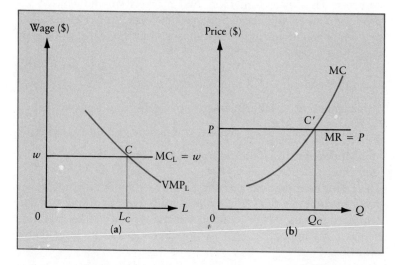

marginal equality at point C in panel a and at point C' in panel b are not two separate conditions but rather two ways of illustrating the same profit-maximizing condition.

Competitor in Labor Market, Monopolist in Output Market

Suppose a firm displays some monopoly power in the sale of its output; that is, it faces a downward-sloping demand curve for its output. At the same time, let the firm face the wage rate as a parameter in the labor market. This firm, like all others, maximizes profit by equating MRP_L and MC_L. The MC_L equals the wage rate as long as the firm is a competitive buyer of labor services. The real interest here is the specification of the firm's MRP_L curve. The most general definition of MRP_L is

$$MRP_L = MP_L \cdot MR \qquad (12.5)$$

The MRP_L measures the additional total revenue arising from the hiring of an extra worker. Two forces exert an influence on the revenue that the last worker contributes: (1) the marginal product of labor, MP_L, and (2) the amount the firm can charge for the added output, MR. If the firm is a price taker, $P = MR$ and $MRP_L = VMP_L$. as shown in Chapter 11.

However, the simple monopolist faces a downward-sloping demand curve for its product and cannot sell the last worker's extra output without lowering the price on the last unit sold as well as on all units sold previously at a higher price. Chapter 7 defined marginal revenue as

$$MR = P + Q\frac{\Delta P}{\Delta Q} \qquad (12.6)$$

Marginal revenue is the algebraic sum of the price received for the marginal unit sold, P, and the reduction in price on all inframarginal units sold previously at a higher price, $Q \cdot (\Delta P/\Delta Q)$. The term $\Delta P/\Delta Q$ is the (negative) slope of the demand curve. The competitive firm faces a demand curve of zero slope; when $\Delta P/\Delta Q = 0$, $MR = P$. But for the monopolist, $MR < P$, because $\Delta P/\Delta Q < 0$. Thus the monopolist receives only the MR as a result of selling an additional unit of output. For the monopolist, MR (instead of P) is used to define the MRP_L curve.

Figure 12.2 illustrates the equivalence of the profit-maximizing rules for input and output in the firm under consideration. Labor use is set by point M in panel a, where

$$MRP_L = MP_L \cdot MR = w \qquad (12.7)$$

Figure 12.2
Profit Maximization for a Competitor in the Labor Market, a Monopolist in the Product Market

(a) In the labor market, $\text{MRP}_L = w$.
(b) In the product market, $\text{MC} = \text{MR}$.

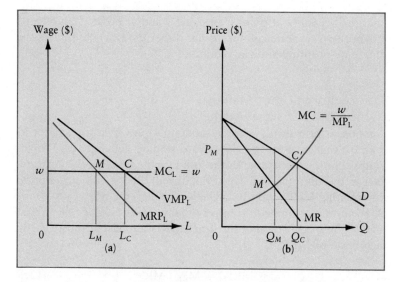

But Equation 12.7 implies that $\text{MR} = w/\text{MP}_L$, which we know from Equation 12.3 also equals MC. Thus output is maximized at point M' in panel b, where

$$\text{MC} \equiv \frac{w}{\text{MP}_L} = \text{MR} \tag{12.8}$$

Points M and M' violate the efficiency conditions because each is derived from the monopoly proposition that $P > \text{MR}$. If the monopolist is forced to equate P and MC, the optimizing points would shift to points C and C'. Output would rise to the competitive level, Q_C; labor use would increase to the competitive optimum, L_C. At L_C and Q_C the efficiency conditions $\text{VMP}_L = w$ and $P = \text{MC}$ are satisfied. Thus equating MC and MR in panel b is equivalent to equating w and MRP_L in panel a. Both represent a misallocation of resources caused by the $P > \text{MR}$ characteristic of monopoly.

Monopsonist in Labor Market, Competitor in Output Market

In speaking of monopolies in factor markets, economists use the term **monopsony**. Just as a monopolist is the only seller in its output market, so the monopsonist is the only buyer of inputs in the factor markets. For example, Kennecott Copper Corporation is a monopsonist in Ruth, Nevada, where the only important industry is copper mining and the only mining company hiring workers is Kennecott. In this section we can assume that the monopsonist is a competitor in the sale of its output. How does the monopsonist select its best labor use?

As always, the firm maximizes profit by selecting labor so that $MRP_L = MC_L$. And MRP_L equals VMP_L by virtue of our present assumption that the firm is a product market competitor. For monopsony, our point of departure is the MC_L curve. The full specification for MC_L is

$$MC_L = w + L \cdot \frac{\Delta w}{\Delta L} \qquad (12.9)$$

Note the similarity between the definitions of MR and MC_L. The additional cost of hiring an extra worker has two components: the higher wage, w, that must be paid the marginal worker as an inducement to enter the work force and the increase in the wages of all inframarginal workers who were previously earning a lower wage, $L \cdot (\Delta w / \Delta L)$. The term $\Delta w / \Delta L$ is the slope of the supply curve for labor. Under labor market competition, the firm can hire any amount of labor at the going wage, so $\Delta w / \Delta L = 0$ and $MC_L = w$. Thus, just as the competitive firm for output faces a horizontal demand curve equal to price, the competitive firm in labor hiring faces a horizontal supply curve of labor equal to the wage. And just as the output monopolist faces the industry demand curve for output, the monopsonist faces the industry supply curve for labor. Abstracting from wage discrimination for the moment—a procedure whereby the firm can pay similar workers different wages—an expansion of the labor force requires bidding up the wage, not just for the last worker hired, but for all workers. Because $\Delta w / \Delta L > 0$ for a positively sloped industry supply curve of labor, $MC_L > w$ for the monopsonist. The analogy between simple monopoly and monopsony is perfect: For monopoly, $MR < P$; for monopsony, $MC_L > w$.

Figure 12.3 exhibits this analysis. The curve labeled S_L in panel a is the upward-sloping supply curve of labor; within the wage range shown, additional workers can be brought into the work force only by raising the wage offer to equal the reservation wages of workers who are increasingly reluctant to work. Just as a demand curve is an average revenue curve, the labor supply curve is the average cost of labor curve. Definitionally and intuitively, the **average cost of labor (AC_L)** is the wage:

$$AC_L = \frac{TC_L}{L} = \frac{w \cdot L}{L} = w \qquad (12.10)$$

Using our knowledge of the average/marginal relationship between curves, we know that, for the average curve to rise, the marginal curve must lie above the average curve. Figure 12.3a shows that, when the firm faces an upward-sloping labor supply

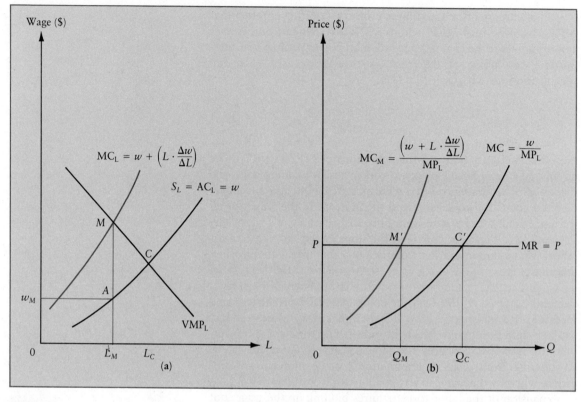

Figure 12.3
Profit Maximization for a Monopsonist in the Labor Market, a Competitor in the Product Market

(a) In the labor market, $VMP_L = MC_L$. (b) In the product market, $MC_M = P$.

curve ($S_L = AC_L = w$), the MC_L curve lies above the AC_L curve for each level of labor employment.

In order to reinforce the conclusion that $MP_L > AC_L$ under monopsony, Table 12.1 presents a numerical example. The first two columns represent the industry labor supply curve facing the firm. Suppose the firm presently has 1 worker at a wage of $0.50 per time period. If the monopsonist wishes to increase its labor force to 2 workers, the increase in labor costs, MC_L, will be

$$MC_L = w + L\frac{\Delta w}{\Delta L} = \$1.00 + 1(\frac{\$0.50}{1}) = \$1.50 \quad (12.11)$$

Table 12.1
MC_L and $AC_L = w$ Compared

Worker	$AC_L = w$	MC_L
1	$0.50	$0.50
2	1.00	1.50
3	1.50	2.50
4	2.00	3.50

Total costs rise by $1.50: the $1.00 wage paid to worker 2 plus the extra $0.50 paid to worker 1. The MC_L figures for all workers are listed in the last column of Table 12.1. Except in the case of the first worker hired, $MC_L > w$. For this reason, the MC_L curve lies above the $S_L = AC_L$ in Figure 12.3a. Whenever the firm must raise the wage to attract more workers, as the monopsonist must do, the MC_L exceeds the wage. The symmetry between the analysis of monopsony and monopoly should be crystal clear.

With reference again to Figure 12.3, the monopsonist achieves the $VMP_L = MC_L$ profit-maximizing condition at point M by hiring L_M units of labor. Note that the maximum wage needed to attract a work force of L_M is $w_M = L_M A$. In other words, the MC_L curve is used to establish optimal labor use, but the $AC_L = S_L$ curve is employed to determine the wage rate (just as the monopolist uses the MR curve to determine output but the $AR = D$ curve to set product price). The marginal worker contributes $L_M \cdot M$ to the revenues of the monopsonist and receives a wage of only $L_M \cdot A$. The difference between the last worker's contribution to revenue and the wage rate, AM, is a measure of the **monopsonistic exploitation of labor.** No political connotation need be attached to this phrase; it is merely used to describe how a firm with monopsonistic power limits employment instead of expanding labor employment to L_C, the competitive level of employment for which workers are paid the value of their marginal product.

Figure 12.3b shows the product market equivalent of the $VMP_L = MC_L$ labor market condition. Up to now, we have concentrated on the production-cost duality contained in Equation 12.3. However, such duality presumes that the firm is a competitive purchaser of labor, in which case $MC_L = w$. Now that we deal with monopsony in the purchase of labor, we need a more careful definition of the firm's marginal cost of output. Under competitive purchasing of labor, the marginal cost of production can increase only by the hiring of more labor. Thus

$$MC = \frac{\Delta TC_L}{\Delta Q} = \frac{w \cdot \Delta L}{\Delta Q} = \frac{w}{MP_L} \qquad (12.12)$$

But the monopsonist must increase the wage to attract more workers. Accordingly, w must be replaced in the duality Equation 12.12 by the complete expression for MC_L contained in Equation 12.9:

$$MC_M = \frac{w + L \cdot \dfrac{\Delta w}{\Delta L}}{MP_L} \qquad (12.13)$$

The term MC_M denotes the monopsonist's marginal cost curve, as distinct from MC, the marginal cost curve of a wage-taking firm. Because the term $\Delta w/\Delta L$ is positive for an upward-sloping labor supply curve, the numerator in the definition of MC_M (Equation 12.13) exceeds the numerator in the definition of MC (Equation 12.12). Thus $MC_M > MC$ at each level of output. The monopsonist's MC_M curve is shown in Figure 12.3b. The MC_M curve lies above the MC curve at each level of output.

We have already seen that the monopsonist that is an output market competitor selects labor so that $VMP_L = MC_L$. But because $MC_L = w + L \cdot (\Delta w/\Delta L)$ for the monopsonist, the rule may be rewritten as

$$VMP_L = MP_L \cdot P = w + L \cdot \frac{\Delta w}{\Delta L} \tag{12.14}$$

Equation 12.14 is equivalent to

$$P = \frac{w + L\dfrac{\Delta w}{\Delta L}}{MP_L} \tag{12.15}$$

The term to the right of the equal sign equals MC_M, as previously shown. Thus the monopsonist selects its output by equating P and MC_M, which occurs at point M' in Figure 12.3b. The monopsonistic output Q_M (instead of the competitive output Q_C) and the monopsonistic labor use L_M (instead of the competitive labor use L_C) are reflections of the same problem: $MC_L > w$ for the monopsonist. The efficiency conditions are manifestly violated by monopsony.

Monopsonist in Labor Market, Monopolist in Output Market

This last case, in which the firm has monopoly power over both its output price and the wage paid to workers, can be handled expeditiously, because we have already covered the necessary analysis. When the firm is a monopolist in both its markets, the profit-maximizing rule is

$$MRP_L = MC_L \tag{12.16}$$

and is achieved at point M in Figure 12.4. The wage rate is $w_M = L_MA$. Labor exploitation is now AB, the difference between the VMP_L (the value that society places on the marginal product of labor) and the wage rate. Labor hiring is now suppressed to L_M by two forces: (1) The firm is a product monopolist, hence it employs

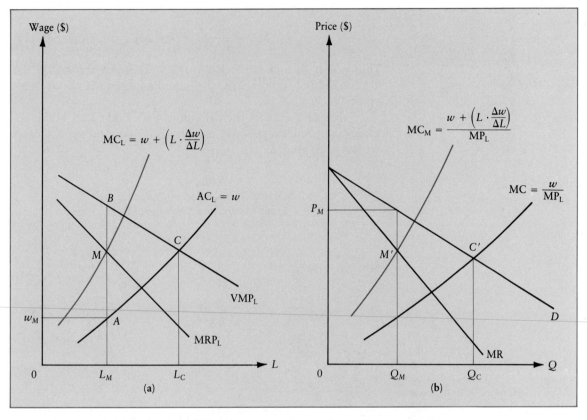

the MRP_L curve in its decisions instead of the VMP_L curve necessary for efficiency; (2) the firm is an input monopsonist and therefore uses the MC_L curve instead of the wage in its decisions. If the firm were forced to equate w and VMP_L, (or equivalently, P and MC), labor use would rise to L_C, the competitive ideal. Thus inefficient labor use, L_M, is the manifestation of monopoly and monopsony combined.

In the product market the firm employs the MR and MC_M curves in its decisionmaking. Thus the firm selects its output by equating MR and MC_M at point M' in Figure 12.4b. Here also the competitive output rate, Q_C, is not obtained, because monopoly and monopsony forces cause the firm to maximize profits with reference to curves that are inconsistent with competition. As before, the profit-maximizing labor use (panel a) and output (panel b) are simultaneously determined. For labor utilization,

$$\text{MRP}_L \equiv \text{MP}_L \cdot \text{MR} = w + L \frac{\Delta w}{\Delta L} \equiv \text{MC}_L \qquad \text{(12.17)}$$

But Equation 12.17 can be rewritten as

Figure 12.4
Profit Maximization for a Monopsonist in the Labor Market, a Monopolist in the Product Market

(a) In the labor market, $\text{MRP}_L = \text{MC}_L$. (b) In the product market, $\text{MC}_M = \text{MR}$.

$$MR = \frac{w + L\frac{\Delta w}{\Delta L}}{MP_L} \equiv MC_M \qquad (12.18)$$

Thus points M and M' in Figure 12.4 are manifestations of the firm's monopoly power: $MR < P$ (monopoly) and $MC_L > w$ (monopsony).

Table 12.2 collects the definitions and Table 12.3 brings together the profit-maximizing conditions for the four general cases we have just studied.

Table 12.2
Marginal Terms Used in Analyzing the
Profit-Maximizing Behavior of Firms

Term	If	Then
$MR = P + Q\frac{\Delta P}{\Delta Q}$	$\frac{\Delta P}{\Delta Q} = 0$	$MR = P$
$MC = \frac{(w + L\frac{\Delta w}{\Delta L})}{MP_L}$	$\frac{\Delta w}{\Delta L} = 0$	$MC = \frac{w}{MP_L}$
$MC_L = w + L\frac{\Delta w}{\Delta L}$	$\frac{\Delta w}{\Delta L} = 0$	$MC_L = w$
$MRP_L = MP_L \cdot MR$	$MR = P$	$MRP_L = VMP_L$

Table 12.3
Profit-Maximizing Conditions under Alternative Market Structures

Product Market	Labor Market	
	Competitor	Monopsonist
Competitor	$VMP_L = w$ or $MC = P$	$VMP_L = MC_L$ or $MC_M = P$
Monopolist	$MRP_L = w$ or $MC = MR$	$MRP_L = MC_L$ or $MC_M = MR$

Labor Demand Curve for the Imperfectly Competitive Firm

Chapter 11 established that the labor demand curve for the competitive firm and industry depends on the shift parameters underlying the firms' VMP_L curves; it also showed how changes in the wage rate affect these shift parameters and in turn the position of the VMP_L curves. The basic building block in deriving the demand for labor is the MRP_L curve, which equals VMP_L for the output competitor.

A similar analysis applies to labor demand for the monopolist or imperfect competitor in output markets. We start with the MRP_L curve (not the VMP_L) and move to the firm's demand curve by proper attention to the shift parameters in the MRP_L curve. For the monopolist, the MRP_L curve may be written

$$MRP_L = MP_L \cdot MR = MRP_L\Big|_{K,\ r} \qquad (12.19)$$

When labor is the only variable input, the MRP_L curve is the labor demand curve, because a change in the wage will not affect capital (K) or the rental rate of capital (r). In contrast, a change in the wage rate will affect K and r if capital is variable, if labor and capital are complementary, and if the supply curve of capital displays a positive elasticity. Thus the MRP_L curve may shift when the wage changes. The monopolist's labor demand curve is the connection of all profit-maximizing wage-labor combinations. Each point on the labor demand curve represents a profit-maximizing amount of labor and therefore satisfies the condition $MRP_L = w$ (if the firm is a wage taker) or $MRP_L = MC_L$ (if the firm is a monopsonist). In other words, the position of the MRP_L curve determines the labor hired at a given wage. If a wage rate change shifts the MRP_L curve, the new quantity of labor demanded at the new wage will be a point on the new curve. Thus each MRP_L curve contributes one point to the labor demand curve.

This analysis is brief because it does not differ from that in Chapter 11—except that the basis for the monopolist's labor demand is the MRP_L curve, not the VMP_L curve. As before, the monopolist's labor demand curve must be negatively sloped. The marginal productivity theory does not make allowance for a "Giffen input"—an input that exhibits a positively sloped demand curve.

Monopsony and Wage Discrimination

In our analysis of monopsony, we have assumed that the firm pays the same wage to all workers. This is a case of "simple monopsony." However, a monopsonist may be able to engage in **monopsonistic wage discrimination,** meaning that it is able to pay different wages to workers. It is useful to study the behavior of the discriminating monopsonist in contrast to the simple monopsonist in order to gain insight into the profit incentives that encourage the firm to discriminate.

The first three columns of Table 12.4 repeat the information in Table 12.1, which we used previously to distinguish between the

Table 12.4
Perfect Wage Discrimination: $MC_L(disc.) = S_L$ and $AC_L < S_L$

Worker	$w = AC_L = S_L$ (No Discrimination)	MC_L (No Discrimination)	MC_L (Discrimination)	TC_L (Discrimination)	AC_L (Discrimination)
1	$0.50	$0.50	$0.50	$0.50	$0.50
2	1.00	1.50	1.00	1.50	0.75
3	1.50	2.50	1.50	3.00	1.00
4	2.00	3.50	2.00	5.00	1.25

AC_L and MC_L curves of the simple monopsonist: MC_L exceeds AC_L $= S_L$ because the nondiscriminating monopsonist cannot pay its workers different wages. How is the labor supply curve related to the MC_L curve for the perfect wage discriminator? The fourth column in Table 12.4 measures the MC_L when it is assumed that each marginal worker can be paid the wage necessary to induce the worker to join the labor force but that the inframarginal workers already employed continue to earn the reservation wages at which they were hired. Thus worker 1 is hired at a wage of $0.50. Worker 2 is hired at a wage of $1.00. and worker 1 continues to earn only $0.50 per time period. Worker 3 is hired at $1.50, but the wages of workers 2 and 1 remain fixed. Under such hiring circumstances, the marginal cost of hiring an additional worker equals the wage rate. Thus the supply of labor equals the MC_L under perfect wage discrimination. In Table 12.4, note that the second and fourth columns are equal. Note too that the AC_L does not equal the wage rate under perfect wage discrimination, as it did before. Because the wages of previously hired workers are kept at initial levels when hiring a new worker, the AC_L is less than the wage paid for the last worker hired. The last two columns in Figure 12.4 complete the arithmetic for TC_L and AC_L. Except for the first worker, $w = MC_L > AC_L$ under the assumptions of perfect wage discrimination.

Figure 12.5 depicts the case of perfect wage discrimination by the monopsonist. Assuming the firm is a competitor in the output market, the VMP_L curve is relevant to the firm's profit maximization. The firm maximizes profit by equating VMP_L and MC_L. But as we have just seen, the MC_L curve of the perfect wage discriminator is equivalent to the labor supply curve! Thus $VMP_L = MC_L(disc.)$ at point C in Figure 12.5. Curiously, perfect wage discrimination results in the competitive wage (w_C) and labor use (L_C) and, by implication, the competitive level of output. If the firm had no power to conduct wage discrimination, the MC_L would equal $MC_L(no\ disc.)$, in which case VMP_L would equal $MC_L(no\ disc.)$ at point M. The inefficient labor use L_M and wage w_M would result, along with the exploitation of labor equal to AM. Thus another

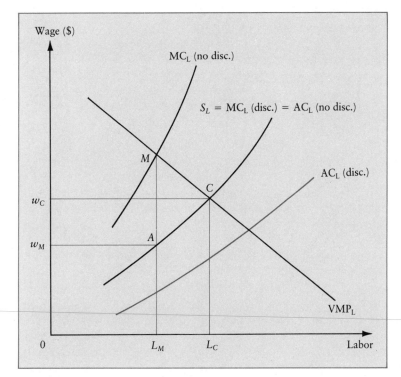

Figure 12.5
Perfect Wage Discrimination

The competitive level L_C is chosen where $VMP_L = MC_L$ (disc.)

interesting aspect of perfect wage discrimination is the elimination of labor exploitation at the margin, because at point C, $VMP_L = w$ for the last worker.

As Table 12.4 discloses, $AC_L < w$ under perfect wage discrimination. Figure 12.5 shows the AC_L(disc.) curve as a colored line; for each level of labor utilization, $AC_L < S_L = w$. Recall from Chapter 9 that perfect monopoly price discrimination breaks the equality between P and AR and that the competitive level of output is produced by the perfect price discriminator. Our present results concerning the perfect monopsonist wage discriminator are the labor market analogues of the monopoly findings.

The principal lesson to be learned here is that the monopsonist has profit incentives to discriminate in its wage policies, because wage discrimination results in lower labor costs for each level of hiring and production. The most self-evident forms of wage discrimination are those based on seniority, sex, age, and race. Less blatant but still profitable wage discrimination may arise if the firm is able to maintain strict secrecy in the work force about wages. (Many private universities have a secrecy code that bars faculty members from discussing their salary structures.) Such practices increase the profits of the monopsonist but, by lowering labor costs, allow the firm to approach the competitive level of labor hiring and output production.

Figure 12.6
Labor Exploitation

AM = monopsonistic exploitation;
MB = monopolistic exploitation.

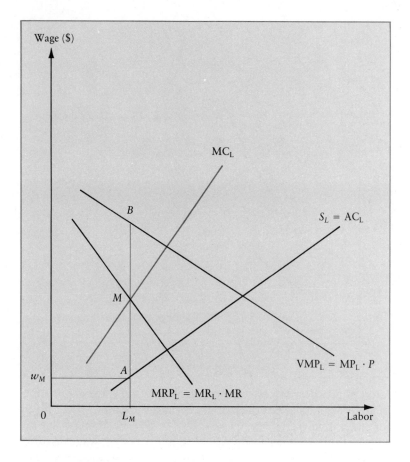

Labor Exploitation

Sprinkled throughout this chapter are several references to the *exploitation* of labor. This is a loaded term, full of political, emotional, and normative connotations. For this reason, we should clarify what is and is not meant by it.

Consider Figure 12.6, which exhibits the various labor cost and revenue curves of a firm that is a simple monopolist in its product market and a simple monopsonist in its labor market. The firm maximizes profit by equating MRP_L and MC_L at point M, hiring L_M units of labor, and paying the wage $w_M = L_M A$. Professor Joan Robinson defines labor exploitation as the difference between the VMP_L of labor and the wage paid the work force.[1] In Figure 12.6, the VMP_L of the L_Mth worker is $L_M B$ and the wage is $L_M A$. Thus labor exploitation is measured by the distance AB. Note that AB can be divided between AM, monopsonistic exploitation, and MB, **monopolistic exploitation.** The full exploitation, AB, is attributable to two monopolistic forces: $MC_L < S_L$, or monopsony, and MRP_L

1. Joan Robinson, *The Economics of Imperfect Competition*, 2nd ed. (London, Macmillan, 1969; originally published 1933).

Monopsony and the Minimum Wage

APPLIED MICRO THEORY

12.1

The conventional analysis of minimum wages holds that employment will be reduced when firms face minimum wages in excess of uncontrolled wages. The reason is that the higher minimum wage forces the firm to move up its demand curve for labor. However, Professor Robinson demonstrated that the minimum wage can increase employment if the firm is a monopsonist.* The accompanying figure illustrates this curious result. Assuming that the monopsonist faces parametric prices for its output and assuming that the firm's labor demand curve is VMP_L, the profit-maximizing level of labor employment is L_M, for which $VMP_L = MC_L$ and the monopsonist's wage is w_M. Suppose a minimum wage of $\bar{w}$ is adopted. The supply curve of labor becomes $\bar{w}AB$ and is kinked at A. Also, the MC_L curve changes. Over the range $\bar{w}A$ of the labor supply curve, $MC_L = S_L = \bar{w}$. At the kink of the S_L curve at A, the MC_L curve is undefined. For labor greater than L_1, the firm pays a wage greater than the minimum wage, $\bar{w}$, and the MC_L segment CE becomes relevant. Thus the MC_L curve is $\bar{w}ACE$. Now the firm maximizes profits by hiring L_1 units of labor at the minimum wage, $\bar{w}$, because $VMP_L = MC_L$ at A. The minimum wage lowers the MC_L of labor even though it raises the wage. Profit incentives induce the firm to expand hiring until the VMP_L equals the lower MC_L. Thus minimum wages increase employment and reduce labor exploitation.

Milton Friedman calls Robinson's analysis a "theoretical curiosum."† Friedman notes that the

*Robinson, *Imperfect Competition*, p. 295.

†Milton Friedman, *Price Theory: A Provisional Text* (Chicago: Aldine, 1962), p. 190.

The Minimum Wage and Employment in a Monopsony

A minimum wage flattens the MC_L curve up to point A. Thus employment rises from L_M to L_1.

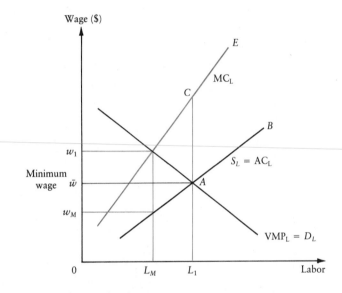

result occurs only if the minimum wage falls between w_M and w_1 and that there is no presumption that the minimum wage will be set in that interval. Also, Friedman doubts that significant degrees of monopsony are likely among firms hiring the kind of inputs affected by minimum-wage rates.

However, Robinson's analysis of minimum wages in monopsony is more than just curious—it is incomplete and misleading. Specifically, the analysis fails to consider the effect of long-run entry and exit. The monopsonist under discussion is a competitor in the output market. If such a firm is earning zero economic profit before the imposition of the minimum wage, the firm needs the monopsony rents to stay in business. When

wage costs rise due to the minimum wage, the firm must exit the industry. For such firms, the minimum wage reduces employment to zero!

In product market competitive equilibrium, the minimum wage drives some previously marginal firms out of business, causing the industry supply curve for output to fall until product price rises enough to cover the increased labor costs of the remaining marginal firms in equilibrium. Thus the effect of minimum wages on employment is uncertain even in the presence of monopsony: Employment may increase in firms that do not require the monopsony rents to break even but will fall among firms that break even previous to the minimum wage.

$< \text{VMP}_L$, or product monopoly. As long as monopoly exists in either the labor or the product market of the firm, the VMP_L will exceed the wage and labor exploitation will exist. Accordingly, labor exploitation is the direct result of monopoly (including monopsony). Eliminate all monopoly forces in all markets, and labor exploitation vanishes.

Bilateral Monopoly

The analysis of monopsony assumed tacitly that the wage and labor employment decisions of the monopsonist would be acceptable to the sellers of labor, who offer their labor services competitively. But suppose a monopsonistic buyer of labor had to deal with a monopoly seller of labor. Such an economic confrontation between monopolists on both sides of the labor market is called **bilateral monopoly**. For example, in Ruth, Nevada, bilateral monopoly in the market for copper-mining employees is in evidence; Kennecott Copper Corporation is the only important buyer of labor services, and the local copper workers' union acts as a monopoly seller of labor. Thus wage and employment decisions must be hammered out in collective bargaining sessions between the union and the firm's management.

Wage and employment variables are indeterminate under bilateral monopoly. In this context, *indeterminate* means that the model is unable to predict the equilibrium values for w and L. It does not mean that the two parties cannot strike a bargain but rather that the actual wage bargain will depend on considerations not included in the profit-maximizing model.

Figure 12.7 contains the bilateral monopoly theoretical apparatus. The supply and demand curves for labor are labeled S and D. The labor supply curve, S, is equivalent to the average cost of labor curve for the monopsonist, which is labeled AC_{buyer}. We have already seen the derivation of the marginal cost of labor curve that is associated with the average cost of labor curve. The curve labeled MC_{buyer} is the monopsonist's marginal cost of labor curve; it lies above the labor supply curve. The arrows in Figure 12.7 reinforce the tie between AC_{buyer} and MC_{buyer}.

The demand curve for labor, D, may or may not be the monopsonist's MRP_L curve. Either way, it measures the marginal revenue that an extra worker provides the firm. Thus the labor demand curve is labeled MR_{buyer}. The monopsonist selects its profit-maximizing labor use, L_{buyer}, by equating MC_{buyer} and MR_{buyer} at point B and paying wage w_{buyer}.

Now let's consider the choices of the union, which we can assume is a monopolist in the selling of labor services. The labor demand curve, D, is equivalent to the average revenue earned per worker. Thus D is labeled AR_{seller}. The curve labeled MR_{seller} is the

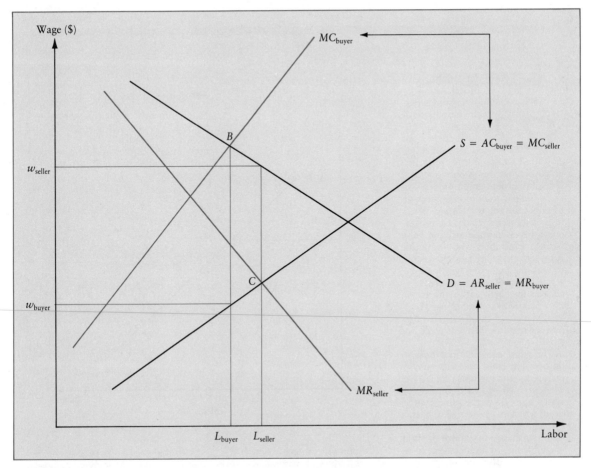

Figure 12.7
Bilateral Monopoly

The equilibrium wage and labor use are indeterminate in a bilateral monopoly.

standard MR curve of the monopolist. This curve measures the additional revenue that union employees receive when employment is expanded by all workers accepting a lower wage. Once again, arrows tie the AR_{seller} and MR_{seller} curves together.

The seller's marginal cost curve, MC_{seller}, is the firm's supply curve. The union will maximize the net benefits of its hired employees (the difference between total wage earnings of workers and the total cost of providing the labor services) by equating MR_{seller} and MC_{seller} at point C. The union will accordingly want to have L_{seller} workers hired at wage w_{seller}. And herein lies the difficulty. The monopolist seller of labor (the union) seeks a higher wage and more employment than the monopsonist (firm management). The most that can be said is that collective bargaining will result in a wage between w_{seller} and w_{buyer}. The actual wage bargain will ultimately depend on such things as the bargaining skills of the negotiators, the political pressure each side can bring to bear on the bargaining process, and public sentiment.

Labor Union Objectives

APPLIED MICRO THEORY

12.2

The analysis of bilateral monopoly assumes that the union's objective is to maximize the net benefits of the employed workers. It is apparent, however, that this is only one of several plausible **union objectives.** For example, the union may want to maximize the total wage earnings of its membership. Or it may instead seek to maximize the number of its members who find work. Another possibility is for the union to seek the highest wages for a select group of union members, such as members with seniority or members with special skills. The achievement of these various objectives requires different wage and employment goals.

The figure exhibits these possibilities. The labor demand curve facing the union employees is D_L. The curve labeled MR_L is associated with D_L in the same manner as all MR curves are tied to their average revenue curves. If the union wishes to maximize the total wage income of its members, it should expand the employment of members until the MR_L of additional employment is zero. In the figure, $MR_L = 0$ and total wage earnings are maximized when L_2 workers are employed at wage w_2.

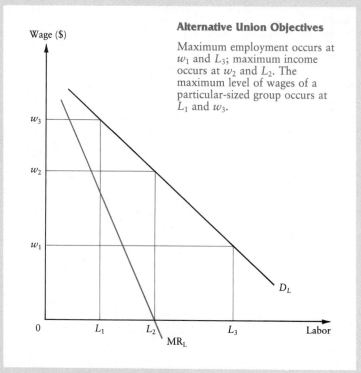

Alternative Union Objectives

Maximum employment occurs at w_1 and L_3; maximum income occurs at w_2 and L_2. The maximum level of wages of a particular-sized group occurs at L_1 and w_3.

If union membership equals L_2, the objectives of maximizing workers' earnings and maximizing employment are consistent. But suppose union membership is L_3. Employing all L_3 workers requires a wage of w_1, which is inconsistent with the wage w_2 needed to maximize earnings. Moreover, suppose the union wants to maximize the wages of a special group of workers, L_1. This policy requires a wage of w_3, which is also inconsistent with the other two goals.

Profit and Rent

The analysis of factor pricing and employment in Chapters 11 and 12 is based on the marginal productivity theory: Inputs receive payments equal to either VMP or MRP as long as monopsony power is absent. The marginal productivity theory assumes implicitly that factors are roughly homogeneous within their own classes. Thus the presence of homogeneous labor inputs and homogeneous capital inputs allows the wages of labor and the implicit rental rate of capital to be determined according to the contributions of the marginal inputs to firms' revenues. However, when an input is specialized and unique (Pete Rose, land with a location advantage, or Beverly Sills), the return to such a factor cannot be determined on the margin. How are the returns to such unique factors determined,

---

Jaw Wars: The Argument over Motion Picture Splits

APPLIED MICRO THEORY

12.3

Motion picture split agreements, which have been used for decades by movie exhibitors, have been challenged by the U.S. Justice Department as violations of the antitrust laws prohibiting restraint of trade. Under such split agreements, exhibitors in a particular market collude to determine which of them has the sole right to negotiate for films offered by distributors. At first blush, the collusion would indeed appear to have the common evil ingredients of a cartel with the resulting higher prices to consumers. Such an analysis has been provided by Professor Gordon:

> It is therefore beyond cavil that splitting interferes with the pricing mechanism by substituting private agreements not to compete for competitive price making. The net effect is a misallocation of some of the na-

tion's economic resources and a distortion of the normal investment pattern. . . . To the extent that the antitrust laws are meant to remedy misallocations of economic resources and the frustration of consumer wants, the motion picture exhibitors' agreement not to compete would seem the paradigm case for the invocation of the per se rule against market division and price fixing.*

The refutation of this approach requires the use of bilateral monopoly theory. The problem should be cast as a bargaining problem among distributors, who offer to rent the film for exhibition, and exhibitors, who use the film to attract customers who rent seats in the theater. Thus, the film is a fac-

*James S. Gordon, "Horizontal and Vertical Restraints of Trade: The Legality of Motion Picture Splits under the Antitrust Laws," *Yale Law Journal* 75 (1965): 239, 250–251.

tor of production for the exhibitor.

The Gordon argument, that splits interfere with competitive efficiency, is apparently misplaced: Competition does not exist in the movie industry, with or without splits, because of the monopoly power of the distributor. The correct comparison is not between competition and collusion but between unilateral distributor monopoly without exhibitor splits and bilateral monopoly with splits. The theory of bilateral monopoly indicates that the splits would provide exhibitors with greater bargaining power and hence the ability to obtain films at a price no higher (because the distributor would not negotiate for a price higher than the profit-maximizing price) and probably much lower than would prevail under unilateral distributor monopoly. Hence the motion picture split system provides a countervailing force to distributor monopoly and helps the consumer by inducing lower prices.

---

and how are these inputs allocated to different firms, industries, and occupations?

We have encountered the economic role of specialized resources once before. Chapter 7 modeled the long-run entry/exit decision of the firm by stating the following definition of economic profit:

$$\text{Economic profit} = \text{total revenue} - \text{explicit costs} - \text{owner's opportunity costs}$$

The process of selecting the best industry to be in is equivalent to choosing the industry with positive economic profits.

Chapter 7 notes that inframarginal firms can earn positive economic profits in long-run competitive equilibrium if they have a specialized resource that gives them a cost advantage over their competitors. Such a positive inframarginal economic profit is a surplus arising from a specialized factor. If the factor becomes widely available to all firms, the positive profit is competed away by market forces. Thus we are already accustomed to thinking of economic profit as a surplus accounted for by the presence of a specialized factor.

Economic Rent

Just as the profits and the entry/exit decision of a firm can be studied by carefully defining economic profits, the earnings and job selection decisions of specialized resources can be analyzed by distinguishing between **net income** and **economic rent,** which are defined as follows:

$$\text{Net Income} = \text{earnings} - \text{expenses}$$

$$\text{Economic Rent} = \text{net income} - \text{highest net income forgone}$$

Net income is the difference between the total payment received by the factor and the total expenses that the factor incurs in providing services. For the factor's economic rent to be positive, net income in the current job (income minus expenses) must exceed the highest forgone net income available in another job. Let's take a concrete example.

Pete Rose is an utterly magnificent and unique baseball player. Nothing is lost and great deal of clarity is gained by regarding Pete Rose as a firm producing a service that becomes an input in the production function of a major league team. Rose's output is a composite of baseball-related services—hits, runs, diving catches, and postgame interviews. Rose's inputs are a composite of natural and acquired attributes and services, such as his arms, legs, strength, time spent jogging, medical supervision, and an experienced masseur. Now suppose Pete Rose has the option of playing baseball in Philadelphia, playing baseball in Kansas City, or playing semiprofessional football in Biloxi. Rose's hypothetical total earnings and business expenses for all three jobs are shown in Table 12.5.

All three jobs result in positive net income (earnings minus expenses), but Rose has an opportunity cost—the forgone net income of playing in another city. When Rose subtracts this opportunity cost from net income, the resulting economic rent is positive in Philadelphia and negative in Kansas City and Biloxi. Rose chooses to play baseball in Philadelphia by selecting the positive economic rent and the highest net income. These rules are equivalent. Note that the net income is quite high in all jobs but that

Table 12.5
Rose's Hypothetical Earnings and Expenses for Three Jobs

Item	Philadelphia (Baseball)	Kansas City (Baseball)	Biloxi (Football)
Total earnings	$500,000	$ 400,000	$ 75,000
Total expenses	100,000	100,000	5,000
Net income	400,000	300,000	70,000
Economic rent	100,000	− 100,000	− 330,000

economic rent is positive only in Philadelphia, because it exhibits the highest net income.

Using our hypothetical numbers, playing baseball in Kansas City is Rose's best forgone option. The economic rent of $100,000 is that portion of Rose's total income of $500,000 in excess of the amount needed to keep him playing in Philadelphia. In other words, the payment to Rose could be reduced by $100,000 without forcing him to change jobs. This brings us to a formal definition: Economic rent is that portion of the total payment made to an input in excess of the amount needed to keep the input employed in its present activity.

By viewing an input factor of production as an output of some prior production, we can see that there is little if any difference between economic profit and economic rent; both are surpluses that arise from the existence of specialized resources. Indeed, Chapter 8 took the liberty of referring to economic profit and economic rent synonymously.

The principal purpose of economic rent is to model the entry/exit decisions of the factors of production. Figure 12.8 helps us gain a deeper understanding of the role of economic rent in the job selection of resources. Panel *a* illustrates a supply curve for

Figure 12.8
Economic Rent of Specialized Resources

(a) With a perfectly inelastic supply, there are still various levels of demand for the input. (b) The supply of the input to one occupation is determined by the demand from other occupations.

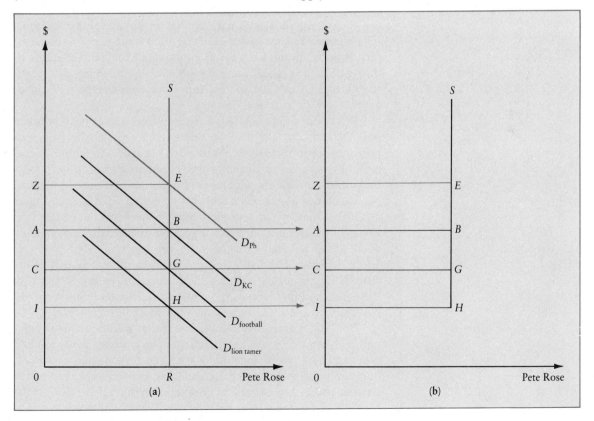

(a)   (b)

inputs with Pete Rose's skills. The supply curve, S, is drawn perfectly inelastic because Rose is one of a kind. Four demand curves for Rose's services are exhibited: (1) the demand for Rose to play baseball in Philadelphia, D_{Ph}; (2) the demand for Rose to play baseball in Kansas City, D_{KC}; (3) the demand for Rose to play football in Biloxi, $D_{football}$; and (4) the demand for Rose as a lion tamer, $D_{lion\ tamer}$. The payments offered to Rose and his selection of jobs are demand-determined. For ease, let's assume that job-related expenses are the same in all jobs. This simplification allows us to define the difference between the total payments in different jobs as economic rent.

Philadelphia will offer Rose an income payment of $R0ZE$ to play baseball. Kansas City, Rose's best forgone option, offers $R0AB$. Thus economic rent is positive only when Rose plays in Philadelphia. This economic rent—the difference between the payments in Philadelphia and the forgone payments in Kansas City—is area $BAZE$. All or any part of rent $BAZE$ could be taxed away or otherwise extracted from Rose's Philadelphia earnings without causing him to leave Philadelphia or the baseball industry.

Figure 12.8b separates the supply curve for Pete Rose's services to Philadelphia from the perfectly inelastic supply curve to all uses, shown in panel a. Rose's supply to Philadelphia is the step function $0ABS$. As long as Rose's net earnings in Philadelphia exceed his possible net earnings in Kansas City, the supply curve to Philadelphia is perfectly inelastic. But if an amount of income in excess of the rent $BAZE$ is taxed from Rose's Philadelphia earnings, Rose will switch to Kansas City and his supply to Philadelphia will fall to zero.

Just as economic rent helps us study Rose's movement between baseball clubs, it can also be employed to model the entry/exit decisions from baseball to nonbaseball occupations. Suppose football is Rose's best forgone nonbaseball option. Because Rose's football offer is $R0CG$, the difference between his best offer in baseball and his best forgone nonbaseball option is area $GCZE$. This surplus is another measure of economic rent; it measures the payment in excess of the amount needed to keep Rose in baseball. Rose's supply curve to the baseball industry is the step function $0CGS$ in Figure 12.8b. If Rose's baseball earnings are taxed, all or any part of the rent $GCZE$ can be extracted without forcing Rose out of baseball. If the baseball tax exceeds the rent $GCZE$, Rose's input supply to baseball becomes zero as he enters the football industry.

But let's assume that a government that would tax away baseball rents would have no compunction about taxing away football rents as well. If we assume that Rose's best forgone nonsport job is lion taming in the circus, Rose's football earnings in excess of the payment needed to assure that he remains in football is $HICG$. If the football tax exceeds this rent surplus, Rose will become a lion tamer. Rose's supply curve to sports—baseball and football combined—is therefore $0IHS$ in panel *b*. If Rose has a reservation wage of $0IHS$ and will not offer any services in the market if his net income falls below this amount, then $0IHS$ is the supply curve to any job.

In effect, in this exercise we are defining various rent components associated with different comparisons of earnings. We have defined the rent associated with being in sports, with playing baseball, and with playing baseball in Philadelphia. You should understand that most authors define the economic rent of a unique resource as the difference between the resource's earnings in its specialty and the best forgone earnings outside its specialty. Professor Paul Samuelson writes,

> Babe Ruth earned $80,00 a year playing baseball, something he liked to do anyway. Outside sports, one doubts he could have counted on earning more than, say, $5,000 a year. Between these limits his supply curve was almost completely inelastic, not affected by tax rates; hence economists can term the excess of his income above the alternative wage he could have earned elsewhere a pure rent.[2]

Samuelson's definition of rent is not wrong, but it is not so general as it might be. We are just as interested—and perhaps more interested—in studying a player's entry/exit between teams as his entry/exit between different occupations. Samuelson's definition of rent is the equivalent of comparing Ruth's earnings as a superstar baseball player with his earnings if he were divested of his talent. But economic rent can be used to study the movement of specialized factors within and between occupations. Thus it is important to be able to determine how an author is using the term *economic rent*.

Quasi Rent

Economic rent is a long-run concept that models the entry/exit employment decisions of inputs. We have seen that economic rent arises from the inelastic supply of the input, rent being that part of the factor's earnings above those needed to keep the factor in its present employment.

The concept of rent has its analogue in short-run analysis. By definition, in the short run the firm's fixed capital inputs cannot be changed or relocated. Capital is totally inelastic in supply and immobile in the short run. The returns to capital in excess of those necessary to keep capital in place in the short run are called **quasi rents**. These quasi rents play an important allocative role in the long run, because the firm makes decisions about the long-run expansion or contraction of capital based on the return to capital.

Consider Figure 12.9*c,* which displays the market supply and demand curves for labor. The wage rate is w_1. Suppose the firm is

2. Paul A. Samuelson, *Economics,* 10th ed. (New York: McGraw-Hill, 1976), p. 581.

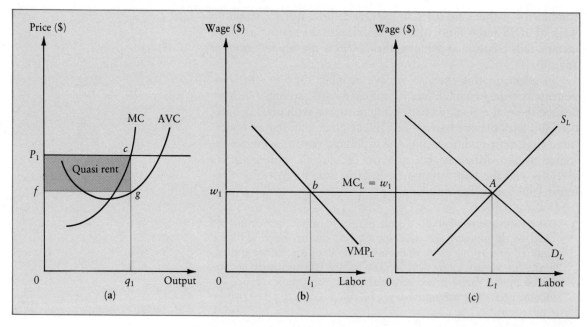

Figure 12.9
Quasi Rent: A Short-Run Payment to Capital

(a) Quasi rent is the surplus over variable costs. (b) Variable costs are determined by the wage taker where $VMP_L = w$. (c) The wage is determined where $S_L = D_L$ at point A.

competitive and takes the wage w_1 as a parameter in its hiring of labor. In the neighborhood of the labor market equilibrium at point A, each worker offers his or her labor services at wage w_1. That is, each worker has the option of working in any of the numerous firms at the going wage. Accordingly, the firm's total wage bill, $0w_1bl_1$ in panel b, is necessary to employ l_1 workers. There is no surplus to labor here as there is to a specialized resource. If the firm does not pay each worker wage w_1, it cannot attract any workers.

The total variable cost, $0fgq_1$ in Figure 12.9a equals the payment needed to hire l_1 workers in the production of q_1 units of output. Any revenue greater than TVC is a return to the fixed capital factor. If product price is P_1, the payment to capital is TR − TVC, or P_1cgf. This is the quasi rent. The firm and its capital will stay put in the short run as long as TR ≥ TVC. Quasi rent is zero when TR = TVC. If TR < TVC, the firm shuts down and sells its capital. Thus quasi rent cannot be negative.

Short-run quasi rent, just like long-run economic rent, has an allocative function. If the quasi rent on the firm's capital exceeds the market earnings on alternative investments, the firm will expand capital investment over time. If the quasi rent equals the return available to alternative earning assets, the firm will maintain its capital stock by replacing worn-out capital. Finally, if the quasi rent is less than the return on alternative investments, the firm will gradually depreciate its capital and close down in the long run. Thus quasi rent determines the course of capital expansion and contraction in the adjustment to long-run equilibrium.

A Potpourri of Surplus Concepts

APPLIED
MICRO
THEORY

12.4

It is useful to pause briefly to collect and demonstrate the unity of three concepts: consumer surplus, economic profit, and economic rent. Each represents the difference between the resources devoted to an economic activity and the resources necessary to that activity. Thus consumer surplus represents the willingness to pay minus the necessity to pay (see Chapter 4). Economic profit is the profit in excess of what is needed to draw resources to the enterprise (see Chapter 7). Economic rent is the payment to productive factors above the payment needed to bring the factors to their rent-generating uses. Although all three surpluses are often called "unearned," and are thus the frequent target of proposed tax levies, each represents an incentive that economic agents have to make value-increasing changes in the way resources are allocated.

Abolishing the Baseball Player Reserve System

APPLIED
MICRO
THEORY

12.5

Professional sports requires well-balanced teams that play exciting games with uncertain outcomes. The professional sports industry has been exempt from prosecution under the antitrust laws because it has been thought that competitive bidding for players would have two effects: Team balance would be jeopardized because the richest teams would buy up all the top players, and some teams would go out of business if forced to pay competitive wages for players.

The antitrust exemption has led to the formation of the "player reserve system," which allows for noncompetitive drafting of amateur players by professional teams. The teams with the poorest records select first, and a contract gives the team owner the right to retain or sell the skills of the player. Clearly, the reserve system gives monopsony bargaining power to team owners in their wage bargaining with players. This monopsony power produces subcompetitive wages for players and equivalent economic rent for owners.

The reserve system is in the process of significant modification. As it is modified or abolished, will league balance and player allocation be affected in the short run? Will some firms be forced to exit in the long run due to the higher wages? And will the incentive to develop players' skills be affected?

League Balance

The reserve system transfers the ownership of players' skills from the players to the team owners. Still, it is easy to show that player trades, and hence league balance, are not affected by the ownership of players' skills—a player will play for the team that places the highest value on his skills whether the reserve system is in place or not.*

The result is also true for the modification of the system that occurred in 1976 and that occurred in settlement of the prolonged baseball strike in 1981. In

*See S. Rottenberg, "The Baseball Players' Labor Market," *Journal of Political Economy* 66 (1956): 242; and H. Demsetz, "When Does the Rule of Liability Matter?" *Journal of Legal Studies* 1 (1972): 13.

1976, the free-agent rule was instituted to eliminate reserved status for players with 5 years or more in the major leagues. The 1981 strike was essentially a response to an attempt by owners to obtain a greater share of the bilateral monopoly profits by requiring a team signing a free agent to compensate the team that the player leaves. Neither of these modifications should affect where the player plays.

Consider a player who is worth $500,000 to Milwaukee, $400,000 to Los Angeles, and less to all other teams. If Milwaukee drafts the player under the reserve system and signs him to a $100,000 contract, the player will not be traded to any other team. Los Angeles's top bid for the contract is $300,000 (it still must honor the $100,000 contractual payment to the player). But the player's contract is worth a net of $400,000 to Milwaukee ($500,00 less the contractual $100,000 wage). Thus no trade is acceptable and the player stays in Milwaukee. If players are allocated to teams competitively, Milwaukee can always exceed Los Angeles's top bid of $400,000. Even if Los

Continued on page 410

Angeles drafts the player originally under the reserve clause, the player will be traded to Milwaukee because the player's contract is worth more to Milwaukee than to Los Angeles. Hence the player ends up in Milwaukee with or without the reserve system, because Milwaukee places a higher value on the player. The reserve system does not affect the willingness of the wealthiest teams to buy up the top players.

Even though the player draft does not affect the ultimate distribution of players, it does distribute money. In our previous example, Milwaukee receives a net payment of $400,000 due to the draft (player valued at $500,000 less the $100,000 wage). But if Los Angeles decides the player is worth $600,000, an offer to Milwaukee of at least $400,000 will induce Milwaukee to trade the player's contract. In the end, Milwaukee receives a money payment of at least $400,000 due to the draft. It may or may not receive a player— player allocation is determined by the relative value that teams place on players, not on the order of drafting. Thus the reserve system in which the worst teams draft first is equivalent to income distribution to poor teams. Some owners may need to have their revenues bolstered by the income transfers associated with the sale of player contracts in order to avoid team dissolution. But such income distribution can be achieved more directly by simple money transfers. Hence it can be concluded that the subcompetitive wages produced by the reserve system cannot be justified as a means of maintaining league balance. Abolition of the reserve system will not affect player trades and league balance if it is replaced by a simple system of money transfers among teams.

The figure contains the graphic equivalent of this argument. Assume that the reserve system is in force initially. The team maximizes its profit on ticket sales by equating MR and MC, thereby selling $0T_1$ tickets at price $0B$. Now let's abolish the reserve system and replace it with an equivalent sys-

tem of income redistribution. The abolition of the reserve system leaves player allocations—and hence ticket sales and prices— constant; this assertion is equivalent to demonstrating that the marginal revenue and marginal cost curves do not shift when the reserve system is abolished. If an equivalent income redistribution system replaces the reserve system, the revenue curves are unaffected. More surprising, the marginal cost curve is also unaffected. This is a surprising result because the marginal cost equals the wage divided by the marginal product of labor, and the abolition increases wages to competitive levels. However, the owner will use the marginal opportunity cost of labor in calculating marginal cost. In the previous example, Milwaukee pays $100,000 to the player but also forgoes the

John Wirges

opportunity to sell the player's contract for $300,000. Thus the full opportunity cost of hiring the player is $400,000, not the $100,000 contractual payment. In other words, the full opportunities forgone in hiring the player equal the competitive wage even though out-of-pocket expenses do not. If the reserve clause is abandoned, competitive bidding raises the player's wage to $400,000 (Los Angeles's top bid). Thus abolishing the reserve system does not shift the MC curve. Pricing, output, and inputs are all unaffected, because marginal cost reflects opportunities forgone at the margin.

Team Exit

The proof that the reserve clause does not affect player trades is valid only if abolition of the clause does not induce team exit. If the higher wages force some cities to lose their teams, player trades are certainly affected, because the players whose teams are dissolved must be traded to other cities. Baseball industry representatives argue that the competitive wages arising from abolition of the reserve system dissolve teams that are only marginally profitable with the help of the reserve-induced monopsony rents. Let's examine this argument in detail.[†]

The team owner can always sell the team—complete with players' contracts—for a value equal to its economic profit. Economic profit equals

$$\pi = R - w^a - E$$

where π = economic profit, R = revenue, w^a = actual (subcompetitive) wages paid to players under the reserve system, and E = profits forgone in the team owner's next most profitable activity. The monopsony rent V bestowed on the entrepreneur is the difference between the players' competitive wage level, w^c, and their actual wage payments, w^a.

[†]This section is based on W. Holahan, "The Long-Run Effects of Abolishing the Baseball Player Reserve System," *Journal of Legal Studies* 7 (1978): 129–137.

$$V = w^c - w^a.$$

Substituting this equation into the first one and subtracting V from each term yields

$$\pi - V = R - (w^c + E)$$

If $\pi < V$, then $R < (w^c + E)$, in which case the firm's revenue is not enough to compensate the owner for the forgone profits of selling the players' contracts, w^c, and of entering his next-best alternative employment, E. If $\pi < V$, the owner is better off dissolving the team and selling players' contracts separately than selling the team intact, because the purchase price will equal the economic profit, π, which is less than $V = w^c - w^a$, the net gain from selling players' contracts separately. Thus team survival requires that $\pi \geq V$; economic profit must be at least as large as the monopsony rent bestowed by the reserve system. If $\pi < V$, the team is dissolved even when the reserve system is in force.

The conclusion that team survival requires $\pi \geq V$ under the reserve system allows us to see immediately the effect on team survival of abolishing the system. Abolition of the reserve system causes a one-time devaluation of the team equal to the monopsony rent, V. But $\pi \geq V$, so there is enough surplus for the loss to be absorbed without producing negative economic profits. Team survival and location therefore are not affected by the reserve system or its abolition. If the firm can survive with the reserve system in effect, it can also survive without it.

A graphic depiction of this argument requires that the average cost curve for the firm in zero-profit equilibrium in the figure not shift when the reserve system is abolished. The average cost curve, AC, is constructed on the basis of full opportunity costs, not just out-of-pocket costs. Thus the full-costs net of monopsony rent, including the forgone opportunity to sell the team, π, are

$$\text{Full cost} = w^c + E + \pi - V$$

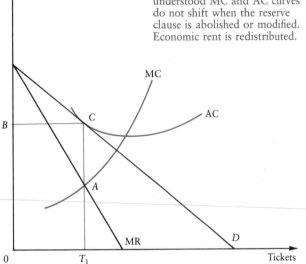

Abolition of the Baseball Player Reserve System

Abolition of the system does not affect player trades or team exit or location. The properly understood MC and AC curves do not shift when the reserve clause is abolished or modified. Economic rent is redistributed.

where E, π, and V are fixed opportunity costs. The AC curve in the figure includes all terms in the previous equation. A zero-profit equilibrium implies that

$$R - w^c - E - \pi + V = 0$$

and is depicted in the figure by the tangency of the average cost curve and the demand curve at point C. Abolition of the reserve clause does not shift the average cost curve, because the loss in monopsony rent, V, is offset by an equivalent reduction in economic profit, π. Abolition of the reserve system will not produce $\pi < 0$. Even after the devaluation equal to V, revenue is sufficient to cover the entrepreneurial opportunity costs, $E + w^c$. The team stays in business in its present location. To be sure, the sale price of the team has fallen because the monopsony rents have been transferred to the players in the form of competitive wages. The owner can sell the club at a lower price or maintain ownership of a depreciated team. But the team will not be dissolved.

Development of New Players

The baseball industry also claims that it needs the monopsony rents bestowed by the reserve system to compensate the firms for investment in new talent and player development. This claim misses the essential question. The key economic concern is whether new talent will be developed, not who will develop it. Under the reserve system, player development is specific training, because the training cannot be marketed to other teams. When the reserve system is abolished, player development is general training, because the player can market his new skills and receive the return to the skill development. Hence the incentive for skill development is unaffected by the reserve clause—in both cases the owner of the players' skills pays for the skill development.

Key Terms

average cost of labor (AC$_L$) 389
bilateral monopoly 400
economic rent 404
monopolistic exploitation 398
monopsonistic exploitation of
    labor 391
monopsonistic wage
    discrimination 395
monopsony 388
net income 404
quasi rents 407
union objectives 402

Summary

Input markets are affected by monopoly power in two general ways. If the buyers of inputs have the power to set input prices, monopsony exists, and the supply side of the input market is altered. If sellers of final output are monopolists, the systematic underproduction of monopoly output results in a diminished demand for inputs. Hence we can observe competition or monopsony in input markets, competition or monopoly in output markets, or any combination in between. Any form of monopoly power distorts the input markets and leads to exploitation of inputs, meaning that inputs will receive payments less than their marginal product. The key analytical concepts are these: VMP > MRP when firms have monopoly power in output markets, and MC_{input} > AC_{input} when firms have monopsony power in buying inputs. Competition in either the input or output markets can then be treated as a special case of the full optimizing conditions presented in this chapter.

Economic rent is defined as the payment that the input receives in excess of the amount needed to keep the input employed in its present activity. There is a close analogy between the excess return to a firm (economic profit) and the excess reward to a factor of production (economic rent). The concept of rent can be applied to the baseball industry; abolishing the reserve system would not result in team bankruptcy and exit, a fear often expressed by apologists for reserve clauses.

Problems

1. A person can earn $50,000 a year as a bank president, $20,000 as a professor of economics, or $10,000 as a high school coach. She chooses to be a professor of economics. What is her economic rent? Discuss the dangers of employing only monetary factors in determining economic rent.

2. If you wish to extract a person's economic rent, do you tax his or her hourly income or annual income? Does it make any difference?

3. If you wish to tax a worker's economic rent without changing his or her economic activity, how could you tell if you were successful?

4. The New York Yankees have an incredibly rich owner, one of the most lucrative TV contracts, and one of the best stadiums—the firm is rich. Furthermore, the owner is not a strict profit maximizer. Still, the Yankees do not have the best player in every position. Using marginal productivity theory, explain why such a team will not buy up all the best superstars from other teams. (Hint: Show that the Yankee's nth superstar is worth less to the Yankees than that player is worth to another team as its first superstar.)

5. Suppose that on noneconomic grounds, a personnel officer does not care whether she hires a man or a woman for an important long-term management post in her firm. She is looking for a 25-to-28-year-old person who will be groomed for top management later on. She knows that if she hires the woman there is a chance that the woman will spend 2 years on leave for family formation, after which she will return permanently. She also knows that a man has an equal chance of suffering from ulcers and heart

attacks and therefore spending a similar period of time away from the firm to recover. Furthermore, she knows that the probability of the woman suffering the man's ailments is equal to the probability of the man having a baby. Retirement age is 65 for both, and productivity increases are the same for each, given the same years of experience. The personnel officer determines that the woman candidate is worth less to the firm than the man and if hired should get a lower wage than the man. How can this decision be justified?

6. Explain how a firm's incentive to discriminate in wages can be exercised.

7. How do market forces erode union seniority rules? (Hint: Focus on firm incentives to migrate.)

8. Major league baseball players are paid an enormous amount. Is it in the interest of league executives to drive those incomes down by allowing more teams into the leagues?

9. "Illegal Mexican emigrants are generally not subject to the minimum-wage laws. This fact drives down the real income of U.S. citizens who work with them." Comment.

10. University professors hired between 1965 and 1969 enjoyed a very tight market due to the great expansion of enrollment that took place then. As a result, high salaries were paid and mobility was great. Tenure systems maintain these high incomes even though market conditions are considerably different now. Did the salaries paid in those glory years include an economic rent component? Do the protected incomes paid now include a rent component? (Contrast the professor who has received job offers from other schools, government, or private industry with those who have not.)

11. What is the impact of the interstate highway system on monopsony power?

12. Explain why northern city labor unions, whose members all make more than the minimum wage, lobby Congress to increase the minimum wage.

13. Does the analysis of motion picture splits discussed in Applied Micro Theory 12.3 apply to block-buster movies such as *E.T. —The Extra-Terrestrial* as it does to less popular movies.

14. Baseball stars such as Pete Rose and Reggie Jackson can earn extra income by appearing in television commercials. However, more of this money is available to stars who play ball in the larger media markets like New York and Los Angeles. Is the reserve clause, discussed in Applied Micro Theory 12.5, necessary to keep these players on the team for which their baseball talents are best suited?

15. The stronger the union bargaining power, the more likely it is to advertise the firm's product. Why?

16. A firm that is well equipped can make a person more productive. For example, a secretary provided with a word-processing computer can do the work of two or three secretaries who don't have computers. Show how the VMP and MRP curves are likely to shift for secretaries as word processors become the norm in business offices.

17. Does the university tenure system referred to in question 19 of Chapter 11 give the university monopsony power over the faculty?

Suggested Readings

Dunlop, J. *Wage Determination under Trade Unions*. New York: Augustus M. Kelley, 1966.

Holahan, W. "The Long-Run Effects of Abolishing the Baseball Player Reserve System." *Journal of Legal Studies* 7 (1978): 129–137.

Kaldor, N. "Alternative Theories of Distribution," *Review of Economic Studies* 23 (1955): 83–100.

Rees, A. *The Economics of Work and Pay*. New York: Harper & Row, 1973.

Stigler, George. *The Theory of Price*. New York: Macmillan, 1966, chaps. 15–17.

Weston, J. F. "The Profit Concept and Theory: A Restatement." *Journal of Political Economy* 62 (1954): 152–170.

Worcester, Dean A., Jr. "A Reconsideration of the Theory of Rent." *American Economic Review* 36 (1946): 258–277.

General Equilibrium, Efficiency, and Economic Welfare

The goal in this chapter is to appraise the economic efficiency of the economy as a whole. We will not be entirely successful, because the topic is so vast and is burdened by great logical impediments. What we can do, however, is construct a framework for thoughts. This ambitious objective requires a more comprehensive analytical structure than used in previous chapters.

Partial Equilibrium versus General Equilibrium Analysis

The primary method of analysis in previous chapters has been "partial equilibrium," in which one market is viewed in isolation from the rest of the economy. With this technique, developed principally by the British economist Alfred Marshall, one market is investigated *ceteris paribus,* holding essential characteristics of other markets constant.[1] **Partial equilibrium analysis** is a powerful conceptual device for getting quickly to the heart of many microeconomic problems, as we have seen repeatedly in previous chapters. Its major benefit lies in enabling us to abstract from the many real-world interrelationships that exist among economic agents and among markets, which as a practical matter are beyond our ability to analyze in a comprehensive fashion anyway. Partial equilibrium analysis is a way of cutting the Gordian knot.[2]

Still, partial equilibrium analysis has a major limitation: It does not describe how the economy fits together as a whole. Whereas we have been content to perform comparative static shifts in the supply and demand curves of a given market and to describe that one market's readjustment to equilibrium, we have had to ignore the effects of such shifts and readjustments on the supply and demand curves of other markets and the resulting feedback of these shifts into the initial market and its equilibrium.

---

1. Alfred Marshall, *Principles of Economics,* 9th ed. (London: Macmillan, 1961).

2. Gordius, ancient king of Phrygia, tied a knot that according to prophecy could be untied only by the person who was to rule Asia. Alexander the Great cut the knot instead of taking the time and effort to untie it.

13

Leon Walras was the principal investigator of **general equilibrium analysis,** a comprehensive method of analysis in which the *ceteris paribus* procedure is discarded and all the economy's interrelationships are taken into account.[3] Conceptually the technique is quite simple. Each market has a supply curve, a demand curve, and a corresponding equilibrium condition that equates the quantities supplied and demanded at a given price. But prices and quantities in each market are shift parameters in the supply and demand curves in other markets. Thus equilibrium must be systemwide; if all markets but one are in equilibrium, the price and quantity adjustments in that one market will disturb equilibrium in other markets. General equilibrium is a comprehensive, simultaneously determined equilibrium in all markets.

Formulating and testing the results of general equilibrium analysis—particularly the mathematical systems that Walras and his successors worked out—often exceed the current state of the art in econometric modeling. The technique is cumbersome because of our inability to gather sufficient data or to solve the necessarily complex set of simultaneous equations that are involved. Thus, microeconomic propositions are testable only in an extremely crude fashion. Economists have generally adopted partial equilibrium analysis in acknowledgment of the unwieldy nature of general equilibrium analysis.

However, general equilibrium analysis is extremely useful in two major areas: macroeconomic modeling and microeconomic analysis of efficiency and welfare. Most macroeconomic models are applications of general equilibrium made possible by aggregating the economy into a manageable number of markets. For example, most macroeconomic textbooks aggregate the economy into an output market, a labor market, a money market, and a bond market. The interrelationships among these markets are of central concern: If output demand falls, how are the equilibrium values in other markets affected, such as interest rates, unemployment rates, and wage rates? And how will these new values feed back to the output market and affect commodity prices and gross national product (GNP)? It is the interrelationships among markets and the general equilibrium solutions that are of primary interest in macroeconomic analysis. This is true also of the multiequation computer models that have been constructed to predict macroeconomic variables.

In microeconomics, general equilibrium analysis is employed principally in deriving the conditions that must exist between consumers in exchange and inputs in production in order to achieve economic efficiency—a precondition to the ultimate goal of maximizing societal welfare. General equilibrium analysis is also employed to appraise the efficiency of alternative economic organ-

3. Leon Walras, *Elements d' Economique Pure* (Lausanne, Switzerland: F. Rouge, 1874).

izations and outcomes. International trade models almost invariably use general equilibrium, as do many modern public finance models, in which the effects of such public interventions as taxes and subsidies in one industry are traced to other segments of the economy.

Efficiency Conditions

What conditions promote economic efficiency, and how do they relate to the price system? These are the questions addressed in the sections that follow. A host of policy implications take on deeper meaning in the light of these efficiency considerations. For example, monopoly rate-of-return regulation, marginal cost pricing, pricing in decreasing-cost industries, and peak-load pricing are natural extensions of the efficiency conditions that emerge from a simple general equilibrium model. But first we must understand these efficiency conditions.

Exchange Efficiency

The following exposition of general equilibrium and economic efficiency is graphic and therefore confined to two dimensions.[4] Thus we will consider a very simple world consisting of two consumers, two final products, and two inputs. Then we can generalize to the more realistic cases of n consumers, products, and inputs.

Pick two heavy eaters at random, named Bill and Steve. Suppose each has an initial endowment of two final goods, meat and vegetables. We can ignore production initially in order to focus attention on the two consumers' exchange (trading) behavior. We seek the answer to the following question: How can Bill and Steve reallocate their initial endowments of meat and vegetables so that each gains if they are free to trade with each other? The answer to this question defines the conditions for **exchange efficiency.**

We are already accustomed to drawing consumer indifference maps in two-dimensional commodity space. Figure 13.1*a* shows separately the meat and vegetable commodity spaces of Bill and Steve. (We can suppress their indifference maps for now.) Bill's axes are black lines and Steve's are colored lines for illustrative purposes. For convenience, let's rotate Steve's axes 180 degrees, so they reappear as shown in panel *b*. Now we can squeeze the two commodity spaces together until the two sets of axes form a box, as illustrated in panel *c*. The result is an **Edgeworth box,** named after its inventor.[5] It is the basic graph used in general equilibrium analysis. The arrows are a reminder of the point of reference for each commodity space.

4. This graphic presentation of general equilibrium closely follows Francis M. Bator, "The Simple Analytics of Welfare Maximization," *American Economic Review* 47 (1959): 22–59.

5. F. Y. Edgeworth, *Mathematical Psychics: An Essay on the Application of Mathematics to the Moral Sciences, 1881* (New York: August M. Kelley, 1953).

Figure 13.1
Constructing the Edgeworth Box

(a) Both consumers have meat and vegetable axes. (b) After a 180-degree rotation, Steve's axes line up with Bill's. (c) The Edgeworth box is formed by fitting the axes together. The length and height of the box equal the sum of the vegetables and meat that Bill and Steve bring to the exchange.

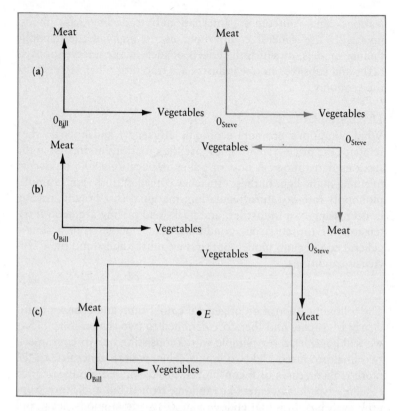

Squeezing the two commodity spaces together into a box could present a problem if the lengths of the vertical and horizontal axes were not fixed. This problem vanishes in our exchange model because of the fixed endowments of meat and vegetables. Thus the length of the vertical axes measures the total amount of meat available (M), which in turn must equal the sum of the two consumers' components: $M = M_B + M_S$. Likewise, the length of the horizontal axes measures the availability of vegetables (V), where $V = V_B + V_S$. Thus any point in the box represents a specific allocation of meat and vegetables between Bill and Steve. For example, point E in Figure 13.1c represents an equal distribution of both goods between the two consumers.

We can now introduce the consumers' indifference maps into the Edgeworth box. In Figure 13.2, Bill's indifference curves are convex to the O_{Bill} origin and are labeled U_B. Likewise, Steve's indifference curves are convex to the O_{Steve} origin and are labeled U_S. You may recall that the slope of an indifference curve equals the marginal rate of substitution, MRS. In our present example, MRS $= \Delta M/\Delta V$ for both Bill and Steve. Thus the slopes of their indifference curves can be compared. But Bill's gain in meat is Steve's loss in meat, because of the fixed meat endowment. The same is true of vegetables.

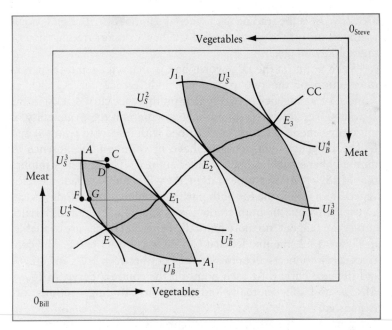

Figure 13.2
The Edgeworth Box and Exchange Efficiency

Pareto optimality in exchange is achieved at positions on the contract curve. Points off the contract curve, such as point A, offer mutually advantageous trading possibilities.

Let the initial distribution of goods be that at point A in Figure 13.2. Are there mutually advantageous trading possibilities? Bill and Steve have an unequal MRS at A because the indifference curves U_B^1 and U_S^3 intersect at A. Whenever $MRS_B \neq MRS_S$, mutually beneficial trades are available. For example, Bill would be willing to give up CE units of meat to obtain AC units of vegetables. Such a trade would move Bill from A to E on the indifference curve U_B^1. But Steve can make such a trade with Bill and come out ahead, because his MRS is less than Bill's. Steve gets CE units of meat for AC units of vegetables, but he only needed CD units of meat to remain at the same utility level, U_S^3. Thus a move from A to E improves Steve's utility without reducing Bill's. Compared to A, point E lies on a higher indifference curve for Steve (U_S^4) and on the same indifference curve for Bill (U_B^1).

The movement from A to E along Bill's indifference curve U_B^1 is of course merely an arbitrary example of how trade can improve one person's utility without reducing the other's. A movement from A to E_1 achieves the same result as a move from A to E but with the names switched. Steve is indifferent between A and E_1. Bill would have remained indifferent by receiving merely FG units of vegetables in trade for AF units of meat; instead he received the larger amount of vegetables, FE_1. Therefore, trading AF meat for FE_1 vegetables increases Bill's utility without reducing Steve's. Points E and E_1 are both superior to A. By analogous reasoning, the entire shaded area AEA_1E, represents the trading area for which one or both consumers' utility can be improved without reducing anyone's utility when the initial commodity distribution is point A. Similarly, area $JE_2J_1E_3$ is the trading area when the initial distribution is point J. Any point off the curve labeled CC has a similar trading area of mutual advantage.

Each point on the Edgeworth box is characterized by either an intersection of the two consumers' indifference curves, such as A and J, or a tangency between their indifference curves, such as the E points. The intersections all have in common the availability of mutually beneficial trades, as described with respect to points A and J. The tangencies, in contrast, have in common the absence of mutually beneficial trades. Consider point E. The tangency implies that $MRS_B = MRS_S$. At the margin, the willingness to trade meat for vegetables is the same for both parties. Trading can no longer yield a surplus to one or both trading partners. When the indifference curves are tangent, no more mutually beneficial trades are available. In Figure 13.2, the line labeled **CC** is the **contract curve**. The contract curve connects all points of tangency between Bill's and Steve's indifference curves. At each point on the contract curve, $MRS_B = MRS_S$, and all mutually advantageous trading options are exhausted.

For any point off the contract curve, such as A, there are superior points on the contract curve, such as the line segment EE_1. Between points E and E_1, both parties are better off than at A; exactly at E or E_1, one party is better off without the other being worse off. Thus there is mutual advantage to trading to a point on the contract curve.

Once the contract curve has been achieved, movements along it result in higher utility for one person and lower utility for the other. For this reason, the contract curve is also referred to as the **conflict curve**; movements along it place the trading parties at odds. We cannot pass judgment on the "worthiness" of movements along the contract curve without making interpersonal comparisons of utility.

We can now formally define the rule for exchange efficiency. Exchange efficiency describes a condition of commodity allocation for which it is not possible to reallocate the goods among consumers and by so doing make some people better off without making any other person worse off. This condition is called **Pareto optimality** in honor of the Italian economist Vilfredo Pareto, who proposed the criterion.[6] Any action that benefits someone without hurting anyone else is termed *Pareto optimal*. When all such actions have been exploited, Pareto optimality is achieved. Note that the Pareto efficiency rule does not apply to actions that help some people and hurt others. Under the Pareto criterion, efficiency is improved unambiguously only when an action benefits some people without harm-

6. Vilfredo Pareto, *Cours d' Economie Politique* (Lausanne, Switzerland: F. Rouge, 1897). Pareto optimality includes more than merely exchange efficiency, as shown in sections that follow.

ing anyone. Pareto optimality is a much weaker efficiency rule than Bentham's, under which efficiency calls for "the greatest good for the greatest number." Pareto optimality avoids such interpersonal utility comparisons.

In our two-person, two-commodity example, exchange efficiency is achieved when

$$MRS_B = MRS_S \qquad (13.1)$$

The contract curve is the collection of all such points of exchange efficiency. Note that exchange efficiency does not occur only at one point but at any of the infinite number of points along the contract curve. Note further that, under the Pareto criterion, all points along the CC are equally efficient but have vastly different consequences for Bill and for Steve.

Figure 13.3 broadens the exchange efficiency discussion. The Edgeworth box is divided into four equal sections. In section I Steve has more of both goods, whereas Bill has more of both goods in section III. In sections II and IV, each has more of one good and less of the other. Thus Steve has an **absolute advantage** in exchange section I. Nevertheless, Bill can have a **comparative advantage** in either good in section I. Consider point R in section I: Bill's comparative advantage exists in the fact that $MRS_B > MRS_S$. At point R it is advantageous for Steve to trade some vegetables to Bill in exchange for some of Bill's meat, even though Steve already has a greater share of both goods. Similarly, at point R Steve can improve his utility by trading meat for vegetables. Trading opportunities exist whenever the contract curve is not attained, regardless of the amounts of commodities that each party owns. This is the key to the theory of comparative advantage in international trade, where free

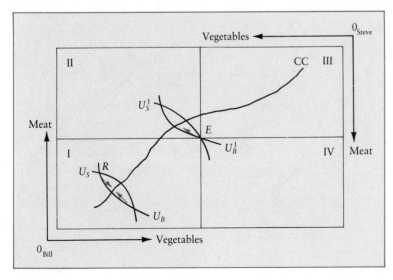

Figure 13.3
Comparative Advantage and Absolute Advantage

Even though Steve has more of both goods at point R, mutually advantageous trade can still take place, because Bill has a comparative advantage in meat. Furthermore, mutually advantageous trading possibilities will usually exist at point E, the point of equal endowments.

trade is argued to be economically efficient because of the gains from trade among nations that may have very unequal endowments of resources.

Also note that point E represents equality between Bill and Steve. But equality is efficient only if point E is on the contract curve, which it is not in Figure 13.3. Thus equality of distribution is not necessarily efficient. In fact, in most cases equality is inefficient. If equality were ever imposed by a "benevolent" social system, it would quickly be eliminated by economic agents trading their way back to the contract curve and away from the imposed equality.

Production Efficiency

Now let's introduce production into the general equilibrium model. We may assume fixed amounts of two inputs, labor and capital. Figure 13.4 illustrates the production isoquant maps in an Edgeworth box that displays the quantity of labor on the horizontal axes and the quantity of capital on the vertical axes. The dimensions of the box are determined by the fixed quantities of inputs available to society. Both inputs are used in the production of both goods, meat and vegetables. The isoquants labeled Q_m are convex to the 0_{meat} origin; these isoquants represent the production function for meat. The isoquants labeled Q_v are convex to the $0_{\text{veg.}}$ origin and portray the production function for vegetables. Note that the input space of vegetable production has been rotated, like our treatment of Steve's output space in the analysis of exchange.

In exchange, efficiency is achieved along the contract curve, where the marginal rates of substitution of both persons are equal.

Figure 13.4
The Edgeworth Box and Production Efficiency

Pareto optimality in production is achieved at positions on the contract curve. Points off the contract curve, such as point B, are inefficient, because more output of one or both goods can be obtained by reallocating capital and labor.

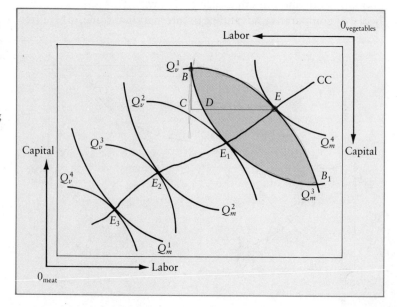

The analogous result in production is that efficiency is attained when the resources are divided among meat and vegetable production so that the marginal rates of technical substitution are equal for both products. Because the marginal rate of technical substitution (MRTS) is the slope of the isoquant, inputs are allocated efficiently between meat and vegetable production when the isoquants of the different production functions are tangent. The connection of all such efficient points defines the production contract curve CC, again like the contract curve in exchange. Production efficiency is achieved by allocating productive resources between the meat and vegetable industries to obtain the production contract curve.

Consider point B in Figure 13.4. At B, $MRTS_{\text{meat}} > MRTS_{\text{veg.}}$. Meat output could be increased without reducing the output of vegetables through the following maneuver: Increase the amount of labor used in producing meat (reduce labor in vegetables) and reduce the capital used in producing meat (increase capital in vegetables) by rearranging inputs from B to E. That is, devote BC fewer units of capital to meat and CE more units of labor to meat. How does this help? Input cominations B and E both lie on isoquant Q_v^1; the switch will not change vegetable production. A reduction of BC units of capital in the production of meat would have required a compensating increase of only CD units of labor in order to remain on isoquant Q_m^3 and keep meat production constant. But this reallocation of inputs frees up the large amount of labor CE, allowing meat production to increase to Q_m^4. Thus when goods' marginal rates of technical substitution are unequal, a rearrangement of resources—a Pareto move—can increase the output of one good without reducing the output of the other. The area of beneficial input reallocation is the shaded lens-shaped area BEB_1E_1 starting from the initial allocation B or B_1. All gains from input reallocation are exhausted once the production contract curve has been reached. Movements along the production contract curve increase the output of one good and reduce the output of the other.

Now we have a formal definition of production efficiency. **Production efficiency** is achieved when inputs are allocated to the production of various final goods so that it is not possible to reallocate the inputs to different uses; such an allocation increases the output of one commodity without reducing the output of any other commodity. This is the production variant of the Pareto criterion. The condition is satisfied in our present example when

$$MRTS_m = MRTS_v \qquad \textbf{(13.2)}$$

The production contract curve is the connection of all such efficient points of production. In production, as in exchange, Pareto optimality does not judge between output levels representing more of one good and less of another. There is no presumption of comparing apples and oranges (meat and vegetables).

Exchange and Production Efficiency Combined

Up to now, exchange and production have been separate so we can focus on the special features of their efficiency conditions. However, the very essence of a general equilibrium model is the interrelationships among all the economy's consumers, resources, and outputs. Much like the orchestra leader who rehearses each section separately before bringing the entire orchestra together, we are now ready to combine the exchange and production activities of our hypothetical (vastly oversimplified) economy.

The first task is to get the exchange and production analysis into a comparable analytical format so that the effects of production on consumption and exchange can be identified. This is done by transforming the production contract curve in Figure 13.4, which is drawn in input space, into a **production possibility (P-P) curve** like that in Figure 13.5, which is drawn in output space. This transformation will help, because the consumers' indifference maps also appear in output space. The production possibility curve—often called the **product transformation curve**—is defined as the various maximum output combinations (of meat and vegetables, in this case) that can be produced from a given set of labor and capital inputs and a given state of technology.

Each point on the production contract curve in Figure 13.4 corresponds to a point on the P-P curve in Figure 13.5. For example,

Figure 13.5
The Production Possibility Curve

The production possibility (P-P) curve is derived in output space from the production contract curve in input space.

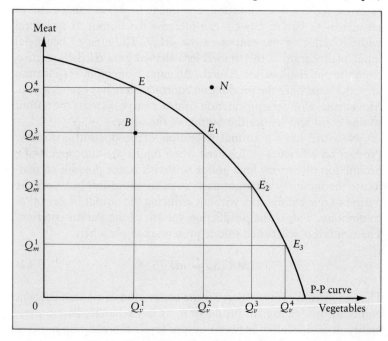

input allocation E in Figure 13.4 yields a production of Q_m^4 units of meat and Q_v^1 vegetables. This output combination is plotted as point E on the P-P curve in Figure 13.5. Thus, all points on the production contract curve correspond to points on the P-P curve, and so each output combination on the P-P curve reflects production efficiency.

Inefficient points in Figure 13.4 also reappear in Figure 13.5. For example, the inefficient point B, off the contract curve in Figure 13.4, is an interior point in output space. Reorganization of inputs could expand the outputs of both commodities along the arc EE_1. Points outside the P-P curve, such as N, are not attainable with the available labor, capital, and technology. These exterior, unattainable points do not have their analogue in the Edgeworth box of Figure 13.4.

The slope of the P-P curve is the **marginal rate of transformation** (**MRT**). The MRT is the change in meat production divided by the associated change in vegetable production, while reallocating inputs along the production contract curve:

$$\text{MRT} = \frac{\Delta M}{\Delta V}\bigg|K, L \text{ along CC} \qquad (13.3)$$

The P-P curve is negatively sloped, which illustrates a basic tenet of scarcity: The production of more meat results in fewer vegetables. Indeed, the opportunity cost of increasing meat production is the forgone vegetable production that makes the added meat output possible. The inability to obtain more of both goods in an efficient society is emphasized by the negative slope of the P-P curve.

Note that the P-P curve in Figure 13.5 is concave from the origin. This characteristic, called the "diminishing marginal rate of transformation," illustrates the principle of increasing costs. When meat production rises by equal increments, the resulting decreases in vegetable production must get larger and larger under the concavity assumption. The cost of obtaining an extra unit of meat is the vegetables that must be given up. A small amount of meat can be produced with labor and capital resources that are specialized in meat and of little use in vegetable production. But as meat production is increased, the economy must divert resources to meat production that are increasingly more valuable in vegetable production and therefore increasingly expensive in terms of vegetables forgone. Thus the concavity of the P-P curve is a plausible assumption.

With the production possibility curve in place, we are ready to define general equilibrium. Ultimately we want the model to show the amounts of labor and capital devoted to meat and vegetable production, the amounts of meat and vegetables produced, the distribution of meat and vegetables between Bill and Steve, and their respective utility levels. Thus the model will give us twelve simultaneously determined equilibrium values: L_m, L_v, K_m, K_v, M, V, M_B, M_S, V_B, V_S, U_B, U_S.

THE SINGLE CONSUMER   One additional dimension of Pareto optimality links exchange and production via the production possibility curve. In order to develop this last efficiency rule, we must temporarily remove Steve from the economy, leaving us with an economy of only one consumer. Here the solution to general equilibrium is straightforward. The production possibilities of the economy are given by the P-P curve, and Bill's preferences for goods are described by his indifference map. These curves are both drawn in commodity space in Figure 13.6. The optimal mix of attainable meat and vegetable production is combination E_1, because it allows Bill to attain the highest indifference curve possible within the resource and technology restraints contained in the P-P curve.

At the welfare maximum point E_1, the following condition holds, which is the **production-exchange efficiency** variant of the Pareto rule:

$$MRT = MRS_B \qquad (13.4)$$

The slope of the P-P curve is society's MRT. The slope of the indifference curve is Bill's MRS_B. The tangency at E_1 satisfies the

Figure 13.6
General Equilibrium in a Two-Good, One-Consumer Model

Production-exchange efficiency is achieved at point E_1, where MRS = MRT.

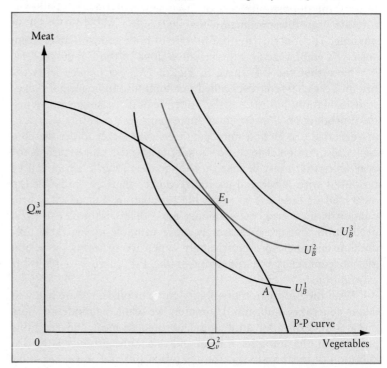

marginal efficiency rule of Equation 13.4. What if MRT $> MRS_B$, as at point A? It would then be possible to rearrange the labor and capital inputs in order to produce a different mix of meat and vegetables (E_1 instead of A) and by so doing raise Bill's utility from U_B^1 to U_B^2. Clearly, maximum consumer utility is obtained at E_1 when MRT $= MRS_B$.

Regarding the list of twelve variables to be determined in general equilibrium, the last six are trivial here, because Bill is the only consumer. Point E_1 determines the output mix Q_m^3 and Q_v^2. To find the amounts of capital and labor resources used in such production, merely locate point E_1 in the production Edgeworth box in Figure 13.4; point E_1 exists in input space. All the general equilibrium values are revealed by doing so.

TWO CONSUMERS   By reducing the world to a single consumer, we were able to ignore the exchange aspect temporarily and study the MRT = MRS efficiency rule. It might seem that a two-person world adds precious little realism over a one-person world. Yet the exchange dimension of general equilibrium introduces problems that a single-consumer economy does not have.

Once Steve is brought back into the model, we can no longer determine a unique output mix for the society. The utilities of Bill and Steve are now in conflict; one output mix may be good for Bill but bad for Steve. And the Pareto efficiency criteria do not allow us to pick and choose between these alternatives. The best we can do is to outline the utility tradeoffs that alternative output mixes yield and appeal to an outside criterion to judge the worthiness of the various positions.

This is all very abstract, so let's become more specific. Consider the production possibility curve in Figure 13.7. Select point Z at random. Before, Bill could obtain the entire utility from any such output mix. Now the output must be shared with Steve. What is the "best" allocation of output mix Z? We have already seen that given amounts of meat and vegetables are efficiently allocated according to the Pareto criterion at all points on the exchange contract curve, CC. In fact, dropping perpendicular lines to the meat and vegetable axes from point Z forms an Edgeworth box bounded by $0MZV$. We can construct the exchange contract curve, CC, in normal fashion. Is there a way to determine which of all the points on the contract curve yields maximum efficiency? That is, all points on the contract curve are exchange-efficient, but are there points on the contract curve that are efficient in both production and exchange?

The answer is yes, and it derives from the efficiency rule MRT = MRS. With two consumers, the rule needs to be expanded to

$$\text{MRT} = MRS_B = MRS_S \qquad (13.5)$$

Figure 13.7
General Equilibrium in a
Two-Good, Two-Consumer Model

Production-exchange efficiency is
achieved when MRT = MRS_B =
MRS_S, as at point Z_1.

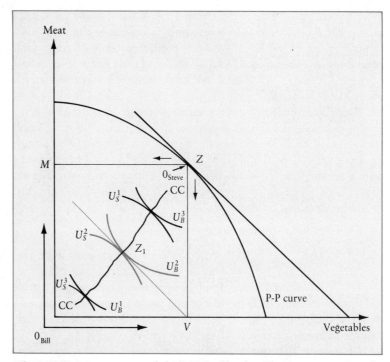

The MRT must now equal the MRS of both (all) consumers. Graphically, the slope of the line tangent to Z equals society's MRT. The slope of the line tangent to the indifference curves U_B^2 and U_S^2 is the equalized MRS of both consumers. When these two tangents are parallel, MRT = MRS_B = MRS_S. Thus at Z_1 the commodity mix Z is efficiently distributed according to the Pareto rule.

A numerical example will help clarify the logic of this assertion. Suppose the MRT of meat for vegetables equals 3; 3 units of meat can be produced by a shift in resources that reduces vegetable production by 1 unit. Assume that each person's MRS of meat for vegetables is 1; each is willing to trade 1 unit of meat for 1 unit of vegetables and remain indifferent. Thus MRT(3) > MRS(1) for both persons. A general equilibrium Pareto optimum is manifestly not acheived.

Now let resources be switched from the production of vegetables to meat at the margin, resulting in 3 more meat units and 1 less vegetable unit. Keep Bill at his original consumption combination. Take the 1-unit vegetable loss away from Steve and compensate him with 1 unit of meat. Both consumers are now as well off as before. But we have 2 units of meat left over! Give them each 1 extra meat unit, and both experience an improvement in utility. Give both meat units to Steve, and his utility rises without making Bill worse off. The presence of such mutually beneficial opportunities means that any production-exchange position for which MRT ≠ MRS of all trading partners is not optimal. All such possibilities are eliminated when MRT $= MRS_B = MRS_S$. In Figure 13.7, this condition is satisfied at Z_1, when Z is the final output selected. Such points as Z_1 (there may be more than one) achieve general Pareto optimality in production and exchange.

The Grand Utility Possibility Frontier and General Equilibrium

We can now map Bill's and Steve's utility levels resulting from various exchange and production decisions and formulate a method for identifying the utilities that correspond to the achievement of consumption and production efficiency.

Figure 13.8 contains a two-dimensional utility space, with Bill's utility measured vertically and Steve's horizontally. These are ordinal utilities; each individual ranks his own preferences, but Bill's rankings cannot be compared to Steve's.

Consider point Z on the production possibility curve in Figure 13.7. Exchange efficiency is achieved at the infinity of points on the contract curve, CC. Given the output combination Z, we can plot Bill's and Steve's utility combinations that would result at various points along CC. These utility combinations form the negatively sloped curve in Figure 13.8, which is called the **utility possibility frontier (UPF)**. The UPF_Z curve in Figure 13.8 slopes downward because movements along the contract curve (or conflict curve) increase one consumer's utility and decrease the other's.

The UPF_Z curve is associated with the specific point Z on the production possibility curve. For every point on the P-P curve, there is a unique Edgeworth box, a unique contract curve, and a unique

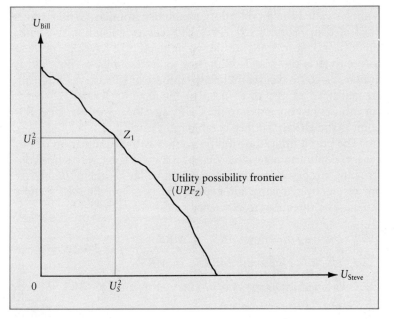

Figure 13.8
The Utility Possibility Frontier (UPF)

The UPF_Z curve corresponds to the contract curve, CC, associated with output mix Z. Utility combination Z_1 is the only point on the CC that achieves exchange and production efficiency for output mix Z.

Figure 13.9
The Grand Utility Possibility Frontier (GUPF)

The GUPF is the envelope of all UPF curves and hence the locus of all Pareto-efficient points, such as Z_1. In theory, the GUPF curve should lie on top of the outermost UPF curve; but for purposes of illustration, we have raised it slightly.

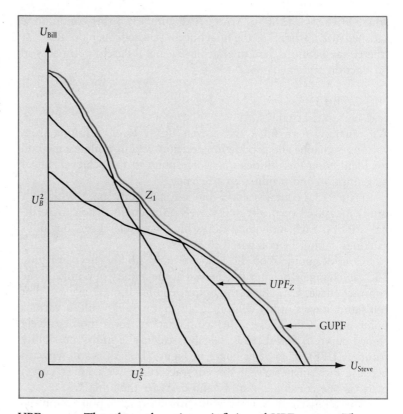

UPF curve. Therefore, there is an infinity of UPF curves. The envelope of all UPF curves is a curve that contains only exchange- and production-efficient points such as Z_1. The envelope of efficient points is called the **grand utility possibility frontier (GUPF)** and is illustrated in Figure 13.9. Three UPF curves, including the UPF_Z curve from Figure 13.8, are shown in black. The envelope of these UPF curves is the grand utility possibility frontier, GUPF, and is drawn as a colored curve. When the infinity of UPF curves is considered, instead of the three used in Figure 13.9, each UPF curve contributes just one point to the GUPF envelope. For each UPF, this point is the efficient utility combination, such as Z_1.

The grand utility possibility frontier is the culmination of our general equilibrium results. We have come a long way since constructing our first Edgeworth box, and it will be useful to summarize our results by retracing our steps. Every point on the $GUPF$ curve satisfies the three Pareto efficiency rules:

1. *Exchange efficiency:* $MRS_B = MRS_S$

2. *Production efficiency:* $MRTS_m = MRTS_v$

3. *Combined exchange and production efficiency:* $MRT = MRS_B = MRS_S$

Beginning at any point on the GUPF in Figure 13.9, all twelve general equilibrium variables can be obtained by reference to the underlying diagrams. Thus U_{Bill} and U_{Steve} appear directly in the *GUPF* in Figure 13.9. The output mix, M and V, and the distribution of the output between Bill and Steve, M_B, M_S, V_B, V_S, are shown in Figure 13.7; the input mix variables L_m, L_v, K_m, K_v are contained in the production Edgeworth box in Figure 13.4. All twelve variables are mutually determined. The only parameters in the model are the fixed quantities of labor and capital inputs.

As noted previously, the grand utility possibility frontier curve is negatively sloped. When all dimensions of efficiency are operating—as they are along the GUPF curve—production and exchange cannot be rearranged to help Bill without hurting Steve, and vice versa. If such mutual benefits were possible, efficiency would not yet have been achieved. Thus redistribution of production and exchange pits one person's utility against the other's. The full Pareto critera, reflected at every point on the GUPF curve, do not allow us to make the interpersonal utility comparisons needed to choose among the points on the GUPF curve. Some higher judgment—outside the weak efficiency rules of Pareto optimality—is required.

Competitive Markets and Economic Efficiency

So far, the description of economic efficiency in this chapter has been utterly devoid of any reference to competitive markets and the price system (except for a brief assertion). Efficiency involves allocating goods and productive services to their most valuable uses. The three-part Pareto criterion for efficiency could presumably be achieved by any omniscient and omnipotent government or social order.

But how close is the fit between the result of competitive markets and the benchmark of economic efficiency? A straightforward approach is to see whether the three efficiency rules are achieved by competitive market forces. If they are achieved, competition is efficient. If they are not, the price system can lay no claims to being an efficient allocator of goods and services.

Competitive Markets Lead to $MRS_B = MRS_S$

Competitive prices are determined by supply and demand. All consumers are price takers and hence face the same relative prices of goods. Each individual maximizes utility by selecting the combination of goods that equates MRS and the price ratio: This is the requirement for individual consumer optimization presented in Chapter 3. Because all consumers face the same ratio of prices, it follows that all consumers will adjust to the same MRS. The exchange efficiency rule is achieved in competitive markets.

Figure 13.10
Identical Price Ratios in Competition

In competition, consumers set the MRS equal to the same price ratio. Hence $MRS_S = MRS_B$, even though the amounts purchased may be very different.

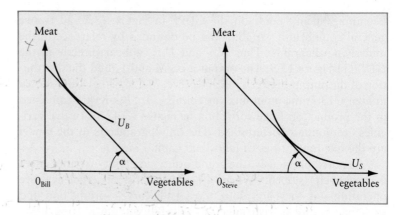

Figure 13.10 shows Bill and Steve adjusting their purchases of meat and vegetables until the MRS of each equals the identical price ratio α they both face. Their commodity bundles differ due to differences in preferences and incomes, but their marginal rates of substitution are equal in equilibrium.

Competitive Markets Lead to $MRTS_m = MRTS_v$

Competitive firms are price takers in all markets, including the input markets. Chapter 7 showed that, for any rate of output, each firm minimizes cost by adjusting input combinations so that the MRTS equals the ratio of input prices. But because all firms face the same input price ratios, they must all adjust to the same MRTS. The production analogy to Figure 13.10 is obvious; simply replace the indifference maps and budget lines with isoquant maps and isocost lines. Competition achieves production efficiency as well.

Competitive Markets Lead to MRT = MRS

The last lap is to see if competitive forces equate society's MRT with consumers' MRS and hence with the ratio of meat and vegetable prices. The MRT is the slope of the production possibility curve, or

$$\text{MRT} = \frac{\Delta M}{\Delta V}\bigg|L, K \text{ on production CC} \qquad (13.5)$$

It is the rate at which the economy can switch from vegetable to meat production while remaining on the production contract curve. We know that the MRS equals the ratio of commodity prices in equilibrium:

$$\text{MRS} = \frac{P_v}{P_m} \qquad (13.6)$$

The profit-maximizing condition for each competitive firm is to equate P and MC. Hence Equation 13.6 can be extended to read

$$\text{MRS} = \frac{P_v}{P_m} = \frac{MC_v}{MC_m} \qquad (13.7)$$

Defining the marginal costs explicitly and rearranging terms yields

$$\frac{MC_v}{MC_m} = \frac{\dfrac{\Delta TC_v}{\Delta V}}{\dfrac{\Delta TC_m}{\Delta M}} = \frac{\Delta M}{\Delta V} \cdot \frac{\Delta TC_v}{\Delta TC_m} \qquad (13.8)$$

Next, let's arbitrarily remove \$1 from the production of meat and add it to the production of vegetables. Note that $\Delta TC_v = +\$1$ and that $\Delta TC_m = -\$1$. Thus Equation 13.8 reveals that the ratio of marginal costs is

$$\frac{MC_v}{MC_m} = -\frac{\Delta M}{\Delta V} = \text{MRT} \qquad (13.9)$$

The MRT equals the ratio of marginal costs. In competitive equilibrium, the ratio of marginal costs is set equal to the ratio of prices by profit-maximizing firms. And consumers adjust their MRS to equal the ratio of prices. Hence the utility- and profit-maximizing signals inherent in the price system lead competitive markets to a Pareto-efficient allocation of productive resources and final goods.

The Social Welfare Function

The weak Pareto criterion—an action is beneficial to society if it helps someone without hurting anyone—is one way to judge between different states of the world without making interpersonal utility comparisons. Yet such efficiency can occur at an infinity of points on the GUPF curve. In short, efficiency defines a function, not a point.

In order to select the "best" of all efficient utility combinations on the GUPF curve—often called the **constrained bliss point**—it is necessary to introduce ethical judgments. We need a statement of social welfare that transcends the society members' private utility considerations. We can deepen our understanding of economic efficiency by studying the implications of a set of ethical judgments.

Judgments about how Bill's and Steve's private utilities are to enter into the measurement of aggregate societal welfare are expressed by the **social welfare function (SWF)**:[7]

$$\text{SWF} = f(U_B, U_S) \qquad (13.10)$$

---

7. The social welfare function was first proposed by Abram Bergson, "A Reformulation of Certain Aspects of Welfare Economics," *Quarterly Journal of Economics* 52 (1938): 310–314.

Social welfare depends on society members' utility levels. But ethical considerations tell us how their various utilities affect aggregate social welfare. Does Bill's utility count more or less than Steve's? We can no longer ignore this question.

The indifference curve–type countours labeled W in Figure 13.11 are a graphic representation of the social welfare function. Movements along a curve do not alter society's welfare. Movements to the northeast, in the direction of the arrow, increase social welfare. Interpersonal utility comparisons are implicit in the social welfare function. The "worthiness" of utilities in social welfare is expressed by the slopes of the welfare contour lines. For example, if the curves were vertical, Bill's utility would be totally disregarded in calculating social welfare. The ethical evaluations of the relative worth of society members' utilities are reflected in the shape of the social welfare function.

Once the notion of social welfare is introduced, a solution to the general equilibrium model can be analyzed. The highest welfare

Figure 13.11
The GUPF and the Social Welfare Function (SWF)

The tangency between the GUPF and the SWF illustrates the ideal constrained bliss point, Ω.

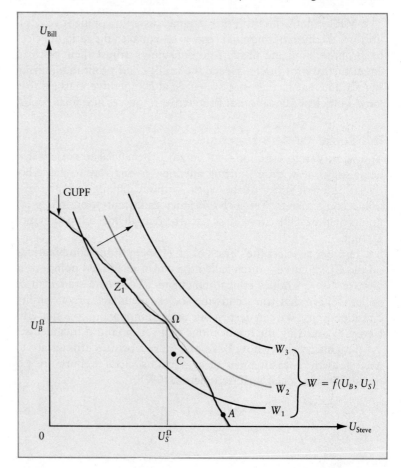

available to society is Ω in Figure 13.11, where the grand utility possibility frontier, GUPF, is tangent to the highest attainable welfare curve. Once the bliss point Ω has been identified, all other general equilibrium values in production and exchange can be determined by retracing our steps, as we have already shown.

The following observations are necessary to put this discussion of welfare economics in the proper light. First, the social welfare function cannot be observed or measured. Voting behavior in democracies and edicts in dictatorships are very imperfect methods of defining the social welfare.[8] Second, the equilibrium at Ω cannot be observed even if it is attained. If we cannot define, measure, or observe a social welfare optimum, does the concept have any usefulness whatever? Yes. As with any model, its value lies in its ability to organize our thoughts. The theoretical apparatus of welfare economics that reaches its culmination in Figure 13.11 shows the following:

1. If we could know the SWF, we could not maximize it at Ω without efficiency in production and exchange. Efficiency is necessary for welfare maximization.

2. Competitive markets in all products and inputs will achieve efficiency but will lead only to a point on the GUPF curve, not necessarily Ω. Competition may instead lead to point A, one of an infinity of stable competitive equilibria. *the highest welfare pt.*

3. Competitive markets lead to efficiency, but efficiency does not require competition. Alternative economic structures could ideally move to the GUPF if equipped with sufficient knowledge and decisionmaking authority. Thus competition is a sufficient but not a necessary condition for economic efficiency.

4. Certain moves can worsen social welfare but increase efficiency, and vice versa. For example, a move from C to A represents a gain in efficiency but a loss in social welfare, because of the extreme maldistribution of income implied by A. Thus increasing efficiency and increasing social welfare are not always compatible objectives.

Thus we have seen what has up to now been little more than an assertion: Competitive markets → efficiency. But note the direction of the arrow. As stated previously, economywide competition is sufficient but not necessary for achieving a point on the GUPF. Furthermore, the point achieved on the GUPF may be an "inequitable" but efficient point, like point A in Figure 13.11, and hence inconsistent with maximization of social welfare.

8. For an extensive discussion of how unlikely it is that a social-choice mechanism based on voting will reflect individual preferences, see K. Arrow, *Social Choice and Individual Values* (New York: Wiley, 1951).

Shopping Malls and Pareto Optimality

APPLIED
MICRO
THEORY

13.1

The Whiteflint Shopping Mall in Montgomery County, Maryland consists of fine shops and department stores, including the famous Bloomingdale's and Lord and Taylor. The mall was completed in 1978 after being blocked for years by local residents. The negotiated settlement between the developer and the residents that led to the required zoning permits serves as a good example of the process of moving toward the contract curve. "Negotiated development" is a modern alternative to expensive confrontation.*

The Whiteflint Mall was first proposed in 1970 to be built on what was then a golf course. Owners of nearby and abutting property opposed construction for fear of lowered property values and of uninhabitability due to night lights, car traffic, inadequate storm drainage, tall buildings

*See these references for more on this and many other examples of negotiated development: Malcolm D. Rivkin, *Negotiated Development: A Breakthrough in Environmental Controversies* (Washington, D.C.: Conservation Foundation, 1977); and L. Susskind and A. Weinstein, "Towards a Theory of Environmental Dispute Resolution," *Boston College Environmental Affairs Law Review* 9, no. 2 (1980/1981).

inconsistent with their bucolic setting, and the detritus accompanying fast-food restaurants.

The outcome of negotiations between the property owners and the developers included several guarantees:

1. A building height limit of 60 feet.
2. Structures set back from the property line.
3. Traffic routes around the neighborhood.
4. A large 14-foot-high hill constructed out of surplus dirt from the excavation. This hill (or berm) was sodded and landscaped to provide a pleasant vista for owners of abutting property. Because of the hill and the shopping center set back, homeowners cannot see the development.
5. Indemnification of the homeowners against lost property value, provided by the developer.

This package led to approval of the zoning changes and thereby demonstrated the efficiency of negotiation versus confrontation. A valuable development was put into place, and homeowners also benefited.

Several basic principles of welfare economics are illustrated in this example:

1. Negotiations will fail unless a package is derived that accomplishes Pareto optimality.

2. The compensation package should exploit the comparative advantages of the developer and the homeowners. This allows the discovery of least-cost methods of compensation and increases the likelihood that a settlement can be found. For example, the berm was built at practically no cost, because surplus dirt had to be gotten rid of in any case. Also, property values do not generally fall when Bloomingdale's locates nearby; in fact, they usually rise. Thus the developer could indemnify the property owners with little risk.

3. Compensation should address the residents' complaints. Unrelated compensations are inefficient, because the marginal rate of substitution rises as the good becomes scarcer. For example, if unsightly night lights are the issue, it is cheaper to reduce the unsightliness than to pay people to accept it. (In addition to the inefficiency of unrelated compensations, people react negatively to bribes unless jaded by a course in intermediate microeconomics.)

4. The compensation package will usually include a mixture of compensations as people negotiate toward the contract curve.

Efficiency and Envy

APPLIED
MICRO
THEORY

13.2

Using a two-good Edgeworth box, we have seen that when commodity allocations are not Pareto optimal, mutually advantageous trading can take place until the parties attain an allocation on the contract curve. We have also seen that once the parties

are on the contract curve, we cannot use the Pareto principle to select among points on the curve. Also, it is possible for a final, efficient allocation to result in one trader ending up with more of both goods, even though the trades that move the parties to the contract curve make both parties better off. This possibility has caused many people to worry

about the equity of exchange allocations. Here we can consider some propositions about envy and efficiency in exchange.

First, **economic envy** is one party's preference for the reversal of allocations. That is, if Bill has 3 pounds of meat and 1 pound of vegetables and Steve has 3 pounds of meat and 2 pounds of vegetables, Bill is envious of Steve because he prefers Steve's commodity bundle to his own. In this example, Steve is not envious of Bill, although we will see later that it is possible for each to prefer the other's bundle.

Consider point E in Figure A, which is the point of equality of both goods and therefore serves as an extreme example of an allocation without envy. Suppose the allocation is changed from E to A. Is either Bill or Steve envious at A? To answer this question, it is necessary to derive the reversal of allocation A. Consider the straight line AEA_1, which is drawn from point A through point E. A and A_1 are equidistant from E, by construction. Thus A_1 is the reversal of A. Similarly, B_1 is the reversal of B, and all points on the line between A_1 and B_1 are the reversals of all points on the contract curve between A and B. Trading from the equality point E to any point on the contract curve between A and B does not engender envy in either party. Because the indifference curves are convex, both parties are better off at any point along AB than at the corresponding allocation reversal along A_1B_1.

It is also easy to see the possibility of going from an inefficient allocation with no envy to an efficient allocation with envy—while the utility of both parties is increased. In Figure B, the initial allocation is A, and its reversal is A_1. At A neither party is envious. There is nothing in the convexity conditions of indifference curves that rules out a move to B, whose reversal is B_1. But Bill prefers B_1 to B. Thus the Pareto move from A to B engenders envy in Bill even though he is better of at B than at A.

Can both parties be envious? Figure C shows that they can indeed, if the reversal of the initial allocation is Pareto-preferred. Both Bill and Steve would prefer the other's allocation instead of their own when A is the given allocation. That is, A_1, the reversal of A, is preferred by both parties. Trade will take place.

Figure A
Envy and Efficiency

Envy is one party's preference for a reversal of allocations.

For any actual allocation between points A and B, neither party prefers the reversal. Hence such allocations entail no envy.

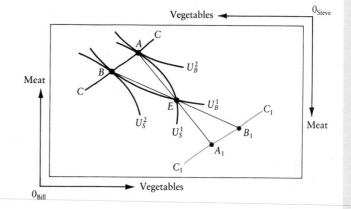

Figure B
Trade with Envy

Allocation A is inefficient, but it engenders no envy. Trade to B yields efficiency and higher levels of utility for both parties. Yet Bill is envious at B, because the reversal, B_1, would increase his utility even more.

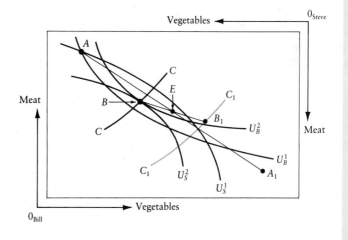

As a final exercise, we can construct an example in which trading among three people can engender envy in one trader, even if all three start with equal allocations. That is, although trade between two parties starting with equality cannot lead to envy, the result does not extend to three or more traders.

For simplicity, assume that Jane and Sally have identical preferences but that Ann has different prefer-

Continued on page 438

ences. All three persons have equal allocations of commodities—3 pounds of meat and 3 pounds of vegetables. Figure D illustrates the trading between Jane and Ann. (Initially there are no mutually beneficial trades between Jane and Sally, because their preferences and endowments are identical.) Let Jane and Ann trade from A to B. The gains from trade are such that both are better off at B than at A. At B, Jane has 4 pounds of meat and 2 pounds of vegetables and achieves a utility level U^1_{Jane}.

We can use the information about allocations contained in Figure D to construct an Edgeworth box for trading between the parties with identical preferences— Jane and Sally. In Figure E, point A represents Jane's original 3 meat, 3 vegetable allocation before trading with Ann, and point B is the starting point for the trading between Jane and Sally. At point B, Jane has a 4 meat, 2 vegetable allocation and a utility level of U^1_{Jane}; Sally has her initial 3, 3 allocation and utility level U^0_{Sally}. Because they have identical preferences, $U^1_{Jane} > U^0_{Sally}$. The prior trade between Jane and Ann has destroyed the equality in allocations and utility between Jane and Sally. Note that Sally is now en-

Figure C
Mutual Envy

Both parties are envious at allocation A, because A_1, the reversal of A, lies on the contract curve.

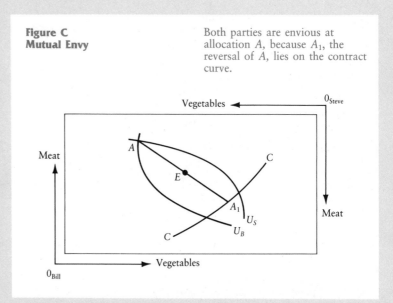

vious of Jane, because point B represents higher utility for Jane than for Sally. Furthermore, trade between Jane and Sally cannot reestablish equal allocations and utility even though the round of trading began with equal allocations and utility levels for both parties. To be sure, Sally can be made better off by trading with Jane because of the prior trade

between Jane and Ann. Trading to a point within the shaded lens-shaped area in Figure E improves the utility of both parties. However, Sally will always prefer Jane's allocation to her own.*

*For a mathematical derivation of these and other results on equity and envy, see A. Feldman and A. Kirman, "Fairness and Envy," *American Economic Review* 64 (1974): 995–1005.

Theory of the Second-Best

Continuing with our simple general equilibrium model, let's assume that the meat industry is monopolized and that vegetables are produced in competitive markets. It is reasonable to think that the maximum attainable efficiency would be achieved by following competitive pricing rules where possible (in the vegetables market) and hoping for the best elsewhere. Surprisingly, when some markets in the system are not competitive, following the competitive pricing rules in those that are generally will not lead to efficiency![9] This is the theory of the second-best; when some markets are not competitive, the **second-best solution** to efficiency involves noncompetitive pricing in all markets.

The following example illustrates the logic of second-best solutions. Monopoly production of meat implies that $P_m > MC_m$, and competitive production of vegetables yields $P_v = MC_v$. Thus

9. R. G. Lipsey and K. Lancaster, "The General Theory of Second Best," *Review of Economic Studies* 24 (1956/1957): 11–32.

Figure D
Envy in a Three-Way Trade

Here Ann and Jane trade away
from the equality point *A* to
point *B*.

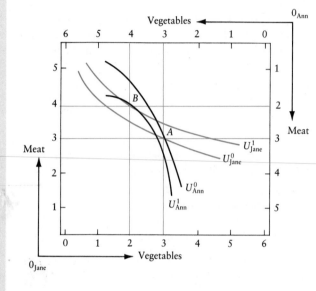

Figure E
Envy in a Three-Way Trade

Here Jane begins with 4 units of meat
and 2 of vegetables; Sally begins with
3 of each. Sally is envious. Furthermore,
there is no Pareto-optimal reallocation
from *B* to relieve Sally's envy.

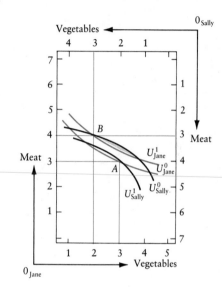

$$\frac{P_m}{P_v} > \frac{MC_m}{MC_v} = \text{MRT} \qquad (13.11)$$

The ratio of prices exceeds the ratio of marginal costs. Recall that
society's MRT is equal to the ratio of marginal costs.

To sharpen the illustration, assume that we are back to an
economy with only one consumer. This assumption permits a
straightforward graphic comparison of the economy's MRT and the
single consumer's MRS. Recall that

$$\text{MRS} = \frac{\Delta M}{\Delta V}\bigg|_{U} = \frac{P_m}{P_v} \qquad (13.12)$$

and that

$$\text{MRT} = \frac{\Delta M}{\Delta V}\bigg|_{L,\ K} = \frac{MC_m}{MC_v} \qquad (13.13)$$

Efficiency requires that MRS = MRT. Such a position is illustrated by point A in Figure 13.12, where the P-P curve is tangent to the highest attainable indifference curve. But a mixed system of competitive-monopoly pricing results in MRS > MRT in our example (Equation 13.11), illustrated as point B. Even if exchange and production efficiency are achieved, the third Pareto criterion—MRS = MRT—will not be. So if $P_m > MC_m$ in the monopoly market, setting $P_v = MC_v$ in the competitive market will not lead to economic inefficiency.

Theoretically, there is a way to get to point A in Figure 13.12 in a mixed competitive-monopoly price system. Suppose both markets set prices so that the ratio of price to marginal cost is the same, or

$$\frac{\hat{P}_m}{MC_m} = \frac{\hat{P}_v}{MC_v} \tag{13.14}$$

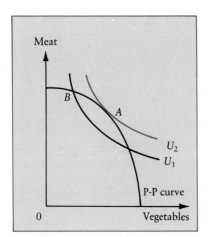

Figure 13.12
The Theory of the Second-Best

When price does not reflect marginal cost in all markets, point A (efficiency) can be achieved by optimal departures from competitive prices in all markets. Point B (inefficiency) is achieved by allowing competitive markets to set price at marginal cost.

where $\hat{P}_m$ and $\hat{P}_v$ are meat and vegetable prices adjusted to equate the ratio of price and marginal cost in both markets. Now MRS = MRT even though $\hat{P} \neq MC$ in each market.

We can rewrite Equation 13.14 as

$$\frac{\hat{P}_m}{MC_m} - 1 = \frac{\hat{P}_v}{MC_v} - 1$$

It in turn can be restated as

$$\frac{\hat{P}_m - MC_m}{MC_m} = \frac{\hat{P}_v - MC_v}{MC_v} \tag{13.15}$$

When competitive pricing cannot be achieved in all markets, efficiency requires that the percentage departure of price from marginal cost be the same for all goods. This condition allows the attainment of point A in Figure 13.12. It is called a second-best solution to efficiency in the presence of noncompetitive markets.

The theory of the second-best gains importance when we realize that some parts of the economy are not competitive. In such cases, prices do not reflect marginal costs. Monopoly markets provide the most striking example, but there are other important reasons why prices may not reflect marginal costs. When the benefits of certain goods are enjoyed collectively (national defense) or when the absence of property rights allows goods to be used as though they had zero cost (bison in the old West), prices will not reflect marginal costs either. Chapter 14 deals with such considerations. Also, the P

= MC equality assumes implicitly that all goods and services are infinitely divisible. Perfect divisibility of products and inputs is required in order to get smooth, well-behaved indifference curves, isoquant curves, cost curves, and production possibility curves. But if commodities are available only in lumps instead of in continuous units, these curves will have discrete discontinuities, and the marginal conditions required for efficiency may not be achievable. Thus the theory of the second-best has a potentially wide range of applications in which prices do not reflect marginal costs.

Monopoly Regulation: Marginal-Cost Pricing versus Average-Cost Pricing

We studied monopoly in Chapter 9 and, within the partial equilibrium framework, used the welfare loss triangle to measure the welfare loss resulting from monopoly pricing. Figure 13.13 shows the nondiscriminating monopolist's equilibrium and the resulting welfare loss triangle ABC. Price is the estimator of marginal benefit, and marginal cost equals the marginal benefit forgone. Monopoly results in too little output produced in the monopoly markets. In

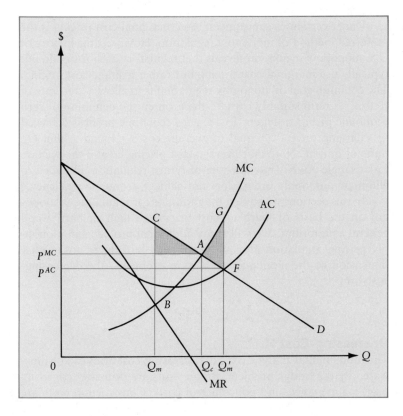

Figure 13.13
The Efficiency of Marginal-Cost Pricing

Production of output greater or less than Q_m creates a welfare loss triangle.

monopoly equilibrium, there are units of output not produced for which $P \equiv \text{MB} > \text{MC} \equiv \text{MB}$ forgone. Each marginal unit not produced when $P > \text{MC}$ involves a welfare loss resulting from a maldistribution of resources. The sum of these welfare losses equals the welfare loss triangle ABC.

If the distortions in the rest of the economy's markets are negligible, so that competition exists as a first approximation elsewhere, **marginal-cost pricing** can be used in monopoly regulation. Requiring the monopoly to charge the competitive, marginal-cost price P^{MC} (and to serve the resulting market quantity demanded, Q_C) is a way of eliminating the welfare loss triangle, a partial equilibrium concept. If the rest of the economy is competitive, marginal-cost pricing regulation has the added feature of attempting to achieve a general equilibrium efficiency, where MRS = MRT.

If the monopolist's maximum price is set at P^{MC}, its marginal revenue equals price P^{MC} up to output Q_C. So regulated, marginal-cost pricing induces the monopolist to equate MR and MC at point A. The partial equilibrium welfare loss disappears and the general equilibrium efficiency is also achieved, because with marginal-cost pricing in the monopoly sector, all markets in the economy price at marginal cost.

Under certain circumstances, then, marginal-cost pricing is the preferred method of monopoly regulation. However, the history of U.S. monopoly regulation reveals that regulatory authorities do not typically use marginal-cost pricing but rather **average-cost pricing.** The common goal of monopoly regulation is to allow a "fair rate of return," a term suitably close to the economist's definition of zero economic profit. In Figure 13.13, zero economic profit is achieved by charging price P^{AC} equal to average cost $Q'_m F$ and selling Q'_m units of output. Note that average-cost pricing creates the welfare loss triangle AGF. Thus fair-rate-of-return regulation, intended to eliminate monopoly profit, does not achieve economic efficiency.

In this section, we studied the rationale for regulating monopolies on the basis of marginal-cost pricing in light of partial and general equilibrium. We will study additional problems in monopoly pricing regulation after we have been introduced to another dimension of the monopoly regulation problem—the decreasing-cost firm.

Decreasing-Cost Firms

The fundamental analytic issue of **decreasing-cost firms** can be illustrated by the bridge problem. Bridge costs are primarily construction, maintenance, and police patrol costs. Construction costs are

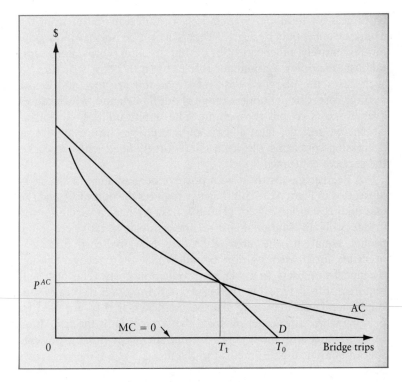

Figure 13.14
The Bridge Problem

Marginal-cost pricing achieves efficiency; average-cost pricing merely covers the cost of financing the bridge.

clearly independent of the number of cars that actually use the bridge—actual volume being independent of planned volume.[10] Even maintenance costs are nearly fixed with respect to car volume, because weather—not car travel—causes the bulk of the damage. Thus the marginal cost of an extra trip across the bridge is virtually zero. The use of bridge services does not use up the bridge. Efficiency calls for a zero (or near zero) price equal to marginal cost.

The bridge problem is shown graphically in Figure 13.14. Assume that all bridge costs are independent of travel. The average cost is thus the rectangular hyperbola AC and the marginal cost is zero (coincident with the horizontal axis). Efficiency requires a zero price, allowing the quantity of trips to rise to point T_0. However, the bridge must be financed somehow. An average-cost price of P^{AC} is required to finance the bridge, provided perhaps by driver tolls. But tolls reduce bridge travel from T_0 to T_1, manifestly inefficient because the forgone trips, $T_0 - T_1$, could have been provided at zero marginal cost. Thus the presence of decreasing costs drives a wedge between efficiency pricing and financing requirements necessary for provision of the services.

Now let's consider a case closer to the firms that may actually

10. In Milwuakee, a bridge over the harbor was planned for 160,000 cars per day, but actual volume is far less. Average cost per car is thus greater than planned.

be targets for monopoly regulation. Certain firms differ from the bridge example only by degree. That is, a firm's costs may be largely, but not entirely, independent of output. In other words, fixed capital costs may play a dominant role in the firm's cost structure. In such cases the marginal costs of expansion are low and below average costs throughout the range of output demand, which causes average costs to fall throughout. The public utilities—including electricity, sewage, natural gas, and telephone—are examples of decreasing-cost firms whose costs are largely fixed with respect to the services consumed.

A decreasing-cost firm with positive but low marginal costs is illustrated in Figure 13.15. Efficiency requires the output Q_e and the marginal cost price $P^{MC} = Q_e A$. But now we have a variant of the bridge problem. Marginal-cost pricing results in negative economic profits equal to the area $P^{MC}CBA$. Marginal-cost pricing—necessary for efficiency—does not allow the firm to recover enough revenue from users to cover all production costs. The firm will require a subsidy equal to the loss $P^{MC}CBA$ in order to break even. But general subsidies may also be inefficient if they are paid by persons who gain no benefit from the service. Thus the regulation of decreasing-cost monopolies by marginal-cost pricing presents special analytical and practical problems.

Figure 13.15
Regulation of Decreasing-Cost Firms

The marginal-cost price P^{MC} results in negative economic profits for the firm.

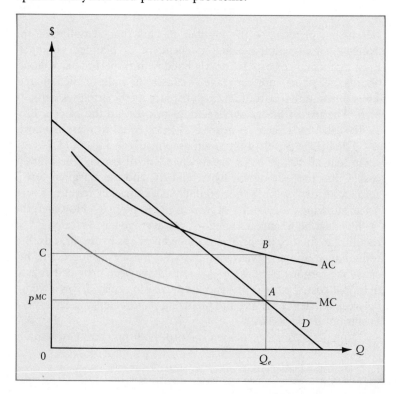

Two-Part Pricing: A Method for Regulating Decreasing-Cost Firms

APPLIED MICRO THEORY

13.3

The two-part tariff is one way to remedy the difficulties that arise from marginal-cost pricing in a decreasing-cost monopoly. Customers are charged in two steps, as Figure 13.15 helps to illustrate:

1. Divide the loss $P^{MC}CBA$ equally among all users and charge them all an "entry" price equal to a per-capital share of the loss. This is a lump-sum payment independent of use; its sole purpose is to recover the firm's loss and allow it to break even.
2. Charge each user the marginal-cost price P^{MC} for each unit purchased.

Such a **two-part pricing** policy has the merit of getting the efficient output Q_e produced (because of the second step) and allowing the firm to cover costs (because of the first step). In Figure 13.15, revenue $0P^{MC}AQ_e$ is received from consumers in user charges and revenue $P^{MC}CBA$ is received as an "entry fee," or a lump sum that gives the individual the "right to purchase" units at marginal cost. (An example is telephone service.) If the entry fee does not reduce any user's quantity demanded to zero, the two-part pricing scheme is Pareto optimal.

However, the two-part tariff has been criticized on equity grounds. Users differ in their incomes and wealth, and the fixed entry fee therefore constitutes a larger percentage of income and wealth for the poor. Thus the entry fee has the same regressive effect as any lump-sum tax or head tax. Also, consumers differ in their use of the service. Even if everyone had equal incomes and wealth, we would still have an equity problem: Consumers who use more face a lower average fixed charge.

Two-part pricing is the perfect solution for regulating decreasing-cost industries if economic efficiency is the only criterion of social welfare. But if equity is also important, the two-part tariff needs modification.

Block Pricing

APPLIED MICRO THEORY

13.4

Block pricing is a first cousin to the two-part tariff. Its purpose is the same: to allow decreasing-cost firms enough revenue to cover costs (the entry fee) but to use marginal-cost pricing to assure efficiency.

Consider the case of electricity. Under block pricing, the customer is charged a high price for the first block of consumption of electricity and is charged lower prices (perhaps equal to marginal cost) for all additional units of electricity purchased. Note that block pricing results in a lower per-unit price for large-scale users. Suppose that Bill uses 200 kilowatts of electricity per month and Steve uses 2000. Let a block price of $10 per charged for the first 100 kilowatts used, or $0.10 per kilowatt, and $0.05 per kilowatt be charged on all units purchased in excess of 100 kilowatts. Bill's total electric bill is thus $15, or $0.075 per kilowatt.

Steve's total bill is $105, or $0.052 per kilowatt. Clearly, block pricing results in lower average prices for those who use more electricity. If use is positively related to income and wealth, block pricing is a regressive pricing policy.

Of course, the government can gain some equity in two-part tariff and block pricing schemes by lowering the entry fee for the poor. However, measurement, reporting, and administrative problems may make such equity gains difficult to implement.

Average-Cost Pricing

APPLIED
MICRO
THEORY

13.5

Regulation of public utilities is beset with another major problem: serving the peak demand. Although public utilities have been described as decreasing-cost industries, sudden increases in demand can put such burdens on production that average and marginal costs rise as the firm expands output on a short-term basis. What kind of price regulation is suitable to handle the problem of serving the peak load?

Let's again use the electric utilities as an example. Electricity-generating capacity typically comes from a variety of plants; for simplicity, we will consider three (and abuse some technical terms in the process):

1. *Primary generators:* These are usually large coal-fired or nuclear-powered steam generators. Primary generators spin constantly because they are too costly to stop and start. Thus additional electricity is available from these generators at very low marginal cost. Within the range of the capacity of the primary generators, electric utilities are certainly decreasing-cost firms.

2. *Secondary generators:* These are typically smaller steam generators and jet turbines that can be stopped and started on short notice. They act as backup capacity for peak-demand periods. The marginal cost of electricity from secondary generators is higher than from the primary generators. When they must be used, costs rise.

3. *Borrowed electricity:* Capacity is borrowed from other regions to meet peak demand and as insurance against brownouts and blackouts. (Borrowing is a form of spreading risks.) This is the most expensive source of electricity because it must be trans-

mitted over long distances and is often produced from inefficient backup generators at its source.

Given these cost characteristics of electric capacity, the cost curves of an electric utility appear like those exhibited in the figure. The off-peak demand is represented by the demand curve $D_{\text{off peak}}$ and the peak demand by D_{peak}. What pricing strategies are available now?

Without attempting a definitive answer, we can at least confront certain issues that follow naturally from welfare economics. Average-cost pricing is the norm in regulating electrical utilities. But because demand fluctuates, the average cost of electricity also changes. Which average-cost price

do regulatory authorities select? Consider the price P^{AC}. When demand is $D_{\text{off peak}}^0$, P^{AC} exceeds the average cost of providing Q_1 units of output by the distance ab. During those off-peak periods, positive economic profits are earned. But during peak demand, the average cost of service rises. If price P^{AC} is kept constant, the utility earns negative economic profit at output Q_4, because average cost now exceeds price P^{AC} by ef. Thus the strategy of using a single price for all times and seasons is a way of shooting for an average normal return over the peak, off-peak cycle. This is the strategy most regulatory authorities adopt. Mathematically speaking,

$$P^{AC} = \frac{[AC(Q_1) \cdot Q_1] + [AC(Q_4) \cdot Q_4]}{Q_1 + Q_4}$$

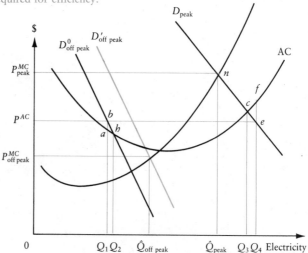

Peak-Load Pricing

Constant prices in the face of fluctuating demand result in inefficient electricity usage. Various schemes can approximate the differential "peak-load" prices required for efficiency.

Seasonal Rates

APPLIED
MICRO
THEORY

13.6

Electricity use is higher on average in the summer than in the winter, primarily because of the energy requirements of air conditioning units. Some regulatory authorities have adopted **seasonal rates** to make consumers pay a higher price for the higher-cost electricity brought on line during peak summer periods. This policy certainly goes in the direction of letting prices reflect the opportunity costs of production. However, seasonal rates cannot reflect marginal-cost pricing very closely. They merely recognize the higher average cost of providing summer electricity due to the greater frequency of summer peaks. Seasonal rates may be viewed as a "floating" average-cost price, which allows prices to rise in the summer months enough to cover the higher average costs of summer electricity. Such prices respond only to seasonal demand fluctuations but not to hourly shifts. In the figure accompanying Applied Micro Theory 13.5, winter (off-peak) rates and output of $Q_2 h$ and Q_2 and summer (peak) rates and output of $Q_3 c$ and Q_3 would allow the utility to earn a fair rate of return year-round and would cut electricity use somewhat during the summer as customers seek substitutes in the face of higher electricity prices.

Comparing year-round average-cost pricing to seasonal average-cost pricing, seasonal rates cause a cutback along the demand curve D_{peak} from e to c at the peak. Thus peak electric capacity needs fall from Q_4 to Q_3. The quantitative difference between Q_4 and Q_3 depends on the price elasticity of demand for peak electricity use, which in turn depends on the availability of substitutes. And here we see the essential weakness of seasonal rates. The price elasticity of demand for electricity under seasonal rates reflects primarily the substitution of electricity for alternative sources of energy. Under seasonal rates, consumers are not given the option of waiting until after the peak to run their electrical appliances. Who can save their dirty dishes and dirty clothes from June to September to wash them in the off-peak period? In short, seasonal rates do not present customers with many money-saving incentives to switch electricity use to the off-peak period. (Of course, customers can sell their electrical appliances and switch to, say, natural gas. But then they would have the wrong appliance when costs are low again.) We should expect very little switch in consumption patterns to result from seasonal rates.

This brings us to another implication of seasonal rates. For technical reasons, an electric utility must have enough reserve capacity to meet the peak—or it must shut down entirely. The system cannot be run on overload for more than a few seconds without resulting in total loss of power. This technological fact limits the usefulness of seasonal rates. Higher summer rates may reduce the use of air conditioning on average, but it may have no effect on the "actual peak." A customer may respond to seasonal rates this way: "I used to turn on the air conditioner to maintain a temperature of 80 degrees or less. With summer rates I will shoot for 85 degrees or less." Seasonal rates may simply alter the average cutomer's breaking point. Average capacity requirements over the summer will be less under seasonal rates, but the utility must have enough excess capacity to handle the one 97-degree day when all air conditioner switches go on regardless of summer rates. Thus summer rates are not so effective as marginal-cost pricing in lowering the excess-capacity requirements of the utility.*

*Sewage systems exhibit the same excess-capacity requirements. Excess capacity must be sufficient to handle the single heaviest rainstorm expected. It only takes one electrical blackout or one basement full of sewage to learn the need for such excess capacity.

Time-of-Day Rates

APPLIED
MICRO
THEORY

13.7

Marginal-cost pricing must allow the consumer the option of saving money by using electricity during off-peak periods. For example, **time-of-day pricing** is a good approximation of marginal-cost pricing. Dishes can be washed in the off-peak evening hours, when electricity is generated at low marginal cost and when the price of electricity is correspondingly low. And consumers may even forgo some daytime air conditioning if they can look forward to some low-cost evening relief.

In the figure in Applied Micro Theory 13.5, the correct marginal-cost price at the peak is P^{MC}_{peak}, because $P = MC$ at point n. The peak capacity, Q_{peak}, is smaller than Q_3, the peak capacity needed under seasonal rates. Again, the quantitative difference between Q_{peak} and Q_3 depends on the price elasticity of electricity under time-of-day pricing, the major determinant of which is the substitutes available to consumers when price rises at the peak. Under time-of-day pricing, we would expect to see considerable shifting of electricity consumption from daytime

Continued on page 448

to nighttime use. Thus the difference between $\hat{Q}_{peak}$ (capacity needed under time-of-day pricing) and Q_3 (capacity needed under seasonal rates) is likely to be quite large, because there is a great deal of discretion in home appliance use. Proper marginal-cost pricing reduces the excess capacity needed to serve peak demand. (Environmentalists should favor marginal-cost pricing, because it implies fewer power plants.)

Time-of-day pricing exhibits another useful feature. The demand for off-peak electricity is a function of, among other things, the prices of substitutes. Under time-of-day rates, peak and off-peak electricity are substitutes. Thus the effect of a marginal-cost price of P^{MC} at the peak tends to increase the off-peak demand to $D'_{off\ peak}$. This demand

shift is beneficial because it increases the use of electricity during off-peak hours, when marginal cost is low. Thus under time-of-day rates, the excess capacity required to serve the peak falls to $\hat{Q}_{peak}$, and the off-peak price $P^{MC}_{off\ peak}$ generates $\hat{Q}_{off\ peak}$ units of electricity consumed, thereby spreading the capacity more evenly over peak and off-peak periods. There are clear economic gains in both of these results. Under seasonal rates, peak and off-peak electricity are not substitutes. Thus seasonal rates do not shift the off-peak demand for electricity, and the excess capacity cannot be as evenly spread over the peak, off-peak cycle.

Time-of-day rates come closer to the marginal-cost pricing ideal than seasonal rates because of the substitutes that time-of-day

rates offer consumers. Of course, time-of-day pricing is not perfect marginal-cost pricing either. Ideally, a home consumer or a plant supervisor should be able to consult a meter that measures the actual marginal cost of use at any given time. Then each customer could compare that marginal cost with the marginal benefit of use. Such a perfectly calibrated information system is not now in place, and time-of-day pricing is an imperfect attempt to convey such information. The technology of marginal-cost metering is now well underway. Meanwhile, many municipalities could benefit by the simple expedient of replacing flat average-cost and seasonal rates with time-of-day pricing.

Key Terms

Summary

This chapter uses a graphic analysis of general equilibrium to outline the various efficiency criteria of Pareto optimality. Even if we could know the social welfare function, the competitive economy would maximize social welfare only by accident. Competition in all markets will get the economy to the grand utility possibility frontier (GUPF) but not necessarily to the best place along it. Once the frontier has been attained, movement along it requires some group to vote against its own interest or a higher power to arrange adjustments in the consumption patterns of society's members.

The general equilibrium model sets the stage for an analysis of the Pareto optimality of competitive marginal-cost pricing. This chapter investigates the role of marginal-cost pricing in several public-policy debates, including the regulation of decreasing-cost firms, two-part pricing, peak-load pricing, seasonal rates, and time-of-day rates. Marginal-cost pricing regulation of utilities captures the efficiency aspects of competitive pricing, even though implementation of such pricing often requires special care in view of the decreasing-cost nature of the regulated firms. If $P = MC$, then $AC > MC$ causes firms to lose money. Two-part pricing policies are designed to promote efficiency while generating sufficient revenue to avoid losses.

Problems

1. a. What is the shape of the contract curve for two identical individuals?
   b. Does this contract curve go through the point of equal allocations?

2. Consider two people with identical preferences but an unequal initial allocation.
   a. Is it possible that they are on the contract curve?
   b. Is it possible that they can trade to the point of equal allocations?

3. Do identical preferences imply identical utility levels for any allocation between partners?

4. Is the position of equal allocations always on the grand utility possibility frontier? Why or why not?

5. Recall from Chapter 8 that marginal cost is equivalent to the marginal benefit forgone. Use this idea to show that the condition $P = MC$ is equivalent to the equality between marginal rates of substitution.

6. Show that the monopolist's result $P > MC$ violates the equality between marginal rates of substitution. Why then do customers not bribe the monopolist to expand output?

7. a. Under peak-load pricing, electric utility customers pay different prices at different times of the day, and yet this does not violate the equality of marginal rates of substitution. Why not?
   b. "If customers paid the same price for electricity at different times of the day, the equality of marginal rates of substitution would be violated." Show that this is true.

8. "Competition leads to Pareto optimality in a sequence of reallocations that themselves may not satisfy the Pareto criterion." Explain.

9. "Prior to construction of a bridge, the entire cost is marginal with respect to the construction decision. Therefore, to satisfy the consumer efficiency conditions, a breakeven price should be charged." Comment.

10. "Two-part tariffs automatically violate the consumer efficiency conditions, because some people pay more per unit sold than others do." Comment.

11. Peak-load pricing will shift peak demand if the prices are not estimated carefully. What considerations are relevant to the problem?

12. "There are no good physical substitutes for electricity. Therefore, peak-load pricing will fail to reduce capacity requirements." Comment.

13. "Peak-load pricing is unfair to peak-load users, because they end up paying more and subsidizing the off-peak user." Comment.

14. Review perfect price discrimination in Chapter 9. Would the monopolist who practices perfect price discrimination impose a violation of the pareto efficiency condition?

15. If a bridge is built that does not generate benefits greater than its cost, what pricing rules should be employed to use it most efficiently?

16. For some public utilities, there is no way to charge the marginal cost price. For example, the typical house is not equipped with a meter to allow measurement of electricity usage at different times of the day, and yet marginal cost varies at different times of the day.

Can you suggest a method to determine the amount of productive capacity to instal in order to approximate the efficiency conditions?

Suggested Readings

Arrow, K. J. *Social Choice and Individual Values*. New York: Wiley, 1951.

Bator, Francis M. "The Simple Analytics of Welfare Maximization." *American Economic Review* 97 (1957): 22–59.

Bergson, A. "A Reformulation of Certain Aspects of Welfare Economics." *Quarterly Journal of Economics* 52 (1938): 310–334.

Dupuit, J. "On the Measurement of the Utility of Public Works." *International Economic Papers* 2 (1952): 83–110.

Hotelling, Harold. "The General Welfare in Relation to Problems of Taxation and of Railway and Utility Rates." *Econometrica* 6 (1938): 242–269.

Vickrey, William S. *Microstatics*. New York: Harcourt Brace Jovanovich, 1964, chaps. 3 and 5.

Joint Products, Public Goods, and Externalities

Previous chapters have made the tacit assumption that all benefits and costs of production and consumption enter into decisionmakers' private comparisons of costs and benefits. Under such circumstances, the parties to a transaction enjoy all the benefits and pay all the costs of their decisions, no more and no less. The models that have already been presented are useful in studying markets characterized strictly by private benefits and costs.

However, many decisions and transactions benefit or injure people who are not voluntary parties to the transactions. Your decision to drive on the freeway during the rush hour increases the time it takes someone else to get to work. If you water your lawn during a windstorm, you also water your neighbors' lawns. Economists call these effects **externalities,** although there are numerous less forbidding and perhaps more descriptive synonyms, including *spillover effects, third-party effects, neighborhood effects,* and *external effects.*

Externalities are costs or benefits that do not enter fully and appropriately into decisionmakers' comparisons of costs and benefits. A key feature of externalities is their involuntary nature. If you contract to have 2 inches of manure spread on your lawn, no externality is present, because you voluntarily incur a cost in anticipation of receiving benefit. But if Farmer Jones spreads 2 inches of manure on his field and the rain washes it onto your lawn, an externality occurs, because it is an involuntary transaction from your viewpoint. If the manure damages your property, you incur an **external cost.** If it enhances your property, perhaps replacing fertilizer that you expected to have to pay for, you receive an **external benefit.** Life is full of such third-party effects, ranging from the trivial (your lunch partner injures you by chewing with his mouth open) to the momentous (an upstream industrial chemical firm kills flora and fauna and accelerates the incidence of cancer by dumping its wastes into a river).

14

When transactions exhibit important external components, free-market production and exchange cannot allocate resources to their most valuable uses, as we are about to see. But questions abound. If the market ceases to send and receive the proper price signals due to externalities, by what means are resources allocated? Can public intervention improve efficiency in such markets? Are there ways to shore up the market mechanisms in order to achieve greater efficiency?

This chapter provides a systematic study of the problems and possible remedies in industries that display important externalities. Because externalities are present in so many public-sector services and because of the public control policies needed to regulate private-sector industries displaying significant externalities, the analysis in this chapter is replete with public-policy implications. The economics of externalities is therefore an exciting subsection of applied microeconomics.

Jointness in Production and Consumption

The beginning point in studying externalities is **jointness,** which may occur in production or consumption activities. A single production process often gives rise to multiple outputs: Steers provide beef and hides; sheep yield mutton and wool; oil wells emit oil and natural gas. In consumption, goods are often consumed jointly by many consumers: A tornado siren alerts everyone within hearing range; a national defense system protects all Americans collectively. Jointness in production or consumption makes these cases fundamentally different from those we have studied so far.

Jointness and Vertical Summation

The analytical tool that captures this difference is **vertical summation** of cost and benefit curves—rather than the horizontal summation used to calculate the market values of most demands and supplies.

Figure 14.1 illustrates the vertical summation of demands, using the beef and hide example.[1] The curve labeled D_b is the demand curve for steers by beef users, and curve D_h is the demand curve for steers by hide users. Our goal is to construct a demand curve for steers, a curve that measures the maximum price that consumers will pay for each steer. Horizontal summation of the two demand curves is not meaningful, because unlike our previous demand analysis, each steer contributes to the benefits of both classes of users. Rather than horizontally summing the number of steers demanded at each price, we must sum vertically the amounts of money that each user is willing to pay for each additional steer.

---

1. Vertical summation was explained in Chapter 8 in the process of describing competitive firms' profit-maximizing behavior when joint production arises. The next two paragraphs repeat that explanation for the benefit of those who have not studied the advanced material in Chapter 8.

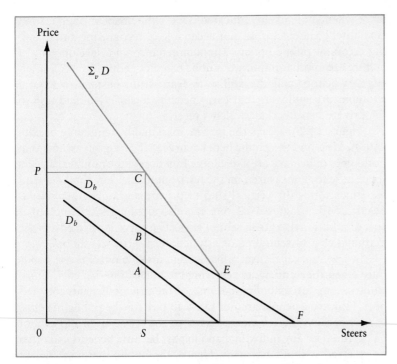

Figure 14.1
Vertical Summation of Demand in Joint Production

For the Sth steer, the total willingness to pay is $\overline{SC} = \overline{SA} + \overline{SB}$.

In Figure 14.1, beef users are willing to pay SA for the Sth steer, and hide users are willing to pay SB for the same Sth steer. Because the two demands are for different components of the same steer, the total price that will be offered for the Sth steer by both classes of users is $0P = SA + SB = SC$. Point C is the vertical summation of points A and B for the Sth steer. Similar vertical summation for all other quantities of steers produces the market demand curve for steers, labeled $\Sigma_v D$. The subscript v with the summation sign signifies vertical summation. The demand curve for steers has a kink at point E, the output at which the beef users' demand vanishes. Line segment EF is a component of the hide users' demand curve and the market demand curve $\Sigma_v D$.

Jointness and Efficiency

Let's apply the joint production model to an industry exhibiting substantial externalities and see how the market outcomes described in previous chapters are affected. Consider education, a service that, much like steers, produces two kinds of benefits to users: private benefits to students and public benefits to society. **Private benefits** are those that accrue directly to the individual attending school. These include the enjoyment derived from training the mind to operate at a high level; the excitement of learning new concepts, teaching them to others, and even discovering new knowledge; and graduates' enhanced streams of income. In contrast, the **public benefits** of education are those that spill over to society at large when students are educated. One public benefit of education is an intelligent electorate that is capable of recognizing and avoiding errors in public policy. The maintenance and development of culture are another important public benefit of education. A knowledge of history and the ability to learn from past mistakes and triumphs are spillovers that carry benefits to society in addition to the private benefits that students receive.

Figure 14.2 displays the private marginal benefit curve of education, MB_p, and the public benefit curve, MB_u. We can assume that both types of benefits are a declining function of the number of years spent in school, measured on the horizontal axis. The total demand for education is the vertical sum of private and public benefit, labeled $\Sigma_v MB$ in Figure 14.2. We can also assume that the marginal cost of additional years in school rises. The curve labeled MC is the marginal cost of schooling as a function of years in school.

In free-market transactions, buyers make payments for goods only when they anticipate receiving commensurate benefits. Thus, students pay for schooling because of the private benefits they expect. However, people are not likely to pay for the public benefits, in part because these benefits accrue to society at large and cannot be captured by any individual and in part because benefits can often be received without payment. Hence, the public marginal benefit curve for education does not represent effective demand for edu-

Figure 14.2
Joint Production and Externalities

Education yields both private and public benefits. These must be vertically summed to aggregate marginal benefit.

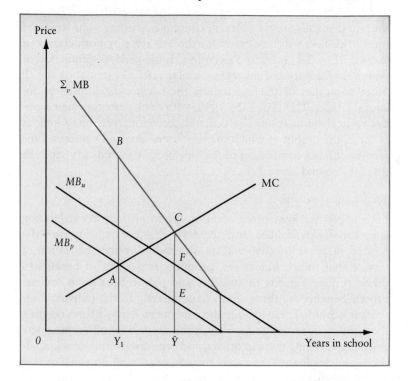

cation. (This problem is discussed in greater detail in later sections.) Thus, only the private marginal benefit curve is relevant to private market decisions.

Private market allocation of education will result in a level of education Y_1, because $MB_p = MC$ at point A. This is a socially inefficient result, because at Y_1, $\Sigma_v MB > MC$. If no public benefit externalities were created by privately purchased education, Y_1 would be efficient. But in the presence of these externalities, efficiency calls for the equality of $\Sigma_v MB$ and MC at point C and an educational output of $\hat{Y}$. When joint production generates external benefits for which there is no effective demand, the efficiency mechanisms of the price system are restrained. Such externalities result in market failure.

One way to establish the efficient level of education $\hat{Y}$, where $\Sigma_v MB = MC$ at point C, is to lower the price that students pay for education from $Y_1 A$ to $\hat{Y} E$. The lower price encourages students to move from A to E along the private marginal benefit curve. For each small increase in schooling between Y_1 and $\hat{Y}$, $\Sigma_v MB > MC$, meaning that the marginal benefit of education, including private and public benefits, exceeds the value of the necessary resources in their most valuable alternative uses. Increasing education by price reductions allows society to capture the valuable external benefits. When $\hat{Y}$ is attained, society is receiving a marginal benefit—private plus public—equal to the marginal cost of resources, and the efficient amount of public benefits is produced. At $\hat{Y}$, $\Sigma_v MB \equiv \hat{Y}E + \hat{Y}F = \hat{Y}C \equiv MC$. The lower price is not a transfer (welfare) payment. It is necessary to induce students to expand education beyond Y_1, to $\hat{Y}$ years, and thereby bestow the optimum public benefits that society desires. Lowering student prices is necessary to capture efficiency, but if lowered accurately, the price difference is not a transfer.[2]

Public Goods

In the previous section, we saw how public benefit externalities interfere with efficiency and how pricing policies may help to restore a better allocation of resources to certain industries. We can become more rigorous about these ideas by distinguishing between private goods and public goods.

Private goods have two essential properties: rivalry and exclusion. **Rivalry** means that private goods are not consumed collectively. If you eat an apple, no one can eat the same apple. Eating one apple uses up that apple, so a new apple is needed each time.

---

2. An excellent article on this subject is E. G. West, "An Economic Analysis of the Law and Politics of Non-Public School 'Aid,' " *Journal of Law and Economics* 19 (1976): 79–102. West extends the analysis to justify public aid to private schools because of their beneficial spillover effects.

Jointness and Mass Transit

APPLIED
MICRO
THEORY

14.1

Consider the benefits that derive from bus service. As in education, benefits are both private and public. Bus riders capture the private benefits of trips, but car drivers also benefit in less-congested roads, lower pollution levels, and a lower probability of accidents. Thus bus service generates joint products: private and public benefits of bus transportation.

The accompanying figure illustrates the two components of benefits resulting from bus transportation. The private benefits to the bus riders are shown in the marginal benefit curve labeled MB_b; the public benefits of bus transportation, which accrue in large measure to car drivers, are shown in the marginal benefit curve MB_c. The vertical summation of these marginal curves is $\Sigma_v MB$.

Because car drivers receive a benefit without making a payment, their demand for bus transportation does not enter into the bargaining process that sets price and quantity. Accordingly, the price system will establish B_1 bus trips at a fare of B_1A, because the private marginal benefit to bus riders equals the marginal cost at A. The

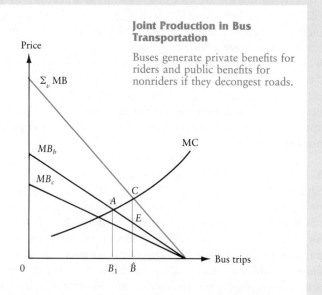

Joint Production in Bus Transportation

Buses generate private benefits for riders and public benefits for nonriders if they decongest roads.

efficient level of bus transportation is $\hat{B}$, at which $\Sigma_v MB = MC$ and at which all benefits of bus ridership enter into the decision. But $\hat{B}$ can be achieved only if the bus fare to riders is lowered from B_1A to $\hat{B}E$, allowing riders to increase their quantities of bus travel demanded in accord with private benefits and thereby bestowing the optimal quantity of public benefits as well.

How should the additional bus service be financed? Because car drivers are major beneficiaries of the additional bus service, some financing should come from automobile-related taxes, such as gasoline taxes and automobile registration taxes. Property taxes can also be appropriate sources of bus financing, expecially if property values are enhanced by bus service.

Exclusion refers to the ability of sellers to limit use to consumers who pay for products. Rivalry and exclusion allow private goods like apples to be produced and exchanged in market transactions because buyers receive benefits for the goods they pay for and sellers can restrict the benefits of products to paying customers.

In contrast, **public goods** exhibit nonrivalry and nonexclusion. **Nonrivalry** means that a good can be consumed collectively. A public good can be shared, and unlike an apple, enjoyment of the good by one does not use up the good for others. Jogging through a park or driving over a bridge does not require the replacement of the bridge after each use. **Nonexclusion** is the inability of sellers to restrict use to people who pay for the services. Private market production and exchange of public goods are not possible, and so some form of public intervention is necessary to divert the efficient amount of resources to their provision.

One important trait of public goods is their extremely low marginal cost of use. The average cost of building a bridge, TC/crossings, may be quite high. But the marginal cost of an additional crossing once the bridge is built, $\Delta TC/\Delta crossings$, is very close to zero. Only a minute change in the bridge's characteristics occur per crossing—perhaps a few cement molecules knocked out of place—surely not worth the measurement and collection costs.

Similarly, one more physical fitness nut jogging through the park or one more viewer enjoying a fireworks display imposes zero marginal cost. Likewise, if a few more people move into a neighborhood that emphasizes education, they enjoy the public benefit of the school spillover at low or zero marginal cost. (Of course, marginal cost is zero in these examples only if the additional consumption does not cause congestion of the park, display grounds, or school system. Congestion costs are considered in Applied Micro Theory 14.2.) So in the absence of congestion costs, efficiency calls for public goods to be provided at a price equal to marginal cost—that is, at a zero price.

Obviously, a zero price creates a problem: The public good must be financed somehow, or it will not be produced in the first place. This is strictly a problem for public goods, and not for private goods, because

1. For a private good, the price is used to finance its production. The revenue per apple enables growers to cover the costs of its production. For public goods, where price is zero, alternative sources of revenue are needed.

2. For private goods, the price system provides information: The price equals the marginal benefit of the last apple sold. Comparing price to costs, growers are guided into growing the efficient number of apples. For public goods, decisions about how much of the goods to provide must be made in the absence of price information. Votes are guides of sorts but are not fine-tuned to public wants.

3. For private goods, there is no incentive for consumers to underdeclare their willingness to pay for the marginal unit. If apples are presently selling for 20¢ apiece and one more apple is worth 21¢ to the eater, the eater would certainly lose by offering only 19¢. The eater who made such an offer would be excluded from buying the apple. But suppose there is no way to exclude an additional consumer from the public good once it is built. Or suppose exclusion is very costly or changes the nature of the good. In these cases, users have an incentive to underdeclare benefits, and there is no market in which consumer benefits can be observed.

Congestion of Public Goods

<table><tr><td>APPLIED
MICRO
THEORY

14.2</td><td>Public goods like bridges, once constructed, allow additional use at near-zero marginal cost because they are not used up at</td></tr></table>

each use. However, if a bridge becomes congested, this congestion imposes opportunity costs on users separate from the negligible number of cement molecules lost from the bridge on each crossing.

To study the effect of congestion on a public good, consider the case of a road built between two points. In Figure A, the horizontal axis measures the volume of cars on the road at any given time. The vertical axis measures time costs. Two demand curves are shown, each negatively sloped with respect to the time cost of driving on the road; along each demand curve drivers will reduce their driving by seeking substitutes when the price of driving, measured in terms of time spent, rises. Curve $D_{off\ peak}$ is the aggregate demand of drivers at off-peak hours; D_{peak} is the aggregate demand of drivers during the peak rush-hour periods.

Figure A also displays two cost curves: the marginal cost of travel, MC, and the average time cost of travel, AC. Over the range of low-volume, off-peak traffic, MC = AC, because an additional car can enter the road without slowing down any other driver. For that range of volumes, the road is a pure public good. For traffic volumes above V_0, an additional driver adds more to the time cost of other drivers than the previous driver because of congestion. Now the marginal and average time costs rise; as always, MC > AC when AC rises. Each extra driver entering the road imposes a small extra delay on every other driver. But no driver has an incentive to incorporate this marginal time cost into the decision to drive during the peak time versus the off-peak

Figure A
Congestion Externalities

Drivers ignore the congestion costs that they impose on other drivers. Excessive traffic volume results.

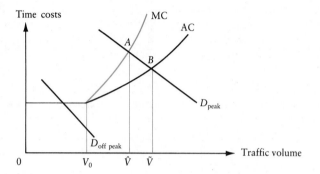

Figure B
Facility Expansion in Response to Congestion

Expansion lowers both the average and marginal time cost during peak use and shifts off-peak demand to the left.

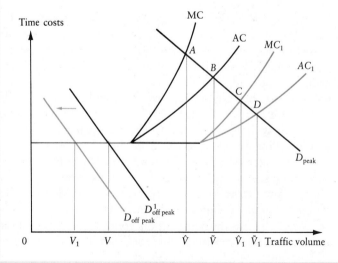

time. To each driver, the marginal time cost imposed on other drivers is an external cost for which the driver does not pay. Instead, each driver compares the private benefits and private costs of driving; that is, each compares the marginal benefit to the average time cost of travel. Drivers add their cars to the roadway whenever the marginal benefit of driving exceeds the average time cost of driving, or $MB > AC$. Equilibrium for all drivers occurs at the inefficient volume $\tilde{V}$, where D_{peak} intersects AC at point B. The efficient volume of peak traffic, $\hat{V}$, at which D_{peak} equals the MC curve at A, is not achieved. The external costs that drivers impose on one another are not internalized. Excessive traffic volume is the result.

What remedies are available for congestion of public goods? Policy options fall into three general divisions: (1) expand capacity, (2) impose tolls, or (3) stagger work hours to smooth out the peak demand.

Expanding Capacity

Figure B demonstrates the effect of expanding road capacity. Two problems arise. Increasing the number of lanes shifts the average and marginal time cost curves down to MC_1 and AC_1. Thus more volume can occur before the external costs of congestion rise. However, drivers now equate their marginal benefits of driving during the peak (points on their demand curve) with their average time costs, points on the new AC_1 curve. The expansion of capacity shifts the equilibrium to traffic volume $\tilde{V}_1$. Given the new road capacity, efficiency occurs at volume $\hat{V}_1$. Thus a larger facility, while reducing the average driving time per driver, still creates excessive congestion, given the size of the facility. Volume increases beyond $\hat{V}_1$, the new efficient level.

Also remember that traveling during peak and off-peak hours are substitutes for many drivers. The expansion of capacity reduces the price of peak travel time from

$\tilde{V}B$ to $\tilde{V}_1D$. The price of peak travel is a shift parameter in the demand for off-peak travel. When the price of peak travel falls, the demand curve for off-peak travel shifts to the left, and off-peak volume falls from V to V_1. Because the facility is larger, the roadway becomes increasingly empty during the off-peak hours, because demand is lower then. Thus a major limitation of facility expansion as a solution to congestion is the off-peak idleness of the public good.

Toll Charges

Instead of expanding capacity, suppose an attempt is made to internalize the external congestion costs by charging an entry price into the roadway—a toll. The proper toll would be enough to bring the total entry price up to full marginal cost. The driver already pays the average time cost; so the toll, if properly calibrated,

would equal CA in Figure C. The driver's total price, average waiting time plus toll, or $\hat{V}C + CA$, equals the marginal time cost of driving during the peak, or $\hat{V}A$. Beginning at point B (volume $\tilde{V}$), imposition of the rush-hour toll AC would increase the total price of driving and reduce the quantity of peak driving demanded from B to A. At A, the efficient traffic volume $\hat{V}$ is achieved; $MB_{peak} =$ MC. This policy also makes better use of the road during off-peak hours. The increase in the price of peak-time driving due to the toll increases the demand for its substitute—driving during the off-peak hours. Hence off-peak demand shifts to $D^1_{off\ peak}$ and off-peak volume rises from V to V_1. Other charges would have the same effect, such as higher parking prices for drivers who arrive downtown during peak hours.

Continued on page 460

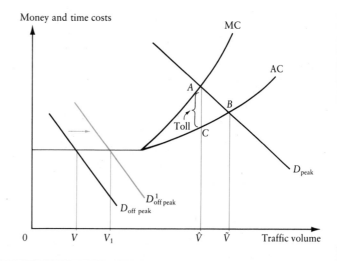

Figure C
Toll Charges in Response to Congestion

Peak-time tolls equal to $\overline{AC}$ produce efficient congestion, increase off-peak use, and provide demand elasticity data as well as revenue.

The toll system also provides information about the elasticity of demand for peak driving between points *B* and *A* in Figure C and hence information about benefits. For example, if demand at the peak is relatively elastic, the toll will reveal that capacity expansion is not warranted. A very inelastic peak demand would provide partial evidence that expansion is necessary. Still, capacity should be enlarged only if the marginal cost of expansion is less than the marginal time cost of drivers.

Staggering Work Hours

Staggering work hours shifts both demand curves: Off-peak demand increases as workers move to different travel hours, and peak demand falls for the same reason. Staggered work hours smooth out the demands for travel over the day. The failure to use a pricing mechanism prohibits the establishment of the efficient volume; yet this policy has the benefit of achieving a more uniform use of the facility, much like the toll method.

Staggering work hours is a move toward efficiency if either of the

**Figure D
Comparison of Three
Congestion-Reducing Strategies**   The effects on traffic volume of tolls, capacity expansion, and staggered work hours are shown here.

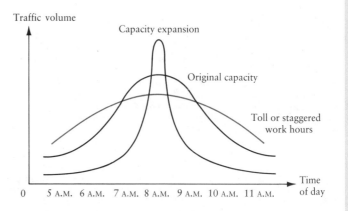

following two relationships is satisfied, where MC_s refers to the marginal cost of staggering the work hours:

$$MC_s < \text{MC of driver} < \text{MC of capacity expansion}$$

or

$$MC_s < \text{MC of capacity expansion} < \text{MC of drivers}$$

Figure D compares the expected results of the various policy options for handling traffic volume.

The Free-Rider Problem

The **free-rider problem** describes the behavior of consumers of collectively consumed public goods and explains why the financing of such public goods on a private-payment basis is so difficult to achieve. To illustrate, suppose that 1000 people will benefit if a park is built. Let the marginal cost per acre of construction be $500, as shown in Figure 14.3. Let the private marginal benefit curve for each participant be MB_i, with an intercept of $1 and a slope of $-(\$1/100)$. The vertical summation of all 1000 MB_i curves produces the curve labeled $\Sigma_v MB_i = 1000\ MB_i$. This is the true marginal social benefit curve, with an intercept of $1000 and a slope of -10. (Figure 14.3 is not drawn to scale.) The efficient acreage for the park is found by equating $\Sigma_v MB$ and MC. Thus

$$\Sigma_v MB \equiv 1000 - 10X = 500 \equiv MC \qquad (14.1)$$

where X = park acreage.

Solving Equation 14.1 for X, the efficient size of the park is 50 acres. Under such "full revelation of benefits," where all consumers

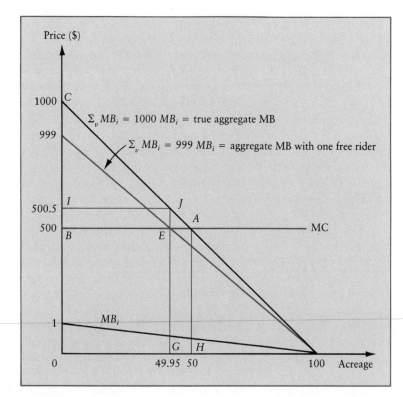

Figure 14.3
The Free-Rider Problem

The incentive to underdeclare the
value of public goods is a hindrance
to efficiency.

participate in the financing of the park according to their identical
marginal benefits, each individual pays 0.001 of the total park cost
and receives 0.001 of the total benefit. The total benefit equals area
$0CAH$, or \$37,500. The total cost of the park is $0BAH$, or \$25,000.
Thus the total net benefit or consumer surplus, area ABC, equals
\$12,500; each individual's share of the net gain is \$12.50.

Now let's see the effect of one person's attempt to get the park
produced without paying his or her share of the total cost. Such a
person is called a *free rider*. Suppose only 999 of the 1000 original
participants reveal their true marginal benefit curves and are willing
to participate in the financing of the park. The new aggregate marginal benefit curve falls ever so slightly to $\Sigma_v MB_i = 999\ MB_i$ in
Figure 14.3. When one individual is a free rider, less than full
revelation of benefits results in a park size of 49.95 acres, fractionally smaller than the efficient size of 50 acres. This new acreage is
derived by setting $\Sigma_v MB = MC$. Thus

$$\Sigma_v MB \equiv 999 - 9.99X = 500 \equiv MC \qquad (14.2)$$

The value of X is now 49.95 acres, a 0.001% reduction in park size.
By not participating in the payment scheme, the free rider saves
\$25.00 in expenses and enjoys the benefit of a park virtually indis-
tinguishable from 50 acres.

But what are the exact benefits and costs of the free rider and of the remaining 999 participants? All 1000 persons now share the total consumer surplus equally, but only 999 participate in the cost. The total benefit of the 49.95-acre park is the area $0CJG$, the area beneath the true aggregate marginal benefit curve, and it equals $37,474.98. Each individual, including the free rider, receives an equal share of the total benefits, or $37.47. Thus the free rider receives $37.47 in benefits at no cost instead of the $12.50 net benefits he or she receives by participating in the payment scheme. Each remaining participant receives a net benefit equal to the total benefit, $37.47, less his or her share of the total cost, which remains at $25.00. Thus each participant receives a consumer surplus or net benefit of $12.47.

The free rider gains $24.97 in net benefits (receiving $37.47 instead of $12.50 if he or she participates), whereas each participant is denied only $0.03 in net benefits ($12.47 instead of $12.50). These results dramatize two facts: the strong incentive to be a free rider and the weak incentive to prevent free riders.

This example makes it clear that financing public goods through voluntary payment schemes according to individual benefits has the same inherent instability problems as cartels do: Each participant is better off when the solution is achieved than when it is not; but while the solution is being arrived at, each member has an incentive to cheat (become a free rider). If there are enough free riders (500 or more in the park example), the private-payment scheme collapses and the public good may not be provided at all. To summarize, the efficient solution calls for public goods to be allocated according to the condition $\Sigma_v MB = MC$; but private-payment schemes may break down in the presence of free riders.

If voluntary contributions cannot be counted on in the financing of public goods, what remedies are available? Compulsory taxation is the most common method of financing public goods. For example, citizens are taxed in order to provide national defense. In this way citizens are denied the option of understating or completely denying the existence of their marginal benefits and becoming in essence free riders. Property, income, and sales taxes are the major sources of tax revenue used to provide public goods.

Club memberships can also provide a solution to the free-rider problem. Memberships must be sold on an all-or-nothing basis. A person cannot buy just the option to use the sauna but must pay a lump sum that purchases access to the entire club. Individual services can then be sold to members at low prices, because the marginal cost of using the facility, once constructed, is low. But this solution is efficient only if the lump-sum membership fee does not exhaust the total consumer surplus of any prospective member of the club who can benefit from membership. Otherwise, such members would not join or the club would be too small. Perhaps it would not be formed at all. Obviously, to achieve the exact MB = MC position is virtually impossible.

Church tithing practices, a system where members have a moral obligation to contribute 10% of their income (or some other arbitrary amount) to the church, is another method of overcoming the free-rider problem. And although not a method of finance, cost-benefit analysis is a social-scientific method of selecting appropriate public-sector projects and of operating such projects at the correct levels. Cost-benefit analysis is a way of replacing the information that a price system fails to provide for public goods.

To sum up, collective enjoyment of public goods gives rise to the free-rider problem, which in turn prohibits the production and financing of public goods by conventional pricing schemes. Alternative methods of measuring benefits and of financing public goods must be found.

External Costs: Pollution as a Factor of Production

Externalities have been defined as costs or benefits of a decision that do not enter into decisionmakers' private comparison of costs and benefits. We have seen the central roles of joint production, non-rivalry, exclusion, and public goods in the generation of external benefits. On the cost side, pollution may be the by-product of the production of an otherwise useful final good. Firms often have access to the waste-assimilating properties of the environment (air, water, land) at zero or very low cost. Such firms produce output at profit-maximizing rates that allow for the firms' private costs and revenues but largely ignore the environmental costs imposed on others. As we will soon see, there is a stong incentive to ignore these cost spillovers.

We can address this problem of external costs analytically by considering pollution a factor of production in the sense that the firm's ability to emit one unit of pollution into the environment allows the firm to avoid some cleanup costs. This means that more capital and labor can be devoted to the production of the useful good out of a fixed cost outlay than would be possible if the pollution unit were not permitted at zero cost. Treating pollution as an input to be combined with labor and capital to produce output leads to the construction of the **marginal product of pollution** (MP_p) curve and the **value of marginal product of pollution** (VMP_p) curve. These pollution curves correspond to the analogous curves for capital and labor, derived in Chapters 5 and 12. Thus $MP_p = \Delta Q/\Delta Y$ and $VMP_p = (\Delta Q/\Delta Y) \cdot P = MP_p \cdot P$, where Q = units of output of a useful final good, P = price of the useful final good, and Y = units of pollution emitted.

The efficient level of pollution is determined by balancing the benefits of pollution to firms, as one component of society, and the costs of the pollution to other members of society. For convenience,

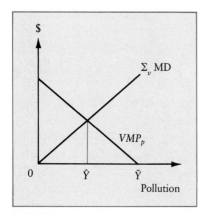

Figure 14.4
Efficient Pollution

Efficient pollution is generally neither zero nor where $VMP_p = 0$. Efficiency requires $VMP_p = \Sigma_v MD$.

let's assume that the firm is competitive in output and input markets. The private benefits to firms of additional pollution are measured by the VMP_p curve. Figure 14.4 shows a downward-sloping VMP_p curve, reflecting the diminishing marginal product of the pollution input. The positively sloped curve, $\Sigma_v MD$, is the marginal cost curve. We can assume that each additional unit of pollution causes more additional cost, in pollution damages, than the preceding unit. Small doses of pollution are assimilated into the environment at low marginal cost, because of the cleansing effect of winds and running streams. But when the air and water are overloaded, additional units of pollution create rising marginal costs (damages) to health and esthetics. Thus the **marginal damage curve** (Σ_v**MD**) measures the costs imposed on members of society; it is the vertical summation of all individual marginal damage curves. Like the external benefits discussed earlier, the external costs of pollution are consumed collectively. A meaningful societal marginal damage curve must therefore add vertically the marginal costs incurred by all damaged parties for each additional unit of pollution.

The optimal "employment" of pollution is $\hat{Y}$, at which $VMP_p = \Sigma_v MD$. But the marginal costs of pollution are external to firms if they are under no obligation to pay for pollution rights or to pay for the damages caused by their pollution. If there is no way to charge firms for their pollution, the price of pollution units is zero; firms will increase pollution as long as VMP_p is positive. Thus actual pollution ($\tilde{Y}$) exceeds the efficient level ($\hat{Y}$).

Note that the efficient pollution level, $\hat{Y}$, is an internal, as opposed to a corner solution; we do not generally wish to set Y equal to zero. The bumper sticker slogan Help Stamp Out Pollution reflects an ignorance of the need to balance benefits and costs at the margin. (But a bumper sticker Help Equate MB = MC would not be likely to motivate the public.)

Of course, there are pollutants that we want virtually none of. For example, there is some evidence that the chlorofluorohydrocarbons, once commonly used in spray-can propellants, rise to the ionosphere and reduce the amount of protective ozone. Too many infrared rays making their way to earth would kill the basic elements of the food chain, thereby starving higher organisms, and cause skin cancer in light-complected people. Because of its highly toxic effects, the "correct" equilibrium of chlorofluorohydrocarbon pollution is virtually zero. In this case, the MC curve for pollution is too high to allow any use of the pollutant. Figure 14.5 illustrates such a corner solution. In a case like this, the damages are so great that an internal solution is ruled out.

Plutonium is another by-product that we virtually cannot tolerate in the environment. Thus plutonium also provides a corner solution at zero levels of pollution. Note that in both examples the zero corner solution arises not because the by-products are pollutants but because $\Sigma_v MD > VMP_p$ for all units of pollution, including the first unit. Note too that $\tilde{Y}$ rather than 0 will be generated if the price system is relied on exclusively to allocate resources; firms will push the VMP_p to zero in an effort to maximize profits.

When firms have free or nearly free access to the environment for pollution, external pollution costs are imposed on damaged parties and a socially excessive level of pollution results. These are inefficient outcomes, because the pollution costs are not borne by polluting firms but by third parties with no say in pollution levels. In effect, polluting firms are free riders that enjoy the benefits of pollution without payment. Thus, the external costs do not influence firm decisions appropriately, and pollution levels are too high.

Internalizing externalities is the process of getting the external costs back into decisionmaking. Are there policy options capable of internalizing externalities and promoting "correct" pollution levels?

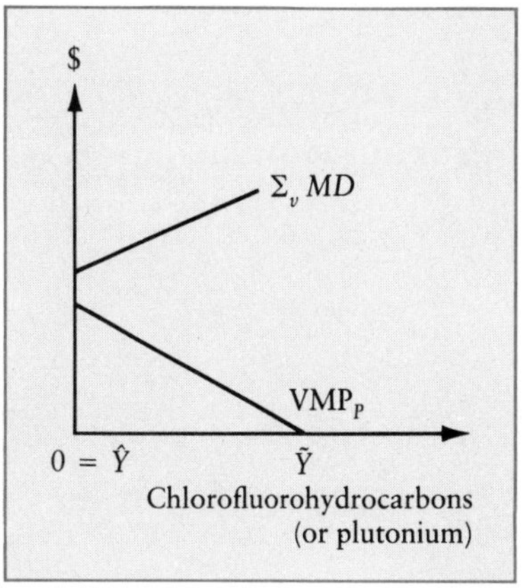

Figure 14.5
The Corner Solution for Pollutants

Some pollutants generate MD > MB at any level.

Assignment of Property Rights:
The Coase Bargaining Solution

One difficulty in the economics of pollution is that neither the polluting firm nor the members of society damaged by pollution have well-defined property rights to the air and water. Specifically, firms have not been given the right to pollute the air, and consumers have not been given the right to clean air. In a classic article, Ronald Coase pointed out that, if property rights are well defined, the emitters and receptors of pollution would bargain and move to the efficient position.[3]

For example, suppose a paper mill and a laundry are in a conflict over air pollution: The paper mill emits into the air pollutants that settle into the clothes of the adjacent laundry, thereby imposing an external cost on the laundry. If the value of the air pollution to the paper mill and the resulting damages to the laundry are measurable and if the environmental pollution rights are well defined, the firms will negotiate the sale of pollution rights until the efficient amount of pollution is established, as Coase demonstrated. It is essential that one party or the other be assigned pollution rights: Either the paper mill is given the right to pollute or the laundry is given the right to clean air. And surprisingly, Coase showed that, if income effects can be ignored, the equilibrium level of pollution will be the same regardless of which firm is assigned the initial pollution rights. Either way, bargaining between the emitter (paper mill) and receptor (laundry) will result ultimately in the same level of pollution. To summarize, the **Coase theorem** asserts that the amount of pollution will be both efficient and independent of the initial assign-

3. Ronald H. Coase, "The Problem of Social Cost," *Journal of Law and Economics* 3 (1960): 1–44.

ment of pollution rights. (Strictly speaking, this result requires that transaction costs between parties be zero and that the bargaining between parties gives rise to no net income effects.)

THE SHORT RUN   The Coase theorem has short-run and long-run implications. Figure 14.6 illustrates the logic of the Coase theorem in the short run. Begin by assuming that the emitter—the paper mill—is given the initial rights to pollution. The VMP_p curve measures the value of additional pollution to the emitter, and the MD curve measures the damages to the receptor—the laundry.

The first step is to show that the equilibrium amount of pollution will be $\hat{Y}$, the efficient level, as long as the pollution rights are marketable. If the emitter is allowed to pollute at zero private cost, it would achieve pollution level $\tilde{Y}$, where $VMP_p = 0$. But the receptor will have an incentive to pay the emitter to reduce pollution from $\tilde{Y}$ to $\hat{Y}$, because for each unit of pollution between $\tilde{Y}$ and $\hat{Y}$, MD $> VMP_p$. This means that the receptor is willing to pay the emitter a sum of money greater than the VMP_p to induce the emitter to stop using those marginal units of pollution, even though the emitter is legally entitled to them. Thus the emitter receives a larger gain in the payments to stop polluting than it receives in revenue from the polluting activity itself for each marginal unit of pollution from $\tilde{Y}$ to $\hat{Y}$, and both parties enjoy a mutual gain from such bargaining. For marginal pollution units less than $\hat{Y}$, $VMP_p >$ MD; for these pollution units, the receptor cannot offer the emitter a payment that is at least as great as the VMP_p. Thus bargaining among parties produces the efficient pollution level, $\hat{Y}$, when the polluter owns the property rights.

Figure 14.6
Coasian Bargaining

Bargaining produces an efficient use of pollution regardless of the initial assignment of pollution rights.

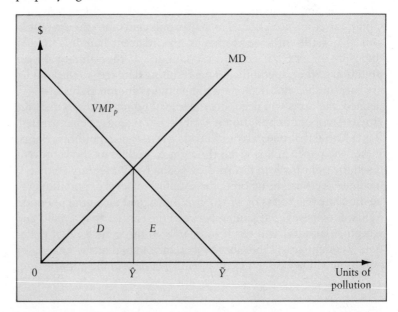

Now assume that the receptor is given the pollution rights, that is, the right to clean air. The receptor would no doubt wish to select a pollution level of zero, prohibiting the paper mill from producing any pollution. However, for all marginal units of pollution between 0 and $\hat{Y}$, $VMP_p > MD$. Now the emitting paper mill can offer the receptor money payments for all its pollution rights in an amount greater than the receptor's MD but smaller than the emitter's VMP_p. In other words, the emitter now has an incentive to buy pollution rights from the receptor, which in turn has an incentive to sell these rights. As before, the bargaining stops when the emitter buys $\hat{Y}$ units of pollution rights.

To summarize, bargaining between parties for pollution rights internalizes the external pollution costs and produces efficient levels of pollution, regardless of the ownership of pollution rights. The Coase theorem is a restatement of market efficiency when property rights are well defined. It also points up the misallocation of resources that can be caused by the failure to establish property rights.[4]

THE LONG RUN   Economists are in general agreement on the short-run aspects of the Coase theorem. There is less agreement about the long run. The main dissenting argument goes like this: Suppose the emitter owns the pollution rights, is producing the efficient level of pollution, $\hat{Y}$, and is just breaking even. If the pollution rights are withdrawn and awarded to the receptor, the emitter will no longer be able to break even. The emitter goes out of business, and the level of pollution drops to zero. But at $Y = 0$, $VMP_p > MD$. Thus long-run entry and exit are affected by the assignment of pollution rights, causing pollution to occur at inefficient levels. It is argued, therefore, that Coasian bargaining breaks down in the long run.

It is time for the cost curves of Chapter 7 to come to the rescue. We can expose the error in the above argument by taking sufficient care to define correctly the entrepreneur's opportunity cost. Refer back to Figure 14.6. Assume that the emitter is awarded the pollution rights initially. If the emitting firm is currently breaking even, it earns a net revenue in its current industry equal to the net revenue it would receive by exiting the industry; that is, the net revenue must equal opportunity cost. When the emitter produces $\hat{Y}$ units of pollution, it is entitled to a net flow of revenue equal to the total revenue on sales of final output, R, minus the resource costs, C, plus the payment, E, received from the receptor as an inducement to reduce pollution from $\tilde{Y}$ to $\hat{Y}$. The area of the triangle E is actually the minimum payment that the emitter would accept, because being the area beneath the VMP_p curve, it equals the total revenue forgone by

---

4. The payments that receptors make to emitters to reduce pollution are sometimes called bribes. But the symmetry of the payments reveals that the direction of payment has no moral significance. Thus the pejorative *bribe* has no place.

cutting pollution from $\tilde{Y}$ to $\hat{Y}$. The emitter may demand payments in excess of area E. For ease, let's assume that the emitter accepts the minimum bid, E. Thus

$$\text{Net revenue from producing at } \hat{Y} = R - C + E \quad \text{(14.3)}$$

If the emitting firm is earning zero economic profit, the net revenue from producing must equal the net revenue from not producing; the firm must be indifferent between remaining in business and exiting. Technically, the breakeven firm must exactly cover its opportunity cost. The opportunity cost equals the net revenue that the firm could receive by exiting the industry and reducing the output of final goods and of pollution to zero. If the emitter stops producing entirely, it can sell the rights to pollution units 0 to $\hat{Y}$ to the receptor for an amount equal to, at most, D, which is the total damages of such pollution to the receptor. In addition, the emitting firm can use the revenue from the sale of pollution units $\hat{Y}$ to $\tilde{Y}$ for something besides pollution control. When the firm produces and emits $\hat{Y}$ units of pollution, the payment E is devoted to abating pollution in order to reduce pollution from $\tilde{Y}$ to $\hat{Y}$. But if the firm exits the industry, the revenue from those pollution units, E, is free and clear. Thus the net revenue available to the emitter from exiting equals the payment that the receptor will make to the emitter to stop polluting: $D + E$.

$$\text{Opportunity cost} = D + E \quad \text{(14.4)}$$

Ignoring the emitter's opportunities as an entrepreneur in another industry and focusing solely on the net revenue in pollution payments forgone by continuing in the present industry, the emitter's opportunity cost equals the sum of the two payment components, D and E. If the emitter is a breakeven entrepreneur, the net revenues to the firm while in the industry must equal the net revenues forgone by not leaving the industry. Thus

$$\underbrace{R - C + E}_{\substack{\text{net} \\ \text{revenue}}} = \underbrace{D + E}_{\substack{\text{opportunity} \\ \text{cost}}} \quad \text{(14.5)}$$

Now let's translate these cost and revenue data into our usual format. In Figure 14.7 the emitter's resource costs are contained in the LAC_1 curve. Payment E from the receptor is shown as a reduction in resource costs. Curve $LAC_1 - E$ is resource costs net of the payment E.

$$R - C + E = abcd - efcd + efgh = abgh \quad \text{(14.6)}$$

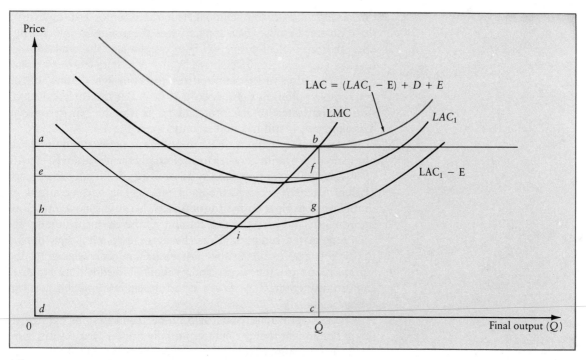

The opportunity cost, $D + E$, also equals $abgh$, or

$$\text{opportunity cost} = D + E = abfe + efgh = abgh \quad (14.7)$$

By producing final output $\hat{Q}$ and by using pollution units $\hat{Y}$, the emitter earns just what could be earned by exiting, which is the firm's opportunity cost.

Now suppose that the pollution rights are withdrawn from the emitter and transferred to the receptor. What changes occur in the emitter's net revenue from producing and in its opportunity cost? The net revenue from producing equals $R - C - D$ because the revenues from the sale of final output, R, must now be reduced by two cost factors in computing net revenue: resource costs (C) and the payment the firm must now make to the receptor for the right to $\hat{Y}$ units of pollution. The payment D is the minimum that the receptor will accept, because it equals the area under the MC curve, or the total damages arising from $\hat{Y}$ pollution. Thus the emitter's net revenue is now

$$\text{Net revenue} = R - C - D = \quad (14.8)$$
$$abcd - efcd - abfe = 0$$

The change in pollution rights has dropped the net revenue to zero. If the opportunity cost is positive, the firm should exit the industry. But the opportunity cost has also fallen to zero. The firm

Figure 14.7
Coasian Bargaining in the Long Run

The assignment of pollution rights does not affect entry or exit.

can no longer receive a payment from the receptor firm by exiting the industry, because it no longer owns the pollution rights. Thus after the reversal in property right assignment, the emitter's net revenue and opportunity cost are both zero. There has been a one-time devaluation in the value of the firm through the loss of the marketable pollution right asset, it is true. But the entry/exit decision is unaffected. If the firm had no reason to exit before the reassignment, it still has no reason to exit.

In Figure 14.7, the reversal in pollution rights simply replaces one form of cost with another form. Initially the pollution payments $D + E$ *(abgh)* were opportunity costs or payments forgone by not exiting. After the reversal, the payments $D + E$ become additions to the firm's explicit costs of production, because it now pays D to the receptor and gives up the amount E, the payment initially received from the receptor. Thus the average resource and opportunity cost curve, LAC, does not shift. The only change is the composition of the cost components imbedded in LAC—opportunity costs $D + E$ are transformed into explicit costs of doing business.

If the opportunity costs of forgone payments are ignored, it might be thought that the emitter initially breaks even at j in Figure 14.7, the minimum of the $LAC_1 - E$ curve. Beginning at j, it would appear that the property right reversals that increase the explicit costs of the firm by $D + E$ would also force the emitter to exit the industry. But the proper specification of opportunity cost makes it clear that the initial breakeven point is b, the minimum point of the LAC curve. Pollution right reversals do not shift the LAC (or LMC) curve, and hence long-run entry and exit is unaffected. The Coase theorem is rescued in the long run by the proper application of cost curves.

Effluent Charges and Quotas

The **effluent charge** is another policy option in pollution control. The polluting firm pays the government a price per unit of pollution emitted into the environment and is thereby encouraged to reduce its waste emissions. Figure 14.8 illustrates how effluent charges can establish the efficient level of pollution. Panel a shows the value of marginal product of pollution (VMP_p) curve of the polluting firm, and panel b contains the marginal damage (MD) curve of such pollution to other members of society. The following steps show how the optimal charge can be established by trial and error:

1. Impose effluent charge f_1 and note the level of pollution that the firm produces. The charge f_1 is the marginal cost that the firm must pay per unit of pollution. The firm will pollute up to the profit-maximizing level where $f_1 = VPM_p$. When the fee is f_1, the firm emits Y_1 units of pollution.

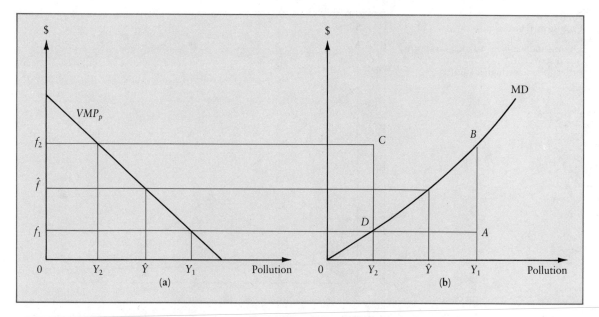

2. Measure the marginal damage at pollution level Y_1 or Y_1B.

3. If marginal damages at Y_1 exceed the charge f_1, we know that $MD(Y_1) > VMP_p(Y_1)$. Thus the effluent charge should be raised to f_2.

4. Measure the pollution level when the fee is f_2 and measure the MD of the pollution level. In Figure 14.8, $f_2 = VMP_p(Y_2) \equiv Y_2C > Y_2D \equiv MD(Y_2)$.

5. Because $f_2 > MD(Y_2)$, lower the effluent fee to f_3, where $f_2 > f_3 > f_1$ (not shown). Repeat the first four steps until a fee is found that equates VMP_p and MD. For fee $\hat{f}$, $VMP_p(\hat{Y}) = MD(\hat{Y})$. Fee $\hat{f}$ is the optimal charge because it produces the efficient level of pollution, $\hat{Y}$.

Figure 14.8
Effluent Charges as a Means of Internalizing Pollution Externalities

(a) The firm will respond to an effluent charge by setting $VMP_p = f$.
(b) The fee should be compared to MD and adjusted until $\hat{f}$ = MD. This results in $VMP_p = \hat{f}$ = MD.

An important advantage of imposing effluent charges is that the regulatory agency responsible for setting fees need not have knowledge of the polluting firm's VMP_p curve but only society's marginal damages. The firm itself will reveal points along its VMP_p curve, because at each fee there is a profit-maximizing level of pollution that equates the VMP_p with the established effluent fee.

The Coasian bargaining method and the effluent charge approach are ways of using the price system to allocate pollution resources. In contrast, the **effluent quota** system is a method by which the regulating agency estimates the proper level of pollution and gives a pollution quota to the firm; the firm can pollute up to the quota and no more.

If the regulatory authority happens to pick the correct quota, that is, the pollution level that equates the firm's VMP_p and society's

Figure 14.9
Pollution Quotas

Quotas induce firms to exaggerate (or not discover) their VMP_p curves in order to receive higher quotas.

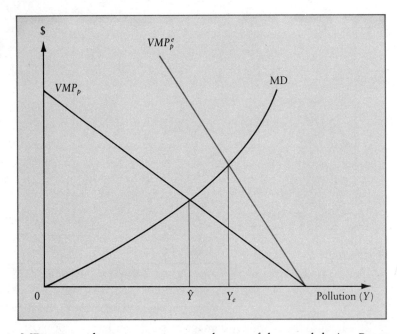

MD curves, the quota system may be a useful control device. But a major weakness of quotas is their inability to approach systematically the efficient pollution levels. For example, the efficient pollution level in Figure 14.9 is $\hat{Y}$, where VMP_p = MD. The regulatory authority thus wants to set the quota at $\hat{Y}$. Even if the authority knows MD with certainty, it typically will not know enough about the internal affairs of the firm to know the firm's VMP_p curve. In sharp contrast to the effluent charge strategy, where the firm was forced by profit incentives to reveal true pollution benefits, the regulatory authority must now seek other ways to estimate the firm's VMP_p curve, starting no doubt with assertions made by the firm itself. But under quotas it is in the profit-maximizing interest of the firm to exaggerate the benefits of pollution as an input and to claim an exaggerated VMP_p, such as VMP_p^e in Figure 14.9. If the true VMP_p curve is VMP_p and the exaggerated curve is VMP_p^e, the firm can increase profit by convincing the authority that Y_e instead of $\hat{Y}$ is the optimal quota. By not using the price system, the firm loses the incentive to provide truthful information about pollution benefits. Also, under quotas the firm has an incentive to hire lawyers to defend VMP_p^e before the regulatory authority; under the effluent charge it has an incentive to hire engineers to clean up its production processes—that is, to find the efficient VMP_p.

Problems in Economic Policy

All three approaches to solving externalities—Coasian bargaining, effluent charges, and quotas—present many practical difficulties, including the following:

Effluent Charges versus Quotas: Multiple Firms

APPLIED MICRO THEORY

14.3

We have seen that effluent charges force firms to reveal the benefits of pollution and that quotas encourage them to exaggerate benefits. Effluent fees have another advantage over quotas when, in a typical case, there is more than one firm to regulate. To illustrate, the accompanying figure shows the VMP_p curves of two firms and the horizontal summation of these curves (in the right-hand panel). The optimal effluent charge is $\hat{f}$, which equates $\Sigma_h VMP_p$ and MD at

$\hat{Y}$. Each firm chooses a pollution level for which the fee equals its VMP_p. And although the firms' amounts of pollution differ, their VMP_p are the same in equilibrium. Thus

$$\hat{f} = VMP_p^1 = VMP_p^2 = MD$$

The is the multifirm efficiency condition.

Under a quota system where firms have unequal production functions and hence unequal VMP_p curves, the quota system would equalize the VMP_p of firms only by accident. Barring such an accident,

the quota system cannot achieve multifirm efficiency.

When a reduction of pollution is called for, the regulatory authority should seek to achieve the efficient level of pollution, $\hat{Y}$, and to achieve $\hat{Y}$ pollution at least cost. Effluent charges have two main advantages over quotas in achieving these goals: true revelation of the firm's VMP_p, allowing the efficient pollution level $\hat{Y}$ to be approached, and equalization of the VMP_p among firms, permitting the efficient pollution level $\hat{Y}$ to be achieved at least cost.

Multifirm Efficiency

Effluent charges achieve multifirm efficiency: $\hat{f} = VMP_p^1 = VMP_p^2 = MD$. The two panels on the left show the VMP_p for two firms. The right-hand panel shows equality of the horizontal sum of the firm's VMP_p and society's marginal damages, MD.

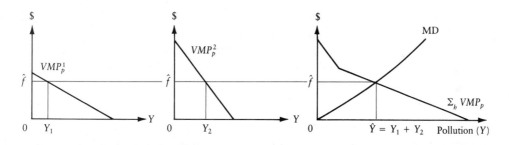

Quotas in a Bubble

APPLIED MICRO THEORY

14.4

The Environmental Protection Agency has adopted a "bubble" policy to make its effluent quota system more efficient. Under this policy, each polluter is placed under an imaginary bubble that limits its total pollution to a quota. The polluter's VMP_p from its various emission points (vents,

stacks, chimneys, and so forth) can then be equated. This system is more efficient than the old system of controlling pollution at each source point.

Firms are also allowed to apply for a bubble merger—two or more firms placed under one bubble. Firms have the incentive to apply for a bubble merger when there is a difference in their VMP_p for their separate bubbles. Mutually advan-

tageous trades of money for pollution rights can take place within the merger bubble; the firm with a low VMP_p sells pollution rights to the firm with a high VMP_p. When the VMP_p are equated, the cost of pollution abatement falls.*

*For an extensive discussion of the "bubble policy," see Richard A. Liroff, *Air Pollution Offsets: Trading, Selling, and Banking* (Washington, D.C.: Conservation Foundation, 1980).

The measurement of pollution at the source.

The measurement of the resulting damages, MD. In measuring both the pollution and the damages, there are engineering and information problems. We need incentive systems that induce the production and revelation of information.

The free-rider problem. All three policy approaches require full participation to lead to efficiency.

Transaction costs. All policies are cumbersome and expensive to implement. If it costs more to set up the regulatory agency, collect information, and organize the participants than is returned in benefits, the transaction costs will prohibit the achievement of efficiency.

External Costs and Interindustry Equilibrium

The presence of external costs in one industry misdirects productive resources and output in that industry as well as in other industries whose products are substitutes. The essential problem is that, when one component of the supply side of an industry imposes external costs on members of society without charge, incorrect information regarding substitutes is communicated to consumers.

Let's consider two industries producing substitute outputs: Naugahyde coats and cowhide coats. Suppose the tanning of cowhides is a highly polluting activity (which it is) but the production of Naugahyde is a clean activity (a surprise to the cows, perhaps, but the Naugas knew it all along). Assume also that the hide-tanning firms do not pay the full opportunity cost of their pollution through effluent charges or Coasian bargaining due to some or all of the weaknesses inherent in these schemes. Then the private costs of firms producing cowhide coats are below the full societal costs of production. What will be the interindustry equilibrium?

Figure 14.10*a* illustrates the cowhide coat industry's supply and demand curves. The black supply curve, S_c, is the industry supply

Figure 14.10
Interindustry Equilibrium

Inefficiencies in one industry spill over into other industries whose products are substitutes. (a) Excess pollution in cowhide coat production is translated into the inefficiently low price P_c. (b) The price of cowhide coats is a shift parameter in the demand for Naugahyde coats. Thus demand is depressed in the Naugahyde coat market due to excess pollution in the cowhide coat market.

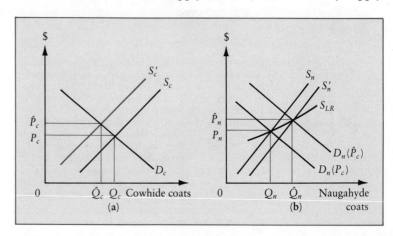

The Control of Externalities through Purchased Injuctions

APPLIED
MICRO
THEORY

14.5

A famous court case illustrates how laws that preserve property rights can allocate resources efficiently by recognizing the role of prices in generating information, the very essence of the Coase theorem. The case involved Del Webb, a residential housing developer, and a cattle feedlot owned by Spur Industries.* Webb developed Sun City, Arizona, a retirement community offering fine homes, clean air, spectacular vistas, community recreation facilities, and an ample amount of college and professional sports exhibitions, including the Arizona State University teams and the Milwaukee Brewers' spring training camp. The feedlot was a profitable business that allowed cattle to finish growing under professional inspection before being sent to market.

Initially, Sun City was some distance from the feedlot, but as the retirement community expanded, it grew toward the feedlot. Soon the feedlot began to impose external costs on the retirees in the form of pungent odors, a large fly population, and the increased potential for disease. Complaints grew, and new homes became harder to sell. Del Webb finally sought a court injunction to force

*Spur Industries v. Del Webb, 108 Ariz. 178, 494 P. 2d 700 (1972).

Spur to cease feedlot operations.

The stage was set for the court's ingenious application of microeconomic theory. Although Webb's development of Sun City responded to a real need for housing and was a very profitable business, the feedlot was also very profitable, and after all, had been there first. Webb wanted to be rid of the feedlot at no cost. The court's solution was to issue a purchased injunction. In effect, the court-issued injunction against operation of the feedlot would become effective only if Webb made a payment to Spur large enough to pay for its exit. Webb would have to pay Spur a price equal to a reasonable estimate of Spur's lost profit due to exit plus moving costs. In other words, if the benefit to Webb of halting the feedlot externalities exceeded the benefit to Spur of continuing operation, Webb could pay Spur to exit and both parties would come out ahead. Such Coasian bargaining mimics the price system's mechanism for facilitating value-increasing exchange and guiding resources to their most valuable uses.

The purchased injunction order forced Webb to reveal, by money payment, that the value to him of Spur's exit was greater than the value to Spur of remaining. Therefore, it eliminated the possibility of Webb's overstating the value of Spur's moving in order to obtain a profitable but inefficient injunction. It also prevented Spur from

overstating its expected lost profit in order to hold out for an inefficient combination of housing and feedlots.

Thus the purchased injunction solves an important information problem by creating a forum in which negotiations between parties force them to reveal benefits and, in the process, to establish the optimum combination of activities. If these activities could be made compatible—perhaps through waste treatment, electronic fly control, the breeding of odorless cows, or the maintenance of an efficient distance between home and feedlots—the incentives would be in place for both parties to discover these mutually profitable techniques instead of having a judge rule whether or not the activities are mutually exclusive. Because the primary parties are in a better position to discover these techniques than the judge is, placing the burden on the parties is an important element of efficiency in the decision. In the end, the feedlot departed Sun City with a payment from Webb. The purchased injunction internalized the feedlot externalities and allowed an efficient result to be achieved via private bargaining.†

†For an extensive discussion of the legal and economic issues touched on here, see Guido Calabresi and A. Douglas Melamed, "Property Rules, Liability Rules, and Inalienability: One View of the Cathedral," *Harvard Law Review* 85 (April 1972):1091–1128.

when all firms ignore environmental costs in their private cost calculations. Thus all firms' marginal cost curves are too low, and the horizontal sum of firms' marginal costs—the industry supply curve—is overstated. If firms were forced to pay all costs of production, including environmental damages, as they must under an effluent charge or Coasian bargaining arrangement, their costs would increase and the industry supply curve would shift to S_c', shown as a colored curve in panel *a*. Thus the presence of external costs understates costs, which in turn leads to excessive output (Q_c) and too low a price (P_c). By allowing firms to ignore the environmental costs of their activities, the price system allocates too many resources to cowhide coat production at too low a price.

If a way could be found to charge firms for the cost of their environmental pollution, thereby making them take environmental costs into account in their decisionmaking, firms initially breaking even would be pushed to negative economic profits, and long-run exit would ensue. The industry supply curve would shift to the left, putting upward pressure on commodity prices. Long-run equilibrium would be reestablished when all firms that earned negative economic profit when forced to pay environmental costs had exited the industry. Some previously inframarginal firms would become marginal firms under the full-cost arrangement. The optimum industry price and output would be $\hat{P}_c$ and $\hat{Q}_c$. Thus the environmental externality allows some firms to produce cowhide coats that could not do so if required to pay for their pollution damage. The presence of such firms keeps industry output above the efficient rates and industry price too low.

But the inefficiencies in the industry experiencing external costs do not remain wholly within the industry. Instead they spill into substitute industries as well—to the Naugahyde coat industry in this example. Figure 14.10b shows the Naugahyde coat industry's supply and demand curves. The two industries are tied together because their products are substitutes in consumption. Thus the price of cowhide coats is a shift parameter in the demand curve for Naugahyde coats. For cowhide coat price P_c (the inefficient price), the demand curve for Naugahyde coats is $D_n(P_c)$, and industry price and output are P_n and Q_n. But if an optimal pollution policy raised the price of cowhide coats to $\hat{P}_c$, the demand curve for Naugahyde coats would increase to $D_n(\hat{P}_c)$, in turn raising the price of Naugahyde coats, attracting into the industry additional entrants whose costs were too high at the previous prices, and expanding industry output. Recall from Chapter 8 that the entry of higher-cost firms produces an upward-sloping long-run supply curve even for constant-cost industries. The optimal price and quantity of Naugahyde coats are $\hat{P}_n$ and $\hat{Q}_n$. But as long as external costs are not internalized in the cowhide coat industry, Naugahyde coat prices and output will be held at the inefficient levels P_n and Q_n.

Thus the inefficiencies of the cowhide coat industry cause inefficiencies in the Naugahayde coat industry as well. The price and quantity of Naugahyde coats are too low because of the external costs in another industry. The lesson to be learned is that industries become interdependent by virtue of the substitutability of their products in consumption. If external costs disturb efficiency in one market, the inefficiencies will spread into related industries via the inefficient pricing of substitutes.[5]

5. For convenience in exposition, the feedback effect of the price of Naugahyde coats on the demand curve for cowhide coats has been ignored. Final general equilibrium between the two markets would be the result of an iterative process.

Interindustry Equilibrium: Effluent Charges versus Quotas

APPLIED
MICRO
THEORY

14.6

Let's examine the effect of effluent charges and quotas on the costs of a polluting industry and, indirectly, on the equilibrium of related industries. To continue the coat example, assume that the Naugas are successful in convincing the regulatory authority that their competitors—firms selling cowhide coats—should be regulated due to the environmental costs of their production. Figure A illustrates the effects of a quota system on the costs of the firm, Figure B the effects of effluent charges.

Under a perfectly calibrated quota system, the optimal quantity of pollution, $\hat{Y}$, must equate the horizontal sum of firms' VMP_p curves, $\Sigma_v VMP_p$, and the vertical sum of individuals' marginal damages, $\Sigma_v MD$. In Figure A such a perfect quota means that the firms' marginal cost per unit of pollution is the discontinuous line $0\hat{Y}MC$. The total cost to firms of a $\hat{Y}$ level of pollution is the area beneath the marginal cost curve, which is zero. Firms do not pay anything for the units of environment used up; they merely face a limit on such use. It is like having a limit on the number of workers that a firm can hire for a zero wage. Naturally, such a subsidy results in an oversupply of final output, too low a product price, and too much quantity demanded. These results affect the industry equilibrium of related industries, as we have seen.

Also, because pollution is priced at zero until the quota is reached and afterward priced at infinity, economic rent is incorrectly assigned under quotas. Firms are

Figure A
Under a quota system, the economic rent on the allowed units of pollution is too large. Excessive entry results.

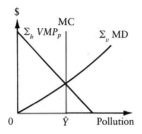

Figure B
Under an effluent charge system, the economic rent is eliminated by the fee $\hat{f}$.

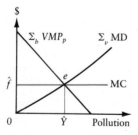

employing pollution units at zero private cost, which results in excess profits for the polluting firms. Thus regulating pollution via quota allocations entails the additional regulatory responsibility of licensing entry in order to restrict the entry that the pollution quotas elicit. One regulation—pollution

quotas—gives birth to a new one—the licensing of entry.

Thus a perfect quota system can regulate the use of the environment optimally only if the licensing of new entrants is also undertaken. And even so, quotas typically will not bring the price and output of the regulated industry and its competitors to efficient levels. A pricing mechanism is needed.

Such a pricing mechanism is available in the effluent charge. By trial and error, the optimal effluent charge $\hat{f}$ may be determined. As shown in Figure B, it equates the horizontal sum of firms' VMP_p curves, $\Sigma_v VMP_p$, and the vertical sum of individuals' marginal damages, $\Sigma_v MD$. The effluent charge is the marginal cost to firms of additional units of pollution. The total cost to firms of $\hat{Y}$ pollution is the area beneath the marginal cost curve up to $\hat{Y}$, or area $0\hat{f}e\hat{Y}$. Comparing the total cost to firms of polluting at the $\hat{Y}$ level under quotas (TC_Q) and effluent charges (TC_{ec}), note that

$$TC_{ec} = 0\hat{f}e\hat{Y} > 0 = TC_Q$$

The effluent charge passes the cost of environmental pollution to the public through higher prices, less output, and less quantity demanded. Also, the substitute industries, such as the Naugahyde coat industry, are allowed to achieve an efficient equilibrium. The pricing mechanism inherent in the effluent charge (as well as Coasian bargaining) can be a useful means of bolstering the market when the pricing signals are otherwise blurred by external costs.

The Common-Pool Problem: Fisheries

APPLIED
MICRO
THEORY

14.7

In the fishing industry, the common-pool problem is unrelenting. Under certain circumstances, competitive market forces lead to the extinction of a biological species. Vernon Smith has provided an excellent example of the power of an interdisciplinary approach to such a problem.*

Let's begin with the biological part of the problem. Curve G in Figure A is a biological replenishment curve for fish. The vertical axis measures the change in fish population per unit of time, ΔF, and the horizontal axis measures the stock of fish at a moment in time, S. Thus the G curve is a rate-of-fish-replenishment curve. Movements along G measure the changes in fish population as a function of the stock of fish already in place. When the stock of fish is less than A, the fish stock is too small to form large enough schools to ward off or survive attack by natural enemies. Thus $\Delta F < 0$. Natural extinction will result if restocking is not undertaken. When the fish stock is between A and B, the stock of fish is sufficient for natural maintenance and growth. Here $\Delta F > 0$. The fish stock will grow until the stock reaches B. When the fish stock exceeds B, it is too large. Insufficient food causes the weak fish to die, and $\Delta F < 0$. As fish die off, B is approached. Thus barring total extinction, stock size B is a stable natural equilibrium.

Now let's introduce a predator of fish: people in fishing fleets. We need a graphic depiction of the reality that a larger stock of fish can sustain more competitive fishing firms, the marginal firms of which break even. Line K in Figure B is a fish kill curve; the K line

*Vernon Smith, "Economics of Production from Natural Resources," *American Economic Review* 68 (1968): 409–431.

Figure A
Fishery Economics

The biological replenishment rate for fish is shown by curve G.

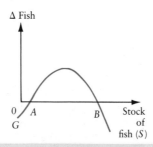

depicts fish kill rates achieved in a competitive market as a function of S, the size of the stock of fish. All along line K, the firms are breaking even; above it there will be entry; below it exit. The K line slopes upward because a larger stock of fish will support a larger fleet of boats, which in turn produces a larger zero-profit kill rate.†

The G curve in Figure A is used to depict the biological replenishment process. The K curve in Figure B describes the economic

†The kill curve, K, need not emanate from the origin, as does the K curve in Figure B. If there is a minimum stock of fish required for any commercial fishing, the K curve would exhibit a positive intercept.

Figure B

The zero-profit kill rate is shown by curve K.

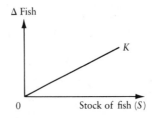

relationship between the size of the fish stock and the quantity of competitive fishing. Now we can put biology and economics together by combining the G and K curves in one diagram. How does the addition of the human predator change the biological equilibrium?

Let technology and costs in the fishing industry result in the kill curve K_1 in Figure C. The addition of the fishing industry changes the steady-state equilibrium stock of fish from B to C. The fishing fleets extract an amount of fish equal to BE per time period. At B the natural fish population is stable $[\Delta F(B) = 0]$, but the fish kill is positive $[\Delta F(B) = BE > 0]$. Thus the stock of fish will shrink and the number of competitive fishing firms will fall. The stock of fish will continue to fall as long as the additional kill exceeds the additional natural replenishment. When the kill rate equals the natural replenishment rate, the stock of fish will remain in equilibrium. This condition is achieved at point C, where $K_1(S_1) = G = S_1C$. The stock of fish S_1 determines the number of competitive fishing firms that can be supported, given present fishing technology and costs.

So far it appears that competition is compatible with the coexistence of people and fish and with an orderly extraction of fish within the limits of natural replacement. But suppose a change in fishing technology makes it possible for previously extramarginal fleets to enter the industry. The kill-rate curve shifts upward. If the kill-rate curve shifts up wholly above the replenishment curve, as K_2 does, there will be no stable equilibrium that satisfies both the profit motives of the fishing fleets and the natural reproduction rates of the fish. For each stock of fish, there is more extraction due to the number of firms in the industry than normal reproduction rates can replace. The end result of such disequilibrium is the complete extinction of the fish

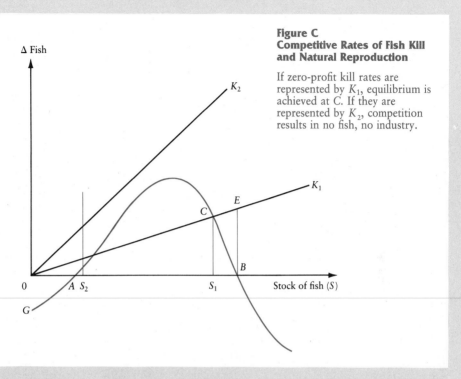

Figure C
Competitive Rates of Fish Kill and Natural Reproduction

If zero-profit kill rates are represented by K_1, equilibrium is achieved at C. If they are represented by K_2, competition results in no fish, no industry.

species and therefore of the fishing industry. Surely, such a result is not efficient; yet it is long-run equilibrium in the absence of intervention when the kill-rate curve is K_2.

Note the central role of the common-pool problem here. Faced with the threat of complete extinction of the species, the individual competitive firm is too small to do anything but participate in the extinction. One firm's output reduction from the common pool cannot save the species, because it is too small to affect the total kill rate. Hence the firm must also hurry its extraction rate in order to profit from the fish while they last. The profit-maximizing decisions of competitive firms operating from a common pool eventually eliminate the biological species and hence the industry.

The competitive industry is powerless, without collusion, to counteract the effect of disease or natural disaster on a fish population. Suppose an economic/biological equilibrium is established at point C when the kill-rate curve is K_1 in Figure C. Now suppose the lamprey eel is introduced to the lake and reduces the fish population to S_2. Even if the eel is conquered before the fish species is killed off, the competitive fishing industry would finish the job that the eel started, because at S_2 the kill rate exceeds reproduction.

Clearly, there is a role for government in the restocking of fisheries, the licensing of fishing firms, and the regulation of their technologies. Duck hunters are licensed and limited to shotguns (plenty would use machine guns if allowed to) as a control on the number of ducks taken from the common pool. Thoughtful duck hunters must welcome this regulation as a means of duck preservation. The externalities implicit in the common pool inhibit the ability of unregulated competitive markets to establish efficient rates of extraction.

Common-Pool Resources

The problem of **common-pool resources** is another intriguing aspect of externality theory. The common-pool problem arises whenever independent economic agents draw a productive resource from a common source. Indeed, it is another manifestation of the absence of property rights. The problem applies to multiple oil wells drawing from large pools of oil; fisheries; woodlands; populations of species, such as bison or beaver, killed for fun or profit; and milkshakes shared through many straws out of one glass. In all such cases, the incentive is to draw out the resource at an inefficiently high rate, because whatever you do not draw out will be extracted by competitors. There is no incentive to store for the future in the common pool. Oil companies draw out the resources and store them in tanks for the future. Kids sharing milkshakes just get sick. But give kids separate glasses, and they will drink at a more enjoyable (efficient) rate. The same principle applies to firms like oil companies, although it is difficult (if not impossible) to give them separate pools to draw from.

Key Terms

Coase theorem 465
common-pool resources 480
effluent charge 470
effluent quota 471
exclusion 456
external benefit 451
external cost 451
externalities 451
free-rider problem 460
jointness 452
marginal damage curve (Σ_vMD) 464
marginal product of pollution (MP_p) 463
nonexclusion 456
nonrivalry 456
private benefits 453
private goods 455
public benefits 453
public goods 456
rivalry 455
value of marginal product of pollution (VMP_p) 463
vertical summation 452

Summary

Bringing the loose ends of this chapter together poses a formidable challenge. Merely to list the concepts shows how vast and interrelated they are: jointness in production and consumption, private versus public goods, externalities, free riders, the common pool, congestion and pollution (public "bads"), congestion and pollution control policies.

The unifying theme of the theory of externalities and public goods is jointness. Externalities, public goods, and all the associated problems and implications arise from jointness in consumption or production. Jointness in consumption is ultimately more relevant. Jointness in production does not by itself generate externalities and public goods. For example, beef and hides are jointly produced by steers but are not public goods, because they are not jointly consumed.

Education produces both private and public goods. But the public-goods aspect of educational benefits is due to the joint consumption of these benefits rather than to the joint nature of their production. The same is true of the public good associated with bus ridership. Even the joint production that gives rise to public "bads," such as congestion and pollution, results in externalities only by virtue of the joint consumption of congestion and pollution.

Thus joint consumption is a chief force underlying public goods. When a good is nonrivalrous, consumption of the good by one person does not use up the good for others. For some public goods, such as national defense, exclusion is not possible. For such goods, the inability to charge a price to users is another aspect of the public good. For public goods such as bridges and public parks, exclusion is possible but inefficient, because marginal cost is less than average cost. Clearly, exclusion or nonexclusion is not the central distinguishing feature of public goods. Instead, jointness of consumption is the key aspect.

Another central theme of the chapter is the appropriateness of the price system in devising control systems in industries with important externalities. Free-market Coasian bargaining internalizes pollution externalities and leads to efficient levels of pollution when property rights are assigned. In the absence of pollution rights, surrogates for market prices in the form of effluent charges have several advantages over regulation by quotas. Similarly, congestion tolls act as surrogates for market prices in allocating highway congestion and exhibit advantages over the engineering device of facility expansion. Correctly applied, user charges and tolls generate information that leads to the same efficient resource allocations that would be provided by a free market in the absence of externalities. In short, control devices that place "prices" on public goods mimic the market in terms of the generation of information and efficiency in resource allocation.

Problems

1. a. Many production processes impose danger on workers. Using graphic analysis, discuss how management and labor would negotiate the "optimal level of danger."
   b. Would you expect the "optimal level of danger" to change with the rate of unemployment?
2. A common winter accident is slipping on the sidewalk and hurting one's back. Therefore, the probability of an accident is a function of caution by the walkers and snow shoveling by the home owner. Discuss the rules a municipality may develop for the optimal shoveling of sidewalks.
3. Suppose that a rancher and a farmer have adjacent property and that the rancher's cattle eat some of the farmer's corn.
   a. Draw a diagram indicating that the optimal number of cattle is 15.
   b. Suppose the state entitles the rancher to 10 cattle. Discuss the bargaining that will ensue.
   c. Calculate the farmer's and the rancher's economic rent inherent in such an entitlement.
   d. Compare this result to an entitlement of 11 cattle; 20 cattle.
4. Until about 40 years ago, buffalo were in danger of extinction, but cattle never were, even though both roamed the range. Use the principle of property rights to explain this observation.
5. Presently in the United States, there is no law preventing the construction of buildings that cast shadows on existing buildings and/or property.
   a. What must a property owner do to prevent such construction?
   b. If there is a potential of a building casting shadows on many surrounding properties, discuss the difficulties in determining the optimum height of the new building.
6. "The preconditions for efficiency in trades of pollution rights are the same as in trades of any other set of goods. Hence the Coase theorem merely restates the results of traditional microeconomic theory." Comment.
7. "Coase trivializes the problem of pollution by assuming away its most nettlesome aspects: the public-good (public-bad) nature of the problem, the high transaction costs, the free-rider problem." Comment.

8. Would a monopolist ever deplete a biological species? If so, under what conditions?

9. Does determination of the most efficient activity for a parcel of land depend on who came first? Assume costless entry and exit.

10. Does the distribution of income depend on the assignment of property rights? (Be careful to consider the distribution of income among people, not occupations.)

11. Consider a fishery. Suppose that the competitive fishing rate threatens to extinguish the fish. Comment on the efficiency of each of the following policies:

    a. Bargaining among boat owners to determine the efficient outcome.

    b. Annual fees sufficient to deter enough entry of boats to bring the catch rate down to the biological replenishment rate.

    c. First-come, first-served licenses sold for a fee just high enough to pay the costs of administering the system. (The number of licenses should be adjusted until the catch rate equals the replenishment rate.)

    d. A fee per fish caught. (The fee should be large enough to reduce the catch rate to the replenishment rate.)

Suggested Readings

Buchanan, J. *The Demand and Supply of Public Goods*. Chicago: Rand-McNally, 1969.

Coase, R. "The Problem of Social Cost." *Journal of Law and Economics* 3 (1960): 1–44.

Head, J. G. "Public Goods and Public Policy." *Public Finance* 17 (1962): 197–219.

Samuelson, P. "The Pure Theory of Public Expenditure." *Review of Economics and Statistics* 36 (1954): 387–389.

Smith, Vernon. "Economics of Production from Natural Resources." *American Economic Review* 58 (1968): 409–431.

Glossary

A

absolute advantage In an Edgeworth box, the endowment of more of both goods to one trading partner.

accounting cost An explicit, historical cost incurred by a firm.

adding-up controversy Whether or not the sum of factor payments equals the value of output produced when all factors are paid the value of their marginal products.

arbitrage Buying at a low price and selling at a higher price. Arbitrage is assumed in the theory of the simple monopolist.

arc elasticity The calculation of elasticity along a small segment, or arc, of the demand curve. The formula, using average bases, is $\varepsilon = \Delta X/\Delta P \cdot [(P_1 + P_2)/2]/[(X_1 + X_2)/2]$.

average cost of labor (AC_L) Total labor costs divided by total labor units.

average-cost pricing Setting the price of a public utility equal to the total cost divided by the total units sold.

average fixed cost (AFC) The short-run average (per-unit) cost of obtaining the fixed factors of production: TFC/Q.

average product of labor The average number of units of output that each worker produces: $AP_L = Q/L|_K$.

average revenue (AR) Average price: TR/Q.

average revenue product of labor Total revenue divided by the amount of labor input.

average tax rate The percentage of total taxable income that a taxpayers pays in taxes.

average total cost (ATC) The short-run average (per-unit) cost of obtaining all variable and fixed factors: TC/Q.

average variable cost (AVC) The short-run average (per-unit) cost of obtaining the variable factors of production: TVC/Q.

Averch-Johnson effect When rate-of-return regulation sets a maximum allowable profit on public utility firms in terms of a percentage return on invested capital, firms are induced to select an inefficient input mix by employing too much capital.

axioms of consumer behavior The assumptions about consumer behavior that are used to make testable predictions.

B

barometric price leadership Price experimentation by one firm in an oligopoly. The term *barometric* signifies that the price experimentation reflects industry cost conditions.

barriers to entry The costs of entry that are not included in required costs. Examples include taxi medallions, licensing restrictions, and trade barriers.

basing-point pricing Cartel pricing of products as if shipped from one location (the basing point).

bilateral monopoly The condition that exists when a monopsonist purchases from a monopolist.

block pricing The practice of charging different prices for successive blocks of services, such as electricity.

breakeven point The minimum point on the firm's LAC curve. Breaking even means earning zero economic profit, or exactly covering opportunity costs.

budget constraints The limits imposed on consumer expenditures by income and product prices: $I = P_Y Y + P_X X$.

C

capital inputs Inputs to production that can be used in several periods.

cardinal utility Utility measured in units ("utils"); a key concept in a theory of consumer behavior. The concept of marginal utility is related.

cartel A group of firms in an industry that collude to set output below competitive levels.

ceteris paribus A Latin phrase meaning "other things constant."

change in demand A shift in the demand curve resulting from a change in the value of one or more shift parameters.

change in quantity demanded Any change in the quantity of a good that consumers are willing to buy in a specified period of time. The prime example is a movement along a stationary demand curve due to a change in price.

change in quantity supplied Any change in the quantity of a good that suppliers are willing to supply in a specified period of time. The prime example is a movement along a stationary supply curve due to a change in price.

change in supply A shift in the supply curve resulting from a change in the value of one or more shift parameters.

choice set The set of commodity bundles that the consumer can purchase, given certain money income and prices.

Coase theorem With well-defined property rights in externalities, bargaining will lead to efficiency.

common-pool resources Resources that people can draw on independently, such as fisheries.

comparative advantage In an Edgeworth box, having a higher marginal rate of substitution compared to the trading partner.

comparative statics A methodology for comparing two market equilibria, before and after a market disturbance.

compensating variation in income According to Hicks, an adjustment in money income that would keep the consumer on the original indifference curve after relative prices change. According to Slutsky, an adjustment in

money income that would permit the consumer to purchase the original commodity bundle after relative prices change.

complement A good or service used with another, as in cameras and film.

compounding The continuous accrual of interest.

conflict curve Another term for a contract curve; reflects the fact that moves along the contract curve reduce the utility of one party.

conjectural variation in output Without knowing what its rivals will do, the oligopolist must choose an output level and thus affect price. The oligopolist must conjecture the rival's response.

conjectural variation in price A variation in price by one firm while it assumes a specific response by its rivals.

constant-cost industry Industrywide expansion does not change factor prices.

constant returns to scale When all inputs are increased (or decreased) by a certain proportion, output increases (or decreases) by the same proportion.

constrained bliss point Maximum social welfare subject to production and exchange efficiency.

consumer optimization Allocating a given level of income among alternative commodity bundles so as to maximize total utility.

consumer surplus The difference between the maximum amount that consumers would be willing to pay for goods and the amount that they actually do pay.

contract curve (CC) The locus of Pareto optimal points in an Edgeworth box.

Cournot equilibrium Occurs when no rival has an incentive to change its output or price because all conjectures are verified in fact.

cross-price elasticity (of demand) The percentage change in the quantity of X demanded due to a percentage change in the price of Y, a substitute or complement of X, *ceteris paribus*.

D

decreasing-cost firm A firm with declining average cost up to the level of output.

decreasing-cost industry Industrywide expansion decreases factor prices and shifts the firms' cost curves downward.

decreasing returns to scale When all inputs are increased (or decreased) by a certain proportion, output increases (or decreases) by a smaller proportion.

demand The multidimensional relationship between the quantity consumed and the factors that determine how much is consumed.

demand curve The relationship between the quantities of a good that consumers are willing to buy and all possible prices, in a specified period of time, *ceteris paribus*.

derived demand Demand for a good or service that is an input to production.

diminishing marginal rate of substitution The units of Y that a consumer can give up to receive one more unit of X and maintain constant utility diminishes as the buyer gets more X and less Y. In this case, the indifference curve is convex from the origin.

diminishing marginal rate of technical substitution Isoquant curves are convex from the origin when inputs are imperfect substitutes.

diminishing marginal utility Each unit of a good consumed adds less to total utility than the last unit did.

discounting The calculation of present value of future amounts.

dominant-firm price leadership The setting of price by the dominant firm in an industry. Competing firms take the price as a parameter.

duopoly A two-firm oligopoly.

E

economic cost The opportunity cost of forgone options.

economic envy The preference of one person for another person's allocation of goods and services.

economic profit Net income minus the highest net income forgone.

economic rent The surplus over what is necessary to bring a factor of production to its current use.

Edgeworth box The analytical device used to illustrate the mutually advantageous trading available when the marginal rates of substitution in exchange or production are unequal.

effluent charge A policy option for the control of pollution by taxing the polluter per unit of pollution.

effluent quota A policy of limiting the amount of pollution by a polluter.

elasticity The percentage change in a dependent variable resulting from a percentage change in a dependent variable, *ceteris paribus*. Elasticity measures responsiveness.

elasticity of substitution The percentage change of the capital labor ratio divided by the percentage change in the rental/wage ratio.

Engel curve The relationship between the units of a good that consumers will buy and all income levels per unit of time, *ceteris paribus*.

entrepreneurial opportunity cost The forgone value of invested capital and the owner's time; the highest earnings that owners could earn in the next-best employment or industry.

entry/exit decision If $P \geq$ LAC, the firm will stay in its current industry, because alternative industries are not more profitable. If $P <$ LAC, the entrepreneur will exit the industry, because opportunity costs are not being covered.

equalizing wage differential Equilibrium wages must be different in order to compensate for differences in working conditions.

equal marginal cost principle The cheapest way to produce a given amount of output is to equate the marginal cost of all factors and in all plants.

equal marginal revenue principle The maximum revenue is derived from different markets by equating marginal revenue in those markets.

equilibrium price The only market price that equates the quantity demanded by consumers with the quantity supplied by sellers. Shortages and surpluses have been eliminated when the equilibrium price is achieved.

equivalent variation in income According to Hicks, an adjustment in money income in response to a relative price change that would allow the consumer paying original prices to reach the same indifference curve that he or she will actually achieve paying the new prices.

excess-capacity theorem The equilibrium of the monopolistically competitive firm results in underutilization of capacity.

exchange efficiency The exhaustion of mutually advantageous trading possibilities.

exclusion The limits that the possessor of a good can place on its use.

expansion path (EP) Shows all least-cost factor combinations for all possible output levels, for a given set of factor prices.

external benefit A benefit of a decision realized by a person who is not a voluntary party to the decision.

external cost A cost of a decision realized by a person who is not a voluntary party to the decision.

externalities The effects of a decision on a person who is not a voluntary party to the decision.

extramarginal firm A firm that is earning positive economic profit at the equilibrium price.

extramarginal units The units that consumers do not purchase because the price exceeds marginal benefit.

F

factor complementarity The increase in the marginal productivity of one factor of production associated with increased amounts of other factors of production.

fallacy of composition The false assumption that what is true of the part must also be true of the whole.

firm's demand curve for labor The two-dimensional relationship between the wage and the amount demanded.

fixed inputs The factors of production that cannot be varied in the short run.

focal-point pricing Pricing around or at an identifiable price.

free-rider problem Inefficient financing of public goods when people who refuse to pay cannot be excluded from using the goods.

G

general equilibrium analysis Analysis based on the assumption of simultaneous equilibrium of all markets.

general training Training that can be transferred from one firm to another.

Giffen good A theoretically possible good in which the income effect is opposite in sign and larger than the substitution effect; depicted by a positively sloped demand curve segment.

grand utility possibility frontier (GUPF) The envelope of all utility possibility frontiers (UPFs). All points on the GUPF express exchange and production efficiency.

H

Herfindahl index The sum of squared market shares; used to evaluate the consequences of merges on competition.

hoarding The accumulation of inventories during shortages to lower the risk of not finding future supplies.

homogeneous production functions A production function is homogeneous to degree j if a proportional increase in all inputs of λ increases output by the jth power of λ.

horizontal summation The process of aggregating individual demand curves into a market demand curve. The quantities demanded of all consumers are summed horizontally at each price level.

Hotelling principle The price of storable nonrenewable resources will rise at the rate of interest.

human capital The skills and training invested in people, which can be used in many future periods.

I

imperfect competition Competition among firms that do not face parametric prices.

implicit rental rate of capital (rental rate of capital) The per-unit price of renting a unit of capital per time period; a measure of the opportunity cost of capital.

income-compensated demand curve According to Hicks, it measures the relationship between price and quantity demanded but includes only the substitution effect. The income effect is eliminated and real income is held constant via the Hicksian compensating variation in income.

income-consumption curve (ICC) Records the commodity bundles that the consumer will buy at various levels of money income, *ceteris paribus.*

income effect of a price change The change in quantity demanded due solely to the change in purchasing power caused by a price change, holding relative prices fixed.

income elasticity (of demand) The percentage change in the quantity of X demanded because of a percentage change in consumer income, *ceteris paribus.*

increasing-cost industry Industrywide expansion increases factor prices and shifts the firms' cost curves upward.

increasing returns to scale When all inputs are increased (or decreased) by a certain proportion, output increases (or decreases) by a larger proportion.

indifference curve Shows all of the commodity bundles that give the consumer equal utility.

indifference map The entire family of indifference curves, each defining a different level of utility.

inferior goods When income rises, *ceteris paribus*, purchases of these goods fall. The income-consumption curve for these goods is negatively sloped.

inflection point The point where the total product curve (or any other curve) stops rising at an increasing rate and begins to rise at a decreasing rate. The marginal product of labor reaches its maximum value at the inflection point.

inframarginal firm A firm that earns positive economic profit in competitive equilibrium.

inframarginal profit Profit earned in equilibrium by an inframarginal firm.

inframarginal rent The surplus over what is needed to bring a factor of production or a firm to its present use.

inframarginal units Units of consumption that bestow consumer surplus; at a given price, the marginal benefit of these units exceeds price.

intertemporal analysis Analysis of economic phenomena over time.

inventory profit Profit earned on stored resources by virtue of an increase in the market price.

isocost line Shows the different combinations of factors that can be purchased for any given cost outlay with given factor prices.

isoprofit curves The locus of points that describe the various combinations of resources that yield equal profits.

isoquant curve A curve showing all labor and capital combinations capable of producing the same quantity of final output. Isoquant curves are negatively sloped in the efficient stage, are nonintersecting, are everywhere dense, and are convex from the origin.

isoquant map A family of isoquant curves, each pertaining to a unique rate of output; expresses the firm's long-run production function.

J

jointness When goods or services are produced together, as beef and hides are produced from steers.

K

kinked demand curve A theoretical description of the reluctance of oligopolists to change prices. The key element is the matching of price reductions— but not the matching of price increases.

L

labor inputs Workers' services in the firm.

Laspeyres price index The ratio of income needed to buy the year 1 commodity bundle at year 2 prices to the actual year 1 income.

law of demand Consumers buy less of a product at high prices than at low prices, *ceteris paribus*.

law of diminishing returns When the intensity of a fixed input is increased by adding more and more units of a variable input to the production process, the resulting increases in output must eventually get smaller and smaller.

law of variable proportions See *law of diminishing returns*.

linear homogeneous production function A production function is homogeneous to degree 1 if a proportional increase in all inputs increases output by the same proportion.

long run An analytic time period in which all inputs are infinitely variable.

long-run average cost (LAC) The average (per-unit) cost of producing a given output when inputs are combined to achieve production at least cost: LTC/Q.

long-run competitive equilibrium P = LAC for all firms; the zero-profit theorem of competitive markets.

long-run marginal cost The change in total long-run costs resulting from a small change in output when all cost-minimizing adjustments in all inputs have been achieved: ΔLTC/ΔQ.

long-run supply curve For the firm, the LMC curve above the minimum LAC. For the industry, there are two: (1) Σ_hLMC above the LAC curve and (2) the price-quantity points that exhibit long-run equilibrium.

The first industry supply curve includes only scale-of-plant adjustments; the second includes entry/exit adjustments as well.

long-run total cost (LTC) The total cost of producing a given output when inputs are combined to achieve production at the least cost: $(w \cdot L)$ + $(r \cdot K)$.

loss minimization In the short run, losses are minimized by producing where MK = SMC if $P \geq$ AVC and by shutting down operations if $P <$ AVC.

lumpy entry Entry by firms that have a large fraction of the capital capacity in the industry.

M

marginal benefit The unit of consumption that is just worthwhile. At a given price, marginal benefit equals price, so no consumer surplus is generated.

marginal cost of labor The cost of hiring an additional unit of labor.

marginal cost of plant openings or closings In the multiplant context, the cost of expanding or contracting output by opening or closing plants.

marginal cost of selling curve The diagrammatic representation of the cost of selling an extra unit of produced output.

marginal-cost pricing Public-utility pricing policy that requires the firm to set the price of the marginal unit equal to its marginal cost.

marginal damage curve (Σ_vMD) The theoretical device used to illustrate the economic harm of an external cost.

marginal firm A firm that is breaking even at a given price.

marginal product of labor The change in output resulting from a one-unit change in labor: $MP_L = \Delta Q/\Delta L|_K$.

marginal product of pollution (MP_p) The theoretical device used to illustrate the use of pollution as a factor of production.

marginal productivity theory of wages The theory of market wage determination in which firms adjust employment until the value of the marginal product equals the wage.

marginal rate of substitution (**MRS**) The slope of the indifference curve; the rate at which the consumer is willing to trade one good for another without altering total utility.

marginal rate of technical substitution (**MRTS**) The rate at which labor can replace capital in the production process without changing the rate of output; the slope of the isoquant curve; equals the negative of the ratio of marginal products of labor and capital: $\Delta K/\Delta L|_Q = -MP_L/MP_K$.

marginal rate of transformation (**MRT**) The rate at which the production of one good can be increased at the expense of another by rearranging resources.

marginal revenue (**MR**) The change in total revenue due to a change in the quantity of X sold: $MR = \Delta TR/\Delta X = P[1 + (1/\varepsilon)]$.

marginal revenue of selling curve The diagrammatic representation of the extra revenue derived from an increase in sales effort.

marginal revenue product (**MRP**) The marginal revenue multiplied by the marginal product of an input.

marginal revenue product of labor The marginal revenue multiplied by the marginal product of labor.

marginal tax rate The tax levied on the last dollar of taxable income.

marginal unit At a given price, this unit is the breakeven unit.

marginal utility The change in total utility resulting from the purchase of one more unit of a good.

market demand curve The horizontal summation of all individual consumers' demand curves.

market share maintenance rule A cartel-stabilizing rule that calls for retaliation against cheaters by maintaining market share, thus reducing cheaters' profits below the cartel level.

midpoint base The average base between initial and ending values; used in calculating arc elasticities.

models Devices used to simplify and summarize relationships and to organize thoughts.

monopolist A firm that faces a downward-sloping demand curve; in the extreme, the sole firm in an industry.

monopolistic competition Nonprice competition in an industry with low entry costs but differentiated products.

monopolistic exploitation The gap between the value of the marginal product and the marginal fixed cost.

monopsonistic exploitation of labor The gap between the marginal revenue product and the wage.

monopsonistic wage discrimination Different wage payments to people performing the same tasks; more generally, wages that differ more than necessary to compensate for differing working conditions.

monopsony The circumstance in which the buyer faces an upward-sloping supply curve; in the extreme, the single buyer.

movement parameter In a two-dimensional diagram, the movement parameter appears on one axis and the independent variable appears on the other axis. A change in the value of the movement parameter causes a movement along the stationary curve. Price is the movement parameter for supply and demand curves.

multiperiod analysis Analysis of economic phenomena over time.

multiplant monopoly A firm with market power that has more than one plant.

mutatis mutandis All necessary changes having been made.

N

natural monopolies (technological monopolies) Firms with decreasing long-run average costs up to the point of intersection with the demand curve.

necessary condition An element of a model that is a prerequisite to, but does not by itself permit, a conclusion.

net income Profit for an individual firm.

n-firm concentration ratio The market share of the top firms in an industry.

nonequalizing wage differential Differences in wages that are due to differences in workers' marginal productivities.

nonexclusion The impossibility of excluding collective use of a good or service.

nonprice rationing Allocating shortages among consumers by means other than price increases, including black markets, discrimination, and queuing.

nonrivalry The possibility of collective use of a good or service.

normal goods Goods that are purchased in greater quantities when income rises, *ceteris paribus*. The income-consumption curve for normal goods is positively sloped.

numeraire A composite of all goods that the consumer buys except for good X. The price of X is stated in terms of the units of the numeraire needed to buy a unit of X. The numeraire is usually considered to be money income.

O

offer curve See *price-consumption curve*.

oligopoly An industry composed of a small number of firms.

opportunity (alternative) cost The cost of a resource measured as its most valuable forgone use.

ordinal utility Consumers' ranking of their preferences for various commodity bundles. The main theoretical concept in ordinal utility theory is the indifference curve.

ordinary demand curve Measures the relationship between price and quantity demanded; includes the substitution and income effects of a price change.

P

Paasche price index The ratio of the consumer's money income used to purchase the year 2 commodity bundle at year 2 prices to the income necessary for the consumer to purchase the year 2 bundle at prices prevailing in year 1.

parametric pricing Setting price according to the industry price. Firms that are too small to influence industry price are considered price takers.

Pareto move A reallocation of resources that improves the welfare of at least one person without harming anyone.

Pareto optimality The condition of efficiency in which no Pareto moves exist.

peak-load pricing Charging a higher price when demand is high than when it is low; encourages more efficient use of fixed capacity.

perfect competition A competitive model that assumes firms are identical.

perfect price discrimination Charging a price equal to the marginal willingness to pay for all units of a good.

point elasticity The elasticity at a single point on the demand curve; the formula: $\varepsilon = (\Delta X/\Delta P) \cdot (P/X)$.

predatory pricing Price cutting with the intent to drive a rival out of business.

present value (discounted value) The present value of a future amount is the amount invested today that will grow at compound interest to the future value.

price-consumption curve (PCC) Records the various commodity bundles that the consumer will buy at various relative prices, *ceteris paribus*.

price-determined cost A cost that changes with changes in product price. Economic rent is a price-determined cost.

price-determining costs Costs that, together with demand factors, determine equilibrium prices. Factor costs and the entrepreneur's opportunity costs are price-determining costs.

price discrimination Charging different prices for different units of a good in a ratio different from the ratio of marginal costs.

price elastic A price change causes total revenue to change in the opposite direction; the elasticity coefficient is less than −1.

price elasticity (of demand) The percentage change in the quantity of X demanded due to a percentage change in the price of X, *ceteris paribus*.

price elasticity of labor demand The percentage change in the demand for labor divided by the percentage change in the wage.

price elasticity of supply The percentage change in quantity supplied resulting from a percentage change in price, *ceteris paribus*.

price indexes Numbers used to compare living standards in different years.

price inelastic A price change causes total revenue to change in the same direction; the elasticity coefficient is between −1 and 0.

price rationing Allocating goods and services by price adjustments, which alter the quantities supplied and demanded until the shortage is eliminated.

price taker See *parametric pricing*.

private benefits Benefits that accrue to the decisionmaker.

private goods Goods that can be held for exclusive use.

producer optimization Producing a given rate of output at least cost; requires $MP_L/MP_K = w/r$, or $MP_L/w = MP_K/r$.

product differentiation Efforts to attract customers to a product by changes in quality or performance characteristics.

Production exchange MRT$_B$ = MRS$_A$ of
Returns to scale.

Q

product exhaustion theorem The assertion that, in competition, the value of output is fully distributed to each factor of production, because each factor is paid its value of marginal product.

product group A collection of monopolistically competitive firms producing similar, although not identical, products.

production efficiency Allocating inputs so that it is not possible to reallocate inputs and thereby increase the production of one good without reducing the production of another good.

production function The amounts of final output that can be produced from various combinations of inputs.

production possibility (P-P) curve The locus of points in output space depicting the combinations of maximum output.

product transformation curve Shows the various maximum output combinations of two goods that can be attained from a given set of inputs with current technology.

profit (π) The difference between total revenue and total cost.

profit-maximizing condition The equating of marginal revenue and marginal cost.

public benefits Benefits realized by the public at large due to nonexcludability.

public goods Goods that, once produced, are by their nature or design not held to exclusive use.

pure competition Competition in an industry of price-taking but nonidentical firms.

quantity demanded The quantity of a good that consumers are willing to buy at a specific price, in a specified time period, *ceteris paribus*.

quantity supplied The quantity of a good that suppliers are willing to supply at a specific price, in a specified time period, *ceteris paribus*.

quasi rents Revenue minus total variable cost; returns to capital in excess of what is necessary to keep capital in place in the short run.

R

rate-of-return regulation Controlling the profits of public utility firms by tying the maximum allowable profits to a percentage of invested capital.

reaction function The diagram representing duopolists' profit-maximizing reactions to changes in output (or price) by rivals.

regional monopoly A firm that faces a downward-sloping demand curve while serving a region that is too small to permit competition by a second firm.

relative factor shares The ratio of payments to the factors of production divided by total revenue.

rent-inclusive long-run average cost (*LAC**) The long-run average cost curve with rent included as a fixed cost.

resale price maintenance The practice of forcing dealers to charge a minimum price to encourage them to compete on the quality of point-of-sale service rather than on price.

ridge lines Lines that separate the inefficient, positively sloped segments of an isoquant map from the efficient, negatively sloped segments.

rivalry The impossibility of collective use of a private good.

S

scales of plant The size of a firm as measured by the amount of its capital. Graphically, total cost and average total cost curves are both referred to as scales of plant.

scarcity A societal condition caused by limited resources and relatively unlimited wants.

seasonal rates Rates that vary from season to season in order to approximate the cost of production in each season.

second-best solution When the equation $P = mc$ is not possible for all goods, efficiency requires an equal percentage departure: $P - mc/mc$.

shift parameter A factor that influences the dependent variable but that is not measured on either axis of a two-dimensional diagram. Shift parameters fix the position of a curve; changes in the shift parameters shift the curve to a new position.

shortage The amount by which the quantity demanded exceeds the quantity supplied, at a given price.

short run An analytic time period in which at least one of the firm's inputs is fixed.

short-run marginal cost (SMC) The change in total cost resulting from a small increase in output, holding capital fixed: $\Delta TC/\Delta Q$.

short-run supply curve For the firm, the short-run marginal cost curve above the minimum average variable cost. For the industry, Σ_hSMC curves above the minimum AVC but corrected for increases in factor prices caused by industrywide short-run expansion.

short-run total cost (TC) The sum of total variable costs and total fixed costs: $(w \cdot L) + r\overline{K}$.

shutdown point The minimum point on the AVC curve. If $P <$ AVC, the firm shuts down to avoid unnecessary losses in excess of fixed costs.

shutdown price The price that just covers average variable cost. Any price below the shutdown price causes the firm to shut down.

shutdown rule When price is less than the AVC, firms shut down in the short run.

simple monopolist The monopolist who must charge the same price for all units sold.

Slutsky approach The income effect is separated from the substitution effect by holding apparent real income constant when prices change. A compensating variation in income anchors the budget line at the original commodity bundle, reflecting the new prices. An equivalent variation anchors the budget line at the new commodity bundle, reflecting the original prices.

social welfare function (SWF) A theoretical construct that measures the level of social well being as a function of the utility levels of society's members.

specific training Training specific to the firm and cannot be marketed or transferred to other firms.

Stackelberg disequilibrium The result of two rival firms attempting to be Stackelberg leaders.

stages of production Stage I exhibits an increasing AP_L and is inefficient. Stage II exhibits a diminishing but positive MP_L and AP_L and is efficient. Stage III exhibits a negative MP_L and is inefficient.

subsidy The difference between the prices that buyers pay and the marginal cost of production.

substitutes Goods that are used in place of each other, such as Big Macs and the Whopper.

substitution effect of a price change The change in quantity demanded due solely to a change in relative prices, holding real income constant.

sufficient condition An element of a model that by itself permits a conclusion.

sunk cost A cost that has already been incurred and does not vary with decisions in the current period; should not influence decisions.

supply The multidimensional relationship between quantity supplied and all of its determinants.

supply curve The two-dimensional relationship between price and quantity supplied, *ceteris paribus*.

surplus The amount by which the quantity supplied exceeds the quantity demanded, at a given price.

T

theories Systematic statements of principles used to explain and predict phenomena.

theory of the firm The theory assuming that firms respond to profit incentives.

time-of-day rates Rates that change over the course of the day to reflect the marginal cost of production compared to fluctuating demand.

total benefit (total value) The sum of all marginal benefits of consuming successive units of a product; measured by the area beneath the income-compensated demand curve.

total effect of a price change The change in quantity demanded due to a price change.

total expenditures (TE) See *total revenue*.

total fixed cost (TFC) Short-run costs that do not change when the firm increases or decreases production: $r \cdot \overline{K}$.

total labor cost Wage times amount of labor employed.

total product curve The relationship between labor inputs and final output for a constant quantity of fixed capital.

total profit curve A curve that measures $\pi = $ TR $-$ TC at each output rate.

total revenue (TR) Price times quantity: TR $= P \cdot X$.

total revenue curve The two-dimensional diagram of total revenue as a function of quantity.

total revenue product of labor The diagrammatic representation of revenue as a function of the labor input.

total utility A measure of cardinal utility equal to the sum of the marginal utilities of units consumed.

total variable cost (TVC) The cost of the variable resources needed to produce a given output: $w \cdot L$.

true price index The ratio of the income needed in year 2 to achieve year 1's indifference curve to the consumer's actual income in year 1.

two-part pricing A pricing strategy entailing a fixed charge and a per-unit fee.

U

union objectives A labor union seeks to provide benefits, sometimes conflicting, to its members: maximum employment, maximum total income, and maximum income to a select group.

unit elastic A change in price leaves price times quantity demanded unchanged.

utility Consumer satisfaction, welfare, happiness, or well-being.

utility possibility frontier (UPF) The locus of utility combinations that are possible through rearrangement of a given array of goods among people.

V

value of marginal product of labor The product price times the marginal product of labor.

value of marginal product of pollution (VMP_p) The theoretical device used to illustrate the economic value, due to cost savings, of a firm's pollution.

variable inputs Factors that the firm can expand or contract in the short run.

vertical integration The substitution of permanent ownership for market exchange.

vertical summation The procedure used to sum the jointly produced benefits or costs associated with units of goods or services.

Viner-Wong envelope curve See *long-run average cost (LAC)*.

W

wage differentials Differences in wages. The most interesting cases are those in which wage differences do not correspond to differing working conditions or skill requirements.

welfare loss triangle The diagrammatic representation of the economic loss resulting from inefficient production.

Index